MW00609336

BACKSTAGE PASS

A SURVEY OF AMERICAN MUSICAL THEATRE

Pamyla Stiehl
St. Catherine University

Bud Coleman
University of Colorado Boulder

Acknowledgments
The authors wish to thank research assistants Nathan Stith and David Sinkler.

Image for "Pulling Back the Curtain" sections © Alexandre17, 2012.
Used under license by Shutterstock, Inc.
Image/icon for "Actor Spotlight" sections © Martin Fischer, 2012.
Used under license by Shutterstock, Inc.

Cover image © Mike Powell/Corbis

Kendall Hunt
publishing company
www.kendallhunt.com
Send all inquiries to:
4050 Westmark Drive
Dubuque, IA 52004-1840

CONTENTS

Chapter 7

The Dawn of a New Millennium
and the Current State of American Musical Theatre

CHAPTER *1*

THE WORLD OF MUSICAL THEATRE: INTRODUCTION, OVERVIEW, THEORY, AND BASICS

In 1904, popular star George M. Cohan strutted across Broadway in the smash hit *Little Johnny Jones*, acquiring iconic status as a "Yankee Doodle Boy," while audiences tapped their toes, hummed along, and reveled in the newly arrived American genre: musical comedy. Flash forward ninety years and American audiences could be found in front of their television sets watching *The Simpsons*, with another pop culture icon, Marge Simpson, singing, dancing, and even flying on stage as Blanche Dubois in *Oh, Streetcar!*, a fictionalized musical adaptation of Tennessee Williams' *A Streetcar Named Desire*. And in the first decade of the new millennium, postmodern America delighted in the animated antics of *Family Guy*'s Peter Griffin as he showboated a football touchdown by launching into *The Music Man*'s "Shipoopi," ultimately inciting a sing-along in the stadium which culminated in dancing in the urinals. These *Simpsons* and *Family Guy* segments represent the many musical theatre references

that have become the highly popular sitcoms' satiric signatures; but more important, they barely scratch the surface in regard to the innumerable send-ups of and references to musical theatre found in all entertainment mediums today, from film to television to web-based (or "new") media. In short, it seems that the musical of Cohan was not just a passing fad, an artifact resigned to yesteryear. Instead, musical theatre is a living art form that has not only passed the test of time, but also continues to find relevancy, with its spirit, heart, content, construct, and value built to last. How else does one explain the prevalence and ubiquity of musical theatre today, either in its legitimate form on the stage (and screen) or in its lampooned form found throughout pop culture? And, in the same vein, one must ponder as to why such musical theatre allusions communicate on visceral and shorthand levels to audiences, even eliciting laughs from some spectators who have never seen a musical. One reason is that the musical has been, and

continues to be, a significant part of America's heritage and culture. Audiences get the joke and even feel a sense of ownership and affection for the lampooned subject because they understand, at a fundamental level, the underlying concept, form, artistry, and history. The fact that the American musical is part of a cultural consciousness, even a cultural DNA, suggests that this art/entertainment form, which represents a common vernacular and promotes a shared dialogue, merits contextual, historical, and analytical interrogation. In short, the phenomenon not only helps illustrate why musical theatre matters, but also demonstrates why it is a fertile field of study.

Musical theatre is a nascent art form, coming to full fruition at the turn of the twentieth century. Further, musical theatre is unique in that it is the only theatrical genre born in and, thus, proprietarily claimed by America. Yet, its roots can be traced to European music and theatre arts, which were transplanted to the United States, as well as a multitude of other racial, ethnic, and indigenous entertainments that evolved on American soil, bespeaking the musical's uniquely hybrid, melting pot nature. In short, musical theatre reflects the nature of its birthplace. Thus, to study musical theatre is to study America, for the genre not only exemplifies the amalgamated spirit and constitution of the nation, it also reflects its culture, society, demography, and history. While musicals may be tuneful, entertaining, visually exciting, and emotionally engaging (and they certainly are), they also reflect an American identity, determined and altered by time, place, and circumstance. Through a musical, we might see a compilation of various music, drama, and art forms/constructs; contextual and historical artistry (including personal, biographical expressions by the author/s); and the influences of surrounding sociopolitical, cultural, and aesthetic movements (e.g., a current *Zeitgeist* and/or major political, social, and cultural developments). In addition, musical theatre is defined by an audience that responds to the content, artistry, and entertainment component based on ever-changing criteria of what is "new," "valuable," and "good." In all these respects, musical theatre represents a realm of diversity, mutability, and complexity, meriting significant scholastic exploration.

As one of the newest genres in the performing arts, musical theatre creatively and innovatively merged theatre (including written text) with musical compositions and dance. To understand musical theatre's unique identity and power, however, one must first grasp what is meant by the term **"genre"** and how it determines the study and practice of the arts. In the most general sense, a genre is a particular species, genus, type, or style. For the purposes of musical theatre study, we often use the fine arts definition of genre, that is, a class or category of artistic output that is bound or grouped by a particular form, content, technique, or the like. Examples of different genres in the performing arts include opera, operetta, symphonic music, ballet, contemporary dance, melodrama, classical tragedy, and farce. Genre distinction and definition plays a crucial role in how we view, study, enjoy, and critique works of art. Audiences want and need a certain degree of familiarity with the rules of the game when viewing a performance and interpreting the works before them; they want to know what to expect and can then evaluate the work based on predetermined rules and defining, codified characteristics. Due to its mixed breeding and amalgamated character, however, musical theatre took a while to be recognized as its own genre and, even today, it sometimes confounds "pure" genre categorization due to its mutated and crossbred nature. (For instance, one might be confused as to why a sung-through musical is not actually categorized as opera.) For this reason, it is necessary to understand that genre is also determined and validated by venue, authors, critics, scholars, performers, and audiences—in other words, positioning a work as a "musical" or presenting the work in a Broadway theater (as opposed to an opera house or dance hall) may be enough to solidify its genre categorization. Most often, however, there are certain distinctive and unifying components, models, and dynamics that signify a genre. In the case of the musical, one of its traditional delineators is a construct that is often termed the **"Golden Triangle."**

The Golden Triangle may be a simple concept, but it is the crux and, some might say, the underlying force of musical theatre. The Triangle represents a model in which three elements—music, words, and action—fuse to create an interactive, intersubjective theatrical entity. Such an idealized construct has also been called a "total work" (or *Gesamtkunstwerk*), first theorized and advocated in the 1850s by German opera composer, theorist, and auteur Richard Wagner. This ideal lauds the dynamic activity between tone (Wagner's term for music), dance (although Wagner mostly referred to stage blocking and movement), and poetry (a heightened version of text), suggesting that when such elements are balanced and mutually bound to each other, the combined "total work" becomes a transcendent phenomenon, promoting a heightened state of being and communal enlightenment for performers and audience members alike. This may sound a bit mysterious and lofty, but it basically suggests that there is great power and potential in the musical as its whole is greater than the sum of its parts. Among all other theatre genres, the musical is the unique form that is most often defined and empowered by the Golden Triangle, that is, an amalgamation of song, dance, *and* text. Further, in addition to the three Golden components, the musical is brought to life and empowered, in all its ephemeral glory, by the actual performance of said components. The performance (which includes the crucial contributions made by the performers) is at the center of the Triangle, for this live, definitive and ever-changing element weaves throughout a work, casting its inimitable spell and connecting the components while fleshing out and breathing life into the overall form. [see fig. 1.1]

It must be noted that the equilateral, fully integrated Golden Triangle is a philosophical concept—a traditional ideal. In reality, musicals rarely, if ever, exemplify such an idyllic balance between the three components. Most often, priority is given to one or two of the elements. And as the musical has moved into the modern and postmodern era, the Triangle has become increasingly warped, with contemporary manifestations isolating and neglecting certain components, redefining the genre overall (e.g., some of today's lauded "musicals" have variously omitted spoken dialogue, original music, live singing, and/or dance). Nonetheless, it is the concept, tradition, and ideal of the three components, combined and working together, that define musical theatre. This melded, multifaceted character makes the genre special and distinct. In fact, the collaborative nature of the musical is a marvel and miracle in its own right, for no other genre in the performing arts is the product of so many pooled resources. If the unsightly camel, as has often been joked, is a horse designed by a committee, the successful musical is a rare breed and exception to this cynical rule; for its "committee" process often results in a work of art: a stallion. Thus, as a starting point for the study of the genre, it is imperative to identify the musical's collaborative make-up, that is, its core components and contributing artists. In some cases, one person may do double duty (the lyricist/composer, for instance), while other times, every component may be provided by a separate artist or multiple artists may work together to supply one component (e.g., co-lyricists or co-librettists).

Figure 1.1

MUSIC

PERFORMANCE

WORDS
• Story
• Dialogue
• Lyrics

ACTION
• Dance
• Physicality

- **Composer**: the person who writes the music
- **Choreography**: the designed dance steps or movement on stage, created by the **choreographer**
- **Libretto (aka Book)**: the story, characters, script (the spoken dialogue), written by the **librettist**

  (Note: Technically, the libretto also includes the lyrics, but often they are not written by the librettist so "book" is more often used to refer to what is actually written by the librettist.)

- **Lyrics**: the words to the songs, written by the **lyricist**
- **Score**: the music and lyrics (also refers to the notation of the music, vocal parts, and instrumentation)

When reviewing the number of individuals and elements that must come together to realize a finished musical, another apt metaphor for the musical is that of a cake, created from critical ingredients and brought to fruition through the baking process (e.g., the performance). And with any baked good, there is a leavening—or rising—that occurs during the baking process. With the traditional musical, this leavening or rising phenomenon is represented by another defining dynamic of the traditional musical. This phenomenon may be referred to as the **Bubble Formula** [see fig. 1.2] and embodies the idea that, in musical theatre, when words can no longer express and contain heightened emotion, the body sings; and when song becomes insufficient, the body dances. The Bubble Formula represents the dynamics of the Golden Triangle. The effervescent progression is a result of the various Triangle elements working together to provide completely lyrical moments on stage ("lyrical" meaning a musicalized, poeticized, danced, or otherwise heightened moment of theatre that moves to a sphere beyond realism). For instance, in a traditional musical, a starry-eyed couple might share a scene in which they declare their love for one another. The orchestra swells under the dialogue and soon their passions cannot be contained by mere words and they begin a soaring duet, only to cap the affair with a dance number (possibly joined by the entire chorus). As such scenes exploit the Bubble trajectory, they also carry the audience along, for music and its expression take all participants to a higher place, quickening pulses and connecting humans emotionally and viscerally to other dimensions of existence, often going beyond sociopolitical and cultural meaning. This is an age-old concept that has been expounded, explored, and exploited universally by esoteric philosophers such as Friedrich Nietzsche, as well as everyday work-out trainers and film directors.

Like the Golden Triangle, the Bubble Formula is a traditional dynamic that has mutated as musical theatre has moved away from conventional constructs and forms. For instance, when a musical is completely sung through, there is no progression from spoken dialogue to song. Many may argue as to the diminished effervescence of musicals that are missing one of the elements that comprise the trajectory; but then again, breaking the rules of convention grabs attention and suggests new frontiers, possibly reinventing and energizing the genre overall.

Along with musical theatre's Triangle components, Bubble dynamic, and core constituents, there are other elementary terms and elements that comprise its musicological aspect (for first and foremost, the genre is a musical entity). And, as with any discipline, it is crucial to understand and use correct terminology when addressing such components and constructs; thus, some general musical terms are listed below, although many more will be broached and defined throughout this textbook:

- **A capella**: vocal music sung without accompaniment
- **Alto**: the lower pitched female or boy's voice; also called contralto
- **Ballad**: a slow, romantic song—or a song, often in a simple form, that tells a story
- **Baritone**: the range between tenor and bass for male voices (mid-range male voice)
- **Bass**: the lowest or deepest male voice
- **Chorus**: the dancing and/or singing ensemble of a musical production, with members having few or no solos and dialogue
- **Contrapuntal**: a song technique in which several characters sing separate melodies simultaneously; the contrapuntal song is structured so that each melody or voice is given the same weight
- **Duet**: a song or section of a song sung by or arranged for two voices
- **Key**: a series of tones forming any given major or minor scale
- **Key Signature**: the sharps (#) or flats (b) at the beginning of a staff, determining the key
- **Mezzo-soprano**: the range between alto and soprano for female voices (mid-range female voice)
- **Orchestration**: the arranging of music for the orchestra, as well as the written set of music with orchestral parts

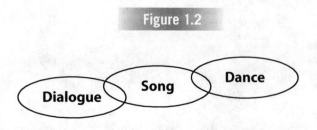

Figure 1.2

MUSIC = EXPRESSION + HEIGHTENED EMOTION

- **Patter Song**: a musical number with lyrics made up of many words, sung at a very rapid tempo (often to comic effect)
- **Recitative**: the sung speech in opera that drives the action forward (musicalized dialogue)
- **Rhythm**: the regular pulsation of music; the division of musical ideas into regular metrical portions
- **Soprano**: the highest pitched female and boy's voice
- **Syncopation**: rhythm characteristic of jazz, in which offbeats are emphasized
- **Tempo**: the speed of the rhythm
- **Tenor**: the high, natural male voice
- **Timbre**: the tone quality of a singing voice or a musical instrument
- **Time Signature**: a sign expressed in fractional figures that indicates the division of beats into measures (4/4, 2/4, 3/4)

In addition to the above-listed technical and musicological terminology, it is also important to understand some broader contextual concepts and terms that help define the overall musical theatre genre and industry. First, as was previously addressed, the locale or venue of a theatre production can determine its genre status, and one of the most potent determiners of musical theatre rank and file is a geographic area in New York City known worldwide as **Broadway**. This theatre district, also nicknamed the "Great White Way" or the "Main Stem," is widely recognized as home to the most prestigious commercial theatre in the English-speaking world. Technically, the district extends north to south from 59th Street to 40th and east to west from 6th Avenue (Avenue of the Americas) to 9th, with the actual street of Broadway running through the area's midsection. A Broadway theatre is considered one of the 40 professional houses in this vicinity (as well as the Lincoln Center) that seats 500 or more in its auditorium. Although New York's theatre district has migrated throughout the city's history, steadily moving uptown, its arrival at the current location coincided with the advent and validation of musical theatre as a genre. Thus, the American musical has often been indelibly tied to the mythos, industry, and geography of Broadway. (At this point, it must also be noted that London is another world capital for theatre, with the city's major commercial theatre district—the **West End**—being Broadway's counterpart across the pond. Musical theatre, however, was almost solely an American product, originating from Broadway, until the late 1970s.) Today, the Great White Way is one of America's top destinations for tourists, theatre lovers, and pop culture connoisseurs alike, with attendance in 2011 topping the 12 million mark. Although much truer in the days before the internet and new media, a musical's success and longevity is still very much determined by its Broadway tenure and reception. The number of Broadway performances (known as the show's "run") is one indicator used by many in the industry to determine value and achievement; another is the garnering of awards allocated by the American Theatre Wing and The Broadway League, known as the **Tony Awards** (officially known as the Antoinette Perry Award for Excellence in Theatre, named after Antoinette Perry, co-founder of the American Theatre Wing). These yearly awards recognize, in designated categories, the best in Broadway theatre (as well as one overall regional theatre award) and are America's professional theatre equivalent to the movie industry's Academy Awards (with the West End's equivalent being the Olivier Awards).

Although a cliché, it is also a truism that Broadway can make or break a new musical; but for many musicals, simply making it to Broadway is an achievement in and of itself. For most of the twentieth century, the road to the Main Stem entailed a period of trial performances, known as "**tryouts**," during which a new musical toured the provinces (any American city outside of New York) and underwent major or minor adjustments (or premature closure) according to initial media and audience reception before its official Broadway opening. Modern variations of the tryout include the development and staging of potential or planned Broadway works in major regional theatres across the country, as well as workshop productions of new musicals in New York City. In addition to the tenuous development, workshop, and tryout hurdles, a musical slated for the Great White Way must also secure and merit financing, as Broadway productions are pricey commercial ventures. Those willing to invest in these private-sector theatrical enterprises are known as "**backers**." Once a new musical finally lands on Broadway, its critical reception and box office success can majorly determine its shelf life, that is, its potential and status in the canon.

At this point, the term "**canon**" should also be explained. In fine arts, a canon is an authoritatively and popularly established (and thereby sanctioned) body or collection of related works. In terms of musical theatre, the canon is the select group of musicals that have stood the test of time; they not only hold noteworthy places in the genre's history but are frequently revived and enjoy an acknowledged place of distinction, suggesting that they will henceforth continue to be performed as signature examples of the genre. It is crucial to note, however, that the canon is not a set entity, for its contents are ever-shifting as musicals variously move in and out of canonical standing. A show may be a major hit in its day, only to fall by the wayside, lost to history as time passes. On the other hand, a production may be a disappointment upon its debut, only to have its book and score rediscovered, revived (and re-envisioned), and positively received, ultimately earning canonical status. Further, long-running Off-Broadway hits and cult favorites may join the established Broadway works in the canon roster, only to fade away again if they cannot attract a wide enough audience. It must also be said that the canon is greatly determined by the opinions of and categorizations made by critics and scholars. Such authoritative voices may deem a musical worthy of survival and permanence, or they may pan a musical, resigning it to the dustbins of history (in fact, there are some originally lauded works that have faded in time but still hold some canonical status in terms of historical significance and merit, often kept alive by musical theatre scholars, historians, and aficionados). Contrarily, the "thumbs down" verdicts by authorities are sometimes defied by public opinion; for example, a show slammed by the critics may, nonetheless, enjoy a healthy box office, continuing to be a popular draw for theatres far into the future. In fact, this tug-of-war between the mass theatre-going populace of America and the system of subjective canonization, categorization and valuation by elite authorities has long influenced the reputation and reception of musical theatre. Cultural elites in America have traditionally designated works or disciplines, according to their subjective benchmarks, as "high art" (or "highbrow"), positioning such as artistically or aesthetically superior to and more viable than the works enjoyed by the common populace, deemed "popular" (and consequently "lowbrow"). Similar divisions are made for the categories of "art" (works which may be non-formulaic, challenging, enlightening, thought-provoking, unique and/or transcendent) and "entertainment" (pleasurable, familiar, engaging, and/or titillating), ignoring the fact that art can be entertaining and entertainment can also be art.

Musical theatre evolved from the popular stage and continues to be a *popular* form of *entertainment*—a lineage and character which has long hindered its acceptance as a high art form. Thus, to study and appreciate the art, entertainment, and highbrow/lowbrow character of musical theatre, it is imperative to put aside the idea that any of these descriptors and categories should be applied as concrete determiners of value and merit. Indeed, the contextualization and categorization of art should be seen as fluid, depending on the historical, sociopolitical, and cultural mores, values, and tastes of a certain time, place, and demographic (e.g., Shakespeare's works were considered popular entertainments in his day, only to be regarded as barbaric artifacts during the Neoclassic theatre reign and then highbrow art in modern times). So, to end this introductory chapter to the world of musical theatre, a potent illustration of the genre's mutability and diversity must be set forth, including lists of canonical examples that will assuredly change over time. Below is a brief overview of the multitude of musical subgenres and variations that variously define (and complicate) the genre today:

- **Book Musical or Integrated Book Musical**: Traditional musical form in which the libretto is integrated with song and dance to tell a linear narrative. The integrated book musical came to its pinnacle and dominated the genre during the mid-twentieth century (often denoted as the musical's Golden Age) but is still seen as the classical musical form and continues to wield great clout, exemplified by contemporary original hits such as *Wicked*, *Memphis*, and *The Book of Mormon*.

- **Rock Musical or Pop Rock Musical**: Modern musical built upon a contemporary music aesthetic (e.g., rock 'n' roll, hip hop, alternative), including heavy amplification and electric instrumentation, centering on themes of youth, counter culture, alienation, and rebellion. Prime examples include *Hair*, *Rent*, *Spring Awakening*, *Rock of Ages*, *In the Heights*, *American Idiot*, and *Spider-Man: Turn Off the Dark*.

- **Concept Musical**: Modern musical in which the theme or idea is more important than plot, that is, songs and dances are connected by a theme to convey an idea instead of relaying a "linear" story. Examples include the many landmark works by composer/lyricist Stephen Sondheim.

- **Sung-Through Musical**: Modern musical form which resembles an opera in that it is mostly sung and underscored, with little or no spoken dialogue. Champions of the form include composer Andrew Lloyd Webber, as well as writing team Boublil and Schönberg.

- **Jukebox Musical ("Disguised Concert" or "Musical Survey")**: A musical consisting of a series of already written songs (often popular hits) connected into a loose storyline. The compiled score can be a collection of songs by one, two, or more composers and the book is sometimes semi-autobiographical. Popular and critically acclaimed contemporary jukebox works include *Mamma Mia!, Jersey Boys, Fela!, Rock of Ages, Movin' Out, Million Dollar Quartet, Priscilla, Queen of the Desert.*

- **Dance Musical ("Dansical")**: A musical that is almost entirely danced, with little or no spoken dialogue and often a jukebox score. Significant examples include *Dancin', Fosse, Contact, Movin' Out*, and *Come Fly Away.*

- **Reflexive Musical**: A postmodern category of self-referential musicals that celebrate and/or poke fun at their own musical identity, alerting the audience to the genre's conventions and character, e.g., *Urinetown, The Producers, Monty Python's Spamalot, Rock of Ages.*

- **Screen-to-Stage Musical**: A musical using the book (and some or all of the score) of an existing film. The category has found dominance on Broadway in the last few decades with past and present hits including *Disney's Beauty and the Beast, The Lion King, The Producers, The Full Monty, Hairspray, The Color Purple, Billy Elliot, Mary Poppins, Shrek the Musical, Sister Act, Newsies*, and *Once.*

- **Revivals**: The restaging of a musical on Broadway after its initial run—revivals can be archival (replicating the original), traditional (restaging in the spirit or style of the original, but with some conceptual reinterpretation), or revisionist (completely reinterpreting the look, feel, sound, and/or concept of the original).

The above categories will be discussed in much greater detail throughout this book, but it is important at this point to recognize that musical theatre is neither a static nor rigidly codified art form (even though there are certain ideal and consistent constructs and components associated with the genre, as earlier detailed). In fact, many contemporary musicals fall into multiple categories (e.g., *Rock of Ages*—a rock musical with a jukebox score that is also reflexive), further demonstrating the flexibility of the genre and the difficulty of pigeon-holing a musical today. And although one might cite traditional constructs and dynamics such as the Golden Triangle and Bubble Formula as starting points and defining elements, rules are also made to be broken. The divergent forms may defy conventional precepts, but they also demonstrate the ever-evolving and dynamic nature of musical theatre.

CHAPTER 2

FORGING THE WAY:
MUSICAL THEATRE ANTECEDENTS

• •

Art never happens in a vacuum. Anything seemingly "new" is actually the offspring of many antecedent forms, movements, genres, precepts, and works. Such is the case with the American musical; for true to its melting pot origins, the genre found its voice and form in mélange fashion, taking a little here, a little there, fusing disparate (or similar) elements, while fine-tuning and editing aspects along the way. In an evolutionary manner, the musical merged Old World genres/constructs with new ideas and entertainment trends in order to effectively speak to a wildly diverse demographic, all the while working to earn and sustain box office profits (a necessary goal, given that American theatre has never received the national funding historically enjoyed in Europe). Within this commercial, "showbiz" arena, artists aimed to please an American audience thirsting for theatrical entertainment reflective of their own milieu and mindset, while imbuing such works with cache and familiarity by referencing and incorporating European genres traditionally revered as legitimate "art" forms. Thus, to fully understand the musical, one must be aware of the antecedents that are not only referenced in musical theatre, but are also a part of its DNA.

Before addressing musical theatre's most significant and definitive antecedents, however, it would be useful to unpack the concept of "genre evolution." Most scholars embrace the idea that a genre is a live, ever-evolving entity. Yet there also exists a pervasive intimation that any new genre or work is more ideally realized than its forbearers, that is, it is a "higher" form of art. Throughout this textbook, one should repeatedly question and challenge this concept, often referred to as "cultural Darwinism," with the understanding that *new* does not automatically equal *better* (or more "highly" evolved). Each movement or work must be contextualized and historicized on its own terms and merits,

taking into account place, time, conventions, and surrounding context in order to assess value, novelty, and contribution. Along these lines, it is also important to recognize the fallacy of framing musical theatre's many developments and innovations as artistic advancements that simultaneously signaled the demotion (or even demise) of previous reigning forms/constructs. Indeed, when the concept musical became all the rage on Broadway in the 1970s, many industry elites predicted the death of the linear book musical which had previously defined and dominated the Golden Age. As we can see today, such a short-sighted declaration missed the mark, for evolutions do not always signal the end of predecessors but, instead, often facilitate a mergence of past and present. Case in point, the traditional book musical is still alive, kicking, and raking in the profits on contemporary Broadway (i.e., *Wicked*, *Memphis*, *The Book of Mormon*, and *Newsies*). Further, these "old school" types sit alongside concept musicals, as well as many other reconfigurations of the conventional form (sung-through musicals, dansicals, jukebox musicals, rock musicals). In short, the evolved musical genre is a vital entity that thrives as a result of its ability to morph, edit, and expand; incorporating its own particular history as it also signals the future. Genre evolution is a fragmented and/or fluid process—never a simple, qualitative linear move. Art is messy—ideas make vital contact with other ideas and works are formed as a result of amalgamation and assimilation. And audiences (as well as learned scholars and critics) often judge works according to their own aesthetics and *Zeitgeist*. In fact, it is difficult to surmise what future audiences will think of spectacles and idiosyncratic works such as *Cats*, *The Lion King*, and *Avenue Q*—all phenomenal hits in their time. A time machine would be a handy way to handle this complicated aspect of musical theatre study; but as time travel is not possible, we must do our best to fully understand and appreciate the history, context, and genealogy of musical theatre. As a starting point, it is helpful to know the genre's for-bearers—those highly influential, inspirational antecedents that shaped this new art form—as well as the types of audiences ready and willing to embrace new developments and genres; for this fomenting, facilitative environment paved the way for the American musical.

OPERA, BALLAD OPERA, COMIC OPERA, AND OPERETTA

Musical theatre is considered to be an American invention, born in the late 1800s and fully realized during the twentieth century. In essence, however, the musical is also considered to be one of theatre's most ancient and universal forms/constructs. While the separation of song, dance, and spoken drama ultimately became an artistically codified and defining aspect of European theatre, this departmentalized model was not always the case or defining rule. In fact, throughout history, many revered forms of theatre around the world employed all three elements in a merged paradigm and placed this construct as the ideal model for stage entertainment and drama. (Asian and African theatre genres traditionally incorporate all entities in holistic fashion, driven by longstanding beliefs that *theatre* is a merged and transformative practice of song/dance/storytelling). Specifically, the birth of Western classical drama is credited to the ancient Greeks who introduced tragedy through Athenian competitions in 534 BCE at the City Dionysia (with the comedy category added in 486 BCE). For centuries, this theatre festival was a cultural pinnacle, resulting in works that have proved timeless, e.g., masterpieces by Aeschylus, Sophocles, Euripides, and Aristophanes. To read the works today, however, one might not realize that the original productions were fully musicalized, with much of the text sung and danced (although, we do not actually know the extent to which the "sung/danced" components would fit our current-day definitions). The Romans continued the musical traditions of the Greeks; for example, the comedies of Plautus (254–184 BCE) could be deemed ancient models of musical comedy, with much of the dialogue written to be sung and physical farce conveyed through dance. Sanctioned theatre waned during the Medieval Age; yet its resurgence happened in the churches, with music playing a major part in the highly theatrical Catholic liturgies and tropes (not to mention

the unauthorized activities of the rural mimes, troubadours, etc.). And at the height of the Renaissance, another titan of Western theatre, William Shakespeare (1564–1616), included song and dance in many of his most popular comedies and romances, often metatheatrically employing musical interpolations, sometimes framed as entertainments within the plot of the play. In the 1660s, another leading figure in the European theatrical world, French playwright Molière (1622–73), actually looked back to the Greeks as he created what he declared to be a novel form of theatre for the court of King Louis XIV: the *comédie-ballet*. Molière's first *comédie-ballet*, *Les Fâcheux* (1661), was born out of necessity when King Louis ordered the playwright to stage both a ballet and a play for a special court celebration. Having too few dancers for a court ballet proper, Molière inserted brief ballet interludes into the play, defending the mash-up as a return to the merged drama/music/dance model of the classical Greek theatre. The new work pleased both King Louis and court audiences; thus, collaborating with powerful court composer Jean-Baptiste Lully (1632–87) and dance master Pierre Beauchamp (1631–c.1719), Molière created twelve more *comédie-ballets* in his lifetime, with one of the most successful being *The Bourgeois Gentleman* (1670).

At this juncture, it must be noted that an overview of musical theatre ancestry, as well as attempts to definitively categorize or reference "musical theatre" antecedents, can become a convoluted project due to issues of place, time, context, convention, authorship, and reception. For instance, both Shakespeare and Molière were playwrights and producers who sought to please public tastes and royal sponsors, incorporating song and dance as necessary, but with no conscious aim and/or design to create a novel form of "musical play." During their lifetimes, however, another theatre genre was introduced and developed in Europe by artists and scholars in a conscious attempt to assert a codified musical form that could artistically and aesthetically reign on the European stage. The genre came to be known as "**opera**;" and despite its beginnings as an exclusive court entertainment, it eventually moved to the public arena and became a prominent, influential form of theatrical and musical art/entertainment for centuries. Given its purposeful "musical drama" design and character in the Renaissance, opera is often cited as the most direct ancestor of musical theatre.

To appreciate the invention and evolution of opera, one must return to the 1400s, during which the Italian Renaissance was fueled by the decline of the Byzantine Empire and fall of Constantinople in 1453, resulting in a Western European rediscovery of ancient Greek culture. In the late 1500s, a cohort of Florentine scholars, humanists, and artists (including composers Iacopo Peri and Giulio Caccini, and poet Ottavio Rinuccini)—known as the Camerata—sought to increase Italy's artistic import and influence by reviving the Greek drama in its purist musical form (or what they perceived to be the sung-through format of the classical Greek tragedy on stage). They attempted an approximation of the Greek aesthetic and construct for their sixteenth-century court entertainment. After the Camerata's first operatic endeavor, Caccini's *Dafne* (1594), the concept was further developed by classical artists such as Claudio Monteverdi, whose *L'Orfeo* (1607) set a new benchmark for the burgeoning genre. Initially termed *"Dramma per musica,"* the new musical form would soon be referred to as *"opera seria,"* a completely sung-through work in which the *da capo* aria became the defining component. Specifically, this style of solo aria is an A-B-A song form in which a first section (A) introduces a musical theme, the second section (B) offers a complementary one, and the third section repeats the first theme (A) with vocal ornamentation provided by the singer (given the artistic liberty allowed the ornamentation of the arias, many of the *opera seria* singers became the "rock stars" of their day). Soon, opera moved beyond the exclusivity of the court, with the first public opera house opening in Venice in 1637. As opera became a highly popular and influential theatre art in Europe, the genre's overall structure continued to adhere to a strict neoclassic formula (aria, variation, duet, recitative, and choral passage) while its material also became highly codified and regimented throughout the 1700s. Numerous works from this period live on today, resulting in the fact that *classical* opera may still be defined according to many of the following traditional characteristics: (1) A classical opera is often dramatically "serious," depicting tragic stories of a noble or mythic nature. (2) An opera is completely sung through, composed of arias, recitatives, duets, and ensemble/choral passages that require virtuosic voices. (3) The instrumental underscoring and accompaniments are grand and orchestral. (4) The productions are staged with opulence and largess. Soon, however, the highly codified nature of opera's format, style, and subject matter (such as its

early preoccupation with royal and/or mythic subjects) not only became perceived as stilted on the "highbrow" stage, but also provided fodder for "lowbrow" satirists. In short, opera was seen as an art form ripe for skewering. And in this revolutionary, irreverent, and artistic spirit, the **ballad opera** was born, a reactionary genre which not only parodied opera but also provided relevant sociopolitical commentary and musical entertainment that spoke to the common man.

John Gay (1685–1732) is credited with creating the first ballad opera, *The Beggar's Opera*, which debuted on January 29, 1728. With musical collaborator Johann Christoph Pepusch and theatre manager John Rich (who debuted the work at the Lincoln's Inn Fields Theatre), Gay presented to London audiences a musical work which lampooned *opera seria* by turning the world of gods, goddesses, and royalty on its head. *The Beggar's Opera* depicts and celebrates a seedy, conniving, and raucous world of street criminals, whores, and beggars, all of whom live according to their own code of morals and honor. The topsy-turvy landscape highlights and excuses gutter behavior—such as the hair-pulling catfight-cum-duet between two "prima donnas" of ill repute competing for the affections of a slimy crook—while framing England's royalty, elites, and legal establishment as the more corrupt

Michael Redgrave and Audry Mildmay in 1940 UK Production of *The Beggar's Opera* © Gwen Watford Collection/Lebrecht Music & Arts/Corbis

and pathetic segments of society. If the subject matter wasn't enough to lure and entertain London commoners, Gay also implemented the concept of using familiar compositions for the score, e.g., popular tavern tunes, folk themes, and classical melodies (such as those by Handel, Purcell, and other well-known composers). Spectators from all walks of society could basically hum along with the melodies while delighting in the creator's witty application of new lyrics. Gay also did away with the burdensome recitative by adding spoken dialogue between the songs. All of which delighted London audiences and the production was a major hit, so much so that an oft-repeated quip of the day was that *Beggar's Opera* "made Gay rich and Rich gay" (referencing John Rich, manager of the theater). Its success led to a profusion of ballad operas by other writers, while drawing the ire of British authorities, who did not take well to the satirical critiques and accused many productions of sedition. Ultimately, in 1737, a highly offended British Prime Minister Robert Walpole led Parliament in banning the theatrical staging of ballad operas. As a result, a sequel to *Beggar's Opera* by Gay and Pepusch, titled *Polly*, could not be produced until 1777, after the ban was lifted. By that time, however, the legal restrictions had greatly weakened the genre, and the production was all but dismissed as "old news."

Importantly, the British ban on ballad opera was impossible to enforce overseas in the American colonies. As early as 1735, the ballad opera *Flora*, or *Hob in the Well* was presented in Charleston, South Carolina, with many historians placing *Flora* as the first staged "musical" production in what would become the United States. Fifteen years later, the American premiere of *The Beggar's Opera* was greeted with wild enthusiasm, debuting on December 3, 1750, in New York City. Its impudent spirit spoke to the colonists; and the show's popularity can be cited as a significant beginning for the development of the musical theatre in America.

Along with ballad opera, other forms of light musical drama were developed throughout Europe during the eighteenth century: the French *opéra comique*, the German *singspiel*, and the Italian *opera buffa*. All of these genres were forms of **comic opera**, another reaction to *opera seria*, containing content that was more audience-friendly, spirited, occasionally satiric, lighthearted, and romantic. As part of their populist demeanor, the forms were written in native languages, as opposed to Italian (the traditional idiom of early opera).

In France, the comic opera, or ***opéra comique***, is said to have developed in the early 1700s out of entertainments performed at fairground theatres in which comic and romantic tales were acted out in pantomime by performers playing stock characters (many borrowed from *commedia dell'arte*). During the scenes, other actors, dressed as cupids, held up placards on which the characters' dialogue and speeches (in verse) were written; and the spectators were invited to sing the sentiments aloud to popular tunes, helped along by other performers planted in the audience. As *opéra comique* evolved, it became more like ballad opera, losing its early improvisational and audience-participation elements and incorporating more satire and sociopolitical content, while moving into legitimate Parisian theaters. The works were written in French; and dialogue was added between songs. Eventually, the scores consisted of original compositions, requiring virtuosic singing voices, and content moved from completely comic/satiric to more sentimental (e.g., George Bizet's *Carmen*).

While the beginnings of *opéra comique* were being enjoyed by audiences at fairgrounds in France, other types of comic operas, written in native languages, were taking root around the continent. Specifically, German audiences were enjoying their own brand of comic opera, the humorous and fanciful ***singspiel***, which provided showcase roles for German actors by incorporating dialogue and colorful character portrayals and combining them with virtuosic vocal work by highly trained singers. The *singspiel* reached great heights in the late 1770s, when Emperor Joseph II sought to expand the form and commissioned composers such as Wolfgang Amadeus Mozart. Mozart's triumphant and fantastical *The Magic Flute*, written in 1791 for the Vienna Folk Theater, proved to be a watershed moment for the form, while changing the face of what would henceforth be considered "classical" opera. Yet, Mozart was not confined to the *singspiel*, for he also created *The Marriage of Figaro* (1786), one of the most celebrated examples of ***opera buffa***, the Italian version of comic opera. *Opera buffa*, like its German and French counterparts, sought to exploit the musicality (and virtuosity) of opera, while appealing to a broad populace. Specifically, the genre exploited the spirit of *commedia dell'arte*, an improvisational Neapolitan form of comedy, romance, and music that flourished in the 1600s, eventually finding prominence in established theatrical venues throughout the 1700s. *Buffa* has also been traced to the *intermezzi*, comic one-act interludes that played as intermission entertainments between the acts of serious Italian operas. *Opera buffa* flourished for centuries, with new works continuing to find great popularity on the nineteenth-century musical stage (e.g., Gioachino Rossini's *The Barber of Seville* and Gaetano Donizetti's *The Elixir of Love*). While *opera buffa*, the *singspiel*, and *opéra comique* demonstrated a more lighthearted, native, and populist style and treatment of opera, the significant impact of the three genres was helped by the fact that many exemplary works were accepted into the repertories of recognized commercial and national theaters. With such public and private support, comic operas flourished and a new canon was established. Furthermore, the spirit and form of the comic opera inspired a new genre which rose to theatrical prominence in the nineteenth and twentieth centuries. The genre was termed **"operetta"** or **"light opera."** Eventually, the operetta reined on the European stage, while it also jumped the pond to become an early American craze.

Most historians and scholars trace the operetta's origins to comic-opera forays by German-born French composer Jacques Offenbach (1819–1880). When *L'Alcove* (1847), one of Offenbach's earliest one-act *opera buffas*, was well-received in Paris, he was inspired to buy a theater near the Champs-Elysées; and in 1855, the composer opened his Théâtre des Bouffes-Parisiens. Using his theater as a showcase, Offenbach exploited the idea of satirical short operas (he called them "musiquettes"), but he eventually wrote the full-length *Orphée aux Enfers* (*Orpheus in the Underworld*), which opened at the Bouffes-Parisiens in 1858. *Orphée aux Enfers* is a cheeky and lively parody of Christoph Gluck's *Orfeo ed Euridice* (1762), one of classical opera's most significant early works. In the ballad-opera and comic-opera vein, Offenbach's production incorporated stinging contemporary satire, clever couplets, and an infectious, melodic score (which has been immortalized due to its introduction of the iconic can-can). The work, now cited as a seminal operetta, was a sensation; and by the time of Offenbach's death, he had composed over 100 operettas, many of which were produced around Europe in musical capitals such as London and Vienna. The genre moved overseas in the 1880s with the New York premiere of Offenbach's *La Vie Parisienne* (1866), setting in motion the operetta craze in America. Offenbach's work also inspired other masters of the new form, including composer Johann Strauss II (1825–1899), whose operettas such as *Die Fledermaus*

(1874), along with numerous others by contemporaries, contributed to what has been deemed the Golden Age of the Operetta, which climaxed in America with the phenomenal popularity of composer Franz Lehár's *The Merry Widow* (1905). Lehár's romantic work set box offices ablaze in 1907 (remaining popular until 1930), with Americans in every segment of society experimenting with the "naughty" dance craze of the waltz, taking partners in their arms and moving in 3/4 time to the show's title song. By this time, the popular European operetta had become somewhat formulaic, with certain genre characteristics becoming codified. Such characteristics include dialogue being used instead of recitative; original scores that include cheerful, lilting, lyrical melodies (a lot of waltzing time signatures) while still requiring vocal virtuosity; decorative sets and costumes, stock characters, and escapist librettos that revolve around comic and/or romantic plots, often set in far-off, fictional lands. The fanciful storylines contain contrived adventures of princes/princesses/nobility (often with one party disguised as a "commoner") that resolve happily when pretexts are dropped and obstacles are overcome. The happy ending usually entails a wedding. At the height of the operetta craze, French and Viennese works had become so ubiquitous and powerful in America that some feared that their popularity might hinder the development of more indigenous musical forms (fears were unfounded, however, as home-grown works soon found their own power and popularity on the American musical stage, as will be seen in the upcoming Victor Herbert section).

W. S. GILBERT AND ARTHUR SULLIVAN

The French and Viennese operettas were not the only foreign, classical genres which dominated and influenced the early American musical arena, for American audiences were also quite smitten with the **light operas** penned by W. S. Gilbert and Arthur Sullivan. The duo's canonical works expanded beyond their native home of Great Britain to theatrically reign in the United States during the late 1800s and early 1900s, serving as powerful antecedents and inspirations in regards to the nation's emerging musical theatre.

William Schwenck Gilbert (1836–1911) was already an established satirist and author in 1871 when he was paired, by powerful theatre impresario Richard D'Oyly

Carte, with prolific classical composer Arthur Sullivan (1842–1900), who was known for his popular hymns, marches, and anthems. The operettas of Gilbert and Sullivan, with Sullivan's compositions inspired by the works of Offenbach and written to match the witty lyrics and librettos penned by Gilbert, would immortalize both men. Beginning with their first collaborative success, the one-act *Trial by Jury* (1875), they produced a prolific canon of 13 full-length light operas (also termed "operettas") that not only triumphed in London and throughout Europe, but in America as well. The trend began with their fourth production, *HMS Pinafore* (a satire revolving around the British imperial navy), which enjoyed international success after opening in London in 1878. That same year, the work debuted in Boston and was such an unprecedented hit that it eventually played simultaneously at eight New York theaters, with approximately one hundred North American touring companies presenting their own "versions" of the show. Unfortunately, the widespread popularity of the work also created artistic and financial headaches for its authors. Many of the New York and touring productions were unlicensed, unauthorized, and liberally adapted interpretations of the original, given the lack of international copyright agreements established with the United States at the time (in short, a "foreign" work received no copyright protection in the United States). Adding further injury to insult, Gilbert and Sullivan were unable to secure royalties from the productions. When the pair wrote their next hit, *Pirates of Penzance*, they tried to remedy this situation by giving the new show a private reading before an audience of 45 in the small English town of Paignton on December 30, 1879, thus securing rights in Europe. Then, in a deft move, they followed the very next day with the "official premiere" of *Pirates* in New York City, which they produced themselves (along with D'Oyly Carte), while they also delayed publishing the score and libretto, keeping it from thieving eyes. When the production opened at New York's Fifth Avenue Theatre, it was greeted enthusiastically; but more importantly, its quality and profits could be controlled by the producers and it was covered under American copyright law. (It must be noted, however, that this still didn't fully prevent American bootleg productions of the show, as well as many other Gilbert/Sullivan works, even though the pair also established "official" U.S. touring companies to combat the problem.) *Pirates* did not open in London until April 3, 1880, where it became the second international hit for the duo. By 1881, the reputation of Gilbert and Sullivan had become so impressive that D'Oyly Carte built the Savoy Theater in London to specifically house their repertoire. Their subsequent string of hits would grow to include other major light operas such as *The Mikado, Ruddigore, The Gondoliers,* and *Iolanthe.* As opposed to many of the European operettas of the Golden Age, much of the Gilbert and Sullivan canon is still produced today, delighting steadfast "G & S" acolytes (known as "Savoyards"), as well new fans who find themselves smitten by the sound, content, and aesthetic of the team's oeuvre. Specifically, the Gilbert and Sullivan body of work can be characterized by certain elements: (1) a significant degree of witty political and social satire in the libretto, which uses both recitative and dialogue; (2) a topsy-turvy worldview in which societies are fantastically imagined, reversing and upending class/power strictures and social norms, with all crises resolved via a "miraculous" tongue-in-cheek ending (what is conventionally termed a *deus ex machina*); (3) a diverse and densely written score that highlights clever, showy lyrics, while requiring virtuosic vocal skills. Here, it must be noted that Sullivan composed to Gilbert's already written rhymes, which could force him into what some musicologists have deemed a "tumpty-tumpty" meter to suit Gilbert's deftly rhymed and strictly measured verse (e.g., a signature G & S patter song such as "I Am the Very Model of a Modern Major-General" from *Pirates*). Yet Sullivan's compositions could also vary greatly, resulting in scores that contain soaring operatic refrains, infectious marches, lyrical ballads, and solemn anthems. Gilbert and Sullivan's partnership lasted from 1871 to 1896. During the twenty-five years, the duo created a light opera canon that has not only proved timeless but has become its own genre, a cross between the ballad opera and European operetta, as well as one of the most significant forerunners of American musical theatre.

MELODRAMA

While classical European opera and its offspring (ballad opera, comic opera, operetta, and light opera) were obvious predecessors to the American musical, other non-operatic types of theatre proved equally influential in the genre's development. Although America's theatre was a mélange and evolution of the European forms carried to its shores, its early survival depended on the ability to thwart Puritan founders' denouncements and prohibitions (given their moral opposition to the stage).

In fact, America's earliest documented theatre performance became an instance of Puritan censorship and legal jeopardy, for when three amateur actors produced and performed *Ye Bare and Ye Cubb* in Virginia in 1665, they were put on trial by citizens for indecency (they were ultimately absolved of wrong-doing by the appointed judge). This situation exemplifies the challenges faced by those determined to bring theatre to the New World, which makes all the more impressive the fact that one dramatic genre was able to overcome such obstacles to win critical approval and widespread fandom. Maybe it was the genre's exploitation of Judeo-Christian concepts in regards to moral certitude and justice, as well as its favored status in Europe, but **melodrama** became the number one choice of theatrical escape for Americans, beginning in the late 1700s and continuing throughout the next century. And as melodrama dominated the stage, it could not help but leave an indelible imprint on the nascent musical.

Many historians believe that melodrama evolved from the French *opéra comique* of the 1780s and '90s, with dialogue added to sentimental storylines that centered on stock characters undergoing dramatic trials and triumphing in a morally absolute world. While the text was increasingly spoken, however, musical elements persisted in the shape of instrumental underscoring (and an occasional ornamental song). Given its fantastic plotlines, with twists and turns that defied logic and upset decorum, melodrama was also seen as a reaction against the strict dictates of Neoclassic theatre, which had ruled the European stage since the early 1600s. The new form soon monopolized the popular theatre on both continents in the 1800s, as the "masses" (especially a burgeoning middle class) embraced the form. The new phenomenon of leisure time during the Industrial Age facilitated a flood of new audiences demanding more and more stage titillation, sentiment, and spectacle, tempered by moral affirmation. Thus, melodramas were churned out almost nonstop by European masters such as French playwright Rene Charles Guilbert de Pixérécourt (1773–1844) and German playwright August von Kotzebue (1761–1819). In America, melodramas were favored over more classical fare, especially the many translations or adaptations by playwrights such as William Dunlap (1766–1838) who is often referred to as the "Father of American Drama." By the mid-1800s, the genre had became the most popular and pervasive in the country, squeezing out other dramatic forms, with prolific playwrights

such as Dion Boucicault (1820–1890), Augustin Daly (1838–1899), and David Belasco (1853–1931) industriously creating a string of hits, each one more elaborate and fantastic than the other, in order to satisfy the growing public demand.

As melodrama's popularity grew, it also became known for its highly codified style and content. Melodrama's formulaic characteristics would also become signature, constitutive components of traditional musical theatre, only to be slowly challenged, altered, and even dismissed as the musical evolved through the Golden Age. Similar to musical theatre, melodrama is a musical entity. Its coined name means **"music drama,"** for the melodrama uses music in a dramatic fashion to heighten dialogue, sentiment, and action (much like a film score). This element includes continuous instrumental underscoring that consists of musical passages termed **"melos,"** often arranged by house musicians in order to support the script (e.g., "pathetics" for tear-jerking scenes or "hurries" for nail-biting action). Along with the melos, played by pit orchestras, onstage pianos, or anything in-between, several incidental songs could also be inserted into the story and performed by the characters. A melodrama's plot is built upon **intrigue** and **suspense**, with a virtuous hero and/or heroine often hounded by a villain but triumphing in the end after undergoing threats to life, reputation, and happiness. Suspense builds as a result of the climactic moments used to end every act (e.g., the heroine being tied to the railroad tracks) and other plot devices such as cases of concealed or mistaken identities, abductions, strange coincidences, and discoveries of hidden documents. Melodrama's thematic foundation and rule of order, a concept termed **"poetic justice,"** guarantees a happy ending for its virtuous characters, as well as its audience. Poetic justice dictates that good folks are rewarded and bad folks always punished. In most melodramas, good and evil are treated as absolutes (no grey areas), and such qualities are rarely affected or determined by circumstances or environment. While the universe of the melodrama is anything but static (for example, the evildoer may ultimately repent and receive redemption or the bereft pauper might reap a great fortune), the actual natures of the characters are most often fixed. These determined characteristics provide melodramas with their conventional cast of archetypes, known as **stock characters**. The lead roles include the **ingénue**, who is a sweet, virginal young woman often put in peril by the **villain** (the bad guy) and saved by her romantic interest, the **hero**, a brave, pure-hearted leading man. Supporting stock roles include the **matron**, who is an older woman, often a spinster or married shrew, depicted as an unattractive butt of jokes, and the male or female **sidekicks**, who contrast the purity of their leading character companions (for example, sidekick types include the saucy, sexualized female and the foolish or dodgy male). Although sidekicks provide comic relief, comedy can also be supplied by minor **servant** roles. Lastly, there is often an **elderly man**, portrayed as a doddering and/or lecherous fool or a source of mature counsel. The final defining characteristic of the melodrama is also indicative of the Industrial Age's obsession with and advances in technology. Specifically, the nineteenth-century melodrama relied heavily upon elaborate stage spectacle, specifically in regard to the "**sensation scenes**." In these climatic scenes, natural disasters such as floods, fires, snow-storms, and avalanches, as well as explosions, oncoming trains, and even chariot horse races, were simulated on stage by use of elaborate stage techniques and devices such as treadmills, moving panoramas, lighting effects, fireworks, thunder boards, and wind machines.

When citing melodrama as a musical theatre antecedent, it should be noted that the most significant melodrama of all time was also one of the most musical. In 1852, Harriet Beecher Stowe's *Uncle Tom's Cabin* made its landmark literary debut, and numerous playwrights immediately sought to adapt the work for the stage. George L. Aiken's version, however, was by far the most successful and lives today as the exemplar of melodrama's import and power in America. Aiken's play, which opened in New York City in 1953, was populated by stock characters, many of whom became iconic (the villainous Simon LeGree and the saintly Uncle Tom) and was built upon suspense and sentiment, continually vacillating between dramatic highs and lows, while scenic spectacle contributed to its epic nature (especially thrilling was the staging of Eliza's river crossing). Most important, however, was the work's strong moral center and purpose. *Uncle Tom's Cabin* not only addressed but also sought to redress a great social ill as the production became a theatrical tool for abolitionist groups across America. (It should be noted that although many melodramas illuminated socioeconomic and class inequities in order to dramatically frame and heighten their plots' crises, threats,

struggles, and fortune reversals, the genre's main goal, overall, was entertainment, not revolution or social change.) Another defining performance aspect of *Uncle Tom's Cabin* was its music, for the play incorporated hymns, spirituals, original character songs ("Uncle Tom's Religion"), and plantation songs by the likes of Stephen Foster (performed by the characters or, sometimes, accompanying choirs), as well as instrumental underscoring (melos) throughout. In time, productions of *Uncle Tom's Cabin* came to resemble revivals; and it became the most popular and produced play of the nineteenth century, with numerous adaptations and versions by other writers staged across the country. After the Civil War, thousands of touring productions became known as "Tom shows," with many growing to mega size (with double-casting of some lead roles to add to the spectacle and largess) and degenerating into more-or-less variety shows that loosely told Stowe's narrative while incorporating dances, novelty acts, animals, and comics. Nonetheless, *Uncle Tom's Cabin* still stands as America's most famous and influential melodrama, representing a significant musical theatre antecedent while becoming an indelible part of the nation's history.

MINSTRELSY

Legend has it that in 1828, a stock touring performer named Thomas D. Rice was waiting outside a New York theater, scheduled to perform a specialty intermission act (or entr'acte) during the evening's program. Suddenly, he saw a black man cross the street, singing to himself and walking with an erratic gate (some reports cite a limp; some say it was a jig step). Inspired, Rice supposedly "borrowed" articles of the man's clothing, "blacked up" (the act of blackening the face with burnt cork), and improvised a new act on stage, performing an eccentric dance and musical ditty as a blackface caricature of the man, calling his character Jim Crow. The act was a hit; and as Rice travelled from New York to frontier stages in the coastal South and the Ohio River valley, the portrayal became his signature. By 1830, Jim Crow had become theatre's newest stock character, as well as a grotesque depiction of race. The negative caricature also signaled the beginnings of a new form of entertainment that would reign in America for decades during the mid-1800s: **minstrelsy**.

Drawing of T.D. Rice singing "Yankee Calculation" © Bettmann/CORBIS

around his character of Jim Crow, calling them "Ethiopian Operas." The "Negro" entertainment form was further developed in 1843 by four white men who called themselves the Virginia Minstrels, led by Dan Emmett (composer of "Dixie"). The quartet appeared in blackface, sat on stools with individual instruments (tambourine, banjo, violin, and castagnettes, dubbed "bones") and traded jokes and dialogue between their songs and dances, posing as derogatory Southern slave stereotypes. In the three short years that followed, the minstrel show grew greatly in size and import, becoming a prominent touring fixture, playing large and small entertainment venues around the country. The most successful and famous companies, notably the Christy Minstrels (formed in 1846 by balladeer Edwin Pearce Christy), had dozens of performers in their casts (ultimately growing to 50 plus men) and were largely responsible for giving the genre its distinctive form.

The blackface stage depiction of the lazy, carefree slave had been a familiar sight on the American theatre and entertainment scene decades before Rice's invention. Further, since black actors were not allowed on the American stage, "Negro" characters had historically been played by whites in blackface and often used for comic "buffoonery" (as could be seen as early as 1787's *The Contrast*, the first professional play written by an American). Around 1800, immigrant comedian Johann Gottlieb Groupner made a name for himself singing and playing the banjo as a blackface character named The Gay Negro Boy. Other white actors followed suit, and Rice became the latest to specialize in this performing tradition. Yet he would elaborate on the concept, building entire song and dance productions

Al. G. Field Greater Minstrels Poster, c. 1900 © CORBIS

At the height of its popularity, the minstrel show could vary in size but was quite formulaic in style, structure, and basic content, typically containing a number of codified components. (1) The preamble to and preview of the production usually included what has been termed a "walk-about." This segment served as an opening song, dance, and parade of the performers in blackface and costume, often as their signature characters. (2) After the introductory procession, the show's official program was divided into three major sections. The first contained an identically dressed blackface chorus who sat in rows (the number of rows determined by the cast size), where they performed songs and choreographed movement, supporting the three featured company members: Mr. Interlocutor, Mr. Tams (or Tambo), and Mr. Bones. Mr. Interlocutor, the only character not in blackface, served as a master of ceremonies and had the prominent seat, front and center of the group. Tams and Bones, also known as the Endmen, were in blackface and held instruments (a tambourine and castanets, respective to their names) which they used to accompany the musical numbers. The two men sat at opposite ends of the first row and traded jokes and comic dialogue with Mr. Interlocutor, most often assuming the manner of the dimwitted "slave" or posturing "wise-guy" (soon to become stereotyped as the "Shuffling Coon" and "Dandy," respectively—two of the many stock types, including the "Mammy," institutionalized by the minstrel show). After this musical extravaganza and jokey repartee, there would often be a spotlighted eccentric dance routine called a "breakdown." (3) As a bridging device for the show, there was a line-up of acts—the "oleo"—performed by soloists, duos, or small groups while scenery was being set up for the upcoming sketches and playlets. The nature of this portion varied, depending on the budget and stage sophistication of the minstrel company, but it could comprise elaborate comic bits, specialty/novelty acts, stump speeches, songs, and/or dances performed in front of a scene-change curtain. (4) After the oleo, the third major portion of the minstrel show comprised a one-act travesty, termed the "afterpiece" or "conclusion," performed entirely in blackface. The travesty was a scripted vignette which originally lampooned plantation life and the behavior of slaves but later evolved into burlesques of Shakespeare and other classic works, populated by minstrel stock types. It is crucial to note that the sketches not only ridiculed blacks, but also exploited and perpetuated existing negative stereotypes of all American ethnic minorities (with gender also being a target, as women were portrayed as shrewish and/or buffoonish types by men in drag). (5) Finally, to signal a celebratory end, the minstrel show would cap its antics with a hoedown, a spirited dance performed by the entire minstrel company.

The minstrel show enthralled white Americans for decades—even though both its performing ranks and audiences were anything but inclusive. From its beginning and throughout its heyday, the minstrel show was a Caucasian male-dominated province; the shows were performed by white men for a white male audience (the show was not seen as appropriate fare for women or children). Although this demographic may have seemed limiting, the minstrel show was the most popular form of entertainment in United States from 1850 to 1870. Given the "slavery question" and concordant tensions in America during this period (culminating in the Civil War), as well as the influx of immigrants landing on its shores, the minstrel show became a place of "acting out," that is, targeting America's Others, be it "Negros" or immigrant populations. Newly landed immigrants may have taken comfort in the fact that they did not see themselves realistically depicted in the blackface grotesquery on the minstrel stage or, possibly, they understood the convention and enjoyed being part of the joke; in any case, they embraced the antics. Shortly after the Emancipation Proclamation in 1863, diversity crept into the minstrel show. Blacks began to form their own minstrel troupes, beginning with the Georgia Minstrels in 1865. Such companies stayed in blackface and subscribed to the minstrel show formula, while billing themselves as "authentic race delineators." By the end of the century, women had joined the minstrel ranks, with 1891's *The Creole Show* being the first to feature a female Interlocutor and chorus. By this time, however, the minstrel show had been usurped by other entertainment forms, losing its popularity and prominence, soon to be consigned to the annals of American entertainment curiosities.

Although now an obscure theatrical artifact, the minstrel show holds great significance as an antecedent of the musical, as well as a potent history lesson in regard to theatrical representations of race and Otherness in America. The entertainment form was, no doubt, a perpetuator of racist and bigoted views; and reverberations of its harmful legacy are still felt today (notably, blackface would remain acceptable on the American entertainment scene far into the twentieth century, in films until the 1940s while amateur minstrel shows were still prevalent in the 1960s). Yet, there were some components introduced and/or disseminated by minstrelsy that have positively contributed to America's music, dance, and theatre. Folk music idioms that originated with black slaves in the South, such as gospel and the blues, as well as syncopated rhythms that would foster ragtime, were deemed only appropriate to be performed by whites in blackface. Thus, minstrelsy enabled these idioms to reach a wider white audience, albeit, the compositions were categorized as "coon songs" and carried a negative racial connotation. (Case in point, popular white composer Stephen Foster spent much of his career exploiting and appropriating the black idioms, writing minstrelsy numbers or "coon songs" such as "Camptown Races," "Oh, Susanna," and "My Old Kentucky Home;" and he was much lambasted and ostracized by peers for his concentration on this type of music.) Another legacy of minstrelsy is tap dance, which was appropriated and evolved from the folk dance traditions of the Southern black slaves (as well as dance idioms brought to New York City by Irish immigrants). Finally, many historians point to the comedic nature of and relationship between Tams and Bones as a seminal model for the bantering duo act that would become a staple of vaudeville and American comedy (e.g., Burns and Allen, Williams and Walker, Laurel and Hardy, Martin and Lewis, The Smothers Brothers, and the numerous mismatched partners found in contemporary television sitcoms and buddy movies).

BURLESQUES, EXTRAVAGANZAS AND *THE BLACK CROOK* (1866)

Americans have always loved the "big show," and no musical theatre antecedents were bigger in size, spectacle, and sass than the burlesques and extravaganzas of the nineteenth century. The **burlesque** was originally a satiric production filled with music and dance which often spoofed famous dramatic works, genres, and artists. The festivities included popular songs that were given new lyrics, as well as linguistic tomfoolery consisting of rhymed couplets and comic puns. In the 1800s, "Shakespeare" burlesques (also known as travesties) became all the rage in London, making the genre one of the top entertainment draws. The popular productions also lampooned current events and well-known persons, while imbuing the activities with a certain element of naughtiness. America had its own love affair with the burlesque when Lydia Thompson and her "British Blondes" landed on its shores in 1868, headlining a big and bold, yet somewhat crudely structured, burlesque that featured Thompson and her troupe of blond dancers in scanty costumes performing songs and dances loosely held together by a convoluted storyline parodying Greek mythology. The overall program was typical British burlesque, comprising satire, parody, musical numbers, cross-dressing, variety acts, some improvisation, and extravagant scenic elements. Given the women's risqué costumes, the show caused a scandal but sold tickets, running for almost six profitable years and making Lydia Thompson and her Blondes the toast of New York (and the United States, given the production's two tours). It also set a precedent as the burlesque became more about the "flesh" than song and dance, evolving into its twentieth-century configuration as vaudeville's disreputable cousin, a variety form that featured mostly strippers and crude comedy.

Two years before the British Blondes caused a sensation in the States, another theatrical blockbuster had taken New York by storm: *The Black Crook* (1866). The production is still cited by some historians as the first musical, although it is more aptly deemed a seminal **extravaganza**, a form similar to the burlesque but with less satire and more spectacle. When a struggling playwright, Charles M. Barras, wrote a weak melodrama with a plot that featured a satanic bargain, black magic, thwarted lovers, and a fairy queen (liberally borrowing from Goethe's *Faust*, as well as two well-known operas, Charles Gounod's *Faust* and Carl Maria von Weber's *Der Freischütz*), his production found a home in Niblo's Garden (3200 seats), one of New York's largest theaters. Niblo's manager, William Wheatley, had serious doubts regarding Barras' convoluted Faustian rehash, however. At the same time, a troupe of Parisian ballet dancers (according to differing reports, the number of dancers ranged anywhere from thirty-five to one hundred) had been signed by American producers Henry C. Jarrett and Harry Palmer for a series of New York performances. Unfortunately, they arrived only to find that their planned venue, the Academy of Music, had burned to the ground. With necessity proving to be the mother of invention, Jarrett and Palmer, in search of a new performance space, approached Wheatley with a plan to save everyone's venture. They would combine the ballet troupe's repertoire with Barras' melodrama, as well as add popular songs to the mix (along with some original compositions by Giuseppe Operti and a hit song, "You Naughty, Naughty Men," written for star Miss Millie Cavendish by composer George Bickwell and lyricist Theodore Kennick). The dance routines and songs were barely integrated with the story, as the entire proceedings were more or less tacked together. As a result, the debut of *The Black Crook* lasted for five and a half hours, but audiences didn't mind. They were smitten by the novel product, especially its lavish scenery and use of "high-tech" stage effects which included walls of mist, an underground grotto, and silver coaches swinging through the air carrying lounging fairies. Indeed, *The Black Crook*'s other major draw was its female contingent, with the ballerinas often dressed in leg-baring costumes for the dances (especially popular were the dancers' flashy "devil" costumes). Even the critics who deemed the play to be "manure" begrudgingly praised the visual splendor of the production, while the original poster promoted the production's outlay of "fifty thousand dollars" as its major attribute. *The Black Crook* was a sensation that ran in New York City for sixteen months (475 performances) and toured the country, earning almost a million dollars; it continued to be revived into the 1920s.

As previously mentioned, *The Black Crook* is often cited as the first musical; but it does not meet the criteria most musical theatre scholars use to define conventional musicals today, given its lack of organic invention and song/dance/story integration. However, the production's size, aesthetic, spectacle, and co-joined presence of the three components foreshadowed the integrated and mega musicals of the future. In addition, *The Black Crook* was early evidence that "sex sells," an adage and ethos that continues to permeate theatre and entertainment industries today. Productions in the mold of *The Black Crook* soon followed on its heels; these extravaganzas were loosely themed or storied productions that included song and dance on a grand scale and emphasized spectacle. Like *The Black Crook*, the productions usually boasted a bevy of lovely ladies in their choruses, thus garnering the "leg show" nickname, a pejorative descriptor that was also applied to the musical in its early days. Mammoth theaters were built to house the outsized shows and their scenic wonders (with many acts of nature replicated on stage); the largest was the Hippodrome (1905), which could seat 5,200 audience members and boasted a 115-foot-deep stage replete with a water feature. Impresarios also began to specialize in the genre. Two such men

KIRALFY BROS. "BLACK CROOK."

Kiralfy Brothers' 1886 production of *The Black Crook* Courtesy of Library of Congress were the Kiralfy Brothers (Imre and Bolossy Kiralfy), Hungarian immigrants who had started as star dancers in their native Europe but successfully turned to producing spectacles in the United States and abroad, including a well-received 1886 revival of *The Black Crook*. The Kiralfy extravaganzas raised the bar in regard to scenery, chorus lines (some productions boasting 250 dancers), and special effects, with two of their most successful and epic productions playing to sold-out audiences in 1877: *Around the World in 80 Days* and *A Trip to the Moon* (both adapted from Jules Verne novels).

VAUDEVILLE

In 1861, theatre impresario Tony Pastor had an enterprising idea. He would find a way to expand the audience for the variety acts playing in the disreputable but popular Bowery establishments on the Lower East Side of Manhattan. The notorious Bowery was once the largest entertainment district in New York but its concert saloons (or honky tonks) were often situated next door to brothels and gambling houses, discouraging respectable folks from attending. The saloons not only offered a variety of entertainments for working-class men, many of whom lacked formal educations, but also became the preferred performance venues for an ever-expanding immigrant population with little command of the English language. Most performers had to compete with their raucous surroundings, that is, the cursing, fighting, and drunken behavior of men in the smoke-filled, spittoon-littered establishments. Regardless, they showcased their specialty acts and Old World talents, many of which were largely nonverbal or transcended verbal communication in order to capture the audience's attention and merit monetary reward. Such talents could include the warbling of Italian arias, flashy execution of eccentric or novelty dances, crooning of sentimental ballads, farcical ethnic impersonations (e.g., Yiddish or Irish), and even sword swallowing, juggling, contortionism, and acrobatics. Pastor saw the appeal of the Bowery acts and envisioned a formula by which the variety show could become "family" entertainment. First, he needed to move the acts out of the seedy saloons. Thus, he opened his own theater on Broadway in 1865 and billed it as a wholesome variety venue, prohibiting cursing, smoking, and drinking in the auditorium, as well as insisting upon a certain degree of decorum and decency on stage. To further appeal to women and children, he initiated the "door

prize" as part of the show, luring this demographic with the possibility of winning household articles or toys. Seeing some success, Pastor continued to assert his brand of "clean" variety entertainment for family audiences, ultimately opening his highly profitable and influential 14th Street Theatre in 1881. With his newest venture, Pastor also cemented his place in history as the "Father of Vaudeville."

As the popularity of Pastor's concept and product grew, more enterprising fellows followed his example, expanding the industry and reaping even greater financial rewards. Two of the most successful were Benjamin Franklin (B. F.) Keith and Edward F. Albee, partners who had built a chain of lavish theaters throughout the Northeast and began putting variety shows in their venues, thus going national with the new theatrical form. Using booking agents as middlemen, Keith and Albee signed performers to tour their circuit of theatrical "palaces" across the nation (the Keith Circuit). Keith and Albee are also credited with instituting "vaudeville" as the name of the newly widespread form of national entertainment. (It should be noted that historians cannot definitively cite the origin of the term "vaudeville." Some sources claim that it came from "vaux de Vire," a collection of fifteenth-century satiric songs originating in the Vire valley of Normandy, while others assert that the term is a convoluted version of "voix de ville," French slang for "songs of the town," and some link the name to a tradition in the Vire valley in which travelling entertainers performed for farmers waiting to have their wheat milled. Nonetheless, these linguistic lineages have little to do with the genre of variety entertainment that took root in America under the "vaudeville" moniker.) Other major circuits by various impresarios soon popped up around the country (e.g., the Orpheum), accompanied by smaller circuits such as Pantages and the Loew. Vaudeville acts travelled from theater to theater (or palace to palace) across the country, according to the circuit for which they were booked. The enterprising efforts and growing industry resulted in vaudeville replacing minstrelsy as America's number one form of popular entertainment, beginning c. 1890 and holding the title until the early 1930s.

The vaudeville show promised "infinite variety" for the spectator, with a program consisting of independent acts, which were called "turns," presented one after another in quick succession. Most vaudeville palaces staged two to three different shows a day, with eight to sixteen turns per show, depending on the particular circuit. Each program varied in content, but the actual line-up formula was a bit codified at the height of the vaudeville vogue. Further, vaudeville fans knew the formula, enticed by the headliners but anticipative and appreciative of the supporting acts. Spectators could plan on seeing "dumb acts" (acrobats, dancers, contortionists, magicians, jugglers, animals, and "eccentrics") at the top of the show, immediately after intermission, or as a finale. Such visually captivating turns didn't need to be heard while an audience was settling and provided a delightful visceral aftertaste as audiences were departing. After the opening "dumb act," there could be a conventional, engaging turn to focus the attention of the audience (e.g., a singing or comic duo, instrumentalist/s, a sister act, or a ventriloquist with dummy) and then an act which varied from the precursors (a sketch comedy or dramatic scene), serving to further engage the audience and set the stage for one of the major headliners. In most cases, the "big punch" was then delivered by a headlining star (singer, comedian, and/or dancer), followed by a secondary act (another top biller, often a celebrity lecturer) which would also serve as an intermission teaser, leaving the audience wanting more. After intermission, another "dumb act" might be followed by a contrasting turn (maybe a child vaudevillian) to further settle the audience and build anticipation for the second major headliner. Finally, the audience could exit while another flamboyant "sight act" (or "dumb act") took the stage (trapeze, dance, acrobatics, animals). This was a basic formula for the most popular and powerful vaudeville programs; yet depending on the talents and acts signed, the program could vary considerably. Such was the exciting and unpredictable art of vaudeville; and most of America's greatest comic, singing and dancing stars of the early to mid-1900s got their starts on vaudeville and toured as headliners (with even greater stardom later realized in film, radio, and television). The roster includes seminal acts such as Weber and Fields, the Four Cohans, Lillian Russell, and Harry Houdini, as well as successive favorites and icons such as Fanny Brice, Eddie Cantor, Will Rogers, Sophie Tucker, W. C. Fields, Bert Lahr, Joe Frisco, Fred and Adelle Astaire, The Marx Brothers, and Burns and Allen. Singers, dancers, and comics were not the only headliners, for a vaudeville show might also feature fading dramatic divas such as Sarah Bernhardt, touring lecturers (e.g., Carrie Nation and Helen Keller with a translator), even celebrity athletes like Babe Ruth (whose vaudeville turn included a recitation of "Casey at the Bat"). The vaudeville show also continued to be censored, guaranteeing its wholesome "family audience" reputation for decades (while burlesque became the variety stage for the risqué acts, soon to decline into a seedy, smalltime forum of strippers and adult comedy). Although there were 3,000 flourishing vaudeville theaters in America in 1913, the trend would slow due to the financial stresses of the Great Depression and, more significantly, the rise of Hollywood "talkies" (beginning with 1927's *The Jazz Singer*), as well as radio, records, and, ultimately, television. The live theatre palaces simply couldn't compete with new technologies that could transport entertainment directly into audiences' homes. Hence, vaudeville was in steady decline by the 1930s and '40s, soon to be declared "dead" by midcentury. Yet, its spirit, legacy and wealth of talent would live on in other mediums (especially the American musical), as well as the collective American psyche.

HARRIGAN AND HART

Musical theatre historians and scholars often attempt to identify an ancestral point of origin for the American musical. Some cite 1866's *The Black Crook*, yet they also concede that the production, given its construction and constitution, more aptly represents America's first significant extravaganza. Some award the "first musical" title to a musical play which debuted thirteen years later, *The Brook* (1879), due to its integration of song and story. *The Brook*'s score was a compilation by several different composers, however, and the show contained no dance. Thus, a significant camp of scholars/historians credit the beginnings of musical comedy to a series of works that dominated the popular stage in the late 1870s and '80s; these were the farcical Mulligan Guard plays by the team of Edward "Ned" Harrigan and Tony Hart.

Edward Harrigan (1844–1911) was an Irish New Yorker who had been raised in the immigrant, working-class neighborhoods of lower Manhattan. Aspiring to a stage career, he got his first break as an actor in San Francisco in 1867 and four years later (1871) formed a fourteen-year theatrical partnership with fellow Irishman Tony Hart, née Anthony Cannon (1855–1891). At the beginning of their soon-to-be renowned career, Harrigan and Hart played vaudeville and minstrel stages, performing comic sketches written by Harrigan which were accompanied by popular songs. In the

Harrigan and Hart in *The Mulligan Guard Ball* (c. 1880) © Bettmann/CORBIS

vignettes, baritone-voiced Harrigan played the dry foil to Hart's many flamboyant and versatile stage personas, which included drag roles embellished by falsetto vocals. As the two men garnered top billing at New York's notable Lower Broadway variety house, Theatre Comique, they capitalized on their headliner status by taking over the management of the theater and forming their own performing stock company of approximately thirty actors and comics. Harrigan correspondingly expanded the duo's sketches into longer pieces which colorfully brought to life the working-class immigrant groups co-existing in New York's hard-pressed ninth ward, now known as the Lower East Side. Having grown up as a tenement dweller in "melting pot" Manhattan, Harrigan wrote about the people and places he knew— focusing on the Irish (his own ancestry and an ethnic group not considered to be fully "white" or American at the time), with secondary attention often paid to the emancipated "Negroes" who had migrated from the South. Harrigan completed the neighborhood milieu by adding other prominent immigrant groups such as the "Dutch" (Germans), Italians, Chinese, and

Eastern European Jews. Although he exploited much of the ethnic/racial stereotyping and grotesquery found in minstrelsy and vaudeville (for the staged Irishman was as negatively caricatured as the blackface "Negro" at the time), Harrigan also innovatively infused the overall proceedings with affection and humor, working to fully realize and individualize his characters by giving them human flaws, prejudices, empathies, ambitions, and desires. (It should be noted, however, that Harrigan's Irish were routinely portrayed more positively than other groups, with their faults usually redeemed at the end of the plays.)

Despite being touted by contemporaries and late nineteenth-century critics as a writer of American "realism," Harrigan was not a social crusader. Instead, he aimed to tell an entertaining story and focus on character interactions within a specified New York locale. And in 1878, Harrigan and Hart landed upon their most successful stage formula, developing a theatrical narrative based on the serial travails and comedic adventures of the Mulligans—an Irish-American family featuring patriarch saloon-owner Dan Mulligan, wife Cordelia, and son Tommy, played by Harrigan, Annie Yeamens, and Hart, respectively. Other company actors took on supporting roles, continuing in their signature parts throughout the Mulligan series, with the extroverted and popular Hart doing double duty as the African American maid, Rebecca Allup (a minstrel "Mammy" type). As the company's actor-manager, Harrigan directed the newly expanded works, which had also become highly musical due to the incorporation of songs written by Harrigan (as lyricist) and composer David Braham (1834–1905). Braham was also Harrigan's father-in-law (Harrigan married Annie Braham in 1876), and their longtime theatrical collaboration resulted in a catalogue of over 200 songs. Significantly, Harrigan and Hart's first full-length hit, *The Mulligan Guard Ball* (1879), was the offshoot of one such Harrigan/Braham song—"The Mulligan Guard." The number first appeared in an early Harrigan and Hart comic act, lampooning the paramilitary social clubs prevalent in New York City at the time. Because immigrants and blacks were not allowed to enlist in the military, numerous ethnic groups formed local societies for the purpose of firearm target practice, evolving into self-appointed quasi military units who mostly marched through neighborhoods in handmade uniforms and held social events (the Mulligan Guard was a fictional Irish-American contingent). The satiric song was such a crowd-pleaser that Harrigan and Hart expanded its concept and content into a ten-minute sketch in 1873 and then a forty-minute playlet in 1878, with the subject matter ultimately finding great popularity in 1879 as a one-act play, *The Mulligan Guard Ball*, with four added Harrigan/Braham songs. The seminal show contained two roughly merged plotlines. First, Dan Mulligan, the blustery and bigoted leader of the social group named after him, finds that his Guards have booked the same venue for their social ball as the Negro Skidmore Guard, inciting conflict between the two groups. Contributing to his travails, Dan discovers that his son Tommy has eloped with the German butcher's daughter, much to the outrage of both fathers. The show ends with the ball, during which the Skidmores, who were relegated to the top floor of the building, party so wildly that they break through the floor onto the Mulligan Guard's festivities, with the curtain lowering on comic confusion and calamity. *The Mulligan Guard Ball* was such a success that it became the first of six consecutive full-length Mulligan Guard musical plays to dominate the New York theatre scene from 1879 to 1884 (*The Mulligan Guard Chowder, The Mulligan Guards' Christmas, The Mulligan Guards' Surprise, The Mulligan Guard Picnic*, and *The Mulligan Guard Nominee*). The ubiquitous theatre presence of the Mulligans during this period included revivals of *The Mulligan Guard Ball* (Harrigan would continue to tinker with and expand the original show) and spin-offs regarding the Mulligan family (*The Mulligans' Silver Wedding, Cordelia's Aspirations*, and *Dan's Tribulations*). Consequently, the Mulligan series became New York's top box office draw, overtaking the previously dominant Gilbert and Sullivan light operas. And in an era when a successful uptown Broadway show played approximately 40 performances, the Mulligan productions ranged from 56 performances (*The Mulligan Guard Ball*) to 176 (*Cordelia's Aspirations*). Not surprisingly, these works also dominated the repertoire of Harrigan and Hart's company, serving as exclusive program fare for three of its five 1879–1884 seasons, with Harrigan and Hart playing in seventeen of the shows.

In the beginning, Harrigan and Hart's audiences were mostly Irish American—a fertile demographic given that New York City's population of just under a million consisted of nearly 500,000 immigrants (or half the population), with two-fifths being Irish. Soon, however, more and more of the city took notice of the Mulligan Guard series; and the company's productions became increasingly "uptown," migrating from the Bowery (Theatre Comique) to venues in Union Square and Herald Square, catering to middle-class and upper-class New Yorkers, although still finding great favor with Manhattan's immigrant population. Thus, during its heyday, the Harrigan and Hart repertoire spoke to immigrants who often delighted in seeing exaggerated versions of their selves on stage, cooperating and competing to improve their lots and achieve the American Dream; while middle/high-class spectators may have enjoyed a sense of voyeurism and superiority regarding a farcical depiction of the American Other. Despite issues of class, ethnicity, and reception, however, audiences were universally hooked by the human stories and serial drama provided by the Mulligan series; for the storylines, along with their characters, continued from play to play, while no absolute closure was provided at the plays' ends (much like television sitcoms). The addictive milieu also included colorful stock types, slangy dialogue comprising various dialects, and interracial, interfamilial conflict, sprinkled with songs, dances, and comic bits. The resulting productions were rarely constructed in the "well made play" mode but, instead, were episodic and character-driven. In regard to musical theatre, the Harrigan and Hart productions were amalgamations of vaudeville, burlesque, minstrelsy, and melodrama, combining the styles, songs, dances, and dramatic structures of the disparate genres with a newly dramatic aesthetic of "realism," providing works that could be viewed as seminal examples of musical comedy. The genre was not completely realized through the works, however, given the crudely applied songs and dances which were rarely integrated with the plots but were more often tacked on for stand-alone atmospheric and entertainment value. Yet one might question how far this concept/construct actually veers from the earliest "official" examples of musical comedy (e.g., the works of George M. Cohan).

Harrigan and Hart split up in 1885, and Hart died six years later at age 36 from complications caused by syphilis. Harrigan, however, continued to write, produce, and perform until 1893, becoming one of the most revered American theatre figures of the late nineteenth century. Overall, Harrigan wrote books and lyrics for more than twenty-five Broadway plays with music and forty extended plays in all. Further, not all of the Harrigan (or Harrigan/Hart) works were centered on the Mulligans or the Irish (e.g., 1882's *Mordecai*

Lyons featured Jews and 1888's *Waddy Googan* centered on Italians). With the premiere of his popular hit *Reilly and the Four Hundred* (1890), Harrigan and his company were accorded ultimate theatre legitimacy as the production debuted in the Herald Square vicinity, christening a brand new showcase theater built by and named after Harrigan. At the height of his career, Harrigan was cited as an influence on other significant late nineteenth-century playwrights and named as the sole indigenous example of American comedy by William Dean Howells (one of the most influential drama critics of the day). To elaborate on Howells' assertion, Harrigan and Hart could also be cited as the originators, in spirit if not construct/content, of the American musical comedy.

AMERICAN OPERETTA AND VICTOR HERBERT

Although the light operas of Gilbert and Sullivan, along with other European works, dominated the American musical stage during the late 1800s and early 1900s, they were not alone in comprising the operetta's Golden Age, for a domestic canon was burgeoning in the States, much of which could be attributed to the "Father of American Operetta," Victor Herbert. During his prolific career, Herbert composed over 40 operettas that combined American idioms with French and Middle European evocations, resulting in scores that featured lilting waltzes, soaring ballads, romantic duets, and rousing marches. Even though he was solely a composer, Herbert was the controlling force behind many of his most popular works, choosing the diverse subject matter, orchestrating his scores (a rarity), and repeatedly teaming with prominent lyricists to realize his vision of classical music merged with popular entertainment, creating fresh and inventive operettas that provided musical escape for the everyday theatergoer. (Specifically, Herbert partnered with the country's most prolific and popular lyricist/librettist, Harry B. Smith, for thirteen works, Glen MacDonough for five, and Robert B. Smith for three, as well as teamed with America's pioneering female lyricist/librettist Rida Johnson Young for one of his most successful works, 1910's *Naughty Marietta*.)

Born in Dublin, Ireland, on February 1, 1859, Victor Herbert received his formal education and musical training in Germany, where the family relocated early

Victor Herbert © Bettmann/CORBIS

on. After studying composition, Herbert embarked on a career as a classical cellist and became a renowned soloist in Europe, as well as a composer and acclaimed conductor, specializing in Viennese waltzes. At the age of twenty-seven, however, his life changed drastically when his wife, opera singer Theresa Forster, received a job offer from New York City's Metropolitan Opera (the company was looking to import European sopranos who could sing the highly specialized and challenging works by composer Richard Wagner). Forster would only sign her contract on the condition that the MET also hire her husband, granting him a principal cellist position in the orchestra. The MET agreed and the couple immigrated to America in 1886, where Herbert's star rose quickly as he established himself once again as an accomplished concert artist. At the same time, Herbert chose not to limit himself to the classical sphere, for he was also an unabashed fan of popular music idioms (e.g., the stirring marches by America's favorite composer at the time, John Phillip Sousa), as well as entertaining music/theatre mediums, forums, and constructs such as military bands, extravaganzas, burlesques, and operettas. In fact, one of Herbert's most famous and telling quips was his assertion that it should not be a "crime" to be "popular."

Demonstrating this mindset, Herbert left his orchestral position in 1892 to take a job as conductor of the 22nd New York National Guard Band, concentrating on what could be deemed the "pop music" of his day. At the same time, however, he continued to compose his own works which mixed classical technique with melodies and styles that appealed to the ear of working-class America. In 1894, his first Broadway operetta, *Prince Ananias*, ran for 55 performances. Encouraged, Herbert left his marching band gig to return to Broadway, scoring a major success with *The Wizard of the Nile* (1895), book and lyrics by Harry B. Smith. The work would be the first of many collaborations with Smith, while fully launching Herbert's historic Broadway career. For the next five years, Herbert churned out operetta hit after operetta hit, often working on multiple projects at the same time. His works during this period ascribed to a winning formula that combined exotic locales, virtuosic vocals, and cliché operetta storylines (e.g., romances between royalties/nobilities, complicated by mistaken or disguised identities, only to end in happy resolution and marriage). They also appealed to New York audiences looking for spectacle, "art," and take-away tunes. Meanwhile, Herbert acquired a degree of celebrity due to his outsized ego, flamboyant manner, and epicurean tastes and appetites. In fact, a highly publicized anecdote recounts how Herbert simultaneously composed *four* operettas for the 1899–1900 Broadway season, setting them in wine regions and reportedly imbibing wine from each operetta's locale for inspiration (often moving between multiple operettas—and wines—in a single work session). Although popular, few of Herbert's early works are notable in regards to his canon. A couple exceptions include *The Gold Bug* (1896), which featured the black comic team of Bert Williams and George Walker, premiering their soon-to-be signature dance craze, the cakewalk, as well as *The Fortune Teller* (1898), which contained the breakout hit, "Gypsy Love Song."

From 1898 to 1904, Herbert also served as conductor of the Pittsburgh Symphony, taking a brief leave of absence from Broadway. The career move incited controversy, however, for strict lines were drawn between "classical" and "popular" music idioms and arenas at the time. As a result, Herbert faced harsh criticism in the local press from elite music critics who were dismayed that a military band leader and specialist of "leg shows" (their words) should represent their city's esteemed orchestra. The grousing finally went too far when an editorial in *The Musical Courier* insinuated that Herbert's operetta compositions contained plagiarisms. Herbert did not take the editor's accusation lightly; he sued the paper for libel and was awarded damages after a highly publicized court trial. Toward the end of his orchestra assignment, Herbert began writing for Broadway again and triumphed in 1903 with *Babes in Toyland* (book and lyrics by Glen MacDonough). The childlike fantasy centers on the nursery-rhyme adventures of orphans Alan and Jane as they flee from their dastardly guardian, Uncle Barnaby, and encounter colorful characters such as Contrary Mary, Tom-Tom, the Moth Queen, and even Old Mother Hubbard. The brother and sister ultimately land in Toyland where they are put in mortal danger by the evil Master Toymaker but escape in the end with the help of their friends and a group of mutinous toys.

With the success of *Babes in Toyland*, Herbert returned to New York City and resumed his operetta career full-time, becoming a prominent fixture on Broadway as he premiered at least one (and often more) new works a season for the next two decades. Over a dozen works topped the 100-performance mark (signifying a major Broadway hit at the time). Audience favorites of the period included 1905's *Mlle. Modiste* (a Cinderella/rags-to-riches story in which a lowly Parisian hat-shop employee is made a stage star) and 1906's *The Red Mill* (detailing the colorful, comic adventures of two Americans in a fictional village in Holland), while most critics consider his best and most iconic work to be 1910's *Naughty Marietta*. This operetta is set in late eighteenth-century New Orleans and details the "naughty" adventures and misadventures of a free-spirited heroine of noble birth who has disguised herself as her maid, Marietta, to avoid an arranged marriage, only to fall in love with the unsuitable Captain Richard Warrington, who repeatedly rescues her from danger and wins her in the end. Not long after *Naughty Marietta*, Herbert enjoyed another success with *Sweethearts* (1913), a formulaic romance set in the fictional kingdom of Zilania between Prince Franz and the lovely peasant Sylvia (who, unbeknownst to him, is actually a princess). Along with providing another collection of popular take-away songs, *Sweethearts* incited an unexpected landmark achievement for Herbert, one that would cement not only his own level of property control and capital, but also that of all other musical industry artists and professionals.

As previously noted, Herbert demanded and enjoyed a significant degree of control over his work. Even though he often created star vehicles, he became frustrated by some headliners' habits of inserting their own specialty songs into his productions. Rejecting this accepted practice, Herman alienated many lead performers who insisted upon the interpolations. Another area of control was his insistence upon orchestrating his own works, for Herbert felt that using an orchestrator was akin to being an artist envisioning a painting, only to have others physically paint it. Finally, with *Sweethearts*, Herbert asserted the ultimate right of authorial control when he not only became one of the nine founders in 1914 of the American Society of Composers, Authors, and Publishers (ASCAP) but also helped legitimize the entity's power and authority, seeking a court decision that would make the organization's copyright and royalty stipulations legally binding. It all began when Herbert happened upon an orchestra in the popular Shanley's Restaurant playing his title song from *Sweethearts* without authorization from or royalty payment to its copyrighted creator, that is, Herbert. Such a situation ran counter to ASCAP, for its rules stipulate that society members (composers, authors, and publishers) are to be paid appropriate royalty percentages when their songs/compositions are used for commercial purpose (that is, performed in any commercial format or venue). Again proving unafraid of a litigious fight, Herbert sued for financial damages. When a local judge ruled against him, Herbert appealed to the Circuit Court of Appeals, but again lost the case. Undeterred, Herman fought the rulings all the way to the U.S. Supreme Court, which ruled favorably in a decision written by Justice Oliver Wendell Holmes. Thus, ASCAP was given legal merit and muscle, with Herbert serving as the organization's Vice President for the next ten years (1914–1924).

When Herbert died of a heart attack on May 26, 1924, he left behind one of Broadway's largest song catalogues. Yet today, he is more closely associated with operetta than musical theatre. Further, much of his extensive repertoire has been relegated to historical archives, with a few works occasionally revived by operetta and light opera companies. *Babes in Toyland* is the rare work that is revived with any frequency on the musical theatre stage (with rewritten librettos),

while excerpts such as "Toyland" and "March of the Toys" resurface during Christmas holidays. Although rarely produced, Herbert's *Naughty Marietta* is often cited as a pinnacle moment for American operetta, with the added distinction of being the first operetta to be set in America. Its score also illustrates the characteristics that defined Herbert's appeal during his heyday, that is, the bouncy, hummable melodies found in numbers such as "Italian Street Song" and the soaring vocal lines and poetic sentiments (by collaborating lyricists) constituting hit ballads such as "Ah! Sweet Mystery of Life" [see fig. 2.1]. In a humorous side note, the latter is one of the few Herbert songs that remains familiar to contemporary audiences, albeit in a much different context. Specifically, Mel Brooks parodied the song in his film *Young Frankenstein* (1975), turning it into a climactic ode to the monster's sexual gifts and prowess, resulting in an iconic moment of modern movie comedy.

Today, Herbert's most significant career achievement is most likely the institution and recognition of ASCAP—an entity still active, powerful, and legally binding in the music and entertainment industries. Further, in terms of his theatrical legacy, Herbert successfully proved that the Old World operetta techniques could be melded with popular theatre subject matter and American idioms. In this respect, his career set the stage for operetta's Silver Age (with some citing *Naughty Marietta* and Franz Lehar's *The Merry Widow* as starting points). This new operetta vogue in America would be dominated by Herbert successors, however: Sigmund Romberg (1887–1951) and Rudolf Friml (1879–1972). Both Romberg and Friml were classically trained émigrés who found great popularity on Broadway, providing a steady flow of operettas during the 1920s, with many successfully adapted to film. Romberg's best-known works include *The Student Prince* (1924), *The Desert Song* (1926), *The New Moon* (1928), and *Rosalie* (a 1928 collaboration with George Gershwin), most of which echoed the sound, aesthetic, and subject matter of Golden Age Viennese operettas (for instance, *The Student Prince* concerns a conflicted romance between a prince and a barmaid). Friml became an audience favorite with hits such as *The Vagabond King* (1926) and *Rose-Marie* (1925), with the latter innovatively including Canadian Mounties and a murder in its plot. Further, *Rose-Marie*'s "Indian Love Call" is still heard today, often used to represent (and parody) classic operetta. Given the contributions of these two Silver Age composers (and others), operetta continued as an integral part of the Broadway scene up through the 1930s, until its mass appeal waned and musical theatre became the dominant genre on the popular American stage.

Figure 2.1

AH! SWEET MYSTERY OF LIFE

Music by Victor Herbert;
Lyrics by Rida Johnson Young (1910)

Ah! Sweet Mystery of Life
At last, I've found thee.
Ah! At last I know the secret of it all.
For the longing, seeking, striving, waiting, yearning,
The burning hopes,
The joy and idle tears that fall.

For 'tis love and love alone,
The world is seeking.
And 'tis love and love alone,
That can repay.
'Tis the answer, 'tis the end and all of living,
For it is love alone that rules for aye.

For 'tis love and love alone,
The world is seeking.
And 'tis love and love alone,
That can repay.
'Tis the answer, 'tis the end and all of living,
For it is love alone
that rules for aye.

CHAPTER 3

EARLY 20TH CENTURY: MUSICAL THEATRE PIONEERS AND BIRTH OF A GENRE

● ●

Historically speaking, Broadway is a paradox. It is a twentieth-century creation—yet, it existed long before the 1900s. To unpack the puzzle, one need only research what Broadway looked like before the twentieth century. It resembled numerous other bustling New York City thoroughfares; for technically speaking, nineteenth-century "Broadway" was little more than the name of a major New York street. It was not yet the district that would acquire the iconic, all-encompassing moniker, for that geographic locale contained no legitimate theatrical venues, much less a musical theatre empire. Instead, the area was a seedy section of town known for its brothels and criminal activity, nicknamed the Tenderloin (officially titled Longacre Square). But it was the dawn of a new theatrical age; and "Broadway," the theatre district, was in the early stages of real estate development, while "Broadway," the myth, icon, and dream machine, was on the cusp of making its imprint on America's cultural consciousness.

Such a monumental progression would begin in the 1890s, when a visionary impresario, Oscar Hammerstein (grandfather to Oscar Hammerstein II), bought several plots of land in the Tenderloin (from 43rd to 45th Street, on the east side of Broadway) and began building theaters where it was once deemed unthinkable. Soon, Hammerstein's Olympia (a conglomeration of entertainment/dining venues built in 1895) and his Victoria Theatre (a grand theater built in 1899) became proof positive that the once "untouchable" Tenderloin could become fertile ground for family-friendly enterprises. Other industry titans soon got into the business of building theaters in Longacre Square. These included the monopolistic theatre management/production group known as The Syndicate (started by partners Marc Klaw and Abraham Lincoln Erlanger), as well as competitors who sought to break the Syndicate's hold on commercial theatre in America, i.e., the Schubert

Brothers (Sam, J.J., and Lee). Thus, by 1910, there were thirty-four theaters in the 42nd Street vicinity, most constructed as a result of the competition between the two organizations.

Once the venues were built, the shows (and audiences) soon followed. Specifically, New York's theatre activity began moving uptown, migrating from its hub in the vicinity of West 37th Street to 40th (including such hotspots as Herald Square, named after the widely read *Herald*, later *Herald-Tribune*) to the newly developed areas around 42nd Street. Further prompting the migration and construction frenzy was the industrial-age marvel planned by New York City in 1900: the subway. When its builder, the Interborough Rapid Transit Company, decided that the line required a major stop at 42nd and Broadway, the surrounding triangle of land became the pulsing "heart" of Manhattan, christened Times Square in 1904 (named for its most influential and dominant tenant, *The New York Times*). And in another synchronistic development, music publishers began setting up shops a few streets away—on West 28th Street, between Broadway and 6th. This area was nicknamed Tin Pan Alley, and its industry was spurred by an emerging consumer demand for songs with populist appeal, a trend jumpstarted in 1892 by the first million-copy hit, "After the Ball," by Charles K. Harris. Tin Pan Alley became the seat of American songwriting and publishing for decades to come, as well as a hotbed of musical creativity and output, enjoying a mutually beneficial and productive relationship with the new "Broadway."

It wasn't all about geography, property development, and industry, however. New York City's demography was also changing by leaps and bounds during the nineteenth century, creating an entirely new and ever-evolving pool of artists, as well as audience members.

Immigrants were flowing into the city during the nineteenth century, with nationalities and ethnicities that included the Irish, Germans, Eastern European Jews, and Italians. The tide surged toward the end of the century and the beginning of the twentieth. In fact, 5.5 million Europeans immigrated to New York in the years between 1880 and 1919, with 1.2 million arriving in 1907 alone (1 million of the immigrants being Jewish). Further, a substantial portion of this population, once through Ellis Island, settled in districts such as the Bowery, Little Italy, and other Lower East Side neighborhoods, as well as Harlem. They often kept to their own nationalities/ethnicities, while entertaining themselves and others with remnants and variations of performance idioms, constructs, and content from their homelands. The forms soon found their way to the New York stage, often filtered through an American lens. Yiddish theatre, with its mixture of song and drama, took root in Jewish neighborhoods, while influencing the evolution and overall character of the newly emerging American musical. Further, the Jewish contingent produced a wellspring of artists who would become the formative pioneers of the musical theatre genre. Alongside such Jewish assertions and influences, other immigrant populations inspired and provided comic and dramatic fodder for the stage (e.g., the Irish antics of Ned Harrigan and Tony Hart's Mulligan Guard, as well as the "Dutch" tomfoolery of vaudevillian team [Joe] Weber and [Lew] Fields). In another significant development, vaudeville not only surpassed minstrelsy as the most popular form of stage entertainment at the turn of the century, but it also absorbed the most crowd-pleasing elements of the minstrel show. Thus, minstrelsy's signature music and dance idioms fully entered the mainstream theatre lexicon, as well as, unfortunately, its negative racial stereotypes and aesthetic (e.g., the cartoonish blackface persona of soon-to-be superstar Al Jolson). However, there were some African American performers, such as Bert Williams, who were able to move from minstrelsy, via vaudeville, to find stardom on the "legitimate" theatre stage (albeit, still within a racially charged, conflicted, and constricted sociocultural context).

Speaking of vaudeville, one might cite it as the era's most telling and illustrative form of entertainment in terms of the embodiment of the American Dream and its "melting pot" ideal on the stage. With little dependency on text and language, the vaudeville show became a cultural and artistic crossroads for the immigrant populace as they shared and showboated acts that ranged from the sublime to the bizarre (with a good deal of mundane mediocrity thrown in). And at the height of vaudeville's popularity, many of its stars, given their lack of formal education and first-generation immigrant status, became living embodiments of America's "rags to riches" mythos. Furthermore, vaudeville, along with Tin Pan Alley, created a platform for the polyphony of diverse voices on America's shores, facilitating invaluable contributions to popular music, e.g., the sounds of Hebraic composition and tone, as well as the syncopation of African American folk rhythms (with the evocative, jazzy "blue note" found in both). Amazingly, these music idioms coexisted on a burgeoning "Broadway" alongside the formal strains of European operetta (e.g., Franz Lehar's *The Merry Widow*, which took the country by storm in 1907), as well as novelty tunes, military marches, lyrical ballads, and saloon ditties. Such sundry sounds were eventually given a glamorous setting and format via a theatrical vehicle called the revue. Coming on the heels of vaudeville, the revue would soon become a reigning Broadway form, due in great part to impresario Florenz Ziegfeld and his editions of *Ziegfeld Follies*, beginning in 1907. The spirit of diversity also shaped a new genre, termed "musical comedy." The nascent musical construct not only contained vestiges of operetta, vaudeville, and minstrelsy, but it also adhered to the idea of narrative linkage between songs, dances, and comic turns, all of which would be written in a contemporary and common American vernacular.

The birth of any genre connotes parenthood. Thus, musical theatre's developmental phase is often defined by the pioneers who are credited with "fathering" its most significant evolutions and formative constructs, i.e., Victor Herbert, a.k.a. "Father of the American Operetta"; George M. Cohan, a.k.a. "Father of the American Musical Comedy"; Florenz Ziegfeld, a.k.a. "Father of the American Musical Revue"; and Jerome Kern, a.k.a. "Father of the American Musical Theatre" (with an unofficial "Father of the American Musical Play" being Oscar Hammerstein II). As the musical found its footing, form, and voice, it succeeded in melding what had previously been deemed "high" and "low" art, somewhat thumbing its American nose at strict delineations, for many of the best works merged the opera house, the dance hall, the melodrama stage, and the vaudeville palace. Furthermore, several exemplary musical productions proved their muscle and merit in the overall theatre arena. Specifically, one might cite *A Trip to Chinatown* (1891) as one of theatre's early blockbusters. The 1891 musical comedy featured a score with music by Percy Gaunt and lyrics co-written by Gaunt and Charles H. Hoyt, who served as the show's librettist, producer, and co-director (with Julian Mitchell, who represents another informal "father"—that of the modern musical theatre director/choreographer). A precursor to *Hello, Dolly!*, the show basically concerns an interfering widow who orchestrates an escapist night on the town for two couples, unbeknownst to their mercantile employer, with all parties farcically ending up at a highbrow restaurant. Upon its debut, *Chinatown* signaled the importance of a strong, appealing narrative, while generating two big takeaway hits: "After the Ball" (written by Charles K. Harris) and "The Bowery" (which became an anthem for New York City's Lower East Side). For twenty-eight years, the show held the record for most continuous performances (totaling 657). Nine years after *Chinatown*, another hit, *Florodora* (1900), further defined the musical theatre genre, while providing America with pop culture icons: the Florodora Girls. Ironically, the show was not American (it was a British import), but along with the highly popular light operas of W. S. Gilbert and Arthur Sullivan, the show predated the "British Invasion" of Andrew Lloyd Webber by running for an astounding (for its time) 533 performances. With a libretto by Owen Hall, music by Leslie Stuart, and lyrics by Stuart, Paul Rubens, and Frank Clements, the show centers around a love triangle, set in a perfumery (Florodora is both the name of the perfume and the Philippine island where it is manufactured). The highlight of the show was its six coquettish, parasol-twirling ingénues, the Florodora Sextette, which became a double sextet; each girl paired with a male partner in a flirty showstopper, "Tell Me, Pretty Maiden."

Along with romance, fantasy was also prevalent on the nascent musical stage, with *The Wizard of Oz* (1903) proving to be a major success. The show's music was by Paul Tietjens and A. Baldwin Sloane, while the book and lyrics were provided by Frank Baum, adapting his own fantastical stories about Dorothy and her trip to Oz. Again, director/choreographer Julian Mitchell spearheaded the early musical spectacle, which ran for 293 performances. Furthermore, the production inspired fantastical ventures by other artists, such as composer Victor Herbert, whose *Babes in Toyland* (1903), again directed and choreographed by Mitchell, resulted in

192 performances, as well as a takeaway song, "Toyland," which lives on today as a holiday favorite. Herbert himself became America's own operetta master at the beginning of the twentieth century, as he began to bridge the gap between European operetta and a more populist, American form of song/dance drama. Given this winning formula, Herbert would merit two of the top hits of the early musical era: *Mlle. Modiste* (1905) and *The Red Mill* (1906). Both operettas featured archetypes, storylines, and surrounding aesthetics that would soon become signposts of the traditional musical. First, *Modiste* (with lyrics and book by Henry Blossom) asserted the "Cinderella" prototype on America's musical stage; for its heroine, a lowly worker in a Parisian hat shop, is discovered and made a singing star. With Herbert's *The Red Mill* (lyrics and book also by Blossom), theatrical promotion and technology took a leap forward, for the show provided Broadway with its first moving, illuminated sign (a revolving, electrically lit red windmill). Further, the show's comedy was based on the concept of American exceptionalism, detailing the adventures of two baffled, broke, but enterprising and highly inventive Americans stranded abroad in the fictional Katwyk-aan-Zee, Holland.

With works such as *Modiste* and *Red Mill*, Herbert would continue in the operetta vein; yet, his productions began to be categorized as more "musical comedy" (and/or "leg show") than "operetta" by classical music elites. Conversely, there was no question as to the musical-comedy nature of works by contemporary George M. Cohan. This son of Irish immigrants would completely reject the operetta formula and create an "all-American" form, replete with the American archetype, the Yankee (or Johnnie). Given the rise and popularity of Cohan's works, the musical comedy became a Broadway staple, inciting further experimentation by future artists (e.g., the intimate and modern Princess Theatre Musicals, beginning in 1915).

With the assassination of Austria-Hungary's Archduke Franz Ferdinand and his wife in Sarajevo on June 28, 1914, Europe plunged into World War I, a devastating conflict that would last until the ceasefire on November 11, 1918. America would not enter the War until its last year. Nonetheless, even while on the sidelines, the nation was greatly affected by the carnage and madness of the conflict overseas (more than 9 million combatants would ultimately be killed). As America mobilized to join the Allies, the War was reflected on the theatrical stage (especially in the revues of the time and through songs written by favorite Broadway sons such as Cohan and Irving Berlin). When the War came to an end, many realized that the world had changed forever. The same could be said for America's musical stage; for the nation was moving into the Jazz Age, with further experimentations in music and a significant expansion of racial and ethnic influence on the content, sound, and aesthetic of the musical. With every progressive movement, the genre was stretched and, at the same time, further defined, with many changes happening in the blink of an eye or, more accurately, with the raising of a curtain. The new art form was still a bit messy, as it reflected its own melting pot origins, replete with inherent tensions, conflicts, and contradictions. Nonetheless, having ascended to great prominence on the newly instituted "Broadway" stage, the twentieth-century American musical was ready to take its place as one of the nation's foremost artistic contributions to the world.

GEORGE M. COHAN

As famously asserted in his iconic, reflexive song "Yankee Doodle Boy," George M. Cohan considered himself to be nothing less than a "real live nephew" of Uncle Sam, "born on the Fourth of July." There was only one thing wrong with this assertion: Cohan was actually born in Providence, Rhode Island, on the *third* of July, 1878. Significantly, this did not deter the brash, self-promoting showman from insisting on the "Fourth of July" birthdate throughout his career. Concurrently, he was able to not only assert his own legendary persona as a theatrical savant, but also as an all-American success story, a musical comedy pioneer. Cohan combined his charismatic, extroverted talents on stage with an uncanny ability to personify some of the most desirable characteristics of America at the turn of the twentieth century. As the star, composer, lyricist, librettist, director, and producer of numerous Broadway productions, Cohan codified the spirit and formula of early American musical comedy, returning again and again to the subject matter and themes closest to his heart and most emblematic of the American ideal: patriotic love of country, importance of family, and entrepreneurial attainment of the American Dream.

Although Cohan, a multifaceted artist and impresario, is commonly referred to as the Father of American Musical Comedy, he is also sometimes (and incorrectly) categorized as simply a song-and-dance man. This reductive definition is understandable, given that he was born into a vaudevillian family, with singing and dancing in his blood. In fact, when Cohan, a natural-born musician with little formal education and training, was disparaged by some critics as a limited composer who only wrote with "four chords," he often rebutted by referencing his song-and-dance stage persona, reiterating the fact that he could write songs better than any dancer and dance better than any songwriter (although, Cohan did, in fact, compose all his songs using only the black piano keys). In short, Cohan was a musical "man of the people," an entertainer whose wisecracking, street-smart manner revolutionized the legitimate Broadway stage, while each of his star-vehicle creations appealed to audiences in a straightforward, visceral, and easily digestible manner. As an antithesis to the European operetta aesthetic, Cohan not only promoted the idea of an authentically "American" musical form (with roots in vaudeville and melodrama), but he was also an emblematic product of the American melting

George M. Cohan as Johnny Jones, c. 1905 © Bettmann/CORBIS

pot paradigm. As a member of the much-maligned Irish-American population, Cohan unapologetically celebrated his heritage while "making good" as a flag-waving patriot and self-made man.

Born into show business, Cohan made his theatrical debut before he could walk, carried onstage in the arms of his vaudevillian parents, Jeremiah (Jerry) and Helen (Nellie) Cohan. Cohan spent his childhood touring the country with his family (Jerry, Nellie, and older sister Josephine). With little time spent in a schoolroom, the theatre became his primary source of education, indelibly shaping him during his formative years. As an 8-year-old, George played violin in the pit orchestra; the next year, he was given a speaking cameo onstage; and at age 11, he was finally allowed, along with his sister, to officially join his parents' act. Thus, The Four Cohans became a fixture on the prominent B. F. Keith vaudeville circuit, delighting audiences with their familial mix of song, Irish dance, and sketch comedy. Little George started to garner attention as a spirited lad, lighting up the stage with his comic antics and dance steps. He was ultimately accorded the title role in an 1891 stage adaptation of the popular novel *Peck's Bad Boy*. Although he performed the pugnacious role so convincingly that he became the target of aggression by local youths, he continued in the production, along with his family, for over a year. Then, The Four Cohans returned to the road, touring the country as vaudeville headliners; yet, young George was not satisfied with this measure of success. He had his sights on bigger lights: Broadway. As he often exclaimed, this was the only "bell" he wanted "to ring." Consequently, at age 14, he attempted to run away, only to be stopped at the last minute by his father, who ultimately acquiesced to George's wishes and secured a premiere engagement for The Four Cohans at Manhattan's Union Square Theater.

The move to New York was not the only evidence of George's power with regard to the family's vaudeville act. While still a teen, Cohan began to write much of the material for The Four Cohans. In addition, at 16, he published his first song ("Why Did Nellie Leave Her Home?"), only to be confronted by the realities of show "business" when he discovered his lyrics had been rewritten by another songwriter to more appropriately reflect the flourished, formal language currently in American songwriting vogue. Furious over this intervention and interference, he determined, from that point forward, to maintain complete control over all his material and assert his own brand of pedestrian verbiage in his songs. George was determined to create songs in which his own "voice" could be heard, loud and clear—not the artificial, heightened, and often stilted poetry associated with operetta. His slangy, conversational style caught on, as well as his straightforward, catchy melodies; and he was soon a Tin Pan Alley favorite, creating a number of hits for other performers. During these same teen years, George took over the role of business manager for The Four Cohans, and they soon became the highest paid foursome in vaudeville. However, after a falling out with their longtime vaudeville boss, B. F. Keith, the family decided to make the transition to the legitimate theatre and, more specifically, enter the nascent arena of integrated musical comedy.

Given this new direction, Cohan approached Louis Behman (of the Hyde and Behman vaudeville circuit) and persuaded him to produce a full-length Broadway musical comedy to be written by Cohan and to star The Four Cohans. Behman agreed, but only on the condition that The Four Cohans tour their act on his circuit for a year before embarking on the Broadway show. Thus, expanding on a vaudeville sketch that he had previously written for his family's vaudeville act, Cohan penned *The Governor's Son* in 1901, officially leaving the vaudeville stage behind and making his Broadway debut as a musical comedy writer, composer, director, and star. Unfortunately, *The Governor's Son* did little to promote Cohan's Broadway career, for the debut was deemed a flop. Contributing to its failure was the fact that Cohan injured his ankle in the first scene. This created a major obstacle; for Cohan, as a director and performer, was known to highlight antic energy in his shows, advocating the following musical comedy formula throughout his career: "Speed! Speed! And lots of it! That's the idea of the thing. Perpetual motion!" As Cohan limped across the stage during his Broadway debut, his physical charm and energy were seriously compromised; the production could not, seemingly, recover. However, Cohan struck a deal with the producer to tour *The Governor's Son* across America; the provincial audiences loved its hearty vaudevillian humor and catchy tunes. Given this road success, Cohan was offered another chance to create a Broadway musical for himself and his family. But his next attempt, *Running for Office* (1903), fared no better than *The Governor's Son*. Thus, he again toured the production, turning another flop into a profitable road show. Significantly, during this period, Cohan was introduced to Sam H. Harris, a boxing promoter with a bit of theatre production experience. With one meeting and a handshake, Cohan took Harris as a producing partner, hoping to delegate much of the day-to-day business dealings to Harris and thereby concentrate on more artistic endeavors, i.e., rewriting and doctoring his shows on the road to improve their Broadway prospects. It was a prescient calculation. Harris and Cohan's partnership proved wildly successful, lasting for 15 years.

Significantly, Cohan's new partnership bore fruit as Harris assumed the role of business manager and Cohan was able to more fully concentrate on making his third Broadway show, *Little Johnny Jones* (1904), a box office success. The path was a bit rocky, however. Echoing past failures, the New York debut of Cohan's latest production was less than auspicious; and the show closed quickly, only to be taken on the road. Yet, this time, Cohan (who was once again the production's producer, director, composer, librettist, lyricist, and star) used the time on tour to revise and fine-tune the show, ultimately returning a new and improved version to Broadway, which soon became a smash success. With his family in supporting roles, Cohan played the title role, Johnny Jones, a jockey who aims to prove his mettle in the English Darby, only to be falsely accused of throwing the race. The production itself incorporated melodrama (stock characters, mistaken identities, hidden evidence, and poetic justice) as well as vaudeville (especially in terms of its humorous banter and comic interpolations). More important, Cohan flooded the score with hummable, memorable tunes that celebrated America; songs such as "Yankee Doodle Boy" [see fig. 3.1] and "Give My Regards to Broadway" have become iconic works not only reflective of the Cohan canon but of American innocence, optimism, and assertiveness at the turn of the century. And Cohan, as Johnny, symbolized the ultimate American Yankee—the heart-of-gold hero who employs his cocky confidence, honest sentiment, and wisecracking street smarts to expose and triumph over the effete, posturing, and phony foreigners (i.e., the British). It was a role that Cohan would exploit and embellish throughout his career. Cohan's performance was also revelatory in that he had a limited singing voice (often delivering numbers in a sing-song speaking manner) but acquired his star power through a physical energy and athletic dance style that embodied a new version of the romantic leading man on Broadway. He was a tap dancer who reverted to his vaudevillian roots, relying on tricks and flashy footwork, often incorporating the side of the proscenium for back flips and other crowd-pleasing acrobatics. George M. Cohan represented a new type of legitimate musical star, a far cry from the static tenors and baritones of operetta who had previously dominated the Broadway stage.

Cohan lost no time in capitalizing on his newly acquired success and notoriety. In 1906, he created hit musicals such as *45 Minutes from Broadway* and *George Washington, Jr.* Both shows again starred Cohan and featured his family. They also contained Cohan librettos promoting American exceptionalism and showcasing America's favorite son, the Yankee. In *45 Minutes*, a woman forfeits her inheritance to keep her sassy, urban Yankee beau (played by Cohan); while *George Washington, Jr.* features a son (again played by Cohan) who changes his name to George Washington, Jr. in protest of his father's infatuation with all things British. Further, the productions contained more samples of catchy melodies and sentiments that appealed to audiences and jointly (and somewhat ironically) celebrated Cohan's own immigrant roots as well as his American identity. For instance, "Mary's a Grand Old Name," from *45 Minutes*, musically exploits an Irish lilt, referencing Cohan's Irish heritage; while "You're a Grand Old Flag," from *George Washington, Jr.*, bespeaks the patriotic fervor that had become a Cohan hallmark (Cohan was once facetiously asked if he could write a song without using the word "flag"). In 1908, he created his last show for the entire Cohan family: *The Yankee Prince*. Here, the self-sure Cohan billed The Four Cohans as "George M. Cohan and his Royal Family," and the popular production once again extolled all things American by lambasting the practice of marrying off rich American daughters to European nobility. With *The Little Millionaire* (1911), Jerry and Nellie Cohan made their last appearance in a Cohan production. Yet, George M. Cohan, as a solo act, continued on his career trajectory.

By 1911, Cohan had opened his own theater, George M. Cohan's Theatre, while continuing to create long-running hits such as an adaptation of the novel *Get Rich Quick Wallingford* (his theater's inaugural production) and the mystery parody *Seven Keys to Baldpate* (1913). He also began to create revues, starting with his first hit, *Hello Broadway* (1914), which wickedly spoofed the contrived practice by contemporary revues of imposing weak, loose plot elements to link musical numbers and sketches. In addition, his influence had spread beyond his own productions. Given his talent for pleasing audiences, he repeatedly assumed the role of what is commonly referred to as a "show doctor." In this capacity, Cohan would be called on to "fix" failing shows created by other artists, applying his expertise, sans credit, in terms of libretto and/or score tweaks and revisions. So prevalent became this practice that he referred to it as "Cohanizing;" and thus, his imprint on the musical comedy genre, whether overt or inconspicuous, was undeniable and ubiquitous during the first decades of the twentieth century. Consequently, by 1918, he had become America's first media giant, a stage superstar and a household name whose songs reverberated throughout the country, especially his World War I anthem "Over There," which used a simple melody and straightforward lyrics to touch the hearts and minds of Americans during the war. This song, riffing on a military bugle call, voiced a timely, patriotic call to "send the word" that the "Yanks are comin'" and they "won't come home till it's over, Over There." Unfortunately, the next year would prove to be a turning point for Cohan, as he found himself vilified by a segment of the New York theatre community. Ironically, this was the same community that had once held him up as an ideal with respect to show business and American/theatrical capitalism.

At the turn of the century, actors were shamelessly exploited by theatre producers and owners, often in terms of workplace safety, hiring/firing practices, working conditions, and pay equity. In 1912, professional stage actors looked to labor movements in other segments of American industry and, subsequently, formed their own union, named the Actors' Equity Association (AEA). Producers and theatre owners ignored this group's demands for safe and equitable working conditions, however, so Actors' Equity proceeded to strike in the summer of 1919, effectively closing down theatres across the country that relied on the employment of professional actors. Given the two hats worn by Cohan—that of an actor and that of a producer/theatre owner—he was caught in the middle of the firestorm. Much to the dismay of the actors and contrary to Cohan's previous track record of fair and supportive treatment of performers, he sided with the producers, voicing a belief that the profession of acting should be above labor unionization and that any refusal to perform ran contrary to an actor's "calling." He also initiated a fierce campaign against Actors' Equity. Cohan was portrayed as an out-of-touch millionaire and traitor by many actors. Cohan felt further betrayed by the overall theatre community when fellow producers (including his longtime partner Harris) foresaw the money that could be lost due to the cancelled productions so they ultimately acquiesced to Equity's demands. After final agreements were reached, a disgruntled Cohan refused to join the union; and given his powerful position in the theatre arena, he was granted an exception from the AEA's hiring regulations, working on Broadway under a special non-Equity contract for the rest of his career.

It was not only the Actors' Equity fracas that served to temper enthusiasm for Cohan's work on Broadway, but also the changing tastes and attitudes of Americans as they moved into the 1920s. Cohan's flag-waving, vaudevillian style and formulaic plots started to seem rehashed and antiquated. Furthermore, popular music was beginning to embrace the dance rhythms/

syncopations and melodic complexity of jazz, a musical idiom somewhat distant from Cohan's simple, tuneful marches and lilting Irish waltzes. Throughout the decade, Cohan had a couple more popular hits but was quickly losing his audience and was repeatedly dismissed by the critics. By 1930, he was considering retirement. He was then lured back to the stage for two crucial performing engagements: Eugene O'Neill's *Ah, Wilderness!* (1933) and Richard Rodgers/Lorenz Hart's *I'd Rather Be Right* (1937). In the former, he invested himself fully in the non-singing, non-dancing role of the amiable patriarch, impressing audiences and critics alike. In the Rodgers and Hart musical, his workmanship proved to be less professional, possibly because he was performing, for the first time, a song/dance role that was not of his own devising. *I'd Rather Be Right* was also an anomaly in that it was a musical featuring Franklin D. Roosevelt, played by Cohan, during Roosevelt's own lifetime. During the development and run of the show, Cohan was openly dismissive of the work by composer Rodgers, lyricist Hart, and librettist Moss Hart, often belittling them during rehearsals and taking liberties with the score and book during his performances. Yet, the production, as well as Cohan's performance, was wildly lauded (receiving positive notices from President Roosevelt himself); and Cohan spent two years in the role, both on Broadway and on tour. In the early '40s, Cohan once again tried his hand at writing, producing, and starring in his own Broadway musicals, only to find his efforts rejected by modern audiences. Further, he had been diagnosed with stomach cancer. As he retired from performing and kept his illness a secret from the public, he oversaw a movie version of his life: *Yankee Doodle Dandy* (1942). Produced by Warner Brothers, Cohan was allowed a great deal of input with regard to casting and content; thus, the film contains many close reproductions of some of Cohan's most famous numbers, as well as a leading man, James Cagney, who was personally approved by Cohan due to Cagney's vaudevillian background, brash persona, and physical dance style (aided by one of Cohan's old dance assistants). Before Cohan died on November 5, 1942, he was able to see his name in lights one last time as the film became a major box office success. With Cagney delighting audiences across the country with his impersonation of Cohan, performing such iconic hits as "Yankee Doodle Boy," "Give My Regards to Broadway," and "Over There," Cohan was once again remembered by America and revered as the nation's musical voice and theatrical ambassador.

Further contributing to the legacy of Cohan is the successful biographic revue, *George M!*, created by Michael Stewart and Cohan's daughter Mary in 1968. Although the songs from Cohan shows have become American classics, the musicals themselves are problematic today due to their unwieldy or dated librettos (for instance, despite a substantial rewrite, *Little Johnny Jones* still closed overnight in its only revival on Broadway in 1982). Yet, Cohan's life story, his accomplishments, and his song canon are irresistible and still speak to American audiences; such was the winning formula of *George M!*. With Joel Grey starring as Cohan and winning rave reviews, the production was one of the major hits of the Broadway season and continues to provide contemporary audiences with a glimpse of the extraordinary talent of this earliest and formative musical comedy pioneer, Broadway's own "Yankee Doodle Boy."

Figure 3.1

YANKEE DOODLE BOY

Music and Lyrics by George M. Cohan (1904)

I'm the kid that's all the candy,
I'm a Yankee Doodle dandy,
I'm glad I am,
So's Uncle Sam.
I'm a real live Yankee Doodle,
Made my name and fame and boodle
Just like Mister Doodle did, by riding on a pony.
I love to listen to the Dixie strain,
I long to see the girl I left behind me;
And that ain't a josh,
She's a Yankee, by gosh,
Oh, say can you see
Anything about a Yankee that's phony?

I'm a Yankee Doodle dandy,
A Yankee Doodle, do or die;
A real live nephew of my Uncle Sam's,
Born on the Fourth of July.
I've got a Yankee Doodle sweetheart,
She's my Yankee Doodle joy.
Yankee Doodle came to London,
Just to ride the ponies,
I am a Yankee Doodle boy.

Father's name was Hezikiah,
Mother's name was Ann Maria,
Yanks through and through,
Red, White and Blue.
Father was so Yankee-hearted,
When the Spanish war was started
He slipped on his uniform and hopped up on a pony.
My mother's mother was a Yankee true,
My father's father was a Yankee too,
And that's going some,
For the Yankees, by gum,
Oh, say can you see
Anything about my pedigree that's phony?

I'm a Yankee Doodle dandy,
A Yankee Doodle, do or die;
A real live nephew of my Uncle Sam's,
Born on the Fourth of July.
I've got a Yankee Doodle sweetheart,
She's my Yankee Doodle joy.
Yankee Doodle came to London,
Just to ride the ponies,
I am a Yankee Doodle boy.

FEATURED PRODUCTION: *Little Johnny Jones* (1904)

Music, Lyrics, and Book by George M. Cohan

Original Broadway Run: Opened November 7, 1904; Liberty Theatre; 52 performances

Promoting and presenting himself as a contemporary representation of America's "native son," that is, a "Yankee Doodle Boy" for the nascent twentieth century, George M. Cohan achieved a level of stardom and theatrical power that would not be equaled by any other artist during his lifetime. And it all began in 1905, with his third musical and first Broadway hit, *Little Johnny Jones*. In the production, Cohan recreated and reinvigorated a quintessential and historic archetype of American theatre: the "Jonathan," i.e., the unpretentious, guileless, and self-sure Yankee hero who uses his innate American ingenuity and country/street smarts to prove himself cerebrally and morally superior to Old World "elites." (The stock type of the Jonathan was first introduced in 1787 by Royall Tyler in his social comedy, *The Contrast*.) Inspired by a contemporary news story about Tod Sloan, an American jockey who was racing in London, Cohan decided to remake the horseracing hero in his own song-and-dance image, fashioning a melodramatic story about a jockey, Johnny Jones, who travels to Britain to race in the English Derby. In the process, Johnny is embroiled in scandal, clears his name, wins the love of the ingénue, loses her to a kidnapper, saves her, and undoes the villain in the end. With his real-life family in supporting roles and his current wife, Ethel Levey, playing the love interest, Cohan created his own version of the Jonathan. Portraying Johnny Jones as a bold, brash, and disconcertingly honest lad who not only races his horse (Yankee Doodle) brilliantly but also charms the English upper classes, Cohan imbued the character with an energized and eccentric brand of song and dance, most notably exemplified by Johnny's opening number in which he introduces himself to British society, proclaiming himself to be a "Yankee Doodle Boy," while listing and celebrating his American attributes. This sterling reputation is soon in jeopardy, however, when Johnny loses the race and is falsely accused of throwing it. Correspondingly, he is in danger of losing Goldie Gates, the American girl abroad with whom he has fallen in love. In an introspective solo number, Johnny muses on his reversal of fortune, offering a quiet moment of song-speech sentiment (unusual for stage musicals at the time): "A Funny Proposition." But, through the efforts of a private detective and reporter, documents come to light that prove Johnny was framed. The revelatory scene is one of the musical's most dramatic; for as Johnny waits on a Southampton pier for word from the departing boat as to his verdict, he begins to sing "Give My Regards to Broadway," a plea to his departed American entourage to send his best wishes to old haunts such as Herald Square and 42nd Street, and to implore his compatriots not to forget about him. However, when he sees the signal from the boat midway through the song, clearing him of all charges, he breaks into a jubilant dance. In the original 1905 production, the scene was also a theatrical highpoint, containing innovative special effects, for the boat was portrayed as an electrically lit model, moving across the backdrop, and the signal was a stage effect that simulated a flare from the boat. In an abrupt plot shift, the third act convolutedly moves to San Francisco's Chinatown, relaying the news that Goldie has been kidnapped. However, Johnny and the private detective soon nab the kidnapper, only to discover that the cad was also the villainous mastermind behind the framing of Johnny in England. With this discovery, all loose ends are neatly tied and Johnny is happily reunited with his love.

When the production debuted at Liberty Theatre, the audience was not overly impressed, and it ran for less than two months. However, Cohan used a road tour of the production to make extensive revisions. Consequently, the show returned to New York twice in 1905, with a total run of twenty weeks and a wildly enthusiastic audience. Given this belated success, the production became iconic in many respects, introducing American audiences to the "everyman" aesthetic of Cohan's songwriting style, which produced classics such as "Yankee Doodle Boy" and "Give My Regards to Broadway," as well as its introduction (via Cohan) of a new breed of musical leading man: the physical, comedic, wry, yet sentimental, leading man who sounded nothing like the heroes of opera or operetta. Furthermore, the many hats worn by Cohan, that of director, producer, librettist, lyricist, composer, and star, was an unprecedented event, never to be repeated in the musical theatre arena. And Cohan himself would see his theatre career skyrocket after *Johnny Jones*, creating (and most often starring in) twenty-one subsequent musicals and twenty plays/melodramas, establishing himself as one of America's first superstars.

Unfortunately, *Johnny Jones* itself is not as timeless as the many songs it contained. Indeed, the production has proved to be extremely difficult to revive. The original work contains awkwardly interpolated songs, vaudevillian comic bits, and seriously offensive and negative/racist stereotypes and musical numbers. Most significant is the caricature of an evil Chinese lottery boss, Sing Song (who helps orchestrate the kidnapping of Goldie), as well as the opening number to Act II, titled "March of the 'Frisco Chinks.'" This is not to suggest that revival attempts have not been made. The production was extensively rewritten by Pulitzer-Prize-winning playwright Alfred Uhry for a 1982 Broadway revival, while its score was embellished with additional Cohan songs. Starring box office draw Donny Osmond as Johnny, the production could not overcome the dated and awkward nature of its material. Given one Broadway performance, which received scathing reviews, the show closed after opening night. Yet, this failure does not change the fact that *Little Johnny Jones* is a pioneering work in musical theatre history, changing the genre in many formidable ways and helping to usher the musical into the twentieth century.

Little Johny Jones cast from 1980 production at Goodspeed Opera. Photo by Jay Thompson. Used by permission of Goodspeed Musicals.

PULLING BACK THE CURTAIN:
Cohan and the Melodic Hook

Have you ever heard a song that you simply couldn't get out of your head? Chances are the song contained what is often termed a melodic "**hook**," i.e., a musical refrain that is easily digestible and often recognizable, therefore memorable. Musicologists have long posited that there are certain formulas present in popular music in which a particular arrangement of and movement between musical notes on the scale make sense to the listener, appealing to the human ear because aural expectations are happily met by the familiar melodic progressions, jumps, shifts, and compilations. Of course, such expectations are a product of one's culture, history, and experience; and the ear itself is trained through repetition and familiarity. It is often said that a "pop" song, at first hearing, makes you feel that you have heard it before. And the "hook" is what signals this familiarity and/or sense of melodic rightness and delight, arriving at an anticipated place of musical pleasure.

George M. Cohan was a master at musically appealing to the populace, often using variations of the hook to speak to his audiences directly. His aim was to have audience members whistling his tunes as they left the theatre. To that end, he employed two important devices by which to musically hook his audience. One was the **riff tune**, and the other was the technique of **sampling**. A riff tune is basically a song that uses a short melodic refrain, then repeats it numerous times until the audience is fully familiar with the repeated "riff" and, consequently, the overall song. Cohan often used a riff when writing his simple melodies, helping imprint the song on his listener's mind while also providing an easy fit for his direct, conversational lyrics. One of the most famous examples is Cohan's World War I hit, "Over There," which uses a three-note riff, referencing a bugle call. He repeats the three-note riff five times in succession to begin the song's chorus. And although he includes some melodic variation after this beginning, he also goes on to repeat these short variations before ultimately returning to the original riff. Riff songs are used often in musical theatre, especially when a composer/lyricist wants to highlight his/her lyrics (rather than a complex melody) or when he or she wants to appeal directly and simply to an audience. Cohan also ingeniously used what can be termed "sampling" to musically communicate with his audience, exploiting familiarity and nostalgia. Sampling is the technique by which short melodic refrains are quoted musically from widely known songs, that is, the refrains are interpolated into an original song, serving as familiar and referential auditory signposts for the first-time listener. One of the more famous Cohan examples is his use of musical snippets from "The Star Spangled Banner," as well as "Dixie" and "Yankee Doodle," all squeezed into the composition of his iconic hit "Yankee Doodle Boy." Importantly, the use of riffing and sampling is still prevalent today in musical theatre and popular music. One might hear one or more purposeful references to a past iconic musical ballad in a contemporary score (not to mention the prevalence of sampling in contemporary rap and hip-hop music). Further, the riff song continues to thrive, for example, in Stephen Sondheim's brilliant Broadway patter songs, as well as the driving melodic repetition often found in Green Day's rock opera, *American Idiot* (in fact, many rock idioms owe much to the riff song, e.g., the punk movement in the 1970s and '80s). What is genius, however, is Cohan's exploitation of and success with such compositional devices as early as 1904.

FLORENZ ZEIGFELD

At the beginning of the twentieth century, vaudeville was the most popular form of theatrical entertainment in America, delighting audiences in New York and across the country with its eclectic and wholesome program content. Another theatrical form, however, was soon to overtake vaudeville in terms of prestige and popularity on the New York stage. Termed a "revue," this new form vaguely resembled vaudeville, for it also incorporated a mix of song, dance, and comedy. Yet, instead of vaudeville palaces, this musical mélange was created for the "legitimate" stage. And as the revue took Broadway by storm, it consolidated vaudeville's haphazard formula of independent acts and performers into a thematically cohesive, aesthetically pleasing musical/theatrical event. The popularization and propagation of the revue within the musical genre can be credited to one of the most powerful, innovative, and larger-than-life impresarios of the twentieth century: Florenz Ziegfeld, Jr. When tracing the history and development of American musical theatre, Ziegfeld is a significant figure, heralded as a visionary who arguably revolutionized the Broadway stage with

not only his annual editions of the *Ziegfeld Follies*, but also his bravado and influence as one of the industry's most resourceful theatre producers and pioneers. Specifically, in addition to his spectacular revues, Ziegfeld helped introduce "serious" musical theatre to Broadway and challenged existing "moral" restrictions, outmaneuvering censors while slyly titillating audiences. In short, fifty years after *The Black Crook*, Ziegfeld reinscribed sex and spectacle as defining elements of showbiz, while concurrently reconfiguring such elements into a novel form of art. And the simultaneous presence of both "biz" and "art" could be found in his numerous productions that captured audiences' imaginations, fed their fantasies, and informed the musical theatre industry for decades.

Born in 1867, young Florenz enjoyed a secure and affluent childhood in Chicago, surrounded by music and theatre (his German immigrant father was a concert pianist who founded the Chicago Musical Academy). Always a dreamer, Florenz had little use for school; and as a teenager, he was allowed to leave his studies to chase his cowboy dreams at a Wyoming cattle ranch. Following this adolescent adventure, he

Florenz Ziegfeld surveying beauty pageant contestants in swim wear, c. 1920s.
© Bettmann/CORBIS

returned to Chicago and took an active interest in his father's ventures within the entertainment business. To bolster the lackluster box office of his father's newly opened nightclub, The Trocadero, Ziegfeld scouted and signed the strongman Eugene Sandow as a novelty act. Significantly, Ziegfeld not only contracted Sandow for the club, but also capitalized on the Chicago World's Fair crowds to publicize his find. Concentrating on Sandow's crowd-pleasing feats of strength and, more importantly, his unusually muscular and defined physique, Ziegfeld dressed his star in miniscule trunks or loincloths, showcasing Sandow's body as the weightlifter flexed and posed for the awed crowds (most notably, the society women of Chicago). Ziegfeld then ventured beyond Chicago, booking Sandow on the vaudeville circuit. During the tour, Ziegfeld cleverly fed and furthered media reports that women, outfitted with "special velvet gloves," were known to faint when touching Sandow's bulging muscles. One might say that Sandow became Ziegfeld's first "sex object," offered up to the American public for a sizable profit.

Given his success with Sandow, America's first male sex object, Ziegfeld looked to New York and, more specifically, to Broadway to further his impresario dreams. By this time, however, Sandow had departed, and Ziegfeld needed new talent. In search of a female star, he travelled overseas in 1895, scouring the music halls of Europe. There he became enamored with current sensation Anna Held. The Polish émigré's coy, faux-French, flirtatious stage persona and stunning figure (her corseted waist was rumored to be eighteen inches) so impressed Ziegfeld that he wasted little time luring her away, both romantically and financially, from her estranged husband and her contract with the famous *Folies Bergère* in Paris. New York anxiously awaited this highly touted import whose stage engagement required a much-publicized payoff of $1,500 from Ziegfeld to the *Folies Bergère* for her release (today's equivalent of $40,000+). Debuting in the 1896 musical version of *A Parlor Match*, Held proved to be a sensation with American audiences, both on Broadway and during the production's nationwide tour. Meanwhile, Ziegfeld not only capitalized on the success of *A Parlor Match's* score, which contained the popular hit "A Bicycle Built for Two," but also on its star, the intriguing, glamorous Held. He spent the next dozen years producing seven Broadway musicals (and consequent tours) for her. In the process, Ziegfeld staged publicity stunts to perpetuate Held's evocative image (e.g., a

media blitz regarding her supposed "milk baths" and his dissatisfaction with the dairy supplying the milk), while exploiting her charming music hall talents and ultimately surrounding her with a troupe of lovely chorus girls, billed as "The Anna Held Girls" (precursors to his soon-to-be-renowned Ziegfeld Girls).

Although Held and Ziegfeld were never married, denoted as "common law spouses" in New York State, their relationship soured and Held sued for "divorce" in 1912, claiming infidelity on Ziegfeld's part (it was widely known that he was repeatedly involved with various actresses and chorus girls, many of whom were in his employ). Although the couple went their separate ways, Held could be said to be responsible for the greatest and most identifiable contribution by Ziegfeld to the twentieth-century Broadway stage: the *Ziegfeld Follies*. Given Held's past association with the *Folies Bergère* in Paris, she persuaded Ziegfeld to create an American version of the show, employing the *Folies* formula of beautiful and scantily clad chorus girls, along with popular music and comic diversions. Referencing a popular newspaper column by Harry B. Smith, titled *Follies of the Day*, which cleverly addressed current events, Ziegfeld named his new show *Follies of 1907* and hired Smith to write material for the show. Financed by theatre owners Marcus Klaw and A. L. Erlanger, Ziegfeld's premiere production included musical numbers, comic sketches (containing impersonations of well-known contemporary figures), and lavish scenic elements, all of which were loosely connected by a thematic thread in which Pocahontas and Captain John Smith are introduced to modern life in America. Terming the 40-minute production a "revue" in homage to its European model, the show debuted in New York City on July 8, 1907, at Klaw and Erlanger's Jardin de Paris, a modest roof garden theater (i.e., a garden area on the rooftop of a theater building that has been converted into an additional performance space—a popular trend in the pre-airconditioned 1900s). Although the production was not the first of its kind, predated by *The Passing Show* in 1894 (also a variety show in a revue format), Ziegfeld's *Follies* was positioned and marketed as an innovative form on the Broadway stage. Further, Ziegfeld widely publicized his role as ultimate architect/creator of the novel production. This is not a completely accurate assertion, however. Indeed, Ziegfeld produced the event and controlled almost every aspect, as he would for every edition of the *Follies*; but in reality, he was also savvy enough to bring in top-notch stage directors, dance arrangers, designers, composers, and star performers to help him realize his vision. Ziegfeld himself was none of these things, but his eye for such talent was thought to be unmatched. In the case of his first show, he not only relied on attractive chorus girls and relevant satire but also hired the gifted director/dance arranger Julian Mitchell, who helped shape the production into an eye-pleasing, cohesive event. And even though the score was lackluster (as opposed to future *Follies* editions, which would profit from premiere tunesmiths who supplied at least one hit song per show), the production was a success, running the entire summer and enjoying a brief, but profitable, tour.

As salaried producer, Ziegfeld made a sizable amount of money from his 1907 *Follies* and saw his new "theatre impresario" role as the ticket to a lucrative future. Thus, he immediately began work on a new *Follies* for 1908. The finished product again featured the beautiful Ziegfeld girls, spectacular sets and costumes, and a star vocalist, Nora Bayes, whose rendition of "Shine On Harvest Moon" helped turn the number into one of the best-selling songs in America that year. Ziegfeld wasted no time in creating another *Follies* in 1909, employing premiere performers such as Sophie Tucker and Eve Tanguay, both of whom sang renditions of the newest *Follies* hit, "By the Light of the Silvery Moon." By 1910, Ziegfeld was adding formidable comic talents, such as vaudevillian stars Fanny Brice and Bert Williams, to his casts. The employment of Williams was a landmark moment for the American musical theatre, for Williams would become the first African American to star on Broadway alongside Caucasian headliners. In fact, his contract so upset Ziegfeld's cast that they threatened to boycott rather than share the stage with him. Once Ziegfeld countered that the only member of his cast he could not easily replace was Williams, they relented, and Williams went on to become one of the most popular stars of the *Follies*, and America, during his lifetime.

By the time Ziegfeld presented the *Ziegfeld Follies of 1913* (the name was officially changed from *Follies* to *Ziegfeld Follies* in 1911), his productions had found a new home on 42nd Street in the New Amsterdam Theatre. This sumptuous setting was a more fitting environment for Ziegfeld's ever more elaborate productions. In addition, Ziegfeld, whose business card was known to read "Impresario Extraordinaire," was becoming

increasingly notorious for his demanding perfectionism, business acumen, profligate appetite for women, gambling ventures, and canny showmanship (often publicizing star controversies and censorship issues to boost box office sales). In 1914, however, he curbed one of those appetites—the womanizing—to marry actress Billie Burke. They would stay married until his death, albeit not with complete fidelity on his part. Along with Ziegfeld's own image, the reputation of the *Ziegfeld Follies* continued to grow, especially with regard to their lavish milieus and star-studded casts. The rosters of A-list performers headlining the yearly editions throughout the 1910s included dancing, singing, and/or comic stars such as Ann Pennington, Eddie Cantor, W. C. Fields, Ed Wynn, Will Rogers, and Marilyn Miller. In addition to the headliners, another defining component and highlight of the *Ziegfeld Follies* was the Ziegfeld Girl. This was the title given the chorine in the revues who embodied Ziegfeld's ideal of beauty and talent; the Ziegfeld Girl could be a short woman who was a good dancer ("pony") or the stunning, statuesque "showgirl" who paraded the elaborate costumes and headdresses. She was young (teens-twenties), single, and cast according to Ziegfeld's own exacting physical criteria. Thus, his Girl might seem, through a twenty-first-century lens, to have been objectified and sexually exploited, yet Ziegfeld explained that he was never looking to sexualize the women but aimed to exalt all that was admirable in the American female. In fact, "Glorifying the American Girl" became the signature motto for Ziegfeld and his *Follies*. Further, the women became celebrities in their own right and were accorded a unique opportunity at the time to achieve financial independence through employment on Broadway.

Along with the stars and the women, the opulent settings of the *Follies* productions contributed immensely to the overall "Ziegfeld" aesthetic and effect. By the mid-1910s, the famous Austrian designer Joseph Urban became Ziegfeld's premier set designer, creating a lavish Art Nouveau look that would elevate the most lowbrow comedy or sexual content onstage, giving decadence and populist entertainment the luster of highbrow glamour and art. The contracting of Urban was not the only example of Ziegfeld's genius with regard to his unique mix of sex, art, and eye-popping theatricality. When censors threatened to close down certain editions of the *Ziegfeld Follies* due to the partial nudity employed in some of the Ziegfeld Girl costuming,

Ziegfeld did not want to risk losing this titillating (and box office–boosting) aspect of his productions. Thus, he and Urban craftily utilized the "tableau vivant," in which a work of art was reproduced onstage, using his beautiful cast in various stages of undress, as deemed necessary in the artwork's reproduction. The curtain would rise and the performers would hold completely still in the tableaux. The audience would be teased by glimpses of flesh, as well as awed by the luxurious, composed beauty of the art scene. Most important, because the performers were not actually "performing" but were stationary "works of art," the censors were disarmed.

Ziegfeld's reach could also be felt beyond the Broadway stage as his *Follies* scores continued to contribute to the popular music canon of America during the 1910s and '20s. As is the case with most revues, the *Follies* editions not only contained sketches written by numerous authors, but their scores were also composite works by various composers, with some numbers achieving more popular success than others. Most notably, a breakout hit written by Irving Berlin for the *Ziegfeld Follies of 1919* was "A Pretty Girl Is Like a Melody," a haunting, hummable song that would not only go on to become a signature hit for Berlin but also develop into the leitmotif for subsequent editions of the *Ziegfeld Follies*.

Given the mega success of his revues, Ziegfeld soon began looking for other ventures by which to increase his impresario prestige and power on Broadway. In 1915, he branched out with a late-night revue, the *Midnight Frolic*, produced on the rooftop garden of the New Amsterdam Theatre. The stage area was remodeled by Urban so that it could retract to reveal a dance floor and was outfitted with glass walkways above the seated audience on which Ziegfeld's glamorous showgirls could parade (rewarding patrons with naughty "underside" views). With a pricey $5 cover charge, Ziegfeld assured his midnight revelers an elegant, yet risqué night that mixed party with quality performance (many of his *Follies* headliners debuted at the *Frolics*). The shows were perfectly in sync with the newly burgeoning jazz age and ran until 1923, when prohibition put a damper on the proceedings and Ziegfeld could no longer profit from the late-night productions.

Despite this defeat, however, the '20s saw Ziegfeld achieve another triumph when he and William Randolph Hearst built a new theater. Designed by Urban, the Ziegfeld Theatre opened in 1927 and was an architectural/decor showcase while providing a home for Ziegfeld to experimentally produce musical works other than the *Follies*. In 1920, he had had great success with *Sally*, a musical vehicle for dance star Marilyn Miller, with a score composed by Jerome Kern. Thus, it was not surprising that Ziegfeld would agree to produce a Kern musical as one of the first in his eponymous theater. What was surprising, however, was that the production was not a conventional musical comedy but a novel type of show that would herald a new direction for the musical genre, one that looked to serious content and integrated components. The work was titled *Show Boat* and introduced the concept of "musical theatre" to an arena that had previously celebrated jokey humor, leggy chorus girls, contrived plotlines, and loosely connected musical numbers. It was a gamble to confound his audience's expectations, but Ziegfeld was a renowned gambler (much to the detriment of his personal fortune), and in the case of *Show Boat,* his instincts paid off. Although Ziegfeld initially feared that he would be bankrupt when the opening night curtain call was greeted by semi silence, he needn't have worried. Indeed, audiences were surprised by the production's storyline, which spans forty years and details the many triumphs and travails of a family in the showboat business, including taboo subject matter such as spousal abandonment, gambling addition, alcoholism, and miscegenation. Yet, they were also enamored with the plot's humanity and melodramatic aspects, as well as its cohesive, brilliant score by Kern and librettist/lyricist Oscar Hammerstein II. The critics lauded *Show Boat* in the press, recognizing the importance of the landmark work, and audiences continued to flock to the Ziegfeld Theatre for the show's lengthy and profitable run of 572 performances. Ziegfeld not only provided a home (and more than twenty elaborate set designs) for this innovative and bold experiment on Broadway, but he also contributed to the overall shape of the production during its out-of-town tryouts; consequently, Ziegfeld, as "Impresario Extraordinaire," should be given a portion of credit for its success. Accordingly, *Show Boat* is considered by many to have been the pinnacle of Ziegfeld's producing career (so much so that he reportedly considered opening a second production in New York to run simultaneously with the first).

Although Ziegfeld enjoyed a string of hit productions at his theater during the late 1920s, including *Rio Rita* (1927), *Rosalie* (1928), and *Whoopee* (1928), the Great

Depression loomed. With the 1929 stock market crash, Ziegfeld's fortunes abruptly changed and his hard-earned, merited theatrical dominance also came to an end. After losing his worth of almost $3 million in the Crash, he also failed at an attempt to enter the nascent movie business. He returned to Broadway, only to embark on a series of failed producing ventures. Even his reliable *Ziegfeld Follies* could no longer draw the large crowds as audiences had either tired of or could no longer relate to the opulent, no-expense-spared aesthetic and content of his revues; specifically, his final attempt, *The Ziegfeld Follies of 1931,* was unprofitable—a sacrilege for Ziegfeld. The next year, Ziegfeld turned to his other legacy—*Show Boat*—to try and rekindle his past glory. He assembled a revival (just five years after the initial production) with most of the original cast. The production was well received by the critics, but box office sales were disappointing, and the production eventually moved from Broadway to a modestly budgeted tour. During this period, Ziegfeld was also suffering from persistent lung infections, which progressed to the point of pneumonia during the revival of *Show Boat.* Florenz Ziegfeld was ultimately denied the comeback he so doggedly pursued; for time ran out, and he succumbed to lung disease, dying on July 22, 1932. His wife, Billie Burke, continued to pay his debts and promote and preserve his legacy for years, facilitating successful film productions centered around the *Ziegfeld Follies,* as well as new editions of the revue on Broadway. With his imprint on the theatrical arena, as well as the American psyche, Florenz Ziegfeld will forever be remembered as the man who not only brought the musical revue to America, but reconfigured the look and feel of Broadway in the process, mixing ideal beauty with naughty sex appeal, highbrow art with populist entertainment, and quality substance with superficial pizzazz. As a result, the "Ziegfeld" formula and form would not only inform Broadway for years to come, but all other mediums of performance and entertainment, including television and film.

FEATURED PRODUCTION: *Ziegfeld Follies of 1918*

Music and Lyrics by various artists
Book (Sketches) by Gene Buck and Rennold Wolf

Original Broadway Run: Opened June 18, 1918; New Amsterdam Theatre; 151 performances

In the decade following its 1907 conception, Florenz Ziegfeld's *Follies* evolved from novel entertainment to one of the premiere theatrical events in any given Broadway season. Thus, by 1918, the *Follies* not only delighted audiences with its cavalcade of stars, sex, and spectacle, but it also served as a communal touchstone for America, musically, comically, and scenically reflecting current events and the overall national *Zeitgeist*. In this regard, the *Ziegfeld Follies of 1918* is often touted as one of the most significant and successful productions in *Follies* history.

The edition cannily combined abundant references to America's recent entry into World War I, as well as overall patriotic material, with a full roster of top stars and soon-to-be audience favorites, including Marilyn Miller, Eddie Cantor, W. C. Fields, Will Rogers, and Ann Pennington. Some numbers and sketches used the stars to reference the war and incite patriotic fervor. For instance, in her *Follies* debut, Miller danced a "Yankee Doodle" number; while pop-eyed comedian Cantor scored in a sketch as a hopeful pilot in a recruiting office. Other moments included less flag waving but still spoke to the audience in contemporary terms, establishing a communal "American" dialogue. America's favorite monologist, Rogers, twirled his signature lariat while dryly musing over current topics; and Fields lampooned trendy national pastimes, posing as a golfer in his famous comic routine.

Further, there was, as usual, no cost spared with regard to spectacle. Staged by one of the leading "dance arrangers" of the day, Ned Wayburn, the production numbers were lively and lavish, while merging modernist Americana with a wartime call to arms. Specifically, the iconic Ziegfeld Girls paraded across the stage, elaborately costumed as the "allied nations," while a staged tableaux, titled "Forward Allies," ended the first act. Finally, the entire production ended with a spirited jazz dance number—jazz being the newest musical/movement craze in the country. Indeed, it might have been difficult to leave the 1918 *Follies* without a patriotic tune ringing in one's ear or a sense of duty resonating in one's heart. A particularly stirring sketch depicted the women on the home front taking on the jobs of deployed men, and two songs by a young Irving Berlin reinforced similar sentiments: "Blue Devils of France" and "I'm Gonna Pin a Medal on the Girl I Left Behind." Overall, the twelfth edition of the *Follies* was a feast for the eyes and ears, a combination of a star-studded, escapist delight and a flag-waving rally for a nation that had entered into a period of wartime uncertainty, communal sacrifice, and national pride.

Edna French (center, nude) with other performers in *Follies of 1918 tableaux* © CORBIS

PULLING BACK THE CURTAIN:
The Revue and Its Prevalence in Early American Musical Theatre

As mentioned in the previous section, Florenz Ziegfeld is often credited with bringing the revue to America; but, in reality, he was beaten to the punch by *The Passing Show,* a three-act production by George Lederer, presented at the Casino Theatre in 1894. While Lederer used the term "revue" to describe the show, he also billed it as a "topical extravaganza," employing musical numbers and sketches to spoof neighboring New York theatre productions, much as *Forbidden Broadway* does today. The original production contained a score predominantly created by composer Ludwig Engländer and librettist/lyricist Sydney Rosenfeld (although songs by other artists were also included). *The Passing Show* proved popular enough with audiences to warrant several more editions before the end of the century. Nevertheless, it wouldn't be until 1907 that the revue really gripped Broadway, spearheaded by the vision and promotional talents of Florenz Ziegfeld. Such was his influence that Ziegfeld is often hailed as the "Father of the American Revue," and his *Follies* provided a template for the multitude of revues that soon graced, and sometimes dominated, Broadway during the 1910s, '20s, and '30s. Here is a sampling of some of the most successful contemporaries of and successors to the *Ziegfeld Follies:*

The Passing Shows: Borrowing the name from Lederer's original Casino "extravaganzas," the Shubert Brothers (theatre producers Lee and Jacob) premiered their own revue in 1912 at the Winter Garden, mainly to provide formative competition for Ziegfeld and interrupt what was beginning to look like his theatrical monopoly. For more than a decade, the thirteen editions of the Shubert Brothers' revue pleased audiences; yet, other than the occasional employment of notable composers (e.g., George Gershwin) and consistent showcasing of notable talent (e.g., comic Ed Wynn, matinee idol Marilyn Miller, and dance team Adele and Fred Astaire), the *Passing Shows* often lacked the distinction and extraordinary style of the *Ziegfeld Follies.*

George White's Scandals: This highly successful revue (thirteen editions in twenty-one years) was the brainchild of former hoofer George White, who not only produced but also directed and choreographed the high-energy, polished productions. Beginning in 1919, the shows were filled with new talent, ear-catching music, and fresh movement, rivaling those of Ziegfeld. The *Scandals* differed from other revues (except for those at Irving Berlin's Music Box) in that White hired only one composer or songwriting team for each edition. Famously, George Gershwin composed for five editions, from 1920 to 1924; while the renowned trio of [B. G.] DeSylva, [Lew] Brown, and [Ray] Henderson created some of America's favorite hits during the late '20s and early '30s for their *Scandals* scores. The *Scandals* editions were also more dance-centered than other revues, setting in motion many dance crazes that swept the nation, e.g., the "Black Bottom," which was introduced by one of White's star dancers (and previous *Ziegfeld Follies* performer), Ann Pennington.

Greenwich Village Follies: In 1919, another *"Follies"* on Broadway proved successful enough that Ziegfeld threatened to sue over its name. The lawsuit never happened, however; and the simple and stylish *Greenwich Village Follies* enjoyed eight editions from 1919 to 1928, all under the guiding hand and vision of director John Murray Anderson. Distinguished by an abundant use of satire, the productions were all originally mounted at the Greenwich Village Theatre but were moved to Broadway during their runs. In addition to comic parodies and song, the *Greenwich Village Follies* were notable for their signature use of highbrow "ballet ballads," based on literary sources, and female impersonators.

Earl Carroll Vanities: There was nothing small, simple, or subtle about the eleven editions of this revue, created by producer Earl Carroll in 1923. To a greater degree than his contemporaries, Carroll pushed the envelope of decency, appealing to tired businessmen with programs filled with racy humor (his comedians were edgier than many of those appearing in neighboring revues) and blatant female sexuality. For instance, the *Vanities* infamously introduced the "living curtain" in which lovely girls were draped across the stage in various degrees of undress. Not only were the productions big, gaudy, and seductive, but Carroll's 1931 edition christened his newly rebuilt Earl Carroll Theatre, famous in its own right for its extravagant 3,000-seat size (and was interestingly bought by Ziegfeld when Carroll could no longer afford to own and run it).

The Music Box Revues: A series of revues with all songs written by hit maker Irving Berlin, the *Music Box Revue* was Berlin's cohesive and sophisticated production, created especially for his privately owned and built New York theater, the Music Box. From 1921 to 1924, the four editions provided some of America's favorite music and some of Broadway's most stylish production numbers, with "Say It with Music" acting as the revue's theme song.

The Garrick Gaieties: What began as a singular showcase of talent in 1925, originally intended as a fundraiser for the Theatre Guild, soon became the surprise hit of the season and made stars of its first songwriting team, Richard Rodgers and Lorenz Hart. The *Gaieties'* content was fresh, young, and irreverent, as were the overall performances (the cast was mostly comprised of lesser-known and/or novice company members who relished the performing opportunity). The popularity of the inaugural performance (a two-night gig which grew into a run of 211 performances) led to two more *Gaieties* editions which also proved to be fertile stomping grounds for young, soon-to-be stars, as well as songwriting talents such as Vernon Duke and Johnny Mercer.

The Blackbirds Revues: After introducing London to some of Harlem's premiere African American performers in *Blackbirds* (1926), producer/director Lew Leslie brought his revue back to America, giving it a new home on Broadway. Originally billed as "A Distinctive and Unique Entertainment with an All-Star Cast of 100 Colored Artists," Leslie's *Blackbirds of 1928* featured talents such as dancer Bill "Bojangles" Robinson (who also reappeared in the 1933 edition). In addition, the 1928 edition showcased the top-notch songwriting team of Jimmy McHugh and Dorothy Fields, who provided such hits as "I Can't Give You Anything but Love." Three subsequent *Blackbirds* editions (1930, 1933, and 1939) continued to introduce formidable talents to Broadway audiences, e.g., Ethel Waters (in 1930) and Lena Horne (1939).

The Revues of Dietz and Schwartz: Beginning with three editions of *The Little Show* (from 1929 to 1931), composer Arthur Schwartz and lyricist Howard Dietz (who also served as frequent sketch-writer and sometime director) captivated audiences with their intimate and sophisticated aesthetic and content, often interspersing dramatic numbers/scenes with comic ones. For instance, in their hugely successful 1929 edition, there appeared a segment, set in a rundown Harlem tenement, that featured a bluesy and carnal vocal performance of "Moanin' Low," followed by a sexually suggestive dance number. After *The Little Show* editions, Dietz and Schwartz created four new revues: *Three's a Crowd* (1930), *The Band Wagon* (1931), *Flying Colors* (1932), and *At Home Abroad* (1935). Of the four works, *The Band Wagon* was the major success, deemed to be one of the most stylish, inventive, and musically notable revues of its time, tightly organized by its small creative team that worked closely together to create a cohesive, signature product, again challenging audiences with both serious and stylized "highbrow" content, as well as satire and silliness. In addition to the memorable scores and chic material, the Dietz/Schwartz revues of the '30s also showcased great performers such as Beatrice Lillie and the brother/sister dance team of Adele and Fred Astaire.

BERT WILLIAMS

In 1910, racial tremors were felt across Broadway when some top-billed performers of the *Follies* staged a revolt against their all-powerful producer, Florenz Ziegfeld. The cause of such turmoil? Ziegfeld's hiring of African American comedy star, writer, and composer Bert Williams to join his cast of all-white performers as a headliner for that year's edition. In the end, Ziegfeld called the bluff of his disgruntled stars, announcing that Williams was the only star he could not replace, so the rest of them were free to leave. They stayed; and Bert Williams became the first African American to top a marquee in a mainstream production on Broadway, adding another landmark triumph to the remarkable career of one of the most versatile, compelling, and popular artists during the early 1900s. Pushing against racial barriers, Williams not only brought comic artistry, dignity, and humanity to the previously mocked and marginalized stock minstrel character of the "shuffling coon," but was instrumental in introducing African American musicals to Broadway, as well as writing and performing signature songs that made him the best-selling black recording artist at the beginning of the twentieth century. Williams' smart, slapstick, and sensitive antics on stage were unparalleled during his time, an achievement that was double edged in an American society burdened and conflicted by racial tensions, prejudices, and constrictions. Although Williams was lauded by a prominent New York critic as "one of the great comedians of the world," he was also poignantly described by fellow *Follies* star W. C. Fields as "the funniest man I ever saw—and the saddest man I ever knew."

Egbert Austin "Bert" Williams was born in Nassau, Bahamas, on November 12, 1874. His family immigrated to America when he was 10 years old, ultimately settling in Riverside, California, where Williams graduated from high school. After graduation, he moved to San Francisco where he gave up his plans to study civil engineering due to financial shortcomings and soon began working as a local performer, ultimately joining The Mastoden Minstrels, a traveling minstrel company in California. By 1893, Williams began to tread the boards of vaudeville, having teamed with an African American partner, George Walker, in San Francisco. In their vaudevillian comedy act, Williams & Walker, Williams routinely played the slow-witted, comic fool to Walker's straight conman. Both men were required

Bert Williams in signature number "Nobody" in 1922. © CORBIS

to perform in the minstrel tradition of blackface, billing themselves as "Two Real Coons" to differentiate themselves from white minstrel performers. They incorporated song and dance with comic banter and sketches in which Williams often succumbed to Walker's conniving schemes while providing humor and pathos through his dexterous physicality and clownish demeanor. By 1896, they had gained enough notoriety on the segregated black vaudeville circuit to be featured in a Victor Herbert work, *The Gold Bug*, thus providing their debut on Broadway. The show was a box office failure; but Williams & Walker were singled out for positive notices. In the production, they also introduced their rendition of the cakewalk (a dance step originally derived from an African circle dance but which became configured by African Americans in the South to lampoon the superficial airs of plantation owners). With Williams & Walker's introduction of the dance on Broadway, the cakewalk soon became a craze throughout America, as well as a signature choreographic move for Bert Williams throughout his career. As the nineteenth century came to an end, Williams & Walker were vaudeville headliners at

Koster and Bial's Music Hall, and Williams had begun making audio recordings of his early compositions. The team also created and appeared in other productions, such as *The Policy Players* (1899), but had still not achieved "legitimate theatre" status until the fall of 1900 when they found great success with *Sons of Ham*. Importantly, with this jovial farce, Williams & Walker, who wrote most of the music and lyrics, moved away from the simplistic and negative African American portrayals found in minstrelsy to provide more innovative humor and less caricature. Furthermore, the production appealed to New York audiences who had, possibly, tired of the easy minstrel formulas; thus, it ran for two years (including a 1901 revival). Capitalizing on their new fame, the duo began recording discs in 1901, resulting in national exposure for Williams as his compositions gained notice. Specifically, one of Williams' best-known songs, "When It's All Going Out and Nothing Coming In," voiced a universal sentiment as it bemoaned financial troubles, and "Good Morning Carrie," rendered by various artists, became a top hit of the year.

Williams & Walker forged new territory when they created *In Dahomey*, with music by Will Marion Cook and lyrics by Paul Laurence Dunbar. When the production debuted in 1903, it was a first for an all-black musical on Broadway, although audiences were still segregated in the theatre. After its run in 1903 (fifty-three performances), the production enjoyed a well-received London engagement in that same year and then a brief New York revival (seventeen performances) in 1904. Having set a landmark precedent for black musicals on Broadway, Williams & Walker followed up *In Dahomey* with a new musical, *Abyssinia*, a comical/musical depiction of two African Americans (Williams and Walker) who win the lottery and tour Ethiopia. Featuring live camels on stage, the production debuted in spectacular style at the Majestic Theatre in 1906. Working again with composer Cook, Williams co-wrote the score with a variety of lyricists. Significantly, one of the songs from the production, "Nobody" [see fig. 3.2], would become a signature tune for Williams; he not only wrote the music for this mournful tune, which laments society's disregard for the unfortunate and marginalized "Nobody," but performed it with his inimitable style of sung speech and wry, poignant "sad clown" pathos. The song would become so identified with Williams that he would be forced to include it in his vaudeville act and *Follies* performances throughout his career. He once stated

that he had begun to "curse" the song (and the "assembler of the tune"), for audiences demanded it of him, no matter how many times he tried to drop it from his repertoire. Topping the sales of Williams' many other recordings, including referential compositions such as "Somebody" and "I'm Neutral," "Nobody" remained active in Columbia's sales catalogue into the 1930s. Furthermore, the song has been echoed in contemporary musicals, such as Kander and Ebb's *Chicago* (1975), which uses the number "Mr. Cellophane" to both reference the stage persona of Williams and his signature song.

The early 1900s continued to see Williams & Walker triumph on Broadway, as well as make significant advancements with regard to African American influence on and presence in the musical theatre genre. In 1908, the duo created *Bandanna Land,* which opened at the Majestic Theatre to positive notices and ran for 89 performances. Not only did Williams once again collaborate with Cook on the score, along with other artists, he once again created an iconic routine for himself: the pantomime poker game. In this signature bit, Williams, as a participant in a poker game, physically and facially communicated to the audience, through his silent, solo performance, the inherent drama experienced in a hand of poker. The sketch would become a staple in his repertoire throughout his career. *Bandanna Land* would also prove to be a turning point in Williams' life, as Walker would become seriously ill during the run and have to leave the show in 1909. Williams & Walker, consequently, disbanded; and Walker died less than two years later. Williams sorely missed his partner, who had often handled their business affairs and public relations. Somewhat adrift, Williams returned to the vaudeville circuit as a solo act, relying on his most popular songs and comic routines, and starred in some less-than-successful productions. Williams was then approached by Florenz Ziegfeld to join the *Ziegfeld Follies of 1910*. The move was unprecedented, as segregation was still the norm in the American theatre (for both audiences and performances), and it was unheard of to have a black headliner share the bill with an otherwise all-white cast in a mainstream Broadway production. Thus, although the Ziegfeld company members were fans of Williams' work, they threatened to walk out on their contracts rather than perform side by side with him in the *Follies*. When Ziegfeld made it clear that Williams was the only irreplaceable performer, the others relented. Williams then basically performed his solo vaudeville act in his *Follies* debut, receiving rave notices and embarking on one of the most significant engagements of his career.

The conflict surrounding Williams' initial engagement with the *Ziegfeld Follies* is significant in many respects. First and foremost, it highlights the racial prejudice with which he dealt throughout his career. Even before the Ziegfeld showdown, Williams had confronted similar situations; specifically, during the run of *Bandanna Land* in 1908, some acts refused to perform at a charity benefit held by George M. Cohan rather than share the stage with Williams & Walker, who had also been asked to be part of the evening's entertainment. In short, Williams may have done more than any African American during his lifetime to achieve legitimacy for the black performer and black material in the musical theatre arena, working to reconfigure and humanize the negative stereotypes and content popularized by minstrelsy. Yet, he was often forced to walk a fine line, balancing his artistic aims against the conventions, norms, and expectations of the white audiences that he sought to entertain. He always performed in blackface; and at the height of his career with the *Ziegfeld Follies*, he continued to confront racist obstruction and make necessary concessions. Williams negotiated his *Ziegfeld Follies of 1910* contract with Ziegfeld to include provisions that he would not appear in shows that toured the South, as well as never appear alone with a white woman on stage due to his concerns over her reputation, the audience reception, and his own safety. Further, when the *Follies* made their annual spring tour engagements throughout America, Williams used rear entrances to all hotels. One of the most emblematic stories of Williams' conflicted status in America, in regard to wealth, fame, and race, is the often told tale in which he entered a bar and ordered a drink, only to be told by the bartender that it would cost him $1,000. Williams deftly opened his jacket and removed a wad of cash, informing the bartender that he would, therefore, like

five of them. In Williams' own words, he wrote, "I have never been able to discover that there was anything disgraceful in being a colored man. But I have often found it inconvenient … in America."

From his debut in 1910 to 1919, Williams found great success with the *Ziegfeld Follies*, appearing in seven editions total. Throughout his *Follies* engagements, he continued to create iconic comic routines and introduce signature songs, which gained nationwide popularity once recorded. Specifically, in 1911, he created another famous comedy routine while popularizing a song called, "Woodman, Spare That Tree." In the number, he appeared as a feathered bird and lampooned the well-known poem by George Pope Morris. Indeed, Williams continued to be a bestselling artist in the recording and music publishing arenas, both during and after his tenure with the *Follies*. His hits included comic songs addressing the new legal scourge of Prohibition (e.g., "The Moon Shines on Moonshine") as well as several records under the alter ego of a corrupt preacher named Elder Eatmore. At the beginning of the 1920s, Williams was indisputably one of America's favorite recording artists, as well as one the highest paid in the world, with sales numbers that topped the charts and a signature rendition style. However, Williams was beginning to have health problems and his career was stalling. Still a popular box office draw, he was appearing in mediocre productions and struggling physically. After a bout of pneumonia in 1921 and a collapse during a road performance in 1922, Williams returned to New York where he suffered fatal health complications, dying on March 4, 1922. Williams was only 46; yet he had revolutionized the position and perception of the African American on the musical stage. Honored with a public funeral in which thousands had to be turned away, it was publically evident that he was loved by both white and black Americans, the sad-sack clown who found a way to negotiate race in America through his unique talent and pioneering spirit.

Figure 3.2

NOBODY

Music by Bert Williams, Lyrics by Alex Rogers (1905)

When life seems full of clouds an' rain
and I am filled with naught but pain,
who soothes my thumpin' bumpin' brain?
Nobody

When winter comes with snow an' sleet,
and me with hunger and cold feet,
who says "Ah, here's two bits, go an' eat!"
Nobody.

I ain't never got nothin' from nobody, no time!
And until I get somethin' from somebody, sometime,
I don't intend to do nothin' for nobody, no time!

When I try hard an' scheme an' plan,
to look as good as I can,
who says "Ah, look at that handsome man!"
Nobody.

When all day long things go amiss,
and I go home to find some bliss,
who hands to me a glowin' kiss?
Nobody.

I ain't never done nothin' to nobody,
I ain't never got nothin' from nobody, no time!
And until I get somethin' from somebody, sometime,
I don't intend to do nothin' for nobody, no time!
Nobody, no time!

FEATURED PRODUCTION: *In Dahomey* (1903)

**Music by Will Marion Cook; Lyrics by Paul Laurence Dunbar;
Book by Jesse A. Shipp**

**Original Broadway Run: Opened February 18, 1903; New York Theater;
53 performances**

At the advent of the twentieth century, the blackface comic act of Williams & Walker was a favorite with both white and black audiences. The two African Americans had become headliners on the black vaudeville circuit and enjoyed a well-received Broadway debut as featured players in *The Gold Bug* (1896), in which they introduced what was soon to become their trademark dance step, the cakewalk. In 1903, they were given starring roles in *In Dahomey*, a production that would also prove to be a landmark in musical theatre: the first full-length African American musical to play Broadway. Williams & Walker's indelible stamp on the production was a major contributing factor in its success; further, the team's subsequent popularity (both nationally and internationally) garnered them additional opportunities to create their own musicals, *Abyssinia* (1906) and *Bandanna Land* (1908), making the first decade of the 1900s a fertile one for African American productions on the musical theatre stage.

Overall, *In Dahomey* has been described as a "road comedy," that is, a farce in which two misfits find themselves in "fish-out-of-water" scenarios during a series of travels, moving through numerous comic mishaps to triumph in the end. Featuring an African American cast and created by African American artists (composer Will Marion Cook, lyricist Paul Laurence Dunbar, and librettist Jesse A. Shipp), *In Dahomey* tells the tale of two characters, Shylock Homestead (played by Williams) and Rareback Pinkerton (played by Walker). The two men, along with a group of others, discover a pot of gold in America and use their newfound riches to travel back to the African land of Dahomey (the present-day West African republic of Benin). Once in Dahomey, the Americans have to finagle their way through multiple plot twists and comic misadventures. Homestead and Pinkerton, however, triumph over the many complications and are ultimately crowned rulers of the land.

With its reinscription of negative minstrel types, *In Dahomey's* libretto could be seen as offensive today; further, as would happen throughout their theatrical career, both Williams' and Walker's characters (Homestead and Pinkerton) were drawn according to the Williams/Walker performative alter-egos, respectively, the "Shuffling Coon" and the "Conman/Dandy." Yet the production also includes an ironic and subversive edge, specifically exemplified in the musical number "Evah Dahkey Is a King" in which the audience is advised to respect the "dahkey," for a return to the African jungle suggests that any lowly black man could actually be a king. In addition to the textual component, the score is one of marked compositional sophistication. Cook was a trained musician, aiming to create an African American opera; and he succeeded in giving the score an "operetta" touch, while merging formal aspects with the many musical idioms found on the popular stages of minstrelsy, vaudeville, and Broadway. In addition, he integrated modern sounds such as ragtime, most apparent in the production's rousing finale, "The Czar of Dixie." Star performers Williams and Walker were also given featured songs, which they embellished and used as show-stopping specialty numbers. Walker brashly led the entire company in the rousing "When Sousa Comes to Coontown," while Williams established himself as the hard-luck clown with one of his earliest signature songs, "The Jonah Man." This number, which anticipated Williams' iconic "Nobody," presents Williams, née Homestead, as the Everyman who is tripped at every turn but continues to rise and stumble along—a musical moment of resistance, born of pathos and comedy. Indicative of the score's impact and import is the fact that it was also published (a first for any black musical production).

Once *In Dahomey* opened on February 18, 1903, at the New York Theater, it ran for a modest, yet critically acclaimed fifty-three performances. An extraordinary four-year run for the production was on the horizon, however. Significantly, after the show closed in New York, it moved to London. There, it became a long-running novelty hit, premiering at the Shaftesbury Theatre (during which a "cakewalk" number had to be added, given the audience anticipation of the Williams/Walker dance specialty). The production then enjoyed a tour throughout the provinces, culminating in a command Buckingham Palace performance for the Prince of Wales' birthday. With *In Dahomey* being declared the musical sensation of London, it continued to tour for another year throughout England and Scotland, then back to New York's Grand Opera House in 1904 for a quick stint, before embarking on a forty-week tour across the United States. All of which resulted in a healthy profit for *In Dahomey's* investors and creators, while also demarcating it as one of the most successful musical comedies of its time. Given these attributes—profits, prestige, portent, star power, and pioneering spirit—it is no wonder that the musical is considered not only a theatrical milestone in black history, but a musical theatre landmark that paved the way for future productions that could further racially integrate and influence the Broadway musical genre.

PULLING BACK THE CURTAIN:
Race and Segregation in America's Early Musical Entertainment

As difficult as it is for a modern reader to understand the degree of racial discrimination that a superstar such as Bert Williams could face throughout his career, it may be even more confounding (and disconcerting) to appreciate how commonplace his situation was and how long such discriminatory practices and paradigms dominated the American live performance scene. Listed below are some illustrative examples of how racial segregation influenced and informed musical/theatrical entertainment in America, in terms of both performance and audience, during the first half of the twentieth century.

TOBA Circuit: One need only look at the segregated Theatre Owners Booking Agency—TOBA Circuit—in vaudeville to comprehend the separation of the races in America and its impact on an entertainment medium that was often celebrated and distinguished by its "melting pot" content and construct. Organized in 1909 as a vaudevillian alternative for the segregated audiences of the North and an antidote to the Jim Crow theatre proscriptions of the South, TOBA (generally known as "Toby Time") was a vaudeville circuit that extended below the Mason-Dixon Line into venues specifically designated for "colored" customers. Although one might see blacks and whites sharing a vaudeville stage in the North, it was a fact that most southern states did not allow blacks in the "whites-only" audiences of mainstream theaters; and even northern states implemented "blacks only" seating in the back (or balconies) of the houses up through the 1920s. Thus, the TOBA Circuit provided all-black vaudeville shows for all-black audiences (while occasionally allowing white audience members in the balcony for a midnight performance). Budgets were tight and conditions were rough, however, due to lower ticket prices (TOBA was referred to as "Tough on Black Asses" by its performers). Further, the circuit was somewhat deemed "second class," as it was excluded from the most prestigious black theaters in Harlem, Philadelphia, and Washington, D.C.; but performers (even those who were vaudeville stars in other venues) took pay decreases to play to enthusiastic black audiences. Such premiere talent included outstanding entertainers, vocal stars, dancers, and musicians such as Williams & Walker, Ethel Waters, Josephine Baker, Ma Rainey, Bessie Smith, Bill "Bojangles" Robinson, Fats Waller, Louis Armstrong, and Duke Ellington. Proving successful throughout the 1920s and into the 1930s, the theaters on the TOBA Circuit stretched from the East Coast into the deep South and as far west as Oklahoma, growing from 31 theaters to over 100 at the peak of its popularity. Like the rest of vaudeville, however, TOBA would ultimately dissolve due to the advent of talking films and the economic pressures of the Great Depression.

Chitlin' Circuit: Providing another outlet for African American musicians, vocalists, comics, and all-around entertainers who wanted to circumvent the racially restrictive and segregated venues in America, the Chitlin' Circuit was a collection of theaters, concert venues, nightclubs, diners, and dives that catered to African American audiences and provided secure and prominent employment for African American performers. Nicknamed after a regional Southern dish, the circuit ranged from the East Coast (including New York City's Cotton Club and Apollo Theater, as well as the Uptown Theatre in Philadelphia) into the most segregated regions of the South. The circuit also veered a bit into the Midwest (Fox Theatre in Detroit) and the Southwest (Victory Grill in Austin, Texas). During the "Jim Crow" era, many of America's most notable African American performers got their start on the Chitlin' Circuit, for other segregated venues were hesitant to hire unknown talent, unsure of their box office appeal for all-white audiences. This impressive roster included Cab Calloway, Dorothy Dandridge, Etta James, Billie Holiday, Duke Ellington, B. B. King, Richard Pryor, and many others.

National Theatre in Washington, D.C.: Prior to the Civil Rights Movement of the 1950s, most of the theaters in the U.S. were segregated, to one degree or another. Ironically, one of the most prestigious American theaters, situated at the historical heart of American democracy, was also one of the last regional theaters in America to be desegregated—and only after much protest and public outcry. During the first half of the twentieth century, black actors were allowed to appear on theatrical stages, but many times, only white audiences were allowed to attend. Washington, D.C.'s National Theatre was no exception. Even as other theatrical venues along the East Coast began to allow African American audience members to sit alongside whites, the National still enforced policies in which blacks were allowed to perform but barred from sitting in the audience. When *Porgy and Bess* (1936) was granted a limited engagement at the National, lead performer Todd Duncan, along with other cast members, threatened to boycott the performance unless black audience members were allowed to attend. Thus, the National relaxed its segregation policies for the run of the show. Yet, the gains were short lived, and the venue soon returned to its discriminatory practices, even though there were other public protests, including an Actors' Equity Association boycott in 1948. Rather than allow blacks to join its audience ranks, however, the theater closed its doors to live performances and remained dark until 1952, when it finally reopened as a desegregated venue.

Shuffle Along (1921): One notable success story (and anomaly) at the height of America's segregationist era was a theatrical production that is often touted as the first majorly successful African American musical on Broadway. Although this credit is not factual, given the popularity of the earlier Williams & Walker musicals at the turn of the century, there is merit to the descriptor; for it had been over a decade since the Williams/Walker works and no African American productions had appeared in the interim. It seemed that segregation had taken hold of the theatre community, with few producers willing to promote and stage African American works on the Great "White" Way. Then, in 1921, a musical with a book by Flournoy Miller, lyrics by Noble Sissle, and music by Eubie Blake took Broadway by storm. The musical was *Shuffle Along*, a political satire and comic romp regarding a mayoral race and political wrangling in fictional Jimtown, USA. One highlight was a twenty-minute comic fight scene in which the mayor and police chief "settle their differences," while a new mayoral candidate sings a sardonic, upbeat song, vowing to end the corruption. Created by an African American writing team, the original production of *Shuffle Along* featured Blake at the piano and Noble in the cast, along with African American musical stars of the day, many having found fame on the TOBA and Chitlin' circuits. The show played for 484 performances, an incredibly successful run. It also enjoyed a profitable national tour up through 1924, producing hit songs such as "I'm Just Wild About Harry" (later adopted by Harry Truman for his presidential campaign). Looking at this musical through a modern lens, much of the material may seem offensive, given its allusions to the minstrel stock type of the "Dandy" (the posturing black conman), as well as its inclusion of sentiments such as a closing assertion that the lighter the skin of an African American woman, the more desirable she is. Yet, *Shuffle Along* also proved to producers that an African American musical could appeal to white audiences and turn a profit on Broadway, reminding everyone that America's black artists were formidable players in the industry. Apparently, the reminder worked, for nine other African American musicals and revues opened on Broadway between 1921 and 1924. In addition, instead of being relegated to the balcony, black audience members were allowed orchestra seats to *Shuffle Along*, where they were able to witness the first nuanced and somewhat realistic African American romance on the Broadway stage (without blackface makeup), as well as fully realized characters who carried the narrative and provided the drama (instead of serving as cartoonish song/dance/comedy diversions). To appreciate the import of the production, it is crucial to note that there are many theatre scholars and historians who credit *Shuffle Along* with launching the Harlem Renaissance—a high honor for a musical comedy, especially given the national climate in which it appeared.

JEROME KERN

At the beginning of the twentieth century, the Broadway musical had something of a split personality. In short, there were two categories of narrative musical entertainments on the "legitimate" New York stage: (1) *operettas:* romantic, fanciful, decorative productions composed of ornate vocals, which included the American works of Victor Herbert, as well as many doctored European imports (capitalizing on the popularity of Franz Lehar's imported *The Merry Widow* in 1907), and (2) *musical comedies:* loosely constructed productions, epitomized by the popular works of George M. Cohan, which contained sentimental and/or melodramatic plots interpolated by generic and catchy songs, dances, and comic diversions. Thus, the musical theatre genre, as defined later in the century by its integrated song/dance/text construct, did not yet exist. This is not to suggest that turn-of-the-century musical entertainments were lacking or lesser forms than the later integrated works, for they were hugely popular and succeeded on their own terms. For instance, early musical comedies may have been textual mishmashes, but it is because they were more actor driven than text driven. Audiences came to see the impressive talents of the beautiful ingénues, dashing leading men, dancing chorus girls, and rubber-faced comedians. But, there did seem to be room for a third form on the American stage, i.e., a musical that could exploit the worlds of operetta and musical comedy, merging the sophistication of the former's musical composition with the latter's pop sensibility, while incorporating a paradigm of theatrical integration between the songs and their librettos. Further, the pioneering realization of such a new form required a creator who was versed in both operetta and musical comedy. Jerome Kern proved to be such an artist. In this regard, Kern is often acclaimed as the "Father of the American *Musical Theatre*" (as opposed to *Musical Comedy*). Specifically, Kern not only deployed his operetta training and experience to innovate songwriting in both musical comedy and American popular music, but he also worked to bring the idea of integration to the Broadway stage in the form of cohesive scores, integrated construct, and innovative subject matter, as well as an uncompromising vision of a new direction for the American musical *theatre.*

Born on January 27, 1885, to an entrepreneurial businessman (Henry Kern) and pianist (Fanny Kern), Jerome David Kern spent most of his childhood in Newark, New Jersey, receiving his first piano lessons from his mother and avidly continuing music studies

Jerome Kern (reclining on couch) collaborating with Ira Gershwin, summer 1943 © Underwood & Underwood/Corbis

throughout high school. After graduation, his father, who worked for a department store, refused to finance Jerome's dream of furthering his music education; instead, he demanded that Jerome join him at the store. The job was short lived, however. A popular tale regarding this career misadventure recounts that Jerome was assigned to represent the store as a buyer, purchasing *2* pianos from a dealer. Unfortunately, he was so enamored with the instruments that he ended up purchasing *200* pianos. Needless to say, it became clear to his father that Jerome did not have a head for business and, more importantly, that his heart stubbornly belonged to the world of music. He was, thus, allowed to attend music school, beginning with the New York College of Music, where he studied piano and composition for about a year, and then in Europe where he furthered his studies in music theory. During this period, Kern found employment in London, often writing songs for musical comedies, operettas, and/ or music hall productions that needed extra numbers inserted into the beginning of the shows, filling time while audience members were finding their seats.

When Kern ultimately returned to New York in 1904, his talent for adding songs to already written scores served him well. As a song-plugger for the Lyceum Publishing Company and then a salesman for T. B. Harms (a leading publisher of theatre scores), Kern was at the hub of the theatrical music business. In this position, he began peddling his own musical talents to his theatre clients, convincing many a producer and director to hire him as a rehearsal pianist for their shows. Once hired, Kern would play his own tunes to the delight of cast members and production staff during rehearsal breaks. So charming were the songs that one or more would often be added to the production's score. Furthermore, these interpolated songs began to be noticed by audience members and singled out by critics in the press. The songs were especially notable when they were added to operettas; for as a composer, Kern had a talent for bringing an American sound and freshness to staid European imports. Because of his formal training and experience in the operetta arena, he could emulate the rich compositional breadth of the genre (unlike Cohan's "four chord" compositions), while integrating (and reinvigorating) such techniques with catchy thematic hooks and refrains, as well as sweet, lilting melodies and some of the popular dance rhythms of the day. All of which resulted in hummable, unified songs that appealed to the populist ear. In addition to

his operetta work, he was able to bring a new degree of songwriting sophistication to the sometimes simplistic and limited scores of Broadway's popular musical comedies. For the next ten years, Kern would make this songsmith labor his career, interpolating numbers that would become musical standouts and prove to be more popular than the shows to which they were added, often topping American pop charts for both sheet music and record sales. Starting with his score revisions and additions for *Mr. Wix of Wickham* (1904), Kern's songs were deemed by critics to be a notch above the typical fare occurring on Broadway at the time—a point substantiated the next year when the song "How'd You Like to Spoon with Me?" (lyrics by Edward Laska) superseded the mediocre show for which it was supplied, becoming Kern's first major song hit.

During the next five years, Kern contributed songs to the scores of almost two dozen Broadway operettas and other musical works. In 1912, he finally composed a complete score, *The Red Petticoat*. With a libretto by Rida Johnson Young, the musical did not perform well at the box office, but it holds a unique historical place as the first musical to deal with the American West. Although Kern continued to provide hallmark songs for imported scores (case in point, the breakout hit "They Didn't Believe Me," supplied for the 1914 English musical *The Girl from Utah*, with lyrics by M. E. Rourke), he was increasingly disillusioned with the haphazard construction of musical comedy and operetta on Broadway. Having devised his own complete score, Kern was beginning to disdain the patchwork scores and disjointed assemblage of components in works that, in his opinion, undermined the artistic potential of the American musical.

The year 1915 would prove to be pivotal for Kern, however. He teamed with a small group of like-minded artists and theatre professionals to realize his vision of a reconfigured, relevant, and cohesive musical on the American stage. In that year, theatre owner F. Ray Comstock was contemplating a new direction for his failing Princess Theatre and sought advice from a notable literary agent, Elisabeth Marbury. Given the Princess Theatre's intimate size (299 seats), Marbury looked beyond mainstream Broadway to the model of the "New Theatre" movement, which had spread from Europe to America. This movement approached theatre with a seriousness of purpose, "elevating" the drama and appealing to select subscription audiences who were supportive of experimental techniques and content. As she exclaimed to Comstock, "Now is the time for someone to do the same thing for musical comedy." Although the Princess Theatre musicals would not be subscription-based, they still relied on discriminating audiences who would be open to innovations in musical comedy. Comstock and co-producer Marbury hired Jerome Kern to provide the music for their experimental musicals, along with English librettist Guy Reginald Bolton. At thirty years of age, Kern was finally given the opportunity to compose, as well as shape musicals that would embody his philosophy of score/libretto cohesion. The Princess musicals would be intimate, humorous, human, modern, and integrated. Due to budget and theater size, the musicals would limit cast size to thirty performers and orchestra size to approximately eleven musicians. Productions would require only two sets, one for the first act and one for the second. This stood in stark contrast to the musical comedies, revues, and operettas of the day that included patchwork scores, dozens of "extras" in supporting choruses, concert-sized orchestras, and numerous extravagant sets capitalizing on variety, diversion, and spectacle.

The first work created by Kern and Bolton, with the aid of various lyricists, was *Nobody Home* (1915). The show was intimate in size but did not completely ascribe to the overall Princess Theatre aspiration of integration and American content/spirit; specifically, it included interpolated songs and was adapted from an English musical. However, Bolton and Kern tried again in December of 1915 and triumphed with the whimsically titled *Very Good Eddie*. With this work, they established the innovative direction of the Princess Theatre, providing a new template for the American musical comedy in general. The small-scale *Eddie* dealt with two modern-day couples on their honeymoons and their comic misadventures as they are separated from one another on a Hudson River steamboat. The production was novel in that its humor was rooted in real-life situations and arose from the characters' psyches and actions, not from clumsily interjected comic bits and funnyman cameos (the current custom). In addition, the score was considered fresh and lively, with songs written specifically for the libretto in ear-pleasing American idioms.

Although bolstered by *Eddie's* positive reception (the show would run for a full year), Kern and Bolton were still working with a variety of lyricists, which undermined their mission to create integrated, unified works. Fortuitously, at the height of *Eddie's* success, Kern reconnected with P. G. Wodehouse, the well-known British writer with whom he had collaborated during Kern's early London days. The reunion happened when Kern ran into Wodehouse at the opening of a Broadway show, and the two struck up a spirited conversation. That same night, he introduced Wodehouse to Bolton, and the threesome continued to talk long into the night, with Kern and Bolton advocating their Princess Theatre mission and imploring Wodehouse to join them. By the next morning, the musical writing team of Kern, Wodehouse, and Bolton had been formed, with Kern serving as composer, Wodehouse as lyricist, and Bolton as co-librettist with Wodehouse. The collaborators set to work right away; and in 1917, they created four musicals, two of which became box office and critical triumphs. Debuting at the Princess Theatre as the follow-up to *Eddie*, the Kern/Bolton/Wodehouse production of *Oh, Boy!* is often asserted to be their greatest achievement. With another madcap libretto composed of romantic/marital misunderstandings and mishaps, the Princess production was also rooted in situation and character; and the score not only contributed to the plot's mood and action but also contained numerous stand-alone gems, including the breakout pop hit "Till the Clouds Roll By." The trio's second success was the comedy *Leave It to Jane*, and its humorous escapades were set in the unique locale (at the time) of a college campus. Unlike *Eddie* and *Oh, Boy!*, *Leave It to Jane* was not produced at the Princess Theatre, but the show still adhered to the Kern/Bolton/Wodehouse formula of dramatically integrated comedy and song, furthering their reputation as pioneers in the musical comedy genre. Given today's expectations with regard to the integrated book musical, their works can seem crudely constructed and somewhat contrived. Yet, in turning their backs on the hodgepodge content/construct of early twentieth-century musical comedy and the ornate machinations of the European operetta, Kern/Wodehouse/Bolton helped the American musical comedy redefine itself, introducing a musical treatment of situational comedy built on modern American content, filled with modern American characters, and integrating modern American songwriting. The last Kern/Bolton/Wodehouse musical at the Princess Theatre was a follow-up to *Oh, Boy!*, titled *Oh, Lady! Lady!!* (1918), set in Long Island and Greenwich

Village, which once again provided a comical take on courtship and marriage. Staying true to his credo that musical numbers should "carry the action of the play" and "be representative of the personalities of the characters," Kern would drop a lovely torch song from *Oh, Lady!* before its opening. The deleted number, "Bill," contained descriptive lyrics that didn't mesh with the actual physical characteristics of the actor playing the character described in the song. (Significantly, "Bill" would be pulled from Kern's "trunk" a decade later and inserted, with alterations, into *Show Boat's* score.)

In 1918, the Princess Theatre's writing team disbanded, and Kern found himself again on his own as a "hired gun" (albeit, one of the most prestigious names in the business), working with numerous lyricists and librettists on the type of empty, lavish, non-integrated productions he had decried in the past. For instance, in 1920 he was hired by Florenz Ziegfeld to provide the music for an elaborate star vehicle created especially for *Follies* dancing star Marilyn Miller. The show was titled *Sally* (1920) and it told a formulaic Cinderella story in which a lowly dishwasher (Miller) becomes a Ziegfeld star. The production was a smash, playing for 570 performances, and increased Miller's superstar status. Kern's status as a songwriter was also reaffirmed, as he wrote one of the most popular radio hits of the day, "Look for the Silver Lining" (lyrics by Buddy DeSylva), introduced by Miller in the show. Exploiting the success of *Sally*, producer Charles Dillingham hired Kern to write the score, with the librettist/lyricist team of Otto Harbach and Oscar Hammerstein II, for another Miller vehicle. The production was similarly titled *Sunny* (1925) and, basically, relied once again on the Cinderella plot, Miller's star power, and the barely integrated songs provided by Kern and company. Dispirited by these glitzy Broadway ventures and concerned that his grand concept of a new breed of American musical would never be realized, Kern often complained to his *Sunny* collaborator, Hammerstein, in whom he found a kindred spirit. Hammerstein had also spent years working on hobbled-together scores for weak operettas and musicals, while envisioning a new potential and purpose for the American musical comedy. As they parted ways, Hammerstein reiterated to Kern that if he ever found material that lent itself to their ideals of musical integration and seriousness of purpose, Hammerstein would be willing to work with him on the project.

Then, while reading the 1926 novel *Show Boat* by Edna Ferber, Kern excitedly hit on the idea of turning the book into a musical. Accordingly, he went looking for collaborators, men with whom he had worked previously who had demonstrated both the willingness and bravado to push the Broadway envelope. Specifically, he reunited with Florenz Ziegfeld, who boldly agreed to produce the show and premiere it at his new Ziegfeld Theatre. As promised, Kern also called lyricist/librettist Oscar Hammerstein II, who dove headfirst into the project, elated to finally tackle unique subject matter and provide lyrics integral to character and plot as well as poetic evocations of mood and atmosphere. Ziegfeld, Kern, and Hammerstein had reason to be nervous, however. Ferber's *Show Boat* was far from conventional source material. Specifically, the novel is a sweeping epic spanning over forty years and deals with such controversial subjects as miscegenation, racism, gambling addiction, spousal abandonment, and alcoholism. Consequently, although Broadway's *Show Boat* was originally billed as "An All-American Musical Comedy," with a plot infused with romance and melodrama, it veered far from the "musical comedy" formula of the day, embracing the serious elements of Ferber's novel as well as employing an innovative construct and tone. There was no celebratory ending, nor were there explicit comic insertions—a departure from the jokey, boy-meets-girl, happy-ending musical comedies currently playing on the Main Stem. Undertaking this massive effort, the group worked closely together, putting the production through numerous adjustments during its out-of-town tryouts. Once it opened in New York City, audiences were not only surprised but also somewhat overwhelmed, initially greeting the final curtain call with silence. Many of *Show Boat's* obvious innovations were the result of Kern's (and Hammerstein's) uncompromising musical vision, e.g., the desegregated choruses of African Americans and Caucasians on stage (a first for Broadway), as well as an opening in which a group of African American dockhands sing labored lamentations while toting bales of cotton (in stark contrast to the usual musical opening in which a chorus of comely females performs a high-energy kick line). Some of Kern's other *Show Boat* innovations were less blatant, such as its diverse score containing 23 musical numbers (including reprises), representative of multiple musical idioms. Further, Kern and Hammerstein's integration of their songs lent coherence and human connection to multiple storylines, timelines, and locales, e.g., the haunting and metaphoric use of the song "Ol' Man River," which became a leit-motif throughout the production, suggesting a larger metaphor of life's all-encompassing challenges and a Hegelian model of humanity's progressive "flow" through history. Happily for Kern and his collaborators, the critics lauded the production as a new concept in musical comedy. Even more important, audiences con-curred, and *Show Boat* played for 575 performances, a rarity at the time. Further, the work would solidify Kern as the "Father of American Musical Theatre;" that is, the man who bravely proposed and then proved that musicals could be something other than "musical comedies" by employing unconventional, sophisticated content and tying it all together with a unified score, reliant on character and situation.

Due to its landmark status, *Show Boat* is often posi-tioned as the beginning of the Golden Age of Musical Theatre, a period that spans 1927–1964, demarcated by the reign of the integrated book musical. However, some scholars and theatre aficionados argue that this period did not really begin with *Show Boat*, citing the fact that most Broadway musicals did not follow *Show Boat*'s example or promote its model for more than a decade. Even Kern failed to carry the torch with regard to the new direction of the serious, integrated book musical. Instead, he reverted to his operetta roots with classically constructed works that were lyrical, romantic, and traditional in tone and content. Signifi-cant among these works are *Cat and the Fiddle* (1931), written with lyricist/librettist Otto Harbach, and *Music in the Air* (1932), written with his *Show Boat* col-laborator, Hammerstein. Both works are set in 1930s Europe and fancifully center on backstage romances;

they also represent a high degree of musical lyricism. Detached from real life (a significant omission, given the turmoil in Europe at the time), the two works use an almost continuous musical score to tell their tales. They also illustrate Kern's move away from contemporary American content (which had been a core principle of his Princess Musicals) as he began to embrace a more Eurocentric aesthetic. And although Kern returned to the American musical comedy with 1933's *Roberta*, the critics were not overly impressed, as the production seemed to be a formulaic throwback, a disappointment given the portent and potential of *Show Boat*. The show, however, was a box office success and provided another iconic hit song for Kern: "Smoke Gets in Your Eyes." This song epitomizes Kern's gift for thematic cohesion, complex melodic expanse, and sweeping use of octaves, all the while supplying a seemingly simple and catchy tune. After moving to Hollywood in the 1930s to compose movie musicals, Kern furthered his reputation as one of America's premier composers (both George Gershwin and Richard Rodgers named him as an idol and inspiration). In 1945, Kern returned to New York to discuss writing a score for a musical biography of Annie Oakley, produced by Richard Rodgers and Oscar Hammerstein. In the midst of this visit, Kern suffered a cerebral hemorrhage while crossing Park Avenue and died four days later on November 11, 1945. The "Oakley" project would soon be given to another American musical genius and icon, Irving Berlin. But the loss of Kern stood as a reminder to the unique strength of American musical composition and the new artistic sensibility in the American musical comedy (or *theatre*) arena as well as a harbinger of all that was left to be done to realize the goals he presciently articu-lated during his career.

FEATURED PRODUCTION: *Very Good Eddie* (1915)

Music by Jerome Kern; Lyrics by Schuyler Greene
Book by Philip Bartholomae and Guy Bolton

**Original Broadway Run: Opened December 23, 1915; Princess Theatre;
341 performances**

While thrilled at being given the chance to re-present and redefine the American musical in 1915, Jerome Kern and company were also most likely daunted at the size and scope of the task. As previously detailed, the idea to create an intimate experiment in musical comedy integration and relevancy was initiated by literary agent Elisabeth Marbury, in response to manager/producer F. Ray Comstock's search for appropriate material (and attendant audiences) for his small 299-seat Princess Theatre. Once they recruited composer Kern (who was similarly committed to the idea of the integrated musical) and British librettist Guy Bolton, the mission of the Princess Theatre became clear: produce "little" musicals (cast size of around 30, orchestra size around 11, only two sets per show) with contemporary plots in which the comedy arises from somewhat believable situations and the human foibles of thoroughly modern characters. Most important to Kern, the scores should no longer contain individual songs by various artists, interposed into the libretto, but should be written specifically for the work, integrated into the storyline to comment on character or further character development.

The team's first effort, *Nobody Home* (1915), was a less-than-successful attempt to realize their innovative vision, but later that year, a second endeavor pleased audiences, critics, and its creators. The musical was *Very Good Eddie,* and its success was the beginning of a prolific three-year run by Kern, Bolton, and eventual writing partner, P.G. Wodehouse, whose collaborative works are commonly referred to as the Princess Theatre Musicals. With its plot and comedy dependent on physical, social, and cultural stereotyping, *Very Good Eddie* may look contrived and clichéd to a twenty-first-century audience, but to its Princess Theatre spectators, it was something new and exciting: a small-scale, character-driven musical comedy, placed within an everyday setting and fueled by everyday mishaps and misunderstandings. To summarize the plot, the eponymous "very good" character, Eddie, is a short, demure man, newly married to tall, bossy Georgina. The mismatched newlyweds are on their honeymoon aboard a Hudson River dayliner, along with another couple, Percy and Elsie. Percy and Elsie happen to be the reverse image of Eddie and Georgina, with Percy as the tall domineering partner and Elsie being the small, timid spouse. When Georgina and Percy are accidently delayed on shore, the boat sails without them, forcing their respective other halves, Eddie and Elsie, into embarrassing "couple" predicaments on the boat, full of comic confusion and compromised situations. Eddie stays "very good," however, and all is resolved in the second act, set on land at the Rip Van Winkle Inn, where the respective couples reunite and clear up all misunderstandings. Further, in the show's final comic resolution, Eddie transforms from mousey spouse to authoritative husband, reigning over his newly deferential wife and restoring order to his household. In addition to the situational comic plot, the show was filled with contemporary hummable tunes and sweet ballads by Kern and various lyricists, including "Babes in the Wood," "Some Sort of Somebody," "Isn't It Great to Be Married?" and "Nodding Roses."

Ultimately the novel Princess Theatre formula proved to be a winning one; and *Eddie*, after a triumphant run of 341 performances, was followed in 1917 and 1918 by three other major hits by the creative team of Kern, Bolton, and added lyricist/librettist Wodehouse: *Oh, Boy!*, *Leave It to Jane*, and *Oh, Lady! Lady!!*. Including *Eddie*, the four works are seen as landmarks in musical theatre history and cited as germinal models for the modern, intimate, and integrated musical comedy.

PULLING BACK THE CURTAIN:
Jerome Kern and Musical Theatre Cohesion

It is difficult today to comprehend a time when the musical had little use for score/libretto cohesion. Yet, the most successful musical comedies during the first few decades of the twentieth century consisted of patchwork scores, in which songs, often provided by several different artists, were loosely strung together, inserted opportunely (and often awkwardly) into the libretto. Jerome Kern sought to shift this paradigm, for he envisioned a day when the musical would be treated as an artistic whole, unified by the solidity and purposeful structure of its components. As a composer, he exploited, popularized, and codified certain unifying constructs and techniques, promoting the idea (and the soon-to-be accepted norm) of an organized musical score. Here are four of his most prevalent and influential innovations:

Regarding classical unity, Kern looked to the past to employ some of opera's more successful compositional devices. Specifically, he employed the (1) **overture**, (2) **leitmotif**, and (3) **reprise**, musically signaling to the audience a melodic, compositional through-line for his works.

The **overture** is a thematic/musical introduction to the production. It is an extended musical composition played by the orchestra before the curtain rises (figuratively speaking), consisting of a medley of the major songs and musical compositions contained in the score. Kern popularized the overture, giving his audiences a preview of the music they would soon hear once the show officially began. The overture continues to be a popular convention in musical theatre today, providing an audience with a connection to the upcoming score, that is, a starting point of cohesion.

Kern implemented **leitmotifs**, which are short, melodic refrains provided as part of the orchestral underscoring and specifically associated with a character and/or a certain dramatic action/development throughout the musical. In many ways, the leitmotif can become the character's signature "theme." Often introduced through an early song, it follows him/her throughout the musical, continuously reconnecting the audience to the character and/or event, while evoking memories of earlier incidents and musically commenting on progressive developments. (Importantly, the leitmotif is used in many other mediums today; one only has to think of Darth Vader from the *Star Wars* series to hear his musical theme or leitmotif.)

Along with the leitmotif, Kern employed and popularized the **reprise**, i.e., a song that is repeatedly performed throughout a musical production. Differing from the leitmotif, which only reappears as a musical refrain, often as underscoring, the reprise is a song or song excerpt (music and lyrics) performed on stage in a different context by one or more characters. But similar to the leitmotif, the reprise also connects the dots of the score, allowing development of characters and the libretto. Further, as the song is repeated, but often with different dramatic intent, response, and/or result, it not only familiarizes the audience with the score, but also takes them on the musical journey of progression for the character and overall plot.

Kern's other cohesive technique, which not only influenced the American musical theatre genre but also American songwriting for decades, was the **AABA song format**. If one were to think of the most formulaic pop hits since the advent of radio, one could not help but spot the dominance of this compositional form. Simply put, AABA is a song formula in which the chorus is organized into three repeated melodic refrains (with varying lyrics; denoted in the formula as "A") and one completely different melody, often denoted as the "bridge" or B section. Thus, the chorus (which in popular music is the predominant portion of the overall song) would be organized as follows: "A" is the completely self-contained melodic refrain with one set of lyrics and the next "A" is the same melody, repeated with new lyrics. Then the

"B" follows with a different melodic refrain (and new lyrics) that provides diversion and bridges the song to its final repeated "A" refrain; thus, after "B," the "A" melody reappears a final time (with closing lyrics and, most likely, a little variation to signal that this is the song's end). A prime example of AABA is the chorus of *Show Boat*'s "Ol' Man River." Given the symmetry of this songwriting technique and the audience's pleasure at understanding and anticipating its cohesive nature, it is not surprising that AABA became one of the most prevalent American song forms in the twentieth century. Of course, songwriters have delighted in complicating and confounding the AABA formula, twisting it into ABBA, ABCBA, AABCDBA, etc. (any time there is a new melodic invention in the chorus, a new alphabetic letter is designated). However, it is fun to continue to look for Kern's AABA today; for many standard pop hits that appeal easily and quickly to the ear employ this songwriting formula.

OSCAR HAMMERSTEIN II

Theatre scholars and historians have long argued over the definitive beginning of the Golden Age of Musical Theatre, some position 1927's *Show Boat* as the defining moment at which the Age began; others have insisted that the Age did not really cohere until the debut of *Oklahoma!* in 1943. Regardless of this somewhat academic dispute, one artist can be placed at and deemed partially responsible for the advent of the Golden Age, as he was the lyricist/librettist for both landmark works. Oscar Hammerstein II's career spanned decades, working with various partners (the most famous being Richard Rodgers) to revolutionize the conceiving, writing, and staging of musicals as he brought his own sense of artistic integrity, experimentation, poesy, and social consciousness to Broadway. There is little disagreement that Oscar Hammerstein II was the guiding force behind the genre's evolution from musical comedy to musical theatre.

Oscar Greeley Clendenning Hammerstein was born on July 12, 1895, in New York City to Helen and William Hammerstein. Named after both of his grandfathers, the famous antislavery newspaper publisher Horace Greeley and the powerful theatre/opera impresario Oscar Hammerstein (while, curiously, "Clendenning" was the minister who married his parents), young Oscar ultimately simplified his lengthy name to Oscar Hammerstein II. He also aimed to follow in the footsteps of his chosen namesake and continue the Hammerstein theatre legacy, for his grandfather is often credited with moving New York's Theatre District north from the Herald Square vicinity at the turn of the twentieth century to its current "Broadway" location around Times Square. Specifically, Hammerstein I, an entrepreneurial Prussian immigrant, bought pieces of land from 43rd Street to 45th Street and began building theaters, defying the common wisdom that family audiences would not venture into this territory (Longacre Square), which was situated at the corner of the Tenderloin, a seedy district known for prostitution and criminal activity. Hammerstein I's visionary gamble paid off, with the most prominent of his theaters being the Victoria Theatre, built in 1899 and ultimately becoming America's largest vaudeville house. Hammerstein I also wielded great power in the New York theatre scene as a producer (and composer, of sorts); especially notable was his successful production of Victor Herbert's *Naughty Marietta* (1910). Oscar Hammerstein II's father, William, was also in show business and managed the Victoria Theatre, while his uncle, Arthur Hammerstein, was a theatre producer.

Given this lineage, it seems reasonable that the young Hammerstein would quickly move into the family business; however, any such theatre "calling" would have to wait. Although he had spent a childhood surrounded by theatre and had been active in school plays, with piano lessons starting at age 9, he was discouraged from pursuing theatre after high school. Instead, his father insisted that he attend Columbia University and study law. Hammerstein's mother had died when he was 15; therefore, his father was the lone parental voice and Hammerstein complied, attending Columbia University as an undergraduate, beginning in 1912, then moving on to Columbia Law School. As a Columbia undergrad, 1914 and 1915 proved to be formative years for Hammerstein in two respects: (1) In 1914, his father died, leaving him free to dabble in theatre, and (2) he joined the Columbia University Players in 1915 and participated as a performer in that year's annual Varsity Show titled *On Your Way*. Throughout his time at Columbia, Hammerstein would consistently work on the Varsity Shows as a performer and, more important, as a writer, penning librettos and lyrics for several editions. He also established lifelong friendships with other musical theatre neophytes at Columbia, including Lorenz Hart and, most significantly, a young Richard Rodgers with whom he wrote a musical number, "There's Always Room for One More," for a Varsity Show in 1920; i.e., the first "Rodgers and Hammerstein" song.

Although young Hammerstein had acquiesced to his late father's wishes by attending law school, he was increasingly consumed by his theatre pursuits; thus, he dropped out of school after a few months in 1919. Looking for work and anxious to start his theatre career, Hammerstein appealed to his uncle, theatre producer Arthur Hammerstein, who gave him his first professional job as stage manager for several musical productions by operetta composer Rudolf Friml. Working for his uncle proved fortuitous; for Hammerstein was able to make important connections with other potential collaborators, even dabbling on librettos during their development phases. Further, Uncle Arthur produced Hammerstein's first two writing projects for the professional stage: *The Light* in 1919 (a nonmusical play) and *Always You* in 1921 (for which Hammerstein wrote the book and lyrics, collaborating with composer

Herbert Stothart). Neither production was successful. Consequently, Arthur suggested to Hammerstein that he sharpen his writing skills by teaming with the more experienced and proven librettist/lyricist Otto Harbach (who had collaborated with Friml on numerous operettas). The partnership proved amazingly successful, both in terms of the box office and as a training ground for Hammerstein as he found his own voice and theatre philosophy, while simultaneously garnering exposure and critical acclaim. From their first success with *Wildflower* in 1922, the Harbach/Hammerstein writing duo collaborated with composers to create eight musicals and operettas, half of which became top hits in the 1920s, including the wildly popular *Rose Marie* in 1924 (with music by past collaborators Stothart and Friml) and the 1925 star vehicle for Marilyn Miller, *Sunny*, where Hammerstein established significant relationships with the show's producer, Florenz Ziegfeld, and its composer, Jerome Kern. His next project, in collaboration with both men, would prove to be the first milestone in Hammerstein's prolific and potent career: *Show Boat*.

As detailed in the previous section, Kern and Hammerstein, while working on the frivolous *Sunny*, had discussed their desire to create an integrated musical work which would constitute a "musical play." After Kern read Edna Ferber's *Show Boat*, he asked Hammerstein if he would like to collaborate on adapting the work for the musical stage; Hammerstein eagerly agreed. Kern and Hammerstein's *Show Boat* would revolutionize the musical genre in many respects. Although the production was subtitled "An All-American Musical Comedy," Hammerstein's libretto dealt seriously with controversial subjects (although he also infused comedy throughout the work). Further, instead of the usual hodgepodge conjoining of librettos to songs, both Kern and Hammerstein envisioned a new type of "musical play" in which the songs were specifically created to further the narrative and enhance character development, an organized work in which all components could function as a seamless whole. As Hammerstein recounted, *Show Boat* represented a "new genre" in which "the play was the thing"; and on this building block there could be a "complete integration of song, humor, and production numbers into a single and inextricable artistic entity." Significantly, *Show Boat* also reflected Hammerstein's personal ideology that men and women are innately good and can aspire to the "angels" of their nature, triumphing over intolerance,

ignorance, and personal demons to contribute to society as newly evolved and enlightened citizens, furthering the development of humankind as a whole. As *Show Boat* illustrated, some characters were able to evolve by rising above bigotries and intolerances to succeed on many fronts and receive second chances, finding both communal and personal places of enlightenment and peace. It is significant that Hammerstein rewrote Ferber's original *Show Boat* ending, offering a more hopeful scenario where Gaylord and Magnolia meet in a sentimental reunion at the stage debut of their beloved daughter who is furthering the family theatre legacy. In such an instance, as Hammerstein asserts, the human experience is ever evolving and progressive, or as he more poetically writes in "Ol' Man River," it "jes keeps rollin' along" [see fig. 3.3]. As potently illustrated in the aforementioned song, Hammerstein's *Show Boat* lyrics easily matched Kern's sweeping and versatile score, as he moved from witty entertainments ("Life Upon the Wicked Stage") to romantic ballads ("Only Make-Believe") and character studies ("Can't Help Lovin' Dat Man").

Show Boat was a tremendous success, heralding great things for the integrated "musical play" or "musical theatre" on Broadway. Successors were slow to emerge, however, as Broadway soon reverted to its old form. Accordingly, Hammerstein returned to works reminiscent of those early in his career. Specifically, his Broadway follow-ups to *Show Boat* included an operetta, *The New Moon* (1928), written with renowned composer Sigmund Romberg, as well as *Sweet Adeline* (1929), a formulaic production written with Kern as a vehicle for their *Show Boat* star Helen Morgan. Hammerstein also reunited with Kern for *Music in the Air* (1932), a romanticized Old World venture in terms of locale, subject matter, and operetta-style music. The Eurocentric backstage romance and musically dominant work had a lengthy run on Broadway; but it would be Hammerstein's last significant stage success for almost a decade—until he received another life-changing proposition by an old Columbia colleague, Richard Rodgers.

Rodgers' proposal came just in time, for Hammerstein had suffered a decade filled with disappointment. After a string of failed productions, including his last collaboration with Kern, *Very Warm for May* (1932), Hammerstein moved to Hollywood in the '30s to write for the movies. Unhappy with and unable to work within the industry's time restraints and factory methods, he returned to New York in 1942 and began an adaptation of Georges Bizet's famous 1875 opera *Carmen*. Using Bizet's music and the basic plotline, Hammerstein rewrote the libretto and lyrics to contemporize the work, setting it in America during World War II and recasting it with African American characters. He titled his revised work *Carmen Jones*. After finishing the libretto, he put the project on hold to begin work with Rodgers, who was looking for a collaborator to musicalize *Green Grow the Lilacs*, a popular 1931 play by Lynn Riggs. Rodgers' longtime partner at the time, Lorenz Hart, had become increasingly difficult to work with and had rejected the project. Before leaving for a "hiatus" in Mexico, however, Hart gave his blessing to the Rodgers and Hammerstein venture (Hammerstein also proved to be a gentleman in the arrangement, having told Rodgers in the past that he would never intrude on the partnership of Rodgers and Hart unless Hart proved unable or unwilling to work with Rodgers on a particular musical). Like *Show Boat, Oklahoma!* was a gamble. Produced by the Theatre Guild, the work tackled unusual subject matter, steeped in nostalgia and Americana, e.g., Oklahoma's emerging statehood, the rural conflicts between "farmers and cowmen," and romantic intrigue regarding a date to the box social. The production would also advance the "integration" ideas and ideals that *Show Boat* promoted in 1927. Hammerstein's libretto and lyrics became important components by which the locale was specified, the tone was poetically set, the narrative was furthered, and characters were differentiated and developed. In fact, Hammerstein would write many of the lyrics before Rodgers would compose the music, somewhat dictating the direction of the score (an unusual position of prominence and power for a lyricist). An oft-told account by Rodgers is illustrative: The composer stated in many interviews that the first lyric he heard from Hammerstein was "there's a bright golden haze on the meadow." From that point, Rodgers knew the music he wanted to compose. To further their vision of a production that integrated all elements of song, text, and dance, Rodgers and Hammerstein worked with director Rouben Mamoulian and prominent ballet choreographer Agnes de Mille. Originally titled *Away We Go,* the show would be renamed *Oklahoma!* before debuting on Broadway on March 31, 1943, where it was accorded great critical and popular acclaim. *Oklahoma!* ran for an unprecedented 2,243 performances, and Hammerstein, along with Rodgers, received a special 1944 Pulitzer Prize for the musical.

Oklahoma! would also signal the beginning of a two-decade-long partnership. After Hammerstein finished *Carmen Jones* (which debuted in December 1943 to positive reviews) and Rodgers attempted one more project with Hart (a revival of their 1927 musical, *A Connecticut Yankee*), the two reunited to become one of the most celebrated and profitable musical theatre writing teams and producers in the genre's history. Their canonical catalogue includes such hits as *Carousel* (1945), *South Pacific* (1949), *The King and I* (1951), *Flower Drum Song* (1958), and *The Sound of Music* (1960), all of which are discussed in detail in the Rodgers and Hammerstein section of Chapter 5. Suffice it to say, Hammerstein's influence on the American musical theatre genre is immense, given the breadth, integrity, and vision of his works, both before and after his partnership with Rodgers. His professionalism and artistry promoted the librettist/lyricist to a place of prominence, yet he also furthered the concept of an integrated work in which all components serve the overall musical play instead of the top-billed stars and/ or individual collaborators. It is no wonder that Hammerstein was often deemed the "poet amongst lyricists" by his peers; for he found a way to write lyrics that were evocative, active, and humorous, while imbuing his writing with poetic sensibility, colloquial language, and heartfelt sincerity that seemed natural to each character and situation. Given his positive and idealistic world view, Hammerstein has often been accused of writing overly sentimental material; yet, if one contextualizes and historicizes the subject matter of his works, one cannot deny the innovations and controversial, socially conscious subject matter he introduced to Broadway and the American musical theatre genre. In short, Hammerstein was not only an experimentalist and revolutionary in terms of musical theatre content and construct, but also an artist who didn't mind wearing his sincere and hopeful heart on his sleeve.

Shortly after the opening of *The Sound of Music* on Broadway in 1959, Hammerstein succumbed to a prolonged battle with stomach cancer and died on August 23, 1960. With a Broadway career spanning almost forty years during which he contributed lyrics to 850 published songs and garnered eight Tony Awards, as well as two Academy Awards for Best Original Song, Hammerstein was considered irreplaceable in the world of musical theatre. In recognition of this fact, theatre districts in New York and London paid him tribute on the eve of his death, with West End theaters respectfully dimming their lights and Broadway turning off all lights for a complete minute in homage to the Broadway legend. It was a poetic metaphor for the passing of one of the brightest American musical theatre talents of the twentieth century.

OL' MAN RIVER

Lyrics by Oscar Hammerstein II

Music by Jerome Kern (1927)

Dere's an ol' man called de Mississippi;
Dat's de ol' man dat I'd like to be!
What does he care if de world's got troubles?
What does he care if de land ain't free?

Ol' Man River,
Dat Ol' Man River,
He mus' know sumpin'
But don't say nuthin',
He jes' keeps rollin',
He keeps on rollin' along.

He don' plant taters,
He don' plant cotton,
An' dem dat plants 'em
Is soon forgotten,
But Ol' Man River,
He jes' keeps rollin' along.

You an' me, we sweat an' strain,
Body all achin' an' wracked wid pain –
Tote dat barge!
Lif' dat bale!
Git a little drunk,
An' you land in jail . . .

Ah gits weary
An' sick of tryin';
Ah'm tired of livin'
An' skeered of dyin',
But Ol' Man River,
He jes' keeps rolling' along.

Niggers all work on de Mississippi,
Niggers all work while de white folks play,
Pullin' dose boats from de dawn to sunset,
Gittin' no rest till de Judgment Day.

Don' look up
An' don' look down –
You don' dast make
De white boss frown.
Bend your knees
An' bow your head,
An' pull dat rope
Until yo' dead.

Let me go 'way from the Mississippi,
Let me go 'way from de white man boss;
Show me dat stream called de river Jordan,
Dat's de ol' stream dat I long to cross.

Ol' Man River,
Dat Ol' Man River,
He mus' know sumpin'
But don' say nuthin',
He jes' keeps rollin',
He keeps on rollin' along.

He don' plant taters,
He don' plant cotton,
An' dem dat plants 'em
Is soon forgotten,
But Ol' Man River,
He jes' keeps rollin' along.

You an' me, we sweat an' strain,
Body all achin' and wracked wid pain–
Tote dat barge!
Lif' dat bale!
Git a little drunk
An' you land in jail . . .

Ah gits weary
An' sick of tryin';
Ah'm tired of livin'
An' skeered o' dyin',
But Ol' Man River,
He jes' keeps rollin' along.

FEATURED PRODUCTION: *Show Boat* (1927)

Music by Jerome Kern; Lyrics by Oscar Hammerstein II
Book by Oscar Hammerstein II

Original Broadway Run: Opened December 27, 1927; Ziegfeld Theatre; 572 performances

Show Boat was a major theatrical gamble. Über producer Florenz Ziegfeld, never one to shy away from a gambling prospect, leveraged his own financial security and professional reputation by agreeing to financially back the risky production, as well as provide a venue for its debut. Nonetheless, it would be up to its creators, composer Jerome Kern and librettist/lyricist Oscar Hammerstein II, to ultimately realize the production on the stage, a "musical comedy" that would upset the conventional wisdom as to what constituted the musical form, as well as how far the traditional formula could be stretched and bent without alienating the theatre establishment and Broadway ticket buyers. All ended happily, however. *Show Boat* enjoyed a triumphant Broadway debut, not only exceeding Ziegfeld, Kern, and Hammerstein's artistic aims and box office hopes, but also suggesting a new potential for the American musical.

Show Boat was originally intended as the inaugural production for Florenz Ziegfeld's new venue, the Ziegfeld Theater; but delays during the show's development necessitated that another more formulaic and innocuous musical, *Rio Rita* (1927), be Ziegfeld's premiere production. When audiences were finally introduced to *Show Boat,* however, they were undoubtedly stunned by its many structural innovations and the unconventional subject matter contained in its storyline. Although Hammerstein consolidated the sprawling narrative of Edna Ferber's novel, he kept his libretto true to much of the novel's content. To begin, *Show Boat* begins with black stevedores on stage, toting bales of cotton and singing a soulful lament about their hard labor on the Mississippi River. This alone was a major innovation, as most musicals at the time began with a spirited female chorus line. In fact, there existed at the time an inside understanding (and joke) that the merit of a Broadway show depended on the "leg" view of the chorines, visible to spectators by the time the opening curtains had risen to a knee-high height. The audience also had to confront a serious discussion of race in the show. Many documented accounts of *Show Boat*'s opening night describe the audible gasps and murmurs by audience members as they witnessed the opening number and a first on the American musical stage: a desegregated chorus. From this starting point, Hammerstein's libretto continued to challenge its audience, including such controversial topics as miscegenation, racism, familial abandonment, gambling addiction, and alcoholism, while depicting the fortunes and misfortunes of a show business family. Given its forty-year span, the plot, with its multiple storylines, basically chronicles the romance between ingénue Magnolia Hawks (whose lovable father, Cap'n Andy, manages the show boat, *Cotton Blossom*) and the boat's newly contracted performer, Gaylord Ravenal. The love story of Magnolia and Gaylord is introduced and cemented on the Natchez levee through their quasi love song "Make Believe," after which they become *Cotton Blossom*'s featured romantic duo. The couple soon marries and moves to Chicago. Once there, Ravenal, tormented by gambling debts and failed aspirations, abandons Magnolia and their young daughter Kim. In a pivotal scene, however, Magnolia emotionally reunites with her father as she performs a New Year's Eve number at the Trocadero nightclub, desperately trying to reinvigorate her performing career and provide for her daughter. Given her father's encouragement, the number is a success, and Magnolia goes on to great stardom in the theatre, with Kim ultimately following in her footsteps. Years later, Magnolia and Ravenal are reunited on the *Cotton Blossom,* with a suggestion that their love story may end in reconciliation (a more idealistic and romantic ending than Ferber's novel, courtesy of Hammerstein). The secondary plot entails the tragic decline of Magnolia's friend and show boat mentor, Julie La Verne, a *Cotton Blossom* star who is discovered to have been "passing" as a white woman (she has an African American mother). Once her mulatto status is uncovered and her marriage to a white *Cotton Blossom* entertainer, Steve Baker, is declared criminal on the basis of miscegenation, the couple is forced to leave the boat. Julie eventually reappears in Chicago, a sad alcoholic who, having been abandoned by Steve, is now bereft and alone, a sentiment conveyed through her bittersweet torch song "Bill." (In a significant side note, "Bill" was originally written by Kern and P. G. Wodehouse for *Oh, Lady! Lady!!* in 1918. Having been pulled from that musical and inserted into *Show Boat* [with crucial lyrics changes by Oscar Hammerstein II] almost ten years later makes the song a "trunk song," that is, a song written for a show/situation other than the subsequent production for which it is resurrected and ultimately used.) However, once Magnolia auditions for a chanteuse job in the same establishment, Julie gives up her singing gig, unknown to Magnolia, to provide an opening for Magnolia while sacrificing her own livelihood.

With its romance, tragedy, familial/domestic drama, social commentary, and comic interludes, Hammerstein's libretto had something for everyone. Furthermore, Kern's compositional output was a match for the epic narrative, consisting of 23 musical numbers in a gamut of historical styles and musical idioms (e.g., operetta, Negro spiritual, jazz/ragtime, minstrel tune, pop ballad, etc.), replete with devices such as leitmotifs, reprises, and trunk songs. (So expansive is the score, however, that it is almost never used in its entirety for revivals.) Importantly, Kern and Hammerstein's score was integrated on a level not previously seen in a major musical on Broadway. It was also used to communicate sophisticated themes to its audience, e.g., the travails and perseverance of the human spirit metaphorically suggested by "Ol' Man River," the questionable idealism of romantic operetta reveries exemplified by "You Are Love," and the whimsical and metatheatrical nature of "Life Upon the Wicked Stage." Lastly, given Ziegfeld's influence and signature aesthetic, the production was a feast for the eyes, employing spectacle in the guise of more than twenty stage settings. In this respect, Ziegfeld worried about recouping

Photo of the 2010 MUNY production of *Show Boat*. Jim Herren. Photo courtesy of MUNY.

his sizable investment in the show, especially given the tepid audience reaction at the opening night curtain call. The worries were unfounded, however, as Broadway patrons and critics were smitten by the innovative musical, fueling a phenomenal run of 572 performances. Ziegfeld staged a revival five years later with most of the original cast members (although Paul Robeson replaced Jules Bledsoe as Joe, an ironic development in that the role had originally been intended for Robeson). The 1932 production was the first of a string of Broadway revivals as well as movie versions. The most recent and successful revival was produced and directed by Hal Prince in 1994. Prince's lavish production had a Broadway run of 947 performances and contained many songs that had been cut in previous revivals, and added one written for the 1936 film version. Prince's production, which paid homage to historical accuracy, also ignited controversy, as he chose to highlight earlier racial/racist aspects in the libretto, as well as in the song lyrics, deemed offensive today (specifically, he resurrected the 1946 lyrics of "Ol' Man River," including the term "colored"). Yet the work reflected much of what was considered revolutionary in its initial configuration. In short, *Show Boat*, which was originally billed as "An All-American *Musical Comedy*" (given that the moniker "musical theatre" did not yet exist), still stands as a theatrical landmark, suggesting to its contemporaries an alternate path for the musical genre, one that integrated an atmospheric, poetic, and dramatic score with a multifaceted, epic libretto. For this reason, *Show Boat* is arguably positioned as the beginning of musical theatre's Golden Age.

PULLING BACK THE CURTAIN:

The Musical as Drama and Hammerstein's Librettist/Lyricist "Musical Play" Devices

Hammerstein believed in the seriousness and purposefulness of the musical text. In this respect, his work as librettist/lyricist is often compared to that of a playwright. Contrary to a playwright, however, a musical theatre writer must adapt the words of the characters, as well as the overall narrative, to unique musical/lyrical demands. Thus, here are four of the major contributions and innovations made by Hammerstein as he reconfigured the librettist/lyricist role to realize the "musical play" and introduce significant dramatic aspects to the once dismissed musical libretto.

1) Quasi Love Song: Instead of using the obvious, and often contrived, techniques of operetta and early musical comedy whereby love is declared simply and blatantly through song, Hammerstein created a type of nuanced love song/scene in which the romance is only suggested, often in fictional or fanciful terms. In the quasi love song, characters never overtly declare their love for one another, but speak in terms of conjecture and/or resistance, e.g., "if I loved you" (*Carousel*), or "people will say we're in love" (*Oklahoma!*), or "only make believe I love you" (*Show Boat*). Yet, by song's end, the romance is ultimately realized and recognized (if not completely by the characters, then, at least, by the audience). It is a sophisticated scenic/musical device and dramatic journey in which a love song is used for character development and psychological/emotional exploration.

2) The Self-Contained Song/Scene: In this innovation, Hammerstein introduced the concept of a self-contained scene that crucially furthers the plot and is also an extended musical number (with a bit of interjected dialogue). One of the earliest and most fully realized examples is *Carousel's* "Bench Scene," a musical interlude, containing a beginning, middle, and end, where song is inextricably intertwined with propulsive dialogue. Specifically, in the "Bench Scene," one sees the courtship of virginal Julie by the brutish Billy, beginning with expositional dialogue, then moving to semi-recitative, and ultimately arriving at the main theme/song, "If I Loved You." Once the refrain is sung by both characters, driven by intermittent dialogue and recitative, the number ultimately resolves in a climactic kiss, concluding the scene and cementing the relationship, all conveyed through a continuous scenic/musical number. This construct was further explored in other musicals by Hammerstein (e.g., a song/scene in *South Pacific* between Emile and Lt. Cable in which Cable's "Carefully Taught" evolves into Emil's "This Nearly Was Mine," with minimal dialogue but continual underscoring, to potently dramatize an argument and bonding between the men as they confront issues of racism and prejudice). As the integrated musical became the norm, the song/scene was further conventionalized and codified, with a notable instance being the "balcony scene" in *West Side Story*, as well as the pervasive occurrences in *Sweeney Todd* (with lyrics/music by Stephen Sondheim, who happens to have been a protégé of Hammerstein).

3) Song-as-Soliloquy: Here, a classic playwriting device is employed by Hammerstein in which a musical theatre character, through song, muses aloud in a solo scene through sung lyrics, dramatically struggling with conflicting thoughts, actions, and circumstances, while often (but not always) coming to a realization or resolution by the end of the song. In the process, the audience is also carried along the journey, witnessing the innermost thoughts and struggles of the character, as well as his internal process. Billy Bigelow's "Soliloquy" in *Carousel* is a fully developed example; yet Hammerstein would continue to use the form in many other musicals, often requiring a *Sprechstimme* (or spoken-sung) style to convey to the audience a character's psyche and consequent actions. Such examples include "A Puzzlement" and "Shall I Tell You What I Think of You?" from *The King and I*. And if one soliloquy was effective,

Hammerstein may have thought that two would be even more so, employing a double soliloquy ("Twin Soliloquies") in *South Pacific*, during which both Emile and Nettie musically voice and wrestle with their inner doubts regarding their budding romance. Regarding the soliloquy's dramatic volatility and immediacy, this type of number also falls under the category of the **active song**, which is a type of song in which a character, thinking aloud and wrestling with a problem, comes to a realization, undergoes a change, and/or progresses emotionally/psychologically throughout his/her vocal performance of the song. This is the opposite of the **reflective song**, which is a static song, in terms of dramatic action, which describes, recollects, or reflects on a situation, condition, concept, or person.

4) Metatheatre: This theatrical concept/theory of "beyond theatre" is, in simple performative terms, the dramatic device of a show within a show or a performance within a performance. Such an occurrence (e.g., the many staged performances and auditions contained in *Show Boat*) is a potent, meaningful moment on many levels; for when the audience in the auditorium watches another audience on stage watching another performance, the actual boundaries of what is theatre and what is life becomes blurred and signifies to the spectators that, as Shakespeare put it, "all the world is a stage" and we are "merely players," or as musical theatre team Kander and Ebb asserted, "life is a cabaret." One can also see the reflexive import and impact of metatheatre in musical theatre. Through it, the genre can address, explore, interrogate, and lampoon its own history, conventions, and defining constructs in many shows. Lastly, a metatheatrical scene or moment can serve a utilitarian purpose. Specifically, a song explicitly and overtly treated as a performance within the show, often termed a **prop song** (e.g., the "let's sing everybody a song" number) can be exploited as an entertaining diversion or as a more complex metaphorical message to the audience. Overall, metatheatre celebrates the fluid nature of life and theatre, merging both and subtly alerting audiences to the powerful paradigm, while possibly commenting on the preceding action or foreshadowing coming events. Beginning with numerous and assorted applications of metatheatre in *Show Boat* (especially the numbers performed onstage at various venues, ranging from the *Cotton Blossom* to the Trocadero), Hammerstein continued to employ the effective device with sophistication throughout his career (e.g., "Honey Bun" in *South Pacific*, "The Small House of Uncle Thomas" in *The King and I*, "Fan Tan Fanny" in *Flower Drum Song*, and "So Long, Farewell," as well as the Trapp Family Singers' concert performance, in *The Sound of Music*). In the process, Hammerstein used such musical moments to contribute elements of metaphor, diversion, and reflexive commentary to the drama aspects of the libretto, while setting an example for a multitude of librettists following in his wake.

DOROTHY FIELDS

Every once and a while, it is a good thing when children don't listen to their parents' advice. Legendary vaudeville star Lew Fields (born Moses Schoenfeld) got his start as a 9-year-old by performing in saloons, eventually becoming a famous headliner, theatre owner, and musical producer. Trying to shield his four children from the emotional and financial rollercoaster of show business, Fields and wife Rose (they remained married their entire lives) created as "normal" a home as could be expected for a performer, albeit a home where guests might include stars like Lillian Russell and Fay Templeton. Despite repeated admonitions to stay clear of the entertainment industry, three of his children became famous in their own right, contributing to the creation of classic American musical theatre. Joseph and Herbert Fields made their mark as librettists, while sister Dorothy's lyrics and librettos would shine on Broadway and in Hollywood from 1924 to 1973, an astonishing forty-nine-year career.

After a short-lived marriage to a doctor, Dorothy Fields (1905–74) began to dabble in lyric writing with pop composer J. Fred Coots. While none of their efforts were published or recorded, their songs did get Dorothy a job at Jack Mills Music, Inc., as a house lyricist, where she earned $50 for each completed lyric. The manager at Mills, the gregarious composer Jimmy McHugh, took a gamble on this new, 22-year-old employee. Their first collaboration, "Collegiana" (1924), became a pop hit, starting a successful decade-long collaboration which resulted in hundreds of songs, including many standards in the American songbook: "On the Sunny Side of the Street," "I Feel a Song Comin' On," "I Must Have That Man," and "I'm in the Mood for Love." Working with McHugh, Fields sounded less like her idols Lorenz Hart and Ira Gershwin, quickly developing her own unique style.

After writing songs for revues performed at the famous Cotton Club in Harlem, Fields and McHugh were asked to write the score for another all-black show, *Blackbirds of 1928,* which opened on Broadway starring Bill "Bojangles" Robinson and Adelaide Hall. The revue's standout hit, "I Can't Give You Anything But Love" [see fig. 3.4], helped propel the production to a run of 519 performances, resulting in the first Broadway show to record an entire album. Inspired by an overheard conversation between a poor couple peering at a

Dorothy Fields, April 1934 © Bettmann/CORBIS

window display at Tiffany's—"Gee, honey. I can't give you anything …"—Fields and McHugh wrote the song, which was to become an even bigger hit after the Stock Market Crash in 1929.

"I Can't Give You Anything But Love" also exemplifies a significant feature of Fields' work, that is, it boasts an easy-going, conversational feel that belies the painstaking construction of its lyric lines. Fields' incorporation of the vernacular ("gee," "swell," "baby") makes the song sound contemporary and young, while the internal rhymes give it a solid structure. Rather than calling attention to itself as poetry, a Field lyric comes across as matter-of-fact. The song was not only a hit in 1928 (rendered by Cliff Edwards, aka "Ukelele Ike"), but subsequent singers sent it back to the pop charts in 1936 (i.e., Billie Holliday and Teddy Wilson) and 1948 (Rose Murphy). It has been sung in at least nine films and made it back to Broadway in the revues *Ain't Misbehavin'* (1978), *Sugar Babies* (1979), and *Jersey Boys* (2005).

The next Fields/McHugh project was a book musical that became a Fields family affair. With a libretto by Herbert Fields, *Hello Daddy!* was also Lew Fields' last appearance on stage and ran for a respectable

197 performances. Dorothy realized she liked writing songs for a book musical, having already found success with revues and pop songs. After two editions of the *Ziegfeld Midnight Frolic* revues, Hollywood called, and Fields and McHugh moved to California in 1930 to work in the new world of sound motion pictures.

The title song of *The Cuban Love Song* (1931) would be Fields and McHugh's first Tinseltown hit. Dorothy was under contract with MGM, while brothers Herbert and Joseph were with Warner Brothers and Republic, respectively, so the three Fields siblings bought a house together and lived in Hollywood for most of the 1930s.

For the grand opening of the 6,200-seat Radio City Music Hall in 1932, Fields and McHugh were the only songwriting team asked to create and perform two songs for the occasion: "With a Feather in Your Cap" and "Hey Young Fella (Close Your Umbrella)," songs that found their way into the movies. (Fields occasionally sang some of her songs for radio programs; she was also an accomplished pianist.) At 27 years of age, Dorothy Fields was starting to become a household name, a rarity for a lyricist.

One of the eight films for which she created songs in 1935 was *Every Night at Eight*; it contained two numbers that became stand-alone hits, "I Feel a Song Comin' On" and "I'm in the Mood for Love." In addition to these collaborations with McHugh, Dorothy had started songwriting with other composers: Fritz Kreisler, Oscar Levant, and *Show Boat*'s Jerome Kern. Working with Kern proved to be most inspirational for Fields, and her writing reached a new level as the two created such standards as "Lovely to Look At," "I Won't Dance," "I Dreamed Too Much," and "A Fine Romance."

As with all of her collaborators, Kern wrote the melody first, then Fields created the lyric. Although nineteen years her senior, Kern felt immediately at ease with Fields, and the two enjoyed a friendly, but professional, relationship until Kern's death in 1945. For their third film together, the team was asked to write a score for the screen sensation of Fred Astaire and Ginger Rogers. The resultant *Swing Time* (1936) not only featured "Pick Yourself Up" and "A Fine Romance" (Fields' only two songs where she wrote the lyrics first), "Never Gonna Dance," and "Bojangles of Harlem," it also garnered the pair an Oscar for Best Original Song with the soon-to-be classic "The Way You Look Tonight." In this iconic number, Fields' lyrics capture the shimmering essence of an Astaire/Rogers movie musical: sophisticated, sexy, and a little bit saucy. This was the first Oscar awarded to a female songwriter.

While Hollywood had been good to Dorothy Fields, she missed New York, and when she married businessman Eli Lahm in 1939, she decided to move back to her hometown. Dorothy and Eli had two children (David in 1940 and Eliza in 1944). In short order, she teamed up with composer Arthur Schwartz for the Ethel Merman and Jimmy Durante musical, *Stars in Your Eyes* (1939). She remained active in the theatre in the 1940s, but not as a lyricist; with brother Herbert, she wrote the books for three hit Cole Porter shows: *Let's Face It* (1941), *Something for the Boys* (1943), and *Mexican Hayride* (1944), the last two again starring Ethel Merman.

After five years away from lyric writing, the chance to team up with legendary operetta composer Sigmund Romberg brought Fields back to songwriting. Their collaborative musical, *Up in Central Park* (1945), was not only a box office hit, but it also featured another Fields song destined to become a pop standard, "Close as Pages in a Book." Fields' next show actually began with her idea that Ethel Merman play Annie Oakley in a musical biography of the sharp-shooter. Merman loved the concept, as did Rodgers and Hammerstein who signed on as producers. Dorothy, partnering with Herbert, set to work on the libretto, while Jerome Kern enthusiastically agreed to write the music, as long as Dorothy penned the lyrics. Unfortunately, all came to a halt when a series of strokes killed the great Kern at the age of 60. After Irving Berlin was talked into writing the score, Dorothy bowed out as lyricist (remaining as co-librettist), for Berlin always wrote both music and lyrics. *Annie Get Your Gun* (1946) was a personal triumph for all involved, running 1,147 performances in New York and 1,304 performances in London.

Reunited with composer Arthur Schwartz in 1951, Dorothy would pen some of her most acclaimed lyrics for *A Tree Grows in Brooklyn*, writing for star Shirley Booth. Based on the bestselling novel, the story is a family drama set at the turn of the twentieth century and tells the tale of a charming drunk, Johnny Nolan, whose wife and daughter fight in vain to keep him from self-destruction. The score features heart-wrenching ballads ("I'll Buy You a Star" and "Make the Man Love Me"), comedy numbers ("Love Is the Reason" and "He Had Refinement"), and rousing ensemble numbers ("Mine 'til Monday" and "Look Who's Dancing").

As the 1950s progressed, however, Fields struggled both personally and professionally. After a brief, unsatisfying sojourn back to Hollywood to work on four films, Fields returned to Broadway to co-write the libretto and pen the lyrics for another Shirley Booth vehicle, *By the Beautiful Sea* (1954). In 1958, Dorothy's beloved brother and long-time collaborator, Herbert Fields, died of a heart attack, and four months later she lost her husband to a stroke. Artistically, things were also difficult. In development for years, *The Works!* had been rewritten for three leading ladies (Celeste Holm, Ethel Merman, and Beatrice Lillie), before being revised again—and retitled *Redhead*—for Gwen Verdon. First-time director Bob Fosse demanded what seemed like endless additional rewrites from *Redhead*'s lyricist (Fields) and composer (Albert Hague), but when the production finally opened on Broadway, the critics raved. *Redhead* took home nine Tony Awards in 1959, including Best Musical and Best Libretto, and stands as the last collaboration of Dorothy and Herbert Fields (who had been working on the project at the time of his untimely death).

With the advent of the '60s, Dorothy Fields found herself alone and adrift. Not only had she lost her husband and brother, but many dear friends and collaborators, such as Jerome Kern and Oscar Hammerstein II, were dead. She had no musical or film in development, and with rock 'n' roll gaining in popularity, she wondered if her time was past. But a chance meeting at a party with the young composer Cy Coleman would change her life.

In 1965, 62-year-old Dorothy Fields teamed up with 37-year-old Cy Coleman to create *Sweet Charity*, the tale of an ingenuous, good-hearted New York dance-hall hostess named Charity who sentimentally seeks true love only to find frustration and disenchantment time after time. Coleman's music was bright, brassy, and irreverent. Field's lyrics, in sync with Neil Simon's libretto, captured the tone of the 1960s. "Hey Big Spender" and "There's Gotta Be Something Better Than This" oozed with world-weary sarcasm, while "Baby, Dream Your Dream" and "Where Am I Going?" were introspective and emotional, making the characters more sympathetic. And "If My Friends Could See Me Now" showed that Fields could still write an upbeat hit like 1930's "On the Sunny Side of the Street."

Working again with star Gwen Verdon and director/choreographer Bob Fosse, Fields had another hit on her hands. *Sweet Charity* took New York by storm, opening with a $1 million advance. Although the critics were lukewarm toward the production and it only garnered one Tony Award out of eight nominations (Best Choreography for Fosse), audiences loved this bittersweet tale. The original Broadway run lasted for 608 performances, then moved to London for 476 performances, followed by a lavish feature film in 1969 (also directed and choreographed by Fosse). *Sweet Charity* has been revived twice on Broadway (1986 and 2005) and remains a favorite in regional theatre.

Coleman and Fields' next project was *Seesaw* (1973), and while its libretto by Michael Bennett, William Gibson, and Neil Simon (uncredited) was not strong, Fields and Coleman, nevertheless, came up with another exceptional score. *Seesaw* is as much about New York City as it is about its two mismatched lovers, and Fields' lyrics caught the verve of the city in the 1970s. "My City," "Nobody Does It Like Me," and "Poor Everybody Else" were as contemporary-sounding as any song being written by younger lyricists at the time. Further, the show produced another optimistic, rousing hit for Fields, "It's Not Where You Start, It's Where You Finish." In short, Fields, who was 68 years old, sounded fresher than ever.

With over fifty cast members and numerous elaborate dance sequences and production numbers, *Seesaw* was an expensive show to run; and it closed after 296 performances. Unfortunately, the writing partnership of Coleman and Fields ended with this musical. She died of a heart attack on the evening of March 28, 1974, after having sat through a rehearsal for the road company production of *Seesaw*.

Dorothy Fields' career, from 1924 to 1973, was not only one of the longest in musical theatre history, but also one of the most varied. A successful lyricist, librettist, and screenwriter who wrote for America's popular songbook as well as Broadway and Hollywood, Fields is one of the few who effortlessly made the crossover from one medium to another and from one decade to another. She worked with eighteen composers during her 48-year-long career, finding particular success with Jimmy McHugh, Jerome Kern, and Cy Coleman. She wrote the lyrics to over 400 published songs, worked on fifteen musicals and revues, and at least twenty-six films. Even though she frequently referred to herself as "just one of the boys," Fields was a trailblazer for women, being the first female lyricist to receive an Oscar (1936), a Tony Award (1959), and membership in the Songwriters Hall of Fame (1971).

This daughter of a vaudevillian never went to college, yet she acquired a virtuosic mastery of the English language. While a Field lyric could steer toward the sardonic and wry, it was undoubtedly her unbridled enthusiasm for life that kept her songs on the pop charts. In summary, Dorothy Fields' autobiography can be written using her song titles, as she was able to boast "I'm Livin' in a Great Big Way," while avowing her belief that "It Doesn't Cost You Anything to Dream" as well as "Who Said That Dreams Don't Come True?"

Figure 3.4

I CAN'T GIVE YOU ANYTHING BUT LOVE (BABY)

Lyrics by Dorothy Fields

Music by Jimmy McHugh (1928)

Gee, but it's tough to be broke, kid,
It's not a joke, kid, it's a curse;
My luck is changing, it's gotten
From simply rotten, to something worse.

Who knows some day I will win too
I'll begin to reach my prime;
Now though I see what our end is
All I can spend is just my time.

I can't give you anything but love, baby,
That's the only thing I've plenty of, baby,
Dream a while, scheme a while,
We're sure to find,
Happiness and I guess
All those things you've always pined for,

Gee, I'd like to see you looking swell, baby,
Diamond bracelets Woolworth's doesn't sell, baby,
Till that lucky day, you know darn well, baby,
I can't give you anything but love.

FEATURED PRODUCTION: *Blackbirds of 1928* (1928)

Music by Jimmy McHugh; Lyrics by Dorothy Fields;
Produced, Directed, and Conceived by Lew Leslie

Original Broadway Run: Opened May 9, 1928; Liberty Theatre;
518 performances

During the mid-1920s, nightclubs and supper clubs began to appear in Harlem which featured black performers and catered to white audiences. These "black and tan" cabarets not only showcased up-and-coming performers, but they also began to serve as "out-of-town" tryout venues for material that would eventually find its way into musical revues on Broadway. With a keen eye for talent, producer/director/librettist Lew Leslie not only created shows for the Harlem clubs, but he also started to produce all-black revues on Broadway: *Plantation Revue* (1922) and *Dixie to Broadway* (1924). His *Blackbirds of 1928* would also span Harlem and Broadway, as well as become an international sensation. Leslie's first version of the *Blackbirds* revue played in Harlem for six sold-out weeks at the Alhambra Theatre. He then took the show to Paris where it ran six months before moving to London in 1926. Before he could bring *Blackbirds* back to the United States, however, one of the stars who he had discovered and around whom he planned to build the show—Florence Mills—died. Consequently, the 1928 American production of *Blackbirds* had a revised cast (along with a new score) that included Aida Ward, Adelaide Hall, Earl "Snakehips" Tucker, and Peg Leg Bates. (Bill "Bojangles" Robinson was hired during the out-of-town tryout and only appeared in one number in Act Two: "Doin' the New Low-Down.") In addition to the standard Broadway 8-show performance week, Leslie added a midnight show on Thursdays, evoking the revue's uptown nightclub roots. This linkage of a Broadway musical revue to the clubs of Harlem added a certain ambiance and distinction to the show, making *Blackbirds of 1928* the must-see revue of the season.

With a cast of over one hundred African American performers, *Blackbirds of 1928* was a high-caliber production. Its stellar score by lyricist Dorothy Fields and composer Jimmy McHugh introduced many new songs into the lexicon of 1920s American popular music: "Doin' the New Low-Down," "I Can't Give You Anything But Love," "I Must Have That Man," "Digga Digga Do," "Porgy," "Here Comes My Blackbird," and "Bandanna Babies." While many songs written (by white and black composers and lyricists) for African American performers in the 1920s reinforced negative stereotypes and/or were quite risqué, the Fields and McHugh score was more elegant than ribald. Due to the previous success of their songs for the black performers at Harlem's Cotton Club, Leslie hired the young team to write the Broadway score for *Blackbirds*. While the rest of the score was written specifically for *Blackbirds of 1928*, the duo decided that this revue was also the perfect home for "I Can't Give You Anything But Love," a song they originally wrote for (and was cut from) an earlier revue, *Delmar's Revels* (1927). But a reviewer who saw *Blackbirds* during its tryout in Atlantic City not only hated the show but he also singled out "I Can't Give You Anything But Love" as particularly weak. Fortunately, producer Leslie liked the song and the rest of the McHugh/Fields score, so he kept the show running and brought it to Broadway, despite an initially weak box office. Eventually, the novelty of the added Thursday midnight shows spurred ticket sales and Aida Ward's rendition of "I Can't Give You Anything But Love" made it the hit of the production. And while the opening number "Dixie" evoked the typical Southern Plantation setting of many minstrel shows, the rest of *Blackbirds of 1928* focused on the urban sophistication of Harlem (even though the male comedians in the revue still appeared in blackface).

Blackbirds of 1928 ended up running an astounding 518 performances, thus becoming the longest running all-black revue in Broadway history. Lew Leslie created three sequels to *Blackbirds* (1930, 1933, 1939), but none recaptured the success of the original 1928 revue. While three songs from *Blackbirds of 1928* were recorded with twenty-five musicians (including Duke Ellington at the piano) in 1928, the entire score was not recorded until 1933. And although this was the first album to feature the full score from a Broadway musical, it was not recorded with performers from the Broadway cast. Nevertheless, *Blackbirds of 1928* spawned dozens of imitators, including Lew Leslie's own *Rhapsody in Black* (1931) which made a star out of Ethel Waters. In this regard, *Blackbirds of 1928* can be seen as crucial in the development and recognition of African American artistry on Broadway.

Actor Spotlights

Anna Held (1872–1918)

Anna Held © CORBIS

Anna Held was a Polish-born beauty who first gained fame by way of the *Folies Bergère* and the variety venues of Europe. In America, she reached stardom through her association with promoter and common-law husband Florenz Ziegfeld, who capitalized on her flirtatious and magnetic stage persona. Born in Warsaw circa 1872 (her documented birth date ranges from 1865 to 1873), Helene Anna Held was the daughter of a Jewish glove maker and his French-Jewish wife. While still an adolescent, her family was forced to flee Poland due to anti-Semitic pogroms, ultimately arriving in Paris. There, young Anna worked in the garment industry to provide income for her struggling family, but she soon turned to the theatre, working as a singer in the Jewish theatres of Paris and London and starring in plays such as Abraham Goldfaden's *Shulamith* (1881). Within a decade, Held moved from the Jewish/Yiddish theatre to major music halls across Europe, achieving headliner status. While performing in London, she caught the eye of American impresario Florenz Ziegfeld. At this time, she was also the estranged wife of a fast-living Uruguayan playboy, Maximo Carrera, whom she had married in 1894, giving birth to their daughter later that same year. Ziegfeld was smitten by Held's coy and effervescent stage presence, as well as her naughty comic sensibility and striking physical attributes (she was famous for her eighteen-inch waist and willingness to show her legs). Thus, the love-struck and showbiz-savvy Ziegfeld persuaded Held to return to New York City with him—a move that necessitated a legal split from both her husband and the *Folies Bergere* (aided by Ziegfeld's much-publicized $1,500 payoff to the famous Parisian company). The couple landed in the Big Apple in 1896, amidst a flurry of media attention, speculation, and titillation.

Once in New York, Held did not disappoint theatre patrons who may have initially wondered what all the fuss was about. Many skeptics became fans after witnessing Held's charming stage persona (although theatre critics were harsher, dismissing her as an artless, inexpert "attraction"). After audiences applauded her American debut in a Broadway musical version of a play titled *A Parlor Match* (1896), she toured the show to further popular acclaim. For the next ten years, Held continued to star in Broadway musicals and tours created for her by Ziegfeld, as well as reign as one of America's top celebrities, due in great part to Ziegfeld's publicity stunts and media embellishments on her behalf (e.g., touting Held's beauty regimen of "milk baths"). At the height of her career, she was flanked by a troupe of lovely chorus girls in her star vehicles, billed as "The Anna Held Girls." And while her star status put money in Ziegfeld's coffers during this period, she also became a millionaire in her own right.

After a decade of American stardom, Held's love affair and professional relationship with Ziegfeld went sour. Their common-law marriage became tabloid fodder when Held sued for "divorce" in 1912, citing Ziegfeld's widely known instances of infidelity. Before this break-up, however, Held made an indelible mark on the American theatre by giving Ziegfeld the idea for his *Follies*, leading to the birth of the American musical revue. Specifically, in 1907, Held had suggested to her "spouse" that he develop his own version of the *Folies Bergère* for American audiences. The rest was history, sealing Ziegfeld's iconic fame. Held, however, saw her career slowly decline after her divorce from Ziegfeld. During World War I, she worked in vaudeville and then returned to Europe to tour the French provinces and entertain French troops, often on the front lines, raising funds for the war effort and garnering praise as a war heroine. Afterwards, she returned to America, but would never regain her past stage stature. Nonetheless, she continued to work, appearing in early silent films and constantly touring the United States, with her health suffering. In 1918, she collapsed onstage, dying months later from multiple myeloma at age 46. Held was mourned by many, while there were also recriminations in the press against Ziegfeld, charging him with neglect in regard to his most famous star, muse, and "wife." While it may seem unfair that Held is often omitted from the chronicles of Ziegfeld and his American revue, it is crucial to note that Held not only facilitated Ziegfeld's career but she also stands as one of America's earliest female icons on the musical stage—a model to be revisited and reinterpreted for years to come.

Fanny Brice (1891–1951)

Against all odds, Fanny Brice became one of the greatest American stars of the early twentieth century. She found stardom and power during an era in which women seeking the limelight often relied on physical attributes, sexual titillation/ flirtation, or "feminine" song-and-dance talents. In this climate, the gawky, brash, and oddball Brice was not only a novelty but also an anomaly. Although turn-of-the-century American theatre featured and celebrated rubber-faced comics, ethnic satirists, eccentric dancers, and "coon-shouters" (all types of entertainment at which Brice excelled), the performers of such popular forms were most often men. But then again, Fanny Brice was used to thumbing her nose at convention, breaking rules, and winning over naysayers.

Fanny Brice © Bettmann/CORBIS

Brice's real name was Fania Borach; and she was born in New York City's Lower East Side in 1891 to Hungarian-Jewish parents. The Borach family moved to Newark, New Jersey, where they ran a chain of successful saloons. But with an increasingly absent (and inebriated) husband, Rose Borach got a divorce and moved her four children to Brooklyn. At age 13, Fania won an amateur contest with a comic song at Keeney's Theatre in Brooklyn. Infatuated with the theatre, she dropped out of school before graduating to work in burlesque, performing songs with her idiosyncratic personality and energy (now as Fanny Brice). As an oft-told story goes, she worked on the burlesque circuit for two years; but after having been fired from a George M. Cohan show, she became discouraged, worried that she had hit a professional dead end. Therefore, in 1909, she approached Tin Pan Alley songsmith Irving Berlin and asked for a specialty number to showcase her comic and mimicry talents. He wrote an "ethnic" Jewish ditty for her, titled "Sadie Salome, Go Home." The song was a parody in which a Jewish girl with a heavy Yiddish dialect implausibly plays one of history's greatest seductresses. Brice's performance of the song at a local benefit performance was a hit (it should be noted here that the Yiddish dialect and persona associated with Brice throughout her career was an act, assumed for theatrical and comic effect; she was unable to speak Yiddish). She soon began to make a name for herself as an eccentric song stylist, satirist, and mimic, ultimately catching the eye of Florenz Ziegfeld's talent scouts. Ziegfeld hired her for a two-year contract as one of his headliners for the 1910 and 1911 editions of *Ziegfeld Follies*, where she further exploited her gift of song and comedy to great acclaim (her repertoire included Yiddish comic songs and blackface "coon-shouting" numbers). She was hired again in 1921 and continued with the *Follies* into the 1930s, becoming a beloved American star in the process as she often spoofed popular trends (ragtime and burlesque fandancing), as well as "high art" (ballet, modern dance, and tragedienne acting), while even good-naturedly making fun of herself. Given her *Follies* exposure and platform, Brice would credit Ziegfeld for her success throughout her career. During this period, she also performed on Broadway in various other musicals, as well as made numerous recordings for Victor and Columbia Records, topping the charts with hits such as "Second Hand Rose" (1921) and her signature song, "My Man" (an English version of the French torch song *Mon Homme*). It may have been Ziegfeld who suggested to Brice that she introduce "My Man" in the 1921 *Follies*, talking her out of playing the song for laughs, but it was Brice who daringly delivered the career-changing performance. She surprised her fans and reinvented herself as a versatile chanteuse as she gave an honest and heartbreaking rendition of a song that refers to spousal brutality in its avowal of longsuffering love and devotion. Brice also posthumously won a Grammy Hall of Fame Award for her 1921 recording of the song.

Significantly, Brice's rendition of "My Man" also reverberated with her audience due to her own highly publicized marital drama and heartbreak. Although she had been briefly married in 1911 to Frank White (a local barber of Springfield, Massachusetts, whom she met while on tour), it was Brice's second marriage that would earn major tabloid attention. During her early rise to stardom, Brice fell in love with the professional gambler Julius W. "Nicky" Arnstein, staying true to him throughout his fourteen-month prison sentence for wiretapping and ultimately marrying him in 1918, after years of living together. Six years later, Arnstein was convicted of bond theft and served three years in a federal penitentiary. Despite her highly public display of moral support and extensive funding of his legal defense, Arnstein abandoned Brice and their children (William and Frances) once released from prison, necessitating that she sign divorce papers in 1927. Two years after this heartbreak, Brice made headlines again when she married famous songwriter and theatre impresario Billy Rose, starring in several productions under his management, only to see their marriage fail as well, divorcing Rose in 1937.

Fanny Brice is a significant predecessor of the many female satirists, impersonators, and comediennes whose careers span live theatre and other mediums such as film, television, and radio, e.g., Lucille Ball, Lily Tomlin, Whoopi Goldberg, and the multitude of female talents who got their starts on *Saturday Night Live*. Brice has often been hailed as a pioneering crossover artist for women, for she not only reigned as a Broadway headliner for decades, but she became a radio favorite via her iconic portrayal of the precocious, impish Baby Snooks (a juvenile role she played far into her fifties). She also played herself in the hit movies *The Great Ziegfeld* (1936) and *Ziegfeld Follies* (1946). For these Hollywood endeavors and many others, Brice received a star on the Hollywood Walk of Fame; yet, her most significant film presence remains a portrayal by another artist. Thirteen years after Brice's death, due to a cerebral hemorrhage in 1951, a (mostly true) musical account of her early career and ill-fated marriage to Nicky Arnstein debuted on Broadway. The show was *Funny Girl* (1964); and in a fiction-meets-reality scenario, the production made a star out of the young performer who portrayed Brice: Barbra Streisand. Streisand reprised her stage role in the 1968 movie version (her film debut) and won an Academy Award for her performance. Streisand's rendition of Brice, as well as the musical itself, may be majorly credited with keeping the memory and legacy of Fanny Brice, America's original "funny girl," alive today.

CHAPTER 4

THE JAZZ AGE AND GREAT DEPRESSION: MUSICAL THEATRE AS AMERICA'S SONGBOOK

• •

Whereas the two decades spanning 1920–40 could easily be categorized as the best and worst of times, the era's musical backdrop reached a level that could only be described as exceptional. As the nation jazzed it up in the 1920s and then soberly confronted the downslide and Great Depression of the 1930s, the musical theatre became a place where the extremes were filtered through artistic lenses, then staged and disseminated to the masses. And those who were responsible for the verve and vision of the period's most popular musicals were correspondingly the leading composers and lyricists of the American songbook, dividing their time between Hollywood, Broadway, and Tin Pan Alley. In short, it was a time when the popular music industry was intertwined with the musical theatre stage, a symbiotic relationship that produced numerous songbook classics that have yet to be equaled in terms of artistry, import, and longevity. The list of men and women contributing to this catalogue is extensive, with many becoming household names throughout the decades, e.g., the Gershwins, Irving Berlin, Jerome Kern, Schwartz and Dietz, Henderson, DeSylva and Brown, Vincent Youmans, Rodgers and Hart, Cole Porter, and Dorothy Fields. These artists would set America's toes to tapping and gain immortality as they, in many respects, became the voice of the nation.

As America celebrated the end of World War I, it also found itself at the cusp of a musical and entertainment revolution. The 1920s were ready to "roar," and the syncopated rhythms of jazz (which had grown out of African American idioms such as ragtime) were soon to become all the rage, luring American youths to the dance floor, kicking and shaking to dance crazes such as the Charleston, the Varsity Drag, and the Black Bottom. In addition to its innovative rhythms, the music's snappy chromatics and harmonic tensions were matched by snazzy, slangy lyrics, resulting in songs that bespoke a sense of modernity and bubbling, hyperkinetic optimism. All combined to define a new musical (and cultural) age for the nation: the Jazz Age. Accordingly, Broadway provided an arena where the current spirit could be exploited and promulgated, and no theatrical form was more conducive to showcasing the modern sights and sounds than the Broadway revue. Specifically, as vaudeville waned in popularity (exacerbated by the advent of the Hollywood "talkie" in the late '20s), the revue took its place; and its flashy and trendy variety format would reign on Broadway during the 1920s and into the '30s. The prototype was the *Ziegfeld Follies*, but a profusion of other popular revues followed on *Follies'* heels, e.g., *George White's Scandals*, Irving Berlin's *Music Box Revue*, and the *Earl Carroll Vanities*, to name a few.

Yet revues were not the only showcases for songwriting excellence and excess, for the zany musical comedies of the day were also vehicles by which one hit song after another could be heard. Most of these musicals paid little heed to the idea of text/song/dance "integration" (a burgeoning concept, significantly advanced and evinced by 1927's *Show Boat*). Instead, they used thinly constructed librettos (e.g., "boy meets girl; boy loses girl; boy gets girl") as a means by which they could loosely link songs, hoping for takeaway hits that could easily be lifted from their original source. The Gershwins excelled at this method during the 1920s, providing a string of popular musicals with scores filled to the brim with soon-to-be classics. Rodgers and Hart were also adept at crafting crowd-pleasing, hit-filled musical comedies (although, to their credit, they did experiment with unusual source material). Joining these two dominant songwriting duos were others, such as the writing team of [B. G.] DeSylva, [Lew] Brown, and [Ray] Henderson who, in addition to providing significant songs for top-notch revues, also wrote numerous musicals, including the genre's first "college" musical, *Good News* (1927). The hit show, which set the formulaic boy-meets-girl storyline on a college campus, had the nation singing "The Best Things in Life Are Free" and dancing "The Varsity Drag," while running for 551 performances. Another favorite composer of the '20s was the prolific Vincent Youmans. His frothy *No, No, Nanette* (1925) is often cited as one of the most popular and prototypical musical comedies of the decade. The show also had all of America humming and soft-shoeing to its ubiquitous takeaway hit, "Tea for Two," as well as the swinging "I Want to Be Happy" (lyrics for both songs by Irving Caesar).

This is not to suggest that the era's musical comedies and revues were frivolous or without import, for there were some Broadway works that signified the slowly changing tides with regard to race and gender in America. While the country was still a place of systemic racial segregation and discrimination, one could see some attempts at African American authenticity on the musical stage (as opposed to persisting minstrelsy paradigms). Al Jolson, with his blackface persona, may have been America's reigning superstar, but musicals with actual African Americans were also playing the boards to great acclaim. Bookending this development were the works *Shuffle Along* (1921) and *Porgy and Bess* (1935), while *Blackbirds of 1928* and Ethel Waters' landmark performance in *As Thousands Cheer* (1933) also asserted the growing presence and influence of African American talent and artistry on the Broadway stage. In terms of gender, the musical theatre industry remained, for the most part, a "boys' club." Nonetheless, American women had finally won the right to vote in 1920, and their voices were to be heard on the musical theatre front as well. Dorothy Fields became a reigning lyricist (and soon-to-be librettist) during the '20s, resulting in a prolific career that lasted until her death in the 1970s. Further, in 1930, Kay Swift became the first female composer to have a musical play on Broadway. The work was a sociopolitical musical comedy titled *Fine and Dandy*; and it was created for star Joe Cook, who played an inept general manager of a tool factory who deals with labor/management disputes. The production ran for 255 performances, while Swift continued to make significant contributions to the musical field for years to come.

In addition to its gender significance, *Fine and Dandy* also illustrated the new sociopolitical climate in America. With the Stock Market Crash of 1929 and the ensuing Great Depression, America went from dancing on the ceiling to "Brother, Can You Spare a Dime?" The fall may have happened with a resounding thud, but its reverberations inspired new directions in musical theatre. The sociopolitical or socioeconomic musical became a vehicle by which artists could reflect, critique, and satirize the nation's sorry state of affairs. One of the more curious hits was a topical revue that was also a grassroots creation: *Pins and Needles* (1937). The production was a pro-union evening of sketches and musical numbers that took swipes at a broad swath of topics and targets, e.g., Nazis, Fascists, Communists, warmongers, and even the labor union itself. The show had been organized as a limited engagement by and for the members of the International Ladies' Garment Workers' Union, but it soon attracted great numbers of Broadway patrons to its modest home, the tiny Labor Stage (formerly the famed Princess Theater), breaking box office records by eventually running for 1,108 performances. *Pins and Needles* also launched the career of its lyricist/composer, Harold Rome, who would go on to create Golden Age hits such as *Call Me Mister* (1946), *Wish You Were Here* (1952), and *Fanny* (1954).

Another "union" musical and theatrical phenomenon, as well as sign of the times, was *The Cradle Will Rock* (1938), with book and score by Marc Blitzstein. In the manner of Bertold Brecht, Blitzstein created a production that was a cross between agitprop and musical theatre. The show was initially part of the WPA's Federal Theatre Project, America's only attempt at subsidized national theatre, providing free live productions for countrywide audiences from 1935–39, as well as paying jobs for theatre artists. *Cradle* was produced by John Houseman, with stage direction by theatrical wunderkind Orson Welles. Blitzstein's abrasive, modernist, and stylized score and libretto tells the allegorical story of a fictional factory town, Steeltown, USA, that is transformed by the determined leadership of a union organizer, Larry Foreman. Foreman works to end the corporate and political corruption and abuse in the town, taking on the autocratic industrialist Mr. Mister. Eventually, the downtrodden workers find strength in numbers, unionizing to fight the exploitative capitalists. The controversial production of *Cradle* was scheduled to open on June 16, 1937; but real life mirrored fiction as Congressional pressure was applied to shut down the show, with its theater, the Maxine Elliott, padlocked on opening night. Further, Actors' Equity caved to the pressure, barring its actors from performing *Cradle* on any stage. Refusing to be silenced, the company marched through the streets to the vacant Venice Theatre, procured by Welles. There they inventively staged the work, with the Equity actors performing their roles from their seats and other areas in the auditorium, while Blitzstein served as a one-man orchestra, playing his score on a stage piano. After 19 performances in this fashion, the show moved to a new home in the Windsor Theatre, opening on January 3, 1938, again with minimal scenery and accompanied solely by Blitzstein.

The Cradle Will Rock ultimately ran for 108 performances but holds a place in American theatre history as a flagship event during the short-lived duration of the Federal Theatre Project, as well as symbolizes the spirit behind the sociopolitical theatre movement of the 1930s. Indeed, *Cradle* was not alone, for it was surrounded by other significant (and often satirical) sociopolitical works on the musical stage, e.g., the Gershwins' *Strike Up the Band* (1930), *Of Thee I Sing* (1931), and *Let "Em Eat Cake* (1933), as well as Irving Berlin's *Face the Music* (1932) and *As Thousands Cheer* (1933), Rodgers and Hart's *I'd Rather Be Right* (1937), Kurt Weill's *Knickerbocker Holiday* (1938), and Cole Porter's *Leave It to Me!* (1938).

Although *Leave It to Me!* is listed above (given its farcical treatment of world politics), it would be misleading to suggest that Cole Porter was a sociopolitical musical writer. Instead, he offered his audiences escapist fare on stage (and screen) during the Great Depression. Specifically, Porter's musicals were effervescent vehicles populated by attractive, well-to-do sophisticates, sipping champagne in lavish places such as cruise ships and New York penthouses on the "90th Floor." Such an escapist category during the '30s also describes much of the Rodgers/Hart oeuvre as well as the ongoing parade of colorful, giddy revues. In fact, the longest running musical of the 1930s was one such giddy work: *Hellzapoppin* (1938). Created by vaudevillian stars Ole Olsen and Chic Johnson, the show was somewhat of an extension of their fourteen-year-old act, filled with their own raucous, comedic sketches and a composite score, performed by the duo and other supporting performers (but no big Broadway names). *Hellzapoppin* opened to poor reviews, but audiences didn't care and flocked to the revue, which, consequently, ran for 1,404 performances, beating the box office record previously held by *Pins and Needles*.

Escapism even claimed Jerome Kern, who was one of the first to address serious and troubling topics on the Broadway stage via his masterwork *Show Boat* (1927). In the '30s, however, Kern would create more romantic and fanciful works, placed beyond America's shores, with music evoking the sound of European operetta, e.g., *The Cat and the Fiddle* (1931) and *Music in the Air* (1932). Such a development is also a reminder that operetta continued to be a force on Broadway throughout the '20s and into the '30s. Specifically, the era has been called operetta's "Silver Age," distinguished by a new generation of composers. At the forefront was Sigmund Romberg, who worked with Oscar Hammerstein II as well as a leading librettist/lyricist of the period, Otto Harbach, to create smash hits such as *The Desert Song* (1926) and *The New Moon* (1928). Matching Romberg in terms of popularity was Rudolf Friml, who also collaborated with Hammerstein and Harbach on box office favorites *Rose-Marie* (1924), *The Vagabond King* (1925), and numerous others.

Despite his successful collaborations with both Romberg and Friml, Hammerstein aspired to more than operetta; and his 1927 work with Kern—*Show Boat*—would make history as the seminal prototype for the integrated book musical. Nonetheless, it would be more than a decade before the new form would really take off (although there were some important exceptions, such as the Gershwins' *Of Thee I Sing*). Even Rodgers and Hart, who would champion the idea of integral dance in *On Your Toes* (1936), would not seriously subscribe to the "integration" concept until *Pal Joey* in 1940. In fact, *Joey*'s dark subject matter and antihero signaled a new age for musical theatre; for it seemed that the Broadway musical was maturing, with its content being viewed as more than a convenient vehicle by which to showcase potential hit songs. Sadly, Hart was unable to further explore this terrain, as he would die a few years after *Pal Joey*'s debut. However, his longtime partner, Rodgers, would find another collaborator, Hammerstein, and the two would become leading figures in the next phase of the Broadway musical—a period that would soon be known as the genre's Golden Age.

GEORGE AND IRA GERSHWIN

Ira Gershowitz didn't really want to play the piano. This came as a disappointment to his parents, who had scraped together enough money to buy the instrument, with hopes that their 14-year-old son would prove to have musical talent. But Ira's little brother, Jacob, couldn't resist the keyboard, and before long, the piano was allocated to him as he became immersed in music lessons, repeatedly surpassing his teachers' skills. The switch would prove to be a momentous and fortuitous development for both boys. Jacob was soon to be known and lauded worldwide as George Gershwin, arguably the most accomplished and versatile American composer of the twentieth century, while Ira fell in love with the written word and stands today as one of the most prolific and celebrated lyricists in the American song canon. Further, it is poignant that the disparate brothers found many of their artistic and popular successes *together* as a symbiotic sibling songwriting team. Making an indelible imprint on the American songbook and musical theatre landscape during the 1920s and '30s, the unique and individual talents of George and Ira merged into a phenomenon known simply as "The Gershwins."

George Gershwin, née Jacob Gershowitz, was born on September 26, 1898, to parents Morris and Rose Gershowitz in Brooklyn, New York. The family soon Americanized their Yiddish name to "Gershwin" and eventually moved to the Lower East Side. Although George was the second of four children, it was his older brother Ira with whom his future would be most entwined. And when George died at the unexpectedly early age of 38 from an advanced brain tumor, his untimely death shook the theatre and musical community, leaving many heartbroken in its wake. No one was more heartbroken, however, than George's sibling and partner, Ira, who would voice heartfelt sentiments while paying tribute to their relationship in the lyrics he supplied to a melody composed by George before his death. The title of the song, which became a Gershwin classic, says it all: "Our Love Is Here to Stay."

It is unsurprising that George Gershwin's death sent such shockwaves through all areas of music, for he was a musical genius whose range of accomplishments has never been surpassed. In short, having started in Tin Pan Alley, he is the only composer from that forum to attain equal degrees of success in both the classical fields (concert and opera) and the popular (radio, movies, and theatre). Further, Gershwin is credited by many with bringing jazz into the mainstream at a time when the idiom was distrusted by many consumers due to its African American connotations and unconventional sound. He introduced and converted pop music listeners to many of jazz's compositional characteristics and innovations, incorporating its ragged, syncopated, hopped-up rhythms, while also playing with discordance and inventive melodic progressions. Throughout his career, Gershwin served as an "ambassador" of jazz, writing about and advocating for it, as well as frequenting Harlem jazz clubs, such as the Cotton Club, to soak up the sound and observe (as well as jam with) the musicians. Importantly, Gershwin's popular music legacy is matched by his classical music contributions as a concert pianist and modernist composer, introducing experimentation and a signature sound to his American concert masterpieces *American in Paris* (1928), *Piano Concerto in F* (1925), and easily the most recognizable and lauded American symphonic work of the twentieth century, *Rhapsody in Blue* (1924). Bridging the two worlds, Gershwin transformed Broadway by bringing a similar degree of musical sophistication and complexity to his show compositions (e.g., it often took two pianists in the orchestra pit to do service to his musical scores).

George Gershwin's formative two-decade journey from aspiring juvenile pianist to world-class composer comprised three years of training as a teen with various piano teachers, including his first significant instructor and mentor, Charles Hambitzer. Around the same time, he took a job as pianist for Jerome H. Remick Music Publishing Company and, at age 15, established himself as the youngest (and the showiest) song plugger in Tin Pan Alley. By 1914 he could no longer reconcile his music ambitions with the drudgery of school, so he dropped out of high school to concentrate on his promising music career. Like his idol Jerome Kern, Gershwin supplemented his Tin Pan Alley work with stints as a vaudeville accompanist and rehearsal pianist (including rehearsals for a show written by Kern), while plugging his own compositions, with hopes that they might be published and/or interpolated into a musical show. After two failed publication attempts, Gershwin finally sold his first song in 1916, a satirical relationship lament titled "When You Want 'Em, You Can't Have 'Em, When You Have 'Em, You Don't Want 'Em" (lyrics by Murray Roth).

After this modest debut, George continued to peddle his songs, seizing any opportunity to put his music before the public. Soon, he caught the attention of publisher Max Dreyfus, who offered George a position as staff composer. Then, in 1918, he wrote his first song with his brother, Ira, a ragtime-referencing number titled "The Real American Folk Song." Previous to this, Ira had discovered his talent for writing lyrics and had been working with a number of composers. In that same year, George wrote his first musical, collaborating with another novice composer, Alex A. Aarons. The mutual Broadway debut of both composers was a bedroom farce titled *La La Lucille* (and subtitled "The New Up-to-the-Minute Musical Comedy of Class and Distinction"). The show only had a modest run, but the 20-year-old Gershwin succeeded in getting his name on a Broadway marquee. Next, 1919 proved to be a momentous year for George as he finally composed a song that would reach almost every American ear. The song was "Swanee," a riff tune that has been described as a ragging one-step; and it was reportedly written in fifteen minutes by Gershwin and lyricist Irving Caesar. After the song was lifted from a failed revue by Al Jolson and added to his popular star vehicle, *Sinbad*, the

catchy number became the biggest hit in the country. Such developments contributed to a growing reputation for the young George Gershwin, culminating in a commission by George White to compose the second edition of the *George White Scandals*. Gershwin was a perfect fit for the revue, for his rhythmic melodies and lush, modern sound matched and served well *Scandals'* youthful spirit and dance-centric aesthetic. Consequently, he was the sole composer for five *Scandals* editions (1920–24). Interestingly, however, out of his forty-five songs written for *Scandals*, none proved to be noteworthy or long lived, except for the lush and bluesy "Stairway to Paradise," written especially for a spectacular staircase production number in the 1922 edition. The other notable composition created by Gershwin for the 1922 *Scandals* was a failed, yet germinal, experiment. Foreshadowing his later masterpiece, *Porgy and Bess*, Gershwin composed *Blue Monday*, billed as an "Opera à la Afro-American." With lyrics by B. G. DeSylva, the tragic, sung-through one-act was set in Harlem, and its plot centered on a community of African Americans (portrayed by white performers in blackface) whose unsavory acts, such as gambling and infidelity, culminate in murder. *Blue Monday* was lengthy for a revue number (approximately thirty minutes), and its gritty and depressing subject matter, as well as its unusual "jazz opera" sound, seemed out of place in the *Scandals* program. Most critics panned the work, with some even feigning outrage over its content, and *Blue Monday* was cut after its opening-night performance. A vocal minority, however, praised the experimental nature of the piece, and the work did not completely disappear; specifically, some excerpts (e.g., "Blue Monday Blues") are still performed today as stand-alone concert pieces.

In 1924, George Gershwin made the fortunate mistake of asking George White for a raise. White refused and Gershwin left *Scandals*. This move freed him for other projects, and the next year would prove to be a creative watershed for him. First, the celebrated orchestra conductor Paul Whiteman approached Gershwin to supply a symphonic work for a concert that he was organizing at Aeolian Hall to showcase American "experiments in modern music." Gershwin accepted the project and worked furiously to prepare a piece for the concert. The result was his modern masterpiece, *Rhapsody in Blue*, and it was the highlight of the evening. Taking on the role of concert pianist, Gershwin debuted the symphony himself, backed by Whiteman's Palais

Royal Orchestra. The overall effect was one of classical symphonic technique merged with jazz and the blues. Indeed, it is no coincidence that the word "blue" is part of the title, for the symphony exploits and plays with the musical construct/sound known as the "blue chord" or "blue note." Technically, the "blue chord" is a chord that contains a flatted third or seventh note; the "blue note" itself is the flatted note used in the moving interval, replacing an expected major interval note. Of course, music theory is not as important to theatre listeners as the emotional and dramatic significance of the "blue note." In short, its use in a melodic progression creates a shifting moment of surprise or lament, suggesting melancholy, loss, and unease/vacillation (i.e., the "blues"). Scholars and musicologists have also pointed to the use of the "blue note/chord" in African American and Jewish folk/cantorial music, both of which figure prominently in Gershwin's own musical legacy and leanings. All of this leads to a crucial point: Gershwin's frequent exploitation of the "blue note" throughout his career has made it a signpost of his compositions, contributing to his uniquely personal sound and his trajectory on the world's concert stage. Yet there existed public accusations throughout Gershwin's career by some in the upper echelon of classical music circles that he could not have possibly composed his symphonies in their entirety, given his background in terms of class (lower), ethnicity (Jewish), and education (limited). Instead, they insinuated that the symphonies may have been "ghostwritten" in part by his arrangers and orchestrators. Importantly, contemporary musicologists point to his signature use of the "blue note," resulting in a sound that is uniquely "Gershwin," as proof that the compositions are completely attributable to him, refuting past accusations of illegitimacy.

As if *Rhapsody in Blue* was not enough of a landmark achievement, George cemented his place in the musical theatre arena by joining Ira for their first Broadway hit, *Lady, Be Good!*, in that same year. With producers Alex Aarons and Vinton Freedley, the team originally aimed to emulate the Princess Musicals, even working with Princess Theatre veterans Bolton and Wodehouse for several librettos. Nonetheless, the Gershwin productions turned out to be more typical of 1920s Broadway, containing simple and often thinly contrived plots by which to string together memorable (yet theatrically generic) songs and to showcase lead performers. However, when one of the most formidable, popular, and stylish songwriting teams of the twentieth century

combines with star talent, as well as a sense of whimsy and madcap adventure, the conventional formula can result in big ticket sales. Point in fact, beginning with *Lady, Be Good!*, the Gershwins produced five of the decade's most popular musical comedies in the short span of six years. The other hits were *Tip-Toes* (1925), *Oh, Kay!* (1926), *Funny Face* (1927), and *Girl Crazy* (1930); a brief overview illustrates their fanciful librettos, hit-laden scores, and key performances that so pleased Broadway audiences. *Lady, Be Good!* originally featured Fred and Adele Astaire (dynamic dance duo and real-life siblings) as down-and-out brother/sister vaudevillians who use friends' homes for refuge and performance opportunities. The siblings also attempt, unsuccessfully, to fraudulently claim an inheritance but ultimately find prosperity through honest means. The show's score introduced such hits as "Fascinating Rhythm" and "Oh, Lady, Be Good!," and the production ran for 330 performances. (Interestingly, "The Man I Love" was initially written for *Lady, Be Good!* but was removed during tryouts. After being dropped from two other musicals, it became a radio hit and Gershwin classic, having never reached Broadway.) Running for 194 performances, *Tip-Toes* provided audiences with another tale of likable vaudevillians assuming false identities in pursuit of wealth. This time, however, the vaudeville team consists of a young girl and her uncles, stranded in Palm Beach; and the girl ultimately wins the heart of a glue industry tycoon. *Oh, Kay!* was initially created as a vehicle for British star and new Broadway sensation Gertrude Lawrence, featuring a plot in which an engaged upper-crust man falls in love with a young woman, Kay, who is posing as a lowly cook in order to protect her brother's bootleg hooch in the wealthy man's cellar. The production, which ran for 256 performances, debuted Gershwin classics such as "Maybe" and "Someone to Watch Over Me." The next year, *Funny Face* again starred Fred and Adele Astaire and treated Broadway audiences to a caper comedy in which a smitten aviator mistakenly steals a bracelet for an engaging young lady, resulting in an extended chase through numerous locales along the East Coast. Running for 244 performances, the show's take-away hits included "'S Wonderful" [see fig. 4.1] and "My One and Only." Finally, *Girl Crazy* capped the successful 1920s streak for the Gershwins, playing for 272 performances and telling the tale of a New York playboy who takes a taxi to Arizona to oversee a ranch for his wealthy father, then turns it into a dude ranch and falls in love with the local gal. Hits from the production included "Embrace-able You" and "I Got Rhythm," the latter introduced by newcomer Ethel Merman, who earned rave notices for her vocal performance that included holding a single belted note through the song's entire second chorus.

The Gershwin partnership not only succeeded on stage but extended behind the scenes, exemplifying a positive, symbiotic relationship that lasted until George's death. Interestingly, the two brothers were opposites in terms of personality: George was a lifelong bachelor and urban playboy; Ira was a steady family man. George was the life of any party, often monopolizing the piano to introduce his new songs, while Ira often stood in the corner, looking on in quiet admiration. Yet, the introvert/extrovert paradigm did not extend to their work, for Ira could easily match George in terms of assertiveness and cleverness. For instance, the whimsy, playfulness, and brashness of George's musical phrases, modern-sounding with their jazz components, were echoed by Ira's snappy, effervescent, and showy lyrics, modern-sounding with his creative use of slang and wordplay. All of which resulted in songs that spoke to the carefree optimism of the Roaring '20s.

The 1930s would present new challenges, however, and require the Gershwins to alter and adjust the character and construct of their theatre work. First, 1927's *Show Boat* had introduced the idea of a more serious and integrated "musical theatre" form on Broadway and was proving to be a growing influence on musical writers. Next, the Great Depression had shifted America's sociopolitical climate from one of lighthearted confidence to disillusioned cynicism. To their credit, the brothers not only met the challenges, but created landmark works during the decade, which not only reflected the current *Zeitgeist* and resonated with audiences, but also revolutionized the musical theatre genre. Their first innovative work in 1930, *Strike Up the Band*, was originally created and slated for Broadway in 1927. Unfortunately, the libretto by George S. Kaufman so displeased producers and alienated audiences with its strident and obdurate antiwar libretto (which grimly ended with America preparing for war with the Soviet Union) that the production closed during out-of-town tryouts. It was rewritten by Morrie Ryskind, who played up the satire and disarmed some of the more barbed elements, placing all the action within a dream and replacing the Soviet Union with innocuous Switzerland

as America's enemy and war threat (over U.S. tariffs on imported Swiss chocolate, no less). The humor hinged on the casting of screwball comedy stars, as well as lampooning easy targets, such as politics, propagandist doublespeak, and ineptitude in national government, echoing the dissatisfaction and dissolution felt by many Americans, while providing enough laughs to ease the pain. Finally reaching Broadway in 1930, the production also boasted a winning score, including soon-to-be Gershwin standards such as the title song, "Strike Up the Band," which was used to parody a patriotic march, and the sweetly tuned "I've Got a Crush on You." Audiences enjoyed the revamped production and *Strike Up the Band* ran for 191 performances. The Gershwins, as well as their *Strike* librettists Kaufman and Ryskind, were dissatisfied with the success, however, feeling they had compromised their vision to placate producers and audiences. Therefore, they were even more determined to realize an innovative and uncompromised political satire with their follow-up musical, *Of Thee I Sing*.

With the wickedly satiric *Of Thee I Sing*, the Gershwins again worked with co-librettists Kaufman (who also directed) and Ryskind, introducing a new level of integration and sociopolitical sophistication to the musical comedy genre, as it humorously reflected and deflected America's Depression-era angst and cynicism regarding previously revered institutions. Opening at the Music Box on December 26, 1931, the work, considered to be a comic opera by its creators, contained an almost through-composed score, the likes of which had not been seen on Broadway to date. Key scenes morphed seamlessly from one musical interlude to another, while the book told the tale of an unqualified United States presidential candidate (John P. Winter-green), who wins the office, along with his dithering running mate (Alexander Throttlebottom), on a calculated campaign of "Love," only to be faced with and forced to reconcile unintended complications and comic crises resulting from his unconventional election. Boldly and creatively matching a Kaufman/Ryskind libretto that lampooned such sacred cows as the Presidential office, Congress, beauty contests, the Supreme Court, international diplomacy, marriage, and motherhood, the Gershwins' score was considered, at the time, to be one of the most sophisticated and diverse to appear on Broadway, combining grand opera, jazz, operetta, and recitative. In the end, audiences approved of the bold experiment, and the Broadway production ran for 441 performances. The critics lauded *Of Thee I Sing*; and the work was accorded the Pulitzer Prize for Drama (a first for a musical). Unfortunately, George Gershwin, as composer, was not named as one of the Pulitzer recipients; thus, Ira initially refused the award, seeing the omission of George as not only an artistic slight but a serious misunderstanding of the constitution of musical theatre (i.e., a musical does not exist by written word only; the composer, as "author" of the music, is a fundamental contributor to the overall dramatic work). Ultimately, he was convinced by George to accept the honor and monetary award. George was ultimately awarded his Pulitzer, posthumously, in 1998. Given the critical and popular success of *Sing*, its follow-up, 1933's *Let 'Em Eat Cake*, by the same Gershwins/Kaufman/Ryskind creative team, proved to be a disappointment, failing at the box office and accused by most critics of having gone too far with its acerbic and alienating libretto, and unsparing satire. Returning to its lead characters, Wintergreen and Throttlebottom, the sequel evolves their narrative, re-presenting Throttlebottom as a fascist Head of State who ultimately orders a capital execution. One bright note, however, was that *Cake's* quick closure freed George Gershwin to devote himself to his newest project, one that had been five years in the making: *Porgy and Bess*.

As early as the 1920s, George Gershwin had been interested in writing an opera. His first consideration was an adaptation of the Yiddish drama classic, *The Dybbuk* (1914). Even though this project never came to fruition, George had convinced powerful brokers in the classical music world that he could compose a modern American opera. Accordingly, he was given open-ended financial backing from a Metropolitan Opera patron, Otto Kahn, to create such a work. In 1926, George read the contemporary hit novel *Porgy* (1925). Written by DuBose Heyward, the book paints a vivid picture of African American life in the South, detailing the lives of numerous black residents, their relationships, and dramatic conflicts in the seedy, fictional Charleston neighborhood of Catfish Row. At the heart of the action is the struggle of a lame beggar, Porgy, who is thwarted in his passionate pursuit of the ambivalent Bess. After George read the book, he reportedly sent a letter to Heyward, asking to turn the material into an opera. Heyward was intrigued; but unfortunately, the novel was already being adapted for the stage by his wife, Dorothy Heyward. As a result, the play *Porgy* (produced by the Theatre Guild and directed by Russian émigré Rouben Mamoulian) debuted in 1927 and

became one of the top hits of the Broadway season. In the meantime, George refused to give up on the "opera" idea. Once *Porgy*'s Broadway run began to wind down, Heyward reconnected with Gershwin, signaling that he was ready to explore the opera project. But this time, George was too busy, immersed in the development of *Let 'Em Eat Cake*. Further, during this period, the Theatre Guild had approached the Heywards with the alluring idea of letting Jerome Kern and Oscar Hammerstein II make a musical of the story, with Al Jolson in the title role. Jolson was also making a personal bid to shape the material into his own "blackface" star vehicle. Gershwin understood that such a venture could be profitable for its creators; so throughout the bidding process, George diplomatically wrote to DuBose that he understood the business sense behind the Jolson choice but that he could provide a more artful, serious approach to the material. The Jolson deal never came to fruition; and in 1933, five days after *Cake* opened, Gershwin commenced writing his long-sought-after opera, *Porgy and Bess* ("Bess" was added to the opera's title to differentiate it from the novel and play).

Finding a producer for the innovative work proved to be even more complicated than the aforementioned contract and development negotiations. A persistent myth holds that the Metropolitan Opera had originally shown interest in commissioning *Porgy and Bess*, but as the Met maintained that it would have to use white performers in blackface, Gershwin refused the offer. In actuality, however, Gershwin insisted from the beginning that the work be performed by African Americans, and no overture was ever made by the Met, given its position that the production was unworkable for its all-white roster of opera singers (while implicitly suggesting that African Americans were ill-suited to the opera genre). Seeing the writing on the wall, George Gershwin bypassed the traditional opera houses and approached the Theatre Guild. Given their success with *Porgy*, the Guild agreed to produce the opera on Broadway, again hiring Mamoulian to direct. This visionary decision was significant and would forever influence perceptions of the production, for the original Broadway venue proved confusing for many in theatrical and classical music circles. Was this new work an opera, a musical, or both? Its blurring of musical theatre and opera boundaries contributed to the notion that *Porgy and Bess* was of indeterminate genre and has caused much debate over the years as to its place in the musical theatre and/or opera canon.

Nonetheless, with a producer on board, the creators could confidently proceed with the writing. Without delay, George asked Ira to join the project as a co-lyricist with Heyward (Ira would handle the score's up-tempo character songs, and Heyward contributed lyrics for the ballads). At certain points, Heyward and the Gershwins worked from separate locations. Heyward left New York City and returned to Charleston, often submitting his writing by mail to the brothers. George also travelled occasionally to Charleston, and he took a hiatus from his New York penthouse to live for five weeks on Folly Island, just off the coast of South Carolina. There, he stayed in a beach shack, living carefree and barefoot as he immersed himself in the culture—especially the rhythms, songs, sounds, and tonalities—of the indigenous black population, the Gullah people. With score in hand, George returned to New York and, refuting the idea that black opera singers were nonexistent, cast Washington, D.C. music professor and baritone Todd Duncan as Porgy and Julliard-trained Anne Brown as Bess. The classical vocalists were offset by the casting of vaudevillian song-and-dance man John Bubbles to play the cocaine-dealing shyster, Sportin' Life. Gershwin proceeded to orchestrate the score himself (a rarity in musical theatre, as well as a reproof to skeptics who questioned his classical composition capacity). Still, the scope of the project demanded an army of arrangers and copyists, with the work continuing up until rehearsals began. With a cast of nearly fifty, *Porgy and Bess* began its out-of-town tryout in Boston, where the opera played more than three hours. Given the musical theatre audience's impatience with the length, Mamoulian asked George Gershwin for cuts; he complied and a more "manageable" and commercial product opened at Broadway's Alvin Theatre on October 10, 1935.

Reactions to *Porgy and Bess'* Broadway debut were mixed, with much criticism aimed at issues beyond the production's actual performance. First, a debate raged over Gershwin's subtitling of *Porgy and Bess* as "An American Folk Opera," necessitating that George justify how his opera qualified as a "folk" work in terms of race, culture, and sound. Specifically, he needed to explain how he had captured the "spirit" of the African American experience by employing and/or approximating many of the African American musical idioms prevalent in the South, reinterpreting them as opera forms (complete with recitative, leitmotifs, and virtuosic vocal requirements). Indeed, Gershwin's richly diverse score spanned the musical spectrum, with styles ranging from bluesy arias ("Summertime" and "My Man's Gone Now") to sweeping love ballads ("Bess, You Is My Woman Now") to jazzy up-tempo numbers ("It Ain't Necessarily So" and "I Got Plenty o' Nuttin'") and gospel ("Oh Lawd, I'm On My Way"). Nevertheless, his use of the term "folk" was met with resistance from those who saw his score as an appropriation of such forms by an interloper, with no claims to legitimacy and authenticity (one of the more vocal critics was Duke Ellington, who was currently working on his own opera). There were also those in the classical music world who dismissed the populist aspects of the score and balked at Gershwin's use of the term "opera." It did not help that there remained prejudicial sentiments by some in the music and theatre establishment who not only disparaged the idea of an "opera" rooted in African American culture and music, but were also discomfited by the overall "melting pot" significance of *Porgy and Bess*, given its channeling and creation through a Jewish filter, i.e., the Gershwins. One of the most vehement critics in this last regard was prestigious composer and music critic Virgil Thomson, who managed to disparage both the African American content (feeling the racial/folk character of the music did not meet the definition of "opera") and what he deemed to be the inexpert treatment by an unsuited "Jewish" composer (interestingly, Thomson was also working on a "Negro folk" opera at the time). All of these factors may have contributed to the production's lackluster Broadway box office: a disappointing 124 performances. *Porgy and Bess* would not find success until 1942, when it was revived on Broadway, with a significantly revised score that cut most of Gershwin's original recitative, replacing it with dialogue. The adjustments succeeded in pleasing a Broadway audience, however, and the work entered the American musical theatre canon. Validation of its "opera" status came in the 1960s and '70s, when the work premiered in European opera houses and ultimately debuted at America's leading opera house, the Met, in 1986, where the original score, including all recitative, was restored. But *Porgy and Bess* continues to be a controversial work in many respects, especially given persistent criticisms that it reinscribes, perpetuates, and glorifies negative African American stereotypes (gambling addicts, promiscuous women, abusive men, beggars, murderers, drug dealers, and petty crooks). And although it has become a staple for many opera houses, as well as musical theatre venues that can meet its production/performance demands, it remains a work confounded by its construct, content, and history. Point in fact, a 2012 Broadway revival caused a great stir as an adaptation of its book by Pulitzer-Prize-winning playwright Susan Lori-Parks contained major changes that were publically condemned by theatre purists and heavyweights (e.g., Stephen Sondheim). The changes were scaled back and ended up being minor; but tempers had once again flared over the 77-year-old work. Nevertheless, audiences have consistently looked past the show's attendant controversies to bask in its sweeping musical score, operatic passions, raucous spirit, and community of marginalized Others who surmount oppressive odds.

Unfortunately, George Gershwin was never to see his beloved "folk opera" become an American classic. In the year following *Porgy and Bess'* disappointing Broadway debut, George and Ira moved to Hollywood to write for the movies. George also engaged in a series of concerts, during which he began having difficulties getting through certain musical passages. Then, the headaches began and accelerated throughout the spring of 1937. Doctors could not find the cause (out of desperation, George also started seeing a psychiatrist). By July, George's condition quickly deteriorated. It was only when he lapsed into a coma that an inoperable brain tumor was discovered. Surgeons tried to intercede, but their efforts were futile; and the 38-year-old George never regained consciousness, dying on July 11, 1937. Not only did the music and theatre community mourn his passing, but all of America grieved as well, with his death announced on the radio, accompanied

by famous strands of *Rhapsody in Blue*. No one would ever master as many musical genres as George Gershwin; and when he teamed with his brother, the two produced a body of work, in song and on stage, that has endured for generations, speaking to contemporary audiences while providing a window to the past and an example of artistic adventure and experimentation that continues to inspire and instruct musical artists today.

figure 4.

'S WONDERFUL

Music by George Gershwin; Lyrics by Ira Gershwin (1927)

Life has just begun:
Jack has found his Jill.
Don't know what you've done,
But I'm all a-thrill.
How can words express
Your divine appeal?
You could never guess
All the love I feel.
From now on, lady, I insist,
For me no other girls exist.

'S wonderful! 'S marvellous –
You should care for me!
'S awful nice! 'S Paradise –
'S what I love to see!
You've made my life so glamorous,
You can't blame me for feeling amorous.
Oh, 's wonderful! 'S marvellous –
That you should care for me!

Don't mind telling you
In my humble fash
That you thrill me through
With a tender pash.
When you said you care,
'Magine my emosh;
I swore, then and there.
Permanent devosh.
You made all other boys seem blah;
Just you alone filled me with AHH.

'S wonderful! 'S marvellous –
You should care for me!
'S awful nice! 'S paradise –
'S what I love to see!
My dear, it's four leaved clover time;
From now on my heart's working overtime,
Oh, 's wonderful! 'S marvellous –
That you should care for me!

FEATURED PRODUCTION: *Of Thee I Sing* (1931)

Music by George Gershwin; Lyrics by Ira Gershwin
Book by George S. Kaufman and Morrie Ryskind

Original Broadway Run: Opened December 26, 1931; Music Box Theatre
441 performances

After the Stock Market Crash of 1929, America would never be the same. Gone was the over-confident optimism, exceptionalism, and carefree giddiness that characterized the 1920s. America entered a decade of economic depression and uncertainty as well as a sociopolitical climate of disillusionment and cynicism, all fueled by President Hoover's seemingly empty promises of imminent prosperity, even as Hoovervilles were cropping up around the country. Further, the country was being rocked by a number of highly publicized political scandals (e.g., the corruption indictments leveled against power-ful, politically connected New York City mayor Jimmy Walker, which resulted in his resignation). The Gershwins, with their finger on the American pulse, made a corresponding artistic shift, redirecting their talents to engage and exploit the current *Zeitgeist*, leaving their Jazz Era positivity to embark on a satirical skewering of socioeconomics, politics, and American culture.

The concept of *Of Thee I Sing* originated with its librettists, George S. Kaufman and Morrie Rys-kind, who were dissatisfied with the watering down of their previous Gershwin musical collaboration, *Strike Up the Band* (1927), which closed out of town. Therefore, they devised the idea of a sharp and timely satire aimed directly at national politics. The initial work, tentatively titled *Tweedledee*, depicted two ineffectual political parties warring over a new national anthem. The material appealed to the Gershwins, who had also been disappointed with the neutering of the original biting satire of *Strike*. Thus, they agreed to reunite with the librettists. When Kaufman and Ryskind could not find enough material in the "anthem" idea to constitute a full-length work, they revised the concept (in the manner of a Marx Brothers comedy), arriving at a straightforward satiric assault on the highest office of America, as well as its surrounding politics. When the Gershwins contributed their musical talents, redefining themselves as "operetta" writers, the result proved to be a significant political satire on the Broadway stage as well as the longest-running Broadway show of George Gershwin's career (441 performances).

To appreciate the brilliance and bravery of *Of Thee I Sing*'s content, one must first understand the tongue-in-cheek plot. When an indeterminate political party nominates innocuous candidate John P. Wintergreen for President, the party bosses decide that, given his bachelor status, he should run on the equally innocuous platform of "Love" (a platform that could offend no one and entice all). To fur-ther exploit the "Love" strategy, it is decided that Wintergreen should embark upon a "wife" search, in the form of a contest. As judge of a national beauty pageant in Atlantic City (a parody of the Miss America Pageant), Wintergreen will not only name the winner but will crown her "Miss White House," his wife-to-be. To the dismay of his political advisors and the contest organizers, he rejects the winner, Diana Devereaux, because he has fallen in love with the pageant organizer, Mary Turner, due, in great part, to her delicious corn muffins (which also sway his party to accept her as the new prospective First Lady). The sweethearts embark on a political tour, with Wintergreen proposing to Mary on the podium in each state, resulting in a landslide Presidential win.

Once Wintergreen wins the election and marries Mary, complications ensue. Devereaux, the spurned pageant winner, sues Wintergreen for reneging on the "marriage" contract; and diplomatic relations with France are strained when it is alleged that Devereaux is of French lineage (it seems that she is, in farcical style, the illegitimate daughter of an illegitimate son of an illegitimate nephew of Napoleon). Given the national disgrace and international turmoil, Congress begins impeachment hearings against Wintergreen, only to relent once Mary announces that she is pregnant (they refuse to impeach an expectant father). Contributing to the comedy are the bumbling antics of Wintergreen's Vice President, Alexander Throttlebottom. (Evidence of *Of Thee I Sing*'s lasting cultural imprint is the fact that the term "Throttlebottom" has entered the political lexicon as a derogatory moniker applied to an ineffectual political servant.) Along with a Supreme Court that is characterized as ancient, addled, and irrelevant, Vice President Throttlebottom is portrayed as a comic fool, so superfluous and vacuous that he is forced to join a tour group to gain access to the White House. Yet, he is also key to the show's resolution, ultimately appeasing the French government, which is now threatening war, by agreeing to marry Devereaux, citing the Constitutional provision that the Vice President must assume any duties that the President is unable to fulfill. In this vein, the 1931 production not only comically tied up loose ends with a *deus ex machina* (miraculous resolution), but also with an irreverent wink and nod to an audience disgruntled with current congressional and political shenanigans, yet searching for a traditional happy ending (punctuated by a final tableaux in which Mary, in bed with her twin babies, is positioned onstage with the political players).

In 1932, *Of Thee I Sing* became the first musical to win the Pulitzer Prize for Drama. Because the committee did not consider music to be part of the "drama," George Gershwin was not named as one of the award recipients, although Ira Gershwin, Kaufman, and Ryskind were named. Consequently, Ira was discomfited and had to be talked into receiving his award and the monetary prize, while George was awarded posthumously in 1998. Taking into account the extent and utility of *Of Thee I Sing*'s music component, the Pulitzer omission of George Gershwin seems ludicrous today. Drawing inspiration from the comic operettas of Gilbert and Sullivan, the Gershwins created a work that is almost completely underscored and tightly integrated, with one number often melding into another in a semi-continuous score, aided by the occasional use of recitative. With approximately thirty musical numbers (a rarity in musical comedy), the show boasts an unusually sophisticated and wide range of musical styles, including stirring marches, sentimental ballads, choral interludes, contrapuntal passages, and arias. Further, while incorporating the sound, aesthetic, and spirit of jazz (e.g., the title song, "Of Thee I Sing," is given a contemporary, snappy, and somewhat irreverent flavor as the word "baby" is added to its patriotic sentiment), the score suggests operetta as filtered through Tin Pan Alley. The Gershwins also used many samplings from popular American folk songs in their musical numbers (a throwback to George M. Cohan and a flash forward to rap and hip hop), connecting to audiences familiar with the sampled themes, while twisting and commenting on them in the context of the show's overall satire. Given the score's complexity and emphasis on integration, it is one of the few hits by the Gershwins to produce only one hit song ("Who Cares"); further, the production is something of a historic curiosity, highly popular and lauded in its time, yet never successfully revived on Broadway (the lone 1952 revival ran for only 72 performances). This is not to suggest, however, that the work does not deserve a significant place in the American musical theatre canon, for it stands today as an exemplary exercise in musical theatre innovation, as well as artistic courage, creativity, and commentary.

PULLING BACK THE CURTAIN:
Tin Pan Alley and the American Songbook

Capitalism and commerce have always been major factors in America, whether in industry or the arts. And when capitalism, commerce, industry, and art merge in a mutually beneficial paradigm, the result may resemble a phenomenon like Tin Pan Alley: the business, street district, and iconic entity that generated most of America's popular music from the late 1800s to the 1950s. In brief, Tin Pan Alley can be described as a songwriting "factory" where popular songs were manufactured, packaged, and pedaled for public consumption. In geographic terms, the "Alley" consisted of a half block on West 28th St., between Broadway and Sixth Ave., dominated by a conglomeration of music publishers' office buildings. Given the import of the music business in America today, it is hard to believe that popular music has not always been a major industry. Even though sheet music has been available in America as long as there has been the ability to disseminate printed materials, there has not always existed a coordinated effort to create "popular" hits and sell them to a vast public. However, given the emergence of million-seller songs at the end of the nineteenth century (beginning with Charles K. Harris' 1892 megahit, "After the Ball"), finding the next million-seller became a more promising and practical pursuit (case in point, there were approximately a hundred million-plus songs in sheet music form by the end of the first decade). Clearly, the American public had become enamored with the idea of transporting songs from the popular stage and music halls into their own households, given that any amateur pianist or vocalist might spend a bit of coinage to own the sheet music and replicate the musical performances around the piano at home. Prominent song publishers such as M. Witmark and Songs, Remick & Co., and T. B. Harms wasted no time in capitalizing on the new phenomenon and began relocating their offices to the West 28th St. location to be in proximity to each other (keeping an eye on the competition) as well as the Broadway theatre district, which could provide customers as well as venues for song promotion and connections to up-and-coming songwriting talent. The formula worked; and by the end of the first decade of the twentieth century, Tin Pan Alley was the place to be if one wanted to get a song published and sold. The Manhattan publishing hub became the dominant force behind a national surge in sheet music ownership, as well as a resultant shared musical experience by Americans across the country. In this respect, Tin Pan Alley was influential and seminal to the evolution of American popular music, as well as the musical theatre and its cross-over artists.

Tin Pan Alley's name is odd, and origins of the moniker are uncertain. One prominent theory credits a 1903 interview conducted by a newspaper reporter with songwriter, Harry Von Tilzer, whose office was in the heart of the district. Thus, the cacophony of all the banging pianos in neighboring publishers' offices could be heard through the open windows and was compared, in the printed interview, to a clatter of "tin pans." Another myth holds that the district was named after the publishers' use of traveling, open-bed trucks that would troll the area, carrying pianists and pianos pedaling new tunes, with rattling tins tied to the back to attract attention. Regardless, publishers worked closely with songwriters (some could be commissioned as "house composers") to exploit current musical trends or proven formulas to create the next big hit. The songwriting output included a variety of musical forms, such as (1) folksy waltzes and other dance fads; (2) "ethnic songs," i.e., reductive songs that centered around embarrassing depictions of the Irish, Italians, Yiddish, and other ethnic, immigrant minorities; (3) sentimental ballads that were often heart-tugging tales of woe and redemption; (4) "coon songs," i.e., songs that perpetuated negative African American stereotypes, meant to be performed in blackface by white singers; (5) ragtime (e.g., Irving Berlin's first million-seller was his 1911 pseudo-ragtime riff, "Alexander's Ragtime Band"); and (6) novelty songs with references to cultural developments and fads (e.g., the country's growing infatuation with baseball resulted in the 1908 megahit "Take Me Out to the Ballgame"). Proximity to Broadway theatres was also key to Tin Pan Alley's influence and success; for in an effort to reach the wider public, original compositions were sold to producers looking for musical numbers for new shows (such as revue impresario Florenz Ziegfeld) or stars looking for fresh material (e.g., Al Jolson), or even a novice vaudevillian, looking for the perfect song to launch him or her into the "big time." The hope was that once the song was incorporated into a show or given the star treatment, it could gain exposure and develop a following.

Of course, Tin Pan Alley had other creative ways to pedal its wares. The most significant was the song plugger, a pianist/performer commissioned by the publisher to "sell" the song through musical demonstrations (in the publisher's offices, backs of trucks, saloons, theatre lobbies, etc.). Often, prime assignments would be given to gifted song arrangers who could "jazz up" or embellish a composition, creating a more marketable and flashy product (e.g., George Gershwin, one of the youngest Tin Pan Alley song pluggers, was also one of its most effective song "jazzers"/arrangers). One of the more humorous plugging jobs was that of the "Stooge," the plugger who poses as an innocent audience member and then becomes so taken with a song's debut that he sings it back to the performer (such was Irving Berlin's first Tin Pan Alley gig). One drawback to the Tin Pan Alley influence on Broadway, however, was the convention of interpolated musical numbers which often foiled early, innovative attempts at integration; for a song was most often inserted into a production based on its stand-alone merit; that is, if it was considered hit-worthy outside the show—not how it served the overall work.

Even as families moved from singing around the piano to listening to their favorite songs on the radio, Tin Pan Alley maintained its central, concentrated influence on the American song catalogue, for most songwriters continued to work in concert with dominant publishers located in the legendary district. Beginning in the 1950s, however, the music industry increasingly decentralized and shifted from an emphasis on the songwriter to the recording artist, the record producer, and studio work; that is, the rendition of a song through the recording studio arrangements and vocal/instrumental stylings, as well as the marketing of the recorded product to the American public. This phenomenon became even more pronounced with the advent of rock 'n' roll, signaling the death knell for the writer/publisher–driven paradigm of Tin Pan Alley. Yet, Tin Pan Alley has never really died. The multitude of songs that came out of the publishing district and industry during its heyday, as well as the influence of its songwriting talent, lives on today, as well as the idea of the "music business" (and its close relative, "show business")—a capitalist approach to art that served both the commercial bottom line and America's enduring songbook.

IRVING BERLIN

"Irving Berlin *is* American music." This was the legendary response given by Jerome Kern when he was asked where he would place Berlin in the American musical canon. Kern's assessment is hard to refute, for Berlin stands as the most successful and impactful songwriter of the twentieth century. And to date, America has yet to encounter an artist of his stature with regard to productivity and popularity. Indeed, the multigenerational impact of Berlin's song output is not only a consequence of his lifespan—101 years—but is also proven by the timelessness and longevity of hits such as "White Christmas" and "God Bless America." A minimally educated, self-trained artist, celebrity, and businessman, Berlin put great faith in his audience, striving for a connection through both words and music to the American Everyman, often considering public opinion of his works to be above that of the highbrow critics. As a Russian Jew who passed through the gates of Ellis Island as a young child, he loved his adopted country and sought its love as well. Fortunately, American audiences returned the affection, embracing the ear-pleasing melodies and heartfelt, straightforward lyrics by the slight, self-depreciating man who worked unceasingly to musically voice their desires, distresses, and delights. They felt that they "knew" Berlin, and he worked to keep the perception alive, a reciprocal relationship that resulted in an astounding 899 published songs, of which 451 were certifiable hits; 282 registered as "Top Ten" on billboard charts; and 35 reached the #1 spot. At his death, some would name him "America's Composer," but he also stands as a theatre visionary, with twenty-one Broadway shows on his résumé (along with seventeen film scores), contributing significantly to the American musical theatre landscape with landmark achievements in areas of musical entertainment, sociopolitical commentary, patriotic mobilization, racial relations, and musical integration. Most amazing is that these were the achievements of a once-impoverished, wide-eyed Jewish immigrant from New York's Lower East Side.

Israel "Izzy" Baline was the youngest of eight children, born in Siberia on May 11, 1888, to parents Moses (a Jewish cantor) and Leah Lipkin Baline. Five years later, Izzy and his family became victims of widespread Jewish persecution, forced to flee as their village was destroyed by the Russian pogroms. They arrived at Ellis Island in 1893, settling in what was considered

the "Jewish ghetto" of New York's Lower East Side. Unable to find work as a cantor, Moses took a job as a kosher meat inspector and teacher, but it remained a struggle to put food on the family table. Thus, the children pitched in; and at eight years of age, Izzy pulled his weight by pedaling wares on the street and working in sweatshops, often at the expense of his schooling. Ultimately, he received approximately two years, in total, of formal education; and when his father died in 1901, the 13-year-old Izzy officially dropped out of school and left home, determined to be one less mouth to feed. Having been immersed in religious music from an early age and growing up in a neighborhood that, as he often recounted, reverberated with the musical sounds and rhythms of Jewish life, Izzy pursued his own musical career as a street singer. Performing for pennies, he wandered the saloon districts of the Bowery and Chinatown, often sleeping on park benches or finding shelter under fire escapes. One of his earliest jobs was that of an occasional song plugger, or a "Stooge," for composer and publisher Harry Von Tilzer. As the Stooge, Izzy posed as an audience member at Tony Pastor's Music Hall. Then, when a new Tilzer song debuted, he "spontaneously" vocalized the song's refrain from his balcony seat, supposedly overcome by the song's appeal. After years of street performing and sporadic song plugging, Izzy finally landed a permanent job as a singing waiter at Chinatown's Pelham Café. Looking younger than his age (given his size and large, innocent eyes), Izzy became a favorite of the café's bawdy immigrant patrons, often putting made-up dirty lyrics to familiar melodies and specializing in ethnic parody numbers. When Pelham's owner heard that the singing waiters of a rival saloon in the Bowery had written a song and gotten it published, he assigned his own waiters the competitive task of one-upping them. With Izzy as designated lyricist and house pianist Mike Nicholson as composer, the result was an ethnic novelty/parody song titled "Marie from Sunny Italy" (1907). Featuring lyrics in a pseudo-Italian dialect, the endeavor proved significant for Baline in two respects: (1) The song launched Izzy into the songwriting business, being his first published work (albeit, he only earned thirty-seven cents for it) and (2) the song was responsible for turning Izzy Baline into "Irving Berlin," for the publisher had mistakenly printed his name on the sheet music as "I. Berlin." Izzy decided the "Berlin" moniker would work well as an American songwriting pseudonym. He then anglicized the "I" to stand for "Irving," instead of "Israel." Thus, "Irving Berlin" started his trajectory to becoming the most popular and prolific American songwriter of the twentieth century.

With a meager thirty-seven-cent earning from "Marie," Berlin realized that he would need to continue waiting tables and singing to supplement his songwriting. While working at Jimmy Kelly's on Union Square in 1908, he impressed publisher Ted Snyder with his song parodies, and Snyder hired him as a staff lyricist. With Snyder as composer, Berlin supplied lyrics to "She Was a Dear Little Girl," which was added to a minor Broadway show. This Broadway debut was inauspicious; yet, Berlin had found a permanent home on Tin Pan Alley and would spend his formative years learning the tools of the trade in the publishing houses of West 28th Street, often returning to his office at two in the morning to work a self-imposed second songwriting shift until dawn. (Throughout his life, Berlin would suffer from insomnia, often turning to songwriting during the late night and early morning hours.) During this period, his evolution from lyricist to lyricist/composer was mostly by accident. Berlin had no musical training; yet, he knew how he wanted his lyrics to be musicalized, that is, what melody best served their sentiments. In an often related account, Berlin had been commissioned to write a song for a vaudevillian performer, who then neglected to purchase it. Thus, Berlin took his work, another pseudo-Italian dialect piece titled "Dorando," to Snyder, who was so taken with the manuscript that he offered Berlin

$25 for the entire song. Because Berlin had only written lyrics, he vocally applied a melody on the spot, while a staff arranger notated it. Thus, in 1908, "Dorando" became the first published song with both words and music by Berlin. It is fascinating to note, however, that Berlin would never learn to read or write music throughout his long and prestigious career; instead, he worked with an amanuensis (secretary) who would transcribe his hummed, whistled, or sung melodies into notated compositions. To create melodies using a keyboard, Berlin taught himself to play the piano in the back rooms of the many saloons in which he worked as a waiter. But, like his idol George M. Cohan, he would only use the black piano keys, placing all his original compositions in the key of F#. Ever ingenious, Berlin eventually had a special piano designed for him that used levers by which he could transpose his songs to different keys. In short, such limitations did not impede Berlin's growth and output as a musical artist. It is widely reported that he composed at least five songs a week (some accounts place his output at a song a day), with only one of ten deemed good enough by Berlin to actually publish. This level of productivity and intense work ethic was evident early on; and Snyder was so impressed with Berlin that he soon made him a full-fledged partner in his publishing firm of Waterson and Snyder in 1911.

In the same year as the Waterson/Snyder publishing promotion, Berlin wrote "Alexander's Ragtime Band," his first million-seller song. As a seasoned Tin Pan Alley artist at the ripe old age of 23, Berlin had already written over fifty songs, often exploiting popular fads such as "ethnic novelty" tunes (e.g., Fanny Brice's 1909 Yiddish breakout hit, "Sadie Salome Go Home") and ragtime experiments including "That Beautiful Rag" (1910). Berlin even cannily combined ethnic parody with ragtime in "Yiddle on Your Fiddle Play Some Rag Time" (1909). Nonetheless, pure ragtime was a tricky musical milieu for any popular artist in 1911. Like jazz after it, the idiom was widely distrusted, even considered indecent (similar to the stigma attached to early rock 'n' roll). The musical style was associated with African Americans (thus, deemed unsuitable for conventional white audiences), and its ragged syncopations and somewhat hyperactive energy discomforted and alienated more conservative listeners. But Berlin, true to form, found an audience-friendly answer to this predicament, creating an allusion to ragtime while also safely appealing to mainstream America. In 1911, as a new member of the exclusive Friars Club, he was asked to provide a song for the first annual *Friars' Follies* revue. Instead of working from scratch, Berlin revamped an earlier unsuccessful song, "Alexander and his Clarinet," giving it a new melody that employed a "bugle call" riff, along with a sampled musical fragment from Stephen Foster's "Old Folks at Home" and a spirited military march meter. With these crowd-pleasing devices built into the music, Berlin also revised the lyrics to reference ragtime, imploring folks to "come on along" and hear the new musical sounds of bandleader Alexander and his ragtime band. After a positive reception by the Friars, "Alexander's Ragtime Band" was discovered by top-billed vaudevillian performers who delivered the tune to a wider, enthusiastic public. The song soon became the biggest hit in the world. While audiences found its melody familiar and infectious, they also believed they were on the cutting edge of music; that is, they had become newly converted "ragtime" connoisseurs (purists would know the truth, however, that "Alexander's" was a swinging march, not a true ragtime number). And in just eighteen months, "Alexander's" sold 2 million copies of sheet music, as well as opened the door for more authentic ragtime in popular music, inspiring numerous dance crazes around the country. As a result, Berlin found himself the hottest songwriter in America, as well as a celebrity, performing occasionally throughout the 1910s in vaudeville and on Broadway. Specifically, with the meteoric rise of "Alexander's," Berlin, himself, sometimes performed the hit on stage, with his signature thin voice and engaging demeanor.

One short year later, Berlin went from the heights of success to the depths of despair. After marrying Dorothy Goetz in 1912, he lost her just five months after their wedding to typhoid fever, contracted on their honeymoon in Havana. In response to her death, he wrote "When I Lost You" (1912). This heartfelt ballad was a departure from Berlin's lighter Tin Pan Alley exploits, but it spoke to audiences, selling 2 million copies. Although it was the only song that Berlin openly admitted to having written from personal experience, much of his song catalogue has been inspired by events in his life (but with sentiments couched in more generic terms). In short, Berlin often wrote with his heart on his sleeve, communicating directly and simply to audiences though his lyrics and music. Unlike some contemporaries, he didn't try to be overly clever or "artsy;" instead, he shared basic, honest sentiments, hoping to find common ground with

his public. Like his idol George M. Cohan, popular approval was paramount in Berlin's work/art philosophy; for instance, he reportedly quipped that he could never hate a song that sold a half-million copies. Fortunately, Berlin had an innate gift for finding melodies that connected with audiences, intuitively arriving at refrains and tonal progressions that just felt "right" and often fulfilled a listener's auditory expectation. Such tunes were also memorable, and Berlin often asserted his aim to have his melodies "linger on" after the song ended. Yet, the accessibility of his music does not mean that Berlin did not experiment with different musical idioms; his catalogue includes sweet ballads, marches, ragtime, jazzy foxtrots, Latin-inspired compositions, novelty tunes, "coon" songs, and lyrical waltzes. He also became known for his use of contrapuntal song structure (that is, the use of two independent musical refrains played simultaneously, with each given equal weight in the composition). The breadth of his hit compositions is unmatched in American popular music, all the more remarkable given his complete lack of formal music training.

In 1914, Berlin had another major success with his first complete score for the Broadway musical *Watch Your Step*. Subtitled "A Syncopated Show in Three Acts," the production was intended as a showcase for star dance duo Vernon and Irene Castle. Even though it had a thin storyline (its program credits Harry B. Smith with providing the "plot, if any"), the production more accurately resembled a dance revue. And given the prevalence of the score, which featured the latest musical idioms and dance rhythms (e.g., ragtime), the show was often lauded as America's first ragtime opera. Regardless of how to categorize it, *Watch Your Step* was a hit with Broadway audiences. One of its stand-out musical numbers was "Play a Simple Melody," and the song highlighted Berlin's genius as a contrapuntal writer. Specifically, during the number, a sweet and lyrical refrain of "Play a Simple Melody" is simultaneously played against a different syncopated refrain with lyrics that extol "ragtime." After *Watch*, Berlin created other Broadway revues, contributed to the revues of others, and continued his Tin Pan Alley songwriting, all serving to increase his popularity in New York's theatre district, as well as throughout the country. And as a pioneering advocate for composer/ author rights, he joined forces with operetta composer Victor Herbert in order to serve on ASCAP's

(American Society of Composers, Authors and Publishers) initial board of directors from 1914 to 1918.

While lighthearted American audiences were tapping their fingers and toes to Berlin's score for *Watch Your Step*, world-changing events were transpiring overseas. Beginning with the assassination of Archduke Franz Ferdinand, Europe plunged into World War I; and in 1917, America entered the conflict. Consequently, as a newly declared citizen, Berlin was drafted into the Army in 1918 (an ironic news headline proclaimed, "United States Takes Berlin"). Stationed in a training camp in Yaphank, Long Island, Private Berlin found army life difficult, especially the early wake-up calls for duty. Given his insomnia and late-night work habits, he tried to find a way by which he could capitalize upon his strengths while also serving his country in uniform. Berlin ultimately approached his commanding officers, offering to create an all-singing, all-dancing, all-military revue, with proceeds going to war charities. Under this special Army commission, Berlin would organize the show and provide the original score; all he asked in return was that he be able to sleep later in the morning so that he could write throughout the night. Soon, Sergeant Berlin and his cast of nearly 300 soldiers were entertaining Broadway audiences with *Yip! Yip! Yaphank*, a musical revue satirizing life in the military. The show, subtitled "A Musical 'Mess' Cooked Up by the Boys of Camp Upton," moved from Upton to Broadway's Century Theater and included drag performances and black-face minstrelsy as part of its lampoonery, as well as a rousing score. On a personal note, Berlin created an autobiographical number titled "Oh! How I Hate to Get Up in the Morning." In this wink and nod to his own predicament, Berlin appeared onstage in a private's uniform, performing a song which laments morning reveille and comically proposes violence toward the offending bugler. Another musical highpoint of *Yip!* was its finale, which provided an emotionally rousing and patriotic merging of reality and theatre as the entire 300-member cast performed "We're On Our Way to France," reminding audiences of their departure orders while marching up the aisles to theatrically board a ship offstage. Interestingly, a solemn ballad titled "God Bless America" was also written for the show but pulled by Berlin before opening. Consequently, audiences would have to wait two decades to hear this "trunk song" which remains, today, one of America's most revered patriotic anthems.

In addition to succeeding on Broadway, *Yip!* accrued $150,000 for wartime charities and verified Berlin's place as America's premier songwriter, entertainer, and patriot. Once the war ended, Berlin was again a private citizen, so he turned his attention to his music business, while furthering his theatre career. In 1919, he founded his own publishing house, Irving Berlin, Inc., a significant undertaking but a savvy business venture, given that normal royalty distribution at the time was 25% for the lyricist, 25% for the composer and 50% for the publisher. From this point forward, Berlin would receive 100% of the royalties for his copyrighted songs. He also continued to write hit songs for other enterprises, including the *Ziegfeld Follies*. Specifically, Berlin's breakout hit from Ziegfeld's 1919 edition, "A Pretty Girl Is Like a Melody," would ultimately become the *Follies* theme song. In 1921, after seeing his songs profit numerous producers, he decided to further his theatrical control over his work. To this end, Berlin partnered with Sam H. Harris to build his own 1,025-seat theater, the Music Box, on West 45th Street (Berlin would become sole owner after Harris' death in 1941). Instead of leasing a building from owners and paying rent, Berlin was able to build a performance space to specifically suit his own revues, comprised completely of his musical material. Such an undertaking was a first for any composer and a feat that has yet to be replicated. Of course, there were detractors. Labeling the venture "Berlin's Folly," many scoffed when costs mounted (e.g., a million dollars for land/building and almost $200,000 for the first production). Yet, the first *Music Box Revue* at the Music Box in 1921 was such a stylish and innovative theatrical event that Berlin and company made up their expenditures in twelve months, though the usual pay back time for a Broadway musical was ten weeks. In the trendy, elegant, and intimate décor of the Music Box, the *Music Box Revues* featured creative design and staging throughout four editions, incorporating such inventive scenic elements as oversized birdcages, trapezes, trap doors, orange trees spraying audiences with orange scent, special lighting effects, and imaginative (and sometimes gimmicky) costumes such as a hoop skirt that filled an entire stage. Uniquely (for a revue), the entire score was written by Berlin, with a myriad of songs hitting the pop charts, including the sweetly tuned "What'll I Do?" and the show's theme song, "Say It with Music" (which became a hit even before its official theatrical debut). Audiences also had their funny bones tickled by comedy sketches, including Robert Benchley's famous "Treasurer's Report," as well as novelty songs by star comediennes (e.g., Fanny Brice's "I Want to Be a Ballet Dancer"). Although the $5.50 ($77 in 2013) ticket price was higher than the norm, audiences seemed willing to pay the extra amount for the fresh and tuneful productions. It was only when the productions started to feel a bit repetitive that audiences began to lose interest. Consequently, Berlin, ever the intuitive showman, decided to end his *Music Box Revues* after the fourth edition in 1924.

As his *Music Box Revues* were coming to an end, Berlin found himself embroiled in a romantic drama that served as one of the top tabloid stories of 1925. Having met and fallen in love with *The New Yorker* journalist, socialite, and heiress Ellin Mackay, Berlin was dismayed when his marriage intentions were rebuffed by her father, Clarence Mackay, the powerful president of Postal Telegraph (the forerunner of AT&T). Specifically, Clarence considered Berlin to be unsuitable for his Catholic, upper-class daughter due to both Berlin's songwriting/theatre profession and Jewish religion/ethnicity. Clarence went so far as to send Ellin to Europe to keep her from Berlin, threatening to disinherit her if she continued their relationship. The press followed the soap opera closely, often spotlighting Berlin's Jewish identity in articles and headlines as the main obstacle to their desired union, affirming the perception that Berlin, regardless of career achievements, would not be a suitable addition to New York's Social Register. All the turmoil ultimately resulted in a highly publicized elopement by Berlin and Ellin on January 4, 1926, at New York's City Hall. With reports that Clarence was planning to disown Ellin, Berlin guaranteed that his new wife would never have to struggle financially by putting the copyright to his smash hit "Always" [see fig. 4.2] in her name, forever granting her the royalties to one of his most successful and timeless songs (fittingly written as his love declaration to her during their forced time apart).

Berlin's first year of marriage to Ellin was a happy one; and in celebration of the birth of their first daughter, Mary Ellin, he wrote "Blue Skies" (1926). After the song was inserted into a minor Rodgers and Hart musical, *Betsy*, it was published and recorded by other artists, becoming a #1 hit. The ebullient and ubiquitous "Blue Skies" was also sung by Al Jolson in Hollywood's first "talkie," *The Jazz Singer* (1927). Subsequently, Berlin moved his family to Hollywood to work on scores for the new all-talking/all-singing movie musicals.

Unfortunately, the Hollywood years during the late 1920s were dark ones for him. First, the movies on which Berlin worked were crude in sound and filming techniques, often handicapping the appeal of his scores and disappointing audiences. Further, Ellin's health was at risk with a second pregnancy, and she returned to New York to deliver a baby boy, Irving Jr., who died a few weeks later of Sudden Infant Death Syndrome. The death occurred on Christmas morning, 1928, bringing about a Berlin family tradition of visiting the grave every Christmas morning, a sadly bittersweet event given that Berlin's most popular and performed song in his canon is the wistful carol "White Christmas" (1942). In 1929, things got worse, as Berlin lost most of his fortune, two decades of songwriting profits/savings, in the Stock Market Crash. It was only through his role as publisher that Berlin was able to recoup losses in a timely fashion, continuing to accrue royalties from past hits. It was also during this time that the Berlins reconnected with Clarence Mackay, bonding over the tragedy of Irving Jr.'s death and the economic hardships of the Crash, which had also affected Mr. Mackay.

Having left Hollywood a bit bruised by perceived failure, Berlin turned his attentions once again to the Broadway stage. But Broadway had also been somewhat chastened and reconfigured by current sociopolitical and economic realities. Times had changed drastically since Berlin's buoyant and lavish *Music Box Revues* of the '20s. Specifically, 1932 and 1933 were the worst years of the Great Depression (with unemployment at 23.6 percent in 1932), and American audiences were despondent and anxious over the nation's present state. Thus, just as the Gershwins adapted their shows to the existing national *Zeitgeist*, Berlin, ever responsive to his public, decided to write revues that would tap into the current consciousness and serve not only as musical reflections but also as reassurances to a country in need of collective dialogue, connection, and comfort. To this end, he wrote *Face the Music* with librettist Moss Hart, a revue that opened in 1932 at the New Amsterdam Theatre and played 165 performances. The timely production dealt with the Depression, in a general sense, and took aim at political corruption and the laundering of money into a sure failure of a show, not unlike the plot of *The Producers* (a theme inspired and underscored by the resignation of indicted New York City Mayor Jimmy Walker). Although reflective of public sentiment, the show still aimed to musically please audiences with hummable tunes and to inspire with hopeful sentiments, epitomized by Berlin's "Let's Have Another Cup o' Coffee."

Given the success of *Face the Music*, Berlin re-teamed with librettist Hart in 1933 for *As Thousands Cheer* at the Music Box. In the new production, however, Berlin and Hart moved past a generic address of contemporary issues and innovatively decided, instead, to use actual articles and headlines from daily newspapers as the source material for songs and sketches. Foreshadowing the topical parody format of contemporary variety shows such as *Saturday Night Live*, Berlin and Hart's revue boldly lampooned real-life figures such as activist/pacifist Mahatma Gandhi, industrial tycoon John D. Rockefeller, and infamous performer Josephine Baker. The latter was given a satirical treatment by Ethel Waters, singing "Harlem on My Mind," a stellar performance that was significant in many respects. First, Waters was an African American star recruited by Berlin from black entertainment venues such as the Cotton Club in Harlem. He insisted that she headline his revue, a situation that caused controversy and excitement in the musical theatre world. In addition to her Baker parody, Waters stopped the show with "Heat Wave," a high-energy number based on the headline "Heat Wave Hits New York." Waters' most potent musical moment in the revue, however, was an unprecedented call to social justice and understanding: "Suppertime." This Berlin song was performed subsequent to the scenic headline of "Unknown Negro Lynched by Frenzied Mob." During the number, Waters, as the widowed "Negro" mother, set a dinner table and musically lamented over how to tell her children that their father would never be coming home. During Philadelphia tryouts, Berlin was pressured by some producers and investors to remove the number. He insisted on keeping it in the show. Waters also famously stated that she felt she was directly conveying to her "comfortable," white Broadway audiences the tragedy and turmoil of her people during the song. Such was a rare moment of pure racial communication between performer and spectator in the midst of a musical revue. The Act One finale was a more conventional number, "Easter Bonnet," reverting back to the upbeat, crowd-pleasing manner of Berlin. Applying new lyrics to a melody written sixteen years earlier; Berlin provided a number that was staged as an informal Easter Parade on Fifth Avenue, nostalgically looking back at brighter and better days in America. The song would go on to become an American seasonal classic, while *As Thou-*

sands Cheer, overall, would enjoy a triumphant run of 400 performances.

In the following years, Berlin returned to Hollywood, this time enjoying success as he composed scores for the movie musical industry, which had matured and become a wildly popular form of American entertainment (three of his film scores were written especially for Fred Astaire and Ginger Rogers). Then, in 1938, Berlin once again served as America's patriotic mouthpiece and conscience, pulling "God Bless America" from his "trunk" of never-performed/published songs and giving it to Kate Smith to sing live on radio on Armistice Day. In "Berlin" fashion, he chose to donate all royalties from the song to charity—in this case, to the Boy Scouts and Girl Guides of America. The number proved to be a defining moment for Berlin, a chance for him to avow, through Smith's vocals and in published form, his love of and allegiance to his adopted country. Yet, incredibly, anti-Semitic anger also greeted the performance, with various newspaper opinion pieces lambasting the idea of a "Jewish immigrant" imploring "God" to bless America; while Smith's agent reportedly received hate mail with similar sentiments. It is gratifying to note, however, that the controversy is confined to the past; for Berlin's song is now widely accepted as one of America's most revered patriotic anthems. Further, Berlin received the 1954 Congressional Medal of Honor (like his hero, Cohan) from President Eisenhower for the song, which was declared a national treasure. Indeed, "God Bless America" was specifically used after the September 11th attacks in 2001 as a rallying cry and musical moment of unity for the nation, with no thought to Jewish authorship, and its overall sentiment proving timeless and inclusive.

Four years later, Berlin again served the country in a musical fashion. After the bombing of Pearl Harbor on December 7, 1941, America entered World War II. Driven by patriotic duty, Berlin contacted General George C. Marshall and offered to create a sequel to *Yip! Yip! Yaphank*, donating all proceeds to the Army Emergency Relief Fund and other wartime charities. Given the go-ahead, Berlin returned to Camp Upton to write the show; 300 servicemen were recruited for Berlin's company, and rehearsals began. The result was a new revue titled *This Is the Army*, which opened at the Broadway Theatre on July 4, 1942. Like *Yip!*, the 1942 show used skits, songs, and dances to satirize life in the Army. One highlight was the show's revival of "Oh! How I Hate to Get Up in the Morning," performed again by Berlin in his World War I uniform. On opening night, the packed Broadway house gave Berlin a standing ovation before he even opened his mouth. In addition, the revue once again employed the sight gag of soldiers in drag and treated audiences to a rousing 300-man production number ("This Is the Army, Mr. Jones"). This is not to suggest, however, that *This Is the Army* lacked innovation. Most significant, instead of blackface minstrelsy (as had been used in *Yip!*), Berlin insisted on casting African American soldiers to perform standout numbers such as "What the Well-Dressed Man in Harlem Will Wear." As a result, Berlin's cast/company became America's first racially integrated Army unit (and the only one during World War II). After 113 Broadway performances to sold-out houses and a special performance for President Roosevelt, the revue toured the nation (often having to make special housing arrangements for its black cast members in segregated parts of the country). It then moved overseas: to London, North Africa, Italy, and, ultimately, the active fronts of the South Pacific, with Berlin still performing and often writing new material for each installation of the show. The entire tour lasted a little over three years (extending two months after the war officially ended) and accrued $9.8 million for the Army Emergency Relief Fund. The work was also made into a feature film in 1943, starring George Murphy, Ronald Reagan, and featuring Berlin performing "Oh! How I Hate to Get Up." Finally, for the extraordinary wartime service provided by *This Is the Army*, Berlin was awarded the military's 1945 Medal for Merit.

Berlin was never one to rest on his laurels, however. A few years after the war, he embarked on a venture that would prove to be his longest-running Broadway hit and the pinnacle of his musical theatre career. Although a Broadway veteran, Berlin had never composed a score for a fully integrated book musical. Yet such works were increasingly popular, given the success of Rodgers and Hammerstein's *Oklahoma!* in 1943 (of course, 1927's *Show Boat* had also been a landmark achievement and seminal event in this respect, but it wasn't until *Oklahoma!* that most of Broadway followed suit). So, when Rodgers and Hammerstein approached Berlin to take on a project originally intended for Jerome Kern (whose untimely death happened while visiting New York to begin work on the show), Berlin not only hesitated but regretfully admitted to Hammerstein that he didn't think he had the capacity to write an integrated

score. The show was to be a musical biography about the life of Wild West sharpshooter Annie Oakley and was originally conceived as a vehicle for Ethel Merman by librettist/lyricist Dorothy Fields (who ultimately co-authored the libretto with her brother, Herbert Fields). Still doubtful of his ability to write in the "new-fangled" integrated style, Berlin asked to take a week to think over the project and experiment with some musical ideas. True to his prolific and agile work ethic, Berlin returned with five songs for Rodgers and Hammerstein, presenting them as his "audition" material. After hearing the numbers, the producers insisted Berlin take the job, convinced that he could write for character and situation, as well as deliver engaging melodies and heartfelt, clever lyrics. Four of the five songs were ultimately used in the show, along with a number that became the ultimate showbiz anthem, "There's No Business Like Show Business." Although summing up Berlin's own love affair with and dedication to the music/entertainment industry, Berlin misread the producers' initially silent response to the song (they recount that they were speechless at its brilliance); and he had to be persuaded to keep it in the show. (This was not a rare occurrence. Given Berlin's genius and unmatched success in songwriting, he was surprisingly plagued by insecurity throughout his career.)

During rehearsals, Berlin had a wonderful time working with Ethel Merman, a performer who could not only play up the comedy of his character songs (e.g., "You Can't Get a Man with a Gun" and "Anything You Can Do"), but also deliver ballads (e.g., "I Got Lost in His Arms") with straightforward emotional honesty. For her part, Merman reported that after all the brash comic types she had played to date, *Annie Get Your Gun* was a pivotal point in her career, with Berlin finally making a "lady" out of her. The public loved the entire enterprise. After opening at the Imperial Theatre on May 16, 1946, the show ran for 1,147 performances. The long run held special meaning for Berlin, for he was an artist who looked to popular approval as the ultimate critique, feeling that he only failed if audiences rejected his material. And although critics applauded the show overall, there were some who questioned the "artistic" merit and/or degree of innovation, claiming it to be a bit "old fashioned"—to which Berlin famously retorted that they were right, it was a "good old-fashioned smash!"

Although not a "smash," Berlin had another popular run on Broadway in 1950 with *Call Me Madam*, his second integrated book musical and vehicle for Ethel Merman. With a book by Howard Lindsay and Russel Crouse, loosely based on real-world events, Merman played a socialite hostess who is named as U.S. Ambassador to the tiny, fictional duchy of Lichtenburg. In the production, the ambassador charms local officials and foreign diplomats, while engaging in straight-talking, folksy phone chats with President Truman. Included in Berlin's ear-pleasing score is one of his more complex contrapuntal compositions, "You're Just in Love," as well as the catchy "They Like Ike" (a song eventually revamped as "I Like Ike" and used by Dwight D. Eisenhower as a campaign song/slogan during his successful 1952 presidential bid). Although *Madam* would successfully run for 644 performances, Berlin did not return to Broadway until twelve years later with the failed *Mr. President* (1962), his last Broadway show, which lasted for only seven months and did not recoup its production costs. With the concurrent cancellation of Berlin's film project, *Say It with Music*, the popular icon felt irrelevant, surmising that audiences were moving away from his traditional songwriting and toward the new sounds/sentiments of rock 'n' roll, for which he had no affinity and/or appreciation. Feeling that the American public had turned its back on him, Berlin reciprocated, ceasing to write songs for public consumption (the exception being the addition of "An Old Fashioned Wedding" to the 1966 revival of *Annie Get Your Gun*, his last published song). He became a recluse in his later years, limiting personal contact to a small circle of friends and conducting business affairs by phone only. Berlin also began to pull publishing rights to much of his catalogue, refusing artists the right to perform or record his songs in any form that he found displeasing, (e.g., he refused to allow Steven Spielberg the use of "Always" for his 1989 film by the same title). His last public performance was in 1973, singing "God Bless America" at the White House for returning Vietnam POWs. Sadly, he lost his lifelong partner in 1988 when his beloved Ellin died after sixty-two years of marriage. One year later, Berlin died in his sleep on September 22, 1989, at their home in New York City. He was 101 years old. In younger and happier days, Berlin had once lamented that the most difficult thing about being a success was the necessity of continuing that success. He needn't have worried. Berlin's unmatched twentieth-century career lives on today through his song catalogue, theatrical contributions, and iconic status—a lifetime achievement that will continue far into the twenty-first century and beyond.

To expand on Jerome Kern's assessment, Irving Berlin not only *is* American music, but *will always be* American music.

 igure 4.

ALWAYS

Music and Lyrics by Irving Berlin (1925)

Ev'rything went wrong,
And the whole day long
I'd feel so blue.
For the longest while
I'd forget to smile;
Then I met you.
Now that my blue days have passed,
Now that I've found you at last:

I'll be loving you
Always,
With a love that's true
Always.

When the things you've planned
Need a helping hand,
I will understand
Always, always.

Days may not be fair
Always;
That's when I'll be there
Always —

Not for just an hour,
Not for just a day,
Not for just a year,
But always.

FEATURED PRODUCTION: *Annie Get Your Gun* (1946)

Music and Lyrics by Irving Berlin
Book by Dorothy Fields and Herbert Fields

Original Broadway Run: Opened May 16, 1946; Imperial Theatre;
1,147 performances

Given that *Annie Get Your Gun* introduced audiences to the iconic song "There's No Business Like Show Business," it is fitting that the story behind the musical similarly exemplifies the age-old adage that "The show must go on!" When lyricist/librettist Dorothy Fields originally thought of creating a musical based on the life of Wild West sharpshooter Annie Oakley, she could think of no one else for the role but Broadway star Ethel Merman. She approached producers Richard Rodgers and Oscar Hammerstein II, who had recently formed their own production company to finance, develop, and control their works as well as outside projects. The team liked the idea, on the condition that they could sign Merman; they also felt that book musical pioneer Jerome Kern (who had worked with Fields in the past) would be a perfect choice as composer. Merman, recovering from a cesarean section, demurred at first but then signed on once she was offered a hefty salary and a cut of the gross profits. Kern was equally ambivalent, not anxious to move back to New York from Hollywood, but was ultimately won over. Lastly, Dorothy's brother, librettist Herbert Fields, joined the group as co-librettist with Dorothy (who would also serve as lyricist).

Once the entire team was in place, however, tragedy struck. Kern, in New York for early development meetings, died suddenly from a cerebral hemorrhage. To salvage the project, Rodgers and Hammerstein turned to the only other artist they felt could accomplish the task, especially given the newly tight timeline: Irving Berlin. Berlin, however, was gun shy (no pun intended) regarding the project. He was not used to working on projects that were not of his own making or under his control; more importantly, Berlin was not sure that he could write an "integrated book musical," having only written scores for revues (or revues masquerading as thinly plotted musical comedies). To help convince Berlin, Rodgers and Hammerstein agreed to give him a week or so to mull over the project; Berlin returned with five songs in hand, four of which were used in the score: "Doin' What Comes Natur'lly," "The Girl That I Marry," "You Can't Get a Man With a Gun" (three songs that basically comprise an almost continuous musical exposition early in the musical's first act), and "They Say It's Wonderful." By the end of Berlin's "audition" with the newly written material, all parties were convinced that Berlin was more than up to the task of writing *Annie Get Your Gun's* score (with Dorothy giving up her lyricist role and concentrating on co-writing the libretto with Herbert). The musical would prove to be Berlin's greatest Broadway triumph and longest running show.

The storyline of *Annie Get Your Gun* is the rise to fame of Annie Oakley, a sharpshooting sensation during the late 1800s. At the show's onset, Annie, as an uneducated hillbilly, emerges from the Ohio backwoods to win an amateur shooting contest in Cincinnati against the current star marksman of Buffalo Bill's Wild West Show, Frank Butler. The earthy, sassy nature of Annie is comically illustrated through her introductory numbers, "Doin' What Comes Natur'lly" and "You Can't Get a Man With a Gun." After being immediately smitten by the suave Butler and being talked into joining Buffalo Bill's company (lured by the overall anthem and leitmotif of the production, "There's No Business Like Show Business"),

Annie soon overtakes Butler in popularity and skill, becoming the star of the show. The eventual top billing of Annie causes a rift in her burgeoning romantic relationship with the jealous Butler, and he leaves Buffalo Bill to join another Wild West tour for showman Pawnee Bill.

In the second act, Annie pines for Butler (conveyed through the lyrical "I Got Lost in His Arms"); and she, along with the rest of Buffalo Bill's troupe, has fallen on hard times, returning to New York from a European tour, financially strapped and forced to ride in the cargo/cattle section of the ship. To restore their fortunes, the company convinces Pawnee to combine his show with theirs. As a plus, Annie and Butler will be reunited through the merger. The plans are scuttled, however, for Annie and Butler cannot reconcile their competitive natures and stubborn egos, ultimately challenging each other to a shooting match to be staged at Governor's Island in New York harbor. Immediately preceding the contest, the two reaffirm their superiority through the duet "Anything You Can Do." Annie, however, has decided to swallow her pride and throw the contest, allowing Frank to win. With a winking nod to his "superior" skill, Annie reaffirms her love for him, and Butler reciprocates. The two Wild West companies successfully merge. All ends with one last reprise of "There's No Business Like Show Business."

The combination of romantic comedy, folksy and nostalgic Americana, colorful metatheatre, a "Cinderella"/rags-to-riches theme, and Berlin's rich, hummable score was a winning formula, delighting audiences and critics alike. Opening May 16, 1946, the show ran for 1,147 performances (proving to be both Berlin's and Merman's longest running Broadway hit in their respective careers). Berlin's trepidation at writing an integrated book score seemed, in retrospect, to be unfounded. In fact, for a 1966 revival, which again starred Merman, he added another effective character duet for Annie and Butler titled "An Old Fashioned Wedding." The song is built on Berlin's famous use of contrapuntal melodies, comprised of an upbeat vamp section in which Annie details her lavish plans for a modern wedding, sung against Butler's languid, lyrical description of his "old fashioned wedding" plans. In addition to the 1966 revival, the musical was filmed in color by MGM in 1950 and taped in B&W for television in 1957. Further, it

has continued throughout the years to be a favorite of regional and community theatres, with adjustments made, to both score and libretto, to temper some of the more dated and offensive aspects of the show (specifically, "I'm an Indian, Too," an ethnic novelty song by Berlin that employs negative stereotypes of Native Americans). A more recent Broadway revival was in 1999, with Bernadette Peters in the starring role. The Fields libretto was given an updated treatment by librettist Peter Stone, playing up the metatheatrical aspect and placing the entire work as a "show within a show," while disarming some of the politically incorrect and awkward book moments. Audiences again cheered the struggles and triumphs of Ms. Oakley; this revival ran for 1,045 performances, winning the Tony Award for Best Revival of a Musical.

Ethel Merman, Irving Berlin, and Dorothy Fields at the piano, 1966 © Bettmann/CORBIS

PULLING BACK THE CURTAIN:
Jewish Identity, Authorship, and Influence in American Musical Theatre

George Gershwin (formerly Jacob Gershowitz) had his first major song success with "Swanee," a cake-walking, two-step homage to the Deep South. The song might have been relegated to obscurity, as its initial debut merited little notice, but it caught the attention of America's top stage entertainer, Al Jolson (formerly Asa Yoelson), who performed the tune to great acclaim in his signature blackface. Thus, the Southern "folk" song (or "coon song"), written by a Jewish composer with an anglicized name, became a top American hit at the hands of another Jewish artist, performing the number as an African American caricature. Such is the convoluted and complex paradigm of Jewish identity and the role of the Jewish artist in the history and development of American musical theatre.

Scholars and historians have long cited the active theatre scenes in the Jewish immigrant districts of New York City during the 1800s as breeding grounds for the Broadway musical and training grounds for its many artists. Early forms of Jewish theatre and entertainment in America included both the Yiddish theatre and its English-speaking counterpart, as well as a plethora of independent musical acts and skits, all of which had been transplanted to urban neighborhoods, such as the Lower East Side and Harlem (originally a Jewish ghetto) by Jewish immigrants who had fled their mostly Eastern European homelands due to persecution and economic hardships. By the first decade of the twentieth century, Jews accounted for nearly one quarter of New York City's population; consequently, their musical heritage and theatrical traditions became more and more integral to the city's entertainment landscape. Thus, it is not surprising that Jewish artists and entrepreneurs started to shape, and soon dominate, the musical theatre industry and genre, a level of influence and power that remains today.

Reflecting the site of its origin, the American musical theatre is a melting pot, that is, a mélange of influences, owing its evolution and content/construct to many cultures and antecedents. Consequently, it is crucial to historicize, contextualize, and analyze the role of Jewish music and culture in the musical theatre arena alongside other idioms/genres, such as African American music/dance and European operetta, all of which combined to spawn and shape the American musical.

With regard to the operetta, many Jews were at the forefront of the genre during its heyday (the late nineteenth and early twentieth centuries), with prominent Jewish composers including Jacques Offenbach as well as American émigrés Sigmund Romberg, Oscar Straus, and Rudolf Friml. And while much of the African American component of musical theatre was initially appropriated by and filtered through white Americans, early Jewish influence on and constitution of musical theatre was engaged, exploited, and developed by Jews themselves, resulting in a significant Jewish presence and authorship on all Broadway fronts. This phenomenon included pioneering impresarios, producers, and theatre owners such as Oscar Hammerstein, who is often credited with establishing the modern-day Broadway district through his theatre proprietorship, and Florenz Ziegfeld, auteur of the *Ziegfeld Follies* and dominant creator/propagator of the Broadway revue in the early twentieth century. The power and influence of Jewish producers and directors would continue throughout the twentieth century into the twenty-first, with controlling production/theatre enterprises exemplified by the Nederlanders, Shuberts, and Minskoffs, and individual producers and directors, including such luminaries as Joseph Papp, Harold Prince, Jerome Robbins, and Julie Taymor.

Jewish performers were also significant and formative fixtures on the burgeoning musical theatre scene at the turn of the century, many of whom came to prominence via another musical antecedent: vaudeville. In this popular form of entertainment, Jewish immigrants could capitalize on their musical, physical, and/ or comic talents, often circumventing the English language to appeal not only to fellow immigrants but also to a diverse and vast American populace. Such early Jewish headliners who rose from the ranks of vaudeville to become Broadway stars included Fanny Brice, Eddie Cantor, Anna Held, Al Jolson, The Marx Brothers, and Sophie Tucker. Behind the scenes, Jewish composers and authors supplied the majority of early musical theatre scores and librettos, while stretching and redefining the genre. Significantly, Jewish composers, lyricists, librettists, and directors such as George Gershwin, Ira Gershwin, Oscar Hammerstein II, Lorenz Hart, George S. Kaufman, Jerome Kern, Richard Rodgers, and Morrie Ryskind pioneered the integrated book musical as seen by their landmark works: *Of Thee I Sing, Oklahoma!, Pal Joey, Porgy and Bess*, and *Show Boat*. Furthermore, throughout the Golden Age and continuing into the new century, the musical theatre canon has been and continues to be largely authored by Jewish composers, lyricists, and librettists. The impressive roster includes Irving Berlin, Leonard Bernstein, Jerry Bock, Mel Brooks, Jason Robert Brown, Betty Comden, Fred Ebb, Harvey Fierstein, Adolph Green, Adam Guettel, Sheldon Harnick, Moss Hart, John Kander, Jonathan Larson, Alan Jay Lerner, Frank Loesser, Frederick Loewe, Stephen Schwartz, Neil Simon, Stephen Sondheim, and David Yazbek—as well as the French creators of *Les Misérables* and *Miss Saigon*, Claude-Michel Schönberg and Alain Boublil.

To date, since the Tony Award for Best Original Score was instituted in 1947, Jewish composers have written approximately 70 percent of nominated scores and constitute 60 percent of the winners. Such overwhelming statistics should beg the question, "Why?" Jews brought a rich tradition of music and theatre to New York, while also becoming a sizable immigrant group in the city. But, musicologists also point to the Jewish tradition of composing music with an emphasis on melody, featuring the solo voice, as a paradigm that translated well to the musical stage and facilitated the musical play (e.g., traditional Jewish religious music is led by the lone singing cantor, as opposed to the choral emphasis of Christian music). The fact that Jewish music/song suited and served musical theatre has long been recognized and exploited by early composers. Jerome Kern, working with Hammerstein II on a musical treatment of Donn Byrne's *Messer Marco Polo*, explained that he would write "good Jewish music" for the Orientalist project, while non-Jewish Cole Porter famously told Richard Rodgers that his musical success was due to his skill at writing "Jewish tunes." Indeed, Porter often used a "Jewish" tonal character; most of his song canon resides in the minor key (concordantly, musicologists categorize almost 90 percent of traditional Jewish folk music as minor keyed). Further, Porter's melodies often include moody, chromatic progressions, a compositional structure reflective of Gershwin's use of the "blue note" (the tweaked pitch of the third or seventh note of the scale), which also served to give the Gershwin tune a bluesy, unsettled quality. And as previously detailed, the "blue note" has been traced back to traditional Jewish secular and religious music, as well as African American folk music. In short, a strong melody, defined by its tonal component and memorable vocal line, is characteristic of Jewish folk music as well as the "standard" song found throughout the American catalogue. Such a melody-dependent work also relies on the single vocal rendition, versus the harmonic combinations of the singing group or the recording studio arrangement. This compositional style also suited prominent Jewish songwriters such as Irving Berlin or Bob Merrill, who often used the plunking of singular piano keys or the whistling of a melody to fashion a song or an entire musical theatre score.

Significantly, Jewish influence is not relegated to the melodic structure/character of the musical theatre score, for the aforementioned Jewish librettists and lyricists also provided much of the genre's most acclaimed and long-lived thematic and dramatic/textual substance. To date, nine musicals have won the Pulitzer Prize in Drama (including the special Pulitzer awarded *Oklahoma!*); of that number, eight winning works were written/adapted by a Jewish librettist, lyricist, or both. In short, most scholars agree that the majority of twentieth-century musicals were written (or adapted) by Jews and that the musical itself has accorded these artists an opportunity by which to explore, interrogate, and illuminate the concept/construct of ethnic/racial identity and complexities of assimilation and marginalization of minority groups within the larger "community" (or "melting pot") of America. Even if the Jewish author did not write an original plot for his or her libretto, it is significant that he or she was drawn to certain material for adaption. Specifically, many musical librettos written/adapted by Jewish authors explore the phenomenon of conflicting cultures, races, or ethnicities (classic examples include *South Pacific*, *The King and I*, *Brigadoon*, *Miss Saigon*) or issues of racial/ethnic identification and marginalization in America (e.g., *Show Boat*, *Porgy and Bess*, *Finian's Rainbow*, *West Side Story*) as well as broader, metaphoric tales of tolerance (or intolerance) and the societal outsider or outlier (from Jud in *Oklahoma!* to the bohemian artists/squatters in *Rent*). As exemplified by Irving Berlin's tragic "Suppertime" in *As Thousands Cheer*, Jewish artists could exploit and disguise their own pain and struggles as they gave voice to other victimized and marginalized groups (specifically, African Americans in Berlin's song).

This leads to another question: Why did the Jewish artists so rely on coding, proxies, and metaphors during much of the Golden Age? To further complicate the issue, these same artists often chose to mask their own Jewish identities through the acquisition of new names: Jacob Gershowitz became George Gershwin; Isreal Baline became Irving Berlin; Basya Cohen became Betty Comden; Jerome Rabbinowitz became Jerome Robbins; and so on. Of course, historically speaking, this was a norm at the time, with most public figures anglicizing immigrant names to appear more "American." And in many respects, the strategy was pragmatic, for a significant degree of anti-Semitism existed in various parts of America throughout the twentieth century, as evidenced by the rejection and repudiation of Irving Berlin by the Social Register when attempting to marry Christian heiress Ellin Mackay. Toward the end of the Golden Age, however, writers and composers started to openly claim, embrace, and explore their heritage on stage, mirroring a nation experiencing a significant wave of antidefamation and civil rights movements. To many, 1964's *Fiddler on the Roof* was the tipping point. Jerome Robbins often recounted that he felt the production finally enabled him to fully "own" his lineage, to "come home" to his own Jewish identity, voicing it directly and communally on stage. Yet, *Fiddler's* producers also worried that the content was *too* Jewish to play beyond New York—an unfounded concern as the musical ultimately enjoyed 30 international productions and, interestingly, became a hit in Japan, with locals marveling at how the authors managed to capture such a "Japanese" cultural/generational conflict.

Subsequent to *Fiddler*, the musical theatre genre has continued to directly address Jewish identity, community, persecution, and assimilation/marginalization, both in America and abroad—a development that includes works such as *Cabaret* (1966), *The Rothschilds* (1970), *Rags* (1986), *Ragtime* (1998), and *Parade* (1998). And in a final, ironic note, the Jewish musical theatre author has also moved beyond theatrical conveyance of Jewish struggle, pain, and triumph to embrace postmodernism, finding outrageous humor in the same paradigm. When Mel Brooks' *The Producers* opened on Broadway in 2001, it had the audacity to lampoon Hitler and the Nazis, taking one of the most tragic episodes in Jewish history and turning the unlikely material into irreverent and reflexive comedy. After 2,502 performances and a record number of twelve Tony Awards, the production was also credited for reinvigorating the Broadway musical comedy, proving that the specter of Jewish identity and influence continues to potently inform the Broadway stage.

COLE PORTER

While many songwriters, librettists, directors, and producers of musical theatre's Golden Age were born into poor, Jewish families in New York City, none of these facts applied to Cole Porter, who was born in Peru, Indiana, on June 9, 1891, to a wealthy Episcopalian family whose money came from lumber and mining interests. As both composer *and* lyricist, he wrote over 800 published songs in his lifetime, although he didn't really start his Broadway career until he was in his late 30s. Porter was a homosexual who was married to a woman for over three decades, a theatre person who was an avid horseman (until sidelined by an accident), and a society playboy who loved being in the press, yet was as disciplined as any tunesmith on Broadway. In short, the life of composer/lyricist Cole Porter was full of seeming contradictions.

With formal training in violin and piano, Porter began writing songs at an early age; his mother saw to it that young Cole's first song was published when he was 11 years old, "Bobolink Waltz." Sent to boarding school at the Worcester Academy in Massachusetts, he later graduated from Yale and briefly attended Harvard Law School. While at Yale, he not only wrote songs for six college theatricals but also wrote several fight songs, some of which are still sung at football games today. Pursuing his dream of being a Broadway songwriter, he was able to get a few of his numbers into two shows before he teamed with fellow Yale alum, librettist T. Lawrason Riggs, to create his first professional musical, *See America First*, with a complete score by Porter.

It opened to dreadful reviews in 1916, and limped along for only fifteen performances.

While his contemporaries would brush themselves off after a defeat in the Big Apple and attack Broadway with another show to prove their mettle, Porter instead moved to Paris, subsidized by an allowance from his family. Living the high life in Venice, London, and on the French Riviera as a member of a glittering expatriate society, Porter was the life of the party. In 1919, he married the wealthy Southern divorceé Linda Lee Thomas (nine years his senior) who lived in Paris. The couple was known for being sophisticated, stylish, and above all, smart. When Porter's grandfather died in 1923, he inherited a small fortune which led to even more extravagant spending and travel.

The biggest surprise to Porter's closest friends was not that Linda was older than him, but that he married at all, for Porter was known for having a rather ferocious sexual appetite for other men. Yet his relationship with Linda, which was to last 35 years, was more than a marriage of convenience; by all accounts, it was a committed and loving partnership between two great friends. The couple tried to have a child, but Linda's one known pregnancy resulted in a miscarriage. With full knowledge of her husband's homosexuality, Linda allowed Porter to have relationships with men, all the while protecting his image and projecting a picture of conventional matrimony to the outside world.

While in Europe, Porter wrote or contributed to three revues after the failure of *See America First*, but it

Cole Porter working on *DuBarry Was a Lady*, 1939.
© Michael Ochs/Archives/Corbis

was not until he agreed to write a star vehicle for the vivacious Irene Bordoni that he returned to Broadway in 1928—twelve years after his first failure—with the musical comedy *Paris*. Written at the Porter home in Venice, the score contained smart and melodic numbers such as "Oh, You Sweet Old Whatcha-May-Call-It," "Two Little Babes in the Woods," and "Don't Look at Me That Way." It also introduced the smash hit "Let's Do It, Let's Fall in Love." Notable for its innuendo and very suggestive lyrics, "Let's Do It" was the first of many of Porter's "list" songs. With favorable reviews and a healthy run of 195 performances, *Paris* was a hit and the Porters left Europe and moved to New York City. Even though he had been writing songs for years, it was only upon returning to the United States that Porter made it big; and at the age of 37, he was hardly a young Broadway talent.

While the newspapers only reported on the A-list parties the Porters attended, Cole was actually writing nonstop since his move back to America. *Wake Up and Dream* debuted in London to rapturous reviews in March 1929, and then he had three productions open within five weeks (two Broadway musicals, *Fifty Million Frenchmen* and *Wake Up and Dream*, and the film *The Battle of Paris*), and this was *after* the stock market crash on October 29, 1929. That producers had faith in Cole Porter to attract a shell-shocked audience during the Depression speaks volumes to the popularity of his tuneful, witty, and upbeat songs. In typical Porter style, he left New York after New Year's Day 1930 with Linda and some friends for a 6-month vacation through the Far East and Europe.

The trip was more like a busman's holiday as Porter had two relatively modest Broadway productions come along in short order upon his return to America: *The New Yorkers* (1930) and *Gay Divorce* (1931), with the latter providing Fred Astaire his first starring role after his sister Adele decided to retire. Porter's following endeavor, the London production of *Nymph Errant* (1933), was deemed a failure, even though the show ultimately ran for 154 performances. Bruised by the reception given this adaptation of the racy 1932 novel (it deals with a young English woman's intention to lose her virginity) and considering it his best score, Porter challenged himself to write scores for future musicals that would appeal to a broader audience. (*Nymph Errant* would not receive its New York debut until 1982.) Indeed, Porter was gaining a reputation for

the sophisticated and but often worldly (and sometimes naughty) sentiments of his work. In fact, "Love for Sale," another Porter song from this period (originating in *The New Yorkers*), was banned from radio play due to its suggestive lyrics, yet it was destined to become a standard in the American songbook. Like Lorenz Hart, some of Porter's lyrics were not only about romantic love, but were also about carnal desire.

Porter's first blockbuster hit on Broadway, *Anything Goes*, actually began with an idea from a producer, not a writer. While on a lengthy ocean cruise, Vinton Freedley starting thinking about a light-hearted romp on the seas starring comedians William Gaxton and Victor Moore, and vocal powerhouse Ethel Merman, with music/lyrics by Cole Porter and libretto by P.G. Wodehouse and Guy Bolton. Based on ideas provided by Freedley, Bolton and Wodehouse penned a comic escapade in which screwball characters react to a shipwreck. But two months before the musical was scheduled to open on Broadway, a ship did sink off the coast of New Jersey, killing over one hundred people. With Bolton and Wodehouse out of the country, Freedley enlisted Howard Lindsey and Russel Crouse to rewrite the libretto—at post haste. Rehearsals started without a second act, and revisions continued daily throughout the show's Boston tryouts (inciting an inside joke amongst its creators that, in the case of the musical's libretto, "anything goes"). The production even had two previous titles before it finally opened on Broadway on November 21, 1934, as the newly christened *Anything Goes*. A brief summary of the libretto is all that is needed to understand the slapdash and spirited nature of the piece. On board the ship is Public Enemy Number 13, hiding from the authorities dressed as a clergyman, who just happens to carry a machine gun around in his saxophone case. Other passengers include Reno Sweeney, a former evangelist turned nightclub singer, and Billy Crocker, a dashing bachelor stowaway (also in disguise), hoping to get closer to his society sweetheart, Hope Harcourt. In musical comedy fashion, all complications are resolved in the end. And although the characters get increasingly entangled in the shenanigans throughout the musical, nothing gets in the way of Porter's brilliant songs. A show that might have been an unmitigated disaster instead became a blockbuster hit, with five of Porter's songs hitting the top of the pop charts: "Blow, Gabriel, Blow," "You're the Top," "All Through the Night," "Anything Goes," and one of his most distinctive classics, "I Get a Kick Out of You" [see fig. 4.3], with its references to champagne, cocaine, and the jet-setting lifestyle. Initially written for *Star Dust* (1931)—a musical that never made it to Broadway—"I Get a Kick Out of You" also originally contained a lyric line referencing Mrs. Lindbergh flying in an airplane. After the kidnapping and murder of her son, Charles Lindbergh, Jr. in 1932, Porter rewrote the lyric to remove this reference, and *Anything Goes* reaped the benefit of having the retailored song added to its score. As the first song in the musical, it is used to set the stage when a world-weary Sweeney (originally played by Ethel Merman) tells her old friend Crocker that although the high life no longer excites her, she still gets a "kick" out of him. Porter also got a "kick" out of Merman, falling in love with her powerful voice, clear enunciations, and overall renditions of his songs; and he would end up writing a total of five musicals for her.

Remarkably, in the middle of the Great Depression, *Anything Goes* ran for 420 performances. Frequently revived, this is one of the few pre-World War II musicals that continues to delight audiences, with a recent 2011 production winning the Tony Award for Best Revival of a Musical. Unfortunately, the musical's two film versions (1936 and 1956) fail to capture the effervescent *joie de vivre* of the stage production.

During a four-and-a-half month long cruise around the world, librettist Moss Hart and composer/lyricist Porter worked on a new musical, *Jubilee* (1935), in which the king and queen of an unnamed country, weary of the daily routine at court, decide to leave their castle to live as ordinary people (Mr. and Mrs. Smith), taking their two eldest children with them. The king is at last able to pursue his beloved hobby of rope tricks while his wife is attracted to a swimming champion who plays a "native" on the silver screen. Their daughter falls in love with a talented playwright while the son finds success on the ballroom dance circuit with his new love. The production's budget, extravagant for the time ($150,000), provided a lush visual treat for audiences; one critic called it the most handsome production since the time of Ziegfeld. In spite of one of Porter's strongest scores (including "Begin the Beguine," "Why Shouldn't I?," "Just One of Those Things," "A Picture of Me Without You") and terrific reviews, *Jubilee* closed after only 169 performances, with producers losing their entire capitalization (including Porter's personal investment of $18,000). The country was still in the grips of the Depression, and Hollywood star Mary Boland,

in the lead role, was not up to the rigor of performing eight times a week. Coupled with her drinking problem, Boland began to miss performances, to the point that the producers bought out her contract after only four months. With high weekly running costs and no star to drive ticket sales, closing the show was the only option. "Begin the Beguine" escaped the show's demise with an instrumental version of the song, arranged by Jerry Gray for clarinetist Artie Shaw's band in 1938, ultimately becoming one of the top radio hits of the decade.

But with *Anything Goes* running strong in both New York and London, and Hollywood calling, Porter had little reason to mope. When MGM offered him $75,000 for twenty weeks of work to write numbers for what was to be *Born to Dance*, the Porters moved west in December of 1935. Starring Eleanor Powell, Jimmy Stewart, and Buddy Ebsen, this "feel good" musical included tap dancing, patriotic flag waving, and irresistible Porter tunes such as "Easy to Love" and "I've Got You Under My Skin."

Porter thrived in the California sun, exploiting his moneyed Yale/Harvard pedigree whenever he was feeling bullied by the movie moguls. Never suffering the "hack for hire" complex and abuse like some of his Broadway contemporaries lured to Tinseltown by the promise of riches, Porter loved writing for a larger audience and therefore ended up living in Hollywood from six to eight months every year for the rest of his life. Linda, on the other hand, was not nearly so enchanted by this movie colony as her husband. She disliked many of the people who worked there and feared that Porter's more public homosexual encounters would damage his reputation and career. Given that Porter, although enamored with Hollywood, was not about to give up on Broadway, the couple maintained two homes for the rest of their married life. In 1935, the Porters moved into a large apartment in New York City's elegant Waldorf Astoria, the largest hotel in the world when it was built in 1931.

For his next stage musical, *Red, Hot, and Blue!* (1936), reuniting with many of the artists associated with *Anything Goes* (Ethel Merman, William Gaxton, Vinton Freedley, Howard Lindsay, and Russel Crouse) and adding comedian Jimmy Durante seemed like a recipe for success, until Gaxton dropped out of the project. Bob Hope was hired to replace him, but the show's woes were far from over. The Broadway production had a respectable run of 183 performances, but critics agreed that no one involved with *Red, Hot, and*

Blue! was operating at their personal best. Nevertheless, Porter's "It's De-Lovely" became popular with its catchy melody and infectiously fun lyrics. With a barrage of "de" words—delightful, delicious, delectable, delirious, dilemma, delimit—the lyrics sounded like they may have been written by Ira Gershwin. Other standards introduced in *Red, Hot, and Blue!* include "Ridin' High" and "Down in the Depths (On the Ninetieth Floor)." While Porter was born into money, married money, and made his own fortune, he sometimes wrote lyrics for characters who came to realize that money could not buy happiness. For Merman's character, Porter wrote about a woman who lived on the 90th floor and was still depressed, even though no buildings in 1936 had an apartment that high up yet. (The Empire State Building, erected in 1931, has 102 floors of offices.)

After completing the rather minor movie musical *Rosalie* in 1937 (although it does contain "In the Still of the Night"), Porter returned to the east coast and accepted an invitation to party on Oyster Bay, Long Island. While horseback riding, Porter's horse inexplicably reared up and fell to its side, crushing one of Porter's legs. In its attempt to right itself, the horse fell onto its other side, shattering Porter's other leg. The prognosis was grim, with amputation recommended, but Porter would not allow it. Instead, Porter would endure more than thirty operations over the next twenty years and consequently suffer chronic pain for the rest of his life, relying more and more on walking aides as he aged (canes, attendants, etc.).

But the forty-five-year-old Porter was in decent physical shape, and as he adhered to his physical therapy, he also used work as a distraction from the pain. In fact, the composer/lyricist turned out not one, but two musicals which opened on Broadway in 1938. With its weak book, *You Never Know* closed after 10 weeks, but *Leave It to Me* ran for 307 performances. And although the hit musical starred Victor Moore and Sophie Tucker, it was newcomer Mary Martin who stopped the show cold with one of Porter's most slyly suggestive ditties, "My Heart Belongs to Daddy."

Pushing through the pain, Porter was more productive than ever; between December 1939 and January 1944, he produced scores for five hit Broadway shows in a row (in a little over four years time), each running over 400 performances each—*DuBarry Was a Lady* (1939), *Panama Hattie* (1940), *Let's Face It!* (1941), *Something for the Boys* (1943), *Mexican Hayride* (1944)—and three film scores: *Broadway Melody of 1940*, *You'll Never Get Rich* (1941), and *Something to Shout About* (1943). Germany invaded Poland in September 1939, and Britain and France declared war two days later. In this climate of international hysteria, it seemed New Yorkers craved the boisterous and bawdy fun delivered to them with that certain Porter flourish. In *DuBarry*, Bert Lahr and Ethel Merman winningly delivered "But in the Morning, No," "Do I Love You?," and "Friendship." Yet again, however, it was a young performer (Betty Grable, making her Broadway debut) who brought down the house with "Well, Did You Evah!," a song that wittily highlighted and satirized high society in inimitable Porter fashion. Porter's fourth musical written for the indomitable Ethel Merman was *Panama Hattie*, in which she played a calloused nightclub singer who falls in love with an American government official in the Canal Zone. Although the score contained more typical world-weary Porter standards ("Make It Another Old-Fashioned, Please"), the score also contained sentimentality, a quality never associated with the songster before (e.g., "Let's Be Buddies" and "My Mother Would Love You"). This did not bother audiences, with *Panama Hattie* running 501 performances on Broadway, 308 in London, and spawned a mediocre film version in 1942. The star power of Danny Kaye in *Let's Face It* (1941) and Ethel Merman in *Something for the Boys* (1943) propelled these musicals to a strong box office, yet neither produced the chart-topping songs which Porter had created earlier in this career. While some critics began to think the magic was over, Porter nevertheless had three more Broadway musicals on his résumé, and saw *Something for the Boys* (1944) adapted for the silver screen.

In the mid-1940s, while he was very much alive, Porter was also immortalized on the big screen. When close friend and colleague Irving Berlin suggested to Warner Bros. that the resilience and continued success of Porter after his horrible accident could prove inspirational, the movie studio offered Porter $300,000 for the rights to his life story. As a result, in 1946, Hollywood created a wildly inaccurate biopic, *Night and Day*, starring Cary Grant, a top-tier star who looked nothing like Porter. (It was not until the 2004 biopic written and filmed by producer-director Irwin Winkler, *De-Lovely*, that Cole Porter—played by Kevin Kline—would be authentically presented on the silver screen, replete with his many complexities.) *Night and Day* was only one example of Porter's fame during this period. With songs on the pop charts, musicals on Broadway, and compositions featured in films, Cole Porter was such a household name that companies such as Rheingold beer and Camel cigarettes paid him handsomely to appear in commercials endorsing their products. And in the late 1940s, five songs by Cole Porter were included among the thirty-five most popular U.S. songs of all time: "What Is This Thing Called Love?," "Night and Day," "I Get a Kick Out of You," "Begin the Beguine," and "Just One of Those Things."

In the first half of the twentieth century, the works of William Shakespeare had had limited success on Broadway as librettos (or adaptations), so when a young stage manager approached the esteemed librettist Bella Spewack about creating a Broadway musical out of *Taming of the Shrew*, she rejected the idea, stating that *Shrew* was Shakespeare's worst play. Six weeks later, however, she had devised a libretto for a new musical: *Kiss Me, Kate* (1948). As composer Burton Lane was not available due to scheduling conflicts, Spewack convinced the producer to ask Cole Porter, as she had worked with him in 1938 on *Leave It to Me!* Initially very skeptical, Porter was eventually sold on Spewack's show-within-a-show libretto which not only concerns the backstage affairs of contemporary actors, but also highlights their transformations into and portrayals of *Shrew* characters. Just as Berlin had written his biggest hit, *Annie Get Your Gun* (1946), when most insiders thought his Broadway career was all but over, so composer/lyricist Porter realized the crowning achievement to his long and illustrious musical career with *Kiss Me, Kate*.

It was not easy raising money for a show with novice producers, only one known star, and a seemingly washed-up Cole Porter; but once *Kate* played before pre-Broadway audiences in Philadelphia, it was clear that it was going to be a major hit. Rave reviews met its New York debut in 1948, and it won several Tony Awards that season: Best Musical Production, Best Book, Best Score (Porter), and Best Costumes.

To celebrate the warm reception given *Kate*, Cole and Linda planned to go to Europe, their first visit there in twelve years (since Porter's horse accident). Unfortunately, Linda couldn't seem to shake a cold, which then turned into pleurisy and congested lungs. With Linda in Arizona (hoping its dry climate would make her

healthy again), Porter returned to California, to write a song for the Katharine Hepburn vehicle *Adam's Rib* (1949) and oversee casting of the national tour of *Kate* (which was to last three years).

Porter's next musical proved to be a disappointing follow-up to *Kiss Me, Kate*. With a weak book that was constantly being rewritten, *Out of This World* (1950) only lasted 157 performances, although its cast album (Porter's second, with *Kate* being his first) ensured that songs like "Use Your Imagination," "Nobody's Chasing Me," and "I Am Loved" entered the American songbook. One of Cole Porter's most famous songs, "From This Moment On," was cut from the show during previews, but singer Doris Day's recording in 1950 not only saved it from obscurity but sent it to the top of the pop charts.

After a severe bout of depression, which resulted in a month-long stay in the hospital and electroshock treatments, Porter returned to work, collaborating with veteran librettist Abe Burrows on *Can-Can* (1953), set in the composer/lyricist's beloved Paris. The lightweight plot focuses on the futile attempts by Paris police to shut down a music hall that features "indecent" dancing by young women, especially Claudine (first performed by Gwen Verdon in a role which was to make her a star). Audiences loved the show, no doubt energized by Michael Kidd's exuberant choreography, making it Porter's second-longest running show (892 performances). The cast album helped put five songs from the show—"I Love Paris," "It's All Right With Me," "C'est Magnifique," "Allez-Vous-En," "I Am in Love"—into *Variety's* list of the year's top songs.

A year before *Can-Can's* debut, Cole Porter's beloved mother Kate died. Then, a year after, in 1954, his wife and best friend, Linda, died of emphysema, leaving Porter her estate, worth almost $2 million. Distraught and depressed, but industrious as ever, Porter traveled the world, moved into a new 9-room apartment in the Waldorf Astoria, and professionally pushed onward. His next Broadway musical, *Silk Stockings* (1955), was based on the popular 1939 film *Ninotchka*, starring Greta Garbo, about an icy Russian operative who travels to Paris to track down a famous composer from the U.S.S.R. who has not returned home. Porter's last score for a Broadway musical elevated this thin plotline, with audiences drawn to "All of You" and "Paris Loves Lovers." The strength of the Broadway run (478 performances) paved the way for an original cast album and for MGM to create a feature film in 1957, starring Fred Astaire and Cyd Charisse.

Porter's next project was another musical adaptation of a famous film (and play), *The Philadelphia Story* (1940), but devised for Hollywood instead of Broadway. The movie musical was titled *High Society* (1956) and MGM loaded it with stars—Grace Kelly, Frank Sinatra, Bing Crosby, Celeste Holm, and Louis Armstrong—while paying Porter $250,000 for his first original film score in eight years. For his part, Porter merited the salary, providing a score that included stellar numbers such as "True Love," "I Love You, Samantha," and "You're Sensational," helping to make the film a financial success, while interpolating a few past hits for atmosphere and popular appeal (e.g., "Well, Did You Evah!"). Considered a high point of the MGM movie musical era, *High Society* was eventually adapted for the Broadway stage in 1998, with added Porter songs, but ran for only 144 performances.

Still in Hollywood, Porter supervised the film version of *Silk Stockings*, wrote a dozen original songs (with only five retained) for 1957's *Les Girls* (a movie musical starring Gene Kelly and Mitzi Gaynor), and devised an original score for a television musical, *Aladdin* (1958). But Porter's health was failing. First a large stomach ulcer required surgery in 1957, and a year later his right leg was finally amputated. Now a depressed recluse seeing only a few select friends, Cole Porter never wrote another song. His declining health resulted in a string of hospitalizations for the next six years; Cole Porter died on October 15, 1964, at the age of seventy-two.

Porter's Associated Press obituary noted that there was not one but three signature types of a "Cole Porter song." (1) With suave, intelligent, and sophisticated lyrics and music which evoked a supple, complex, and often dark mood, Porter penned suggestive and atmospheric songs that were often seemingly obsessed with sexual romanticism (i.e., "Love for Sale," "What Is This Thing Called Love?," "Night and Day," "Let's Misbehave," "Please Don't Make Me Be Good," and "Begin the Beguine"). (2) Further, while he did not invent the form, Porter took the list song to new heights, often combining the high and the low, citing popular culture references, and name-dropping everyone from Mickey Mouse to Fred Astaire (i.e., "Let's Do It," "Friendship," "You're the Top," "Too Darn Hot").

(3) Embracing the exclamatory songs written by George M. Cohen and Irving Berlin, Porter also put his stamp on the extroverted musical showstopper, exploiting the quintessential Broadway "belt," epitomized by many of the songs which appear in the five musicals he wrote for Ethel Merman (i.e., "Blow, Gabriel, Blow," "Just One of Those Things," "From This Moment On").

It is worth recalling that Cole Porter is one of only a handful of Broadway songwriters who wrote both music and lyrics. This gave many of his compositions an organic unity which often does not come when the lyrics and music are written by different artists. (In fact, Porter once joked upon hearing the score of *Oklahoma!* that it was very good, but a shame that it took *two* men to write it.) For example, in addition to its musky lyrics, "Love for Sale" features a plaintive melody wrapped in an accompaniment which moves back and forth between major and minor keys. Most western popular songs are composed in a major key; for instance, if you were sitting at a piano, starting at middle C, and played the white keys up to the next C note (with no flats or sharps: C-D-E-F-G-A-B-C), you would have a C Major scale. C Minor, however, is composed of C-D-Eb-F-G-Ab-Bb-C (the notes E, A, and B are flatted). In languages which assign gender to objects and ideas, major keys are masculine and minor keys are feminine. In German, major is called *durus* ("hard") and minor, *moll* ("soft"). Nevertheless, to most ears, a minor chord has a darker, more melancholic feel to it than its major chord equivalent. Ironically, the Episcopalian Porter felt like one of the reasons for his success with the public was his writing of "Jewish tunes" (his words), reasoning that since many of the popular tunes of the early twentieth century were written by composers of Jewish descent (Jerome Kern, Irving Berlin, George Gershwin, Richard Rodgers, Sigmund Romberg, etc.), he would also be popular if he wrote in their style. And as traditional Jewish music often sits in a minor key, so do most of Porter's compositions. (In point of fact, a composer's race or ethnicity has nothing to do with the type or style of music they are capable of writing.)

Another element of Porter's genius was his ability to absorb musical influences from around the world, gleaned from his many travels, and create new hybrid forms, palatable to the American ear. For example, "Love for Sale" (*The New Yorkers*) evokes an eastern Mediterranean sound, "Night and Day" (*Gay Divorce*) recalls the Islamic call for prayers Porter heard on his trip to Morocco, and "Begin the Beguine" (*Jubilee*) evokes a slow rumba, popular in the islands of Martinique and Guadeloupe in the 1930s. It is somewhat ironic that many American musical songwriters in the twentieth century were foreign-born and often strove to distance themselves from their European roots in order to sound "American," while the Indiana-born Porter, a thoroughbred American if there was one, wrote songs which embraced an international feel in terms of words and music. Further, it is this attribute that musically set his songs apart from most of the popular radio hits of the day.

Porter was also adept at writing to the strengths (and avoiding the vocal weaknesses) of the stars in his productions. The better they sounded, the more likely the critics and audiences would fall in love with a Cole Porter song. For example, while a brilliant dancer, Fred Astaire was only a mediocre singer. Thus, most of "Night and Day," introduced by Astaire, creatively exploits three notes only a half step apart. Writing for Bert Lahr (a star comedian who was known for his exaggerated diction and is still renowned today as the Cowardly Lion in MGM's *The Wizard of Oz*), Porter penned lyrics full of sibilants (hissing consonants/ sounds, e.g., "s") and plosive consonants (consonants sounded by a release of air through initially closed lips, e.g., a hard "p"). And for the seemingly infinite vocal power of Ethel Merman, Porter composed the rousing, brassy anthem "Blow, Gabriel, Blow."

While Cole Porter's songs have enjoyed a healthy life in cabarets and innumerable recordings, producers Leigh Blake and John Carlin brought his work to a new generation of listeners with the album and video RED HOT + BLUE in 1990. Supported by new orchestrations (many with a rock or soul feel), pop stars like Sinead O'Connor, David Byrne, U2, k. d. lang, Annie Lennox, and Tom Waits presented their interpretations of Porter classics. In more recent times, two of Porter's musicals have enjoyed a number of award-winning, popular revivals on Broadway and in London: *Anything Goes* (NYC: 1987, 2011; London: 1969, 1989, 2002) and *Kiss Me, Kate* (NYC: 1999; London: 1978, 2001, 2012). About Cole Porter's music, written for twenty-six Broadway shows and eighteen films, people still seemed to be saying, "You've Got That Thing," "You Do Something to Me," "I Get a Kick Out of You," and "I've Got You Under My Skin"—which just happen to be titles of his songs.

I GET A KICK OUT OF YOU

Music and Lyrics by Cole Porter (1934)

My story is much too sad to be told,
But practically everything leaves me totally cold.
The only exception I know is the case
When I'm out on a quiet spree
Fighting vainly the old ennui
And I suddenly turn and see
Your fabulous face.

I get no kick from champagne,
Mere alcohol doesn't thrill me at all
So tell me why should it be true
That I get a kick out of you?

Some get a kick from cocaine.
I'm sure that if i took even one sniff
That would bore me terrific'ly too
Yet I get a kick out of you.

I get a kick ev'ry time I see
You're standing there before me.
I get a kick though it's clear to me
You obviously don't adore me.

I get no kick in a plane.
Flying too high with some guy in the sky
Is my idea of nothing to do,
Yet I get a kick out of you.

Note: Due to the Hays Code, Porter was required to remove the mention of cocaine in the 1936 film version, changing the line to "Some like the perfume in Spain."

PULLING BACK THE CURTAIN:
The List Song

There are times when a single reference or turn of phrase feels insufficient—especially if you are a self-expressive lyricist, intent on flexing your literate, linguistic muscle. Such a philosophy and practice had much to do with the advent of the "list song"—a type of song which consists of a barrage of wittily rhyming lyrics in the form of a list. Generally, these lyrics are a series of parallel lines and phrases adding up to the same concept, often including recognizable names, places, and events, as well as illustrative examples, incidents, and arguments that support the song's central story or theme. The list song spotlights the lyricist (for the plot is often halted and the composer has probably written a simple tune, possibly in riff fashion, to keep out of the way of the lyrics). Not unique to musical theatre, list songs can be found in other genres of music, such as operetta. In fact, light opera lyricist/librettist W. S. Gilbert is given credit for starting the form on the popular musical stage with the appropriately titled "I've Got a Little List" from *The Mikado*. (A landmark precursor to this overt list song is Gilbert and Sullivan's iconic patter-styled "I Am the Model of a Modern Major-General" song from *The Pirates of Penzance*.)

It is worth noting that most patter songs are list songs, but not all list songs are patter songs, that is, not all list songs are composed to be sung at a very fast tempo. In Ira Gershwin and Kurt Weill's "Tchaikovsky," the character sings the names of fifty Russian composers (list song) at breakneck speed (patter song), but in Sondheim's *Follies*, when Sally remembers her long-ago love in "In Buddy's Eyes" (list song), the tempo is slow as it is written as a ballad. (Sondheim is considered a contemporary master of both the patter and the list song, expanding and exploring both forms throughout his career.) As musical theatre developed, the genre provided an ideal format for this extroverted type of songwriting, with two undisputed masters of the list song being Cole Porter ("You're the Top," "I Get A Kick Out of You," "Let's Do It," "Too Darn Hot," "Friendship") and Noel Coward ("Don't Put Your Daughter on the Stage, Mrs. Worthington," "Why Do the Wrong People Travel?"). Other notable musical theatre examples include:

- Rodgers and Hart's "The Lady Is a Tramp" (*Babes in Arms*)
- Weill and Gershwin's "Tchaikovsky" (*Lady in the Dark*)
- Lerner and Loewe's "Wouldn't It Be Loverly?" (*My Fair Lady*)
- Rodgers and Hammerstein's "My Favorite Things" (*The Sound of Music*)
- Bernstein and Sondheim's "Gee, Officer Krupke" (*West Side Story*)
- Bock and Harnick's "Tonight at Eight" (*She Loves Me*)
- Webber and Rice's "Rainbow High" (*Evita*)
- Sondheim's "A Little Priest" (*Sweeney Todd*)
- Menken and Ashman's "Be Our Guest" (*Beauty and the Beast*)
- Jonathan Larson's "La Vie Boheme" (*Rent*)

The list song also extends far beyond the musical theatre genre, for the song form is used by a wide range of popular music artists:

- Bobby Troup's "(Get Your Kicks on) Route 66" (recorded and popularized by Nat King Cole)
- Beatles' "I've Just Seen a Face"
- Neil Diamond's "Done Too Soon"

- Billy Joel's "We Didn't Start the Fire"
- Gary Burr's "I Try to Think About Elvis" (recorded by Patti Loveless)
- Butthole Surfers' "Pepper"
- R.E.M.'s "It's the End of the World as We Know It (And I Feel Fine)"
- Barenaked Ladies' "One Week"
- Green Day's "American Idiot" (which also became the title song of their hit rock musical)
- Radiohead's "A Wolf at the Door"
- Flobot's "Handlebars"

FEATURED PRODUCTION: *Kiss Me, Kate* (1948)

Music and Lyrics by Cole Porter

Book by Samuel and Bella Spewack

Original Broadway Run: Opened December 30, 1948; New Century Theatre; 1,077 performances

Most of Cole Porter's Broadway work was done before the era of the integrated musical, so while his songs often say a great deal about the character/s singing them, they are not uniquely tailored to a specific sound or overall temperament of a particular musical. Indeed, Porter songs are easily interpolated into revivals of his other works. Porter the man believed in living and celebrating a philosophy of "anything goes" in penthouse style, and Porter the lyricist was remarkably consistent with this point of view, whether he was writing in the Roaring Twenties, the Depression, the unsettling war years, or post-war euphoria. But after reading the libretto by Sam and Bella Spewack for *Kiss Me, Kate*—and no doubt very aware of the new vogue for integrated musicals—Porter wrote his first score that is expertly joined with a book and its characters.

Written between 1590 and 1591, Shakespeare's *The Taming of the Shrew* tells the story of two head-strong, combative characters who ultimately fall in love. A nobleman from Verona, Petruchio, takes on the challenge of wooing the angry and obstinate Katherina. While the idea that a woman needs to be "tamed" by a man strikes many contemporary viewers as misogynistic, this trope was popular in medieval and Elizabethan literature. Throughout time, it has been constantly adapted and re-imagined (e.g., the basic *Shrew* storyline was set in a modern-day high school for the 1999 film *10 Things I Hate About You*).

Most Cole Porter musicals are set in contemporary New York City, while others are set in exotic locales like Panama, Russia, and Paris (his favorite). Porter first rejected the idea of writing about something so outside of his norm, that is, classical Shakespeare, but once he decided to embrace *Kiss Me, Kate*, his fifteenth Broadway musical would prove to be his most enduring.

Written as a show-within-a-show, *Kate*'s plot centers on the complications and fireworks that occur when producer/director/star Fred Graham not only casts himself as the male lead, Petruchio, but also hires his ex-wife, Lilli Vanessi, to appear as Kate in his musical adaptation of *The Taming of the Shrew*. Also in the company is a flirtatious actress, Lois Lane, playing Kate's sister, Bianca, and her boyfriend, Bill, who plays Lucentio (one of Bianca's many suitors). Lilli and Fred are always arguing, especially when she realizes that he is smitten with Lois. And as if trying to stage a new musical is not enough, Fred doesn't realize that Bill has been gambling and signed an IOU for $10,000 in Fred's name. A bewildered Fred is soon confronted at the theatre by two gangsters who intend to collect their $10K. In addition, Lilli wants to leave the show to be with her fiancé, Harrison Howell. Fred craftily tells the gangsters that if Lilli departs, he won't be able to repay the ten grand; and to keep a constant eye on Lilli, the gangsters insert themselves into the show, dressing up in Elizabethan garb so they can "blend in." At one performance, they find themselves alone on stage, so they make up a song ("Brush Up Your Shakespeare") during which they instruct men to use Shakespeare when attempting to woo women. By the end of the show, Lilli realizes that Fred is her soul mate and Bill forgives Lois for her numerous male admirers. In musical comedy fashion, spectators are left with the prospect of a double wedding at the final curtain.

Given the nature of this dual-world musical (the modern backstage and the Elizabethan musical performed by the troupe), Porter was inspired to devise two very distinct types of songs, both musically and verbally. Taking Shakespeare's verses as his cue, Porter wrote "I've Come to Wive It Weathily in Padua," "I Am Ashamed That Women Are So Simple," "Were Thine That Special Face," and "Where Is the Life That Late I Led?" With Shakespeare and his plays as inspiration, he also devised "Brush Up Your Shakespeare," "Tom, Dick, or Harry," and "I Hate Men." And although the songs were linked by Shakespearean source material and references, they varied greatly in musical style, ranging from strutting march ("Wive It Wealthily") to soft-shoe ("Brush Up Your Shakespeare"), pop ditty ("Tom, Dick, or Harry"), and operatic aria ("I Hate Men"). Of course, Porter would never neglect standard Broadway fare, e.g., a witty list song such as "Always True to You in My Fashion," a torchy character number such as "Why Can't You Behave?" and a lush, longing ballad such as "So in Love." He also uncharacteristically (for him) wrote two rousing valentines to show business: "Another Op'nin', Another Show" and "We Open in Venice." Along with the highbrow, literate allusions to Shakespeare and evocations of Broadway, Porter diversified his score even further by referencing operetta. With "Wunderbar," he created a mock Viennese waltz whereby Fred and Lilli reminisce about when they were (briefly) happily married.

It is worth remembering that a riding accident in 1937 severely injured both of Porter's legs and left him in chronic pain for the rest of his life (another twenty-seven years). But this personal disaster did not stop him from writing the crowning achievement of his career, *Kiss Me, Kate*, in 1948. The sunny, incandescent score does not sound like it was penned by someone who had been in chronic pain for many years. And not only did the production win four Tony Awards upon its debut, but Cole Porter saw himself on the on the cover of *Time* magazine on January 31, 1949.

North Shore Music Theatre's 2004 production of *Kiss Me, Kate* © Paul Lyden. Used by permission of Paul Lyden.

RICHARD RODGERS
AND LORENZ HART

In musical theatre, as in any other arena, the maxim that "opposites attract" often rings true and can yield momentous results. When a 16-year-old would-be composer by the name of Richard Rodgers arranged a meeting with an aspiring lyricist seven years his senior, Lorenz (Larry) Hart, the differing ages and temperaments should have been enough to discourage any future get-togethers, much less a partnership. Yet, the meeting proved to be serendipitous. Suggested by a mutual friend and occurring in Hart's Upper West Side apartment, coincidentally not far from Rodgers' home, the brief introductory chat turned into an intense and lengthy discussion concerning literature, theatre, and music. By the end, the preternaturally gifted and disciplined Rodgers and the brilliant, troubled, impetuous Hart found that they shared a fierce passion for musical theatre and the musical song, as well as an aspiration to further develop and challenge the genre and form. In short, as Rodgers often recounted, he left Hart's home that afternoon having gained a partner, best friend, career, and "constant source of irritation." Predating Rodgers and Hammerstein by two decades (Hammerstein being Rodgers' second long-term collaborator),

Rodgers and Hart became the "golden" writing team of the 1920s and '30s on Broadway, radio, and film, with their prestigious, prolific, and for the most part, exclusive partnership lasting for over two decades.

Early in the twentieth century, it was the composer who received most of the credit for musical theatre songwriting, with the lyricist receiving little acclaim or acknowledgment. In a significant development, however, Rodgers and Hart became the first writing duo to be acknowledged as a "team"—with both parties receiving equal recognition for authorship (preceding the Gershwins, Rodgers and Hammerstein, Lerner and Loewe, et. al.). Although Rodgers often supplied the music first and Hart's contribution was sometimes produced after prolonged procrastination and under occasional duress, their compositions were surprisingly symbiotic and reflected the sound and spirit of the times, often serving as mutual showcases. On one hand, Hart's brilliantly rhymed and sassy lyrics found their perfect accompaniment and complement in Rodgers' jazzy, up-tempo riffs; on the other, Rodgers could provide sweet, lyrical melodies to subtly counter (or soften) Hart's more sardonic and/or melancholy lyrics. Most of the Rodgers and Hart musicals are not tightly crafted, integrated works, however. This is because they were written according to the fashion of the day, with

more attention paid to the "stand-alone" potential of a song within a musical than its ability to further the plot, illustrate character, or reflect place/time. In this regard, Rodgers and Hart were phenomenally successful, with a multitude of songs, such as "Lady Is a Tramp," "My Romance," and "My Funny Valentine," moving from their Broadway origins to become American song classics. This is not to say, however, that Rodgers and Hart did not challenge certain conventions of musical comedy, for they were adventurous and creative in their choice of diverse and fantastical subject matter and theatrical concepts, tackling Shakespeare, Mark Twain, dreams, angels, bicycle races, circuses, classical ballet, and Roman Gods. Along with their librettists, they did much to change the face of Broadway during their partnership, imparting a fresh and modern spirit through their musicals as well as their songs.

In the first forty years of Richard Rodgers' career, he only had two major partners, Hart and Hammerstein, with each partner differing substantially in working process, writing style, preferred subject matter, and collaborative temperament. As a composer, Rodgers had a unique ability to fuse his music to the disparate verbiage, writing methods, and worldviews of his two major collaborators. Rodgers could exploit a plethora of musical idioms to speak to audiences, while also shaping (and sometimes compromising) his compositions to seamlessly serve the overall process, always putting the product and the collaboration first. He was born Richard Charles Rodgers on June 28, 1902, to a well-to-do Jewish family in New York City. His mother, Mamie, was a polished pianist, and his father, William, was a doctor and amateur baritone. Rodgers' musical upbringing included amateur concerts in their Manhattan apartment, during which he joined his family in performing current musical theatre and operetta hits for neighbors and friends. The young Rodgers was a natural, for he had begun plunking out recognizable tunes on the piano at age 4; and by 6, he was playing with both hands. As opposed to his future partner, Hammerstein II, Rodgers was encouraged and supported by his father in his musical and theatrical aspirations. Along with his nurturing home environment, he was influenced by the works of Jerome Kern (in Rodgers' words, he "worshipped" the composer), seeing *Very Good Eddie* at the Princess Theatre over a dozen times as a 14-year-old. At that same young age, he composed, printed, and distributed his first copyrighted song, "Auto Show Girl" (with lyrics by David Dyrenforth). Given his precocious talent, he was given the opportunity, at age 15, to write for the theatre by his brother, Mortimer. Mortimer belonged to the Akron Club, a New York social organization, and when the Club proposed a fundraising revue, Mortimer suggested that the group hire Rodgers to write the score. Rodgers' songs (music and lyrics) were so successful that he was asked to write for a second Akron production. This time, Rodgers' score was so well-received that he was encouraged to publish five of the songs. Unfortunately, Tin Pan Alley publishers were not interested; but Rodgers' ever-supportive father came to his aide, paying to have the songs published. By the time Rodgers was 16, he decided that he needed to solely concentrate on composing music; thus, he needed a lyricist. History was then made when he agreed, per mutual friend Phillip Leavitt's suggestion, to meet with Larry Hart.

Hart, for his part, had also been waiting for the perfect creative partner, someone who was dedicated to the "serious" and "adventurous" nature of songwriting and musical theatre. Rodgers proved to be this artist, as well as a facilitative collaborator who could temper and mediate Hart's self-destructive excesses and complicated genius. Lorenz Milton Hart was born on May 2, 1895, in New York City to Jewish parents, Max and Frieda Hart. Obsessed with literature, poetry, and drama (he was a descendent of German poet Heinrich Heine), he attended Columbia University, participated in the varsity shows, and left after three years to work as a play translator for the Shubert organization. Hart also continued to dabble in lyric writing, believing that audiences were capable of appreciating challenging wordplay, unconventional rhyme schemes, and sophisticated sentiments in popular song. Such a belief shaped his songwriting, as he pushed the limits of imaginative polysyllabic rhymes (e.g., the end-line rhymes of "turkey"/"Albuquerque" in "The Lady Is a Tramp"), alliteration ("Bewitched, Bothered and Bewildered"), and a preponderance of internal rhymes. Hart also exploited unusual external rhymes that were often not the actual end of an overall sentence or thought (sometimes, a word was even hyphenated, with its completion at the start of the next line, to facilitate an external rhyme). In addition to the technical plumage of his work, Hart imbued his lyrics with a worldview that was highly personal, often presenting love in a carnal, cynical, satirical, or despairing manner, reflective of his own anxiety and depression over his closeted homosexuality and seeming inability to realize an enduring romantic relationship in his personal life. In both the exhibitionist nature of his craft and the semi confessional nature of his themes, Hart can be termed a *self-expressive* lyricist, that is, a lyricist who shows off and calls attention to himself or herself as the "artist" behind the words, sometimes at the expense of character development and/or plot integration. The *self-expressive* approach to lyric writing can also result in standalone songs independent of show context, situation, and character, and are, thereby, capable of moving beyond their show origins to become popular hits, as well as timeless classics (in many respects, Cole Porter and Ira Gershwin also represent this paradigm).

Once Hart teamed with Rodgers, the new partners immediately set to work. In 1919, they were introduced (by Leavitt, once again) to the star comedian and producer Lew Fields. Fields, who rose to fame as part of the renowned vaudeville/revue comic team Weber and Fields, auditioned the novice songwriting team and decided to incorporate one of their songs, "Any Old Place with You," into his star vehicle *A Lonely Romeo* (1919). Thus, at 17, Rodgers was one of the youngest composers to have a song performed on Broadway. That same year, while still working professionally with Hart, Rodgers entered Columbia, lured by the opportunity to compose for the Varsity Shows. Accordingly, Rodgers and alum Hart wrote songs for Varsity's *Fly with Me*, through which they also met and worked with a young Oscar Hammerstein II. Their work on the revue pleased audiences as well as Fields, who commissioned them to write the score for his next musical, *Poor Little Ritz Girl*. Of the twelve songs written by Rodgers and Hart, however, eight were replaced by works written by established operetta composer Sigmund Romberg and lyricist Alex Gerber. The young songwriters were unaware of the changes until they attended the show's Broadway premiere on July 27, 1920. Demoralized by the turn of events, Rodgers heretofore vowed to maintain creative control over his future endeavors. After a second Varsity Show, *You'll Never Know*, again written with Hart and directed by Hammerstein, Rodgers enrolled at the Institute of Musical Art (now, Julliard School of Music). For the next five years, Rodgers and Hart continued to write for any organization or amateur show that would have them, while teaming with Lew Fields' son, Herbert, as librettist. A five-year dry period ensued, however, and the early promise of their greatness suddenly seemed exaggerated. Acknowledging

the lack of work, both men considered giving up the musical theatre business altogether (Rodgers actually contemplated taking a job selling children's underwear). Just then, another Rodgers family friend came to their aid, suggesting that they compose some songs for a modest amateur revue he was helping to organize for a group of young, novice Theatre Guild actors. The performers were working on their own showcase and had appealed to the Theatre Guild for sponsorship. The Guild agreed, seeing a win-win situation of showcasing talented unknowns while raising money for theatre curtains; and Rodgers and Hart were officially hired to provide some songs, with Fields serving as dance director. Staged at the Garrick Theatre and scheduled for only two performances, beginning on May 17, 1925, *The Garrick Gaieties* quickly sold out, necessitating six extra performances. Audiences still demanded more, however; and the "little show that could" ultimately ran for six months. Featuring irreverent, spontaneous, and youthful material, the *Gaieties* specialized in spoofs and satire, much of which was aimed at the Theatre Guild itself and its "serious" drama repertoire. Rodgers and Hart's score also reflected the modern, fresh spirit, with "Manhattan" becoming the show's break-out hit, putting them on the map. The song, originally performed as a duet by a young couple in the show, cheerfully lists timely New York references and romantic sentiments, all expressed through intricate rhyme schemes and put to a lilting melody redolent of a leisurely stroll. Consequently, given the first revue's popularity, Rodgers and Hart created another *Gaieties* in 1926, again irreverently burlesquing "stuffy" and formulaic idioms and genres such as love ballads and operettas. The second edition also spawned a hit song, "Mountain Greenery," which details and extols rural pleasures as opposed to the urban joys of "Manhattan."

From 1925–31, in addition to the *Gaieties*, Rodgers and Hart wrote scores for a remarkable eighteen Broadway shows (including revues). Even more amazing is the fact that the majority of the musicals were hits. As Rodgers has recounted, the team purposefully set out to work against formulaic expectations and to never repeat themselves, all of which resulted in fresh and sassy productions that spanned a gamut of subject matter and contained loosely integrated, yet highly appealing and memorable songs. Eight productions were written with Herbert Fields as librettist, including their first Broadway book musical *Dearest Enemy* (1925), which is set in 1776 and tells the comic tale of a group of crafty females who deflect British troops during the Revolutionary War. The next year, they scored hits with *The Girl Friend*, a boy-meets-girl romance against the backdrop of a six-day bicycle race, and *Peggy-Ann*, which depicts the travails of the eponymous heroine who visits 5th Avenue, travels aboard a yacht, falls overboard, floats on a raft, and attends a horserace in Havana, only to find that all has been a dream. In addition to its imaginative premise, the Broadway production of *Peggy-Ann* contained many theatrical innovations, including a fifteen-minute opening without song, as well as costume/scenery changes that occurred in full view of the audience. On a creative roll, Rodgers, Hart and Fields had their biggest hit of the 1920s in 1927 with a musicalization of Mark Twain's *A Connecticut Yankee in King Arthur's Court*, which they titled *A Connecticut Yankee*. Another "dreamscape" musical, it played for 418 performances and introduced the hit songs "Thou Swell" and "My Heart Stood Still." In the following years, Rodgers and Hart were permanent fixtures on Broadway, teaming with other librettists, as well as Fields, to achieve mostly hit musicals (a notable and rare flop was 1928's *Chee-Chee*, which may have pushed the envelope too far in terms of subject matter, centering on the machinations of the son of the Grand Eunuch of ancient China). After 1931's *America's Sweetheart*, a spoof of Hollywood and the last Rodgers/Hart/Fields collaboration, Rodgers (now married and a new father) was worried about the economics of Broadway, given the onset of the Depression. He suggested to Hart that they leave New York to try their hand at writing movie musicals. Thus, they spent the next 3½ years working in Hollywood, where Hart enjoyed the Tinseltown lifestyle and nightlife (although his alcoholic binges often resulted in missed deadlines), while Rodgers became increasingly homesick for New York City and, most of all, Broadway. Disillusioned by the movie studio system and missing the stage, in 1935 Rodgers decided to return to New York, and Hart, given some arm-twisting by Rodgers, agreed to join him.

Back in New York, the team felt the need to catch up with the changing times and tastes of Broadway as well as the new sophisticated and complicated work of their peers (e.g., the Gershwins' *Of Thee I Sing* and Irving Berlin's *As Thousands Cheer*). They didn't start small, collaborating in 1935 on what could be considered a precursor to the contemporary mega musical: *Jumbo*. This "circus musical" was the brainchild of showman/producer Billy Rose and was staged in the Hippodrome,

a 4,600-seat theatre for extravaganzas that had been vacant for years. Due to the fact that the space had to be reconstructed to house an actual circus, *Jumbo* opened at an unprecedented price tag of $340,000 (costs were never recouped). Complete with animals and three-ring acts, the production was co-directed by George Abbott in his first musical directing role (he would soon become the legendary "Mr. Abbott," director of thirty-four Broadway musicals). *Jumbo's* thin plot revolves around an inept publicity manager trying to save a circus in debt. Although the score by Rodgers and Hart introduced standalone hits such as "My Romance," it was overwhelmed by the attendant hoopla. The team's next project, however, would not only reignite their Broadway careers but change the role and potential of dance within the musical genre.

One might divide the musical theatre careers of Rodgers and Hart into two periods: (1) the aforementioned musical comedies of the 1920s and (2) the eleven works of the '30s and early '40s, some of which they co-produced as well. *On Your Toes* (1936) is often cited as the true artistic beginning of Rodgers and Hart's second phase. In an unprecedented move, the duo co-wrote the show's libretto with George Abbott, who had also originally signed on as director but had to leave before rehearsals began, only to return and "doctor" the show during its out-of-town tryouts. Originally conceived by Rodgers and Hart as a movie musical for Fred Astaire (who rejected it), the work was reconfigured for the stage and served as a dance vehicle for vaudevillian "eccentric" dance star Ray Bolger (who would gain lasting fame as the Scarecrow in the MGM film version of *The Wizard of Oz*). Bolger played Junior Dolan, an ex-vaudevillian hoofer and music teacher who tries to persuade a visiting Russian ballet company to stage a "jazz" ballet using his friend's original composition, "Slaughter on Tenth Avenue." In the process, Dolan's relationship with his girlfriend is complicated by his infatuation with a prima ballerina, Vera, while his own dancing skills are put to a farcical test as he is inadvertently required to perform in the company's ballets. He ultimately stars in the premiere of "Slaughter," and Vera's jealous suitor hires two gangsters to kill him. To avoid the murder, Dolan improvises at the ballet's end, dancing for his life until the police arrive and arrest the killers. With the work centering on the classical dance, the creators knew they needed to hire a "legitimate" ballet artist as choreographer. They wisely hired Russian émigré and ballet choreographer George Balanchine (an artist often positioned as the father of classical/neoclassical ballet in the United States, credited with developing America's first ballet company and school). In addition to his extensive dance sequences, Balanchine and *On Your Toes* introduced the term "choreography" to musical theatre, instead of the usual Broadway description of "dance arrangement." Balanchine would choreograph three more hit Rodgers/Hart musicals in the '30s. Another contribution made by Balanchine, along with Rodgers and Hart, was the new degree of dance integration represented by "Slaughter," for the show's libretto/plot depended on the choreographed segment. This was the earliest notable instance of dance being used as an integral dramatic component in a musical, instead of an interpolated or diversionary element. Further, the score exemplified a new sophistication by Rodgers and Hart, especially Rodgers' lengthy "Slaughter" composition, which used a brassy, wailing combination of jazz and blues to convey the ballet's drama and storyline.

For their next project, *Babes in Arms* (1937), Rodgers and Hart again supplied both the book and the score. The plot was in the formulaic "let's put on a show" vein, centering on the teen children of unemployed vaudevillians. Once the youths are threatened with being taken from their families, they put on their own show, raising funds to keep their households solvent. The production was not completely formulaic, however; for the cast consisted of age-appropriate unknowns. This was an unparalleled situation, all the more remarkable given that the young talent was asked to sing, arguably, the greatest collection of American song standards ever produced for a musical score (e.g., "Where or When," "My Funny Valentine," "I Wish I Were in Love Again," and "The Lady Is a Tramp"). That same year, Rodgers and Hart jumped on the sociopolitical bandwagon with *I'd Rather Be Right*; but in another unprecedented move, they chose to spoof a sitting president, Franklin D. Roosevelt. In a libretto by George S. Kaufman and Moss Hart, Roosevelt (in real life a disabled man who had no use of his legs) was represented on stage as a song-and-dance man, portrayed by the venerable George M. Cohan. In short, the libretto loosely revolves around an engaged couple who can only marry once the national budget is balanced; and in a dream, Roosevelt agrees to help in this respect, setting off a sequence of actions that lampoons a gamut of government institutions. Unfortunately, Cohan was not professionally

respectful of Rodgers and Hart during rehearsals, disparagingly referring to the duo as "Gilbert and Sullivan" and going so far as to tinker with Hart's lyrics, until he was forced to stop by the creators and producers. Regardless of the behind-the-scenes tension, the show was not only a success but was immediately followed by another hit, *I Married an Angel* (1938). Employing another fantastical premise, the musical comically explores the myriad of problems that arise when a despondent, cynical, modern hero fancies that only an angel can meet his marital criteria and is granted the heavenly spouse. Choreographed again by Balanchine, the production featured extended fantasy dance sequences, as well as catchy Rodgers and Hart numbers (specifically, the title song) that became pop chart hits. In 1938, Rodgers and Hart tackled Shakespeare with *The Boys from Syracuse* (1938): a musical comedy version of the Bard's *The Comedy of Errors*. Although it was the first musical to be based on a Shakespeare work, it was also contemporary in wit and song, with a highlight being "Sing for Your Supper," sung by a girl trio reminiscent of big band vocal groups (e.g., The Andrews Sisters). Rodgers and Hart ended the 1930s on a career high note; but Hart was steadily declining, with his alcoholism culminating in hospitalization, and Rodgers arranged for a piano to be delivered to the medical suite so that they might finish writing the songs together. Although a younger Rodgers used to quip that Hart would most likely show up on Friday for a meeting that had been scheduled for Tuesday, such debilitating circumstances did not bode well for their continued partnership. Neither did it portend that Rodgers and Hart had their biggest artistic achievement ahead of them. But, Hart's depression and disillusionment may have been the contributing factors behind their most sophisticated and significant Broadway work: *Pal Joey* (1940).

Considered by Rodgers to be a mature musical that dealt with the more sordid "facts of life," *Pal Joey* presents a dark world in which all the leading characters are, in Rodgers' words, "rotten" (an exception, in his opinion, is the ingénue, who is just "stupid"). The musical began as a collection of John O'Hara short stories that appeared in *The New Yorker* from 1939–41, which depicted a Chicago nightclub milieu and its seedy cast of characters, especially a two-bit player and song-and-dance man named Joey Evans. O'Hara approached Rodgers and Hart to turn the material into a musical, feeling that Hart, especially, could do service to his jaded characters and cynical themes of life and love. George Abbott signed on as producer and director but also became an uncredited librettist, as O'Hara's heavy drinking made him unreliable during the show's development. Regardless of its patchwork authorship, *Pal Joey* was ahead of its time and revolutionary in many respects. Its plot concerns the nightclub hoofer Joey who, in search of a financial benefactress, becomes a gigolo for a wealthy, older married woman, Vera, while carrying on with other girls in and around the club. Given this atypical musical comedy fare, Joey stands as the genre's first significant "antihero" leading man, while Vera is a new configuration of the matron, reinventing the stock character as a sexual, powerful woman (instead of the usual spinster, fool, or shrew). In addition to the groundbreaking subject matter, Rodgers and Hart's score was the most integrated of their career, as they explicitly tried to make every song reflect place/time/mood and further plot and character development. The score was one of their most diverse and lush, ranging from jazzy, saucy show tunes for the metatheatrical club numbers to sweeping and confessional ballads such as the classic "Bewitched, Bothered, and Bewildered" [see fig. 4.4]. *Pal Joey* ran for 374 performances but critics were split on their assessments. Many took umbrage at the material, with critic Brooks Atkinson of *The New York Times* lamenting that no matter the pleasing score, the overall experience was like trying to draw "sweet water" from a "foul well."

In 1941, Hart was exhausted and dispirited due to the mixed reception given *Pal Joey*; so he was not in the mood to consider a new project proposed by Rodgers, that is, to turn a play titled *Green Grow the Lilacs* into a musical for the Theatre Guild. Given the play's subject matter, i.e., the plight of settlers in Oklahoma Territory during its bid for statehood, Hart was even more disinterested; for he was drawn to modern, urban, and edgy material, not turn-of-the-century cowboys, farmers, and box socials.

Thus, he gave Rodgers the go-ahead to work with another partner on the show (Hammerstein II), while Hart headed to Mexico for a much-needed vacation. As will be addressed in the following "Golden Age" chapter, Rodgers and Hammerstein's subsequent collaboration, titled *Oklahoma!*, made musical theatre history.

In March 1943, Hart returned to New York for the opening night of *Oklahoma!* and saw its writing team become the toast of Broadway. Genuinely impressed with Rodgers' new work, Hart vowed to remain sober in order to reteam with him. Rodgers agreed to renew the partnership, and the next Rodgers and Hart project was a 1943 revival, with an expanded score, of *A Connecticut Yankee*. The outcome of their reunion was tragic, however, as Hart "fell off the wagon," attending opening night both drunk and disruptive, singing along with the actors onstage. Even more heartbreaking was the fact that Rodgers had arranged to have Hart removed from the theater should he show up; accordingly, he was ejected from the theater. After much searching by Rodgers and others, Hart was finally found two days later sitting drunk in a gutter. He was incoherent and in a state of undress, suffering from acute pneumonia, and was immediately hospitalized. Once admitted to the hospital, with Rodgers continually by his bedside, Hart slipped into unconsciousness and died three days later on November 22, 1943. Thus, the musical world lost a tortured 48-year-old genius who not only imbued his works with a uniquely modern sensibility and sophisticated worldview, but tickled and challenged audiences with brilliant wordplay and poesy, inspiring future generations of lyricists and other musical theatre artists. Although heartbroken over Hart's death, Rodgers also knew he had fortuitously discovered another kindred spirit and symbiotic writing partner in Hammerstein and readied himself for the next phase of his legendary career.

Figure 4.4

BEWITCHED, BOTHERED, AND BEWILDERED

Music by Richard Rodgers; Lyrics by Lorenz Hart (1940)

He's a fool, and don't I know it –
But a fool can have his charms;
I'm in love and don't I show it,
Like a babe in arms.

After one whole quart of brandy
Like a daisy I awake
With no Bromo Seltzer handy,
I don't even shake.

Men are not a new sensation;
I've done pretty well, I think.
But this half-pint imitation
Put me on the blink.

REFRAIN 1

I'm wild again,
Beguiled again,
A simpering, whimpering child again–
Bewitched, bothered and bewildered
am I.

Couldn't sleep
And wouldn't sleep
Until I could sleep where I shouldn't
sleep–
Bewitched, bothered and bewildered
am I.

Lost my heart, but what of it?
My mistake, I agree.
He's a laugh, but I love it
Because the laugh's on me.

A pill he is,
But still he is
All mine and I'll keep him until he is
Bewitched, bothered and bewildered
Like me.

REFRAIN 2

Seen a lot–
I mean a lot–
But now I'm like sweet seventeen a
lot–

Bewitched, bothered and bewildered
am I.

I'll sing to him,
Each spring to him,
And worship the trousers that cling
to him–
Bewitched, bothered and bewildered
am I.

When he talks, he is seeking
Words to get off his chest.
Horizontally speaking,
He's at his very best.

Vexed again,
Perplexed again,
Thank God I can be oversexed again–
Bewitched, bothered and bewildered
am I.

REFRAIN 3

Sweet again,
Petite again,
And on my proverbial seat again–
Bewitched, bothered and bewildered
am I.

What am I?
Half shot am I.
To think that he loves me
So hot am I–
Bewitched, bothered and bewildered
am I.

Though at first we said, "No, sire,"
Now we're two little dears.
You might say we are closer
Than Roebuck is to Sears.

I'm dumb again
And numb again,
A rich, ready, ripe little plum again–
Bewitched, bothered and bewildered
am I.

ENCORE

You know,
It is really quite funny
Just how quickly he learns
How to spend all the money
That Mr. Simpson earns.

He's kept enough,
He's slept enough,
And yet where it counts
He's adept enough–
Bewitched, bothered and bewildered
am I.

REPRISE (at the end of the show)

Wise at last,
My eyes at last
Are cutting you down to your size
at last–
Bewitched, bothered and bewildered
no more.

Burned a lot,
But learned a lot,
And now you are broke, though you
earned a lot–
Bewitched, bothered and bewildered
no more.

Couldn't eat–
Was dyspeptic.
Life was so hard to bear;
Now my heart's antiseptic,
Since you moved out of there.

Romance-finis;
Your chance-finis;
Those ants that invaded my
pants-finis–
Bewitched, bothered and bewildered
no more.

FEATURED PRODUCTION: *Pal Joey* (1940)

Music by Richard Rodgers; Lyrics by Lorenz Hart
Book by John O'Hara (and George Abbott, uncredited)

Original Broadway Run: Opened December 25, 1940; Ethel Barrymore Theatre; 374 performances

Today, an antihero seems almost commonplace, while flaw-ridden characters populate and dominate popular television shows, films, and musicals. Not so in 1940—especially on the musical stage. Thus, when *Pal Joey* debuted on Broadway, no one quite knew what to make of its roster of "nasty" characters and its particularly dark take on human nature and relationships. Fortunately, *Pal Joey*'s mature content eventually "spoke" to audiences, proving that the 1940 work was simply ahead of its time. Specifically, after its lukewarm debut, the musical enjoyed successful Broadway revivals, finally arriving at its current revered and affirmed place within the contemporary musical theatre canon.

Based on a series of *New Yorker* short stories by John O'Hara, the show features the swaggering, street-smart, and manipulative (yet charming) song-and-dance man, Joey Evans, who enjoys women and is unburdened by a moral compass. Early on, the audience is made fully aware that this Rodgers and Hart work is anything but the typical "boy meets girl/poetic justice/happy ending" musical. After Joey gets a gig in a seedy Chicago nightclub, Mike's Club, he sets his sights on the naïve ingénue (who he terms a "mouse"), Linda, while also playing around with numerous chorus girls. The club milieu, itself, is a metaphor for and microcosm of *Pal Joey*'s larger paradigm of moral relativity and exploitation—exemplified by a scene in which Joey is asked by the manager of Mike's whether he's into girls, little boys, booze, and/or cocaine. In short, welcome to the world of *Joey*. Next, the budding romance between Joey and Linda takes a darkly unconventional turn when Joey decides to two-time her by pursuing a sexual relationship with a wealthy and married older woman, Vera. The affair is mutually beneficial; Joey becomes a kept man for Vera, while she agrees to financially back him in his quest for his own nightclub, Chez Joey. (This club-ownership fantasy also morphs into a dream ballet for Joey.) After actually turning Mike's Club into Joey's establishment, however, Vera decides that Joey is more trouble that he is worth, having been tipped off by Linda that blackmailers are plotting to ruin the two adulterers. During the women's exchange, Vera offers to "give" Joey to Linda, who is reluctant to take her "gift." Finally, having been dumped by Vera and suffering a brush with the blackmailers, Joey relents to having dinner with Linda and her family. Realizing that he could never settle into domesticity or lead a "legit" life, Joey decides to leave town in search of new pastures and "patsies." Thus, Joey metaphorically strolls off into the sunset, an antihero who is neither chagrined nor enlightened.

When developing *Pal Joey*, Rodgers and Hart worked with librettists O'Hara and George Abbott (uncredited) to more fully realize an integrated Broadway work. They mostly succeeded in this endeavor, at least with regard to their score reflecting and illustrating O'Hara's milieu, as well as providing authentic musical voices for their characters. This is not to suggest, however, that the score is completely without extraneous, interpolated numbers. For instance, the clever, up-tempo "Zip" was basically written as a diversionary novelty song for a news reporter and does little to further the plot or help develop her character. Nonetheless, many other musical "diversions" in the score are dramatically effective, as they metatheatrically and/or musically reflect and espouse, in sound and sentiment, the mocking and bawdy world and worldview of *Joey*. Specifically, Rodgers and Hart created an auditory portrait of the nightclub and its characters via brassy and extroverted show tunes, replete with satirical and suggestive lyrics. Such numbers serve as part of the club's entertainment and character exchanges (e.g., "You Mustn't Kick It Around," "The Flower Garden of My Heart," "Happy Hunting Horn," and "Plant Ya Now, Dig Ya Later"). Further, the numbers remain true to place and time while also slyly commenting on the characters' psyches, philosophies, and offstage shenanigans. Also innovative is the score's employment of sexually suggestive lyrics and blatant address of adultery, as well as its cynical view of love—all of which is especially evident in Vera and Joey's duet, "Den of Iniquity." During the number, they unapologetically and cheerfully sing of their illicit affair. Although the show's overall content might have seemed a bit edgy, the score, nonetheless, generated numerous mainstream hits. One such number was "I Could Write a Book" which, ironically taken out of context, became a top-selling sentimental pop song in America. In a similar vein, Rodgers' deft touch with a ballad and Hart's genius with lyrics had all of America singing Vera's torch ballad, "Bewitched, Bothered, and Bewildered." The song, in the context of the play, is sardonic and carnal; yet Rodgers' sweet, sweeping melody counters Hart's dark sentiments, and together, the two components worked to veil the true intent/content of the song just enough to appeal, outside the musical, to the general public who read the number as a longing ode to the joys and frustrations of romantic love.

"Bewitched" also underlines *Pal Joey*'s groundbreaking depiction of women. Although Joey views females as exploitable and disposable objects, many of the lead characters in *Pal Joey* are actually strong and forceful women. These include a female reporter who almost undoes him and, most of all, Vera, who is self-aware enough to not confuse sex with love, espousing such sentiments in "Bewitched." In the end, it is Vera, not Joey, who pulls the strings in their relationship, representing an abrupt departure from the past "matron" stereotype, who was often the pathetic or nasty butt of a joke. Even the ingénue, Linda, at *Joey*'s end, shows more brain and moral fortitude than Joey; and in her duet with Vera, "Take Him," she counters Vera's suggestion to "take back" Joey with her own sarcastic and savvy argument.

When looking at the *Joey* score, one must also consider a number that didn't actually make it onto the Broadway stage in 1940, for it is arguably the most thematic and symbolic of the entire show. Cut during the Philadelphia try-outs, Joey's last song, "I'm Talkin' to My Pal," was deemed too melancholy even for *Pal Joey*, with Hart's antihero declaring that he is fine being alone again, as he is the only person he can trust and he is his only true friend. Even without this morbid closing, the Broadway premiere of *Pal Joey* confused and discomfited some audience members and critics, generating mixed reviews. In short, 1940 audiences expected to leave a musical comedy feeling lightened and exhilarated, not challenged and demoralized. But twelve years later, in 1952, *Pal Joey* was revived on Broadway; and this time, the production was lauded by critics as Rodgers and Hart's ultimate masterpiece. Audiences awarded it with a run of 540 performances. In short, the work was prescient, as its mature "realism" was not only appreciated in time but was also exploited by later works in the musical canon, so much so that the antihero and his dark world no longer seem taboo, or even novel, on Broadway today.

PULLING BACK THE CURTAIN:

Rodgers/Hart/Balanchine: Evolution of the "Choreographer" and "Dream Ballet"

As late as 1933, there were no ballet companies in America. Although past tours by celebrity Russian and/or British ballet dancers had proven highly popular, the actual art of ballet was neither appreciated nor particularly understood in the States. It was received by American audiences as spectacle, a curiosity, and with its female dancers, somewhat akin to the old musical theatre leg show/extravaganza (e.g., *The Black Crook*). The lack of a ballet and/or a serious concert dance tradition in America also affected the prestige, import, and overall role of dance on Broadway. All of this changed in 1933, when Russian expatriate George Balanchine arrived in New York City to help found an American ballet company under the sponsorship of Lincoln Kirstein (a young balletomane and aspiring arts impresario) and his producing partner Edward M. Warburg. Balanchine's reputation preceded him, for he had already risen to dance fame as a ballet soloist and resident choreographer for impresario Sergei Diaghilev and his company, Les Ballets Russes, creating masterpieces such as *Apollon Musagète* (1928) and *The Prodigal Son* (1929). Once in New York, Balanchine quickly joined Kirstein and Warburg in founding the School of American Ballet, then a resident ballet company, the American Ballet (which would eventually become the New York City Ballet). Yet, the establishment of classical ballet in America was a slow and obstacle-laden process; thus, Balanchine looked to the theatre as a temporary, supplemental, and lucrative source of employment.

His first Broadway project was the creation of some ballet dances for the *Ziegfeld Follies* in 1936. The work brought Balanchine to the attention of Broadway producer Dwight Deere Wiman who was starting a new project with Rodgers and Hart. The musical was called *On Your Toes* and would establish George Balanchine as, technically, the first "choreographer" on the Broadway stage, for the term "choreography" was used, at Balanchine's insistence, to describe the show's dance numbers in all billing and press materials. This was a first; previously, a show's choreography was denoted as "dances arranged by" or "staged by." The term "choreography" (formerly applied only to "highbrow" concert dance) also signified a new level of prestige and power for the dance component and dance creator of a musical. The concept of dance integration introduced by Balanchine's work in *On Your Toes* was equally significant. Of course, it helped that the libretto by Rodgers, Hart and director George Abbott largely dealt with the backstage travails of a touring Russian ballet company; thus, the use of dance as part of the narrative may have seemed a logical development. Balanchine, however, went a step further as he not only used dance as part of the action but also used it, in certain moments, to advance the plot and develop character. To do so, he choreographed two extended dance segments for the musical. The first number occurred in Act I during which Junior Dolan, a music teacher and hoofer, attempts to impress the ballet company's prima ballerina by performing alongside her in "La Princess Zenobia" (a satirical spoof of Mikhail Fokine's famous ballet, *Schéhérazade*). Comedy ensues as Dolan, taking the role of a Nubian slave, fakes his way through the performance, clumsily attempting the classical choreography. The number was brilliantly designed by Balanchine, who was intimately familiar with the idiom. In Act II's "Slaughter on Tenth Avenue," Balanchine (with the aid of African American tap dancer Herbert Harper) further developed the concept of dance integration. In the libretto, Dolan is ultimately chosen to star in the narrative jazz ballet ("Slaughter"); but after discovering that hit men are planning to shoot him once the number is over, he desperately improvises with more tap dance, extending the number until the police can arrive. Balanchine's number was a tour de force that represented a "danced" climax of a libretto; it not only further developed and illustrated Dolan's character but also complicated, and ultimately resolved, the overall plot.

The next year, Balanchine pioneered what was to become a landmark dance device in musical theatre choreography. On his third Broadway musical, *Babes in Arms* (1937), Balanchine found himself again working with Rodgers and Hart. And while complementing the superlative score and the libretto's thin premise, he presented Broadway's first "dream ballet." In the musical, the lead character, Peter, fantasizes about having $500 and travelling the world. Using on-hand materials in a theatrically obvious way, Balanchine had Peter dance through locales represented by cardboard skyscrapers, cellophane palm trees, and a cloth ocean. It was one of the first times that the term "dream ballet" had been applied to an extended dance sequence in a Broadway book musical, and the entire concept of the fanciful dance number, integrated and legitimized by its use as a fantastical or dream sequence, soon became almost *de rigueur* for any integrated book musical during the Golden Age. Of course, it is important to note that "dream" sequences in musicals had appeared prior to *Babes in Arms*, e.g., *Tilly's Nightmare* in 1910 and Rodgers and Hart's early work, *Peggy-Ann* (1926). Yet, these sequences consisted of mostly mimed action set to music. They were not formally danced or presented as "ballets" within the musical.

Having created an effective choreographic device, Balanchine worked to refine it in his next Rodgers and Hart musical, *I Married an Angel* (1938). With its fantastical premise of mortal-angel nuptials, Balanchine was given more leeway to embellish and develop his choreographic experiments. Specifically, Act I contained the lengthy and flamboyant "Honeymoon Ballet," a dream ballet in which the angel and her new spouse visit a zoo where the animals proceed to dance. The couple then journeyed to Norway for a heavenly snow ballet, travelling by a sled drawn by real huskies. Critics were delighted by this mini *Nutcracker* on Broadway, as well as a show-stopping number in the production's second act: "At the Roxy Music Hall." In Balanchine's dance extravaganza, the angel was seen performing in a Radio City Music Hall spoof. The number alternated between a typical Broadway chorus line and a symbolic ballet, in which the angel scenically (and satirically) rose from the sea in a papiér maché oyster shell. Although not as integrated as "Slaughter on Tenth Avenue," *Angel's* dance numbers, nonetheless, reaffirmed the import of choreography/dance in a musical, for much of the show's comedic and lyrical content was supplied by and depended on the choreographed sequences. Further, the show cemented Balanchine's title as the "first choreographer of Broadway" while his "dream ballet" invention proved that diversionary dance in a musical could further develop, metaphorically address, and/or satirically comment on narrative, character, and theme. With regard to the dream ballet and musical theatre integration, however, one must also examine the paradox of this choreographic convention. The extended dance sequence exploits and promotes dance as an integral, integrated component within the overall "golden triangle" of the traditional book musical. Yet, it may simultaneously break the flow of the overall show, calling attention to the choreographer and promoting the dance above the other musical components. This delicate balance of power and position inherent in the "dream ballet" continues to create challenges, as well as opportunities, for musical theatre choreographers.

By the time Balanchine joined Rodgers and Hart for the fourth and last time on 1938's *The Boys from Syracuse*, there was no question that the Russian ballet master had firmly established himself in the American musical theatre community. In fact, there was a brief period that year in which he had three shows playing simultaneously on Broadway (*I Married an Angel*, *The Boys from Syracuse*, and a failed Frederick Loewe musical titled *Great Lady*). Soon after his stint as director/choreographer for *Cabin in the Sky* (1940), during which he became the first choreographer to also assume a directorial role on Broadway, Balanchine left the musical theatre to resume his concert dance career and devote his energies to running and developing works for the New York City Ballet, ultimately becoming the most powerful and prestigious ballet choreographer and director in modern times. His contributions to musical theatre, however, influenced and informed Broadway long after his departure, providing templates and inspiration for future choreographer/directors such as Agnes de Mille, Jerome Robbins, Onna White, Bob Fosse, Michael Bennett, Tommy Tune, Gower Champion, Susan Stroman, Kathleen Marshall, Rob Marshall, Twyla Tharp, and Bill T. Jones. All of these artists have continued to develop and evolve the role of dance in the musical by exploring, reconfiguring, and furthering choreographic devices such as Balanchine's dream ballet, while experimenting with paradigms of dance integration or dominance within the musical theatre genre.

Actor Spotlights

Al Jolson (1886–1950)

Al Jolson was America's first superstar, dubbed "The World's Greatest Entertainer" at the height of his career. Known for his blackface alter ego, hyperkinetic performing style, and melodramatic song delivery, Jolson reigned on stage and screen throughout much of the early twentieth century. With unabashed sentiment, playful adlibs, and nonstop physicality (clapping/gesturing hands, rolling eyes, mugging face, bouncing feet, and undulating body), Jolson could put his indelible stamp on any song, while his brassy, expressive vocals often became the sound most identified with hits such as "Toot, Toot, Tootsie," "You Made Me Love You (I Didn't Want to Do It)," "Swanee," "My Mammy," "Liza," "Blue Skies," "Rock-A-Bye Your Baby with a Dixie Melody," "April Showers," and "Sonny Boy." And such songs are only the tip of the iceberg when it comes to the Jolson hit parade. Between 1911 and 1928 alone, he had more than 80 top-selling records. But a recorded Jolson song did not do justice to his distinctive talent; for it was his live stage performances that set him apart and made him the favorite of audiences worldwide. During his shows, he "worked" the audience, using specially designed runways to gain proximity to the spectators as he exhaustingly charmed, implored, and teased them directly (going so far as to dare reserved audiences to try and "have a good time"). This up-close-and-personal style would be imitated for years to come, especially by future rock 'n' roll stars and other performing icons. Lauded as the consummate singer/actor/comedian, Jolson had nine sell-out Winter Garden shows in a row during the 1910s and '20s, as well as 16 national and international tours.

Al Jolson in blackface, c. 1920s
© Underwood & Underwood/Corbis

Jolson's voice was as unique as his performing style; thus, it was only fitting that he would star in the first Hollywood "talkie," 1927's *The Jazz Singer*, giving him a legendary place in film history, as well as theatre. He would go on to star in many other movies, and by end of the '20s, Jolson was the most famous and highest paid entertainer in America. His signature use of blackface was applauded in its day as a means by which ragtime, blues, jazz, and other African American music idioms could be disseminated to white audiences. Through a contemporary lens, however, it is difficult to see the grotesquery of Jolson's blackface exaggerations in a positive light; nonetheless, he reflected the cultural norms of his day and can be legitimately credited with exposing mainstream audiences to diverse musical styles. Further, Jolson's biographers have often addressed his almost "religious" devotion to blackface (holding on to the convention long past its heyday), citing it as a "mask" behind which Jolson could present a highly emotional and extroverted character to audiences, practically begging for their approval and love. It may also be seen as a depiction of marginalized and persecuted Otherness that mirrored and included vestiges of Jolson's own Jewishness (Jolson never denied his Jewish roots and religion). While Jolson may have exploited a racist paradigm on stage, biographers have never noted racist behavior by Jolson in his personal life; he often befriended and openly supported fellow performers who were black. As evidenced by his blackface paradox, Jolson was a complicated character: egomaniacal and driven, living a celebrity highlife that would rival that of today's most public and extravagant stars. Yet, he was also a neurotic and difficult talent, threatened by anyone who could possibly steal (or even share) his limelight. (A famous story tells of Jolson running water backstage when fellow performers were onstage, trying to drown out any laughter and applause.) In every respect, he was a true original; and when Jolson wanted to inject a new number into otherwise scripted performances, he used to tease his fans with a catchphrase that was also the title of one of his hit songs: "You Ain't Heard Nothin' Yet" (1920). True to this prediction, Jolson stretched the boundaries of music and performance style on the American stage, never failing to deliver on his promise to top himself repeatedly as he captured and thrilled American audiences for decades.

The career of Al Jolson has been the subject of numerous books, films, and stage works, which contain extensive and exhaustive details. Thus, this biography offers a condensed snapshot of his lifetime achievements, mostly in regard to musical theatre. Jolson's real name was Asa Yoelson, and he was born in 1886 in an obscure Jewish village in Lithuania, then part of the Russian Empire. He was the fifth and youngest child of Moses and Naomi Yoelson. In 1891, Moses—a nomadic, struggling rabbi and cantor: immigrated to America to secure a better future for the family, sending for Naomi and the children in 1894. The family reunited in Washington, D.C. where Moses made a meager living at a neighborhood synagogue. Unfortunately, Naomi died in 1895, shortly after arriving at their new home, with eight-year-old Asa in the next room (biographers often cite his mother's death as the pivotal event that would haunt Jolson throughout his life). After a period of shock and inconsolable mourning, the adolescent Asa discovered a passion for performing and was soon singing with his brother, Hirsch, for coins on street corners and in amateur venues (at this time, Asa also changed his name to "Al"). From this humble start, Al became obsessed with making it in showbiz, running away to join a travelling circus in 1899, then progressing to burlesque in 1901 and, ultimately, vaudeville, where he performed as a solo vocalist during his late teens and early twenties, while also teaming again with his brother (now known as "Harry") and a wheelchair-bound comic, Joe Palmer. It was during his vaudeville period that he, along with Harry, changed his last name to Jolson and began to perform in blackface, using the gimmick to create his soon-to-be signature look and a performing style that was uninhibited, bold, and expressive (qualities that Jolson had failed to exhibit previously). By 1908, Jolson caught the attention of Lew Dockstader, who offered him a featured role in the Dockstader's Minstrels troupe, after which Jolson became synonymous with blackface performance. And after his successful 1909 booking at Hammerstein's Victoria Theatre (vaudeville's premier palace), Jolson secured his place as New York's newest sensation.

After paying his dues in burlesque, vaudeville, and minstrelsy, Jolson finally arrived on Broadway. On March 20, 1911, Jolson was featured in his first Winter Garden Theatre revue, *La Belle Paree*, singing Stephen Foster plantation songs in blackface. After a slow start, Jolson used his wily stage smarts (and adlibbed audience appeals) to woo the crowd; and within a month, the twenty-five-year-old became a Broadway star. After the show closed (104 performances), Jolson proceeded to light up the Broadway stage in an unbroken series of hits until he mostly retired from theatre in 1926. His theatre roster includes *Vera Violetta* (1911), *The Whirl of Society* (1912), *The Honeymoon Express* (1913), *Dancing Around* (1914), *Robinson Crusoe, Jr.* (1916), *Sinbad* (1918), *Bombo* (1921), *Artists and Models* (1925), and *Big Boy* (1925, with a revival in 1926). Never one to rest on his laurels, he also performed one-man "recitals" at the Winter Garden on his Sunday nights off (circumventing the New York City prohibition of Sunday performances at the time). In 1912's *Whirl of Society*, Jolson debuted his signature blackface character "Gus," a clever, comic slave who always outsmarts his master. The play was so successful that Jolson was awarded a seven-year Winter Garden Theatre contract with a salary of $1,000 a week, where he reprised the role of "Gus" in future plays. As "Gus," he was afforded great flexibility in his stage vehicles, often choosing to break with the scripted proceedings and interpolate new potential hit songs. Such was the case when he injected George Gershwin's "Swanee" into his Broadway smash *Sinbad*—the top Broadway draw of 1918 and 1919—making the song Gershwin's first hit. By 1920, Jolson was the biggest star on Broadway, and his popularity led producer and theater owner Lee Schubert to name his newly built venue after the entertainer. Thus, Jolson's Fifty-Ninth Street Theatre opened in 1921 with a seating capacity of 1,700, and its inaugural production was Jolson's *Bombo*, which moved beyond Broadway to become a national sensation. On a curious side note, Jolson struggled with performance anxiety throughout his life; and he had a paralyzing case of stage fright on *Bombo*'s opening night, having to be physically pushed onstage by his brother, Harry. Thirty-seven curtain calls later, the audience affirmed his superstar status and Jolson expressed his gratitude to the auditorium. *Bombo* became a high point of Jolson's stage career for other reasons as well; in 1922, he gave a special benefit performance of the show to aid injured Jewish veterans of World War I and then took the show on the road, delighting fans across the nation. He ultimately returned with the production to his original Broadway home, the Winter Garden Theatre, where he reaffirmed his love affair with New York audiences, prolonging the show's curtain call with an adlibbed, extended encore consisting of old and new songs. As a singer, Jolson could hold an audience rapt, often working to elicit sobs via his heart-wrenching ballads. As a comic genius, Jolson knew how to directly appeal to his audiences and pull forth laughs, creating pure vitality and fun on stage. And as an ultimate control freak, he often insisted that he be billed as co-lyricist for many of the songs that he performed (and ultimately made famous). Thus, his repertoire often included songs by lesser-known songwriters as they were more apt to acquiesce to his demands.

After his landmark film performance in the first full-length talking movie, *The Jazz Singer* (1927), Jolson turned his talents to Hollywood, mostly leaving the stage to star in over a dozen successful full-length and short-subject musical films throughout the 1930s. During the early '40s, Jolson became somewhat inactive. His star power was then revived and affirmed through two biographical films: the Oscar-winning *The*

Jolson Story (1946) and its sequel, *Jolson Sings Again* (1949), nominated for three Oscars. (Jolson did not star in the movies but songs were dubbed with his voice.) Toward the end of his life, Jolson enhanced his iconic status with exemplary, sacrificial patriotic service, becoming the first star to entertain troops overseas during World War II, and again in Korea in 1950, doing 42 shows in 16 days. When he died just weeks after returning to the United States, partly attributed to physical exhaustion, his family was awarded the Medal for Merit from Defense Secretary George Marshall. In many ways, his death was a testament to his love of audience and country, as well as his need of and gratitude for their love in return.

Ethel Waters (1896–1977)

Ethel Waters may have brought the blues to Broadway, but to classify her solely as a blues artist would be a gross oversight. Waters' vocal oeuvre included jazz, gospel, big band, and pop music, while her lauded acting credits comprised film as well as stage. She was a chart-topping artist who broke racial barriers, introducing and immortalizing such mainstream classics as "Dinah," "Stormy Weather," "Taking a Chance on Love," "Heat Wave," "Supper Time," and "Am I Blue?" (often cited as her signature song), with three of her recordings ("Dinah," "Stormy Weather," and "Am I Blue?") inducted into the Grammy Hall of Fame. Waters was also the second African American to be nominated for an Academy Award (Best Supporting Actress for 1949's *Pinky*), and she won the New York Drama Critics Circle Award in 1950 for her performance in the nonmusical Broadway play *The Member of the Wedding*. With a sob in her voice, she could break her audiences' hearts; with a wink of her eye, she could have them laughing; and with a shimmy in her hips, have them moving in their seats. In short, this queen of the blues was one of America's most diverse artists and national treasures, and in 1994, the U.S. Postal Service honored her as such, issuing a commemorative "Ethel Waters" postage stamp.

Ethel Waters performing in the Cotton Club Revue © Bettmann/CORBIS

Waters not only sang the blues, she lived the blues. Born to teen mother Louise Anderson in Chester, Pennsylvania, circa 1900 (records of her birth year vary), she was the result of Louise's rape by a family acquaintance and pianist, John Waters. Given that John Waters took no parental responsibility and Louise was a mostly absent mother, young Ethel was shuttled between various relatives in the poorest and most violent section of Philadelphia known as the "Bloody Eighth Ward," living in no household longer than fifteen months at a time. After leaving an early abusive marriage (she was thirteen at the time of the nuptials), Waters was working as a maid in a Philadelphia hotel when she found success on stage at the age of seventeen, singing two impromptu songs in a local nightclub. The patrons were so impressed with her soulful song renditions that she was eventually offered a job singing at the Lincoln Theatre in Baltimore,

Maryland, where she was able to make a modest living (although she recounted that the managers stole her tips). Scarred by an early life of brutality, poverty, abandonment, and exploitation, Waters was distrustful of emotional intimacy and had acquired a protective shell that would remain far into her adulthood; yet, she also discovered an emotional outlet and connection to others through music. She soon became known for her poignant, gritty, and spirited song renditions and was featured on the segregated vaudeville circuit for black performers, TOBA (Theatre Owners Booking Agency). She recounted working from morning until "unconscious" on the TOBA circuit, where she was billed as Sweet Mama Stringbean (a nod to her slim figure, accentuated by her 5'9" height). In addition to TOBA, Waters took almost any gig that came her way, touring with the carnival and performing at all-black venues via the Chitlin Circuit (another series of segregated venues that featured black performers).

By 1920, Waters had moved to Harlem where she became a major figure in a burgeoning African American cultural movement historically known as the Harlem Renaissance. With numerous vocalist engagements in black clubs and acting roles in all-black stage comedies, Waters also began making a splash in the recording industry, becoming only the fifth black woman at the time to have made a record (for the modest Cardinal Records label), ultimately landing at Columbia Records in 1925. Throughout her career, she would periodically migrate to other prominent labels, but she initially established herself as a top-selling artist with Columbia, recording mainstream pop hits such as "Dinah," "Heebie Jeebies," "Sweet Georgia Brown," "Someday, Sweetheart," and "Am I Blue?" while continuing to record more authentic blues for Columbia's specialized "race" division (e.g., "West End Blues"). Given Waters' growing status, she was unsurprisingly courted by producers looking to transport the current vogue of black entertainment to the Broadway theatres of midtown Manhattan. Waters did not trust the siren call of "white theatre," however, worrying that her art would be misinterpreted or that she would be exploited. Nonetheless, in 1927, she made her Broadway debut in an unsuccessful black revue, *Africana*, followed by appearances in other Broadway revues, including *Rhapsody in Black* (1931), as well as headlining in "white time" vaudeville (e.g., Keith Vaudeville Circuit). In these venues, Waters entertained white audiences with her mix of blues, pop ballads, jazzy numbers, and novelty songs. It wouldn't be until 1933, however, that Waters would truly transform the Great White Way with her unique talent.

In 1933, America's favorite songwriter, Irving Berlin, was planning a new Broadway revue based on contemporary newspaper headlines and wanted to add a touch of seriousness to his show. By this time, Waters had shown film promise, appearing in the movie musical *On with the Show* (1929) and an all-black satirical short titled *Rufus Jones for President* (1933); and she was currently starring at Harlem's infamous Cotton Club where she introduced, to great acclaim, Harold Arlen's *Stormy Weather*. Berlin went to Harlem to see her notorious performance of the torch song and offered her a starring role in his new revue, soon to be titled *As Thousands Cheer* (1933). She would be the first black woman in an otherwise white Broadway show and some racial tensions ensued, including a brief refusal by the other stars to take their final bows with her—that is, until Berlin threatened to entirely remove the curtain call. Maybe the other performers were a bit jealous, given Waters' standout contributions to the show, e.g., a saucy, entertaining rendition of Berlin's "Heat Wave," a hilarious spoof of expatriate star Josephine Baker ("Harlem on My Mind"), and a controversial, gut-wrenching performance of "Suppertime." The last song was set against a projected headline that read "Unknown Negro Lynched by Frenzied Mob" and a silhouette of a lynched man hanging from a tree. Waters uncompromisingly sang the lament as a mother setting the dinner table for her children, knowing that her husband has been lynched. There were many who tried to dissuade Berlin from keeping "Suppertime" in the show, but he persisted and Waters' performance made an indelible mark on musical theatre which has been felt far into the future. As stated in numerous interviews, Waters recognized the power inherent in bringing "her people's" story to "comfortable" white theatre audiences.

After *As Thousands Cheer*, Waters became a Broadway fixture, starring in numerous musical works (mostly revues) and nonmusical plays. When she played the lead role of Petunia in her only book musical, *Cabin in the Sky* (1940), she introduced another song classic, "Taking a Chance on Love," and became the highest paid performer on Broadway. During the same period, she headlined a national radio program and continued to work in nightclubs. She also expanded her film career. In 1942, she reprised her stage role in MGM's film version of *Cabin in the Sky*, garnering positive reviews. For her supporting role in *Pinky* (1949), she was nominated for an Oscar. In 1950, she won great acclaim and critical awards for her Broadway performance in a Carson McCullers play, *The Member of the Wedding*, reprising her role in the well-received 1952 film adaptation. During the '50s, Waters also dabbled in live television, but she was never completely happy with the nascent medium's quality, format, and material. In addition to her celebrated performances during the decade, which included the Broadway showcase *An Evening with Ethel Waters* (1957), Waters wrote a candid autobiography, *His Eye Is on the Sparrow* (1950). The work, co-written with Charles Samuels, was later turned into a stage production.

Despite her star status, Waters' later years were daunted by financial difficulties, complicated by a major robbery of her cash and jewels, as well as conflicts with the IRS. She also stopped singing commercially, turning her energies toward Christian evangelical charities, including touring with Billy Graham on his crusades. In the '70s, Waters' health suffered, and she worked only sporadically; yet, she was able to author a second autobiography: *To Me, It's Wonderful* (1972). Ethel Waters died in Chatsworth, California, on September 1, 1977, from uterine cancer, kidney failure, and other ailments. The nation, as well as the world, mourned the loss of this great musical/theatrical artist and American cultural icon.

CHAPTER 5

MIDCENTURY AMERICA: THE GOLDEN AGE OF AMERICAN MUSICAL THEATRE

In two, industrious decades, the American musical became forever altered in terms of content, structure, and critical reception. Some might say that the genre matured or "came of age" in the years spanning 1943–64 (a period bookended by *Oklahoma!* and *Fiddler on the Roof*), as the "musical play" and its concept of song/dance/text integration became the accepted, codified, and institutionalized ideal of the era. Yet, one must be careful not to apply a value or aesthetic judgment to the midcentury evolution of the form, framing the newly dominant integrated book musical as superior to those successful works that had previously reigned on Broadway, for the earlier musical comedies and revues may have been less integrated but achieved great aesthetic success in their own right. Nevertheless, there can be no denying that a heightened degree of experimentation and a plethora of sophisticated, groundbreaking, and highly popular works distinguished the Golden Age, while the genre evolved to a point that it could no longer be singularly termed "musical comedy." Instead, it was to be known, henceforth, as "musical theatre." This new term denoted the greater diversity of the musical's content and construct, as well as an increased attempt at dramatic efficacy and a note of artistic "seriousness," a development recognized and lauded by the musical's audience and the broader theatre community.

Although the Golden Age can be viewed as a revolutionary period in musical theatre history, one characteristic of the era remained unchanged: the dominance of its songwriters. Most of the prominent artists of the age were more concerned with devising comprehensive, cohesive, and evocative scores that potently merged song/music with libretto than they were with providing delightful standalone songs for America's hit parade. As a result, the era saw a procession of legendary songwriting partnerships comprised of "integrationist" pioneers, many of whom have become canonical icons, e.g., Rodgers and Hammerstein, Lerner and Loewe,

and Bock and Harnick (not to mention Comden and Green, who were not composers but, as Broadway's most successful and enduring lyricist/librettist team, collaborated with the leading composers of the time, resulting in some of the canon's most prized integrated musical comedies). In addition to the writing teams, midcentury Broadway also espoused an impressive array of composers who lent their concert and popular music credentials to the Broadway stage, while diligently working to adapt their art and craft to the particular needs of the integrated musical. The results were wide-ranging—from symphonic scores by Leonard Bernstein and Kurt Weill to the more populist sounds of Jule Styne, Frank Loesser, and Meredith Willson, all of whom furthered the complexity and dramatic efficacy/integration of the show tune, as well as the codification of the midcentury musical form. Some significant American composers did not achieve the level of theatrical success attained by the aforementioned artists, but they, nonetheless, steadily composed for the stage, imprinting the genre with their impressive, esteemed talent, while creating works that contributed greatly to the American songbook. Prominent among these artists are composers Harold Arlen and Burton Lane, both of whom teamed with venerable lyricists to create works that were both sophisticated and experimental in sound and content. Specifically, Arlen teamed with the prolific Johnny Mercer in 1946 to create *St. Louis Woman*, a musical focusing on the gritty adventures of a group of African Americans in St. Louis at the end of the nineteenth century (the show was a box office disappointment but generated the song standard "Come Rain or Come Shine"). Arlen also wrote with the respected lyricist/librettist E. Y. Harburg, creating the score for 1944's successful *Bloomer Girl* (a Civil War musical that focuses on the women of the era and the liberating fashion statement made by the advent of "bloomer" undergarments), as well as the 1957 hit, *Jamaica* (a metaphoric, romantic tale set in a mythical Caribbean island). Burton Lane also found success with Harburg, creating the idiosyncratic *Finian's Rainbow*, a romantic and fantastic work that mixes Irish mythos (leprechauns and pots of gold) with American sociopolitical issues, all set in the fictional Southern town of Missitucky. The popular musical not only featured a critique of racism in which a Caucasian, prejudiced U.S. Senator is turned "black" (per the power of a magical crock of gold), but also a score boasting such classics as "Look to the Rainbow," "How Are Things in Glocca Morra?" and "Old Devil Moon," while running for 725 performances.

Importantly, however, songwriters did not completely monopolize the upper echelon of power during the Golden Age, for the era also saw the emergence of the commanding stage director, e.g., George Abbott, Rouben Mamoulian, Jerome Robbins, Moss Hart, Joshua Logan, and Gower Champion. Significantly, the ascension of the director could be tied to the rise of the integrated book musical, for the concept of the "total work" could only become reality under the direction of visionary artists who could shape and merge the work's disparate elements into a unified whole on stage. Further, as dance began to be considered a crucial component in the merged song/dance/text paradigm, it was given increased "artistic" weight, which facilitated a new degree of legitimacy and authority for the musical theatre choreographer. This development was exemplified by the influential and recognized work of Agnes de Mille and the aforementioned Robbins and Champion, along with other choreographic powerhouses such as Michael Kidd, Bob Fosse, Onna White, Helen Tamiris, and Hanya Holm.

Along with dance, the musical's libretto received a new degree of attention, treatment, and scrutiny during the Golden Age, moving from an often negligible, perfunctory, and formulaic device to a more potent and complex literary component (it is no coincidence that the musical won the Pulitzer Prize for Drama several times during this period). As a result, the musical libretto exemplified great diversity as it ran the gamut from mythic fantasy to folksy Americana to literary adaptation to urban-contemporary commentary. Regarding fantasy, musical theatre has always been a genre of escapist fare; and the Golden Age writers continued in this vein, often referencing or adapting famous literary sources as they took audiences on fantastical and imaginative adventures that included

goddesses, magical villages, leprechauns, devils, Arabian wizards, Lost Boys, fairy tales, and the legends of King Arthur (respectively, *One Touch of Venus, Brigadoon, Finian's Rainbow, Damn Yankees, Kismet, Peter Pan, Once Upon a Mattress,* and *Camelot*). And as the writers of the musical became more adventurous in their subject matter, they also took the musical beyond America's borders. In short, the Golden Age musical went global as writers looked to other cultures and continents for their musical milieus and content (e.g., *Brigadoon, The King and I, My Fair Lady, Lost in the Stars, Fanny, Silk Stockings, Jamaica, Redhead, The Sound of Music, Irma La Douce, Milk and Honey,* and *Fiddler on the Roof*). This expansion of the musical, as it sought to extend beyond the shores of America, also included *The Boy Friend and Oliver!*. Both were hits that travelled from England to Broadway, predating the British musical invasion of the late 1970s and '80s.

This is not to suggest, however, that a more universal focus diminished the musical's longstanding and defining tradition of addressing its American identity and context/history. (In fact, many works placed in other lands still obliquely referenced American issues and ideologies.) Given the enormity of the national events and evolutions that occurred mid-century (e.g., World War II and the postwar recovery, as well as the country's move into modernity), the musical could not help but reflect such seismic sociopolitical and cultural shifts, as well as exploit a self-congratulatory climate, celebrating America's affirmed world power status. At the beginning of the Golden Age, the musical became a place of refuge and reflection with regard to the country's involvement in World War II. Although there were blackouts on Broadway, wartime America still found its way to the musical stage, both during the engagement and in the years that followed, with hits that included *This Is the Army, Follow the Girls, On the Town,* and *Call Me Mister*. In a blurring of fiction and reality, both *This is the Army* and *Call Me Mister* used real-life servicemen as performers in the shows (as well as ex-GIs and ex-USO performers, in the case of *Call Me Mister*). And as the 1940s came to an end, a musical set in World War II took Broadway by storm: *South Pacific*. This Pulitzer Prize-winner arrived four years after the War, allowing Americans a look backward, while bravely speaking to contemporary issues of race and bigotry.

Indeed, the self-reflective nature of the musical during the Golden Age entailed a great deal of looking back, as a number of musicals used the milieu of early America, with its Americana aesthetic, to showcase the folksy can-do spirit and strength of early Americans. Such works not only mythologized the nation's past, but also celebrated its current rise on the world stage. Beginning with *Oklahoma!*, this trend included successive hits such as *Bloomer Girl, Annie Get Your Gun, Paint Your Wagon, The Golden Apple, The Music Man, Destry Rides Again,* and *The Unsinkable Molly Brown.* This midcentury navel-gazing and mythologizing also fostered the biographical and metatheatrical musicals that came to prominence during the era. A selective list includes musicalized biographies such as *Annie Get Your Gun, The King and I, Gypsy, The Sound of Music, Fiorello!,* and *Funny Girl,* as well as a plethora of backstage musicals (including most of the aforementioned biographical works, as well as *Kiss Me, Kate; Me and Juliet; Mr. Wonderful; Flower Drum Song; Say, Darling;* and *Carnival*). Both categories canonized historical and iconic figures, while invoking the "no business like show business" ethos and again celebrating the American Dream and its promise of success for the enduring spirit. (Note that even the characters that were not American were still treated and viewed as embodiments of such attributes, appearing in works that promoted themes of American exceptionalism.) In a significant development, the Broadway theatre community inaugurated a means whereby it could officially celebrate itself and its artistry, establishing the Tony Awards in 1947. Given this new institution, musical theatre could now recognize, award, and canonize its works and artists, establishing its theatrical legitimacy and assert a documented history of achievement and esteem, while asserting its prominent and valid place in the American Dream machine.

Not all Golden Age portraits of America were of a mythologizing, self-congratulatory nature, however; for the nation was also experiencing domestic tensions and conflicts as it negotiated industrial growth and prosperity alongside new calls for equality by those who were still being denied their piece of the American pie. Accordingly, several significant musicals on Broadway during the Golden Age were set in contemporary times and included librettos that addressed such relevant topics as race/ethnicity, corporatism, youth culture, and gender. Some prescient productions (and soon-to-be canonical works) contained specific critiques and indictments of racism, predating and/or reflecting the burgeoning Civil Rights Movement, as well as examinations of America's "melting pot" paradigm. This roster includes *Finian's Rainbow, South Pacific, West Side Story, Flower Drum Song, No Strings,* and *Golden Boy.* The musical also took a probing and often satiric look at American capitalism, lampooning the country's corporatist culture in hit musicals such as *The Pajama Game, Do Re Mi,* and *How to Succeed in Business Without Really Trying.* The growing youth movement and its accompanying concept of a "generation gap" were addressed during the Golden Age, as some musicals made early attempts to speak to youthful conflicts, concerns, and crazes via works such as *West Side Story, Flower Drum Song,* and *Bye Bye Birdie.* Lastly, female characters became more than chirping ingénues and winking soubrettes as the musical began to look more closely at the experience of women in America (both historically and contemporaneously), while chronicling their trials and triumphs. Predating the Women's Liberation movement of the late 1960s, '70s, and '80s, some musicals featured spirited, self-determined, and idiosyncratic women who bucked traditional gender roles, struggling, strategizing, and most often succeeding, albeit on patriarchal terms, in a male-dominated world, e.g., *Lady in the Dark; On the Town; Bloomer Girl; Annie Get Your Gun; Kiss Me, Kate; Wonderful Town; Call Me Madam; Redhead; My Fair Lady; Once Upon a Mattress; Gypsy; Funny Girl;* and *Hello, Dolly!.*

As detailed above, this was the era in which the popularity of the revue waned while the integrated book musical took over. This does not suggest, however, that the predominance of the integrated musical play stifled experimentation in terms of form, sound, and structure on the Broadway stage. Early manifestations and suggestions of new musical forms also characterized the Golden Age, while the scores of such works were similarly diverse and innovative. These novel forms would not be fully realized at the time but asserted a wide range of possibilities for the genre going forward. They include the concept musical (e.g., *Allegro, Love Life,* and *Candide*); the sung-through musical and operatic musical (*Carmen Jones, The Golden Apple, Candide, The Most Happy Fella, Street Scene,* and *Lost in the Stars*); the dance musical (*Ballet Ballads, West Side Story*); the chamber musical (*She Loves Me* and *The Fantasticks*); and the rock 'n' roll musical (*Bye Bye Birdie*). And even though the good old musical comedy remained a Broadway staple, its form was further developed by artists who aspired to musical integration while experimenting with a blend of popular and classical sounds that would not only appeal to the ear but also develop characters and storylines. Thus, the musical comedy acquired an impressive degree of sophistication and smartness, with the form hitting new heights during the Golden Age, exemplified by works that have since been deemed some of the best in the canon: *On the Town*; *Kiss Me, Kate*; *Guys and Dolls*; *The Pajama Game*; *Damn Yankees*; *Bells Are Ringing*; *The Music Man*; *How to Succeed in Business Without Really Trying*; *A Funny Thing Happened on the Way to the Forum*; and *Little Me*, to name a few.

Ironically, it would be only a few years after *Fiddler on the Roof* that the musical theatre community would bemoan the death of the book musical (and its concurrent Golden Age), seeing the rise and import of the "concept musical" and other non-integrative forms. The mourners were not only rash, however, but wrong in their predictions and assumptions. To date, the integrated book musical is very much alive, while many of its most accomplished examples sired on Broadway from 1943–64 continue to reign on the musical stage. Such a current state of the industry and genre testifies to the timelessness of the Golden Age works, as well as the era's pervasive presence, relevancy, and power in American musical theatre.

RICHARD RODGERS AND OSCAR HAMMERSTEIN II

Richard Rodgers was often asked to name the first lyric given to him by Oscar Hammerstein II. He consistently cited the opening line of the groundbreaking 1943 musical that began their ascendant career on Broadway. The lyric is from "Oh, What a Beautiful Mornin'"; the musical is *Oklahoma!*. Whether it was actually the first contribution by Hammerstein to the Rodgers/Hammerstein oeuvre, the citation by Rodgers proved savvy and prescient, for rarely has one musical number so changed and influenced the entire musical theatre genre. Specifically, *Oklahoma!* defied conventional wisdom that a successful musical comedy should open with a lively chorus-line number performed by shapely chorines. Instead, a lone cowboy, Curly, begins *Oklahoma!* by singing a capella offstage. He saunters onto the stage (where a lone woman sits churning butter) and continues his waltz-tempo reverie, extolling the meadow, the corn, the cattle, and all that is good on a lovely, rural morning in Oklahoma Territory. Regardless of the fact that corn was not domestically grown in Oklahoma at the turn of the century, Hammerstein's poetry was riveting; and by the end of "Oh, What a Beautiful Mornin'," audiences could practically see the crop that reached up to an "elephant's eye." Similarly, Rodgers reported that he was so buoyed by the descriptive nature of Hammerstein's lines that he felt sweet, lyrical music pouring out of him, in symbiotic response to Hammerstein's sweet, lyrical language. The landmark number not only revolutionized the content/ structure of musical comedy, it also facilitated a career shift for Rodgers, as he reversed his previous method (with Hart) of writing music first and, instead, often composed music to Hammerstein's already written lyrics, with both men creating some of the most beloved, revolutionary, and enduring works in the musical theatre canon.

Rodgers may have spent the first two decades of his career in a successful partnership with Larry Hart, but he was also a colleague of Oscar Hammerstein II. They had worked together on the Varsity Shows at Columbia and their careers often crossed paths in the 1920s and '30s. Thus, it was not completely unanticipated when Rodgers joined with Hammerstein to write *Oklahoma!* (after Hart rejected the project). Coincidentally, the first Rodgers/Hammerstein collaboration was for the

Hammerstein with Rodgers (at piano), working on *Me and Juliet*, c. 1953 © Bettmann/CORBIS

Theatre Guild, the same producing entity that brought Rodgers/Hart to fame. Specifically, it was Guild producers Theresa Helburn and Lawrence Langner who proposed the idea to Rodgers of turning a twelve-year-old play by Lynn Riggs, *Green Grow the Lilacs*, into a musical. The Guild was in financial straits and needed another hit to redeem its reputation and bank balance. Likewise, Hammerstein had suffered a string of flops over the past decade and felt the pressure to revive his career by creating another significant work to serve as a worthy, yet belated, successor to *Show Boat*. Hammerstein was also excited to finally team with Rodgers, an artist of similar temperament, discipline, and experimental courage.

With Rodgers and Hammerstein on board, the Guild secured other prestigious talents, such as director Rouben Mamoulian, whose previous credits included *Porgy and Bess* (also for the Guild), and ballet choreographer Agnes de Mille. Investors were a little harder to find, but rehearsals finally began on what was soon to be a milestone musical. Most notable was the new degree of integration employed in *Oklahoma!*, for both Rodgers and Hammerstein were devoted to the idea of the "musical play," a construct that could best be realized and artistically rendered if all songs and dances were specific to character, reflective of place/ time, and served or advanced the plot. Rodgers and Hammerstein employed sophisticated song/dance/text integration while complicating a basic rural melodrama in which the hero, Curly, defeats the villainous Jud to win the hand of the ingénue, Laurey. For the most part,

Oklahoma!'s songs are not only integral to the action and specific to a dramatic scene (such as "People Will Say We're in Love," "Pore Jud," and "All er Nothin'"), they also provide moments of character development and elucidation (e.g., "I Cain't Say No," "Many a New Day," and "Lonely Room"). As opposed to much of the Rodgers/Hart oeuvre, Rodgers and Hammerstein steered away from the conventional use of generic numbers that could be interchangeably applied to any situation or character. Agnes de Mille contributed substantially to the paradigm. As a concert dance choreographer who had just come off a major success with her ballet *Rodeo* (1942), she used her ballet clout to promote dance as a substantial dramatic element in the show. In this regard, de Mille followed in the footsteps of Balanchine; however, she was also able to one-up the Rodgers/Hart choreographer by expanding the function of the dream ballet, choreographing an indispensable dance segment that probed the psychological, sexual struggle of Laurey, set in an elaborate Freudian dreamscape. Finally, as an example of Rodgers/Hammerstein's future writing philosophy and production dictum that the show must always come first, *Oklahoma!* had a cast of relatively new performers in the lead roles, with the show positioned as the ultimate star.

The new duo, however, was anything but confident that they had a "star show" on their hands. Originally titled *Away We Go* and receiving a tepid reception at its Boston tryout, Rodgers and Hammerstein renamed the musical *Oklahoma!* once they heard orchestrator Russell Bennett's stirring arrangement for an ensemble number, titled "Oklahoma," belatedly added to the second act. Still, the musical's advance notices were lukewarm. When *Oklahoma!* debuted on Broadway on March 31, 1943, audience members awaited the opening curtain with curiosities only slightly piqued. Then, as recounted by Hammerstein, the "magic" of theatre happened and one could feel a growing "glow" throughout the theatre as spectators warmed to the show, charmed by every component. Critics were also impressed, adding to the show's aura with glowing reviews in all New York papers the following day. In no time, *Oklahoma!* became an unprecedented box office smash and cultural phenomenon, ultimately running for 2,212 performances at a time when 500 performances denoted a hit.

Both Rodgers (40) and Hammerstein (47) were middle-aged when *Oklahoma!* made their partnership a hot new commodity on Broadway, as well as a household name throughout America. Indeed, the two artists found they were a winning team, complementary in their writing processes, work philosophies, and theatrical pursuits. Rodgers not only reversed his composing process but also evolved his overall compositions, in sound and scope, to reflect the sentimentality, poetry, and lyricism of Hammerstein's written material, with a new emphasis on classical sounds and techniques. The output of Rodgers in the second phase of his career progressively moved away from the swinging, jazzy tunes that epitomized the Rodgers and Hart catalogue; specifically, he increasingly embraced such operetta forms as the waltz (Rodgers is often deemed musical theatre's "waltz king"), while providing a more lush musical character and experimenting with the tonalities, sounds, and folk idioms of other world cultures. This multicultural aspect of Rodgers' work also created tension with regard to accompanying charges of cultural appropriation, with the term "appropriation" often framed as a pejorative by some theatre scholars, critics, and artists. In his attempt to incorporate music styles and sounds that effectively depicted and reflected a libretto's place and time, Rodgers often admitted that he did not feel the need to actually research and incorporate authentic tonal structures, idioms, and techniques from other cultures or races but felt it adequate to approximate and evoke such sounds using Western composition. For example, *South Pacific*, *The King and I*, and *Flower Drum Song* contain songs and musical interludes that merely evoke Asian idioms, but do not actually adhere to the technical structure and tonalities of East and Southeast Asian music. Yet Rodgers' compositions were revolutionary and bravely experimental in their use of untraditional sounds and melodies in the musical genre, regardless of their "authenticity," while also introducing a global sound (or an approximation thereof) to the previously insular American musical stage. Further, there were occasions when Rodgers was extraordinarily successful in this capacity; for instance, the sweetly simple "Edelweiss" from *The Sound of Music* was mistakenly thought by many to be an actual Austrian folk tune, much to Rodgers' ironic dismay, given that he wanted credit for having fashioned such a convincing folk variation.

In accord with Rodgers' evolution and experimentation, Hammerstein also fine-tuned and further developed his craft. The "poet amongst lyricists" continued to resist self-expressive plumage in his lyrics, sublimating any tendency toward cleverness for cleverness' sake. Instead, he wrote for character and situation, with lyrics reflecting personality, place, and time, while providing atmosphere and furthering the dramatic action. And echoing the paradox of Rodgers, Hammerstein went to great lengths to employ dialects and regional idiosyncrasies in his writing; yet, this attempt at authenticity sometimes confounded his best intentions. Specifically, such dialects were not authentically researched but were written as phonetic approximations, often employing negative clichés, e.g., pidginization in musicals such as *South Pacific*, *The King and I*, and *Flower Drum Song*. But when viewed through a historical, contextual lens, Hammerstein's aim may be seen as pure and positive. Given the glaring absence of non-Caucasian material in musical theatre during the team's heydays (1940s and '50s), Hammerstein was attempting to bring the voice of the "Other" to the musical stage, however crudely his linguistic approximations may appear today. Together, Rodgers and Hammerstein persisted in creating works redolent of Hammerstein's positive and sentimental worldview. Sometimes accused of "preaching," the duo unashamedly addressed humanist matters of inequity, conflict, and assimilation in every show, with their exploration of such sociocultural dynamics expanding from small-town Oklahoma to the larger global community. And while the emotional and sensory appeal of Rodgers' melodies and Hammerstein's poesy has been simultaneously revered and criticized by the musical theatre community, the artists themselves had confidence in their work. Rodgers once quipped that there was nothing wrong with "sweetness and light" and asserted that the truths found in "clichés" are often appreciated by audiences. Similarly, Hammerstein stated that he was not interested in "kicking sentiment around" and, while he was a fan of satire, he never felt comfortable writing it. Yet both men were brave enough to challenge audiences with unconventional (and often subversive) subject matter and inconvenient truths, while using sweet melody and sentimental language to make a bitter pill easier to swallow and digest.

Curiously, the triumph of *Oklahoma!* was not enough to spur an exclusive teaming between Rodgers and Hammerstein, for they both resumed independent careers following the show: Rodgers rejoined Hart for a 1943 revival of *A Connecticut Yankee* and Hammerstein completed writing a new libretto and lyrics for *Carmen Jones* (1943). However, with Hart's untimely death, a cemented partnership between Rodgers and Hammerstein was all but inevitable. In search of new source material, the duo began looking at *Liliom*, a 1909 sentimental drama by Ferenc Molnar, which had been suggested to the men by Theresa Helburn. Although the team liked the prospects of the unconventional, somber play, they were concerned that Molnar's tragic ending would prove too depressing for Broadway. So Hammerstein reconfigured the story by adding a more hopeful, redemptive ending. He also moved the play from Budapest to a small mill and fishing village on the New England coast, morphing the rural Americana of *Oklahoma!* into the saltwater, early industrial Americana of the East Coast. The new work, titled *Carousel*, was also produced by the Guild—as was *Oklahoma!*—with Mamoulian and de Mille again hired as director and choreographer. Yet, *Carousel*'s story is a departure from the corn-fed cheeriness of *Oklahoma!*, for it deals with the destructive actions of an antihero, along with themes of domestic abuse, death, and the afterlife. In short, *Carousel* centers on the ill-fated romance and marriage between a rakish carnival barker, Billy Bigalow, and an innocent young woman, Julie Jordan. After Billy is killed in a botched robbery, leaving Julie pregnant and alone, he attempts to redeem his mortal failings by returning to earth and helping his daughter, who has become a lonely and ostracized teen. In their second project, Rodgers and Hammerstein furthered their attempts at compositional integration and sophistication, introducing new score devices to further plot, evoke mood and tone, and reveal characters' psyches and motivations. Specifically, with Billy's "Soliloquy," the team created a merger of active song and musical monologue in which a character moves through a gamut of emotions, dramatically grappling with a dilemma, challenge, and/or choice, while an internal turmoil is externalized in song (Billy actively wrestles with the prospects of fatherhood). In the "Bench Scene," Rodgers and Hammerstein created an amalgamation of self-contained dramatic scene and musical number in which an operatic quasi love song between Billy and Julie, titled "If I Loved You," is interspersed with underscored dialogue, ultimately ending with a climactic kiss to signal the coupling of the two mismatched characters. In addition to the expansive compositions of "Soliloquy" and the "Bench Scene," the overall score of

Carousel is deemed by many to be Rodgers' most complex and lush, often employing operetta and classical stylings and forms, with solemn anthems placed alongside up-tempo ensemble numbers. *Carousel* opened on April 19, 1945, at the Majestic Theatre (across the street from the St. James Theatre where *Oklahoma!* was still running) and was a box office success, proving that even the most unorthodox material could be "sweetened" by the sounds and sentiments of Rodgers and Hammerstein.

Encouraged and, possibly, emboldened by their unconventional triumphs on Broadway, Rodgers and Hammerstein decided to push the envelope even further with their next Theatre Guild production: *Allegro* (1947). Although the show proved to be the team's first disappointment, it represented an artistic leap in many respects. First, the production was directed by Agnes de Mille, marking the first time that a woman was put at the helm of a Broadway musical, although Hammerstein reportedly helped stage some of the book scenes, due to the scale of the production. Second, the libretto was not an adaptation of already-written material but was, instead, an original book by Hammerstein (a first for the duo). For *Allegro*, he created a modern-day morality tale that spans the life of a 35-year-old doctor who leaves his small town to embark on a city career where he is slowly corrupted by money and success. After the final disillusionment of his wife's extramarital affair, the doctor moves back to his town to resume his modest medical practice, chagrined and newly committed to serve others. Although *Allegro's* book seemed trite to many, the show itself was innovative in performance concept and staging. Specifically, instead of representational sets, there were large abstract playing areas (such as revolves and platforms) for the many scenes/locales and ensemble numbers. Further, the actors played their characters as children as well as adults, and a contemporary Greek chorus commented on the action, as well as the tragic fall of the doctor/hero (redolent of classical Greek tragedy). The undertaking was immense. When both critics and audiences were lukewarm to the production, resulting in a disappointing run of 315 performances, Rodgers and Hammerstein partially blamed de Mille. The duo suggested in later accounts that she did not serve the material as well as they had hoped (although Hammerstein also conceded that his libretto may have been a bit too preachy and unwieldy). It would be the last

time the three worked together. Coincidentally, the next Rodgers and Hammerstein project contained very little choreographed dance—a departure from their previous shows. Yet the work did not apparently suffer from its lack of formal choreography, for it was a lyrical journey of sweeping sentiment and emotion, as well as one of Rodgers and Hammerstein's most tightly organized and potent "message" productions: *South Pacific* (1949).

Before the development of *South Pacific*, Rodgers and Hammerstein had become producers, as well as writers, forming their own production and publishing company. Soon they established a successful track record in this capacity (e.g., *Annie Get Your Gun*). Going forward, Rodgers and Hammerstein would produce (or co-produce) all of their works, making a reality of Rodgers' youthful vow to retain as much control over his properties as possible. In this respect, Rodgers remained hands-on with his productions throughout his career, as both producer and composer, often travelling with the shows to oversee rehearsals and out-of-town tryouts. *South Pacific* was the first Rodgers and Hammerstein creation to be co-produced by the team, but the idea to turn James Michener's *Tales of the South Pacific* (1947) into a musical originated with director Josh Logan (based on a suggestion made by a friend who had rejected the property for film adaptation). Logan then approached producer Leland Hayward who liked the idea and thought that the unusual subject matter would be a good fit for Rodgers and Hammerstein. They agreed, signing on as both the writers and co-producers with Hayward. Logan would direct the production, while assisting Hammerstein with the libretto (thus, Logan is also credited as co-author). The collaborators decided to combine two Michener tales, both of which concern Americans stationed on a Polynesian island during World War II and their romantic entanglements with the island inhabitants. The musical's main love story involves a U.S. Navy nurse, Nellie Forbush, and a French plantation owner on the island, Emile de Becque, while its subplot depicts a star-crossed affair between an American lieutenant, Joe Cable, and an indigenous Polynesian girl, Liat.

Rodgers envisioned an expansive score for the production that would reflect both musical comedy and opera/operetta, the first being emblematic of the earthy, all-American Seabees and Nellie, while the second underpinning the conflicted Nellie/Emile love affair and the ill-fated Cable/Liat romance (reminiscent of *Madame Butterfly*). Thus reflecting the two musical worlds on stage, the production team cast musical comedy star Mary Martin as Nellie and opera star (and Broadway newbie) Ezio Pinza as Emile. Given the disparate casting, Rodgers and Hammerstein created songs that were especially suited to character, with vocal styles varying accordingly. For example, Nellie sings up-tempo show tunes such as "I'm Gonna Wash That Man Right Outa My Hair" and "A Wonderful Guy," while Emile operatically expresses his emotions through arias (e.g., "This Nearly Was Mine" and "Some Enchanted Evening"). The Seabees entertain with comic numbers such as "There Is Nothin' Like a Dame." All the while, multicultural approximations color the proceedings, especially the haunting and minor-toned "island" folk song, "Bali Ha'i" (which was reportedly written by Rodgers during a lunch break). In operetta fashion, Cable is also given songs that reflect his romantic nature, such as the lyrical "Younger Than Springtime"; yet he also sings one of the most pointed and controversial songs in the show. The significance of the song lies in the fact that *South Pacific* is more than its two love stories, for both relationships are complicated by issues of race and racism. Nellie, who refers to herself as a naive gal from Little Rock, can't accept that Emile has two mulatto children and breaks off their relationship. Cable anguishes over the fact that it would not be feasible to marry Liat and bring her back to the States. Both racially charged plot complications are highlighted by Cable's fevered rendering of "Carefully Taught" [see fig. 5.1], in which he exposes and laments the ingrained and learned roots of racism. The song was considered incendiary by some Broadway investors who pleaded with Hammerstein to cut it during out-of-town tryouts. Hammerstein, however, wouldn't pull or revise it, feeling that it contained the main theme of the show, as well as a personal plea to humankind to recognize racism and other forms of intolerance as learned behaviors that can be eliminated with enlightenment, resolve, and compassion. The brief song still stands as one of the most potent elucidations of Hammerstein's humanist worldview in terms of the dangers and costs of bigotry. Regardless of Hammerstein's belief in the merits and mission of the song, "Carefully Taught" continued to be a sore spot for some audiences during *South Pacific*'s run, especially when the show toured the country. The song, the production, and its creators were pointedly denounced in 1953 on the floor of Georgia's State Legislature as promoting interracial marriage and "impure blood lines"; in addition, the legislators tried to ban performances of the song when it played Atlanta theaters.

Regardless of the controversy, most audience members loved *South Pacific*, which is all the more surprising given that the work contained an ending that reminded a country still smarting from World War II of the dark realities and costs of war. Specifically, in a tragic plot twist, Cable is killed while on a special military mission with Emile. Along happier lines, however, Nellie tends to Emile's children while he is gone, and he returns to find that she has not only bonded with them but is also ready to further her relationship with Emile. Embracing the tears and smiles at the end of the production, audiences rewarded *South Pacific* with an outstanding run of 1,925 performances. The Broadway production held the record for largest box office gross until 1956's *My Fair Lady*, while also generating a best-selling cast album and garnering the 1950 Pulitzer Prize for Drama, becoming the second musical to win the award.

Having demonstrated that a musical dealing with serious racial and cultural issues and set in an exotic non-Western locale could succeed not only artistically but also financially on Broadway, Rodgers and Hammerstein once again embarked on a "world musical" project that highlighted Eastern/Western disparities. In addition, the work provided a teaching moment with regard to tolerance, understanding, communication, multiculturalism, humanism, and the power of love. For this new production, *The King and I* (1951), Rodgers and Hammerstein travelled back in time to nineteenth-century Bangkok (then known as Siam), musically adapting Margaret Landon's *Anna and the King of Siam* (1944). Landon's novel is a biographical account of British widow Anna Leonowen and her time spent in Siam during the 1860s as governess and court teacher to the children of King Mongkut. The idea to create a musical version of the novel was suggested to Rodgers and Hammerstein by musical theatre star Gertrude Lawrence (after Kurt Weill and Cole Porter turned down the idea); Lawrence also felt she would be perfect in the role of Anna. Rodgers and Hammerstein agreed to not only write the show but, as was now their custom, to produce it, inspired by its universal theme of multiculturalism as shown through the microcosm of a specific, intimate human relationship. With Lawrence already cast as Anna and John van Druten hired as director, the team searched for the perfect actor to play King Mongkut. They ultimately found a charismatic, little-known actor of Russian lineage named Yul Brynner. Lawrence balked at Rodgers and Hammerstein's revised title for the musical, which gave the King first billing. Ironically, with the casting of Brynner, she would find herself taking a secondary role as she was overshadowed by the novice actor. Brynner put his indelible stamp on the role, playing it throughout his life and winning an Academy Award for the 1956 film version. (Sadly, Gertrude Lawrence struggled with health problems during the Broadway run and ultimately had to be replaced, succumbing to liver cancer before the show closed.)

When *The King and I* debuted on March 29, 1951, it was enthusiastically received by audience members and critics alike, ultimately running for 1,246 performances. The success was not unexpected given the appeal of the score and the show's elaborate scenery and costumes. Nonetheless, given the unconventional relationship at its core, the musical's long-lived popularity is also testament to Rodgers and Hammerstein's mastery of sophisticated, nuanced drama. In an interesting twist, *The King and I* expanded the concept of Hammerstein's quasi love song into a quasi love musical. Specifically, the writers recounted that one of the biggest challenges of *The King and I* was how to dramatize the "intangibility" of the feelings between the king and Anna, especially as the couple emotionally evolves from mutual irritation and puzzlement to softened moments of discovery, respect, and most possibly, love. Thus, Rodgers and Hammerstein could not write traditional love songs for the leads, or even quasi love songs, but had to obliquely suggest the possibility of romance between the two. Such creative maneuvering is highlighted in "Shall We Dance?," a highly charged song and dance scene in which Anna's waist is potently encircled by the king as she teaches him a Western polka. Further, instead of love ballads, the intensity of the couple's feelings is most often relayed through "frustration" songs—"A Puzzlement" and "Shall I Tell You What I Think of You?"—both of which are composed in *Sprechstimme* fashion (i.e., musicalized speech), circumventing the romantic suggestion of a sweetly sung Rodgers melody, but still implying passion.

Of course, the production was not completely without sentiment and romantic numbers, for more overt declarations and addresses of love are supplied in operetta style by star-crossed, adulterous lovers Tuptim and Lun Tha (e.g., "We Kiss in a Shadow"). And when Anna threatens to leave the court, unable to accept some of the more autocratic and barbaric actions of the king, an older wife, Lady Thiang, sings one of the more lush love songs in the score, "Something Wonderful," extolling the complicated nature and virtues of the king and ultimately persuading Anna to stay. With Anna's decision to remain at court, she outlives the king and sees not only his son's succession but also the boy's desire to implement some of the democratic principles she has instilled in him. (One must also appreciate the authorial courage of Hammerstein to repeatedly kill off lead characters in his librettos.) In addition to the tuneful and diverse score, Rodgers and Hammerstein reemployed dance in *The King and I*, collaborating again with a recognized concert ballet choreographer, Jerome Robbins. One of the most theatrical and potent numbers in the show is "The Small House of Uncle Thomas," a metatheatrical ballet rendition of Harriet Beecher Stowe's *Uncle Tom's Cabin* (1952). In this elaborate and lengthy narrative dance segment, Stowe's tale is reinterpreted and presented by Siamese court performers under the direction of Anna for the king's British visitors. Using a variety of Asian dance idioms and theatre techniques, the ballet metaphorically addresses the evils of slavery and, thus, the king's own abuses of power, reiterating the show's overall humanist theme.

Although *The King and I* was another triumph for Rodgers and Hammerstein (the fourth longest running show of the 1950s), the duo suffered a couple of surprising failures in the years that followed. First, *Me and Juliet* (1953), with an original libretto by Hammerstein that features a backstage relationship triangle during a theatrical performance, merited an unsatisfactory run of only 358 performances. Their next venture, *Pipe Dream* (1955), proved even more disappointing. The libretto, based on a John Steinbeck novel, takes an affectionate look at a skid row community in Monterrey, California. The Broadway production, however, missed with audiences and only lasted for 246 performances. As the decade came to a close, however, Rodgers and Hammerstein regained their footing and enjoyed several more hits. In 1957, Rodgers and Hammerstein explored a new medium, creating a musical version of

Cinderella for television. The production was originally broadcast live on CBS as a vehicle for Julie Andrews, who played the title role. The musical was seen by over 100 million people and proved to be so popular that it was subsequently expanded and remade for television twice, in 1965 and 1997, and was ultimately adapted for the stage. The next year, they teamed with librettist Joseph Fields to write and co-produce *Flower Drum Song* (1958). Fields initially acquired the rights to the 1957 novel *Flower Drum Song,* by Chin Y. Lee, and brought the idea to Rodgers and Hammerstein. Once on board, the team created a work that comically and sentimentally highlights the generational gap between older, established Chinese-Americans in San Francisco's Chinatown and the younger American-born residents who are eager to assimilate and put aside old world rules and customs. Set amid this generational and cultural conflict is the predicament of Mei Li, a "picture bride" who has been brought to San Francisco to marry an "Americanized" nightclub owner, Sammy Fong. Comedy ensues as Fong finds Mei Li to be too traditional for him; further, he is enamored with his nightclub star, the sassy and modern Linda Low. All ends well, however, when Wang Ta, friend of Fong, falls for the timidity and old-fashioned charms of Mei Li. Directed by Gene Kelly, the production played 600 performances at the St. James Theatre, due in great part to an ear-pleasing and diverse score, which includes easily digestible Orientalist approximations by Rodgers (e.g., "A Hundred Million Miracles"), as well as catchy tunes that reflect not only the production's nightclub milieu but also the modish, assimilated attitudes of the younger Chinese-American generation. Such numbers include the bubbly, syncopated "I Enjoy Being a Girl," a midcentury celebration of modern (for late 1950s) femininity, which became another popular hit for the team.

After the successes of '57 and '58, Rodgers and Hammerstein began work on a new project. However, both men were battling health problems. Rodgers had had to have a cancerous portion of his jaw removed in 1955. In 1959, Hammerstein was diagnosed with incurable stomach cancer. Thus, *The Sound of Music* (1959) was a bittersweet victory for the team, ending the decade on a career high note, yet proving to be the final work in their canon (and the last of Hammerstein's thirty-five Broadway productions). Although not considered their greatest artistic achievement, the work scored highly with audiences, running for 1,443 performances (the second longest running show of the decade). In many ways, *The Sound of Music* is another overt representation and fitting culmination of Hammerstein's sentimental, sincere, and socially conscious artistry. As most of Hammerstein's works bespeak his integral belief in the worth and innate goodness of humankind, *The Sound of Music* stands as a living testament to his hopeful and determined spirit, for he wrote much of the material as he battled his terminal illness and faced death, dying only nine months after the show opened. Thus, it is difficult to read the simple sentiments of "Edelweiss," his final lyrics, and not hear Hammerstein's voice espousing life's small beauties, while affirming the possibilities of transformation and regeneration.

As was often the case throughout their partnership, Rodgers and Hammerstein were not the initial instigators behind the creation of *The Sound of Music.* Having been impressed by Maria Von Trapp's autobiography, *The Trapp Family Singers*, and its German film adaptation, director Vincent J. Donehue believed that a Broadway musical adaptation would serve as an ideal star vehicle for audience favorite Mary Martin. Martin not only agreed but brought her husband, producer Richard Halliday, to the project; he teamed with Leland Hayward to co-produce the show. Originally, Halliday and Hayward intended to compile a score using actual folk songs that had been performed by the Von Trapps, but they also asked Rodgers and Hammerstein if they would supply a few numbers. The duo bristled at the idea of trying to merge their original compositions with the folk numbers, opting, instead, to write a completely original score to suit the libretto (supplied by Howard Lindsey and Russel Crouse). In addition to writing the score, they became co-producers with Halliday and Hayward. The resulting musical is set in Salzburg, Austria, just before the Nazi occupation (1938) and presents a novice, Maria Rainer, who initially causes concern in her Abbey due to her free spirit and adventurous nature. The Mother Abbess sends Maria to serve as a governess to seven difficult, love-starved children; in addition, she must deal with their stern, widowed father, Captain Georg Von Trapp. With determination, empathy, and song, she wins their affections and reunites children and father, as well as uncovers their musical talents (all is portrayed through signature numbers such as "Do-Re-Mi," "So Long, Farewell," "Edelweiss," and "The Lonely Goatherd"). In the process, Maria falls in love with Georg, inciting a personal crisis, given her vows.

However, Mother Abbess ultimately gives the romance her blessing through the song "Climb Ev'ry Mountain," an inspirational anthem that implores one to surmount obstacles in pursuit of hopes and dreams. The second half of the musical details the travails of the family as they confront the new reality of Nazi occupation, especially troubling given Georg's refusal to serve under the new regime. Instead, the family orchestrates an escape from the country; and under the cover of a concert performance at a celebrated Austrian music festival, they flee in the dark of night over the Alps into the neutral haven of Switzerland. Although audiences rewarded the heartwarming and triumphant tale with a healthy box office, the theatre critics were not as impressed, describing it as traditional and saccharine. Yet, this "high brow" drubbing did not consider some of the more innovative musical aspects of *The Sound of Music*, such as its use of "Preludium" (an alleluia chorus) performed a capella by the nuns as the production's opening number, as well as songs throughout the production that so closely replicate Austrian folk music as to be cited as such by uninformed reviewers. In addition, the stage musical includes social critiques such as "No Way to Stop It," a troubling, yet clear-eyed, argument for Nazi collaboration by close associates of George, musically highlighting the tricky (and revolutionary, for its time) Nazi subject matter at the center of the show. Critical swipes notwithstanding, the wildly popular and Academy Award–winning film version in 1965 with Julie Andrews ensured the work's place as the most renowned in the Rodgers and Hammerstein canon.

After Hammerstein's death, Rodgers never found a third exclusive partner but, instead, worked for the first time as both composer and lyricist for *No Strings* (1962), a daring experiment predicated on the musical premise of no strings, with mostly brass and woodwinds in the orchestration. The production put the instrumental combo on stage, while having cast members move set pieces and change scenery, all of which supported an equally daring libretto by playwright Samuel Taylor. The story centers on an affair between an African American high fashion model (a role designed for up-and-coming star Diahann Carroll) and an expatriate white novelist living the bohemian life in Monte Carlo. Critics rewarded the innovations, and the show ran for 580 performances. Future works by Rodgers would not fare as well, however; ill-fated collaborations included *Do I Hear a Waltz?* (1965) with lyricist Stephen Sondheim, *Rex* (1976) with lyricist Sheldon Harnick, and a 1979 musical version of John Van Druten's *I Remember Mama* with lyricist Martin Charnin (the original play was produced by Rodgers and Hammerstein in 1944). Unfortunately, Rodgers was never to recreate his earlier stage successes in his later years; yet, his contributions to popular music and theatre were revered and celebrated up until his death on December 30, 1979, at age 77. With the theatre's (and America's) loss of Richard Rodgers, the import and impressiveness of his legendary career were even more evident, especially given his longtime partnerships, which helped create the American songbook, while defining and revolutionizing the Broadway musical during the Golden Age. Cole Porter was once asked to name the most significant evolution in American musical theatre and his answer was, reportedly, "Rodgers and Hammerstein." Porter's case is hard to refute, for the men were true revolutionaries, rooted in and bound by their integral belief in the sociocultural function, transformational potential, and artistic power of musical theatre. Thus, they fully believed in and backed the integrity and sincerity of their Broadway works. During rehearsals of *The Sound of Music*, Mary Martin, along with producers Halliday and Hayward, thought it might be funny if she, as Maria, climbed a tree in the opening scene and, as a sight gag, had her bloomers catch on branches when she jumped down. Rodgers and Hammerstein vetoed the gratuitous moment, which seemed to serve the star more than the story. In argument, Halliday and Hayward testily declared that the writers' "problem" was that nothing else mattered to them but the show. Little did the producers know that in the eyes of Rodgers and Hammerstein, no greater praise could have been given.

Figure 5.1

CAREFULLY TAUGHT

Music by Richard Rodgers
Lyrics by Oscar Hammerstein II (1949)

You've got to be taught to hate and fear,
You've got to be taught from year to year,
It's got to be drummed in your dear little ear –
You've got to be carefully taught!

You've got to be taught to be afraid
Of people whose eyes are oddly made,
And people whose skin is a different shade –
You've got to be carefully taught.

You've got to be taught before it's too late,
Before you are six or seven or eight,
To hate all the people your relatives hate –
You've got to be carefully taught!
You've got to be carefully taught!

FEATURED PRODUCTION: *Oklahoma!* (1943)

Music by Richard Rodgers; Lyrics and Book by Oscar Hammerstein II

Original Broadway Run: Opened March 31, 1943; St. James Theatre; 2,212 performances

Lynn Riggs' rural drama, *Green Grow the Lilacs*, had been a modest stage success for the Theatre Guild in 1930. But that was when the Guild was a leading and lucrative player in New York's theatre scene. By the early 1940s, however, the Guild had suffered a string of setbacks, reducing its bank account to a paltry $30,000. Consequently, Guild producers Theresa Helburn and Lawrence Langner gambled heavily on Rodgers and Hammerstein (partnering for the first time) to turn Riggs' material into a musical hit that would keep the Theatre Guild solvent and reassert its artistic credentials. Unfortunately, investors were not lining up at the door, regardless of the sterling résumés of the musical's creative team, which included not only top composer Rodgers and greatly respected lyricist/librettist Hammerstein but also seasoned director Rouben Mamoulian, who had courageously tackled the Guild's *Porgy and Bess*, and celebrated concert choreographer Agnes de Mille. The common wisdom in the musical theatre community was that neither the content nor construct of the new project, originally titled *Away We Go*, held much promise. Specifically, "no gags, no gals, no chance" was the legendary assessment made by industry insiders and repeated in musical theatre circles before the show's Broadway debut. However, those who did gamble on the Rodgers and Hammerstein production reaped great rewards, for one estimate holds that a comparably modest investment in *Oklahoma!* of $1,000 ultimately earned its investor a whopping $2.5 million. In another regard, the investment in and support of the new musical may have been priceless, given its soon-to-be milestone status in the musical theatre genre.

While it is true that *Oklahoma!* does not exploit gals and gags, the production features a warm and folksy plot with romantic, melodramatic underpinnings—a formula that should have been foreseen as a winner, given the American audience's fondness for melodrama and romantic operettas. However, hindsight is always 20/20; and naysayers may have been blinded by the work's unconventional rural milieu and the insistence of Rodgers and Hammerstein (as well as director Mamoulian and choreographer de Mille) that the work feature no stars; be tightly integrated, with no interpolated, stand-alone songs; and feature integral, intricate dance numbers. With *Oklahoma!*, all parts were designed to serve the whole. First, as previously detailed, the musical begins with a soaring vocal line sung offstage by its cowboy hero, Curly. Further, the simple opening contains no splashy chorus line or "I Am" number but, instead, consists of "Oh, What a Beautiful Mornin'," rendered solely by Curly, accompanied by the silent pantomime of Aunt Eller churning butter. From this evocative and unprecedented beginning, the original Broadway production continued to surprise and challenge audiences in the way it merged formulaic melodramatic components (that is, a sardonic hero, a virginal ingénue, and an antisocial villain, in romantic/moral conflict) with a newly tightened and dramatic musical treatment of the material. The libretto itself had little to say, basically presenting a teasing romance between Curly and the headstrong farm girl, Laurey, a coupling complicated by seedy farmhand Jud and his attempt to take Laurey to the box social. Instead of directly spelling out the Curly/Laurey relationship for the audience, however, Rodgers and Hammerstein provided character-driven duets early in the production to playfully inform audiences of the couple's romantic inclinations (even though, in a nuanced treatment, the characters themselves did not seem to recognize or overtly declare such feelings). The numbers included "Surrey with the Fringe on the Top" and the quasi love song "People Will Say We're in Love."

In another effective move, Rodgers and Hammerstein used secondary couples and supporting characters to enhance the drama and add color, supplying humor as well as gravitas. In a bold shift away from the weak, foolish, or shrewish stock matron, Aunt Eller is presented as the wise and warm matriarch of the community, a voice of reason and authority who runs her own farm and facilitates the eventual union of Laurey and Curly. On an even more serious and complex note, Jud's internal turmoil is explored and explained in the oppressive, minor-toned "Lonely Room," through which he moves from traditional, clichéd villain to socially and psychologically tortured and sympathetic victim. (It is also important to note that Jud is killed as an act of poetic justice at the end of *Oklahoma!* when his violent nature and actions come in direct conflict with the overall safety and health of the community.) As the comic sidekicks, Ado Annie and Will Parker provide bawdy humor, with the character of Ado reconfiguring the female sidekick as a winning ingénue with an active libido and sexual power (a noted departure from sexual innuendo being relegated to male sidekicks at the time). In song, Ado charms with her unapologetic homage to the fickle joys and temptations of carnal pleasure in "I Cain't Say No" and outwits Will in "All er Nuthin'." (Interestingly, Ado is written as a nondescript wallflower character in Riggs' original play and was given her libido and extroverted character by Hammerstein.) Similar to Eller and Ado, Laurey is presented as a contrast to the typical ingénue. Not only does she have an independent spirit, as evidenced in "Many a New Day," but she is also a complicated young woman torn by carnal urges. This groundbreaking contribution to Laurey's characterization was provided by de Mille. The choreographer was very familiar with Freudian analysis; and when Hammerstein proposed to her his libretto concept for the ballet in which Laurey visits the circus in a dream, de Mille firmly resisted the idea. Instead, de Mille insisted that the dream ballet address Laurey's ambivalence regarding her virginal, romanticized ideal of love (represented by Curly) and her repressed curiosity about and desire for sex (represented by Jud). The segment evolved into an extended psychoanalysis of Laurey in which she is tormented by and torn between the two worlds. The ballet set a new standard for dance sequences in musicals, while providing a sophisticated metaphor for personal and social ideals. Such conflicts are resolved at the musical's end, as Laurey realizes her ideal romance with Curly, territorial residents embrace the ideal of American statehood, and Jud is punished, through death, for his sins against the ideal of an ethical, cohesive community.

E. Faye Butler as Aunt Eller in Arena Stage production of *Oklahoma!* Courtesy of Arena Stage.

Ironically, *Oklahoma!* may have attempted an integrationist ideal, in that all songs were dependent upon the show's context and content, but Rodgers and Hammerstein's score was so engaging that many of its songs quickly became popular radio hits, with "People Will Say We're in Love" hitting #1 in 1943. Further, the production itself became a cultural sensation, with an unprecedented run of sold-out performances, inspiring national jokes about the impossibility of getting tickets to the Broadway show. In terms of street influence, de Mille's dream ballet inspired a popular fad in which wide petticoat skirts with ballerina slippers became a fashion statement throughout the country. Most significant, in terms of contemporary significance and American import, *Oklahoma!* arrived on Broadway when the country was in the midst of World War II, a time when anxious citizens were yearning for signs and affirmations of American exceptionalism. Thus, *Oklahoma!*'s Broadway run could not have been more serendipitous and semiotic, given the show's exploitation of Americana, nostalgia, and national identity. When the cast, in full voice, extolled the virtues of achieving statehood in the inspirational rendition of "Oklahoma" in Act II, audiences at the time could not help but be reminded of who they were as Americans, where they had come from, and what they were fighting for on a global front. And in another significant development, special Broadway performances of *Oklahoma!* were held for soldiers on leave, with those who couldn't get tickets smuggled into the wings, standing three and four deep in the limited backstage space (against the theater's fire code). Tellingly, de Mille often recounted those electric performances in which she would survey the audience of young fighting men, who reacted to the rousing strains of the title song with tears streaming down their cheeks. All of America seemed to be similarly taken with the rich and engaging score, so much so that it was recorded on 78 rpm discs, becoming one of the first recordings of a Broadway cast album for public consumption. In addition to receiving a special, belated Pulitzer Prize in 1944, the show also held the record for longest running Broadway show until *My Fair Lady* (1956) surpassed it thirteen years later. In short, the gamble made by Rodgers, Hammerstein, Mamoulien, de Mille, and the Theatre Guild more than paid off, for the work not only became a momentous turning point in musical theatre history but has also proved to be timeless as it continues to be revived as a twenty-first-century favorite by theatre companies and treasured by contemporary audiences.

PULLING BACK THE CURTAIN:

Orchestrators and Arrangers:
"Unsung" Heroes of the Musical Theatre

As detailed earlier in this section, Rodgers and Hammerstein did not think of changing *Away We Go*'s title to *Oklahoma!* until they heard Russell Bennett's stirring musical arrangement of a last-minute song addition to the second act, "Oklahoma." Given this telling anecdote, one might ask, "Who was this Russell Bennett?" Further, how could the musical tinkering of a man whose name is virtually unknown by the wider public have had such sway with musical theatre giants such as Rodgers and Hammerstein? In answer, Russell Bennett was the greatest orchestrator of his time, often referred to as the "dean of Broadway orchestration" and belonged to a significant group of musical theatre collaborators known as orchestrators and arrangers. These musical artists are, in great part, responsible for almost every signature sound heard on the Broadway stage. To briefly define these artists and their duties, the **arranger** is the musician who expands and/or completes a simple song notation or suggestion of a melody by introducing harmonies, embellishments, riffs, repeats, syncopations, meter variations, countermelodies/contrapuntal devices, and accompaniment (piano) arrangements. He or she may also devise and design interpolations, reprises, leitmotifs, dance music, underscoring, and other connective tissue that comprise a fully realized score. The **orchestrator** then takes the completed arrangements and sets them for instrumentation, often continuing in the vein of the arranger by adding embellishments, riffs, repeats, syncopations, et al. In the process, orchestrators use instruments as dramatic and visceral communicators, to bespeak place/time/atmosphere (e.g., a slide trombone or brassy trumpet may depict a seedy locale or suggest the jazz era); character psyches, emotions, and relations (e.g., lush strings may intensify a love ballad or romantic scene); or a scene's tone/mood (e.g., the low wail of an oboe can evoke loneliness or somberness). Lastly, orchestrations may also inform and influence stage performances of songs and musical numbers; for example, drums reinforce rhythms for dancers (highlighting the choreography), other instruments may double vocal lines to aid a singer and/or strengthen the power of a song's melodic hook. One need only comprehend the import of the orchestrator and his or her orchestrations by listening to a well-loved musical in simple piano form, minus its orchestral color and nuance. For instance, original cast members of *Kiss Me, Kate* recounted that they despaired the lackluster quality of Cole Porter's score during rehearsals until they heard the first orchestrations by Russell Bennett; it was then that they felt *Kate* was something special.

The place and role of the orchestrator/arranger in the musical theatre genre is difficult to address, however, as composers of canonical Broadway musicals are revered alongside their works. Thus, there is difficulty in admitting that the work's *complete* musical tapestry is not the product of its "acclaimed" composer but, instead, may belong to a team of other artists. While this compositional paradigm is not exactly a secret, the extent and significance of the orchestrator/arranger's work on Broadway is not well known by many outside the industry. Specifically, most of the iconic names during the musical theatre's Golden Age wrote only the basic tunes of their iconic songs (and some just whistled or hummed them). Then they delivered the melodic refrains or "lead sheets" (the melodies simply notated on paper with possibly some roughly drafted harmonies) to others to be expanded, arranged, orchestrated, and otherwise crafted into complete compositions ready for the stage. The prevalence of this practice was mostly a consequence of musical theatre's evolution, because at the turn of century, the musical arena was roughly divided into two camps. First, there were the highly popular operetta composers who came out of classical schools and orchestrated most of their own compositions (such as Victor Herbert). Next, there were the untrained composers of genres such as vaudeville, revues, and early musical comedies—artists who had never learned to read or write music but had instinctual talent for devising ear-catching songs (e.g., George M. Cohan and Irving Berlin). Tin Pan Alley was even more populated with these self-taught songsters who could plunk out a pleasing melody (or simply hum or whistle it) but were unversed in any sort of music theory or accomplished on any musical instrument, often hiring others to transcribe the notes to paper, add harmonies, arrange for vocals, and provide orchestration charts. In fact, there was actually a Tin Pan Alley term for these popular songwriters who played by ear and could roughly render their tunes in one key only: "fakers."

As the twentieth century progressed, the new working climate of the musical theatre industry became adversarial to the composer who tried to arrange and/or orchestrate his/her own works. With the advent of vaudeville voices on Broadway (versus classically trained singers), songs often had to be transposed to compensate for the performer's vocal limitations or idiosyncrasies, with little lead time. As the performers in integrated book musicals were required to not only sing but also act (and sometimes dance), songs frequently had to be transposed or rearranged to meet such special demands. As other collaborators (directors, producers, and choreographers) became more authorial and authoritative on Broadway, they started dictating changes to scores to meet their staging requirements, often during rehearsals and requiring immediate turn-around time. Due to these developments, scores were continuously revised, rearranged, and re-orchestrated. This was practically impossible for one artist to accomplish, given the tight rehearsal timelines and production deadlines. Thus, even the most accomplished composer necessarily relied on arrangers and orchestrators (sometimes, teams of such artists) to meet Broadway's demands. And given the expectation that songs/music be specific to time, place, character, and action, orchestrators and arrangers could no longer be hired guns with generic toolkits (that is, standard orchestrations sent by mail to composers with no explicit association to place or purpose in a show). Instead, these artists became more invested in the process and product, working in tandem with the composer, trying to make their work evocative, integrated, and communicative. In short, orchestrators and arrangers became not-so-silent partners in realizing the score and overall production on stage: the unsung heroes. To wit, here are some of these notable heroes and heroines, as well as some crucial historical and contextual facts regarding the art of orchestration and musical arrangement in the musical theatre genre.

As previously mentioned, **Robert Russell Bennett** (1894–1981) was the most esteemed and accomplished orchestrator and arranger of musical theatre's Golden Age (and beyond). He was preceded, however, by another pioneer: **Frank Saddler** (1864–1921). Saddler worked closely with Jerome Kern to orchestrate the Princess Theatre musicals, essentially creating the musical character of the staged works, thereby fueling scholastic arguments that Saddler's orchestrations and connective musical treatments should be noted alongside the writings of Kern, Bolton, and Wodehouse as crucial Princess Theatre innovations in musical theatre integration. Upon Saddler's death, Bennett became Kern's orchestrator, helping to realize Kern's most canonical works. For example, Bennett was often required to take down Kern's songs from piano renderings to provide voice and piano rehearsal arrangements. In a specific *Show Boat* anecdote, Bennett recounted that he was only given a rough thirty-two-bar melodic sketch of "Ol' Man River," sans title or lyrics. He didn't know what to do with the song until he received Hammerstein's lyrics; then Bennett was able to shape the song into its current form and arrangement. Bennett was uniquely qualified for his line of work; he was a classically trained musician with a natural ability to play and compose for multiple instruments. He also understood the culture of "fakers" and "two-fingered" composers on Broadway, as he had gotten his start in Tin Pan Alley, writing out accompaniments for lead sheets and supplementing his career by playing in orchestra pits and composing incidental music for Broadway plays. Soon, he became the crucial musical partner to almost every composer on Broadway, orchestrating some 300 shows from 1920–70. Bennett was not simply a worker behind the scenes; he was also a composer in his own right, with over 175 works to his credit: everything from symphonies to suites, operas and choral works. With regard to musical theatre, Bennett is the unaccredited genius behind some of the most canonical musical moments on Broadway. For instance, he composed and orchestrated *The King and I*'s well-known overture (in only twenty-five hours before the show's out-of-town preview) as well as the signature orchestral trio of three bass notes ("bum, bum, bum") to "Shall We Dance," which are used to punctuate the opening lines of the song. In addition to his long-term collaborations with Kern and Rodgers, Bennett worked with almost every other musical theatre legend (e.g., Berlin, Gershwin, and Porter) to develop, enhance, and complete their canonical scores.

Along with orchestrators such as Bennett, arrangers are also the go-to artists and craftsmen for most musical theatre composers when creating fully realized scores from song ideas and lead sheets. Emblematic of the symbiotic relationship between the composer and arranger is Cole Porter's longtime relationship with **Dr. Albert Sirmay**, a German expatriate and classically trained composer who spent much of his American career assisting Porter, supplying the harmonies and chord work (although, it is reported that Porter worked with other musicians who prepared his piano and vocal copies). Further, Simay was often at Porter's side as he edited his compositions. Simay acted as Porter's orchestral liaison, passing along his wishes and revisions to orchestrators and music directors. As another example, Irving Berlin relied on a series of arrangers who were often loyal and enterprising assistants and scribes. When one such fellow, **Will Irwin**, couldn't quite decipher a composition for *As Thousands Cheer*, as erratically played by Berlin on the piano, he suggested that Berlin just sing the song to him for transcription. Another longtime amanuensis, **Helmy Kresa**, transcribed Berlin's melodies as sung to him over the phone.

One of those orchestrators with whom Porter and Sirmay worked was **Hans Spialek** (1894–1983), the Austrian-born American who worked on 147 musicals, many in collaboration with Robert Russell Bennett. Primarily associated with Porter (12 musicals) and Rodgers & Hart (12 musicals), Spialek orchestrated such iconic productions as *The New Yorkers*, *Anything Goes*, *Stirke Up the Band*, *Pal Joey*, and *Where's Charley?*. Spialek was especially celebrated for his orchestrations for the ballets in *On Your Toes*, *The Boys from Syracuse*, and *Babes in Arms*. Many historians give Bennett and Spialek credit for creating the classic "Broadway sound" in the 1930s and '40s.

In addition to piano and instrumental arrangers, vocal arrangers have made a significant imprint on Broadway scores—artists such as **Hugh Martin**, who was responsible for putting down on paper the tricky harmonic vocals envisioned by Rodgers and Hart for "Sing for Your Supper" (*The Boys from Syracuse*), as well as **Herbert Greene**, who did many of the vocal arrangements for Frank Loesser (specifically, *Guys and Dolls* and *The Most Happy Fella*).

Another "arranger" is the dance arranger, who creates the musical montages (and sometimes original compositions) for the dance and extended movement segments of a production. In this capacity, one woman ruled Broadway for thirty years: **Trude Rittman** (1908–2005). This classically trained artist was Agnes de Mille's preferred dance accompanist and worked alongside Rodgers longer than Hammerstein, arranging much of his incidental and movement compositions. In addition, Rittman collaborated with other brilliant and trained composers such as Leonard Bernstein and Frederick Loewe, not only reprising and compiling existing songs into dance scores but also composing original accompaniments, often unaccredited. For instance, Rittman composed the sixteen minutes of original ballet music for "The Small House of Uncle Thomas" (*The King and I*), a composition that was not publically credited to her for years. In another example, when Leonard Bernstein could not complete his score for *Peter Pan* (1950) due to work conflicts, Rittman composed the dance music as well as the final songs, all anonymously.

The above artists are only a small sampling of musical theatre's roster of impressive orchestrators and arrangers; furthermore, the place of these collaborators in the musical theatre has not diminished. For instance, Mel Brooks, Tony-awarded composer of the phenomenally successful *The Producers* (2001), freely admitted that he hummed his song ideas to music arranger Glen Kelly who, along with vocal arranger/music conductor Patrick Brady, notated and completed the songs for production. (In a witty and reflective homage to historic Broadway and Tin Pan Alley, Brooks embraced and publicized this "old school" style of collaboration.) Further, Stephen Sondheim, probably the most revered contemporary composer today, writes most of his complex and often contrapuntal chorus parts but then has his conductor (frequently Paul Gemignani) tweak them for actual performance. In addition, Sondheim notates detailed piano scores, but then passes them to his longtime collaborative orchestrator, Jonathan Tunick, to orchestrate and realize the full score for the staged productions.

Given the above data, history, and context, it is necessary to caution against viewing the orchestrator/arranger paradigm as an unmasking and dethroning of musical theatre's noted composers and a devaluing of their signature contributions to the genre. Importantly, one must not discount the ear that first "heard" the song or melody and directed the creation and realization of that musical idea, compensating for and circumventing a lack of education, technique, time, and/or manpower to fully translate his or her vision to the page and stage. Regarding this point, most musical theatre arrangers have been in agreement, often signing legal contracts stating that their compositional efforts be considered the "property" of the composer. Thus, given the murkiness of the collaborative process, along with the significant and defining contributions of arrangers and orchestrators, the composer is still positioned today as the artist ultimately responsible for the creation and realization of his or her musical work on stage. Meanwhile, the fully realized composition becomes a more multifaceted and appreciated entity when one understands the working model and artists behind its musical arrangement/orchestration.

AGNES DE MILLE

Agnes de Mille not only loved to dance, she loved to write, chronicling both her art and fruitful career in a series of autobiographies. Through her writings, she repeatedly avowed that she did not believe in dance for its own sake, but saw steps, gestures, and rhythms as conduits to drama, action, and characterizations on stage. De Mille was a pioneer in implementing narrative and dramatic dance in the concert arena, often with a uniquely American aesthetic; and her choreographic philosophy, mission, and methodology had an unprecedented influence on the musical theatre world, moving dance to a new position of prominence and potential within the genre.

Born on September 18, 1905, to a prosperous, theatrical family (her father was writer and film producer William C. de Mille and her uncle was the infamous film director Cecil B. DeMille). Young Agnes displayed a passion and precocious talent for dance and performance as a child, spending much of her adolescence indulging her artistic whims on two coasts, shuttled between family members in New York City and Hollywood. As an adult, she began her professional dancing career in earnest but was discouraged from her initial pursuits in classical ballet, as her movement style and body type were not that of the traditional ballerina. Soon she began experimenting with what she called "character dances," uniquely personal combinations of pantomime and formal dance technique. During the 1920s, de Mille gained recognition for her own solo concert pieces in which she portrayed such disparate characters as a determined waif dancer (*Stage Fright*), a sassy Gold Rush gal (*'49*), and an Algerian belly-dancing prostitute (*Ouled Nail*). She moved to Europe during the 1930s and further explored the integration of dance with drama and psychodrama. In London, she choreographed Cole Porter's *Nymph Errant* (1933), and studied with Antony Tudor, the British ballet choreographer famous for his overt psychological approach to dance, appearing in his premiere of *Dark Elegies* (1937). Although Tudor's psychologically infused form inspired de Mille, she rejected the "dramatic" state as an "internal" process or mindset, but instead, aimed to create an "external" expression of emotion, that is, a danced, corporeal vocabulary, even looking to the nineteenth-century studies of Charles Darwin and mental hospital chronicles to codify gestural, physical, and emotional expression on stage.

Agnes de Mille, 1952 © Bettmann/CORBIS

When de Mille returned to New York in 1939, she joined a group working with the wealthy ballerina Lucia Chase to form a new American ballet company, Ballet Theatre (now American Ballet Theatre). Chase was its founder and patron, but de Mille was instrumental in bringing Tudor to the United States as a company choreographer as well as promoting a young dancer from its ranks to choreographer, Jerome Robbins. Consequently, the team of de Mille, Tudor, and Robbins helped build and define the American Ballet Theatre, still reigning today alongside the New York City Ballet as America's foremost concert dance/classical ballet company and school. During the early years, de Mille's dance philosophy was expressed and realized through concert pieces choreographed for Ballet Theatre, as well as other companies. The crux of her choreography was found in gesture and character, rooted in natural movement (walks, postures, hand gestures, habitual ticks) that were then reconfigured as dance steps, reflecting not only character traits and emotional states, but also evoked atmosphere, tone, and mood.

In 1942, de Mille debuted her most famous ballet of this period, *Rodeo*, which was created for Ballet Russe de Monte Carlo to a score by Aaron Copland. The ballet tells the story of the Cowgirl, a young tomboy who seeks love among the cowboys of the American

West. At first, she is rejected by the men in favor of the more "feminine" women from town; however, she soon changes into a dress, excites the men into fighting over her, and wins the Champion Roper in an energetic hoe-down finale. *Rodeo*'s uniquely American style and subject matter, as well as de Mille's use of nostalgia, iconography, and communicative choreography, made it a hit with general audiences as well as balletomanes. Further, her celebrated treatment of the "cowboy" and their rural milieu made de Mille a natural choice to choreograph Rodgers and Hammerstein's *Oklahoma!* one year later.

In her new role as a musical theatre choreographer, de Mille embarked on a mission to position dance as an integral and integrated component of a production. While seeming to view musical theatre integration not as a matter of question or possibility but one of necessity, she recognized the demands of such a task and steeled herself to adjusting her dances to serve the book and the score—a different paradigm than that of concert dance in which the choreographer autocratically reigns supreme. She also positioned the choreographer as an equal in the creation and operation of the intricate musical machine, seeing her role as the indispensable artist who melds and/or converts the sentiments of song and text into visceral, kinetic expression. Given this lofty task, de Mille proved to be a perfectionist when it came to her beliefs and craft, sometimes alienating collaborators who disagreed with her (although she could be harder on herself than any other team member). Beginning with *Oklahoma!*, de Mille asserted her formidable resolve, butting heads with powerful male collaborators to get her way. For instance, she insisted, against director Rouben Mamoulian's wishes, that her favorite dancers be cast in *Oklahoma!*, including women who were not stereotypical chorus-line cuties but were somewhat quirky and strong de Mille prototypes. Further, with conscious design and precision, de Mille positioned the dream ballet as a means by which a dance drama could be grafted to the plot as an extension of a character's personality and psyche. Most impressive is the fact that "Laurey Makes Up Her Mind," the groundbreaking dream ballet of *Oklahoma!*, was a subversive triumph for de Mille, as her storyline/concept overrode Hammerstein's original libretto idea (he had initially dictated a circus scenario for the dream section). As a result, it was de Mille's concept and choreography for the ballet that ultimately made musical history.

Although dream ballets were not new to musical theatre in 1943, "Laurey Makes Up Her Mind" was novel by delving into the female character's subconscious as well as symbolically reiterating the psychological and emotional crises arising from plot complications. De Mille's ballet portrayed a young woman torn between her desire for romantic love and her awakening sexual appetite; an internal conflict to which the other components of the show only modestly alluded. Specifically, Laurey drifts into a dreamscape in which she is marrying Curly in an idealized setting, only to have the wedding interrupted by Jud, who brutally steals her away to his world of dance hall girls, reminiscent of the French postcards (nineteenth-century pornography) which Jud has posted in his room in real life. Laurey's dream ultimately comes to a heated climax with the murder of Curly by Jud. De Mille's ballet was a tour de force; for instead of commenting on an already-prescribed story, it added entirely new interpretative possibilities regarding Laurey's relationships with Curly and Jud as well as a graphic depiction of her internal conflict regarding sex, marriage, and love. Included in the choreographed dreamscape was the gestural vocabulary of de Mille, e.g., Laurey's fluttering hands, signaling, as explained by de Mille, the beating of her heart and the free flight of birds. Furthermore, the ballet was emblematic of the successfully integrated nature of the rest of the show, with other dance segments featured throughout, such as the gestural defiance danced by the chorus women in "Many a New Day" as well as the folk reiterations evoked in "Kansas City" and "The Farmer and the Cowman." Many scholars cite de Mille's work on *Oklahoma!* as being equal to that of Rodgers and Hammerstein with regard to the energized advancement of and advocacy for the integrated (song/dance/text) musical on Broadway. Nevertheless, at the time, de Mille's contributions were not deemed as valuable. Originally contracted to make all the dances in *Oklahoma!* for $1500, she convinced the Theatre Guild to pay her $50 a week in royalties once the show was deemed a blockbuster success. Nevertheless, de Mille was not able to get royalties for the use of her *Oklahoma!* choreography until the 1980 Broadway revival.

Following *Oklahoma!*, de Mille continued to promote a musical theatre paradigm in which dance contributed to character and plot development, often using her considerable clout with directors, composers, lyricists, and librettists to incorporate lengthy and dramatic ballets. As choreographer, De Mille triumphed with works such as 1943's *One Touch of Venus* (with a score by composer Kurt Weill and lyricist Ogden Nash), as well as *Bloomer Girl* in 1944 (with music by Harold Arlen and lyrics by E. Y. Harburg). Both productions illustrated choreographic integration and dream ballets (especially notable was the "Civil War Ballet" in *Bloomer Girl*, which depicted through dance the pain of war experienced by the "war widows" left at home). In 1945, she worked again with Rodgers and Hammerstein. Regarding this new project, *Carousel*, de Mille reported that she felt particularly challenged, given that the production's Act II ballet required a level of dramatic invention that approximated "playwriting." By choreographing another musical theatre ballet as a dance scenario, she articulated an additional plot point, all told through dance. In the *Carousel* ballet, Billy views his daughter Louise from a heavenly vantage point; years have passed since his death, and she is now a lonely and confused teen. Wandering alone on a beach, Louise is rejected by the townspeople due to Billy's thievery and ignominious demise. She is seduced by a young ruffian who has arrived in town with a touring carnival troupe. The ballet depicts a passionate affair between the two, only to end when the young man deserts Louise, leaving her alone on the beach to again be taunted and dismissed by the local villagers. The fifteen-minute *Carousel* ballet (shortened against de Mille's wishes from its original length of almost an hour) constituted another "act" in the play, but it did so completely through underscoring and dance. Along with the ballet, de Mille added drama via dance throughout the production, moving from her gestural character pieces to folk movement (found in up-tempo numbers such as "June Is Bustin' Out All Over" and "Blow High, Blow Low"). *Carousel* was another triumph for de Mille, Rodgers, and Hammerstein. When the production opened in 1945, de Mille had four musicals running on Broadway simultaneously: *Oklahoma!*, *One Touch of Venus*, *Bloomer Girl*, and *Carousel*. Ironically, her highly acclaimed integrationist work, which often demanded a degree of sublimation to other collaborative elements in order to meld her choreography with music and narrative, had moved the dance and her name to a new place of prominence. Coincidentally, she garnered personal and professional attention and praise, while she moved dance to a position of equal (or at least crucially supportive) footing with song in the musical.

De Mille continued her Broadway ascension throughout the 1940s. In 1947, she collaborated with Alan Jay Lerner and Frederick Loewe on *Brigadoon*, a hit production for which the dances were as crucial to the overall mood and theme as they were to plot and character. Not just one ballet, but two were included in the production: (1) the meticulously researched "Sword Dance," a showy and visceral evocation of a Scottish folk dance performed with actual swords at a wedding ceremony, and (2) "The Funeral Dance," in which the Brigadoon community mourns through gestural, expressive movement the tragic, accidental death of a fellow townsperson. Most critics concurred that *Brigadoon* represented de Mille's most successful endeavor at musical theatre integration, as she effectively blurred the lines between story, song, and dance while pushing the idea of choreographic power and potential within the musical theatre arena.

In the same year, de Mille expanded her role on Broadway by becoming a stage director as well as a choreographer for Rodgers and Hammerstein's *Allegro*. With this groundbreaking move for women and choreographers alike (although Balanchine had already pioneered the director/choreographer duty with his work on 1940's *Cabin in the Sky*), she paved the way for future director/choreographers such as Jerome Robbins, Bob Fosse, Michael Bennett, Tommy Tune, Susan Stroman, Twyla Tharp, and Kathleen Marshall. Hammerstein's libretto tells the tale of a country doctor who is corrupted by money and fame in the "big city," ultimately returning to his humble roots and rural calling. By making the choice to use choreography to tell much of the story, de Mille took on a significant task, given the musical's epic scope and content. In addition, she had to overcome logistical complications due to the large size of the cast (41 principal characters and almost 100 more dancer/singers in the chorus) and the elaborate scenic design (approximately sixty sets requiring forty stagehands to move via a circular track onto a stage that included three levels of shifting platforms). All of this required much in the way of dramatic, suggestive lyricism and movement to provide a unifying framework for the show. Thus, de Mille not only choreographed the production's dance but also traffic-directed the massive scenery shifts and created large-scale stage tableaus, as well as provided pedestrian movement to evoke age, relationships, conflicts, and time periods. Such an undertaking was described by some musical theatre insiders as "Herculean." Unfortunately, given the extreme effort, *Allegro* was neither the critical nor commercial success de Mille's previous collaborations with Rodgers and Hammerstein had been. Specifically, when tensions peaked three weeks before *Allegro*'s out-of-town tryouts, Hammerstein took over the scene-directing duties; Rodgers assumed the role of song-stager; and de Mille was relegated to handling the dance choreography, although she was still billed as the director/choreographer when the show opened. This credit, however, did not make up for what she considered to be a humiliating demotion, and the shifting of duties did not improve most critics' overall negative assessments of the finished production. Furthermore, while Rodgers praised de Mille's choreography in the press, he was blunt in his assessment that she lacked the capacity to take on the additional chores of scene/song direction. Nevertheless, the book received the harshest criticism, with critics labeling it as didactic, pretentious, and simplistic. De Mille still managed to garner some praise for her attempt to give the show form and substance, as well as recognition of her pioneering efforts as a female director/choreographer.

Unfortunately, *Allegro* was not de Mille's only directorial disappointment on Broadway. In 1950, she was hired as director of Cole Porter's *Out of This World* (working with modern dance auteur Hanya Holm as the show's choreographer), only to be fired during rehearsals. Her third and last stint as director/choreographer came in the late 1960s with a conventional book musical and vehicle for dancer Ray Bolger called *Come Summer*; the production lasted only a week after opening March 18, 1969. This is not to suggest that these directing failures deterred de Mille from further choreographic pursuits on both the Broadway and concert stage (in addition, she choreographed the 1955 film adaptation of *Oklahoma!*). Throughout her Broadway career, de Mille continued to work in the field of classical ballet for companies such as Ballet Theatre. In 1948, she scored another triumph with her Lizzie Borden saga, *Fall River Legend*, a story ballet (like *Rodeo*), which depended on plot and character. She would also continue to choreograph for the theatre, for example, Jule Styne's *Gentlemen Prefer Blondes* (1949) and Lerner & Loewe's *Paint Your Wagon* (1951), but neither show lent itself to the degree of dance she had provided (and formatively featured) in her earlier landmark productions. During the 1950s and until her death, de Mille extended her narrative talents to another medium: writing. Wielding the pen, de Mille authored over a dozen books, including several autobiographies and an extensive biography of modern dance icon Martha Graham. With so much to say, her books ignited yet another career for de Mille as a popular lecturer. In addition to promoting and elucidating the crucial role and history of dance and choreography in the arts, she used the platform to fight for choreographic recognition and rights of ownership. In 1959, as a result of her tireless efforts, de Mille facilitated the entry of choreographers into what became the Society of Stage Directors and Choreographers (SSDC); the legitimacy of which was officially recognized by the League of New York Producers in 1962. These events paved the way for the copyrighting of dances by choreographers through the U.S. Copyright Office in 1976. Given these accomplishments, along with her receipt of lifetime achievement awards such as the National Medal of Arts in 1986, de Mille's legacy was firmly established by the time of her death on October 7, 1993. Furthermore, dance, as an integral and integrated component of the musical, would never again be relegated to secondary musical theatre status, thanks to her pioneering and persevering spirit.

FEATURED PRODUCTION: *Carousel* (1945)

Music by Richard Rodgers; Lyrics and Book by Oscar Hammerstein II

Original Broadway Run: Opened April 19, 1945; Majestic Theatre; 890 performances

When Rodgers and Hammerstein, at the suggestion of Theatre Guild's Theresa Helburn, decided to tackle a 1909 play by Ferenc Molnar and create a musical from its sentimental tale that mixes domestic and metaphysical drama, the two men took comfort in the fact that they would be re-teaming with those who had helped make their first effort, *Oklahoma!*, such a landmark success: director Rouben Mamoulian, choreographer Agnes de Mille, and producing entity Theatre Guild. After Hammerstein moved Molnar's locale from Budapest to New England, changed the name of the cocky, bullying carnival barker from Liliom to Billy Bigelow, and added a more positive ending, all parties felt that the work would translate well onto the Broadway stage, despite the antihero at the center of the story and plot points that include spousal abuse, thievery, sexual misconduct, and death. In addition, the musical, titled *Carousel*, would feature numerous musical innovations by Rodgers and Hammerstein. In fact, some musicologists consider *Carousel*'s score to be the most sophisticated and adventuresome of Rodgers and Hammerstein's entire *oeuvre*, a distinction that Rodgers often affirmed, citing it as his personal favorite.

In an unprecedented fashion, the musical opens with an extended instrumental number, "The Carousel Waltz," in which the main characters are introduced, through pantomime, to the audience as they encounter the visiting carnival. Most notable in this segment are the carousel barker, Billy Bigelow, shown in his natural, disreputable habitat, along with the wide-eyed Julie Jordan and her best friend, Carrie, seeking adventure and respite from their dreary textile mill jobs. Such an orchestral/dramatic device was a departure from the traditional overture, typically played while the curtain is down to preview the show's upcoming numbers. After this unique "overture," the score moves effortlessly to an oblique "I Am" song for the two girls, in which the audience learns of their work in the mill, of the "still waters" of Julie Jordan ("You're a Queer One, Julie Jordan"), and of Carrie's current infatuation ("Mr. Snow"). From this continuously sung and underscored opening number, the production flows into the "Bench Scene," during which Julie and Billy share an extended confrontation that evolves into mutual captivation—a self-contained scene that moves between the operetta-styled "If I Loved You" (in which each character takes turns imagining his or her life in love with the other), and underscored dialogue that transitions in and out of the sung segments. All culminates in a final kiss. In the following scene, Billy and Julie are presented as a married couple. In short, the "Bench Scene" takes the place of a traditional textual scene that would normally have provided pure dialogue to develop the plot and then ended with a song to musically punctuate the spoken scene. In addition, the "Bench Scene" was not the only pioneering musical moment in *Carousel*, for the rest of the musical contains a myriad of musical inventions and compositions. Included are the folksy sea ditties ("Blow High, Blow Low") and celebratory group numbers "June Is Bustin' Out All Over"), both of which are used to paint a picture of coastal life in the small, industrial village, placed alongside more lyrical, lush ballads such as "When the Children Are Asleep," depicting the idealized imaginings of Carrie and her beau, and "What's the Use of Wonderin'?," a plea made by Julie as she defends her decision to stay with Billy, despite his brutish temperament, abuse, and other failings. This aspect of Billy and Julie's marriage also provides one of the more troubling components of the musical. In many ways, *Carousel* may be seen as a "problem play" for modern audiences, given its treatment of spousal abuse, which is seen by some as re-inscribing and excusing Billy's acts (especially given Julie's explanation that it is sometimes possible not to feel a "hit" by someone, if you love them enough). It is a conundrum that continues to vex producers, directors, and artists today; yet many have found ways to circumvent the dated treatment by addressing the spousal abuse in terms of a unique and specific situation between two flawed human beings in a particular place and moment of time, not a universal belief or justification of abusive human behavior.

In this regard, "Soliloquy," another musical innovation introduced in *Carousel*, could be seen as a device by which Billy's rougher edges may be softened for the audience, as his internal conflicts and frustrations are elucidated. Upon learning that Julie is pregnant, Billy performs a soliloquy that is sung, instead of spoken (as in Shakespeare), expressing his pride at having a male heir, then the shocking realization that the expected child may be a girl, then his hopeful vision of "Daddy's little girl," then the desperate realization that he cannot provide for a family, and finally his determination to do whatever is necessary to correct the situation. Unfortunately, the song also leads him to his ill-fated participation in a botched robbery, during which he accidentally falls on his own knife and dies. This unconventional libretto development (early death of a lead character) lends itself to a moment in which the "matron" of *Carousel*, Cousin Nettie, offers, as advice to Julie, one of Rodgers and Hammerstein's most inspirational anthems: "You'll Never Walk Alone." From this point, the musical explores Billy's mental, emotional, and metaphysical crisis as he arrives at the gates of heaven and is barred entrance due to his failings on earth. In the original 1945 production, choreographer

Shelly Cox Robie and Wayne Kennedy in Boulder's Dinner Theatre's production of *Carousel*. Used by permission of Boulder's Dinner Theater.

Agnes de Mille was able to lend her hand as a narrative dance auteur and make an indelible imprint on the musical, advocating for and ultimately choreographing a fifteen-minute ballet depiction of life on earth as seen through Billy's eyes as he hangs in limbo. Because of de Mille's efforts, the ballet remains an integral part of the libretto, while providing a unique exploration of female sexuality as it depicts the coming-of-age physical and emotional turmoil experienced by Billy's daughter, Louise. In the dance scenario, the vulnerable teen-age Louise is ostracized by others in her town and seduced by a young worker from the visiting carnival, who then cruelly rejects her, further making her an object of ridicule. Although Billy anguishes over seeing his sins replayed through the daughter and pleads for a chance to help her, he falls prey yet again to another angry fit as she is mistrustful of his earthly presence and will not accept his help. He slaps her, repeating his own history and seeing his chance at redemption slip through his grasp. However, Billy does not give up, and as an unearthly spirit, he is able to encourage Louise to lead the singing at her graduation with a reprise of "You'll Never Walk Alone," while voicing an emphatic avowal to Julie that he always loved her. At this emotional high point, he is led, finally, through the gates of heaven.

Carousel opened on April 19, 1945, at the Majestic; and although it did not merit the phenomenal box office of *Oklahoma!*, it was popular enough to warrant a run of 890 performances—a significant second hit for the team of Rodgers, Hammerstein, de Mille, and Mamoulian. The production has been repeatedly revived, often receiving creative treatments to address some of its more troublesome aspects. For instance, the most recent 1994 revival of the production on Broadway, originally produced by and staged at the Royal National Theatre, won five Tony Awards, including Best Revival of a Musical, Best Direction of a Musical, and Best Choreography, while bringing the work into the latter part of the twentieth century by giving the production a metaphoric staging and refusing to soften or romanticize the darker elements of the New England milieu (which also lent some brutal truth and significance to the relationship of Billy and Julie). Crucially, the production incorporated nontraditional casting, e.g., Carrie was played by African American Audra McDonald in her Broadway lead debut (she won a Tony for the role). It was a decisive triumph, proving that *Carousel* not only "had legs," but could still speak to contemporary audiences.

PULLING BACK THE CURTAIN:
Evolution of the Female Director in American Musical Theatre

When one surveys American musical theatre, it is apparent that most directors of Broadway musicals have been male. It is an inconvenient truth that much of the genre has been shaped, codified, and canonized under a patriarchal hand. But then again, this phenomenon is not unique to the theatre. It is emblematic of America's socioeconomic structure and climate during much of the twentieth century, an era in which most women were relegated to subservient, underpaid, and unacknowledged roles. What is exciting, however, is that the twenty-first century saw a major paradigm shift regarding gender and musical theatre direction, and the female director has now become a defining force in the industry. Nonetheless, the path to prominence and power was a long and arduous one for women. Almost a full century of musical theatre transpired before women took their rightful and accredited place at the helm of a Broadway production.

During the formative days of musical theatre, women mainly had one role, that of the comely, talented, and/or charismatic performer. Further, these performers were directed, choreographed, managed, and promoted by men. One early pioneer, however, broke this mold: **Albertina Rasch** (1891–1967). Rasch was an Austrian who immigrated to the United States as a teen, trained as a classical ballerina, and became the earliest reigning female in staging Broadway musicals. As a premiere "dance director" (the billing given to early choreographers, before Balanchine officially changed the job title), Rasch merged ballet with popular precision dance trends and chorus-line techniques, combining classical steps with showy stage pictures and patterns. The intricate movements and designs were set to the new jazz sounds of Broadway, while the incorporation of props and other scenic and costume devices made the dances appear even more innovative. Rasch trained troupes of female dancers in her style (which she termed "American ballet"); she called them the "Albertina Rasch Girls," touring them abroad as well as including them in many Broadway shows. Although her numbers were mostly treated as nonintegrated divertissements, they were featured in many top shows of the late 1920s up through the early '40s (as well as movie musicals), including the popular *Rio Rita* (1927) which opened Florenz Ziegfeld's theater, Jerome Kern's *Cat and the Fiddle* (1931), Irving Berlin's *Face the Music* (1932), Cole Porter's *Jubilee* (1935), Kurt Weill's *Lady in the Dark* (1941), and most of the Schwartz and Dietz revues, including their most critically acclaimed *The Band Wagon* (1931). Rasch's career slowed in the '40s, due in part to the new popularity of integrated musicals. Nonetheless, she continues to hold the distinction of trailblazer with regard to the acquisition and assertion of "staging" power on Broadway; further, she is credited with opening the door for the onslaught of female choreographers who succeeded her during the Golden Age.

Agnes de Mille was easily the most powerful and prolific choreographer during the Golden Age. However, she was not alone in bringing a serious dance aesthetic to Broadway and asserting a place of influence and industry for women in the staging of musical theatre works. Like de Mille, many of these women came from the concert dance field, merging their formal training and artistic methodology to musical theatre dance. Further, many of them had their own students and dance companies, so they were accustomed to a certain degree of autonomy and authority, which they brought with them to Broadway. As a member of this elite group of women, modern dance performer/choreographer **Helen Tamiris** (1905–66) choreographed everything from operetta (Sigmund Romberg's *Up in Central Park* in 1945) to the 1946 revival of *Show Boat* and the folksy smash *Annie Get Your Gun* (1946). Another modern dance pioneer who figured prominently was **Hanya Holm** (1893–1992), who worked to find free expression of inner states through her modern dance technique, while researching and resurrecting folk idioms for her show choreography, making her dances especially reflective of place, time, and character. Her impressive, diverse roster included *Kiss Me, Kate* (1948), *The Golden Apple* (1954), for which she took over much of the directing for Norman Lloyd but was not officially credited, and the Lerner and Loewe masterpiece *My Fair Lady* (1956), along with its successor, *Camelot* (1960). Representing the younger generation was **Onna White** (1922–2005) and **Carol Haney** (1924–64). When White won an Honorary Academy Award for her choreography of *Oliver!*, it was one of the very few times the film industry has celebrated choreography for film. Her prolific and lauded Broadway work during the '50s, '60s, and '70s included *The Music Man, Take Me Along, Irma La Duce, Mame,* and *1776.* Haney was a Broadway gypsy and star performer with a background in ballet as well as nightclub and concert jazz dance (as a disciple of Jack Cole, schooled in his technique, which he termed "ethnic jazz"). As a choreographer, Haney brought her own "show dance" blend of classical ballet and jazz to shows such as *Flower Drum Song* (1958), *She Loves Me* (1963), and *Funny Girl* (1964). Except for de Mille, none of these women worked as Broadway directors. Instead, they used their roles as choreographers to assert power and, occasionally, to indirectly control much of the stage production. Recent scholarship and personal accounts are uncovering the degree to which these women shaped the overall productions for which they only received "choreography" credit. When de Mille finally made the directorial leap with *Allegro* in 1947, it was unfortunate that her landmark opportunity, so loaded with potential, resulted in perceived failure, possibly stalling advancement into and realization of the director's role for her female contemporaries and successors. After *Allegro*, Broadway saw no women at the helm of a significant musical until the late twentieth century.

Even when women started to be accepted into the musical theatre directing ranks, the floodgates were slow to open, with the first female after de Mille to direct a prominent Broadway musical being contemporary dance artist **Twyla Tharp**. Tharp served as director/choreographer for the moderately successful 1985 stage version of *Singin' in the Rain*, almost 40 years after *Allegro*. This "screen-to-stage musical" was, curiously, Tharp's first major venture within the musical theatre arena, but it did not automatically launch her career as a musical director. She would have to wait nearly two decades to fully realize musical theatre success, conceiving, choreographing, and directing critical and popular Broadway works such as the "jukebox dansicals" *Movin' Out* (2002) and *Come Fly Away* (2010). Furthermore, after *Singin' in the Rain*, it would take five years for another woman, **Graciela Daniele**, to successfully claim the director's chair on Broadway, working as director/choreographer for the highly acclaimed *Once on This Island* (1990). This exuberant musical treatment of an Afro-Caribbean mythic tale came on the heels of Daniele's much-touted choreographic work on *The Pirates of Penzance* (1981) and *The Mystery of Edwin Drood* (1985). Even given the positive reception of *Once on this Island*, Daniele, like Tharp, would not find success again as a director until the end of the century, with the popular, reconceived revival of *Annie Get Your Gun* in 1999. In fact, the late '90s proved to be a fertile period for the female director, including a milestone in Broadway recognition, the first Tony Award for Best Director of a Musical awarded to a woman. This distinction belongs to visionary artist and auteur **Julie Taymor** for her transcendent production of *The Lion King* (1997), a musical that continues to thrill audiences today with its anthropomorphic stage depiction of the original Disney movie, which uses scenic spectacle as well as puppetry and masks designed by its director, Taymor. To date, Taymor continues to push the Broadway envelope, having most recently faced significant challenges when attempting a visionary, conceptual staging of *Spider-Man: Turn Off the Dark* (2011), the rock musical with a score by U2's Bono and The Edge. As director, as well as co-writer, Taymor spearheaded a troubled production that incurred an unprecedented $75 million price tag due to her use of cutting-edge technology to create a Broadway spectacle for a techno-savvy twenty-first-century audience (due to a catastrophic preview period, Taymor was ultimately released from the project, with a new director brought in to "fix" the show before opening).

Recently, **Diane Paulus** has burst onto the musical theatre scene, following in Taymor's footsteps as she won the directing Tony for her conceptual treatment of the 2013 revival of *Pippin*. Her kinetic, effervescent, and circus-inspired translation of the Stephen Schwartz/Bob Fosse classic featured a female

Leading Player, aerial effects by ZFX, and circus acts designed by Gypsy Snider. This work capped a current string of notable and visionary revivals spearheaded by Paulus, including the bold, award-winning 2009 remount of *Hair* and her 2012 "revisal," *The Gershwins' Porgy and Bess* (for which she weathered a firestorm of criticism over her revisionary efforts).

In many ways, however, Taymor and Paulus stand as musical theatre anomalies; for most of their female peers began as choreographers and have evolved into choreographer/directors (an auteur position once claimed solely by male artists such as Jerome Robbins, Bob Fosse, Gower Champion, Michael Bennett, and Tommy Tune). Owing much to the choreographic legacy of female predecessors such as de Mille, Holm, and Tamiris, Broadway's current generation of choreographer/directors represent a hybrid of Broadway "show biz" and concert dance. The group includes aforementioned Twyla Tharp and Graciela Daniele, as well as **Ann Reinking**, a classically trained dancer who gained Broadway fame as a star and muse for Bob Fosse. She can also be credited with renewing interest in and reinvigorating Fosse's work a decade after his death, providing the "Fosse-style" choreography for the still-running 1996 revival of *Chicago*, and co-directing/co-choreographing the hit *Fosse* in 1999. Reinking's colleague, the concert dance choreographer **Lynne Taylor-Corbett**, also found a receptive Broadway audience when she directed and choreographed the dansical *Swing!* (1999). Taylor-Corbett's production was nominated for the Tony Award for Best Musical alongside another dansical that year: *Contact*. It so happened that *Contact* was also directed and choreographed (as well as conceived) by an ascendant female talent on the Broadway scene, **Susan Stroman**. Of the current crop of female choreographer/directors, Stroman stands today as the most awarded and prolific. *Contact*, a collection of three "dance plays," beat Taylor-Corbett's *Swing!* for the coveted Best Musical Tony and was a defining moment for Stroman. Having achieved notice and acclaim for her choreography for previous dance-heavy productions such as *Crazy for You* (1992), Hal Prince's *Show Boat* revival in 1994, and the celebrated revival of *Oklahoma!* by the Royal National Theatre (for which she received permission from de Mille's estate to alter, for the first time, the original choreography), she was given almost free reign to create *Contact*. Immediately thereafter, she directed and choreographed a popular revival of *The Music Man* (2000), as well as one of the most successful musical comedies in recent years, *The Producers* (2001). While also tackling concert dance pieces, smaller shows, and some failed Broadway experiments, she has continued to make her presence felt on the Main Stem with *Young Frankenstein* (2007) and Kander and Ebb's last original production on Broadway, *The Scottsboro Boys* (2010). Lastly, whereas Stroman has mostly made her directing mark with original productions, director/choreographer **Kathleen Marshall** has become a director of note by re-envisioning and revitalizing past works, with contemporary hit Broadway revivals of *Wonderful Town* (2003), *Pajama Game* (2006), *Grease* (2007), and *Anything Goes* (2011), as well as a new Gershwin jukebox musical, *Nice Work If You Can Get It* (2012). In summary, given this impressive roster of artists and their output, the female director, along with her talent, artistry, and vision, appears to be the new norm in the musical theatre arena.

ALAN JAY LERNER AND FREDERICK LOEWE

The legendary partnership of Lerner and Loewe did not happen by chance, nor was it a gradual evolution. When composer Frederick Loewe legendarily introduced himself to Alan Jay Lerner in 1942, over drinks at New York City's Lambs Club, he did so with the sole intent of recruiting Lerner as a librettist/lyricist for an upcoming project. Once Lerner agreed, their long and fruitful collaboration officially took root. For almost two decades, Lerner and Loewe created Broadway musicals ideally suited to a postwar nation receptive to their renderings of exceptional societies rooted in traditional values and romantic ideals of love, honor, duty, and sacrifice—all tinged with humor, warmth, and sometimes, a touch of fantasy. These Lerner and Loewe productions celebrated a romanticized past, while cannily playing to the idealism and can-do spirit of midcentury America, re-inscribing such ideals and suggesting parallels for a modern audience. In this respect, Lerner and Loewe are often hailed as "the last romantics" of Broadway. Although they are responsible for only four canonical works, the musicals themselves are impressively diverse in their settings and content, i.e., a Scottish highland fantasy, rustic Gold Rush chronicle, British comedy of manners, and mythic King Arthur tale. While Lerner and Loewe looked to the past and legend for content, they looked to the future for form, pushing forward an integrationist agenda on Broadway. In fact, in addition to being termed "romantics," they could also be deemed the team responsible for "Integration 2.0" in the musical world, further adhering to and popularizing the musical theatre trend previously evolved and advocated by Rodgers and Hammerstein, thereby setting a new benchmark for integration during the Golden Age.

The structure and philosophy of the Lerner and Loewe works appear to loosely parallel, reflect, and/or respond to the works of Rodgers and Hammerstein (a comparison often made due to the coincident timing of their Broadway shows). Lerner and Loewe's collaboration, however, differed from that of the earlier pair in many respects. In fact, one might see more similarities between the team of Lerner and Loewe to that of Rodgers and Hart, with regard to their working relationship and contrasting personalities (interestingly, Lerner had actually been taken under Hart's wing as a young member of the Lambs Club). Specifically, like Rodgers and

Hart, Lerner and Loewe were seemingly mismatched partners, that is, different nationalities, ages (fourteen years apart), backgrounds, and temperaments, but they fortunately came together during a specific moment in musical theatre history when audiences embraced their vision, style, and content. Loewe was a stern, disciplined professional, emotionally distant, who was versed in classical composition and operetta. Like Rodgers, he worked diligently to find a unique, carefully structured sound, sweetly and lushly melodic, to reflect a specific place, time, and character. In contrast to the stoic Loewe, Alan Jay Lerner was a wild card, with a colorful biography riddled with scandal and speculation (including a longtime amphetamine addiction). While Lerner seemingly channeled Hammerstein in his use of evocative poetry and romantic sentiment (he often admitted to being a "hopeless romantic" and was married eight times), he was also a caustic wit, in the manner of Hart, working intently on intrinsic, smart lyrics that often entailed sassy, humorous expression. Both aspects of Lerner's craft (Hammerstein/Hart) meticulously reflected the "voice" of his characters; and he embraced the idea of the musical play, creating librettos that told stories as evocatively, colorfully, truthfully, yet theatrically as possible. (He once railed at the idea of "realism" in the theatre, stating that any such notion is a "myth.") The Lerner and Loewe partnership is also rare in that Lerner, the lyricist/librettist, received top billing (up to this point, composers were usually named first). The name order is fitting, however, because Lerner was the dominant partner, often implementing and shaping projects (as well as writing all the librettos). He also served as the mouthpiece for the team, partly because Loewe struggled with a thick Austrian accent throughout his life in the United States. Their songwriting, however, was more of a shared process. Per Lerner's accounts, the two men decided together where songs should go in their stories and the general content and mood. With a working title supplied by Lerner, Loewe would compose the melody, after which Lerner wrote the lyrics. Interestingly, given this writing method, the relationship between the two men wasn't an especially close or warm one, but the two opposites were able to overcome their differences and form a unique bond to become one of the most celebrated teams during the height of the Golden Age.

It was a long road to Broadway, however, especially for Frederick (Fritz) Loewe. Loewe was born into a musical family in Berlin on June 10, 1904. His father, Edmund Loewe, was a renowned Viennese operetta tenor, and young Fritz soon found his own European fame. At an early age, he was declared a prodigy, picking out and composing melodies on a piano by age 7. He subsequently studied with leading piano instructors and attended a conservatory in Berlin, ultimately playing, at age 13, with the Berlin Symphony, the youngest soloist to have ever appeared with the orchestra. Two years later, at the ripe age of 15, Fritz wrote a top European pop hit, "Katrina." Riding high on his "boy wonder" status and looking to provide for his mother after his father's death, Loewe immigrated to the United States in 1924. He had planned to write for Broadway, but when he landed in New York City, he found that jazz was the new sound of theatre and popular music. As a product of classical training and accomplished in operetta, Loewe had little aptitude for or familiarity with the syncopated American idiom. To further complicate matters, Loewe was not fluent in English and struggled to make connections in the entertainment and music industry. In short, he was something of a fish out of water and had trouble finding the level of musical employment, not to mention recognition, that he had

enjoyed in his homeland. As a result, Loewe spent his first decade in America as a jack of all trades, playing piano for various nightclub revues but also travelling the East Coast and West Coast, taking odd jobs such as riding instructor, prize fighter, gold miner, cowpuncher, and horseback mail deliverer.

Once Loewe returned to New York City, he also returned to music, eventually working as a pianist at a nightclub that catered to German patrons. Back in the city, he became a member of the prestigious Lambs Club, a social organization of professional and aspiring artists working in the theatre and music industries. Through the Lambs, he started to make connections in the Broadway community. Ultimately, he met his first lyricist (and the only close collaborator he would have other than Lerner), Earle Crooker, a writer with a Hollywood and radio background. Together, they wrote their first song, "A Waltz Was Born in Vienna," which was added to a failed Broadway revue. Not wanting to let a good song go to waste, the partners decided to expand their venture by writing an entire musical, *Salute to Spring*, which was commissioned by the St. Louis Opera Association. Included in the score was their original song, along with enough additional crowd-pleasing numbers that *Salute to Spring* was a top draw in St. Louis throughout the summer of 1937. Even though the work was not staged in New York City, it brought the creators to the notice of Broadway producer Dwight Deere Wiman, who signed the team to write a new operetta, *Great Lady*, which premiered on Broadway in 1938. The production featured a stellar cast of musical comedy favorites and talented newcomers (including Jerome Robbins in his first dance chorus role); but, overall, the show was not impressive enough to stay on Broadway longer than twenty performances. At this point, Loewe said goodbye to Crooker and returned to his piano-playing gigs in New York nightclubs; that is, until 1942, when he introduced himself to another Lambs Club member, a young writer named Alan Jay Lerner.

Lerner was of a different generation and background than Loewe. He was born on August 31, 1918, and grew up wealthy and privileged in New York City as a son of Joseph J. Lerner, the entrepreneur who founded Lerner Shops, a prominent chain of women's apparel stores. Even though the young Lerner did not grow up in a theatrical or musical family like Loewe, he aspired to be a writer at an early age, and his ambitious, determined nature was cautiously nurtured and pragmatically facilitated by his family. He also loved music, taking lessons and playing piano as a child. Consequently, Lerner's family connections (and wealth), along with his own drive and talent, resulted in his enrollment and education in private prep schools (e.g., Choate) throughout his youth. Pursuing his music studies, he took courses at Julliard School of Music during the summers of 1936 and '37. Following these musical summers, Lerner was accepted into Harvard as an undergraduate, where he not only dabbled in theatre but also boxing, ultimately losing the sight in one eye. (Another intriguing fact of Lerner's educational history is that he was a classmate of John F. Kennedy, first at Choate, then Harvard, actually working with the future president on the Choate yearbook.) While at Harvard, Lerner wrote scores (both lyrics and music) for two Hasty Pudding shows, resulting in two songs, "Chance to Dream" (1938) and "From Me to You" (1939), which were commercially published. After graduation, Lerner became a prolific radio script-writer (producing 500 scripts in two years), while also meriting a modest degree of critical notice in New York City as a writer of sketches and lyrics for *The Lambs Gambol*, a high-profile revue presented by the members of the Lambs Club.

All of which leads to the infamous and seminal events of 1942, when producer Henry Duffy approached Loewe in search of an original musical comedy for a theatre venue he owned in Detroit. Duffy was mostly interested in a new treatment of a previously produced libretto, an adaptation of Barry Conners' *The Patsy* (1928). Duffy wanted to revise the production and set its story to Loewe and Crooker's *Salute to Spring* score. He also wanted the librettist of the new treatment to be able to rewrite Crooker's *Salute to Spring* song lyrics to match them to the new storyline (this may sound convoluted but the patchwork process was not uncommon at the time). In short, Loewe had an opportunity to have his music appear once again in another prominent work, but he needed to find someone to supply a new libretto and lyrics. Thus, when Loewe saw Lerner playing cards at the Lambs Club, knowing that both he and Duffy were impressed with Lerner's lyrics for the Lambs' revues, he introduced himself, admitted his knowledge of Lerner's work, and with a brusque compliment, suggested they work together. (Throughout their partnership, Loewe would continue to be the distant and rigid partner, never effusive and extroverted; the extrovert role would be played by Lerner.) Two

days later, the pair embarked by train for Detroit and premiered their first work, *Life of the Party* (the Lerner and Loewe reconfiguration/merger of *The Patsy* and *Salute to Spring*), which was widely enjoyed by Detroit audiences.

The next year, they created their first work for the Broadway stage, *What's Up?* (1943), with music by Loewe, book/lyrics by Lerner, and direction by George Balanchine. The musical failed, lasting only 63 performances; but the writing team was undeterred, embarking on a new musical with another original story by Lerner: *The Day Before Spring* (1945). The new production did somewhat better, running on Broadway for 167 performances and receiving some positive notices for its fanciful material and aesthetic. In 1947, Lerner and Loewe finally hit the mark with *Brigadoon*, a Scottish fantasy inspired by Loewe's reference, during the rehearsals of *The Day Before Spring*, to the miraculous concept of faith moving mountains. Accordingly, the writers began exploring ideas of miracles and fantastical happenings based on faith, love, and other idealized virtues. The two men came up with the premise of faith moving a town, along with the concept that love's power could transform communities and individuals. Building on this idea, they created their third Broadway musical and first hit, taking inspiration from the works of James M. Barrie (celebrated author of *Peter Pan*) and a popular German story, *Germelshausen*.

To summarize, *Brigadoon* tells the tale of two cynical New Yorkers on a hunting trip in Scotland: the soon-to-be-married Tommy Albright and his rakish, hard-drinking best friend, Jeff Douglas. The men see an unmapped village, Brigadoon, appear in the mists of the Highlands and go to explore its environs, only to find a town populated with archaic villagers preparing for a wedding. Tommy soon falls for the prospective bride's sister, Fiona (they become the primary romantic couple); and Jeff realizes a more earthy relationship with a lusty village maiden, Meg (they become the comic secondary couple). Tommy and Jeff soon learn, however, that the town is not what it seems; it exists under a spell that puts the villagers to sleep, only to be awakened for one day every 100 years. The catch to this miraculous protection against the polluting forces of modernization is that Brigadoon may continue to exist on the condition that no outsider enters its ranks and no insider ever leaves. If either situation occurs, the town and its inhabitants will permanently vanish. Calamity ensues at the wedding, however, when a spurned suitor of the bride threatens to leave Brigadoon and is accidentally killed. After Tommy and Jeff realize that they may have set this tragedy in motion, they return to New York City; but Tommy cannot forget Fiona. He cancels his engagement and returns to the Highlands, only to find that the village has disappeared. Tommy loudly bemoans his lost opportunity at true love; and his display of faith, devotion, passion, and enlightenment is so pronounced that it awakens the town before its time. Consequently, he is given permission to reunite with Fiona and forever remain in Brigadoon. Lerner's highly romantic libretto is matched by many atmospheric and character numbers in the score, including lush love songs, given operetta-style musical treatment by Loewe (e.g., "The Heather on the Hill," "Waitin' for My Dearie," and "Come to Me, Bend to Me"). The romantic milieu of *Brigadoon* is also imbued with folksy optimism and innocence, exemplified by Lerner and Loewe's ebullient homage to love that became one of the show's many popular hits, "Almost Like Being in Love." While the atmosphere and mood of the entire piece is conveyed through the haunting "Brigadoon," Lerner's snappy and irreverent wit is also on full display in the score. Specifically, a number of the songs contain naughty humor and wordplay, celebrating the bawdy side of romance (e.g., "Go Home with Bonnie Jean," "My Mother's Wedding Day," and "The Love of My Life"). The original production also incorporated and exploited dramatic lyricism through movement; not surprising, given that its choreographer was Agnes de Mille. Notably, the dances of de Mille were instrumental to the cohesive nature and lyrical structure/ character of the musical. Integration of extensive dramatic ballets and movement numbers, à la "The Sword Dance," "The Chase," and "The Funeral Dance," provided an almost completely choreographed series of scenes that appeared to "dance" many of the most emotional moments of the show. In the end, Broadway audiences embraced the lyrical integration and the escapist, romantic world of *Brigadoon*, making it one of the top hits of the late 1940s, ultimately running for 581 performances.

After the success of *Brigadoon*, Lerner embarked on a new project with composer Kurt Weill, writing the libretto and lyrics for *Love Life*, which debuted on Broadway in 1948. Lerner's book features a married couple with two children who are depicted in various eras, from 1791 to the present. The portrayal of the family in different periods shows the changes in domestic and marital relationships, conveyed through a series of individual scenes and vaudevillian musical numbers, instead of a linear, musically integrated plot. The musical was actually billed as "A Vaudeville." Accordingly, *Love Life*, which ran for only 252 performances, is notable in that it is considered by many to be Broadway's first concept musical.

Lerner rejoined Loewe in 1951 for *Paint Your Wagon*, which looked to America for its "mythic" material, focusing on the California gold rush of the mid-1800s and the idealistic (and foolhardy) optimism and grit of the miners during this fertile time in America's history. While the libretto is an original work by Lerner, he incorporated historic diary accounts into the dialogue and factual incidents into his storyline, which is set in 1853 and centers on a gruff, hard-living prospector and his daughter. They discover gold near their California settlement, and the discovery leads to the boomtown of Rumson, with a surge of miners into the area and their accompanying stories/dramas. One of the major dramatic conflicts concerns a romance between the prospector's daughter and a young Mexican prospector. Their relationship is taboo, however; and she leaves Rumson to attend school in the East, only to return to her love. She finds that the gold strike has dried up and Rumson is all but deserted, with her father once again living on pioneer grit and optimism. True to Lerner and Loewe's integrationist mission, *Paint Your Wagon*'s score boasts an early American, frontier folk sound, including hoe-downs ("Hand Me Down That Can o' Beans") and country ballads ("Wand'rin' Star" and "I Talk to the Trees"). Loewe was able to occasionally conjoin an operetta sound with Lerner's plaintive Americana sentiment, most effectively exemplified by "They Call the Wind Maria," a sweeping aria that voices the passion and pain of the wild frontier. Along with the work of Lerner and Loewe, spirited dances were provided by Agnes de Mille, with attention paid once again to reflecting character as she authentically replicated historic folk dance idioms. To the disappointment of Lerner and Loewe, *Paint Your Wagon* was not a significant hit, running for only 289 performances after its opening on November 12, 1951. Audiences, as critics implied, may have found the production a bit too authentic and unvarnished in its depiction of a specific population, place, and time, missing the glamour, pizzazz, and visual charisma found in neighboring Broadway shows (for instance, the biggest hits at the time were colorful, lavish productions such as *Guys and Dolls* and *The King and I*). Yet, the work continues to be staged by both professional and amateur theatre companies throughout America today, ensuring its place in the musical theatre canon.

If *Brigadoon* and *Paint Your Wagon* garnered Lerner and Loewe a considerable degree of notice, their next musical would change their fortunes forever, cementing their names as musical theatre pioneers and legends. To begin, *My Fair Lady* differs from earlier Lerner/Loewe efforts in that it does not contain an original libretto (although, there are those who think Lerner generously "borrowed" from various folktale and literature sources for his "original" *Brigadoon* book). Instead, *My Fair Lady* is an adaptation of an already-proven property, *Pygmalion* (1912), which is one of the most popular and performed social comedies penned by Irish playwright, philosopher, critic, socioeconomic theorist, and Nobel Prize-winner George Bernard Shaw (1856–1950). The musical adaptation had been a longtime goal of movie producer and Shaw aficionado Gabriel Pascal, who had previously won an Academy Award for his collaboration with Shaw on a 1938 film version of the play. Unfortunately, Pascal faced numerous roadblocks in his attempt to turn the material into a musical, not the least of which was the belligerent refusal by Shaw to grant the rights to the play's musicalization (which he saw as an "outrage" and an undermining of the innate musicality of his written/spoken language). After Shaw's death in 1950, Pascal was still thwarted in his attempt as the project was turned down by such venerable musical theatre songwriters as Cole Porter, Dietz and Schwartz, and Rodgers and Hammerstein. Pascal finally appealed to Lerner and Loewe, who agreed to tackle the task. Unfortunately, the pair soon floundered, unable to find a way to musicalize Shaw's material. After three months, the pair felt they had exhausted all creative options and decided to give up on the project. Furthermore, the experience had proved to be so contentious and draining that Lerner and Loewe separated for two years, with both men working on minor or failed projects until they reteamed in 1954, agreeing to restart work on the Shaw project under a new producer (Pascal had died in the interim).

In a nutshell, the story of *My Fair Lady* features a sassy and disheveled Cockney flower peddler in Covent Garden, Eliza Doolittle, and a professor of phonetics, Professor Henry Higgins. He wagers a compatriot that he can transform her into a "lady" by simply teaching her to speak proper English. In many ways, both the professor and flower girl win: Eliza becomes a refined, enlightened, and independent woman, and Higgins takes the credit for her transformation, while possibly falling in love with her. Finding the right performers to play the 19-year-old Eliza and the older Higgins was a time-consuming challenge for its creators. Ultimately, British Shakespearean actor Rex Harrison was talked into taking the role of the phonetician. Harrison was hesitant at first, given that he had never done a musical, but the creators were confident that he could believably bring the maddeningly impervious Higgins to life. Eliza was even more difficult to cast, as Lerner and Loewe wanted to follow Shaw's stage instructions that she be played by an age-appropriate actress. The team auditioned almost one hundred young women from both the United States and Britain. Finally, they cast a young English import, Julie Andrews, who had just found success on Broadway as the lead in *The Boy Friend* (1954), a British send-up of early musical comedies.

Throughout 1955, Lerner and Loewe continued to work on their new musical, with the addition of significant collaborators. First, the celebrated writer/director Moss Hart came on board, helping to further refine the book while putting his theatrical stamp on the content. Next, modern dance artist Hanya Holm joined the project as choreographer, supplying tightly integrated dramatic and atmospheric dance numbers. When rehearsals began in 1956, the musical's title had been changed from *My Lady Liza* to *My Fair Lady*. It opened in New Haven, with some uncertainty regarding the youth and relative inexperience of Andrews and some drama regarding Harrison, who had never performed in a musical, reportedly suffered last-minute stage fright and was legendarily threatened with public exposure and/or legal action by director Moss Hart to get him out of his dressing room on opening night. The fears were unfounded, for the New Haven tryouts thrilled audiences; and when the show premiered in New York on March 15, 1956 at the Mark Hellinger Theatre, audiences and critics alike felt they were experiencing something special. The production not only boasted a lovely score, but it was also lovely to look at. Costumes, which included Eliza's transformational gowns, as well as the lavish apparel worn by those attending the Embassy Ball and the Ascot races, were designed by celebrated designer/costumer Cecil Beaton. Elaborate and numerous sets graced the stage, courtesy of popular and acclaimed scenic designer Oliver Smith. Along with the transcendent depiction of Eliza by Andrews and pitch-perfect performances by the rest of the stellar cast, Lerner and Loewe's lush score may have been the ultimate key to the production's success. It includes melodically rich and engaging compositions such as "I Could Have Danced All Night," "Show Me" [see fig. 5.2], "I've Grown Accustomed to Her Face," and "On the Street Where You Live," all of which have become American standards. The score also contains an impressive degree of wit and drama, especially exemplified by character/novelty numbers such as "I'm an Ordinary Man," "With a Little Bit of Luck," "The Ascot Gavotte," "Wouldn't It Be Loverly?" and "The Rain in Spain." Reflecting the authors' attention to drama and narrative, many of the musical numbers in *My Fair Lady* are active songs (including the use of *Sprechstimme*, or "sung speech," a vocal strategy necessitated by the casting of non-singer Harrison), which further the plot by illustrating dramatic struggles, reconciliations, and discoveries while providing dramatic impetus for the characters.

My Fair Lady was a theatre success the likes of which had not been seen since *Oklahoma!*. The show not only made Lerner and Loewe household names, but also celebrities. Everyone clamored to know what they would do next. Finally, they chose a retelling of the King Arthur legend. They wrote and produced it themselves, titling the musical *Camelot*. Given the triumph of *My Fair Lady*, hopes were astronomically high for the new production. Contributing to such expectations was the fact that many other *My Fair Lady* contributors reunited to work on *Camelot*, for example, scenic designer Smith, choreographer Holm, leading lady Andrews, and director Hart (who also became a co-producer with Lerner and Loewe). The show was in need of star power for the leading role of Arthur, however. Taking a cue from *My Fair Lady*, the creative team cast a prestigious Shakespearean actor and British import, Richard Burton, in the role. Like Rex Harrison, Burton was a musical theatre novice but a charismatic, powerful stage actor with an innate talent for musical speech; therefore, Arthur's numbers in *Camelot*, specifically written for Burton, also employ *Sprechstimme* (spoken song).

With all parties in place, further development and rehearsals of *Camelot* ensued. Based on T. H. White's *The Once and Future King* Parts III and IV (1958), Lerner's libretto again looks to mythic and historical subject matter, while providing a legendary, conflicted tale of love and idealism. The early scenes in the book detail Arthur's arranged marriage to the maiden Guinevere, whom he ultimately grows to love, and his creation of the Knights of the Round Table to bring peace, nobility, and civility to Camelot. Many supporting characters are pulled from the Arthurian legend and incorporated into the libretto, including Lancelot, a celebrated knight who instigates *Camelot*'s major plot complication and crisis. Although a model of virtue and chivalry, Lancelot falls in love with the married Guinevere. She returns the affection; and the two proceed with an affair, breaking the heart of Arthur, who loves them both but must abide by his own rules of governance for Camelot, thereby, punishing their adultery with death. In the end, however, Lancelot rescues Guinevere from being burned at the stake (with Arthur's complicity); and the lovers flee Camelot. Arthur remains to defend his embattled land, telling a young boy in the musical's last moments to remember the tale of Camelot and spread the word of its ideals and its noble moment in history.

Prior to *Camelot*'s opening, the much-anticipated production was troubled, with Lerner hospitalized for bleeding ulcers during out-of-town tryouts and Hart suffering a heart attack (he would die one year after the show's opening). Once recuperated, Lerner assumed the role of director, cutting *Camelot*'s length from four hours to a little over three. Further, as co-producer, Lerner attempted to keep the mounting production costs in check, for the project had amassed a price tag of $635,000. His efforts were not enough, however. *Camelot* opened on December 3, 1960, at the Majestic Theatre, to a disappointed audience, given the unprecedented pre-ticket box office which topped $3 million—the highest pre-opening box office to date. Reviews were mixed, with much blame placed on *Camelot*'s sprawling, ineffective libretto (versus the tight and smart book of *My Fair Lady*). Two auspicious events occurred, however, that helped to fine tune the production and sell the show. First, Hart came back to the reins of *Camelot* immediately after its opening and tightened the production, working with Lerner to continue rewriting the libretto, making cuts (although the show was still close to three hours long), and revising the ending to contain a more hopeful conclusion. Second, Lerner and Loewe appeared on CBS' *The Ed Sullivan Show*, presumably to celebrate the fifth anniversary of *My Fair Lady*. In a canny marketing move, the team used the time to "market" Camelot to a nationwide audience, presenting four excerpts from the new musical. Audiences liked what they saw and ticket sales surged, with the show ultimately running for 873 performances. The television appearance also stimulated sales of the cast recording, with much of the nation singing along with the tuneful integrated and diverse Lerner and Loewe score. As with past productions, Camelot contained lush operetta-style ballads ("If Ever I Would Leave You" and "I Loved You Once in Silence") as well as smart and witty character songs ("The Simple Joys of Maidenhood," "C'est Moi," "How to Handle a Woman," and "What Do the Simple Folk Do?") and folk-inspired ensemble numbers ("The Lusty Month of May"). One of the cast album's biggest fans was President John F. Kennedy—a fact that only emerged after his assassination. In an interview, Jacqueline Kennedy recounted that the President enjoyed listening to the record before retiring to bed and that his favorite song was the stirring title number, especially its last lines, which express the need to remember the court's "brief shining moment." From that time on, the musical would forever be linked to President Kennedy, with his administration acquiring the "Camelot" moniker.

Given the struggles and disappointments of Camelot, Lerner and Loewe parted ways after the show. Loewe embarked on a period of semiretirement, while Lerner created the moderately successful On a Clear Day You Can See Forever (1965) with composer Burton Lane. Lerner then went through a series of unsuccessful musicals with such composers as André Previn (Coco in 1969), Leonard Bernstein (1600 Pennsylvania Avenue in 1976), and Burton Lane (reuniting for the failed Carmelina in 1979). During this unfruitful period, Lerner talked Loewe into coming out of retirement to work on a stage adaptation of their award-winning movie musical Gigi (1958). The production debuted on Broadway in 1973 but only ran for 103 performances. The next year, the two collaborated again on another movie musical, The Little Prince, based on the classic children's book by Antoine de Saint-Exupéry. Although the movie features a pleasant score and Broadway choreographer/director Bob Fosse in his last filmed performance as the Snake, it was a critical and box office failure. Loewe returned to his retirement in Palm Springs, and the partnership of Lerner and Loewe was, at long last, dissolved. Lerner, however, continued to work in musical theatre. In 1978, he turned to writing books, penning a well-received autobiography, The Street Where I Live; and in 1986, he authored a theatre history tome, The Musical Theatre: A Celebration, punctuated by his personal experiences, recollections, and witty observations (it was published in 1989 to positive reviews). The publications did not mean, however, that Lerner had stopped writing for live theatre; he worked in this capacity up until his death. In his last year of life, he agreed to work with Andrew Lloyd Webber as lyricist for The Phantom of the Opera (1986). After providing lyrics for "Masquerade," he informed Lloyd Webber that he needed to leave the project, as he was losing his memory (due to an undiagnosed brain tumor). Due to health problems, Lerner also turned down an invitation to write English lyrics for the 1980s mega–musical Les Misérables. On June 14, 1986, Lerner died of lung cancer at the age of 67. Loewe would follow two years later, dying in Palm Springs on February 14, 1988. With Loewe's death, the musical theatre community bid final farewell to the "last romantics," an ending that ironically occurred on Valentine's Day. Today, the Lerner and Loewe canon is resilient and pervasive, with their works playing on Broadway, as well as regional, community, and educational stages across America and worldwide, affirming the appeal of their aesthetic, sound, and message for contemporary audiences. Lerner and Loewe may have urged the preservation and assertion of past traditions and ideals (whether rooted in fact or legend), but the continued popularity of their musicals also suggests that such historic and mythic tales contain messages that speak to the realities of the present.

Figure 5.2

SHOW ME

Music by Frederick Loewe;
Lyrics by Alan Jay Lerner (1956)

Words! Words! Words!
I'm so sick of words!
I get words all day through;
First from him, now from you.
Is that all you blighters can do?

Don't talk of stars
Burning above;
If you're in love,
Show me!
Tell me no dreams
Filled with desire.
If you're on fire,
Show me!

Here we are together in the middle of the night!
Don't talk of spring! Just hold me tight!
Anyone who's ever been in love'll tell you that
This is no time for a chat!

Haven't your lips
Longed for my touch?
Don't say how much,
Show me!
Show me!
Don't talk of love lasting through time.
Make me no undying vow.
Show me now!

Sing me no song!
Read me no rhyme!
Don't waste my time,
Show me!
Don't talk of June,
Don't talk of fall!
Don't talk at all!
Show me!

Never do I ever want to hear another word.
There isn't one I haven't heard.
Here we are together in what ought to be a dream;
Say one more word and I'll scream!

Haven't your arms
Hungered for mine?
Please don't expl'ine,
Show me!
Show me!
Don't wait until wrinkles and lines
Pop out all over my brow,
Show me now!

FEATURED PRODUCTION: *My Fair Lady* (1956)

Music by Frederick Loewe; Lyrics and Book by Alan Jay Lerner

Original Broadway Run: Opened March 15, 1956; Mark Hellinger Theatre; 2,717 performances

My Fair Lady was an exercise in perseverance, flexibility, and literally "thinking outside the box." When librettist/lyricist Alan Jay Lerner ran into Oscar Hammerstein at a 1952 Democratic rally, the older man empathized with Lerner's current frustration over the seemingly impossible task of musically adapting George Bernard Shaw's *Pygmalion* for the musical theatre. Hammerstein admitted that he and Rodgers had given up on adapting the material years earlier. Little did he know that Lerner and Loewe would soon follow suit, throwing in the towel on the project. Yet, after a two-year hiatus from *Pygmalion* and each other, Lerner and Loewe reunited and decided to give the adaptation one more try. The resulting musical was an enormous hit, often deemed to be Broadway's first real blockbuster. Specifically, *My Fair Lady* dominated the stage on multiple continents during the latter half of the 1950s, running more than six years on Broadway (2,717 performances) and winning seven 1957 Tony Awards (including Best Musical, Best Director, Best Lead Actor, Best Costumes, and Best Scenery). In 1958, the production went global, setting London abuzz when it landed at the West End with its original New York cast, ultimately running for four years at the Drury Lane Theatre, while playing in other European countries, as well as South America. Further, *My Fair Lady* was a phenomenon in the record industry. After Columbia Records secured recording rights, the score was recorded in numerous languages, grossing $800 million for the company and its creators in the ensuing two decades.

My Fair Lady even had its own Hollywood tabloid moment. When the musical was sold to Warner Bros. for $5 million, the studio hired Rex Harrison to repeat his portrayal of Henry Higgins in the film but cast Audrey Hepburn as Eliza Doolittle, instead of Julie Andrews. Andrews had not only originated the role on Broadway but had echoed the Cinderella story of the musical, as she achieved stardom via her acclaimed portrayal. Much was written in the press about the controversial leading lady choice, especially given that Hepburn's songs were ultimately dubbed by studio vocalist Marni Nixon. The brouhaha did not seem to hurt the film's reception once it debuted in 1964, however, as it was one of the top box office draws of the decade and won eight Academy Awards, including Best Film. (Andrews did not suffer professionally; she was cast as the magical nanny in Disney's *Mary Poppins* the same year and won the Academy Award for Best Actress, with the film ultimately out-grossing *My Fair Lady*).

One of the main reasons that so many musical artists (including Lerner and Loewe, initially) gave up on Shaw's source material was because it was considered to be incompatible with the conventions and traditional substance of the musical stage. Thus, it is a wonder and a triumph that the lovely-looking and -sounding *My Fair Lady* greatly retains the complex, multileveled themes and content of Shaw's play, *Pygmalion*. To understand and appreciate the achievement, distinctiveness, and density of *My Fair Lady*, one must also know something of George Bernard Shaw.

Shaw was a philosopher and social critic, as well as a legendary man of the theatre. Further, he was an avowed and outspoken proponent of Fabian Socialism, a form of socialism that advocates working within current economic systems, through progressive health and education programs, to overturn capitalism and class strictures, evolving an economic system and a society based on shared means of production and prosperity. In *Pygmalion*, Shaw's philosophical precepts and social criticisms are comically espoused in a number of ways. First, the play presents Eliza's journey as a metaphor for Shaw's theory of the "life force." This concept asserts that human beings have an innate "force" within them that determines behavior and development. If the "force" is nurtured and grown (often through the Fabian Socialist ideals of education and environment—not handouts), one can fully realize one's potential, a progressive journey to a superior human existence. Shaw saw class restrictions as obstructions to such an evolution; thus, *Pygmalion* explores and deconstructs class boundaries and the conundrums of societal/cultural inequities. The play was never considered by Shaw to be a "romantic" comedy. (In fact, the autocratic Shaw was so upset that audiences misread his play as a romance between Eliza and Higgins that he wrote an extensive, detailed epilogue in which he elaborated why Eliza and Higgins were never, and could never be, romantically inclined and/or involved.)

Pygmalion's romantic denial, philosophical underpinning, and social critique undoubtedly contributed to the frustrations felt by Loewe and, especially, Lerner when they undertook adapting the work for the musical stage (not to mention the fact that the play's humor lies in verbal sparring placed in interior scenes, instead of being conveyed through extroverted, external action). Eventually Lerner hit on the idea of dramatizing the events that were only described as having happened offstage in the original play. Therefore, he was able to expand *Pygmalion* into a musical that retained Shaw's sophisticated wordplay and pointed themes, while embellishing the material with lavish musical numbers and scenic spectacle. For instance, Lerner chose to show Eliza at the Embassy Ball (an event only described after the fact in the play), with award-winning costumer Cecil Beaton's stunning gowns sparkling in a lavish set designed by Oliver Smith. Further, instead of Eliza's first high society outing occurring at a tea party, as happens in the play, Lerner placed it at the Ascot races, allowing for a highly public (and comic) gaffe by Eliza, as well as lavish Edwardian costumes by Beaton and an elaborately staged song and dance number by choreographer Hanya Holm ("Ascot Gavotte"). Director Moss Hart was also instrumental; for having directed and studied Shaw in the past, he was a source of knowledge and insight regarding changes to and/or adaptations of Shaw's work. While Hart worked closely with Lerner to realize the musical on stage, Lerner continued to take creative license in writing the expanded libretto. Although Lerner stated that he finally conquered Shaw's material by realizing that they should do the musical by "simply doing *Pygmalion*," he ultimately provided a libretto that was at times contrary to Shaw's original instructions and demands, notably romanticizing the playwright's social commentary. Most significant was the alteration of Shaw's original ending: Lerner had Eliza retrieve slippers for Higgins, ending the production on a hopeful note that the two could eventually become a pair. Lerner's work as lyricist also softened and romanticized Higgins. With Loewe, Lerner created an active soliloquy for Higgins, "I've Grown Accustomed to Her Face," that may be viewed as a quasi love song. The song not only comprises abrupt changes in time signatures and dynamics as Higgins struggles with his feelings for Eliza, but also *Sprechstimme* (created especially for Harrison to compensate for his lack of singing ability and to exploit his dexterity with words, meter, dynamics, and range).

As illustrated by the use of *Sprechstimme* in Higgins' songs, the diversity of Lerner and Loewe's score (as well as its integrative efficacy in furthering character and plot development) is another key to *My Fair Lady*'s appeal and artistry. When the audience meets Eliza, she is a scruffy Cockney flower peddler in Covent Garden. Surrounded by her peers, she envisions a better life with the lilting "Wouldn't It Be Luverly?" In contrast to Eliza's charming wistfulness, the pomposity and chauvinism of Professor Henry Higgins are made clear in "Why Can't the English?," his classist and belligerent rant regarding the butchery of the English language. The songs prompt a wager between Higgins and his friend, Colonel Pickering, that the phonetician can make a lady of Eliza. As the experiment progresses, Higgins, Pickering, and Eliza begin to bond; and the musical moves forward with Eliza's diction lesson, which evolves into the tango-influenced "The Rain in Spain" (which, according to Lerner, took ten minutes to write). Other characters are introduced, performing songs specific to their status and role in the libretto. For instance, Eliza's father, Alfred P. Doolittle, romps through music hall numbers such as "With a Little Bit of Luck" and "Get Me to the Church on Time." (Doolittle also embodies a Fabian Socialist philosophy regarding the dangers of handouts and the inscription of the lower class into a corrupting capitalist paradigm.) Freddy, as Eliza's aspiring suitor, is given "On the Street Where You Live," an operatic tenor song suited to the romantic lead. In answer to this sweeping ballad, Eliza demonstrates her strength and assertiveness in "Show Me" (one of the more unlikely numbers sung by an ingénue in a burgeoning romance, yet the active nature of the song is the perfect musical illustration of her "life force," begging to evolve). Indeed, Eliza's songs echo her own multifaceted and conflicted character, ranging from "I Could Have Danced All Night" to "Show Me," that is, from rhapsodic operetta reflection to active dramatic expression.

My Fair Lady represents the rare instance when both the out-of-town tryouts and Broadway run of a new musical were greeted by ecstatic audiences. Its New Haven debut in February 1956 was greeted by a cheering, standing ovation. On its opening night on Broadway, audience expectations were exceptionally high, which caused much anxiety on the part of most production team members. Loewe, however, was calm at the theatre lobby bar, confident that he had written the "best musical on Broadway." Not only did audiences confirm Loewe's view with an unprecedented box office, but critics also agreed, unabashedly telling patrons in their reviews the next morning to buy their tickets posthaste. And incredibly, more than half a century later, the show continues to be greeted by similar audience enthusiasm and fandom, whether revived on Broadway or produced by a community theatre in a small Midwest town. In short, Lerner and Loewe's *My Fair Lady* is a musical placed in the past that continues to speak potently to modern-day audiences.

North Shore Music Theatre's production of *My Fair Lady* © Paul Lyden. Used by permission of Paul Lyden.

PULLING BACK THE CURTAIN:
The Pervasive Pygmalion Myth in American Musical Theatre

As illustrated by the phenomenal success of *My Fair Lady*, Broadway loves a good "Pygmalion" tale. Pygmalion is a figure from ancient Greek mythology, a male sculptor who creates an ideal statue, Galatea, and falls in love with her, forsaking all mortal women because they are incapable of attaining Galatea's perfection (bestowed on her by the sculptor). In the twentieth and twenty-first century, reconfigurations of and thematic variations on the Pygmalion myth comprise and inform much of the musical theatre canon. Specifically, many canonical musicals contain librettos centered on the notion that a woman can be molded into a male-determined ideal—a transformation that also results in a degree of power, enlightenment, and potential for the woman. Such a journey is often cheered by the audience, whether it be a rags-to-riches fable (e.g., a female version of Horatio Alger), a showbiz saga that culminates with the woman finding stardom ("a star is born"), a Cinderella tale in which the downtrodden ingénue is rescued and transformed by a Prince (signifying the idealized concept of romance and true love), or the makeover of a transgressive woman (e.g., a shrew, misfit, spinster, tomboy, etc.). In all these configurations, the woman is transformed, most often to her advantage, through her association with a man, be it a romantic interest, paternal or fraternal figure, financial or professional benefactor, instructor, taskmaster, or Svengali. She also finds her new self by working within and acquiescing to a male-dominated/ordered system. To see the prevalence and potency of the Pygmalion myth (or variations thereof) in the musical theatre genre, one need only survey the many Broadway hits based on that myth.

At the beginning of the twentieth century, many of the most successful early musicals could attribute their success to the appeal of their rags-to-riches, star-is-born, or other female-transformation tales, for example, *Mlle. Modiste*; *Irene*; *Sally*; *Sunny*; *Lady, Be Good!*; *Tip-Toes*; *Peggy-Ann*; and even *Show Boat* (given the rise of Magnolia and Kim). Moving into the Golden Age, works continued to celebrate stories of women who find stardom, fame, riches, and transformational love; such shows include *Annie Get Your Gun*; *Kiss Me, Kate* (although Shakespeare provided the source material for this "shrew" transformation prototype); *The Sound of Music*; *My Fair Lady*; *Gypsy* (especially if one looks at Gypsy Rose Lee's star transformation as not only a result of her mother's obsessive control, but also as an acquiescence to a male-controlled burlesque industry); *Funny Girl*; *Applause*; *The Unsinkable Molly Brown*; and *Little Me*. After the Golden Age, the transformed female prototype continued to triumph on the Broadway stage, taking a variety of guises: the girl from the wrong side of the Argentinean tracks who rises to fame and power in *Evita*, the ingénue who goes bad to win her man in *Grease*, the orphan who finds her Daddy Warbucks in *Annie*, the opera singer who achieves stardom under the hand of a disfigured Svengali in *Phantom of the Opera*, and the woman who becomes a star as a cross-dressing man in *Victor/Victoria*. This period also saw a successful trend in creating new works that were throwbacks to Broadway's earlier musicals of the 1920s and '30s, purposefully exploiting the Pygmalion/Cinderella archetype, while simultaneously re-presenting the stereotype as a newly liberated woman and/or source of referential comedy, e.g., *Dames at Sea*, *42nd Street*, and *Thoroughly Modern Millie*. Most recent configurations of the Pygmalion tale include transformed women who are less "controlled" by dominant male figures, but who are still strongly influenced and driven by their pursuit of a man and who ultimately prove themselves in male-dominated arenas/climates. Such works include *Hairspray* and *Legally Blonde*. Significantly, the above list of musicals does not take into account all the minor and failed shows that have also exploited the Pygmalion/Cinderella themes, not to mention actual musical versions of fairy tales such as *Cinderella* and *The Little Mermaid*.

To further address the Pygmalion paradigm, one might argue that there are musicals that feature a similarly transformed man. Such an argument is tenuous, however, as the occurrence of the Pygmalion trajectory for the male lead in a musical is rare. Some of the limited examples include *Oliver!*, *Starlight Express*, *Tommy*, and *Golden Boy*; but even these rags-to-riches, stardom-achieving, transformational tales do not entail facilitation or sponsorship by a formative, dominant female figure, neither do their stories occur within a matriarchal system (one exception is *Billy Elliot*, as Billy is taught by a female dance teacher). The closest one might get to the musical transformation of a man under a woman's hand is found in those works in which the man is changed by an ethereal female who appears to influence, romantically complicate, and/or instruct his life. However, the woman is still a version of the Pygmalion myth. She is the celestial, mythic, or other-worldly female taking human shape and, in many cases, taking on the ideal characteristics of the "eternal feminine" or femme-fatale (in other words, she embodies the male sculptor's fantasy). Such lead fantastical females are found in *I Married an Angel*, *One Touch of Venus*, *Damn Yankees*, *Xanadu*, *Mary Poppins*, *Kiss of the Spider Woman*, and even *Contact* (Girl in the Yellow Dress).

Given that such a powerful paradigm is seemingly embedded in musical theatre's DNA, it is interesting and invigorating that musicals that showcase a different type of female trajectory have also succeeded on Broadway and are prominent in the musical canon. These works feature women who are not idealized versions of the Pygmalion/Cinderella myth. Instead, they are flawed, multidimensional characters finding their own way on their own terms (even if by questionable means) to their own definitions of success. Such definitions are often nuanced, dark, and contrary; and do not include the traditional Pygmalion (male-dominated) transformation into the glittery star, rescued romantic, or triumphant femme fatale. With male characters placed firmly in the background, the anti-Pygmalion women struggle towards self-realization, refusing to succumb to the patriarchal strictures in their lives. Such women are found in *Mame*, *Chicago*, *Ragtime*, *Grey Gardens*, *Wicked*, *The Color Purple*, and *Next to Normal*, to name a few. So while the themes and concepts of the Pygmalion tale and its variations definitely underpin much of the musical canon, there are antithetical female characters in numerous works who energize the musical theatre genre by either renegotiating the myth, confrontationally and/or ironically re-engaging it, or overtly refuting it.

GEORGE ABBOTT

He is the only American musical theatre artist to have been predominantly addressed by an honorific and surname: "Mr. Abbott." Specifically, friends, contemporaries, and colleagues (as well as legions of subordinates who worked under him) respectfully and deferentially used the formal title when addressing and referring to George Abbott. In essence, they acknowledged the institutional knowledge and craft exemplified and exercised by the man who had been an active theatre pioneer and practitioner for eight decades. Yet, there was a snappier showbiz nickname also applied to Abbott: "Mr. Broadway." Indeed, Abbott was a guiding force behind the popularity and profitability of the twentieth-century musical, while giving his works the sheen of respectability and serious craftsmanship. And while Abbott's professional, perfectionist, and patrician nature was seen as bestowing "class" on the "lowbrow" musical comedy, his directorial and authorial eye also helped transform the overall genre into a model of cohesion, smartness, and artistic purpose. Abbott was, simply put, a theatrical genius and modern-day Renaissance man, making indelible marks on both the stage and screen as a director, librettist, playwright, screenwriter, producer, and actor. The musical theatre community owes a great debt to his vision and workmanship, for Abbott not only wrote (or co-wrote) some of the most popular librettos in the musical canon, but he also produced and directed some of Broadway's most formative musical works, imbuing the genre with a methodology and philosophy that has been described and celebrated as the "Abbott Touch."

George Francis Abbott was born on January 25, 1887, in Forrestville, New York. The family soon moved to the town of Salamanca where George's father was twice elected mayor. In 1898, they left the East Coast, relocating to Cheyenne, Wyoming, where George attended Kearney Military Academy. Once the family returned to New York, young Abbott finished his high school education at Hamburg High School and then attended University of Rochester, where he not only obtained a Bachelor's degree in 1911, but also wrote his first play, a comic farce titled *Perfectly Harmless* (1910), performed by the University Drama Club. Although trained as an actor, Abbott continued to be interested in writing. He attended Harvard University where he studied playwriting under George Pierce Baker as a member of Baker's celebrated 47 Workshop. Under Baker's tutelage, Abbott wrote *The Head of the Family*, which was performed by the Harvard Dramatic Club in 1912. In search of a professional career, Abbott next worked for a year as an assistant stage manager at the Bijou Theatre in Boston, where his play, *The Man in the Manhole*, won a contest. It was not long before Abbott returned to New York City, starting his career in 1913 as a professional actor on Broadway as a drunken college boy in *The Misleading Lady*. The next year he married his first wife, Ednah Levis, with whom he had a daughter, Judith. (After Ednah's death in 1930, Abbott married two more times: in 1946 to Mary Sinclair, which ended in divorce five years later, and in 1983, at age 96, to Joy Valderrama.) In the dozen years that followed his Broadway debut, Abbott was steadily employed as an actor, performing in nine Broadway productions. He finally achieved professional notice for his other passion—writing—as he co-penned a comic melodrama with James Gleason, *The Fall Guy*, which premiered on Broadway in 1925. (We should note that, from the very beginning, Abbott was an adroit and prolific collaborator. Throughout his career, he worked with co-writers for many of his most successful plays and librettos, in addition to sharing directing duties for some of his hit musicals.) The next year, 1926, Abbott branched into directing, a vocation that would cement his legacy as one of the formative pioneers of the Broadway musical theatre. The production, which he co-wrote with John V. A. Weaver, was a comedy titled *Love 'Em and Leave 'Em*. The same year, Abbott enjoyed his first big hit: *Broadway* (1926). The backstage crime drama, which grittily depicts a seamy and illicit side of New York City during Prohibition, was originally written by Philip Dunning but was so thoroughly doctored by Abbott that he was credited as a co-author. The production was co-directed by Abbott and Dunning; and when it opened on September 16, 1926, it proved to be a hit with jazz-era audiences who reveled in the play's current and street-smart atmosphere, content, and language. *Broadway* ran for a remarkable 603 performances. Interestingly, sixty-one years later, Abbott would remount *Broadway* on Broadway, serving once again, at age 100, as the production's director. Unfortunately, even as an archival curiosity, the play was hopelessly archaic, and the production closed after only four nights.

In the 1930s, Abbott began to produce Broadway shows as well as write and direct them. The first was *Lilly Turner* (1932), co-produced with his previous writing and directing partner, Phillip Dunning (by this time, the two had formed the business partnership of Abbott-Dunning, Inc., producing two other plays during the decade). His musical comedy career also began in the mid-1930s, when he co-directed (with John Murray Anderson) Richard Rodgers and Lorenz Hart's epic-scale circus musical, *Jumbo* (1935). He worked on three more Rodgers and Hart hits, staging (uncredited) and co-authoring the libretto for *On Your Toes* (1936); producing, directing, and writing *The Boys From Syracuse* (1938); and producing and directing *Pal Joey* (1940), while working as the show's uncredited librettist. In just over two decades (1913–35), Abbott had progressed from actor-for-hire to a powerful Broadway force: creating, directing, and producing formative works in every theatrical genre. Further, there was rarely a year on Broadway from the mid-1920s to the 1980s that did not see a production directed and/or written by Abbott. Below is a representative sampling of the more than one hundred Broadway works that were written, directed, and/or produced (solely or collaboratively) by Abbott during the seventy years that followed his 1925 writing debut, not including his uncredited efforts as a show or libretto/script doctor. (If counting Broadway productions in which he performed, the exhaustive list expands to

over 130 works.) The necessity of a condensed chronological overview illustrates the unprecedented and yet-to-be-replicated extent and expanse of Abbott's contributions to the theatre.

1926   *Love 'Em and Leave 'Em* (playwright, director)

1926   *Chicago* (director)

1926   *Broadway* (playwright, director)

1927   *Four Walls* (playwright, director)

1928   *Gentlemen of the Press* (director)

1930   *Those We Love* (playwright, director, performer)

1932   *Lilly Turner* (playwright, director, producer)

1932   *Twentieth Century* (director, producer)

1934   *Kill That Story* (director, producer)

1935   *Three Men on a Horse* (playwright, director)

1935   *Jumbo* (director)

1936   *On Your Toes* (librettist)

1937   *Room Service* (director, producer)

1938   *The Boys from Syracuse* (librettist, director, producer)

1939   *Too Many Girls* (director, producer)

1940   *Pal Joey* (director, producer)

1941   *Best Foot Forward* (director, producer)

1942   *Beat the Band* (librettist, director, producer)

1943   *Kiss and Tell* (director, producer)

1944   *On the Town* (director)

1945   *Billion Dollar Baby* (director)

1947   *High Button Shoes* (director)

1948   *Where's Charley?* (librettist, director)

1948   *Look Ma, I'm Dancin'!* (producer, director)

1949   *Mrs. Gibbons' Boys* (producer, director)

1950   *Call Me Madam* (director)

1951   *A Tree Grows in Brooklyn* (librettist, director, producer)

1953   *Wonderful Town* (director)

1953   *Me and Juliet* (director)

1954   *The Pajama Game* (librettist, director)

1955   *Damn Yankees* (librettist, director)

1957   *New Girl in Town* (librettist, director)

1959   *Once Upon a Mattress* (director)

1959   *Fiorello!* (librettist, director)

1960   *Tenderloin* (librettist, director)

1962   *A Funny Thing Happened on the Way to the Forum* (director)

1964   *Fade Out–Fade In* (director)

1965   *Flora, The Red Menace* (librettist, director)

1965   *Anya* (librettist, director)

1967   *How Now, Dow Jones* (director)

1968   *The Education of H*Y*M*A*N K*A*P*L*A*N* (director)

1969   *The Fig Leaves Are Falling* (director)

1970   *Norman, Is That You?* (director)

1973   *The Pajama Game* (revival, librettist, director)

1976   *Music Is* (librettist, director)

1983   *On Your Toes* (revival, librettist, director)

1987   *Broadway* (revival, playwright, director)

1994   *Damn Yankees* (revival, librettist, creative consultant, script revisions)

To further highlight and contextualize this overwhelming body of work—the longest showbiz career of the twentieth century—one might examine Abbott's Broadway activities during the 1950s, treating the period as a microcosm of Abbott's influence and practice on Broadway. It was during this decade, at the height of the Golden Age, that the man who had come to be addressed as "Mr. Abbott" created some of the era's most memorable and emblematic musical comedies. Although he continued his efforts as a producer in the early '50s (e.g., *A Tree Grows in Brooklyn* in 1951, which he also co-wrote and directed), he stopped producing Broadway works after a 1954 revival of *On Your Toes* (which he again directed). Instead, he concentrated on directing, writing, and doctoring librettos and plays for the remainder of his theatrical career. It is significant to note that during the '50s, the musical theatre industry had begun to change, reflecting the more contemporary Broadway model in which original musicals have extensive development periods and, if successful, enjoy lengthy runs. Thus, the number of new works appearing on Broadway each season was diminishing. Yet, there was only one year during the '50s (1956) that did not see a Broadway debut of a show associated with Abbott. Further, there were numerous years in which Abbott had multiple shows opening and running simultaneously. Of course, there were a number of failures, but his successes during the decade, which started with Irving Berlin's *Call Me Madam* in 1950, included *Wonderful Town* (1953), *The Pajama Game* (1954), *Damn Yankees* (1955), *New Girl in Town* (1957), *Once Upon a Mattress* (1959), and *Fiorello!* (1958).

During this period, Abbott continued to codify a style and methodology that was soon to be admired as the Abbott Touch. In short, the Abbott Touch was a Midas Touch (or, to overwork the metaphor, a golden touch for the Golden Age). Due to his literary/writing education and acumen, Abbott, as a director, knew how to amuse and entertain audiences by streamlining and sharpening a show's textual and musical material, then translating all to the stage in an honest, cohesive, propelled manner, able to manipulate a work's disparate mechanics into a smoothly running musical theatre machine. He reportedly referred to his legacy of directorial editing, collaborating, refining, and staging as simply bringing "common sense" and "plot" to the musical comedy. Abbott's theatrical pace was often brisk, but only when it served the necessary comic tempo of a show. He also knew how to juxtapose snappy dialogue, comic antics, and catchy songs with scenes of quiet emotion, sweet sentiment, duets, and ballads. In short, Abbott had a knack for finding the laughs, as well as the poignancy, in a libretto, while displaying an instinct for communicating the moments most effectively and efficiently to an audience. In the process, he sometimes gave his cast members "line readings" (i.e., instructing them on how to say their lines)—a practice frowned upon by experienced, formally trained actors. Nonetheless, some of his untrained and novice performers appreciated Abbott's eye and meticulous instruction, crediting the director for helping them realize winning performances. Even the top stars who worked with him (a roster that included Ethel Merman, Zero Mostel, Chita Rivera, Gwen Verdon, John Raitt, Carol Lawrence, and Ray Bolger) often deferred to his wishes, conceding that an acting choice "suggested" by Mr. Abbott was most often the "right" one. In a self-deprecating—or simply pragmatic—fashion, Abbott asserted in interviews that his successful directing formula consisted of making his actors say their "final syllables," a conscious adherence by the writer/director to the purity and efficacy of a well-crafted libretto and score. And although he may have been controlling in terms of performances and other aspects of a musical's development, he also sought to become invisible once the production played to an audience. He preferred that the flow, cleverness, and cohesion of the staged show speak for itself, with no intrusive or self-expressive showboating (by himself or others) to disrupt the theatrical experience for an audience. Mr. Abbott had little patience for "artsy" indulgences or show-stopping exhibitions that did not serve, first and foremost, the story and integrated forward thrust of the show. It was a philosophy and practice that Abbott further exploited while serving as one of Broadway's most called-on show and script doctors, credited for invaluable contributions and improvements made to weak or failing productions during their rehearsal periods, out-of-town tryouts, or workshops. The Abbott Touch also entailed an eye for and trust of new talent, as Mr. Abbott often gambled on beginners, casting or collaborating with novices who, under his professional guidance and example, eventually found their own voices and careers in the theatre. Always the pragmatist, Abbott cheekily cited the money-saving advantages of working with young, pliable unknowns, as well as the lack of strain on his "nervous system." Among those performers, writers, directors, composers, and producers who were either given their first big Broadway breaks by Abbott or worked closely with him on their initial Broadway outings were Desi Arnaz, Gene Kelly, Comden and Green, Hal Prince, Leonard Bernstein, Jule Styne, Stephen Sondheim (as composer), Bock and Harnick, Tom Bosley, Carol Burnett, Elaine Stritch, Kander and Ebb, and Liza Minnelli. Also included in this group are the iconic choreographers George Balanchine, Jerome Robbins, and Bob Fosse; for Abbott was instrumental, as writer and/or director, in the creation of their initial Broadway choreographic triumphs, which redefined the role of dance in the musical (e.g., *On Your Toes*, *On the Town*, and *Pajama Game*), as well as follow-up works by these artists that further advanced the choreographer's import and presence in the genre. By way of association and facilitation, therefore, one might cite Abbott as a force behind the expanded and codified role of integrated musical theatre dance.

To best appreciate the model of the Abbott Touch, it is useful to look at the method and madness behind Abbott's biggest box office hit of the 1950s: *The Pajama Game* (1954). This musical adaptation of Richard Bissell's 1953 novel, *7½ Cents*, was directed by Abbott, who, in his usual collaborative and multitasking method, co-wrote the libretto with Bissell. In short, *Pajama Game* is a musical comedy that depicts a battle between management and employees in a pajama factory over a 7½-cent wage increase, resulting in a strike by the workers. The crux of the show, however, is the relationship between the new plant supervisor (Sid) and the union organizer (Babe), a budding romance complicated by the labor dispute. In musical comedy fashion, however, both the strike and the love story are resolved in the end. Abbott was talked into working on the project by his frequent stage manager, Robert Griffith, and his assistant, Harold Prince—two men who had dreams of becoming Broadway producers, along with their third partner, Frederick Brisson. The trio had secured rights to the book and financing, on the condition that Abbott helm the project. Abbott agreed to not only direct but to also help Bissell adapt his book. Abbott asked past collaborator Frank Loesser (whose first Broadway musical, *Where's Charley?*, was written and directed by Abbott) to write the score. When Loesser turned him down, Abbott and his producers took a characteristic chance on Broadway neophytes by hiring Loesser's Tin Pan Alley protégés, Richard Adler and Jerry Ross (songwriting partners who wrote music and lyrics together). With *Pajama Game*'s score being written by an unproven Broadway team, Abbott and the producers felt that the musical needed a proven and lauded choreographer to design its dances, that is, Jerome Robbins (whose Broadway choreographic debut, *On the Town*, had not only been facilitated and directed by Abbott but had also resulted in Robbins' working with Abbott on four consecutive Broadway shows). Robbins, however, wanted to move past the singular role of choreographer and break into directing. Fortunately, Abbott's friend, Broadway dancer Joan McCracken, suggested that he hire her husband, a young dancer and novice choreographer named Bob Fosse. Abbott viewed a forty-eight-second dance duet (featuring Fosse and Carol Haney) that Fosse had choreographed for the 1953 film version of *Kiss Me, Kate*. Ever-appreciative of new and exciting talent, Abbott liked what he saw, but he still wanted Robbins to oversee Fosse's choreography. Shrewdly, Robbins agreed to supervise Fosse's work, but only if he could partner with Abbott as an official co-director of the show. Abbott, no stranger to collaboration and secure in his own abilities and authority, agreed to the arrangement.

Happily, the gambles taken on *Pajama Game*'s novice talent paid off. The score by newcomers Adler and Ross proved to be diverse, theatrical, reflective of plot and character and rooted in the Tin Pan Alley ethos of chart-topping pop music. Their ballad "Hey There" became a radio hit before the show even opened. Other musical standouts, as well as standalone hits, included a tango spoof, "Hernando's Hideaway," a novelty number, "Steam Heat," a big ensemble/production number, "Once a Year Day," and a hillbilly-style duet, "There Once Was a Man." Abbott's belief in Fosse's nascent talent proved equally prescient, even though the two men were at odds regarding Fosse's biggest choreographic triumph in the production, "Steam Heat." According to reports, Abbott was not happy with the number as it interrupted the show's forward thrust, as well as the fact that it seemed to be a stand-alone choreographic exhibition (danced by three abstract performers) that had little to do with the story. Robbins and Prince, however, supported Fosse; and the number stayed in the show, proving to be the showstopper that Abbott feared, yet garnering great critical acclaim for Fosse. In fact, most of the numbers in *Pajama Game* pleased audiences immensely, even though the creators initially worried that the work would be a flop, given the meager résumés belonging to some production team members, as well as the lackluster advance ticket sales. But when the show opened on May 13, 1954, all fears were put to rest, due in great part to Abbott's fashioning of an unlikely "labor" musical into a tight, energetic, warm romantic comedy. This was even more of an achievement given that the "labor" content and context of *Pajama Game* had initially discouraged financial backers who were worried about a "McCarthy era" backlash (i.e., unions were negatively tied to communism at the time). The apolitical Abbott, who had little patience for such nonsense, added a prologue to the show in which a character directly addresses the audience, informing them of the musical romp to follow and making light of any attempt to read a sociopolitical message into the musical. When pressed by the media to name which side *Pajama Game* was on (organized labor or capitalism), Abbott stayed true to his "Mr. Broadway" reputation, answering that the musical was on the side of "the audience." (In another attempt to lighten the plot and create a diversion from the labor versus capitalist debate, while creating opportunities for more diverse musical numbers, Abbott provided the libretto's comic subplot, tailored to the talents of character actor Eddie Foy, Jr. and idiosyncratic dancer/actor Carol Haney.)

On opening night, applause stopped *Pajama Game* after almost every number, adding ten minutes to the production's running time (one of the few cases when Abbott may have forgiven such stoppages). The musical itself won the Tony Award for Best Musical and ran for 1,063 performances. Furthermore, three of the most important and innovative artists in musical theatre jumpstarted their careers by working with Abbott on *Pajama Game*: Robbins (premiere director/choreographer of the Golden Age), Fosse (who would follow Robbins' example, proving to be a choreographic/directorial icon and innovator during the 1960s and '70s), and Abbott's early assistant and frequent young producer, Hal Prince (who would move into directing in the 1960s and soon become the most celebrated musical theatre director of the contemporary era). All three men, especially Prince, credited Abbott as their mentor, as well as the seminal influence on and facilitator of their directing careers.

In the year following *The Pajama Game*, Prince/Griffith/Brisson (producers), Adler/Ross (songwriters), Abbott (co-librettist/director), and Fosse (choreographer) reteamed to create *Damn Yankees* (1955), another hit musical comedy of the 1950s. The show is a Faustian tale in which a middle-aged, rabid baseball fan barters his soul to the devil in order to be made into a young, gifted player who becomes the star of his beloved team, the Washington Senators. Ultimately, he must choose between winning the Pennant against the "damn" Yankees or returning to his old life with his loving wife. *Damn Yankees* sounded a chord with musical comedy lovers, baseball lovers, New Yorkers, and Americans in general. The tightly crafted comic delight, helmed by Abbott, ran for 1,019 performances and won the Tony Award for Best Musical (Abbott's second in two years).

It is significant that up until the late 1950s, Abbott also worked in Hollywood as a writer and director. Specifically, Abbott was not only nominated for a screenwriting Academy Award for the classic *All Quiet on the Western Front* (1930); but overall, he had approximately forty Hollywood works to his credit from 1918 to 1958, many being film versions of his musicals and plays (including his direction of hit adaptations of *The Pajama Game* and *Damn Yankees*). Abbott ended the 1950s on another artistic high note on Broadway, triumphantly co-writing and directing the Pulitzer Prize-winning *Fiorello!* (1959).

As Abbott moved into the 1960s and beyond, many of his original musicals and plays were disappointments (and some were out-and-out flops). One exception was *A Funny Thing Happened on the Way to the Forum* (1962)—his last original hit—which contained the first score with both lyrics and music by Stephen Sondheim to play on Broadway. Abbott won another Tony Award for his direction of *Forum* (even though he called on Jerome Robbins to heavily "doctor" the production—an ironic turn of events, given Abbott's past role as Robbins' superior and mentor, as well as Abbott's own notoriety as a show doctor). In 1964, Abbott's direction of *Fade Out–Fade In* (1964) was critically praised, and the show would have been another success but for its premature closure due to the exit of its star, Carol Burnett (whom Abbott initially directed in her stellar 1959 Broadway debut, *Once Upon a Mattress*). Toward the end of his career, Abbott's hits were limited to revivals of earlier triumphs. For instance, he surprised the Broadway community in 1983 when he directed (in his nineties) an acclaimed revival of his 1936 hit, *On Your Toes*, breathing new life into a musical almost fifty years old, with the new production running longer

(505 performances) than the original. Until his death, Abbott continued to be a prominent voice and presence on the theatre scene, developing projects and serving as an esteemed advisor to up-and-coming directors and librettists. In 1993, at the age of 106, Mr. Abbott was still actively at work, advising director Jack O'Brien on book revisions for a 1994 Broadway revival of *Damn Yankees*. Further, it was reported that, when walking down the aisle on *Damn Yankees*' opening night, the 107-year-old Abbott was given a standing ovation, to which he was overheard musing that someone of importance must be in attendance that night. (The revival was also a hit, running 533 performances and enjoying a successful national tour featuring comedy star Jerry Lewis.) The revival of *Damn Yankees* was Abbott's last theatrical triumph.

On January 31, 1995, in Miami Beach, Abbott died of a stroke. The untraditional setting was appropriate, for Abbott, the ultimate Broadway insider, had been an industry anomaly, preferring to reside in Florida over the Big Apple, living modestly (he was notoriously frugal) and spending his free time perfecting his ballroom dance skills and golf game. His patrician allure set him apart from his peers: Mr. Abbott was an erudite professional who was never seen at work in anything other than a suit and tie. In the course of his career, he not only had a Broadway theater named after him (the 54th Street Theatre was renamed the George Abbott Theatre in 1965, but was demolished in 1970) but also a section of West 45th Street in New York City (George Abbott Way). He received a Tony for lifetime achievement (Laurence Langer Award) in 1976 and a Special Tony Award in 1987 in honor of his 100th birthday, along with five directing/writing Tonys during his career. Other awards included the 1959 Pulitzer Prize for Drama, the 1982 Kennedy Center Lifetime Achievement Award, and the 1990 National Medal of Arts. It is no wonder why, on the evening of his death, the lights on Broadway were dimmed in tribute; for there would never be another artist in the modern theatre era to match the career, legacy, and influence of Mr. Abbott.

FEATURED PRODUCTION: *Fiorello!* (1959)

Music by Jerry Bock; Lyrics by Sheldon Harnick
Book by Jerome Weidman and George Abbott

Original Broadway Run: Opened November 23, 1959; Broadhurst Theatre; 795 performances

Musical biographies are not rare and constitute an impressive segment of the musical theatre canon (e.g., *Annie Get Your Gun, The King and I, Gypsy, The Sound of Music, The Unsinkable Molly Brown, Funny Girl, George M!, Evita, Barnum, The Will Rogers Follies, Jelly's Last Jam, The Boy from Oz, Jersey Boys, Grey Gardens, Fela!*, etc.). Musicals rooted in American politics are less common, with the significant portion created during the politically restless and reformist era of the 1930s (e.g., *Of Thee I Sing, Pins and Needles, The Cradle Will Rock, Leave It to Me!, Louisiana Purchase*). Thus, a late-1950s musical biography of a historic mayor, underpinned by an examination of early twentieth-century New York City politics, was a gamble. Even with a colorful, magnetic character at its center, such a show could become mired in local politics and cold historical data and, therefore, alienate a contemporary musical theatre audience. Aware of this conundrum, the creators of *Fiorello!* (composer Jerry Bock, lyricist Sheldon Harnick, co-librettists Jerome Weidman/George Abbott, and director Abbott) decided to address not only the political rise of longtime New York City mayor Fiorello LaGuardia, but also his personal love life. Their experiment, originally produced by Robert Griffith and Harold Prince, proved more than successful, with the songwriting team of Bock and Harnick realizing their first Broadway hit. All in all, *Fiorello!* ran for 795 performances, winning not only the Tony Award for Best Musical (sharing the prize with *The Sound of Music*) but also the Pulitzer Prize for Drama.

Weidman and Abbott's libretto is mostly drawn from Ernest Cuneo's *Life with Fiorello* (1955), a biography of the reformist Republican who battled Tammany Hall, ultimately becoming one of New York City's most famous and powerful mayors. The show starts with a flashback in which pre-mayoral Fiorello, in his modest 1915 law office, attends to all clients, regardless of their ability to pay, and vows to help the New York City female shirtwaist strikers, as well as their champion, Thea Almerigotti, who was arrested on their behalf. Then, with the aid of his trusted secretary, Marie, Fiorello decides to put his hat into the ring for the office of U.S. Congressman, once it appears that Congressional district leader Ben and his poker-playing politicos are having little luck finding anyone gullible enough to be the Republican candidate for the district ("Politics and Poker"). Next, while working for the striking women, Fiorello accepts a dinner date to plan "strategy" with Thea, newly released from prison, forcing him to break his date with Marie, who angrily and comically rants in a song, declaring new rules for courtship and marriage ("Marie's Law"). In the next year, Fiorello campaigns for Congress with Thea at his side, while Marie continues to assist his efforts. He aims to destroy the corruption and power of the political New York City machine, Tammany Hall ("The Name's LaGuardia"). After Fiorello wins, the political establishment is stunned ("The Bum Won"). One year later, he enlists in the Air Force to serve in World War I, proposing marriage to Thea before he leaves and bidding farewell to the steadfast Marie, who still loves him ("Till Tomorrow"). The war is presented through stage montages and film projections. After the war, Fiorello returns to marry Thea, and the ever-faithful Marie, who has also awaited his return, is brokenhearted. The musical's second act jumps almost a decade to 1929. Fiorello is now running for mayor of New York City, but Thea is seriously ill, even though, after a doctor's visit, she still revels in her feelings for Fiorello ("When Did I Fall in Love?"). Meanwhile, corrupt backers of Fiorello's mayoral opponent, Jimmy Walker, have met; one gang member wants to have Fiorello killed during a public speech—a plot discovered by Marie. To further complicate matters, Fiorello's campaign is not going well, due in part to the firing of district leader Ben. Even more troubling is the fact that Thea's health is quickly deteriorating. Ultimately, the plot to kill Fiorello is foiled; but his life is still turned upside down as Thea dies and the race for mayor is won by Walker. Nonetheless, the tragedy serves to strengthen Fiorello's resolve to triumph over political corruption, although he is shaken by his defeat. In 1933, Ben and cronies are again playing poker ("Little Tin Box"). Marie arrives and, after announcing in a fit of bluster that she will quit her job and marry "The Very Next Man" who asks her, she convinces Ben to help Fiorello remount a mayoral campaign. After recruiting Ben, she talks Fiorello into overcoming his fears and running again. With Ben's help, Fiorello finally becomes mayor. He also proposes to Marie, who happily accepts his hand in marriage.

In many respects, *Fiorello!*'s libretto plays fast and loose with historical facts. For instance, in real life, Thea only lived for three years after marrying Fiorello, and Fiorello was not as much of an outsider in New York politics as the libretto paints him. Yet, the authors' artistic license was dramatically effective in 1959, as was their ability to balance their depiction of the inner workings of New York City politics with humor and romance. Equally successful was their rendering of Fiorello, portraying him as an appealing, brash, and energetic showman/reformer (given great pizzazz and authenticity by Tom Bosley in his first Broadway role, winning a Tony and becoming a star in the process). Looking at the libretto and score today, a repeated comic highlight is the musical and sardonic treatment of early New York City politicos and their corrupt political machinery. First, during a poker game and song, "Politics and Poker," a group of political power-brokers satirically and cynically tries to pick a Republican candidate gullible enough to run in a futile district, all the while comparing politics to poker, with their political machinations underscored by a waltz tempo and lilting melody. Later, in "The Bum Won," the same politicians curse Fiorello, who ran and won, without their support, on a platform of cleaning up the city's corruption. Capping the comic depiction of the politicos is their last number, "Little Tin Box," during which they again sit around a poker table, this time imagining scenarios in which Tammany politicians stand before a judge and spin ridiculous tales to justify their ill-gotten wealth (due, in actuality, to having had their hands in the tills, or "little tin boxes," for years). Yet *Fiorello!* is not all satire and sociopolitical commentary; there are also gentle, lyrical numbers, rich in melody and warm sentiment (e.g., "When Did I Fall in Love?" and "Till Tomorrow"). In addition, dance rhythms abound in the Bock/Harnick score, e.g., the gentrified, demure waltz of "Till Tomorrow," the heavier, driving waltz of "Politics and Poker," the vigorous march-time of Fiorello's campaign number, "The Name's LaGuardia," and the use of a jazzy Charleston for "Gentleman Jimmy" (a number about infamous mayor Jimmy Walker). In short, the bouncy, diverse, and richly pleasing score, joined with the smart, tight libretto, made *Fiorello!* a hit when it opened on Broadway in 1959. The musical was showered with critical praise, enjoyed a healthy box office, spawned a best-selling original cast album, and won top awards. Curiously, however, to date the work has not been revived on Broadway. The closest approximations have been concert productions, performed by *Encores!* at the New York City Center in 1994 and 2013. Thus, reflecting the fickle and fluid nature of the musical theatre canon, *Fiorello!*, one of the most critically acclaimed works during the Golden Age, is rarely produced in America today and has practically fallen into obscurity. Nonetheless, the work may be ripe for rediscovery by contemporary musical theatre audiences, given its political satire, warm romance, and classically pleasing score, all created by luminaries of the musical theatre.

PULLING BACK THE CURTAIN:
Putting It Together: The Musical Theatre Director

A musical is an epic undertaking, given its disparate components supplied by various artists. Further, the collaborative nature of the musical sometimes makes it difficult to recognize the specific role played by the director in the overall process. In most cases, the director neither wrote nor designed the show's content; yet, he or she is responsible for the production of the material for an audience. To appreciate the role of the contemporary director, below is a quick summary of his or her duties:

Casting: There is a theatrical adage that the largest percentage of a show's success lies in astute casting. The director is the person most responsible for this task, although he or she works closely with the music director, choreographer, producer, and possibly, casting agents/directors. In the end, however, the show director usually has the final say as to the performers who will bring the production to life on stage. (The exception to this rule is the occasional case in which a producer has cast the show before the director has been hired.)

Production Concept: The director is the visionary who decides on the interpretation of a book and score, providing the overarching concept and intent (sometimes in terms of an image, theme, message, or metaphor) to guide and cohere all aspects of the production's staging and design. In this respect, the director can be an *interpretative artist*, faithful to material as written and aiming to present it on stage as close to the authors' intentions as possible; a *translator*, aiming to capture the "spirit" of the written work but departing from the authors' original specifications (directors of revivals frequently work in this manner); or *auteur*, a principal creative force behind the production, often free to reshape material as he or she sees fit.

Show Development and Rehearsal: In the case of original musicals, the director sometimes serves as an authorial collaborator during workshops, try-outs, and other early production stages. In this role, the director may work with the musical creators to suggest cuts and alterations to help with the show's staging, dramatic flow, and theatrical efficacy. Another crucial part of the development process is the period during which the director, with the choreographer and music director, rehearses the performers. The director serves as the master coordinator and primary "eye" for the production during the rehearsal period. His or her rehearsals include coaching and facilitating actors' insights and interpretative choices with regard to character development, along with the designing of stage pictures/images (e.g., tableaus, spatial relationships, levels, patterns, and focal points) and "blocking" of actors (i.e., movement, gesture, and stage business) to convey situation, emotion, and relationships in scenes and songs, providing visual interest and cues to aid in storytelling. (In a musical, much of the blocking crosses over into choreography.)

Design Guidance: Except for the rare circumstance, the director does not design the scenery, costumes, lighting, or technical sound of a musical. However, the director does work closely with designers to see that his or her concept is accurately represented in scenery, costume, light, and sound. During a show's development, a director may even dictate initial design ideas, while providing commanding images, style choices, technical requirements, and aesthetics to be employed by the designers.

Integrator/Overseer: The musical theatre director must integrate the many disparate elements (song, dialogue, dance, tech/design) into a finished product. In short, the contemporary musical theatre director is the theatrical overseer who provides creative vision and management, coordinating all the elements of a production into a representation of his or her artistic concept.

Even though by the 1900s the nonmusical theatre had already ushered in the era of the modern director, the American musical theatre was slow to follow. Up until the Golden Age, the director of a musical was mostly a "hired gun"; that is, an able functionary whose efforts were often at the mercy and whim of the show's producer/impresario (who had hired him/her), the star (who could have him/her fired), and/or the composer (who saw the musical as, first and foremost, a song showcase). Thus, the director was often billed as a "stager" of the musical, suggesting only the rudimentary mechanics of moving bodies and scenery around the stage. There were, however, those who foreshadowed the modern musical theatre director. In many cases, it was because such men wore more than one hat with regard to their work on musicals (and it is important to note that until Agnes de Mille, men dominated the role of Broadway stage musical director). For instance, **Julian Mitchell** (1854–1926) is often cited as the first director/dance-arranger to wield significant power on Broadway. Having started his professional career as a dancer, he began arranging dance numbers for Broadway shows, demanding an unprecedented degree of professionalism and discipline from his dancers, while raising dance standards on Broadway overall. Once he became a director, he was able to combine the staging of scenes and songs with his choreographic talents, employing the same expectations of technical skill and exactitude from all performers. He was known for the brisk, fluid, and energetic quality of his shows, as well as his entertaining and intricately designed production numbers (industry insiders assert that the character of Julian Marsh in *42nd Street* is a fictional homage to Julian Mitchell). As one of the most prolific directors on Broadway, Mitchell staged everything from *Ziegfeld Follies* editions to hit operettas, ultimately overseeing more than eighty works during his lifetime. Sixteen years younger than Mitchell, **Edward Royce** (1870–1964) was also an early stage director/dance-arranger (and producer) who worked almost constantly on Broadway from 1913–29. In addition to staging most of the groundbreaking Princess Theatre musicals, Royce helmed one of the biggest box office hits of the nascent musical theatre era, *Irene* (1919), as well as numerous revues and a smash star vehicle, *Sally* (1920). Another directing pioneer was **Hassard Short** (1877–1956), who was not only a director but a set and lighting designer in musical theatre. He directed more than fifty Broadway and West End shows from 1920–53. After 25 years as a successful actor, Short turned to directing and designing, exploiting his talents in both areas to realize his conceptual "vision" of a production (foreshadowing artists such as Julie Taymor). He has been described as one of Broadway's greatest lighting designers and a groundbreaking musical theatre director, with credited innovations that include, in 1921, the first permanent lighting bridge (*Music Box Revue*) and in 1931, the first use of a revolving stage in a Broadway musical (*The Band Wagon*).

The careers of Mitchell, Royce, and Short were anomalies, however, until the librettos of musical comedies became more sophisticated and integrated, requiring directors who could not only design and stage a flashy production number alongside a well-delivered comic scene but also create a theatrical experience as a dramatic whole. It may be no coincidence that the earliest powerful, prolific, influential and innovative musical theatre directors were in the vein of celebrated master **George Abbott** (1887–1995); that is, they were significant American playwrights and librettists who evolved into stage directors. In the process, they elevated the import, profile, and craft of musical theatre direction. In addition to Mr. Abbott, the most significant examples are **George S. Kaufman** (1889–1961) and **Moss Hart** (1904–61), who not only staged their own musical librettos with serious attention paid to theatrical flow, entertainment, cohesion, and storytelling, but also directed masterpieces written by others, for example, *Guys and Dolls* (1950) and *My Fair Lady* (1956), respectively. At the onset of the Golden Age, the newly respected dramatic potential of the musical drew other artists to the medium. One such artist was **Rouben Mamoulian** (1897–1987), a director of film, opera, and plays who brought a prodigious technique and willingness to experiment with innovative material to the musical stage, spearheading such canonical groundbreakers as *Porgy and Bess* (1935), *Oklahoma!* (1943), and *Carousel* (1945). Thus, by mid-twentieth century, the director of musical theatre had "caught up" with the nonmusical modern director, in terms of power, import, technique, and function.

To completely appreciate the advance and redefinition of the musical theatre director's role during the twentieth century and beyond, one must look to several factors and developments that not only helped spark and facilitate such an evolution but also continue to inform the director's role in today's musical theater arena. First, as dance became a more sophisticated and integrated component during musical theatre's Golden Age, the choreographer correspondingly became more important and recognized with regard to the success of a musical production, ultimately suggesting that a choreographer may be well suited to the role of director, that is, a "choreographer/director." In this new capacity, the single artist could direct, coordinate, and design all aspects of staging a musical production, with duties no longer being divided between a "stage director" and "choreographer." Further, such choreographer/directors could employ their own concepts for musicals, in terms of visuals/kinetics (to the point of dictating scenic and costume designs), as they wielded higher degrees of power and more hands-on control, somewhat serving as directorial auteurs. The ultimate realization of such directorial and choreographic pursuits would result in dance-centric musicals such as *West Side Story* and *A Chorus Line* or, toward the end of the twentieth century, the "dansical" (e.g., *Contact* and *Movin' Out*), which sublimated the role of the score and text to the choreographer/director's medium of dance and staging. Of course, there had been early and/or semi-realized exemplars of choreographer/directors before the Golden Age (e.g., Julian Mitchell and George Balanchine), but the dominant stars in the choreographer/director paradigm who helped usher in a new musical theatre model that exploited dance, staging, and overall visual/kinetic components were Jerome Robbins, Bob Fosse, Michael Bennett, Gower Champion, and Tommy Tune. And these formative artists set the stage for a contemporary crop of directorial/choreographic powerhouses that includes Susan Stroman, Kathleen Marshall, Graciela Daniele, Jerry Mitchell, Twyla Tharp, and Bill T. Jones.

Another significant development that contributed to the evolution of the musical theatre director was the advent of the concept musical. As this musical theatre form proliferated in the late 1960s, its thematic and conceptual focus (as opposed to a strict adherence to a linear and representational story) allowed for more freedom, creativity, and control with regard to the director's vision, interpretation, and depiction of the material on stage. This musical form relied on a director who could use his or her production concept to manifest the work's crucial linking theme via staging, design, performances, and all other aspects of the production, relaying the information clearly and cohesively to an audience. A prominent example of such a director, who also happens to be the most lauded director of the contemporary musical era, is Harold Prince. Specifically, Prince proved visionary in both the staging and design oversight of iconic concept musicals such as 1966's *Cabaret* (employing a giant mirror behind the action on stage to suggest the alienating, performative aesthetic of the piece, while reflecting the audience's complacency in its brutal, dehumanizing proceedings), as well as 1970's *Company* (staging the detached scenes and songs within designer Boris Aronson's cold, skeletal metal set to suggest the emotional disconnection and ambivalent nature of modern, urban relationships). Again illustrating the flexibility, fluidity, and director-friendly aspect of concept musicals are the later revivals of *Cabaret* (1998) and *Company* (2006), as both were re-interpreted, reconfigured, and redefined by directors Sam Mendes and John Doyle, respectively, who brought new production concepts, constructs, and guiding metaphors to the works. For example, Mendes merged the stage score of *Cabaret* with its film version score, restructured the original libretto (with permission from the authors), and reconfigured the key role of the Emcee into that of a powerful Mephistophelean hedonist who morphs into a deteriorating victim of the Jewish "solution." Doyle worked in the auteur mode as he converted *Company* into an intimate and highly presentational depiction of conflicted urban relationships, all performed by actor/musicians (i.e., actors who not only assumed their roles on stage but also served as musicians in the onstage chamber orchestra). Such conceptual freedom and control for directors carried over into the book musical, including canonical masterpieces that had previously seemed cemented in their original, archival configurations and presentations, for example, director Nicholas Hytner's dark, symbolic, and other-worldly revival of *Carousel* in 1994 and Trevor Nunn's rurally realistic (as opposed to folksy sentimentalist) revival of *Oklahoma!* in 1998.

One last crucial aspect contributing to the increased import and expanded role of the musical theatre director is the rising cost of the contemporary Broadway musical, coinciding with the heightened degree of spectacle and technical demands. The technical sophistication and cost of musical productions sky-rocketed during the rise of the mega–musical in the 1980s. Such a paradigm necessitated a powerful steward to coordinate and facilitate the complex and numerous staging elements, while also serving as a responsible overseer of production costs and the ever-important profit margins. Further, such musicals demanded a new level of technical expertise by the musical theatre director; for instance, when direct-ing mega–musicals *Cats* (1982), *Starlight Express* (1987), and *Sunset Boulevard* (1994), director Trevor Nunn was required to attend as much to the spectacle and coordination of the technical elements (given John Napier's epic set designs) as to the actors. Nicholas Hytner faced similar challenges with 1991's *Miss Saigon*, including the task of coordinating frenetic crowd scenes with the landing of a helicopter on stage. Numerous other visionary and avant-garde directors have used, and continue to exploit, the postmodern energy, sophistication, hyper-theatricality, and multidisciplinary potential of technology and multimedia to provide the American musical with a fresh, forward-looking, cutting-edge aesthetic. For instance, the punk and media-driven world of 2010's *American Idiot* was suggested by director/co-librettist Michael Mayer as he employed concert-style vocal performances, hyperkinetic staging, and an on-stage band, reinforced by a wall of television monitors (designed by Christine Jones), along with other high-tech effects. Regarding this paradigm, one must not fail to mention the epic stage production of Disney's *The Lion King* in 1997, conceived and realized by its director/auteur Julie Taymor, who also designed much of the show's visual aspects—most notably, the anthropomorphic costuming and masks. With this ground-breaking work, Taymor garnered universal acclaim and prestigious awards for her visionary reconfiguring of the American musical. Yet, as she chose to push the musical theatre envelope even further with her 2011 Broadway musical follow-up, the high-tech *Spider-Man: Turn Off the Dark*, she faced challenges and failure, ultimately being replaced as the troubled work's director. Such a disparate directorial experi-ence illuminates the degree of risk inherent in the new level of power and artistic control enjoyed—and suffered—by the contemporary musical theater director. Yet, there is no going back to the simpler days of early musical comedy "staging," for the sophisticated demands and expectations of the modern-day musi-cal have placed the contemporary director in the role of crucial collaborator—no longer a perfunctory hired hand but, instead, an artist versed in acting, movement, and technical design as well as a visionary with regard to production concept and theatrical interpretation.

JEROME ROBBINS

When praising the luminary Broadway career of choreographer/director Jerome Robbins, scholars, critics, historians, and peers often assert that he, more than any other artist working in musical theatre during the 1950s and '60s, sought to create the ideal of a unified, symbiotic song/dance/text theatrical experience—an integrated musical form also termed the *Gesamtkunstwerk* (loosely translated as "total theatre"). In addition to Robbins' advocacy and pursuit of the ideally integrated book musical on Broadway, like Agnes de Mille before him, he paradoxically brought dance and choreography to the forefront of the musical genre. He furthered the power and prestige of the choreographer on Broadway, resulting in the elevation of choreographer to an "über director" who ultimately controls all components of a production to fit his or her artistic stage vision, often determined by a choreographic sense of storytelling through song, movement, and lyrical expression. In the course of this theatrical trajectory, Robbins was able to translate his dance training and background into a remarkable career that, today, places him as one of the foremost visionaries and creators of musical theatre in the twentieth century.

Jerome Robbins was born Jerome Wilson Rabinowitz to a Russian-Jewish immigrant family in New York City in 1918 (his family history included flights from Russian pogroms; this autobiographical fact would assert itself in Robbins' adult masterpiece *Fiddler on the Roof*). He was a precociously talented child, playing the piano and violin as a youth. When he accompanied his sister to her interpretative dance classes, Robbins discovered his own passion for dance. He started his professional career as a teen with the Yiddish Art Theatre, then worked as a song-and-dance man at the resort hotel Camp Tamiment and as a Broadway "gypsy" dancer in various mediocre revues, while also continuing classical dance training in various New York studios. As a young member of the newly formed Ballet Theatre (with Agnes de Mille as one of the founders and choreographers), Robbins danced amid a confluence of new ideas and methods that would shape his future ballet career as well as his approach to dance as an acting and storytelling medium. Robbins studied under the "psychodramatic" dance choreographer Antony Tudor and also came under the influence of de Mille, originating the character of The Youth in her ballet *Three Virgins and a Devil* (1940). Most significant was de Mille's

introduction of Robbins to her childhood friend Mary Hunter, who had a small theatre and acting company. Hunter's studio used improvisation and psychological ("method") techniques in its actor training; by 1941, Robbins had become a devout student of Hunter as well as a close friend. According to various accounts, it was Hunter who suggested that Robbins choreograph a ballet based on *The Fleet's In*, a 1934 painting by Paul Cadmus. This idea materialized as *Fancy Free* (1944), a ballet that would change Robbins' life and begin his journey toward theatrically inspired and integrated choreography.

In *Fancy Free*, Robbins conceived a story line for the painting's sailors: Three men on shore leave compete for the affections of New York City women. Teaming up with neophyte composer Leonard Bernstein, who wrote the ballet's jazz-influenced score, Robbins merged gesture, pantomime, and colloquial dance steps with classical ballet to tell a story and create colorful characters. Such juxtaposition and merging of forms with a balletic foundation would characterize Robbins' choreography throughout his musical career. For instance, at the beginning of *Fancy Free*, Robbins had his sailors cartwheel onto stage, underscored by rim shots on a snare drum, a revolutionary beginning to a "classical" ballet. His choreography for the couples incorporated trendy dance crazes, such as boogie-woogie and jitterbug (an especially effective choreographic device, given the "jukebox joint" setting of the piece). Audiences adored the fresh and timely *Fancy Free*, and due to the ballet's sensational popularity, Robbins and Bernstein were approached to turn it into a musical (Robbins was suddenly fielding numerous offers to choreograph other musicals as well). The two men were initially reticent but were convinced by set designer and eventual producer Oliver Smith to tackle the project. Once lyricists/librettists Adolph Green and Betty Comden joined the team, writing an original book and contributing to the completely new score by Bernstein, *On the Town* (1944) came to fruition on the Broadway stage. And although it was guided by the hand of celebrated director George Abbott, the production acquired its landmark "dance musical" character and status from its choreographer, Robbins. *On the Town* was not only designed by its creators to be a prime example of integration, but it also became a novel work that positioned dance as a facilitative communicator of plot and character, principally conveying the adventures of three sailors on twenty-four-hour leave as they chase and experience fleeting romance in New York City. In fact, the original production contained almost thirty minutes of dancing, more than either *Oklahoma!* or *Carousel*. The number of extensive dance numbers (around eight) in a two-act musical was unprecedented. Included in its choreographic component were showy and athletic numbers by the sailors (e.g., the explosive opening number, "New York, New York"), as well as a dream ballet in Act II, titled "Gabey in the Playground of the Rich," in which the young, infatuated sailor Gabey, asleep on a subway train, dreams of himself as a great lover, having discovered his fantasy girl, "Miss Turnstiles," on a subway poster.

After *On the Town* and throughout the '40s, Robbins choreographed more Broadway shows, some more successful than others. He rejoined Comden and Green to work on his next project, *Billion Dollar Baby* (1945), with music by concert composer Morton Gould. The musical tells the story of a gold-digging New Jersey housewife who manipulates her way into high society and a more luxurious lifestyle. The collaborators again aimed at total integration of the components—score, libretto, and dance—so that all were integral to plot and character development. Robbins supplied another dream ballet, "Life with Rocky," in which the antiheroine, Maribelle, imagines her new life with a moneyed gangster. Despite the creators' aspirations, *Billion Dollar Baby* was a commercial failure, a rare occurrence in Robbins' career. Robbins followed *Billion Dollar Baby* with a smash hit, *High Button Shoes* (1947), which made up for the preceding disappointment, running for

727 performances (one of the year's top sellers). With music and lyrics by the estimable writing team of Jule Styne and Sammy Cahn, the musical is a comic caper set in New Jersey in 1913, detailing the ups and downs of a bumbling conman who swindles a family after selling their worthless real estate. Robbins worked once again with director George Abbott (who also rewrote, uncredited, the original libretto by Stephen Longstreet); and one of the highlights of the critically acclaimed production was a ballet conceived solely by Robbins: "On a Sunday by the Sea." In this number, most often referred to as the "Mack Sennett Ballet," set designer Oliver Smith provided a row of bathhouses set in Atlantic City through which numerous bathing beauties, bungling burglars, Keystone Kops, and a gorilla chase one another, flying in and out of doors, hilariously depicting a perfect example of carefully choreographed chaos. In their laudatory reviews of the production, critics singled out Robbins and his choreography for praise, calling his "Sennett" ballet a comic masterpiece of the contemporary musical theatre. Even at this early stage, Robbins realized the worth of his choreographic contributions and the necessity of protecting his property, while furthering its value and prestige. Thus, in a move unheard of at the time, he negotiated to own the rights to his choreography for *High Button Shoes*. Going forward, Robbins would continue to copyright all his Broadway choreography.

During this period, Robbins also furthered his studies in method acting at the Actors Studio. Possibly, the process of self-analysis used in this acting school inspired him to create his fourth musical, *Look Ma, I'm Dancin'!* (1948). With a score by composer/lyricist Hugh Martin, this semi-autobiographical work was conceived and choreographed by Robbins as well as co-directed by him with producer George Abbott. So at this early stage in his Broadway career, Robbins was acquiring the (shared) status of director, while also originating musicals with his "conceived" ideas (e.g., *On the Town*, *Look Ma*, and later, *West Side Story*). For *Look Ma*, he supplied librettists Jerome Lawrence and Robert E. Lee with a thin premise in which a brewery heiress and ex-vaudevillian, Lily Molloy, bails out a struggling ballet company, comically takes it over, and helps out her old dance pal, Eddie, by giving him a job as company choreographer. Ultimately, Eddie updates the old-fashioned classical ballet repertory with his own modern version of *Swan Lake*, which proves to be a hit. As "conceiver/co-director/choreographer," Robbins helped create a musical that reflected his own experiences as a "gypsy" dancer who had worked in both musical theatre and classical ballet, while providing numerous showy and metatheatrical dance numbers (e.g., the jazzy update of *Swan Lake*). Ultimately, *Look Ma* was not a major success (only 188 performances), but it did manage to make a profit.

The next year, Robbins served as choreographer for Irving Berlin's disappointing *Miss Liberty* (1949) and then for Berlin's popular hit, *Call Me Madam* (1950), neither of which provided much opportunity for Robbins to showcase his choreographic talent. In a more significant venture, Robbins followed up the Berlin productions by working with another Broadway institution, Rodgers and Hammerstein, as he choreographed 1951's *The King and I*. In this musical, Robbins pushed integrative techniques to new levels of storytelling, character depiction, subtext, and even symbolism and metaphor. He used various dance idioms, such as the polka in "Shall We Dance" and the childlike folk movement in "Getting to Know You," to show the cultural and informational exchange between Anna and the court, as well as the evolving relationship between Anna and King Mongkut. But highest praise regarding Robbins' work on *The King and I* was reserved for his ballet, "The Small House of Uncle Thomas." For this lengthy, narrative, and metatheatrical dance number, Robbins used Asian theatre devices (most notably, Kabuki) and Southeast Asian and Thai dance idioms to choreographically depict the plot of the Harriet Beecher Stowe novel, *Uncle Tom's Cabin*, while illustrating the disparity between two cultures (Siam and England) and metaphorically addressing the King's abuses of power and slavery.

In addition to Robbins' output on Broadway during this period, he continued to create significant works in the ballet/concert arena. In 1949, he joined New York City Ballet (NYCB) as associate artistic director with George Balanchine and created numerous canonical ballet masterpieces such as *The Cage* (1951) and *Afternoon of a Faun* (1953). Back on Broadway, Robbins' choreographic services could not save a 1952 flop, *Two's Company*, a revue built around movie star Bette Davis, which quickly closed when Davis had to leave the show for back surgery. In 1953, he worked behind the scenes to "doctor" *Wonderful Town*, finessing the work of the official choreographer, Donald Saddler, and working with director George Abbott on the staging.

(Robbins often played the Broadway "doctor" role, for example, working with director Abbott and composer/lyricist Stephen Sondheim in 1962 to improve *A Funny Thing Happened on the Way to the Forum* during its out-of-town tryout.) After two years with no significant Broadway work to his credit, Robbins' career went into high gear in 1954 as he, in the capacity of director, steered two hit canonical musicals to their Broadway debuts. First, he was approached by director George Abbott to collaborate on a musical adaptation of Richard Bissell's novel *7½ Cents*, titled *The Pajama Game*. Abbott had been persuaded to hire a young dancer-turned-choreographer named Bob Fosse for the production, and given Fosse's inexperience (this would be his first choreographic assignment for a fully staged musical production, Broadway or otherwise), Abbott appealed to his old compatriot Robbins to oversee the proceedings as co-choreographer, taking over all duties, if necessary. The ambitious Robbins, however, had his sights set on direction; therefore, he only agreed to supervise Fosse's work if given the role of "co-director" with Abbott. (Worries about Fosse's abilities were unfounded, and Robbins strongly supported Fosse's novel and unconventional choreography for the show.) With a score provided by the composer/lyricist team of Richard Adler and Jerry Ross, *Pajama Game* tells of a blossoming romance between a male factory supervisor and a pro-union female employee/activist in a pajama factory. Their relationship is jeopardized when the workers strike for higher wages, only to be resolved, romantically and labor-wise, in the end. With quick-paced comedy, catchy tunes, and novel dance numbers, the production reflected the high spirits and optimism of the mid-1950s, running for 1,063 performances and proving that Robbins was capable of taking the helm of big Broadway shows.

In his next 1954 endeavor, Robbins wielded a stronger controlling and proprietary hand. The show was *Peter Pan*, and Robbins not only directed and choreographed (his first time doing both solo), he also helped develop the show, adapting some of James M. Barrie's original play himself for the musical's libretto. Robbins' *Peter Pan* is usually recognized as the official musical version, coming four years after Bernstein's musical play. Interestingly though, like Bernstein, Robbins originally envisioned his production as a new staging of Barrie's play, starring Broadway leading lady Mary Martin, with only a handful of incidental songs by composer Mark Charlap and lyricist Carolyn Leigh. Soon it became apparent that the show had the potential to become a full-fledged musical. Given this new goal, Robbins wanted a more experienced and proven musical writing team to expand on Charlap and Leigh's initial song contributions. He approached old friends/collaborators Styne (*High Button Shoes*) and Comden and Green (*On the Town*). The new songwriting team added numbers and a complete underscoring treatment, with some material added to specifically highlight Martin's vocal talents (e.g., "Mysterious Lady"). In addition to a full score, Robbins envisioned a type of airborne choreography to create the fantasy world of *Peter Pan*. To that end, he contracted a company that had recently devised a system of stage pulleys, riggings, and harnesses to fly actors in complex aerial patterns on stage. The company, Flying by Foy, worked closely with Robbins to design and codify flight sequences to distinguish the musical *Peter Pan* from previous productions. The show opened on October 20, 1954, at Winter Garden Theatre to great fanfare (given the star quality of Martin), but ran for only 152 performances. *Peter Pan*, however, was broadcast in a 1955 color telecast, and has found more of a box office as young audiences have discovered Broadway and become major fans of musicals. Now, the production is a staple in the musical theatre canon, with songs such as "Neverland" and "I'm Flying" entering the American songbook, while the show's treatment of childhood fantasy and adventure, not to mention the flight sequences, charms audiences around the world.

During this period, Robbins also faced personal challenges that would affect him for the rest of his life. As a young man, between 1943–47, he had been a registered member of the American Communist Party. He was never a vocal advocate of the Party, however; and after leaving it, Robbins remained mostly apolitical. Nonetheless, in the early 1950s, he was called to testify before the House Committee on Un-American Activities (HUAC). In fear of being "outed" as a homosexual by the committee and other red-baiting parties (publicly, Robbins kept his homosexuality a secret throughout his life), he appeared under subpoena. There, as a "friendly witness," he named eight theatre/Hollywood artists who were thought to be members of, or affiliated in some way with, the Communist Party in exchange for having his own name cleared. Robbins' career did not visibly suffer and he was not blacklisted. Sadly, the same could not be said for many of those whom he named; consequently, he was blamed and

disparaged by many in the industry for his complicity. Many theatre collaborators perceived a change in Robbins after this period. He had always been a difficult and autocratic artist; but after the HUAC hearings, he became even more unpredictable and volatile during project development and rehearsals.

One past collaborator who seemed immune to Robbins' prickly personality, as well as his HUAC involvement, was composer Jule Styne (further, he was one of the few artists who stood up to Robbins' intimidating, dominating, and bullying tactics, earning the director's professional respect and a rare degree of deference). Robbins and Styne eventually worked together on five successful Broadway shows, so it is not surprising that in 1956 Robbins ventured into safe and familiar territory by re-teaming with Styne, as well as lyricists/librettists Comden/Green, for his first significant Broadway outing after the stressful HUAC years. The show was *Bells Are Ringing*, a charming musical comedy that details the romantic tales and travails of a telephone answering service operator in New York City (the production was also a star vehicle for Comden and Green's friend and early performing collaborator, Judy Holliday). Robbins was the production's sole director, as well as co-choreographer with Bob Fosse, and steered the show to box office success (924 performances).

A year later, Robbins began work on *West Side Story*, where he fine-tuned the art of integration, with dance playing a major role in the process, as well as promoted his own role as a musical production "auteur." The musical had been a project-in-the-making since the late 1940s, when Robbins and Bernstein first toyed with the idea of *East Side Story* (a contemporary *Romeo and Juliet* musical set in New York City). Once the collaborators Robbins, Bernstein, Stephen Sondheim, and Arthur Laurents came to the table to seriously develop the work, the basic premise (and locale) had been revised to focus on warring gangs on New York's West Side.

Robbins was responsible for turning *West Side Story* into a lyrical, danced drama, successfully illustrating the powerful dramatic function dance could serve when integrated with character and plot. The show opens with the five-minute "Prologue," a scene in which the story is introduced through choreography instead of dialogue, all set to haunting whistles, finger snaps, and jazzy dissonance. Robbins meticulously choreographed the gangs' movement from playful taunting to all-out war in this opening scene by using ballet, gesture, sport, and pedestrian movement. Thereafter, per Robbins' original influence, vision, and choreographic contributions, the dance and lyrical movement in *West Side Story* never seemed to stop. To paint a picture of the characters' ethnicity and youth as well as their angst, anger, and playfulness, Robbins incorporated dance idioms such as the cha-cha-cha, mambo, jitterbug/swing, and contemporary jazz, merging them with classical ballet for numbers such as "America," "Dance at the Gym," and "Cool." The violence of gang warfare was portrayed through gestural and visceral choreography ("Rumble"), while the romantic ideal embodied by Tony and Maria found physical expression in the Utopian dream ballet performed by the united gangs in "Somewhere." In short, *West Side Story* created a lyrical theatre experience for audiences in 1957, the likes of which had never been seen on Broadway, opening the door for even more dance-centric musicals.

When *West Side Story* opened, Robbins insisted that the show's billing read, "Entire production conceived, choreographed and directed by Jerome Robbins," suggesting a new place of prominence for the choreographer/director, even though some critics disparaged the credit as an unnecessary vanity. But no one could dispute Robbins' power and clout on Broadway. In 1959, Robbins directed and choreographed another landmark musical: *Gypsy*. Again working with Styne, Laurents, and Sondheim (composer, librettist, and lyricist, respectively), Robbins originally planned the musical, based on the memoirs of burlesque star Gypsy Rose Lee, to be another theatre experience shaped and determined by its choreographer/director. He envisioned the production as a concept musical with the story told through a procession of vaudeville acts, including jugglers, trapeze artists, dance specialists, and animal acts. (The "vaudeville" framing and staging concept would be exploited in future musicals such as *Chicago* and *The Will Rogers Follies*). The producers did not agree with Robbins' vision, however, and the work was staged as a conventional book musical. Nonetheless, his choreography was a visual and atmospheric element integral to the plot and character as well as to the vaudeville and burlesque environment of the play. Many musical theatre scholars and aficionados point to *Gypsy* as a pinnacle with regard to the integrated musical; its book, lyrics, music, choreography, design, and cast (with Ethel Merman as Gypsy Rose Lee's controlling stage mother, Rose) combined to create a work in which one component depended on another, all acting in concert to create a whole greater than the sum of its parts, that is, a *Gesamtkunstwerk*.

Robbins entered the 1960s disgruntled by the necessity of compromising his concept for *Gypsy*, especially having earlier experienced full control in the ballet arena. In 1958 Robbins established Ballets: U.S.A., a touring company more popular in Europe than America, which lasted four years and inspired Robbins to profess that he was "happiest" when fully in charge of his "own company." This attitude was at the crux of his disappointing venture as movie director/choreographer of the 1961 film version of *West Side Story*. He refused to compromise his working methods, spending so much time and money on his meticulous staging of the dance numbers that after the dances were finished, the studio replaced him with director Robert Wise (Robbins still received "co-director" credit, however, sharing with Wise the Academy Award for Best Director). Another development for Robbins during the early '60s was his Broadway forays as the director of nonmusical projects, for example, the 1962 Off-Broadway premiere of Arthur Kopit's avant-garde play *Oh Dad, Poor Dad, Mama's Hung You in the Closet and I'm Feelin' So Sad* (which transferred to Broadway the next year) and a 1963 Broadway staging of Bertolt Brecht's *Mother Courage and Her Children*. Then, in 1964, Robbins returned to musical theatre, spearheading a production that still stands today as an artistic masterpiece and supreme exercise in musical integration. Hoping to stage a musical adaption of Sholem Aleichem's *Tevye and His Daughters* (or *Tevye the Milkman and Other Tales*), composer Jerry Bock, lyricist Sheldon Harnick, and librettist Joseph Stein brought the material (at the suggestion of producer Hal Prince) to Robbins, imploring him to direct/choreograph. The project would soon become the landmark musical *Fiddler on the Roof*. Although it was not a dance show, it was informed by its dance aesthetic, with ethnic and dramatic movement infusing almost every musical moment on stage. The show also provided Robbins the chance to finally claim and embrace his Jewish heritage, something that he admitted in several interviews to having rejected and denied out of shame and discomfort as a young man (e.g., his name change from Rabinowitz to Robbins).

Set in a fictional shtetl (Anatevka) in 1905's Tsarist Russia, *Fiddler* paints a picture of orthodox Jewish life, disrupted by the troubling incursion of religious persecution and generational change. Such wide-sweeping themes, however, are dramatized through the intimate struggles of milkman Tevye and his family, as well as the other villagers of Anatevka. To create an integrated and genuine Jewish milieu for *Fiddler*, Robbins decided to use fewer classical dance idioms, turning almost completely to authentic folk movement. Accordingly, he resisted staging any of his dances as overt production numbers (even the "dream ballet," i.e., "Tevye's Dream," is staged more as a pantomime and theatrical sequence, not as a traditionally danced ballet). He also wove movement into the daily rhythms of Jewish life, incorporating dance for ceremonies (such as weddings) to organically and dramatically enhance communal moments of celebration and conflict, as might happen in real life. Robbins did a great deal of research, reading about shtetl life and observing Jewish weddings and other ceremonies in New York, specifically noting the codified movement, gestures, and behavioral rules used in religious observances by Hasidic Jews. And as a result, the musical seemed to dance and move lyrically, yet the choreography never called attention to itself as "dance" but, instead, underpinned and informed the old-world Jewish life depicted on stage, in harmony with the score and libretto. In addition, Robbins again employed "method" techniques during rehearsals by which he led the cast through exercises aimed at helping them "experience" a real-life sense of marginalization and persecution. All the work paid off. When *Fiddler* opened on September 22, 1964, it was the theatrical event of the season. Running for 3,242 performances, the work also held the title of "longest running Broadway show" until 1979; furthermore, it became one of the first international blockbusters, finding success worldwide with its universal messages of faith, family, community, and persecution, as well as its unique and evocative world created on stage.

After the triumph of *Fiddler*, Robbins all but left the musical theatre world, voicing fatigue over the collaborative working dynamic that defines the industry (correspondingly, many cite *Fiddler* as the end of musical theatre's Golden Age). Looking to completely control his own projects, Robbins began his American Theater Laboratory in 1966 with a $300,000 grant from the National Endowment of the Arts, a project that lasted two years but generated no productions. Ultimately, Robbins began to focus solely on his classical ballet career, especially with New York City Ballet (NYCB),

creating a plethora of canonical concert works, including *Dances at a Gathering* (1969), *The Goldberg Variations* (1971), *Watermill* (1972), *The Dybbuk Variations* (1974), and *I'm Old Fashioned* (1983). After Balanchine's death in 1983, Robbins became co-ballet master in chief of NYCB with Peter Martins. In 1989, Robbins returned to the Broadway stage with *Jerome Robbins' Broadway*, a collection and celebration of his past musical theatre choreography. Here, he uncharacteristically created a nonintegrated musical (a dance revue), reviving Broadway numbers from two decades' worth of past hit shows. The only connecting tissue was that Robbins had originally staged/choreographed the numbers; thus, the show was also an early example of the dansical. The Broadway community enthusiastically welcomed Robbins back, bestowing on him the Tony Award for Best Direction of a Musical. *Broadway* was also a nostalgic hit with audiences, running for 633 performances. Two years later, Robbins began work on an experimental theatre piece that had grown out of an earlier autobiographic soliloquy, *My Name Is Rabinowitz*, which he conceived in the 1960s. He named the new work *The Poppa Piece*. It was planned for the Lincoln Center Theatre season and envisioned by Robbins as a unique musical telling of his own life through dance, song, dialogue, and suggestive imagery. After months of work by the production team and cast, Robbins simply stopped the rehearsal process, giving no reason for its termination. After *Broadway* and the unfinished *Poppa*, Robbins spent the remainder of his life working in the ballet world.

As Robbins entered his twilight years, he did not seem to regret having left Broadway, often reporting in interviews that he preferred to simply work with dancers in his own, authorial way instead of having to "suit" or meet the "needs" of collaborators. In the mid-1990s, Robbins suffered a multitude of physical ailments, including heart-valve surgery, loss of hearing, and symptoms suggesting Parkinson's disease. He continued to work, however, staging in 1998 a revival of his 1965 ballet masterpiece, *Les Noces*. Soon after, he suffered a massive stroke and died in New York City on July 29, 1998. Robbins was neither a composer nor lyricist/librettist. Yet he had made his art—dance/choreography—as decisive a musical theatre component as the score and libretto, while elevating his own role, director/choreographer, to that of authorial auteur. He paved the way for future "director/choreographer/conceivers" on Broadway, while powerfully pushing forward the integrated musical (that is, the interactive triumvirate of song, text, and especially, dance). He was a perfectionist, tortured by personal demons, but fierce in his artistic vision, realizing works that transformed the genres of both theatre and concert dance. His achievements merited five Tony Awards, two Academy Awards, and the Kennedy Center Honor, among other distinctions. For all these reasons and more, lights were dimmed on Broadway on the evening of Robbins' death in tribute to the man who had worked uncompromisingly to realize the *Gesamtkunstwerk* ideal in American musical theatre.

FEATURED PRODUCTION: *West Side Story* (1957)

**Music by Leonard Bernstein; Lyrics by Stephen Sondheim;
Book by Arthur Laurents**

**Original Broadway Run: Opened September 26, 1957; Winter Garden Theatre;
732 performances**

It was a September evening at the Winter Garden in 1957. As orchestral bells tolled and members of two warring gangs, in an impromptu funeral procession, carried the slain hero offstage, audience members sat still, not sure what to make of the new musical they had just seen. Was it an artistic masterpiece, an exercise in indulgent excess, a depressing and sorry way to spend a night at the theatre, or musical theatre history in the making? The questions would persist for a while, and it was not until years later that *West Side Story* secured its canonical status, as it was declared a landmark work in the American musical theatre genre. (Lyricist Stephen Sondheim likes to joke that he occasionally meets people who boast that they were members of *West Side Story*'s original Broadway audience, awed at having witnessed musical theatre history. Sondheim resists asking them whether they were part of the large contingent of "awed" audience members who left at intermission during those initial Broadway performances.) In any case, *West Side Story* proved to be a phenomenon and a harbinger of a new direction for musical theatre, changing forever the idea of what could be deemed suitable content for a Broadway musical as well as how a musical might be constructed, developed, and realized on stage.

As early as 1948, Robbins had been intrigued by the prospect of a contemporary *Romeo and Juliet* musical, suggested to him by his Actors Studio classmate and lover, Montgomery Clift (who eventually achieved stardom in films). Looking to develop the concept, Robbins approached his *Fancy Free* and *On the Town* collaborator, Leonard Bernstein, and the two cultivated the idea of an ill-fated Jewish-Catholic love affair set on the Lower East Side. Soon playwright Arthur Laurents joined as librettist (this would be his first Broadway musical), but the conflicting schedules of the three men necessitated that the project be put on hold for six years. Once they returned to the show, originally titled *East Side Story*, the religious angle seemed outdated. Coincidentally, current newspapers were filled with stories detailing waves of gang violence among ethnic groups in both Los Angeles and New York. The collaborators were inspired by the social/cultural unrest and changed their Romeo and Juliet story to that of star-crossed lovers who are caught in the crosshairs of warring ethnic gangs. As a result, *West Side Story*'s libretto reads as follows: Maria is a Puerto Rican ingénue newly arrived in Manhattan and the sister of Bernardo, leader of a Puerto Rican gang, the Sharks. Tony is an American-born Pole and a former leader of the Jets, a gang composed of American-born children of white, European immigrants. The Sharks and Jets are warring over "turf" in Manhattan's West Side, yet Tony is trying to put his gang activities behind him. Reminiscent of Shakespeare's play, Tony and Maria fall in love at first sight at a dance that was intended to calm hostilities between the two gangs. Tony and Maria are warned to break off their clandestine relationship by family members and friends, but they dream of a life and world where they can marry and live in peace. When Tony tries to broker a truce between the gangs and stop a rumble at the end of the first act, the violence, instead, escalates and he stabs Bernardo in a blind fit of rage (after his best friend, Riff, is killed). Tension builds in the second act, as Tony must tell Maria that he unintentionally killed her brother. Their love for one another transcends the tragedy and they plan to run away together. At their arranged meeting place, however, a rejected and hostile suitor of Maria, who also wants to avenge Bernardo's death, shoots and kills Tony just as Maria arrives.

From the shadows, the rest of the gang members materialize and see the senselessly bloody result of their actions; while Maria, in a desperate and traumatized state, berates them all for their cycle of hate and violence. Then, in a poignant and transformational moment, the two gangs work together to carry Tony offstage, with Maria following.

When developing the musical, it became clear to the team of Robbins, Bernstein, and Laurents that they were working on something unique, venturing into new territory. Robbins often said that *West Side Story* provided an opportunity by which he, Bernstein, and Laurents could write a ballet, opera, and play, respectively, without working in separate genres. Soon to join this formidable team was a young lyricist named Stephen Sondheim. Previously, Bernstein had planned to write both the music and lyrics; but he realized that the score's musical composition demanded all his efforts and time. Sondheim was not eager to take the job, however, for he preferred the role of composer (plus, his feelings were still raw, having just seen the musical *Saturday Night*, with his first complete score, fail to make it to Broadway). Eventually he was convinced by his mentor, Oscar Hammerstein, that *West Side Story* would be a stellar learning opportunity, especially working alongside Bernstein. Sondheim, with Bernstein, collaborated closely with Laurents. For instance, they created Tony's opening song, "Something's Coming," by reconfiguring material that had originally been written by Laurents as an opening monologue. Further, Sondheim incorporated the slang terms and brusque dialogic style that Laurents had invented for the youths (especially notable in the Jets' terse and chilly jazz/pop anthem, "Cool"). Today Sondheim admits to not being completely satisfied with his lyrics for the show, feeling that some of his rhymes were too "precious" and didn't always sound like the voices of the characters. Regardless, he diplomatically rejected the periodic offerings of Bernstein, who initially tried to exercise his influence as co-lyricist. Later Bernstein gave Sondheim sole lyricist credit.

Given the libretto/score of *West Side Story*, which includes three deaths, a sexual assault, ethnic slurs, and other graphic language as well as a culture of bigotry that indicts all players (even authority figures such as Lieutenant Schrank and Officer Krupke), it is not surprising that original producer, Cheryl Crawford, could not find financial backers for the show. Most thought the material was too depressing. Crawford gave up trying to secure funds, leaving the project just a few weeks before rehearsals were scheduled to begin. When Sondheim lamented to his friend, the newly successful producer Harold Prince, that *Gangway* (the show's working title) might be put on hold again due to lack of funding, Prince expressed interest. After listening to a portion of the score, the thoroughly impressed Prince and his partner, Robert Griffith, signed on as producers. But before rehearsals could commence, Robbins had to be talked into choreographing the show (as originally planned) as well as directing. Next, he presented the producers with numerous demands, including an unprecedented eight-week rehearsal period, three rehearsal pianos, and choreographic assistance. Prince acquiesced to all but the pianos; funding the extended rehearsal period as well as hiring Peter Gennaro as an associate choreographer for Robbins. In a final show of clout and authorship, Robbins insisted that he receive official credit in all press and billing materials for having directed, choreographed, and "conceived" *West Side Story*.

Once in rehearsal, Robbins created a novel atmosphere, employing "method" techniques and strategies, which included segregating cast members according to gang affiliation during their offstage time and posting newspaper clippings detailing current real-life gang violence, all to help the actors stay "in character" by internalizing and living their roles throughout the entire rehearsal period. Further, every character was given a name in the libretto (instead of being grouped as "chorus"), and Robbins expected a back story from each actor to bring his or her character to life. In addition to the method acting demands, cast members were required to sing *and* dance, instead of being hired as specialists, that is, relegated to the dancer chorus or the singer chorus. Thus began the era of the "triple threat," in which the ability to excel in all three (acting, singing, and dancing) became a necessity for any "gypsy" hoping to work on Broadway or in musical theatre in general. Given these innovations, *West Side Story* raised the "gypsy" performer to a new level of prominence and prestige, setting the stage for future dance musicals and "gypsy" showcases on Broadway, such as *A Chorus Line*.

If the performance approach to *West Side Story* was unique, it was because the material itself was exceptional for its time. Bernstein employed compositional structures and devices to create a score of symphonic complexity, depth, and unity, while Robbins responded to the score by introducing a lyrical dance reconfiguration of musical theatre. The integration, variety, and dramatic integrity of Bernstein and Robbins' music and dance idioms resulted in lyrical expressions of romantic, combative, combustive, tragic, and darkly comic sentiments and themes. Bernstein's score contains arias, character numbers, contrapuntal group compositions, Latin rhythms and forms, symphonic ballet music, cool and bebop jazz—all unified by thematic repetition and variations. Robbins' copyrighted choreography veers from ballet to lyrical jazz, to choreographed gesture and pantomime as well as colloquial (swing) and Latin dance idioms. Further, the seriousness and dark social commentary of Laurents' 1957 libretto stood in stark contrast to the feel-good, escapist musical plots of the day. Laurents often reported that the villain of *West Side Story* is "society," as well as the dark side of the American Dream, a villainy that includes indoctrinated hate and hostilities between groups warring over "turf" as symbols of community, identity, and pride. Laurents' libretto espouses tolerance and acceptance of the "Other," not only in terms of ethnicity, race, nativism, and age, but gender as well (e.g., the struggle of Anybodys and the sexual assault of Anita). In his attempt to give voice to youth angst and solidarity, Laurents created original slang, hoping to make *West Side Story*'s conflicts timeless. In fact, given Laurents' themes of alienation, rebellion, tribal affiliation, and self-identity, and pleas for tolerance, one might view *West Side Story* as a thematic precursor to the modern rock musical. (It is ironic that some terms, such as "cool," were adopted by the youth of the time and, consequently, date the piece today.) Finally, the unusual content provided by Laurents, Bernstein, Sondheim, and Robbins was given a novel stage setting by scenic designer Oliver Smith, who created a gritty mix of urban artifacts and dreamscape, often using movable scenery pieces against an atmospheric backdrop to evoke locales instead of realistically replicating them. The lighting design was flexible, moving between and isolating the different locales and scenes. This design concept is often described as "cinematic," that is, sets, combined with lighting, that enable one scene or locale to flow into another without lengthy set changes, full blackouts, and/or lowering of the stage curtains.

Emblematic of *West Side Story*'s atypical content and construct as well as its subversion of audience expectations is the musical's poignant ending. Initially, the authors had intended to replicate the ending of *Romeo and Juliet*; that is, they planned for Maria to die alongside Tony. When composer Richard Rodgers attended a rehearsal, however, he recommended to the creators that Maria need not literally die, for she had already suffered to the point of death with her soul shattered. And as Rodgers deduced, the final scene, even without Maria's death, is devastating as it suggests the death of romantic idealism and the social destruction of two individuals' true love. With regard to the same scene, Bernstein originally planned an aria for Maria after Tony's death but decided to end with an orchestral denouement and the final tolling of bells, refusing to soften the gritty realism of the murder for the audience by providing an escapist moment of vocal virtuosity. Sure enough, audiences were ambivalent about the show at its debut, especially given its dancing gangs and biting social critique. Ticket buyers did not immediately flock to the box office, and although most reviews were positive, some critics also lamented the new seamy and serious direction of modern musicals. Robbins won a Tony Award for his choreography, but the production itself lost all other major awards to *The Music Man* for the 1957–58 theatre season. In the end, however, *West Side Story* ran for nearly two years, enjoyed a brief national tour, and then returned to Broadway for another year. It eventually found a prominent place in the American consciousness via its popular 1961 United Artists film version. The movie, which won an unprecedented ten Academy Awards, was choreographed by Robbins (who had to settle for a co-direction credit once he was let go from the production due to budget and time constraints). It seemed that by 1961 the time was right for the groundbreaking musical, as America was feeling the reverberations of a burgeoning cultural revolution and youth movement. Further, *West Side Story* has continued to enjoy numerous Broadway revivals, the latest being a 2009 production, directed by Laurents, who revised his original libretto, aided by Lin-Manuel Miranda who revised some lyrics, to incorporate Spanish dialogue for the Sharks. The show won the 2009 Tony Award for Best Revival of a Musical. It ran for 748 performances, offering definitive proof that the work continues to speak, musically, choreographically, bilingually, to contemporary audiences. *West Side Story* asserts a potent and unresolved vision of America, given the complexities and tensions of the nation's "melting pot" ideal versus the realities of a diverse, challenging, and emotional mélange of peoples.

Photo of the 2005 MUNY production of *West Side Story.* Jim Herren. Photo courtesy of MUNY.

PULLING BACK THE CURTAIN:

McCarthyism, HUAC, and the American Musical Theatre

The late 1940s and '50s were times of great prosperity in America; yet, according to some, all was not yet quiet or safe on the American front. The United States had emerged victorious from World War II, resulting in a heightened sense of can-do spirit and optimism; however, sociopolitical and economic developments across the seas, most notably the rise and dominance of communism in the Soviet Union, Eastern Europe, and mainland China led to fears of similar developments and subversive sympathies at home. In its heightened state of anxiety, America witnessed what is referred to as the age of McCarthyism. McCarthyism itself is the catch-all term used to describe the hunt for disloyal, treasonous communist American sympathizers and activists, leveling false and fevered accusations at such people without proof of subversion. The term was coined as a negative descriptor of the red-baiting actions of Senator Joseph McCarthy; yet, its meaning was broadened to describe much of the communist-hunting hysteria that occurred in the government as well as government-sanctioned activities inspired and incited by McCarthy. The "hunt" resulted in thousands of Americans, accused of Communist Party affiliation or sympathies, being subjected to investigations, harassments, loss of careers, and/or trials. If the accused parties chose to cooperate with authorities (a "friendly witness"), offering up names of other suspected communists ("naming names"), they might save their own reputations and careers (or stay out of prison, in the most extreme cases), most often sacrificing others in the process. (This witch hunt always ignored the fact that membership in the Communist Party was not ever an illegal activity in America's democratic multiparty system. Furthermore, given the disillusionment over the seemingly failed capitalist system that resulted in the Great Depression, communism had found a number of advocates in America.) The primary targets of the hunts were government employees, artists, educators, union organizers, professionals in the entertainment industry, and "deviants" such as homosexuals, with the accusations and convictions of most parties based on inconclusive evidence and, often, hearsay (most of the verdicts would be overturned years later, with the procedures deemed illegal, unconstitutional, or lacking legal foundation).

While notable examples of McCarthyism included Senator McCarthy's own probes and hearings, there were other senatorial committees and FBI anticommunist activities. The musical theatre community was most affected by the actions of the House Committee on Un-American Activities (HUAC). HUAC was formed in 1938 and known as the Dies Committee until 1944. In its early days, it investigated treasonous or suspicious activities but soon evolved into the most prominent and active government committee involved in anticommunist investigations, beginning with a 1938 probe into suspected communist activity within the Federal Theatre Project. In October 1947, the committee achieved notoriety when members of the Hollywood community (actors, screenwriters, directors, etc.) were subpoenaed and asked to testify regarding their Communist Party affiliation and provide information about other suspected communists. Among the earliest witnesses, ten film industry professionals refused to cooperate; they became known as the "Hollywood Ten." Although they believed they were protected by their First Amendment rights, they were sentenced to prison for contempt of Congress. After their conviction, the heads of the major studios prepared a joint statement in which they avowed, as a matter of national interest, to fire or refuse employment to any member of the Communist Party. Thus, the term "blacklist" came into being, and hundreds of HUAC witnesses or "named" parties in Hollywood were "blacklisted"; that is, denied employment once the accusation and refusal to cooperate were made public. (Although publications such as *Red Channels*, *Counterattack*, and other newsletters kept track of communist and leftist organizations and individuals who had been targeted by private investigative committees, HUAC claimed there was no official "list" at the time.) In contrast to Hollywood, Broadway outwardly prohibited the practice of blacklisting due to the strength of Actors' Equity and other theatre unions, as well as the fact that Broadway projects were backed by independent producers as opposed to corporations. Nonetheless, hundreds in the theatre community suffered legal harassment and FBI surveillance; many were called to testify before HUAC, with careers put into jeopardy, especially if they wanted to work in Hollywood (which included radio and television). In short, when asked the infamous question in Congressional hearings, "Are you now or have you ever been a member of the Communist Party of the United States?" witnesses had the option of answering in the affirmative, and following up with a repudiation and disavowal of their past "errors in judgment," along with a redemptive naming of others who they knew, by association, were also communists. Another option was to take the "Fifth," claiming Fifth Amendment protection against self-incrimination, thereby avoiding a Congressional contempt citation for refusal to name names. However, employers considered such a plea grounds for dismissal, and the defendant became known as a "Fifth Amendment Communist," an implicit "guilty" verdict.

During this period, even film icon Charlie Chaplin saw his movie career in the United States end as he refused to testify and contest charges brought against him; thus, he was blacklisted in Hollywood for decades. While some film artists refused to cooperate (and were, thereby, assumed guilty), others gave "friendly" testimony, but all activities left an indelible mark on the entertainment industry, with repercussions that would be felt for decades. Many of the Hollywood witnesses were prominent names in the theatre, with musical theatre contributions on their résumés as well. For instance, renowned German theatre auteur Bertolt Brecht (lyricist/librettist of *The Threepenny Opera*) willingly gave rehearsed testimony in 1947, stopping short of naming names. He was allowed to leave America to return to Europe. Celebrated American playwright Lillian Hellman (original librettist for *Candide*) stood before HUAC in 1950 and refused to testify, reading a prepared statement in which she vowed that she would not "cut her conscience" to satisfy the current "fashion" of the day. Although there is uncertainty regarding the facts of this defiance, she was blacklisted for years. Famous American director Elia Kazan (who ventured into musical theatre by directing *One Touch of Venus*) did name names in 1952, to the incredulity and despair of his peers, a controversy that would resurface in 1999, as many industry insiders decried the decision to bestow an Academy Honorary Award for Lifetime Achievement to Kazan. In the case of Jerome Robbins, the ramifications of his testimony were potent and long-felt. In fear of being exposed as a homosexual and damaging his career, Robbins appeared before HUAC and offered eight names. In light of the many other targeted artists who refused to name names to clear their own, such as Leonard Bernstein and Arthur Laurents (both of whom were harassed by the FBI—to the extent that their passports were revoked), Robbins found himself ostracized by many in the theatre community. Specifically, Laurents reportedly never forgave Robbins who, he felt, capitulated to HUAC for the sake of his own career at the expense of others. Many other musical theatre artists who suffered the slings, arrows, and blacklists of McCarthyism found it difficult to excuse Robbins, but they also found themselves working for him years later, often in a sort of unspoken truce. For instance, theatre and film star Zero Mostel, after refusing to name names before HUAC, was blacklisted throughout most of the '50s. Once he regained stardom, Mostel recounted to others that he could barely swallow his contempt for Robbins, but still managed to originate the iconic *Fiddler* role of Tevye under his direction. Musical comedy star Jack Gilford, whose wife (Madeline Lee Gilford) was actually named by Robbins, with both being blacklisted for years, had to work with Robbins almost a decade later in *A Funny Thing Happened on the Way to Forum*. In the cases of Mostel and Gilford, however, it seems that hostilities were put aside and the work became the prime focus. In many ways, it was this work ethic and determination by many to maintain the art and artistic integrity of the theatre that finally overcame the years of anger and stigma caused by McCarthyism.

LEONARD BERNSTEIN

Friends called him "Lenny," a casual nickname for one of the most renowned artists and advocates of "formal" music in America. Leonard (Lenny) Bernstein was a celebrated composer, lecturer, pianist, music director, and writer, while serving as one of the nation's most famous and acclaimed symphony conductors, especially during his 1957–69 tenure as music director for the New York Philharmonic. Even though his composition catalog includes numerous symphonies, concertos, chamber pieces, operas, and choral works, his talents were not limited to the concert sphere; Bernstein also found popular and critical success on the musical theatre stage, composing tightly integrated, symphonic scores for *On the Town*, *Wonderful Town*, *Candide*, and *West Side Story*. In short, Bernstein was the epitome of a crossover concert/theatre artist, the likes of which had not been seen in America since Victor Herbert and George Gershwin.

Bernstein's musical theatre statistics are impressive. Although he wrote only six musicals in thirty-three years, four are considered popular masterpieces. And given his technical mastery of classical composition, Bernstein is often considered a "composer" among Broadway composers. He added to this distinction by refusing to pander to musical theatre audiences who may have preferred simpler, more hummable scores on the Broadway stage than those which he created. In short, Bernstein never "dumbed down" his scores, even for the most conventional musical comedies. Instead, he chose to challenge audiences with numbers that contained dizzying and shifting arrays of complex time and key signatures, while unifying the overall work with the symphonic application of thematic repetition, variation, and leitmotifs. He believed in and relished the challenge of creating musical scores with different sounds for different situations, locales, and time periods, asserting that he never composed with "Tin Pan Alley" standalone hits in mind, but aimed to create compositions that were "an integral part" of a musical narrative. Bernstein's reputation is that of an eclectic composer, whose sound is hard to categorize. Bernstein could move between the playfulness of swing, the dissonance of bebop jazz, the rhythmic flavor of Latin dance, the lush romanticism of operetta, and the hummable hook of popular music, often merging all forms in the same score. He felt that his eclecticism served the theatricality of the works (his sense of music *as*

Leonard Bernstein hugs Debbie Allen (left) and Chita Rivera at *West Side Story* revival, 2/15/1980 © Bettmann/CORBIS

drama also influenced his highly theatrical style of conducting, with his dramatic expression at the podium sometimes criticized as being excessive and indulgent). Bernstein was also seen as the controlling proprietor of his lush theatrical scores on Broadway in the 1940s and '50s. Unlike most of his contemporaries, he was hands-on with regard to orchestral arrangements, occasionally writing or co-writing his own to create a world of evocative, atmospheric sound on stage. In doing so, he brought the world of classical, symphonic music to Broadway, just as he brought the concert genre to much of America during his lifetime, not only advocating a place for classical music in America's pop culture but also working to nurture a new generation of classical music patrons through his televised *Young People's Concerts*. In the process, Bernstein took the "celebrity" conductor to new heights, exploiting new mediums, such as television, while establishing his name forever in the great American songbook through his musical theatre endeavors.

Lenny was born Louis Bernstein on August 25, 1918, in Lawrence, Massachusetts, to Jewish parents, Jennie and Samuel Bernstein. His Ukrainian immigrant father was a wholesaler of hair products, and the family was not especially musical; however, Jennie and Samuel took their son to symphonic concerts occasionally, which triggered his immediate love and appreciation of music. When "Leonard" (the nickname used by his parents) was 10, his aunt gave the family an old piano and he, like the young George Gershwin, became obsessed with the instrument and showed early proficiency. He pleaded with his father to take lessons, and although Sam was not initially fond of his son's wish to become a musician, he eventually overcame his hesitation and arranged for private lessons. The gifted and studious Leonard (officially changing his name when he was 15) was accepted into Harvard in 1935, at age

17, where he majored in music and took numerous art and philosophy classes. While at Harvard, Bernstein practiced his craft, accompanying the Harvard Glee Club for a short time as well as writing and conducting the musical score for a production of Aristophanes' *The Birds*. It was during this time that Bernstein met esteemed conductor and composer Dimitri Mitropoulos who was impressed with the young man and recommended that he more seriously focus on conducting. Another crucial influence during his Harvard years was the premiere American composer Aaron Copland, with whom Bernstein developed a relationship, regularly seeking advice and later citing the older man as his only "real" composition instructor. Bernstein graduated (*cum laude*) in 1939, then furthered his studies at the Curtis Institute of Music in Philadelphia, where he took advanced courses in conducting as well as piano, orchestration, counterpoint, and score analysis. The following year, Bernstein spent the summer at Tanglewood, the Boston Symphony Orchestra's prestigious institute and music festival held in Lenox, Massachusetts, where he was admitted into a master conducting class taught by the orchestra's conductor, Serge Koussevitzky (purportedly, he was accepted into the select class based on the recommendations of Copland and Mitropoulos). Bernstein was soon hired as Koussevitzky's assistant; and the affection between the two men was mutual, with Koussevitzky serving as a father figure to the twenty-two-year-old Bernstein. (In 1949, Bernstein would dedicate his *2nd Symphony: The Age of Anxiety* to his Tanglewood mentor.) Bernstein returned to Tanglewood in the following summers, although he had also relocated to New York City to further his professional music career.

Bernstein's first jobs in New York were modest, transcribing and arranging music for publishing firms. Before long, however, he found work with the New York Philharmonic, where his promising talent once again impressed a powerful musical director, Artur Rodzinski, who, like Koussevitsky before him, hired the young man to be his assistant. Then, Bernstein's career made a fantastic and unforeseen leap forward, making the twenty-five-year-old conductor America's concert-world wunderkind overnight. On November 14, 1943, scheduled guest conductor Bruno Walter suddenly fell ill and had to be immediately replaced for the Philharmonic's concert that afternoon at Carnegie Hall. With no time for rehearsal and Rodzinski out of town, the job fell to Bernstein,

who stepped onto the podium and conducted the most famous and celebrated orchestra in America. So impressive was his conducting and the circumstances of his debut that the story made the front page of *The New York Times*; further, the concert had been nationally broadcast. Overnight, Bernstein became a household name. (Here it is important to note that Bernstein came to fame during an era in which orchestra conductors were well known and celebrated all across America, instead of being relegated to the formal music sphere, as they are today.) As his career gathered steam throughout the '40s, Bernstein was offered numerous musical commissions, recordings, and guest conducting engagements, finding fame on the world stage (especially significant was his 1947 conducting debut in Tel Aviv, beginning a lifelong professional and personal association with the State of Israel).

In addition to Bernstein's conducting celebrity, he started to receive widespread notice for his compositions, with 1944 proving to be a watershed year as he not only conducted the debut of his Symphony No. 1 *Jeremiah* (written in 1942), but also teamed with a young ballet dancer/choreographer, Jerome Robbins, to compose the score for a new ballet for Ballet Theatre (American Ballet Theatre). The work was titled *Fancy Free*; and when it debuted in April 1944, its contemporary content was like nothing that had previously been seen on the national ballet stage. In short, *Fancy Free*'s scenario depicts the antics of three sailors on twenty-four-hour leave in New York City, spiritedly vying for the affections of women. The ballet's unusual milieu was made even more unconventional by Robbins' balletic use of pedestrian movement and Bernstein's score, which incorporates popular elements of jazz and swing to reflect the time and place of the ballet's action. *Fancy Free* was a phenomenal hit, inspiring scenic designer Oliver Smith to approach Bernstein and Robbins with the idea that they turn the ballet into a full-length Broadway musical.

Bernstein and Robbins were swayed by Smith's proposal (as well as his offer to produce the show); and Bernstein knew of the perfect pair to create fresh, youthful material for an *au courant* Broadway project. He suggested to Smith and co-producer, Paul Feigay, that they sign his old friend Adolph Green and Green's writing partner, Betty Comden, to write the book and lyrics. Bernstein and Green's friendship had begun in 1937, when Bernstein was a music counselor at a summer theatre camp where Green was a lead performer. The two men shared a Greenwich Village apartment during Bernstein's early days in New York, and they had stayed close as the years passed. As Bernstein was achieving fame in the classical/concert sphere, Green, Comden, and comedic performer Judy Holliday were garnering notice by writing and performing their own nightclub act, The Revuers, with Bernstein regularly attending their shows at the Village Vanguard. Comden and Green agreed to join Bernstein and Robbins as collaborators on the new musical. With all of the major contributors being in their twenties, the work would be underpinned and defined by their youthful spirit; yet the production would also require experience and proven know-how at the helm to bring it to fruition. The group chose venerable director George Abbott to oversee and help shape the proceedings.

The resulting musical comedy was titled *On the Town* and dealt with the same plot and theme material as *Fancy Free*, that is, one day of shore leave in New York City for three wide-eyed and randy sailors looking for women and adventure. The musical was not a *Fancy Free* reprise, however; for Bernstein chose to discard his previous ballet compositions and provide all new music for the score to fully mesh with the clever and situation/character-driven lyrics by Comden and Green as well as their witty, fresh, and timely libretto. The new score and libretto were crucially supported and supplemented by Robbins' expansive narrative dance segments. And as the collaborators aimed to create a fully integrated work, Bernstein's tuneful and intricate, yet deceptively simple score can be seen as the cohesive element; it employs idiom-specific compositions for each character and dramatic episode, along with recurring and reconfigured leitmotifs and other unifying symphonic techniques throughout. At the top of the show, Bernstein's overture paints an aural picture of New York, with horns blaring and a muscular, cacophonous, dissonant orchestration that evolves into "New York, New York," the jittery, swing-inspired ode to the city sung by the three sailors. Such a symphonic approach to musical composition is further evidenced by recycling the opening song's major theme, which, at a slower tempo, appears in a later song, "Lonely Town," sung by a sailor who offers a more introspective and less romantic view of the Big Apple. Bernstein's catchy tunes are prevalent in the score, as he provided melodic hooks and beguiling rhythms for narrative character songs such as "I Get Carried Away," in which one of the couples (originally played on Broadway by Comden and Green) lament their overwhelming desire for and acquiescence to passion and drama, as well as "I Can Cook Too," a groundbreaking affirmation of culinary and sexual prowess by another sailor's romantic interest, Hildy.

Given the production's positive attributes and its timeliness, it is not surprising that *On the Town* was a critical and popular success, joining *Oklahoma!* to advance a new, integrated direction in musical theatre. Opening on December 28, 1944, audiences, still enduring wartime anxieties and hardships, had their spirits buoyed by the high-energy antics and sentimental positivity expressed by the work, resulting in a box office run of 462 performances.

Although *On the Town* was a major Broadway achievement for Bernstein, his conducting commissions and concert career limited the time and effort he could expend on immediate theatrical follow-ups. (Interestingly, he lamented in later life that his conducting and music director duties had also compromised his output as a "serious" composer.) *Peter Pan* was the exception, debuting on Broadway on March 24, 1950, and running for 321 performances. Bernstein added musical interludes and some dramatic songs (both music and lyrics) to the 1905 play by James M. Barrie; thus, his musicalized version of the children's classic was considered more of a "play with music" than a full-fledged musical. (The work has somewhat fallen into obscurity today, replaced in the canon by the more popular and conventional Styne/Comden/Green/Leigh/Charlap musical rendition.) The next year, Bernstein wed Chilean actress Felicia Cohn Montealegre; and although Bernstein had had, and would continue to have, numerous affairs with men throughout his life (a fact known and accepted by all those close to him), their marriage appeared to be a contented one, resulting in three children and lasting until her death. Meanwhile, his concert career continued apace. A snapshot of this period includes Bernstein's becoming head of Tanglewood's orchestral and conducting departments in 1951, his guest conductor engagements with symphonic and opera orchestras worldwide (in 1953 becoming the first U.S. conductor to appear at Italy's premiere opera house, La Scala), and his visiting professorship from 1951–56 at Brandeis University, founding its Creative Arts Festival where he premiered his opera *Trouble in Tahiti* (1952). Further, he continued to compose symphony, chamber, and vocal works, as well as a film score for 1954's *On the Waterfront*. (He turned the *Waterfront* compositions into a symphonic suite the next year, a practice that became habitual as Bernstein also converted his *Fancy Free* and *West Side Story* ballet music and *Candide's* overture into orchestral concert works in later years.) That same year, 1954, Bernstein reentered the musical theatre arena, working again with old friends and collaborators Comden, Green, Abbott, and Robbins as he composed the music for *Wonderful Town*.

Given the complexity and charm of *Wonderful Town's* score, it is especially impressive that the work was written in only five weeks, exemplifying the adage that necessity is the mother of invention. *Wonderful Town* was originally devised by librettists Joseph Fields and Jerome Chodorov, who wanted to adapt their successful play, *My Sister Eileen* (1940), into a musical with the collaborative efforts of composer Leroy Anderson and lyricist Arnold Horwitt. However, tensions flared between the librettists and the composer/lyricist team, with Anderson and Horwitt quitting the project five weeks before rehearsals were to start. The producer, Robert Fryer, could not afford a delay. He had cast Broadway star Rosalind Russell, who could take another job if the production did not begin on schedule. Fryer looked to his director, George Abbott, to save the day. True to form, Abbott called in some favors and used his serious clout and connections by talking Comden and Green into coming on board as the production's lyricists. Their collaboration, however, was conditioned on Bernstein supplying the music (they felt that only a composer of his ilk could tackle such an undertaking on such short notice). So after almost a decade away from Broadway, Bernstein reunited with old friends to work on a musical comedy. (Robbins would join the team later, doctoring the work of the official choreographer, Donald Saddler, and working with Abbott on the stage direction.)

Although Comden and Green were less than enthusiastic about *Wonderful Town's* time and locale, Bernstein was excited about the 1930 Greenwich Village setting, which would require a score that could reflect the specific sounds and spirit of that period. (Bernstein was vocal about his love of New York City and its impact on his work throughout his career.) *Wonderful Town* tells the story of two sisters from Ohio who come to New York City in search of career and romance. The older sister, Ruth (played by Russell), is a wisecracking,

independent, and aspiring journalist, while her younger sister, Eileen, is a dreamy ingénue who drives men wild, but is searching for true love. As the two wide-eyed women enjoy adventures in their quirky Greenwich Village bohemian neighborhood, they both find their dreams realized: Ruth finds writing success while winning the affections of a magazine editor, and Eileen finds romance with an unassuming, sincere suitor. The tale is simplistic, while the score is anything but. Bernstein exploited the music and rhythmic trends of the time and locale, playing with a big band jazz sound and meter for "Swing!," as well as an Afro-Caribbean reference for "Conga" and a dissonant bebop jazz component for "Wrong Note Rag." In terms of narrative, he infused the character songs with informative compositional techniques. For instance, the music to Ruth's "One Hundred Easy Ways" is bluesy with a bit of bawd, including a saucy vamp under her list of gender grievances, while Eileen's "A Little Bit in Love" is romantic and melodically lush, embellished with a notated sigh (i.e., her sung "mmmmm"). "Conversation Piece" is a musicalized treatment of awkward chit-chat between the sisters and various suitors, replete with starts, stops, stutters, and sputters, building to contrapuntal cacophony. Bernstein again unified his score with symphonic use of leitmotifs and the recycling of thematic phrases from one song to another. Whether or not audience members actually noted the complex use of themes, rhythms, idioms, etc., they were charmed by the rich and pleasing score, the warm and humorous libretto/lyrics, and the appeal of the show's star, Rosalind Russell. Consequently, *Wonderful Town* was a major hit of the early '50s, running for 559 performances.

In addition to his *Wonderful Town* success, Bernstein further strengthened his reputation as America's leading concert artist, advocate, and envoy by conducting a series of television lectures from 1954–58 on CBS titled *Omnibus*, which culminated in a series of fifty-three televised *Young People's Concerts* throughout the '60s and early '70s. The shows featured lecturer/conductor Bernstein as he explained the components, structures, histories, and meanings of musical genres, artists, and techniques, using visual aids (e.g., oversized notated pages of music, covering the floor) and live orchestral demonstrations. Another career milestone during this period was his taking on the role of music director of the New York Philharmonic in 1957, holding the title until 1969 (although he continued to conduct and make recordings with the orchestra throughout his life, ultimately being named "Laureate Conductor"). Prior to taking over the New York Philharmonic, Bernstein embarked on a theatre project that he had long envisioned: a musical adaptation of Voltaire's satiric 1759 novella, *Candide*. Postponing work with Robbins on their long-planned *Romeo and Juliet* musical, Bernstein first wanted to complete the score for his pet Voltaire project. In doing so, he pushed the envelope of what is normally heard on Broadway, choosing to adopt the style of baroque composition and early classical music, while referencing *opéra comique* in terms of content and aesthetic. The story is a parable in which a naive hero, Candide, resides in Westphalia with his equally naive love, Cunegonde, both of whom idealistically believe in the superior goodness of their world. Candide, however, is forced to leave his safe and simple life to search for Cunegonde, who has been kidnapped and prostituted in lands beyond Westphalia. After they both experience the seductions, barbarities, and evils of the outside world, they realize there is no such thing as "perfection," but that realistic expectations and putting forth one's best efforts may be enough to attain peace and happiness.

Bernstein pulled out all the stops to exploit complex techniques and aesthetics in the score, which includes parodies of classical vocal styles, intricate compositional devices, and numerous musical and rhythmic idioms. In fact, such a significant degree of integration, underscoring, and continuous composition is found in *Candide* that many have categorized it as an operetta. Yet, the challenging content and sound of *Candide* may have been too much for audiences in 1956; the production lasted only 73 performances. The failure may also have been the fault of the libretto, penned by celebrated American playwright Lillian Hellman, who neglected to capture Volaire's winking mischievousness and whimsical satire. (Lyrics were contributed by multiple artists, after the original lyricist, John Latouche, died early in the writing process.) The production, however, found a second life in the 1970s, with a creatively staged remount by director Hal Prince and a significant rewrite of libretto/lyrics by Hugh Wheeler and Stephen Sondheim, eventually pleasing audiences and entering into the musical theatre and opera canons. The ultimate success of *Candide* also affirmed Bernstein's belief, predating the sung-through musicals of the 1970s and beyond, that musical theatre was a genre capable of evolving a new type of populist, "intelligible" opera for the twentieth century.

Although demoralized by *Candide's* initially dismal reception, Bernstein put it behind him in 1957 to concentrate on a musical that had been a decade in the making. The musical was *West Side Story*; and the genesis of this landmark production can be traced back to discussions between Bernstein and Robbins in the late '40s regarding a possible *Romeo and Juliet* musical adaptation. In 1949, at Robbins' suggestion, they brought in playwright Arthur Laurents and began work on the tale of an ill-fated romance set on the Lower East Side of Manhattan between a Jewish girl and an Italian Catholic boy, titled *East Side Story*. When scheduling conflicts and other commitments interrupted the writing process, the collaborators parted ways but vowed to return to the project as soon as they could, which turned out to be six long years later. (Bernstein's busy international schedule was especially problematic, given that he was going to serve as both lyricist and composer.) When the men re-teamed, they felt their original libretto idea was dated. They changed the star-crossed lovers to a Puerto Rican girl, Maria, and American-born Caucasian boy, Tony, both tangentially affiliated with and restricted by warring gangs on Manhattan's West Side, a conflict that ends in Tony's death. It was also decided that the project would be better served by bringing in a lyricist, so they hired a young, aspiring composer/lyricist named Stephen Sondheim for his first Broadway venture. Bernstein was named co-lyricist, but in the end, the show's lyrics were primarily Sondheim's, and most of Bernstein's lyrics were dropped. Consequently, Bernstein relinquished his lyricist credit once the show opened. Before any of this could happen, however, Bernstein's commitment to *Candide* necessitated that the actual writing of *West Side Story* had to wait one more year, but the resulting musical is considered the highlight of Bernstein's Broadway career as well as his most lasting and popular score.

Bernstein brought his symphonic sense of unified and evocative composition to the musical. For instance, the first notes whistled in the "Prologue" introduce a three-note interval that is quoted throughout the score (e.g., "Maria"). It is a subtle strategy, but works on an almost subliminal level to bind the musical world of *West Side Story*. Further, there is a lot of symphonic underscoring and dance music that facilitates the active and narrative movement and classical choreography supplied by Robbins as well as communicates the drama of specific scenes (e.g., "Prologue," "Rumble," "Dance at the Gym," and the dream ballet to "Somewhere"). Not all Bernstein's work was pure orchestral composition; he also wrote for character, place, time, and dramatic situation, employing an array of musical idioms and strategies to do so (for some songs, Sondheim supplied lyrics first; for others, Bernstein supplied the music first). For instance, the Latin-inspired sound of "America" and the mambo in "Dance at the Gym" indicate the Puerto Ricans' heredity, while also fueling a fire under the competitive and argumentative nature of the songs and dances. The tragic romance of Tony and Maria is treated operatically, with the lovers singing arias and virtuosic duets such as "Maria," "One Hand, One Heart," "Tonight," and "I Have a Love" (which grows out of what could be deemed an impassioned and active recitative between Anita and Maria in "A Boy Like That"). In contrast, the Jets enjoy a comic specialty number, "Gee, Officer Krupke," with an almost vaude-villian riff used to assert comedy into an otherwise tragic story, as well as a jazz number, "Cool," which uses a contemporary sound to evoke the gang's youthful rebellion and angst. Interestingly, audiences weren't sure what to think when *West Side Story* debuted at the Winter Garden Theatre on September 26, 1957, given the challenging score, the lyrical aesthetic, and the dark, probing subject matter. Reviews were mixed, and although nominated for a Tony Award for Best Musical, the show was beaten that year by a more sunny and optimistic vision of America, Meredith Willson's *The Music Man*. Although *West Side Story* would eventually gain an audience, running for 732 performances, *The Music Man* would see a run of 1,375. Nevertheless, *West Side Story* entered the upper echelon of the musical theatre canon, and is now declared a modern masterpiece.

After *West Side Story*, Bernstein all but said goodbye to Broadway, the exception being one failed musical, *1600 Pennsylvania Avenue*. With book and lyrics by Alan Jay Lerner, this 1976 musical was panned by critics and ignored by audiences, lasting only seven performances. Bernstein remained active in the classical/concert music forums, however. Not only did he compose numerous orchestral and choral works during the '60s, '70s, and '80s, he also wrote ballets (1974's *Dybbuk*), operas (1983's *A Quiet Place*), and other theatrical pieces (1971's *Mass*), most of which are still performed on concert, ballet, and opera stages today. This is not to suggest, however, that Bernstein should be mainly categorized as a composer of symphonic pieces instead of a songwriter; for he wrote 221 songs during his lifetime, including both music and lyrics for some. He also remained a venerated conductor up until his death, often working in poor physical health (including a bout with lung cancer in 1989). When Bernstein died of a heart attack on October 14, 1990, at 72 years old, the concert and theatre communities mourned, as did music-lovers across America and overseas, acknowledging that the music world had lost a uniquely American artist and icon.

FEATURED PRODUCTION: *Candide* (1956)

Music by Leonard Bernstein, Original Lyrics by Richard Wilbur et. al., Original Book by Lillian Hellman

Original Broadway Run: Opened December 1, 1956; Martin Beck Theatre; 73 performances

The musical theatre canon is peppered with works that detail the coming-of-age journey of an adolescent male, who is searching for happiness, identity, and self-realization. The journey is often theatrically presented as a contemporary parable or morality tale (e.g., *Pippin*, *Spring Awakening*, and *The Book of Mormon*). Such is the basic content of *Candide*, which is a musical version of the famous 1759 satire by Voltaire. The adaptation was a longtime pet project of composer Leonard Bernstein, who collaborated in 1956 with lyricist John Latouche (who died during the work's development and was replaced by Richard Wilbur) and American playwright Lillian Hellman. Since its disappointing debut, *Candide* has undergone numerous rewrites, ultimately finding its place in the musical theatre canon. Because of the revised, dropped, and added material, current staged versions of *Candide* may vary, depending on the material chosen for a particular production; but this segment will outline the basic story and the most commonly included songs from the score.

As *Candide* opens, a narrator (Voltaire, in the original production) introduces the main characters and sets the scene for the ensuing story, as the main players give thanks for the conditions of their blessed existence in the contrapuntal "Life Is Happiness Indeed." The central story concerns the eponymous hero, Candide, who is a paragon of innocence, having been raised as a bastard child in the idyllic land of Westphalia. With his peers, he has been indoctrinated in the philosophy of humanist "optimism" by his professor, Dr. Pangloss, who preaches, through a semi-patter song, that all happens for the best in their "Best of All Possible Worlds." Candide is in love with the beautiful and virginal Cunegonde. Soon, their innocent flirtation turns to carnal exploration, at the suggestion of Cunegonde, who witnessed Pangloss and the serving maid Paquette in a comprising sexual act and was charmed by Pangloss' improvised "advanced physics" explanation. As Candide and Cunegonde being to explore the physical "law of attraction," they sing an operatic duet, "Oh Happy We," in which Candide envisions their future as a rural married couple with livestock, produce, and babies, while Cunegonde trills about jewels, servants, and a palatial residence (the song is a brilliant compositional construct in which they sing together, each in a reverie, paying no attention to the other's divergent sentiments). Candide is soon banished, due to the discovery of his physical relationship with Cunegonde. He departs Westphalia with the plaintive aria "It Must Be So," in which he avows his belief in Pangloss' optimistic philosophy that all happens for the best. Unfortunately, his departure leads to his capture by Bulgarians who are on their way to invade Westphalia. They savage and kill many in the court, but keep Cunegonde alive in order to prostitute her to soldiers. As the battle wages on, Candide's captors are killed, and he is rescued by a troupe of traveling players. Cunegonde, meanwhile, becomes a sought-after prostitute and eventually the "shared mistress" in Paris of both a "tremendously rich" Jew and the Cardinal Arch Bishop of Notre Dame (the Grand Inquisitor). As she laments her situation, vacillating between moral shame and material greed, she sings the trilling and thrilling coloratura aria "Glitter and Be Gay."

The remaining plot involves Candide's search for and rescue of Cunegonde. He once again encounters Dr. Pangloss, who has lost his nose as a result of syphilis but is relentless in his "mindless" optimism, landing them both in a Lisbon jail charged as heretics. Pangloss is ultimately hanged but Candide escapes after a whipping and is rescued and revived by an Old Lady, who also reunites him with Cunegonde. (The Old Lady proves to be the ultimate survivor, espousing her adaptive philosophy in the tango aria "I Am Easily Assimilated.") After Candide kills the Jew (by accident) and the Grand Inquisitor (in a jealous rage), he and Cunegonde, plus the Old Lady, embark on a ship to the New World. Further adventures ensue, including more attacks, rapes, accidental deaths, and murders.

The plot becomes even more surreal as Candide once again loses Cunegonde, this time to pirates, but frees the enslaved Paquette and escapes with her to the jungles of South America, finding gold, jewels, and singing animals in the mythic city of El Dorado. Finally, Candide tracks down Cunegonde in Constantinople and uses all his newfound riches to buy her freedom from the pirates. Once again penniless and back in Westphalia, Candide and Cunegonde decide to follow a new creed, embarking on a simple rural life, chopping wood, growing a garden, and doing the "best they know." This final sentiment is voiced through the folk ballad, "Make Our Garden Grow," which grows into a majestic choral work of baroque proportion, sung by the entire *Candide* cast.

Candide is an almost through-composed work by Bernstein, with reoccurring themes and motifs as well as reprises and variations woven through the musical. In addition to virtuosic operetta vocal stylings and ornate orchestrations, the score contains appealing melodic hooks and lilting meters, written in almost every significant compositional rhythm of pre-twentieth-century music, for example, barcarolle, gavotte, mazurka, polka, schottische, tango, and waltz. The unity of *Candide's* score is even more impressive given the mélange of lyricists collaborating on the work, that is, Latouche, followed by Wilbur, along with contributions by Dorothy Parker, librettist Hellman ("Eldorado") and Bernstein ("I Am Easily Assimilated"). The collective writing became even more pronounced as *Candide* received a significant reworking in 1973, mostly as an effort to resurrect and rescue the production which experienced a dismal box office (73 performances) on its original debut. But in the early '70s, there were those in the musical world, especially Bernstein, who still believed the work held great promise; accordingly, Hugh Wheeler wrote a new libretto and Stephen Sondheim contributed new lyrics. Almost as important was the environmental staging concept employed by director Hal Prince: The musicians were placed around the auditorium with the audience at center, surrounded by ten separate performance spaces, all connected and activated by bridges, ramps, platforms and trap doors. Audiences were charmed by both the content and theatrical experience of *Candide* the second time around, and the 1973 revival at Broadway Theatre ran for 740 performances. Given its Broadway success, the work entered the musical theatre canon, and in 1982 *Candide* was added to the New York City Opera repertory. Thus, *Candide* has become one of musical theatre's cross-over hits, performed in both musical and opera venues. It has also been performed on the concert circuit, recently receiving an elaborate Live on Broadway concert version in 2005, performed at Lincoln Center's Avery Fisher Hall by the Westminster Symphonic Choir and the New York Philharmonic, starring Tony Award winners Kristin Chenoweth and Patti LuPone.

PULLING BACK THE CURTAIN:

Intersections of Classical and Concert Music and the American Musical Theatre

The relationship between concert and classical music and the musical theatre has sometimes been a tenuous and terse one. From the earliest confluence of the two genres, there appeared an elitist dismissal of and distaste for the art and artists of the "leg show" by those in the concert community. This was most apparent in the loud resistance met by successful Broadway operetta composer Victor Herbert when he became conductor of the Pittsburgh Symphony in 1898. The bias sometimes worked both ways, with musical theatre composers purposefully distancing themselves from "elites" in the classical and concert arena, espousing that they, not the concert composers, most effectively spoke to and for the American music-loving public (e.g., George M. Cohan's pride in his lack of formal training and anticlassical compositions). The disparity and distance between the two music camps, however, is a simplistic and manufactured distinction, useful for publicity, but not reflective of reality.

From its earliest days, the musical theatre genre has been influenced by classical forms, since operetta is one of the genre's most significant and formative antecedents. At the turn of the century, Franz Lehar's *The Merry Widow* (1905) became America's first blockbuster, and the popularity of Victor Herbert's many Broadway operettas resulted in a conflation of operetta with musicals/leg shows. Later, the lines were more clearly drawn as operettas by classically trained composers, such as Sigmund Romberg and Rudolph Friml, continued to be popular on Broadway but would be formally categorized as "operettas," as opposed to "musical comedies." Nevertheless, the musical theatre genre, as evidenced by the preceding Leonard Bernstein section, is ripe with cross-over artists, as well as classical borrowings and influences.

Following Herbert, George Gershwin was one of the earliest composers to move between the American musical theatre and the concert/classical worlds. While he suffered some slings and arrows in the concert world at the time (often due to his ethnicity and educational background as well as his solid affiliation with musical theatre, jazz, and Tin Pan Alley), he still found major success on both fronts. Other musical theatre composers found acceptance in the concert field, often because they, unlike Gershwin, could boast formal training. For instance, by the time Bernstein found fame as both a symphony conductor and musical theatre composer, there was no longer a stigma associated with the crossover musical artist as that faced by Herbert. Yet even Bernstein lamented to friends that the popularity of his Broadway shows might have hindered the reception given his "serious" concert works. The intersections of musical theatre and classical/concert music may always contain some tension; yet, there are many crossover musical theatre composers who have not felt hindered in either area, and the extent of their parallel concert careers might surprise many of their Broadway fans.

Kurt Weill (1900–50) stands as one of the most acclaimed theatre composers who merged a concert career with musical theatre, not only writing hit musical plays and comedies, for example, *The Threepenny Opera* (1928) and *Lady in the Dark* (1941), but also a full catalogue of operas, a handful of cantatas, a dozen orchestral works (symphonies, suites, concertos, etc.), more than twenty concert vocal pieces (e.g., song cycles), and numerous chamber and piano compositions. In addition, many of Weill's works originally written as Broadway musicals are categorized and performed as "operas" today, such as *Street Scene* (1947) and *Lost in the Stars*

(1949), both of which were adopted into the repertoire of the New York City Opera in the late 1950s. Weill is also notable in that he is one of the few musical theatre composers who did his own orchestrations.

Marc Blitzstein (1905–64) was considered by many to be a troubled genius, acquiring notoriety with his rallying pro-union musical *The Cradle Will Rock* (1938) and providing the English translation to *The Threepenny Opera* (1954). By the latter half of his career, he moved to composing operas as well as other instrumental and orchestral works such as *Symphony: The Airborne* (1948).

Russian émigré **Vernon Duke** (1903–69), née Vladimir Dukelsky, not only wrote acclaimed ballet, classical, and concert music, but also Broadway and film scores as well as radio song hits (many pulled from his contributions to various *Ziegfeld Follies*). In some ways, he was more prolific as a concert composer than a Broadway musical composer, with his most successful book musical score being the moderately successful *Cabin in the Sky* (1940), while his classical catalogue includes works such as *First Symphony* (1928), *Second Symphony* (1930), and *Third Symphony* (1946), as well as frequently performed concertos and oratorios.

Harold Arlen (1905–86) is deemed, along with Irving Berlin, George Gershwin, Cole Porter, and Richard Rodgers, to be one of the leading composers of the American songbook, writing more than 500 songs, including such standards as "Over the Rainbow," "That Old Black Magic," and "Come Rain or Come Shine." His Broadway output includes numerous revues as well as *Bloomer Girl* (1944) and *St. Louis Woman* (1946). Yet, this popular music icon also wrote concert piano works such as *Mood in Six Minutes* (1935), *American Minuet* (1939), *Bon-Bon* (1960), and *Ode* (1960), and vocal pieces such as *American Negro Suite: Four Spirituals, a Dream and a Lullaby* (1941).

The composer of one of America's favorite musicals, *The Music Man* (1957), **Meredith Willson** (1902–84) was a versatile musician, not only writing musicals, film scores, and radio hits, but also composing concert works as well as conducting bands and orchestras. Throughout his prolific concert career, he wrote two well-received symphonies, Symphony No. 1 in F minor, *A Symphony of San Francisco* (1936) and Symphony No. 2 in E Minor, *Missions of California* (1940), as well as orchestral suites, chamber pieces, and symphonic poems.

Contemporary composer **Andrew Lloyd Webber** not only pioneered the modern sung-through musical (a musical theatre reconfiguration of opera) with megahits such as *Cats* (1981) and *The Phantom of the Opera* (1986), but he also dabbled in classical composition for the concert stage, creating *Variations* (1978), a set of musical variations on Niccolò Paganini's Caprice in A Minor, as well as *Requiem* (1985), a concert piece for orchestra, choir, and solo vocals.

In 1979, Lloyd Webber expanded *Variations* into a song cycle, *Tell Me on a Sunday*, which he later evolved into a full score for his popular West End musical *Song and Dance*, premiering on Broadway in 1985. Such a phenomenon presents another aspect of classical/concert music and its influence on and appearance in musical theatre; that is, borrowing or quoting classical leitmotifs and themes in musicals or using classical compositions as the actual content of musical scores. Of course, when such a borrowing or homage is not overtly declared by the composer, it can result in accusations of plagiarism (e.g., some have accused Lloyd Webber of plagiarizing elements of Puccini's opera compositions in *Phantom of the Opera*). However, most musical theatre composers are candid and artistically purposeful in their referential application and appropriation of classical compositions. Along with *Song and Dance*, other examples include the use of Bizet's *Carmen* score for Hammerstein's *Carmen Jones* (1943), the adaptation of themes by classical composer Edvard Greig for *Song of Norway* (1944), Alexander Borodin for the score of *Kismet* (1953), Sergei Rachmaninoff for *Anya* (1965), and Jonathan Larson's musical references to and thematic variations of Puccini's opera *La Bohème* in 1996's *Rent*.

Another variation on this practice is the number of works introduced as "musicals" on Broadway (even if deemed folk "operas" by their creators), only to be embraced later by the opera community, incorporated into their repertoires and appropriated as classical works, being performed more often in an opera house or in concert version than in a theatrical venue, presented as a Broadway musical. Examples include the previously mentioned Kurt Weill works as well as Gershwin's *Porgy and Bess* (1935), Bernstein's *Candide* (1956), Frank Loesser's *The Most Happy Fella* (1956), and Stephen Sondheim's *A Little Night Music* (1973) and *Sweeney Todd* (1979). Given the above-cited artists, works, and practices, it is evident that the intersection of the Broadway musical and the concert/classical music genre is a continually evolving and potent paradigm of the American musical stage.

BETTY COMDEN AND ADOLPH GREEN

Betty Comden and Adolph Green never met a New Yorker or showbiz type they didn't like. At least, that is the impression one might take away from many of their most celebrated Broadway musicals, e.g., *On the Town, Wonderful Town, Bells Are Ringing, On the Twentieth Century*, and *The Will Rogers Follies*. Comden and Green both grew up in New York and retained a fondness for the city, its boroughs, and its inhabitants, viewing the locale as well as its defining entertainment industry through the lens of aspiring and ultimately successful performers and writers. The entire showbiz milieu, including its geographical signposts of New York City and Hollywood, held excitement and promise for the lyricist/librettist team, as well as a sense of community and kinship. Their early impressions, experiences, and attitudes provided a strong foundation for their partnership, which not only stands as the longest collaboration in musical theatre but also one of the closest. For over 60 years, Comden and Green were joined at the pen and referred to as a single entity; in short, one never wrote without the other. In addition to their warm, celebratory treatment of the theatre and film worlds and urban America, they brought an actor's sensibility to lyric writing. With their backgrounds in satiric musical revues, they created some of Broadway's most memorable specialty numbers. These numbers were often the highlights of their eighteen completed musicals, most of which showcase lovable, comic, and larger-than-life characters who often find themselves in life-changing situations, but tackle the challenges with spunk, idealism, and humor. The formula frequently paid off, as Comden and Green became an iconic Broadway institution, with seven Tony Awards to their credit. Further, they hold esteemed places in Hollywood history as significant screenwriters during the gilded movie musical era, nominated twice for Academy Awards. The musical theatre canon, as well as the movie musical genre and American songbook, owes a debt to the witty and collective genius of this writing team.

Adolph Green was a boy from the Bronx, born to Hungarian-Jewish immigrants Daniel and Helen Weiss Green on December 2, 1914. His humble upbringing in New York would flavor and inform his writing career, imbuing his works with a mischievous sensibility, street-smart humor, energetic tempo, and

unpretentious warmth. Green briefly attended college but soon dropped out, working, instead, as a runner on Wall Street to finance his primary dream, which was to be a professional actor. In pursuit of his acting aspirations, Green worked regionally at various summer theatres (where he became fast friends with a young musician named Leonard Bernstein).

Meanwhile, Betty Comden was on her way to graduating with a Bachelor's degree in drama from New York University. Comden grew up as Basya Cohen in Brooklyn, where she was born circa 1917 (reported dates vary) to an attorney father and English teacher mother. (Although her birth name was Basya, it was changed it to Elizabeth, or Betty, at age 5; and the family changed its last name to Comden while she was still young.) From age 6, Betty studied the piano and acted in school plays, then began writing in high school. Like Green, she aspired to a career in theatre and musical performance. In 1938, Comden met Green through mutual friends, and upon Comden's graduation from NYU, the two performer/writers formed a troupe called the Revuers (along with collaborators Al Hammer, John Frank, and Judith Tuvim, later to be known as Judy Holliday). The troupe performed at the Village Vanguard in Greenwich Village, and eventually received a movie offer to appear in the 1944 *Greenwich Village*. The Revuers traveled to Hollywood to find fame, but their roles barely merited notice in the film. Disillusioned, they returned to New York. Their return would be fortuitous, for they were not discovered through the Hollywood system but on the Broadway boards.

Even though Comden and Green were savvy writer/performers and practically defined the term "show-business veterans," their work meshed with the classical world, too. This collective interest in highbrow culture was often reflected in their musicals. Specifically, three of their collaborators—Jule Styne, Morton Gould, and Cy Coleman—started as child prodigies and classically trained pianists before pursuing popular music. Most notably, Comden and Green wrote two of their most successful shows with Leonard Bernstein. The first was *On the Town* (1944), and it marked Comden and Green's Broadway debut. They not only wrote the book and lyrics for *On the Town*, but they originated two of the leads, Ozzie and Claire; they wrote for their particular talents as well as for the overall show (a unique situation rarely seen since the days of George M. Cohan). The musical features the exploits of three sailors on shore leave who have one day to absorb as many of the sights, sounds, and women of New York as possible. The combined talents, youthful outlook, and integrative mission of Broadway newcomers Bernstein, Comden/Green, and choreographer Jerome Robbins, along with fine tuning by veteran director George Abbott, made *On the Town* a historically notable musical. Comden and Green's material especially delighted audiences with its New York milieu, dizzy silliness, and satiric humor. The lyrics for both sexes contain clever double entendres, sentimental expression, and colloquial patter (with the fast-paced list song eventually becoming a Comden/Green staple), all painting a picture of contemporary male-female relationships and wartime flirtations with romance and adventure. And although the show revolves around the sailors and their exploits, it also features women who perform songs, such as "Come Up to My Place" [see fig. 5.3] and "I Can Cook Too," with lyrics by Green and, especially, Comden that showcase female strengths and smarts, as well as healthy libidos (a novel trait for women in musicals at that time).

Comden and Green's next two shows fell short of *On the Town*'s success. For *Billion Dollar Baby* (1945), they collaborated with Morton Gould, who, like Bernstein,

was known primarily as a classical music composer, pianist, and conductor. In this Roaring '20s musical, the main character, Maribelle, is a newly crowned Miss New York from Staten Island. She loses a highly satirized Miss America pageant and reveals her gold-digging, amoral aspirations, singing of being the object of everyone's envy once she marries money and owns "chateaus" as well as "gigolos" (a clever polysyllabic rhyme by the lyricists, another trademark of their work). Despite such sincerely titled songs as "Dreams Come True" and "I'm Sure of Your Love," the duo subverted the standard musical comedy pattern by having the ever-conniving Maribelle choose a wealthy and crooked paramour over a nice-guy suitor. Further exaggerating the dark humor of the show, the final scene shows Maribelle's wedding, during which the stock market has crashed, financially wiping out her new husband. Blissfully unaware, Maribelle throws bracelets to her wedding guests, and the curtain comes down as the groom scrambles to stop her. Even though choreographer Jerome Robbins supplied numerous dance numbers, including an energetic "Charleston," *Billion Dollar Baby* failed to sustain a long run, with only 220 performances. Perhaps critics and audiences in 1945 were unwilling to embrace a she-heel lead (just as in 1940 when *Pal Joey* was initially reviled because of its unsympathetic protagonist). *Billion Dollar Baby* was a smash, however, compared to Comden and Green's next project, *Bonanza Bound!* (1947). With music by Saul Chaplin and libretto/lyrics by Comden and Green, the musical is set during the 1898 Alaska Gold Rush and its libretto includes shady business dealings, social climbing, and show business—often-travelled thematic territory by the duo. Panned by critics, the production never made it to Broadway, closing in Philadelphia.

After the disappointment of *Billion Dollar Baby* and the out-and-out failure of *Bonanza Bound!* (in which Green was also a cast member), Comden and Green headed once again to Hollywood and found another prominent career as screenwriters for movie musicals, many of which are considered the best of MGM's Golden Age. First they wrote the screenplays for 1947's *Good News* (an adaptation of the 1927 DeSylva/Brown/Henderson Broadway smash) and 1949's *The Barkleys of Broadway* (an original Fred Astaire/Ginger Rogers vehicle). They then adapted their Broadway success, *On the Town*, for the movies, fitting it to the talents of stars Frank Sinatra and Gene Kelly, reworking their original lyrics to fit new compositions and songs. (Producer Arthur Freed felt that Bernstein's original music was not audience-friendly enough for his movie and replaced all but a couple of the Broadway songs, "New York, New York" being the only significant number that remained.) The team became a bicoastal commodity during this period, splitting their time between New York and Hollywood, as they returned to Broadway in 1951 with *Two on the Aisle*. Notably, this revue marked the first of nine collaborations with Jule Styne, but *Two* ran for a modest 281 performances. The next year, 1952, Comden and Green reunited with MGM producer Freed and star Gene Kelly, screenwriting their most successful movie musical: *Singin' in the Rain*. Comden and Green did not supply the lyrics, as the score was mostly a composite of already-published songs by Nacio Herb Brown and Arthur Freed (an exception is the original song "Moses Supposes," with lyrics supplied by Comden/Green), but they contributed their sensibility and humor regarding showbiz types and the Hollywood system. The film is a traditional boy-meets-girl musical that boasts a modern, satiric flavor, as it lampoons Hollywood during its famously awkward transition from silent films to talkies.

Comden and Green followed their *Singin'* success with another movie hit, *The Band Wagon* (1953). Mostly using the Schwartz/Dietz score from the original 1931 Broadway revue, the pair had to substantially rewrite the original stage libretto for the screen to showcase the talents of Fred Astaire. For this, Comden and Green were nominated for an Academy Award for the screenplay (as well as their screenplay for 1955's *It's Always Fair Weather*), adding to their collection of three Screenwriters Guild Awards (*The Band Wagon*, *It's Always Fair Weather*, and *On the Town*). Further, *The Band Wagon* and *Singin' in the Rain* are cited in a number of surveys and studies as the two best musicals in movie history, while *Singin'* is also cited on various lists as one of the top ten American films of the twentieth century.

Despite their flim triumphs, Comden and Green had not gone completely "Hollywood," for they remained active on the theatre front in their hometown. And after nine years of moderate-at-best success on Broadway after *On the Town*, the pair was eager to collaborate again with their friend Leonard Bernstein on *Wonderful Town* in 1953, even though they were given only four weeks to write the lyrics (the libretto was already written by Joseph Fields and Jerome Chodorov, based

on their original play, *My Sister Eileen*). This hit, which ran for 559 performances and won the Tony Award for Best Musical, tells the story of sisters Ruth and Eileen, who move from Ohio to Greenwich Village in the 1930s in search of independence, romance, and "big city" success. As opposed to the male perspective of *On the Town*, *Wonderful Town* focused on the world of two females (romantic male-magnet Eileen and savvy career-gal Ruth), giving Comden her best opportunity to date to express herself as a woman. In her writing and employing her performer sensibility, Comden, with Green, was able to write specifically for the musical's star, the brash, talented Rosalind Russell. Russell's spot-on comic timing qualified her to sell such songs as "One Hundred Easy Ways." In this active song, the character Ruth delivers a bluesy, tongue-in-cheek reenactment of how the smart, assertive gal often says or does the wrong thing (such as correcting the man on his baseball expertise or being able to fix a car with a bobby pin), which guarantees the man's loss of interest. The song depicts Ruth's free-speaking urges that must be suppressed if she is ever to catch a husband in the Big Apple. The sisters are given many such character songs, through which the Comden/Green lyrics illustrate the women's inner psyches and external struggles. Examples include Eileen's romantic yearnings, expressed by the sung "mmmm" in her ballad "A Little Bit in Love," in contrast to Ruth's comic patter as she struggles to interview overzealous and amorous Brazilian naval cadets in "Conga!," and finally, the girls' wistful lament over "why oh why oh why oh" they ever left their home in Ohio. Like *On the Town*, *Wonderful Town* is as much about the "town" (New York) as its newcomers; but in this case, the women come out on top, conquering the city and winning their men.

Comden and Green's next assignment was the opposite of *Wonderful Town*; that is, it originated in California, with the action taking place in "Never Never Land." Although it would eventually become a family favorite, its initial Broadway run only merited 149 performances. *Peter Pan* (1954) began with out-of-town problems in San Francisco, as director/choreographer Jerome Robbins decided to expand the work into a full-fledged musical but didn't want to continue using neophytes Carolyn Leigh (lyricist) and Moose Charlap (composer). Thus, Comden/Green and composer Jule Styne were summoned to write numbers to supplement the ten Leigh/Charlap songs. As part of their significant contribution, Comden and Green wrote lyrics to an enchanting song, "Never Never Land." With childlike, simple rhymes and allusions, the song establishes the mood early in the show. They gave their two stars their only duet, "Mysterious Lady," and showed their characteristic comic edge with songs such as "Captain Hook's Waltz," in which the villainous pirate shows an incongruent "dandy" side as he plays with affected poetic alliteration and rhymes, accentuating the sweet/sour contrast of his nature.

Two years later, Comden and Green reunited with Styne and another old friend, Judy Holliday, for *Bells are Ringing* (1956), a charming musical comedy in which Holliday played an answering-service operator, Ella Peterson, who cares about her clients, especially the procrastinating playwright Jeff Moss. As Ella inserts herself into her clients' lives, she takes on different personas over the phone, which is unfortunate given her romantic feelings for Moss, who thinks she is a little old lady he calls Mom. Everything sorts itself out in the end, of course, as Ella discovers that Jeff loves the real her, not the alter egos she has invented and assumed to get close to him. Besides two pop hits, "Just in Time" and "The Party's Over," the score includes numerous songs that provide delightful comic relief. For instance, "It's a Simple Little System" describes a code by which thuggish bookies use composers' names to denote race tracks (e.g., "Beethoven" for "Belmont Park"); and "Drop That Name" (another Comden/Green list song) spotlights oh-so-sophisticated partygoers who cite every celebrity known to 1956 man, while unpolished Ella can only cite the movie star dog, Rin-Tin-Tin. Given Comden and Green's familiarity with their star, Holliday, they were able to write delightful specialty numbers for her unique comic talents and voice, including Ella's plaintive threat to return to her old job in a brassiere company in "I'm Going Back." With help from Styne/Comden/Green, Judy Holiday won the Tony Award over Julie Andrews' performance in *My Fair Lady*. In short, *Bells Are Ringing* combines an entertaining, hummable score with a sweet natured storyline, which again paints New York City as a small, close-knit community with lovable, quirky residents. The Broadway production ran nearly as long as Comden and Green's previous four musicals combined, a whopping 924 performances.

After writing the libretto for *Bells are Ringing* in 1957, the pair returned to writing lyrics only, this time for *Say, Darling*, an adaptation of Richard Bissell's novel of the same title. The plot—another showbiz saga—chronicles the author's experience in adapting his novel, *7½ Cents*, into the 1954 musical *The Pajama Game*. The show, for which Comden, Green, and Styne supplied songs, is therefore a musical play about the making of a musical, adapted from a novel about the making of another musical based on another novel—a dizzy mix of metatheatre and metafiction. Various renamed characters in *Say, "Mysterious Lady," Darling* represent the real-life parties (producer, director, author, songwriter, star) who were involved with *Pajama Game*. Although *Say, Darling* had a respectable run (333 performances), it is virtually forgotten today. This is most likely because much of the show's popularity was based on an appreciative audience of Broadway insiders who, at the time, understood and enjoyed the behind-the-scenes soap opera and, especially, the thinly disguised portrayals of contemporary well-known theatre personalities. Without this relevant context, the show, today, seems little more than a mediocre backstage musical with nine less-than-memorable songs.

The 1950s were fertile years for the trio of Comden, Green, and Styne; the streak continued into the '60s, with some musicals faring better than others. At the beginning of the decade, the team wrote a straightforward star vehicle for popular comedian Phil Silvers. In the show, titled *Do Re Mi* (1960), Silvers played no-goodnik Hubie Cram, with Nancy Walker (a comic star in her own right) as his long-suffering wife, Kay. Based on a novella by Garson Kanin, who wrote the libretto, *Do Re Mi* is yet another showbiz/underworld concoction, involving a get-rich-quick scheme placed within the jukebox industry. Given the show's comic star power, clever antics, and impressive string of solid tunes, including the instant song classic, "Make Someone Happy," *Do Re Mi* ran for 400 performances. The following year, Comden and Green returned to writing both book and lyrics to Styne's music for *Subways Are for Sleeping* (1961). The foray was a disappointment for all involved. The musical was to be an adaption of Edmund G. Love's same-titled book about his experiences and the people he met as a vagrant, sleeping on New York's subway trains. However, Comden and Green were confounded by the material and the book's structure. Instead of using the book's initial form (i.e., a collection of vignettes), the librettist team concocted a linear romance narrative between a homeless former businessman and a successful magazine writer, plus a colorful subplot that details a relationship between a man who mooches meals from friends and a woman who wears only a towel to thwart evictions by hotel managements. The score includes a few good tunes; but the show was not among Comden and Green's best efforts, even though it once again affectionately depicts New York City as a quirky small town. When it debuted on Broadway, the reviews were negative, and the production closed after 205 performances, despite the Tony Award won by Phillis Newman over Barbra Streisand for Best Featured Actress in a Musical. (*Subways Are for Sleeping* has a place in musical theatre lore, however, due to the devious lengths gone to by its legendary producer, David Merrick, to boost ticket sales. After the scathing reviews, Merrick and the show's publicist found New Yorkers with the same names as prominent media critics, invited them to the show and used their "rave" comments in the show's ads. The ruse was soon uncovered, but the publicity stunt did extend the show's run for a while.)

In their next show, the three partners returned to the *Do Re Mi* formula (show business, comedy, star vehicle) with *Fade Out—Fade In*. Like Comden and Green's *Singin' in the Rain*, this show poked fun at early Hollywood. In its portrait of a gawky movie usherette who, through mistaken identity, is picked for stardom by a movie mogul, *Fade Out* satirizes such 1930s Tinseltown clichés as egomaniacal stars, nepotism, corporate backstabbing, and psychoanalysis. The fast-paced production was punctuated by lively numbers, including a list song chronicling the name changes of famous actors. Further, the show's material was specifically suited to its original star, Carol Burnett (as the usherette), who was given specialty songs such as "Call Me Savage," during which she vainly tried to emulate famous vamps (e.g., Mata Hari), as well as a memorable Shirley Temple impersonation in "You Mustn't Feel Discouraged." In the libretto, the usherette eventually succeeds at stardom and gets the boy; although in *Fade Out*'s final scene, she farcically gets her face stuck in the cement when casting her impression in front of Grauman's Chinese Theatre. Even though the show received good reviews, the irreplaceable Burnett began missing performances, hurting the box office, and then became pregnant when the show re-opened after a hiatus. The production closed prematurely after 271 performances.

At this point in their career, Comden and Green had written ten book musicals in twenty years. Half of the shows were set at least one generation in the past, and the present-day plots of the others hewed closely to the white, middle-class experience of the audience. In 1967, the writing team, with Jule Styne and librettist Arthur Laurents, tried something new by writing about an African American heroine in *Hallelujah, Baby!* In the "concept" libretto, the lead character, Georgina (played by young television singer Leslie Uggams), and three other characters live through the century without aging. Each episode shows Georgina striving to become a success while dealing with racism. The inevitable question, however, is how four affluent Jews could present the African American experience authentically in words, music, and dance to a largely white audience. There was, and still is, criticism that characteristic idioms such as blues, jazz, gospel, and spirituals were either missing from *Hallejuah*'s score or given Tin Pan Alley treatments, being weak approximations of authentic African American music and expression. Overall, the score is conventional Comden/Green/Styne showbiz, with little specificity about blacks' struggles in America. Surprisingly, the show won the Tony Award for Best Musical, even though reviews ranged from negative to antagonistic. The creators were disheartened by both the critical response and audience's disinterest; the show closed after only 293 performances. It seems most likely that Comden, Green, and their colleagues were trying to write a topical show without straying from what they thought would please a predominantly white audience, failing on both accounts.

Comden and Green returned to firmer footing in *Applause* (1970). With a score by composer Charles Strouse and lyricist Lee Adams, the musical is an adaptation of the backstage film *All About Eve* (1950). The writers came into the project late to replace an unsatisfactory libretto and faced the daunting task of adapting one of the most brilliantly written films of all time. Film star Lauren Bacall stepped into Bette Davis' shoes as Margo Channing, the aging stage star whose career and personal life are undermined by her conniving understudy, Eve. Fortunately, Comden/Green's libretto retains the edge of the original screenplay, with biting and sophisticated wordplay that complements the backstage intrigue. The storyline also gave Comden another chance to provide a voice for strong, independent, sexual women. However, the show fell short of breaking new feminist ground, which is surprising given the period in which it was written (on the cusp of the Women's Rights Movement of the '70s) and the fact that Comden was one of the few women to have reached the top in a male-dominated industry. Instead, Comden and Green supplied an ending to the show in which Margo smugly thanks Eve for having stolen her starring role, claiming the loss saved her marriage. In other words, the ending became a traditional, antifeminist affirmation of the superiority of romance/domesticity over career/stardom for women. (Comden, who has often been called a "one-of-the-guys" type of "gal," never wrote overtly feminist lyrics/books, choosing to give her female protagonists traditional values, but significantly girded and enhanced by strong senses of identity, humor, and agency.)

After the success of *Applause*, which ran for 896 performances, Comden and Green made no significant stage contributions for eight years. The period included a disappointing stint in which they provided lyrics for four new Jule Styne songs for *Lorelei* (1974), a failed remake of 1949's *Gentlemen Prefer Blondes*. But their return to Broadway as both lyricists and librettists in 1978 was triumphant, with the ambitious and critically acclaimed *On the Twentieth Century*. A reworking of the 1932 Ben Hecht/Charles MacArthur play and 1934 Howard Hawks film of the same title, the musical presents the love-hate relationship and devious machinations of an egotistical film star, Lily, and an over-the-top, floundering theatrical producer, Oscar, as they are reunited and share a train ride to New York. As Oscar attempts to restart his career by signing the hyper-emotional Lily (whom he discovered and romanced in the past) to his latest stage project, he must contend with her current lover and a rival producer, both of whom are also on the train. For the project, Comden and Green's new music collaborator was Cy Coleman, heretofore known mainly for jazz and pop scores. Yet, with *Twentieth Century*, the team aspired to a "screwball" comic opera, creating a score that spoofs operetta and even grand opera, comprising heavily ironic, contrapuntal, and convoluted spins on various song forms from the classical genres. Such a musical gave Comden and Green a great opportunity to play out their highbrow proclivities within yet another show-business setting, with highly theatrical performances at the center. The lyrics' clever colloquial banter and character expression, combined with brilliant internal and polysyllabic rhymes, represent Comden and Green at the top of their game. Two significant examples are "Never" and "I've Got It All," the point

and counterpoint songs for Lily and Oscar, respectively, which contain some of the funniest and most hyperbolic sentiments found on 1970s Broadway as the two argue over her prospective appearance in Oscar's play. By contrast, "Our Private World," a lovely, romantic barcarolle—with more than a nodding resemblance to Victor Herbert and Rida Johnson Young's operetta classic "Ah! Sweet Mystery of Life"—provides layers of irony to an essentially unromantic musical. *Twentieth Century* allowed Comden and Green to draw on their lifelong interests in show business, movies, classical music, and opera. The musical was enhanced by the spirited directing of Hal Prince and Robin Wagner's elaborate, state-of-the-art scenic design, which recreated the luxury train on stage. *Twentieth Century* won five Tony Awards, with Comden and Green garnering one for the score and one for the book. Although the musical was not a blockbuster (running 449 performances) and is not often revived or staged by regional theatres (there are cost issues with regard to its train setting), it deserves to become one of the pair's more enduring works.

In contrast to *Twentieth Century*, Comden and Green's follow-up project, *A Doll's Life* (1982), was one of their most conspicuous failures. Built on a dramatic classic, the lyricists/librettists, along with composer Larry Grossman, wrote a musical drama that tried to answer the often-asked question about Ibsen's *A Doll's House* (1879): What happens after the stifled wife and mother, Nora, slams the door on her domestic life? The creators, including director Hal Prince, chose to frame the story within a contemporary rehearsal of Ibsen's play, with the actors reappearing in the story of Nora's post-walkout life. In the narrative, Nora goes through several menial jobs, becomes a feminist, and then, as a rich man's mistress, pawns and saves to buy her own company. At the end, she returns to her abandoned home as a successful, independent woman; but her domestic situation remains unresolved. *A Doll's Life* received uniformly poor reviews and closed after five performances, although Comden and Green received Tony nominations for both the score and book. Comden and Green's next stage project, *Singin' in the Rain* (1985), was another career disappointment. The stage adaptation of their classic film debuted in London in 1983 as a star vehicle for British song-and-dance performer Tommy Steele. Songs by other songwriters were added, including the Gershwins' "Fascinating Rhythm" and Cole Porter's "Be a Clown." To rework the show for an

American audience, Comden and Green were asked to restore their original script; and director Twyla Tharp (heretofore known only as a ballet choreographer) brought back the original score and removed the London interpolations, choosing to reproduce the film literally on stage. Due to poor reviews, the show nearly closed on opening night but survived for ten months through an effective advertising campaign and, possibly, the attraction of its actual rainstorm onstage for the iconic title number.

The Will Rogers Follies, A Life in Revue (1991) was Comden and Green's final musical. With a book by Peter Stone, music by Cy Coleman (his second collaboration with Comden/Green), and the overall concept, creative vision, and staging by director/choreographer Tommy Tune, *Will Rogers Follies* turned out to be as bright and hopeful as *A Doll's Life* was dark and brooding. The musical chronicles the life of *Ziegfeld Follies* star and American treasure Will Rogers, tracing his rise from vaudeville houses to national stardom, a trajectory cut short by his 1935 death in a plane crash. The biography is treated as a concept musical, with Rogers serving as the narrator of his life story, chatting with the audience throughout the show via his signature wry commentaries. Each life-changing event for Rogers is presented as a vaudevillian turn or elaborate *Follies* production number, all colorfully and referentially reproduced, often with a touch of irony. Wiley Post (who died with Rogers in the 1935 crash) appears sporadically to remind the audience of the protagonist's untimely end; and a certain Ziegfeld Girl ("Ziegfeld's Favorite"), in various stages of undress, shares the stage with Rogers periodically to assist in the show's narration and stage management. For their part, Comden and Green began the project by writing "Never Met a Man I Didn't Like," the signature number for Rogers in which he declares his egalitarian worldview, that is, he likes everyone, regardless of their station in life. Even though the show belongs to Rogers, it features a strong woman in the character of his wife, Betty Blake. Here Comden had another opportunity to bring her spirited, humorous woman's point of view to the production. Yet, Blake is also framed as a traditional ingénue, then wife, in most ways. Through the Comden/Green lyrics in "My Big Mistake," Blake assumes the role of neglected and plaintive wife who stands by her man, knowing that it may be foolish to love such a public figure but can't help loving her "mistake." In another song, "No Man Left for Me," Blake wryly comments on the challenges of life with Will Rogers; yet her positive wit and spirit keep the song from devolving into self-pity. Overall, however, the show is clearly another Comden/Green paean to showbiz and an affectionate rendering of one of the industry's most beloved figures. The 1991 audiences fell in love with Rogers; the show ran for 982 performances, winning six Tony Awards, including Best Musical and Best Score (Comden and Green's seventh and last Tony Award).

The Will Rogers Follies was a fitting swan song for Comden and Green, encapsulating many signature characteristics of their most successful and celebrated shows. After this "cherry" atop a most delightful "sundae" of a career, the partners, in their mid-to-late 70s, unofficially retired from active writing and enjoyed their final chapter as titans of the industry, being named Kennedy Center Honorees while garnering other awards and career accolades. When Adolph Green died on October 23, 2002, he was given a showbiz-style send-off with a Broadway memorial held at Shubert Theatre, attended by numerous luminaries and, of course, Betty Comden. Comden lived four years longer, until she succumbed to heart failure on November 23, 2006. The American theatre may never see another partnership remotely approaching that of Comden and Green for longevity, consistency, and enthusiastic contribution to the American Dream machine. They took audiences inside the theatre, Hollywood, and the neighborhoods of New York, making these milieus appear glamorous, real, and attainable. Time after time, they playfully referenced the classics, and created characters—male and female—striving to succeed in worlds filled with lovable cons, kooks, and creative types. As a bonus, Comden and Green were also accomplished performers. Not only did they appear in several stage musicals and films, they also performed two-person concerts, which they aptly called "Parties" (two of which ended up on Broadway, in 1958 and 1977). In the shows, the pair chronicled their careers by performing their own previously written sketches and songs in inimitable style. The concerts allowed Comden and Green to basically do what they did best; that is, celebrate their lives in showbiz while paying homage to the cities and communities that fostered their success. Their shows allowed the writers to communicate and connect personally with their many fans and musical theatre aficionados, who could, in turn, thank them firsthand for their contributions to the musical theatre genre for the better part of the twentieth century.

Figure 5.3

COME UP TO MY PLACE

Music by Leonard Bernstein;
Lyrics by Betty Comden and Adolph Green (1944)

CHIP
My father told me, "Chip, my boy,
There'll come a time when you leave home;
If you should ever hit New York,
Be sure to see the Hippodrome."

HILDY
The Hippodrome?

CHIP
The Hippodrome.

HILDY
Did I hear right?
Did you say the Hippodrome?

CHIP
Yes, you heard right.
Yes, I said the Hip-

[Hildy brakes.]

Hey, what did you stop for?

HILDY
It ain't there anymore-
Aida sang an "A"
And blew the place away!

CHIP
Ah, I wanted to see the Hippodrome!

HILDY
Give me a chance, kid;
I haven't got 5,000 seats, but the one I have is a honey!
Come up to my place.

CHIP
Oh no, lady; the Forrest The-a-tre.

When I was home I saw the plays
The Ladies Drama Circle showed.
Now I'm here, I want to get
Some tickets for "Tobacco Road."

HILDY
"Tobacco Road?"

CHIP
"Tobacco Road."

HILDY
Did I dig that?
Did you say "Tobacco Road"?

CHIP
Yes, you dug that,
Sure, I said "Tobac-"

[Hildy brakes again.]

Hey what for did you stop?

HILDY
That show has closed up shop.
The actors washed their feet
And called it "Angel Street."

CHIP
I wanted to see "Tobacco Road."

HILDY
Stick with me, kid, and I'll show you the road to ruin.
Come up to my place.

CHIP
Oh no, Battery Park.

Back home I dreamt of catching fish
So big I couldn't carry 'em.
They told me that they have my size
Right here in the Aquarium.

HILDY
Aquarium?

CHIP
Aquarium.

HILDY
Hold the phone, Joe-
Did you say Aquarium?

CHIP
I'm still ringing;
Yes I said Aquar-

[She brakes again.]

Did you stop for what, hey?

HILDY
The fish have flown away-
They're in the Bronx instead-
They might as well be dead-
Come up to my place!

CHIP
No, Chambers Street.

They told me I could see New York
In all its spreading strength and power
From the city's highest spot,
Atop the famous Woolworth Tower.

HILDY
The Woolworth Tower?

CHIP
The Woolworth Tower.

HILDY
Beat me, Daddy-
Did you say the Woolworth Tower?

CHIP
I won't beat you,
But I said the Wool-

[Hildy brakes again.]

Did you stop for hey what?

HILDY
That ain't the highest spot-
You're just a little late,
We got the Empire State!
Let's go to my place!

CHIP
Let's go to Cleopatra's Needle.
Let's see Wanamaker's Store.
Let's go to Lindy's, go to Luchow's;
Let's see Radio City and Herald Square.
Go to Reuben's! Go to Macy's!
Roxy! Cloisters! Gimbel's!
Flatiron Building! Hippodrome!!

HILDY
My place!!!

FEATURED PRODUCTION: *On the Town* (1944)

Music by Leonard Bernstein
Lyrics and Book by Betty Comden and Adolph Green

Original Broadway Run: Opened December 28, 1944; Adelphi Theatre; 463 performances

When two wunderkinds, a composer and choreographer, joined to create a ballet, which surprisingly became a popular sensation, they broke even more new ground by turning that ballet into a hit musical. The ballet was *Fancy Free* (debuted in 1944 by Ballet Theatre); and the artists were composer Leonard Bernstein and choreographer Jerome Robbins, two twenty-somethings who set the concert dance world afire with their jazzy, timely, and character-driven debut work. Given the ballet's appeal (and box office), they were quickly approached by Broadway producer who solicited the two men's talents for the musical stage. They were talked into transforming *Fancy Free* into a musical by scenic designer (and producer) Oliver Smith. And with two more wunderkinds added to the creative team—lyricists/librettists Betty Comden and Adolph Green—all parties proceeded posthaste to create a fresh and timely musical comedy titled *On the Town*. The task was impressive; for although *On the Town* had grown out of *Fancy Free*, Bernstein wrote all new music for the Broadway production. Comden and Green not only fleshed out the ballet's thin premise into a fast-paced twenty-four-hour adventure, complete with fleeting romance and screwball antics, but also wrote lyrics to the many character-driven songs, often colloquial in nature but filled with clever rhyme schemes and references. On top of these duties, the pair also assumed two of the lead roles—almost unheard of at the time. The show was given smart and energetic staging by veteran director George Abbott, while a major portion of the story was told through Robbins' dance numbers; the production contained more choreography and extended dance numbers than *Oklahoma!*.

Speaking of the landmark Rodgers and Hammerstein musical, *On the Town* is often deemed the "urban" *Oklahoma!*. *On the Town* debuted just one year later than the Rodgers and Hammerstein milestone, while also presenting to Broadway a unique concept in terms of plot (twenty-four hours of shore leave for three sailors in New York City), plus a sophisticated, unified musical score and a choreographic merger of ballet and show dance. All was skillfully blended to create a fully integrated work; in fact, Bernstein, Robbins, Comden, and Green wrote a "manifesto" that asserted their overriding goal in this respect. Opening on December 28, 1944, the quick and bright musical was also redolent of *Oklahoma!* in that it provided a positive and patriotic picture of America, this time in urban garb. The show reflected a city experiencing real-life encounters with wide-eyed and randy sailors on leave, as well as a country mired in war, but sensing victory on the horizon. It was the right moment for a musical that could assert relevancy while finding a bright spot in the wartime climate.

The show, in basic terms, is a "buddy musical," as three sailors spend a day of adventure in the city, seeing the sights and, literally, chasing the women. Its simplicity is deceiving, as evidenced by the many classical techniques found in its symphonic score by Bernstein as well as Robbins' concert dance, and the highbrow references satirically employed by Comden and Green. The opening number, "New York, New York," spells out the sailors' many desires, while paying homage to the city and providing an opening to the musical that uses jazz and symphonic power to suggest the cacophony and energy of the urban milieu and the sailors. All three sailors succeed in finding a short-term mate, some sooner than others. Ozzie (originally played by Green) meets anthropologist Claire de Loon (originally played by Comden), who admires the shape and size of his head. (Claire's name is, of course, a loony homonym of Debussy's piano classic.) The two find that they are simpatico due to their passionate and dramatic personalities, illustrated through their duet "I Get Carried Away," which musically borrows from and lampoons the grandiosity of operatic arias. Chip, another sailor, is picked up (literally and figuratively) by cabby Hildy, whose full name, Brunhilde Esterhazy, is also a play on classical opera, referencing the name of Richard Wagner's warrior maiden in *Die Walküre* (1870), and the family name of the ruling house of Hungary. Hildy aggressively seduces the naïve sailor in "Come Up to My Place," a fast-paced list song that refers to numerous New York attractions, past and present. The song, through which Hildy and Chip argue the merits of tourist attractions versus her apartment, abruptly shifts in keys and time signatures for each voice, creating a complex musical number that provides a scene rich in comedy and character. They eventually end up at "her place," where their relationship takes a romantic turn, as she boasts of not only her domesticity but her "other" talents in "I Can Cook Too." At the center of the plot is the plight of the third sailor, Gabey, who idealistically pursues Ivy Smith, the winner of the "Miss Turn-stiles" subway beauty contest, with whose picture he has fallen in love. This plot point not only inspires a dream ballet for lovelorn Gabey, but also incites the heavily danced search for her by all three sailors throughout various New York City locations. And although the musical comedy conventions are followed by having Gabey find and win over Ivy in the end, the fact that all three sailors must return to their ship without knowing whether they will ever see their women again creates a bittersweet ending. Two of the most heartfelt and expressive ballads in the score, "Lonely Town" and "Lucky to Be Me," along with the final resigned "farewell" sung by all the characters in "Some Other Time," reflect the longings, fears, disillusionment, and hopes of wartime America, lending substance and relevance to the show and giving poignancy to otherwise escapist fare.

The talents of Broadway newcomers Bernstein, Robbins, and Comden/Green combined to make *On the Town* a historically notable musical. Since its debut, there have been Broadway and Off-Broadway revivals, including a 1998 New York *Encores!* concert version of the show, which proved so popular that the New York Shakespeare Festival mounted a full-scale Broadway staging. To the surprise of many, this most recent revival failed. Nevertheless, the show holds an esteemed place in the musical theatre canon as a showcase of phenomenal talents, coming together at a unique moment in America's and musical theatre's history to create a work that both reflected the spirit and mood of the nation while furthering the codification and sophistication of the integrated book musical.

The cast of Goodspeed Musicals' *On The Town* at the Goodspeed Opera House, 1993. Photo by Diane Sobolewski. Used by permission of Goodspeed Musicals.

PULLING BACK THE CURTAIN:
The Specialty Song

Audiences, performers, and box offices love a "showstopper," i.e., a musical number that literally stops the flow of a show due to an overwhelming audience reaction. Thus, it is no surprise that one of the most often-used "showstoppers" is the specialty number, a number that, when written well, serves equally the performer, show, and audience. Given its efficacy and popularity, the specialty song has been an institution in musical theatre since the genre's beginnings. It is described as a unique number in a show's score by which a performer is given a chance to shine and showcase his or her distinctive and signature talent. The two-fold nature of the specialty song is theatrically potent; for audiences can recognize the star's own performing persona, as well as see his/her character further developed and highlighted in the show. In many contemporary configurations, the specialty song is comic and referential (that is, it employs a wink and a nod to the audience, alerting them to the "star turn" in the song). If not completely laugh-out-loud funny, the number is still extroverted, performative, and presentational—a throwback to the days of vaudeville.

One can trace the evolution of the specialty act from its earliest days in musical comedy through its sophisticated development in the Golden Age. The term "specialty" denotes a specific talent and/or act for which a performer becomes known and celebrated (e.g., the insult-throwing comic, the double-talking/patter-song conman, the "highbrow" satirist, the rubber-faced eccentric dancer, the celebrity impersonator, the slapstick drunk, etc.). Originally, the specialty act was crudely interpolated into a musical comedy, often with no attempt to integrate the material. Due to the early musical's close ties to vaudeville, it did not seem unusual for an independent act (or turn) to be inserted into a show to entertain audiences who were thrilled to see one of their favorite performers or a show-stopping, exhibitionistic talent, regardless of whether the added segment (or "character" played by the featured entertainer) furthered, or even had anything to do with the plot. For instance, in their Broadway debut, Williams & Walker were extraneously featured in Victor Herbert's *The Gold Bug* (1896), during which they performed a cakewalk number, introducing their soon-to-be signature dance step. One of the more humorous examples of early specialties in musical comedy occurred in 1925's *Sunny* (score by Jerome Kern and Oscar Hammerstein II). The producers cast "Ukulele Ike" (a singing vaudevillian who accompanied himself on the ukulele); his contract stipulated that he could only perform at some point between 10:00 and 10:15 p.m. in the musical, the exact time varying from performance to performance. Thus, the writers and stage performers had to accommodate this unpredictable performance slot in their book musical, no matter how it might break the continuity of the narrative. This is not to suggest that variety acts were the only musical comedy interpolations. Stars often added their own specialty numbers to productions, leaving their character portrayals periodically to indulge in personal showcases. Megastar Al Jolson was famous for this practice, literally interrupting his shows with "You don't want to hear the rest of this, do ya? Don't you just want to hear me sing?" Then he would sing old hits and introduce potential new ones, e.g., his addition of Gershwin's "Swanee" to *Sinbad* (1918).

As the Golden Age progressed and the integrated book musical became all the rage, the specialty song became better situated within and suited to the libretto. Gifted writers worked within the parameters of the new cohesive form, limiting the obviousness of the interpolation. This did not mean that show creators stopped serving specific stars and exploiting their talents, capitalizing on trademark strengths and celebrity. Sometimes, the number was written into the production as a song performed in a show-within-the-show (metatheatrical "prop" song). Such was the case with the show-stopping turn by Ethel Merman, who had a secondary role as an "entertainer" in 1930's *Girl Crazy*. In this instance, the Gershwins gave Merman "I Got Rhythm," a number not really fashioned to serve the plot or her character but to specifically showcase Merman's stage presence and vocal talent, including her exceptional lung power (holding one note for an entire chorus). Such moments became highlights in popular musicals, even while adhering to "integrationist" style. Examples include "Tschaikowsky" from *Lady in the Dark* (1941), which provided hyperkinetic talent Danny Kaye a virtuosic comic turn, and "I Can Cook Too" from *On the Town* (1944), which gave aggressive comic/vocalist Nancy Walker a chance to use sexual double entendre to sell her character's "domestic" talents. In short, many supporting performers, otherwise known for their comic stage antics, could strut their stuff through specialty songs; for example, Eddie Foy, Jr.'s befuddled "I'll Never Be Jealous Again" (*Pajama Game*, 1954); Ray Walston's vaudevillian "Those Were the Good Old Days" (*Damn Yankees*, 1955), Stanley Holloway's music hall treatment of "With a Little Bit of Luck" (*My Fair Lady*, 1956), and Stubby Kaye's ironically angelic "Sit Down You're Rockin' the Boat" (*Guys and Dolls*, 1950).

As audiences responded favorably to the specialty number performed by supporting characters (often played by familiar character or comic actors), musical theatre writers became even more comfortable with and savvy at working specialty songs into the integrated musical, supplying such moments for leads as well. This became especially easy when the lead role was originated by a performer who had a specific talent, performance quality, or celebrity persona for which she/he was known. Given their own performing sensibilities, Comden and Green were masters at writing special material for the stars of some of their most popular musicals (Rosalind Russell in *Wonderful Town*, Judy Holliday in *Bells Are Ringing*, and Lauren Bacall in *Applause*). One might see the "star vehicle" as the ultimate extension of this paradigm, a show in which almost every number has been written to suit the specific talents of the leading lady or man. For instance, once Barbra Streisand was cast as Fanny Brice in *Funny Girl* (1964), the score and libretto were designed to not only tell the story of Brice's rise to stardom but to also showcase Streisand's unique voice and comic sensibility. Like the earlier *Lady in the Dark* (1941), starring Gertrude Lawrence, these musicals became so identified with and defined by their stars, they have not been revived on Broadway.

It is significant to note that even though specialty songs are not written as a matter of course in modern musicals, they are definitely not relics of the past. To wit, one could cite "Where You Are" (*Kiss of the Spider Woman*, 1993), a referential song and dance showcase originally performed by and created for living legend Chita Rivera, as well as the delightful, yet conspicuously interpolated "Timeless to Me" (*Hairspray*, 2002). The *Hairspray* "in-one" number (a number performed in front of a closed curtain) was given a vaudevillian, soft-shoe treatment by Harvey Fierstein who, as Edna Turnblad dancing with husband Wilber (Dick Latessa), could further exploit his wink-and-nod drag turn, delighting audiences with his unique singing style (the voice is definitely one of a kind) and campy, wisecracking humor. The number was not only a throwback to the in-one specialty songs of yesteryear but also a reminder as to their special theatrical appeal, be it 1902 or 2002.

FRANK LOESSER

Not since George M. Cohan had a Broadway artist worn so many hats: composer, lyricist, librettist, producer, publisher, mentor. Yet, contrary to Cohan, Frank Loesser gradually assumed those roles. Starting as a lyricist, Loesser decided that he could best serve his smart and expressive lyrics by using his own compositions; thus, the self-taught pianist evolved into that rare musical theatre breed, the composer/lyricist (joining the ranks of predecessors Cohan, Irving Berlin, and Cole Porter, as well as successors Stephen Sondheim, Jonathan Larson, William Finn, Adam Guettel, and Jason Robert Brown). In pursuit of even more artistic power and proprietary control over his works, Loesser acquired music industry cachet as president of the Frank Music Corporation, his own company which became one of the country's top music publishers. This achievement was in addition to Loesser's prodigious pop music career and remarkable track record on Broadway, e.g., four out of his five Broadway musicals were hits, with three deemed masterpieces of the 1950s and early '60s. Further, he was able to use his artistic instinct, meticulous ear for talent, business acumen, and industry connections to further the careers of many other theatre songwriters during the '50s and '60s.

Like Cohan and Berlin (Loesser's idol), Loesser came from immigrant roots and progressed from self-made tunesmith to musical Renaissance man. He put poetic witticisms in the mouths of slick-talking racketeers, hard-bitten dames, fallen ingénues, love-struck elders, conniving opportunists, and immoral corporatists as well as providing them with a litany of musical styles and compositional techniques to underscore such sentiments. On one hand, Loesser's words and music could be symbiotic; on the other, they could be comically and meaningfully incongruent (e.g., Baroque fugues and gospel chorales sung by lowbrow gamblers or a love ballad sung to one's own mirror reflection). Much has been made of the contrasting personalities that constitute musical theatre writing teams such as the Gershwins, Rodgers and Hart, and Lerner and Loewe. With Frank Loesser, such opposites were contained in one artist: the abrasive/charming, restless/cool, romantic/earthy, casual/meticulous, artistic/lowbrow guy who spoke from the heart and the libido. He could use the simplest of slang, often elevated to poetic heights, while employing pop hooks, jazz references, gospel riffs,

Frank Loesser, at dinner with Jo Sullivan
© Bettmann/CORBIS

and operatic motifs to express the diverse, ironic, and contradictory sentiments of his characters.

Loesser, who often slept only four hours a night and returned to work before dawn with a cigarette and coffee (or scotch) in hand, once remarked that his ideal work surroundings were a half-written song, a list of financial or industry figures, and a business dilemma. Such a combo was the essence of Frank Henry Loesser. He was born in New York City on June 29, 1910, a first-generation American born to German immigrant parents, Henry Loesser and Julia Ehrlich Loesser. (In an interesting twist, Henry had originally been married to Julia's sister, Bertha, who gave him a son, Arthur, then died in a second childbirth. After Julia joined the household to help Henry with Arthur, the two married.) Henry Loesser was a piano teacher and a rigid classicalist who had no use for popular music. Frank's brother, Arthur, adhered to his father's philosophy and wishes, studying only classical music and ultimately acquiring his own national fame as a concert pianist, critic, and music educator. Although young Frank was also interested in music, plunking out piano tunes by ear at age 3, he resisted the idea of studying classical music, for he loved the pop music of the day. As his father allowed only classical music in the house, Frank refused to take piano lessons, not wanting to be relegated to the classics. This does not mean, however, that Frank did not fill his days with music. As early as 6, he devised simple songs and often spent hours sitting under the family piano, soaking up the music being played by his father and older brother. He taught himself how to play when he was in his early teens, aspiring to someday join the ranks of Tin Pan Alley. He had good reason to want to jumpstart his music career, for his father died suddenly when Frank was 16, leaving Frank and Arthur to support their mother. As a brief detour, he attended City College of New York but flunked out before finishing his first year. Those closest to Loesser also recount that during these formative years, he acquired the persona for which he would become known (much to his highbrow family's annoyance): a brash New Yorker who could be charming or abrasive, famous for his wise-guy flamboyance and fiery temper. The years following his failed college attempt were lean ones for Loesser, as he took a variety of odd jobs to supplement his songwriting career, stints that ranged from screwing lids onto insecticide bottles to working as a reporter. While writing for vaudeville acts and radio, Loesser made inroads into Tin Pan Alley, working as a lyricist with various composers. His first published song was "In Love with a Memory of You" (written in 1931, with music by William Schuman, who was later to become a classical composer). A few years later, while singing and accompanying himself on the piano in a 52nd Street nightclub, he met his first wife, a club singer by the name of Lynn Garland (originally Mary Alice Blankenbaker). For his original songs, written with composer Irving Actman, he also caught the attention of Broadway producers. Consequently, five of their songs were used in 1936's *The Illustrator's Show*. This Broadway debut was anything but auspicious, for the revue closed after five performances. Nevertheless, there was an upside in that the numbers by Loesser and Actman impressed Hollywood powers-that-be, and the duo was given a Universal Pictures contract.

Embarking on their Hollywood careers, Loesser and Actman moved to California; and Lynn followed shortly after, marrying Loesser in 1936. The next year, Loesser left Universal to begin a successful stint as a contract lyricist for Paramount Pictures, remaining with the studio until 1949. Here, Loesser became adept at working within the Hollywood studio system, where he was most often put in a room with a composer and instructed to write songs on spec, meeting the dictates of producers, studio heads, directors, dance arrangers, and roughly outlined screenplay scenarios—all under a tight deadline. In this environment, Loesser churned out song after song, learning to be quick and clever, specializing in novelty songs, and infusing his lyrics with his own mix of sophistication, simplicity, poetry, straight talk, humor, romance, and sex. These

attributes would carry over to his Broadway years, as he was sometimes compared to Cole Porter; that is, Porter minus the champagne. Loesser's list of collaborators during this period included top composers such as Burton Lane, Hoagy Carmichael, Jimmy McHugh, Jule Styne, and Arthur Schwartz, with numerous songs lifted from mediocre films to become radio hits (e.g., "I Don't Want to Walk Without You," written with Styne, and the ubiquitous "Heart and Soul," written with Carmichael, which remains a favorite duet played by amateur pianists everywhere).

As Loesser became a top lyricist in the Hollywood studio system, he also became more demanding of his collaborators. Often, he wrote words to his songs before the composers had written the music. In the process, he would compose what he called "dummy" tunes, made-up melodies to fit his lyrics. Frank's wife, Lynn, was often frustrated when the melodies provided by the official composers were not as strong as her husband's initial musings. Even without the Loesser "dummies," the construction of his lyrics often dictated how they should sound musically (Jerome Kern once exclaimed to Loesser that his lyrics inspired melodies that practically wrote themselves); many of his collaborators urged Loesser to write his own music. Loesser's first attempt at writing both the music and lyrics was "Seventeen" in 1940, the title song for a B movie comedy of the same name. The song became a modest radio hit; yet it would not be until Loesser enlisted in the Army Air Force during World War II that he would hit his stride as a composer/lyricist. As part of the Radio Productions Unit, Loesser was given a special commission by the Army to write patriotic and diversionary songs that celebrated military life and boosted American morale on the home front (a career development reminiscent of Loesser's hero, Berlin). In this capacity, Loesser wrote one of the biggest hits of the war: "Praise the Lord and Pass the Ammunition" (1942). Selling over 2 million records, with sheet music sales topping 1 million, the song was a rousing combination of battle cry and gospel tune that rivaled the significance and popularity of Cohan's "Over There" during World War I. Loesser's Army service, which included numerous other military-themed songs, instilled in him the confidence to write all his own music from that point forward. Returning to Hollywood, he proceeded to write hit song after hit song for movies. One of his most popular was "Baby, It's Cold Outside," which is now a Christmas favorite. Loesser wrote the song in 1944 as a personal duet to be sung with Lynn as they entertained friends at their frequent parties. In 1948, to Lynn's dismay, Loesser was talked into selling the song rights to MGM, which inserted it into a 1949 motion picture, *Neptune's Daughter*. The song not only won the Academy Award that year (after numerous nominations and losses by Loesser in the past), but its structure became a Loesser trademark; i.e., the dialogic, contrapuntal number, often between two characters in a relationship, who converse and argue in sung counterpoint.

Given his level of success in Hollywood and in popular music, Loesser was restless (as was his nature) and looking for new fields to conquer. Broadway seemed the ultimate challenge and held the most allure for the native New Yorker. Conveniently, Loesser had movie and music industry friends who had recently partnered as musical theatre producers: Cy Feuer and Ernest Martin. Feuer and Martin had secured rights to a popular Victorian farce by Brandon Thomas titled *Charley's Aunt* (1892). On his initial Broadway foray, Loesser was hired to write lyrics to music provided by seasoned composer Harold Arlen. When Arlen's house burned to the ground before writing began, he was too distraught to work. By default, Loesser became both lyricist and composer for his first Broadway show. He didn't disappoint, providing a catchy and charming score to serve the adapted libretto penned by the musical's director, George Abbott. Specifically, the musical, titled *Where's Charley?*, is a "drag" farce in which an Oxford undergraduate, Charley, poses as his own rich "aunt" and chaperone in order to entertain his virginal and proper amour, Amy, in his room, a deceit that incites madcap complications. The musical was originally devised as a star vehicle for eccentric dancer and comic Ray Bolger (as Charley). *Where's Charley?* opened October 11, 1946, to pleasant reviews. Given Bolger's over-the-top performance, as well as the ear-pleasing score and contrived comedy, the show was a hit with audiences, running for 792 performances. Feuer and Martin would go on to produce five successful musicals in a row (including the next iconic Loesser hit, *Guys and Dolls*). On his first try, Loesser earned his Broadway stripes by providing a score that not only contained simple and directly appealing ballads, such as "My Darling, My Darling," and an eventual pop hit, "Once in Love with Amy," but also more complex musical constructs, e.g., the song "Make a Miracle," in which Charley vainly attempts to capture Amy's attention while she vocally meanders into daydreams. This contrapuntal/

counterpoint song, which is also a self-contained relationship scene exemplifies the classic Loesser duet. Further, *Where's Charlie?* illustrates the beginnings of Loesser's signature methodology as a musical theatre composer—to employ a variety of music constructs and idioms, some sophisticated and challenging, then adapt and reconfigure those constructs and idioms to reflect a more traditional musical theatre sound, as well as serve the characters and further the plot.

Loesser's next musical would reunite him with Feuer and Martin, while establishing him as one of the premier musical theatre writers of the 1950s. Given his fondness for the colorful New York stories and characters of Damon Runyon, Loesser was the perfect choice to write the score for a new musical based on the 1933 Runyon short story *The Idyll of Miss Sarah Brown*. (Loesser was often described as Runyonesque; that is, an urban mix of energized, brusque wise-guy and idealistic charmer.) Producers Feuer and Martin had agreed on a working title, *Guys and Dolls*, but were having trouble finding their librettist. Originally, the book was to be authored by Hollywood writer Jo Swerling, but he failed to capture the engaging spirit of Runyon's world. The producers searched for a replacement and, after considering eleven authors, they decided on a radio scriptwriter named Abe Burrows (due to Swerling's binding contract, however, he is still named on all billings and program materials as a co-author). Once Burrows joined Loesser, director George S. Kaufman, and choreographer Michael Kidd, the show developed with almost magical synchronicity. Burrows was able to expose and exploit the humor and hearts of gold found in Runyan's world of gamblers, racketeers, and showgirls, while believably establishing the unconventional romance between cynical, conniving gambler Sky Masterson and idealistic Salvation Army-type soldier Sarah Brown (a courtship initially predicated on a bet between Sky and his gambling buddy Nathan Detroit). Further, Burrows presented the secondary couple—Detroit and his longtime fiancée, Adelaide—as more than comic foils; instead, the characters were fleshed out as humans with foibles and desires. Although numerous plot complications threaten to thwart both romances, given the criminal activities of Masterson and his fellow racketeers alongside the religious convictions of Brown and her Save-A-Soul missionaries, all ends in true musical comedy fashion: a double wedding.

Loesser's score melds completely with Burrows' libretto, capturing the Runyonesque spirit and providing patterns of stylized speech for the lowlifes, while suggesting their aspirations to highbrow expression through such compositional forms as the fugue, chorale, gospel, ballad, and aria. This diversity provides incongruous humor as well as a window to the soft centers of the hardboiled characters. Loesser's array of compositions range from the extensive prologue, "Runyonland" (which underscores the show's opening depiction of Times Square shenanigans) to nightclub show tunes, active duets, character and novelty numbers, atmospheric and emotional ballads, and all-hands-on-deck production numbers, such as "Luck Be a Lady" and "Sit Down, You're Rockin' the Boat," designed to bring down the house. And bring down the house they did; for audiences rewarded *Guys and Dolls* with a run of 1,200 performances. In addition, the show won five Tony Awards and is often cited as the most tightly integrated musical comedy in the canon, with every song and dance contributing to and furthering the story and its characters.

Prior to the smash success of *Guys and Dolls*, Loesser had followed in the footsteps of Irving Berlin by founding his own publishing company, Frank Music Corporation. As Loesser's career skyrocketed in the 1950s, his company also became influential and significant, due in much part to Loesser's business savvy and aptitude for discovering and nurturing talent. As he was now able to control his own properties and capture his royalties and profits, he saw a need to help others or, as he often put it, to "improve the breed." Thus, he fostered a new generation of songwriters and published their works, mentoring artists such as Meredith Willson, Richard Adler and Jerry Ross, and Robert Waldman and Alfred Urhy, and facilitating the production of their stage works. Lynn Loesser had an active role in running the business end of her husband's corporation, ultimately becoming co-producer with Kermit Bloomgaarden of Loesser's next project, originally titled *Project 3*, but soon to be known as *The Most Happy Fella*. It would be considered by many (Loesser included) to be the most complex and, possibly, definitive work of his career.

The Most Happy Fella began in 1952 when Loesser, at the suggestion of a friend, decided to musically adapt a 1924 Pulitzer Prize–winning play by Sidney Howard, *They Knew What They Wanted*. The musical version was not to be an ordinary song-and-dance outing.

Some Loesser biographers ascribe the musical's epic scale to the fact that, previous to its creation, Frank's brother and music critic, Arthur, had written a particularly condescending and critical article in which he declared musical theatre scores to be populist pandering and diversionary, as opposed to the "serious" musical compositions found in opera and the concert arena. Of course, this criticism was obliquely aimed at his brother as well as other musical theatre composers. There is wide consensus that Loesser aspired to his operatic score for *The Most Happy Fella*, in part, as a rebuttal to his brother's claims as well as a chance to "artistically" prove himself to a family that had never ceased being disappointed in his popular pursuits, regardless of the significant mark he had made in American music. And, indeed, Loesser exhausted himself in his efforts to realize a rich, complex musical rendering of unconventional subject matter, acting as lyricist, composer and librettist. His libretto, adhering closely to the original play, depicts the tale of an elderly Italian and Napa Valley vineyard owner, Tony Esposito, who falls in love at first sight with a young San Francisco waitress, Rosabella. He tricks her with love letters and a bogus self-portrait (using the photo of his handsome, young foreman Joe) into moving to Napa and marrying him. The disappointments, desperation, and dramatic fallouts continue as the wedding turns into a tragic farce. An emotional Tony flees the vineyard and suffers injury in a car accident prior to the nuptials. Rosabella, out of anger and sadness over Tony's deception, finds sexual comfort with Joe. Once Tony returns home, begins to recuperate, and finally earns Rosabella's affection, she finds she is pregnant with Joe's child. In an unusual musical theatre ending, especially for the 1950s, out of love for Rosabella, Tony agrees to raise the child as his own.

Loesser devoted four years to *Most Happy Fella*, with periods of writer's block and depression followed by bursts of inspiration and productivity. The original draft consisted of roughly fifteen minutes of dialogue and several hours of music, conveying dark, weak, and compromising aspects of human emotion and behavior, alongside folksy good humor, romance, forgiveness, and acceptance. The material was unconventional, to say the least. Given its expansive and diverse score, the musical required operatic virtuosity for the roles of Tony and Rosabella. Loesser was personally involved in the search for and casting of the lead performers, looking for big, articulate, classically trained voices. (As a side note, Loesser was famously hands-on, picky, and temperamental regarding the rendering of his songs, placing the accurate and audible performance of his words and music as a top priority. A famous anecdote relates an incident at the opening of *Where's Charley?* when the exhausted Bolger collapsed in his dressing room after the final curtain and required medical attention, only to have Loesser barge in and berate him for his inattention to some of his tempos and melodies. Loesser was unceremoniously ushered out and banned from the room.) In the case of *Most Happy Fella*, Loesser's intimate involvement in the show's casting and rehearsals forever altered his personal life. During auditions, Lynn Loesser served as a talent scout (part of her co-producer role) and found a young soprano named Jo Sullivan for Rosabella, introducing her to Loesser, who agreed that her voice suited the role. Loesser then fell in love with Sullivan, while Lynn, from her producing perch, watched this romance unfold. Frank and Lynn Loesser divorced soon after the musical's opening; and he married his leading lady, Sullivan.

It was not the real-life soap opera unfolding behind the scenes of *Most Happy Fella*, however, that captured the attention of audiences and critics once the show opened on May 5, 1956. It was the musically rendered and human melodrama. The score itself wowed most critics; and the musical is still considered to be one of Broadway's most ambitiously operatic works, containing more than thirty individual musical numbers (connected by a healthy dose of recitative) that range from classical to pop, all designed to further the plot, reflect the emotional journeys of the characters, and suit the commercial musical theatre arena. Loesser provided his leads with arias such as Tony's "Rosabella," as well as passionate duets, such as Tony and Rosabella's "My Heart Is So Full of You" (a number that would not have sounded out of place in *La Bohème*). Some arias were given a popular music treatment, but still evoked grand emotion such as Rosabella's "Somebody Somewhere" [see fig. 5.4] which dramatically shifts from major key to minor key, surging to an emotional climax as she imagines, through simple, heartfelt lyrics, the joys of being desired and loved. And alongside the classical extravagances in *Most Happy Fella* are the novelty numbers, including approximations of Italian folk songs ("Abbondanza" and "Benvenuta"), interspersed with conventional Broadway production numbers (such as "Big D," in which "Dallas" becomes a cleverly spelled and cheered slogan in the lyrics, supported by an infectious country swing rhythm and twang-filled melody). Loesser did not forsake pop music, however, providing catchy tunes like "Standing on the Corner," performed by four farm workers who sing in tight harmony, reflecting the "guy group" quartets heard on the radio at the time. Loesser also employed his signature technique of dialogic counterpoint, especially evident in the charming duet "Happy to Make Your Acquaintance," during which Rosabella softens toward Tony as she helps him improve his English. Due to the score's seamless, operatic integration, *Most Happy Fella*'s program did not list the individual songs when it opened. Yet Loesser never officially deemed the work an "opera," instead, he referred to it as "dominantly musical." Due to such mixed signals, some audiences had trouble reconciling the ambitious score with its Broadway environs, including Loesser's mother and brother, who never acknowledged his operatic achievement. Regardless, *Most Happy Fella* stands as one of the most popular operatic works to debut on Broadway, enjoying the longest run (676 performances) of an operatic musical for three decades.

Loesser's next project, although commendable on its creative merits, was a failure, his first and only on the Broadway stage. *Greenwillow* (1960), an adaptation of the 1956 novel by B. J. Chute, spins a whimsical and fantastical tale concerning a young man, Gideon, who lives in a bucolic village and is subject to a family curse under which he, as the eldest son, may be called at any time to "wander," leaving loved ones behind, with no certainty of return. Gideon loves his girlfriend and wants a normal domestic life with her. He enlists the help of a newly arrived reverend to help him realize his dream and evade the wandering "call." Loesser wrote the entire score and co-wrote the libretto with Lesser Samuels, again controlling the entire production. The score alone has been praised, as it exemplifies Loesser's gift for writing ear-pleasing tunes and his facility with diverse musical idioms (English ballads, church hymns, holiday carols, folk tunes, and songs of love and romantic conflict are all found in the show). However, *Greenwillow*'s libretto, score, and staging did not mesh in its 1960 Broadway incarnation; and the musical struck many as a trite, forced attempt at folklore (a second-rate *Brigadoon*). The production closed after only 97 performances. On honeymoon with his new wife, Loesser sent the cast and crew a shorthanded "oops" apology via telegram.

Upon Loesser's return to the States, he set to work on a new Broadway show, *How to Succeed in Business Without Really Trying* (1961), once again teaming with producers Feuer and Martin, as well as librettist Burrows. Interestingly, given the production's success, Loesser had to be talked into the project by the producers, as he did not want to return to simply writing a score, without a hand in the libretto. Once on board, however, he was given much say and control over the show's creation (even though Burrows was also the director). Using Shepherd Mead's tongue-in-cheek 1952 guidebook as a template, as well as an unproduced play by Jack Weinstock and Willie Gilbert based on the satirical manual, Loesser and Burrows spent a lot of time mulling over the look, feel, sound, and character of the musical, concentrating on the dramatic integrity and purpose of its content. After drafting numerous musical numbers, even though they were unsure where the songs would fit or how they would be used, the two began to write the book and full score, devoting a year to the process.

Burrow's libretto smartly captures a time in America when corporate ladders, boardroom dramas, women in the workplace, coffee breaks, and executive washrooms had become part of the national dialogue and landscape. The libretto lampoons corporate culture and its mores, morals, and mischief, presenting a musical theatre antihero in the character of J. Pierpont Finch, who rises from window-washer to chairman of the board of the World Wide Wicket Company as he indelicately exploits the weaknesses of his coworkers and superiors, including nepotism, college cronyism, misogyny, sycophancy, and adultery. No one is spared in Finch's conquest of World Wide Wicket, and 1960s conventions and white-collar culture are lampooned in song and dance. In the end, as his office machinations are revealed, Finch is exposed and indicted; although he still manages to work his manipulative magic as he enlists his coworkers in an ironic celebration of corporate kinship during the final production number, "Brotherhood of Man." This hyperkinetic "eleven o'clock" (standing for 11:00 p.m.) number is emblematic of Loesser's use of integration, alongside ironic incongruity throughout the score. The rousing revivalist anthem is performed by the office clones in their stiff business suits, cutting loose as they are overtaken by the spirit of comradeship. Other compositions propel the storyline and fit the corporate milieu as well as satirically comment on its culture and environs; for example, "Coffee Break" and "A Secretary Is Not a Toy" employ staccato and syncopated rhythms, with equally metrical and contrapuntal vocal lines, imitating the sounds of typewriters, coffee percolators, and general office hubbub. Loesser's use of the lyrical ballad reached satiric and reflective heights in "I Believe in You," as Finch sings the hummable number's flattering sentiments to his own reflection in the executive washroom mirror. In 1961, the show made a star out of audacious newcomer Robert Morse in the role of Finch and has continued to serve as a Broadway star vehicle for the likes of Matthew Broderick in 1995 and *Harry Potter*'s Daniel Radcliffe, *Glee*'s Darren Criss, and singing star Nick Jonas in 2011–12. Further, the original production enlisted star Rudy Vallee to play J. B. Biggley, president of World Wide Wicket. (Significantly, the liberties taken with the score by Vallee, who hadn't been on Broadway since 1936, so angered Loesser that he briefly quit the show, feeling that his complaints were not being seriously addressed or supported by the producers.)

In the end, *How to Succeed*, with its refreshingly modern libretto and score, as well as the cartoonish choreography by Bob Fosse, delighted both audiences and critics when it opened on October 14, 1961. Ultimately running for 1,417 performances, the musical won the Pulitzer Prize for Drama. *How to Succeed* matched the sentiment of a nation that may have been pre-Vietnam/Watergate, but was, nevertheless, experiencing growing pains as it moved into a new phase of modernity, resulting in a growing climate of cynicism and reflective humor. Its content still speaks to contemporary audiences and has had several successful Broadway revivals, providing both a nostalgic look at the corporate culture of yesteryear (warts and all) and a hard-eyed look at the American capitalist environment.

How to Succeed was Loesser's last Broadway musical, even though he continued to write. In 1965, he provided music and lyrics and co-wrote the book for *Pleasures and Palaces*, a work placed in historic Russia, looking at the reign and affairs of Catherine the Great. The production, directed and choreographed by Fosse, received harsh reviews in its Detroit tryout; and Loesser, not wanting to spend more money and time on a show that he believed to be unfixable, decided to cancel the rest of its out-of-town tryouts and Broadway debut. Next, Loesser began work on a musical version of the Budd Schulberg short story *Señor Discretion Himself* in 1966, but stopped working on it after two years. (A version of Loesser's *Señor Discretion Himself* was produced posthumously in 1985 in workshop form at the New York Musical Theatre Works and then as a full production in 2004 at Washington, D.C.'s Arena Stage.) Unfortunately, Loesser never had a chance to follow up his two disappointing endeavors with another Broadway hit, for he was diagnosed with lung cancer and died in New York City on July 28, 1969. Loesser was only 59 years old, still at the peak of his career. Colleagues and musical aficionados cannot help but wonder what works he still had in his arsenal and the additional contributions he could have made to the musical genre had he not died so young. Loesser was a unique talent, a creative force, and a living contradiction, a combination of clear-eyed businessman and visionary artist. He managed to balance romance, pragmatism, and cynicism, creating works that gave a lyrical voice to the common man, while offering clever observations on human nature. Given this potent mix, it is no wonder that Loesser's words and music, so representative of the Golden Age of American songwriting and musical theatre, have remained part of the nation's musical landscape, continuing to find appreciative audiences today.

SOMEBODY SOMEWHERE

Music and Lyrics by Frank Loesser (1956)

Somebody, somewhere
Wants me and needs me;
That's very wonderful to know
Somebody lonely
Wants me to care,
Wants me of all people
To notice him there.
Well, I want to be wanted,
Need to be needed,
And I'll admit I'm all aglow,
'Cause somebody, somewhere
Wants me and needs me,
Wants lonely me to smile
And say hello.
Somebody, somewhere
Wants me and needs me
And that's very wonderful to know.

FEATURED PRODUCTION: *Guys and Dolls* (1950)

Music and Lyrics by Frank Loesser; Book by Abe Burrows

Original Broadway Run: Opened November 24, 1950; 46ᵗʰ Street Theatre; 1,200 performances

From the show's prologue, "Runyonland" (which segues into the blustery and elegantly composed "Fugue for Tinhorns"), to the final dual weddings (attended by gamblers who had been chastened and converted via a raucous spiritual, "Sit Down, You're Rockin' the Boat"), audiences in 1950 could tell that *Guys and Dolls* was not your typical musical comedy. For the time, the show took integration to new heights: *Guys and Dolls* proved to be one of the most tightly coordinated musicals ever created, with song, dance, comedy, and romance springing from fleshed-out characters and complicated situations, all placed within a complete, idiosyncratic world—Runyonland—created on stage. Much of the credit can be attributed to lyricist/composer Frank Loesser, whose score effectively brings the colorful, larger-than-life Damon Runyon characters to life. Loesser was not alone in creating the unique milieu and aesthetic of the "Musical Fable of Broadway" (the show's subtitle), as he was joined by librettist Abe Burrows, who took over the job from Jo Swerling. Burrows immediately set about writing a book to fit Loesser's already-written score (one of the few musicals written in this manner). Together, the collaborators combined Runyon's *The Idyll of Miss Sarah Brown* (a short story about an unlikely romance between a gambler and a religious reformer) with other Runyon stories and characters. The duo turned the material into a charming, comic romp, placing the action in the back alleys, sewers, missions, and seedy nightclubs of Times Square and populating it with gamblers, cons, cops, missionaries, and showgirls. All the characters were assigned specific personalities and moral codes, and in the case of the gamblers, their own awkwardly formalized style of speech. Master of comedy, director George S. Kaufman, devised an animated, almost cartoonish look and feel to the festivities (a staging/visual concept that has defined the musical throughout the years). The musical's extensive, spirited dance numbers were choreographed by Michael Kidd, a classically trained dancer who depicted the society, activity, and attitude of Times Square in the lengthy opening dance/mime segment ("Runyonland") as well as designed diverse movement that ranged from showgirl chorus lines to an athletically danced game of craps.

Guys and Dolls' plot centers on the romantic and comedic complications arising from a wager between gambler Nathan Detroit, who is responsible for organizing "the oldest established permanent floating crap game in New York," and the high-rolling Sky Masterson, who has come to town for the big game. Detroit has yet to find a clandestine location for the crap game and needs money to secure one; so he places a can't-lose bet with Masterson. In the wager, Masterson must woo the next girl he sees and take her to Havana. The girl (no surprise to Detroit) turns out to be Sarah Brown, proselytizing soldier of the Save-A-Soul Mission. She is tricked into the date by Masterson, who promises her a dozen sinners for her mission, which is in danger of being closed due to the branch's low turnout. The two travel to Havana, and the evening devolves into a drunken fling for Sarah as she unknowingly swills rum drinks and shares a passionate kiss with Masterson. Meanwhile, Detroit and the boys use the empty mission for their illegal gaming activities. The game is busted; and Brown, who thinks Masterson was part of the scam, angrily spurns him. Of course, the two have fallen in love by this time, and Masterson, desperate to redeem himself, bets everything he has on one high-stakes dice roll against the "souls" of the guys in a climactic craps game ("Luck Be a Lady"). In other words, if he wins, the losing gamblers must attend services at the mission. Just as Brown and her compatriots are bemoaning the empty chairs at their mission service, attended by their superior, General Cartwright, Masterson arrives with his gang of grumbling lowlifes in tow. After a spiritual conversion of the men, incited by gambler Nicely-Nicely Johnson's revivalist rendition of "Sit Down, You're Rockin' the Boat," the mission is saved. By this time, Brown has also discovered that Masterson did not disclose their liaison and forfeited the bet to Detroit, preserving her honor and showing his affection for her. The two are married and Masterson joins the Save-A-Soul mission. Their ceremony inspires the marriage of newly legit Detroit and his fiancée of fourteen years, Adelaide. Throughout the show, Detroit had continually found reasons to back out of marrying Adelaide, who is a nightclub singer at the Hot Box and suffers from psychosomatic cold symptoms due to her unmarried status. (In a humorous side note, Adelaide was originally to have been a stripper, suffering colds from constant exposure to the elements, but Loesser thought she would be more sympathetic as a singer, with her colds resulting from being repeatedly jilted at the altar.)

Adelaide's job at the Hot Box allows for numerous metatheatrical and highly satiric numbers, which feature the Hot Box Girls as cornpone cuties in brief farm-girl outfits who squeal "Bushel and a Peck" and as tongue-in-cheek innocents who strip as they tell any moneyed suitor with impure motives to "Take Back Your Mink." These numbers are the tip of the iceberg with regard to the score's clever-ness, tunefulness, and sophistication. Numbers such as "Fugue for Tinhorns" (which incongruously has the racketeers of Times Square sing as Baroque classicalists), "Sit Down, You're Rockin' the Boat" (a hallelujah gospel number for the unlikeliest of converts), and "Luck Be a Lady" (a classic that is still one of the most recognized showbiz songs of all time) are part of Loesser's diverse, integrated, and dramatically effective score. *Guys and Dolls* also includes longing ballads for Brown and Masterson ("I'll Know" and "My Time of Day"), a sweet swinging jazz number for Brown ("If I Were a Bell"), an active soliloquy for Adelaide ("Adelaide's Lament"), an operatic argument in streetwise vernacular ("Sue Me"), and a Baroque cantata for wise guys ("The Oldest Established").

Photo of the 2004 MUNY production of *Guys and Dolls*. Jim Herren. Photo courtesy of MUNY.

Along with numerous accolades, including a score of Tony Awards, *Guys and Dolls* reigns as the fifth-longest-running musical of the 1950s. Further, it was made into a major Hollywood film in 1955. Curiously, the studio signed non-singing stars Marlon Brando and Jean Simmons for the roles of Sky Masterson and Sarah Brown; and both insisted on doing their own singing (no dubbing). Concerned about this situation, Loesser became hands-on throughout rehearsals and filming, while supplying a number of new songs for the movie (with some dropped from the stage version). Reportedly, he got along famously with Brando, mostly because Brando adhered to his note-by-note musical coaching. The same could not be said for Loesser's relationship with Frank Sinatra, who was cast as Nathan Detroit. Due to Loesser's irritation over Sinatra's persistent "stylings" of his songs and refusal to take notes or corrections, the two hot-tempered men almost came to blows. Sinatra subsequently vowed he would never sing another Loesser song (only to relent later in his career). Since the 1950s, one could make the argument that *Guys and Dolls* has become one of the most, if not the most, performed and attended musicals in the American canon. It is definitely one of the most frequently revived musicals on Broadway; there have been five revivals since its debut (the latest being in 2009), with the productions repeatedly winning Tony Awards (including Best Revival of a Musical in 1992). Of course, the musical theatre genre is bigger than Broadway. Part of the significance, longevity, and continued relevance of *Guys and Dolls* is its beloved and much-performed status in theatres across America. No doubt, if one were to survey educational and community theatres across the nation, a production of *Guys and Dolls* would most likely be playing in a number of them, with audiences humming along with Loesser's iconic tunes and warmly revisiting the comic adventures of the citizens of Runyonland.

PULLING BACK THE CURTAIN:
The Crucial Role of the Mentor in the Musical Theatre

What is a mentor? Technically, he or she is an advisor, instructor, example, or guru. In the musical theatre field, such a person has proven indispensable to the early careers of many of the industry's most formidable artists, who, in turn, have served as mentors to other artists—a passing of the torch, so to speak—creating a tradition that is built on facilitation, education, and inspiration. Not all mentoring processes are the same, however, and throughout the history of musical theatre, the mentor has taken various forms: (1) the first-person teacher/trainer/facilitator who purposefully imparts advice, skills, and career opportunities to a promising novice, student, apprentice, or protégé; (2) the "boss" who teaches by example in the workplace and inspires the careers of those working under him or her (this can also include muse-artist relationships); and (3) the iconic pioneer whose career serves as a specific inspiration and template for future artists, even without a personal, direct relationship. Given the prevalence of these three main models in musical theatre, it is common practice to trace the mentors or mentoring examples in the careers of many of the industry's leading figures, historically and contextually citing and exploring a line of influence and instruction.

Examples of **first-person, hands-on mentoring** are common in musical theatre history. One might even ask whether some careers would have found their footings or, at least, their accelerated rates of success without the direct assistance and advice of mentors. History shows that Jerome Kern was impressed by the talents of a young George Gershwin (who sought to fashion his musical theatre career after Kern's, even serving as a rehearsal pianist for a Kern show); Kern worked to advance Gershwin's Broadway career, opening doors for him as a musical theatre composer. Then, passing on the favor, Gershwin helped popular 1920s composer Vincent Youmans get his first Broadway assignment. During this period, celebrated and prolific lyricist/librettist Otto Harbach also took the young lyricist/librettist Oscar Hammerstein II under his wing, grooming him in the ways of dramatically effective and poetically evocative musical theatre authorship and suggesting that he stop wasting his time on musical composition and focus his innate talents on writing lyrics and librettos. In a later decade, Larry Hart would catch a glimpse of his own self-expressive lyricist talent in a young Lambs Club member, Alan Jay Lerner, and mentor the younger man; consequently, one can see vestiges of Hart's wit and rhyming facility in Lerner's works, even though Lerner preferred to write for tightly integrated musicals. Moving into midcentury, Hammerstein passed his own mentoring forward as he was not only a neighbor to an adolescent Stephen Sondheim but met often with the youth, giving him advice on his earliest attempts at writing for the musical theatre. Once Sondheim entered the professional ranks, he credited Hammerstein for talking him into accepting both the *West Side Story* and *Gypsy* lyricist assignments, for the older man assured Sondheim of the career advancement and artistic growth he would gain by working with distinguished composers such as Leonard Bernstein and Jule Styne. Sondheim has also recounted that Hammerstein instilled in him the concept that every song should be a little play, with a beginning, middle, and end—a philosophy evident in Sondheim's songwriting, even though the context and content of his modern musicals frequently veer far from Hammerstein's positive worldview. Another example of this mentoring model is contemporary tap dancer extraordinaire Savion Glover. As a youth, he was a dance protégé, training under tap legends of yesteryear and performing alongside them in shows such as *Black and Blue* and *Jelly's Last Jam*.

Studying and absorbing their craft, Savion's career came full circle when he created his own musical, *Bring in 'Da Noise, Bring in 'Da Funk*, which contained dance segments that paid literal homage to his legendary tap mentors.

With regard to the purposeful mentor, one of the most significant examples is Frank Loesser, who, in his mission to evolve the songwriter "breed," surveyed Tin Pan Alley to find new talent to promote and publish. In the process, he contracted a novice songwriting team, Richard Adler and Jerry Ross. When Loesser had to turn down the offer to write the score for George Abbott's *The Pajama Game* (1954), he suggested Adler and Ross as his replacement. The musical became one of the biggest hits of the 1950s, followed by Adler and Ross' second big hit, again with Abbott: *Damn Yankees* (1955). Both musicals topped 1,000 performances, and their commercial successes garnered unanimous critical praise, due in great part to Adler and Ross' clever, tight, and tuneful scores, generating pop hits such as "Hey, There," "Hernando's Hideaway," "Heart," and "Whatever Lola Wants." Both works continued in the tradition of *Guys and Dolls*; that is, they raised the musical comedy genre to new heights in terms of artistic merit and popular appeal (the promise of the team was cut short, however, when Ross died prematurely, at age 29, from lung disease). Loesser's mentoring of Meredith Willson may have been even more significant, however, as it was at Loesser's urging that the classically trained Willson turned his Iowa boyhood memories into a musical. As lyricist, composer, and librettist, Willson created the nostalgic *The Music Man* (1957), winner of numerous theatre awards and an epic crowd-pleaser, which has become no less than an American institution. Although producers Cy Feuer and Ernest Martin initially planned to back the show after being introduced to Willson by Loesser, their plans fell through. Loesser's Frank Productions stepped in to produce the musical with Kermit Bloomgarden. Willson's musical tells the story of a fast-talking huckster, Harold Hill, who cons a small Midwestern town into believing that he can turn their sons and daughters into musicians in order to form a marching band, only to find his heart softened and his ways changed by the community and, especially, the local spinster librarian, Marian. In addition to its feel-good plot, the musical boasts a tightly integrated score, with numbers that reflect character, place, and time and are diverse, ranging from patter song ("Trouble") to barbershop quartet ("Lida Rose") to spirited dance number ("Shipoopi") to military marching band ("Seventy-Six Trombones") to lyrical ballads ("Goodnight, My Someone" and "Till There Was You"). In addition, the score features Willson's sophisticated use of counterpoint and repeated/reconfigured themes; for example, a duet between Hill and Marian juxtaposes reprises of "Goodnight My Someone" and "Seventy-Six Trombones," illustrating how the songs are cleverly built on the same melodic refrain. Running for 1,375 performances, the musical won numerous Tony Awards, while Frank Music published the score, making enormous profits off the many songs that became major hits and iconic entries in the American songbook. As a musical theatre high point for Willson and profitable mentoring investment by Loesser, *The Music Man* remains a masterpiece and priceless example of musical Americana.

In conjunction with the conscious, hands-on mentoring of future artists by practiced experts, there is the less direct mentoring model by which **professionals teach others through on-the-job influence and example**. In this process, a more experienced artist often makes an indelible imprint on a novice or up-and-comer while delegating, advising, overseeing, and collaborating in the workplace. For example, Jerome Robbins, Bob Fosse, and Hal Prince have cited their experiences with the venerable George Abbott (Robbins and Fosse as choreographers, Prince as producer) to have been instructive and formative with regard to their own directing careers. The men learned by proximity and osmosis the "Abbott touch"; that is, Abbott's gift for tight construction, effective storytelling, economy, stage composition, and dramatic flow. Then, in a passing of the torch, director Hal Prince inspired the young choreographer Michael Bennett, tutoring him in the school of concept musicals as the two worked together on such groundbreaking works as *Company* and *Follies*. Bennett ultimately graduated from his informal classroom to conceive and create his own iconic concept musicals (*A Chorus Line* and *Dreamgirls*). And in another progression, Bennett significantly influenced the career of director/choreographer Tommy Tune (*Nine, My One and Only, Grand Hotel*, and *The Will Rogers Follies*), who got his big break as a dancer in Bennett's *Seesaw*, learning much from the older choreographer/director regarding the concept/dance-centric musical, a form that Tune exploited mightily on Broadway. One of the most celebrated choreographer/directors today, Susan Stroman (*Contact, The Producers, Young Frankenstein*, and *The Scottsboro Boys*) had a significant mentor as she moved from choreographer to Broadway director/choreographer: her late husband and director, Mike Ockrent. Stroman and Ockrent first joined forces for *Crazy for You*, with Stroman as choreographer and Ockrent as seasoned director. Stroman has recounted that she learned the essential tools of the directing craft from Ockrent, working with him on numerous Broadway shows from that first experience until his untimely death. (She had to be talked into helming *The Producers* solo by Mel Brooks after Ockrent's death, as the project had originally been conceived as an Ockrent/Stroman undertaking.)

In addition to Stroman, the career paths of many other director/choreographers illustrate the less direct, on-the-job mentoring paradigm. Specifically, choreographic assistants, associates, and dance captains frequently go on to establish independent identities and careers, while keeping alive the theatrical imprints and legacies of their bosses. For instance, Bob Avian was a longtime choreographic associate of Bennett (e.g., Bennett's co-choreographer of *A Chorus Line*), who became a lauded director/choreographer in his own right, then came full circle as he directed the successful 2006 revival of *A Chorus Line* on Broadway. Dancers Thommie Walsh, Baayork Lee, and Wayne Cilento received much recognition and acclaim for their work on *A Chorus Line*, originating and helping to create the roles of Bobby, Connie Wong, and Mike, respectively; all then found success as choreographers and directors after their formative experiences with Bennett, as well as Tommy Tune (Walsh, especially, worked closely with Tune). Even the distant and difficult Jerome Robbins gave special attention to promising young performers in his shows, shaping their craft and informing their later directing/choreographing careers on Broadway. Two prominent examples are Grover Dale and Joey McKneely. Grover was a novice Broadway dancer in the original production of *West Side Story*, who evolved into a successful choreographer/director, ultimately co-directing *Jerome Robbins' Broadway* with Robbins. McKneely got his big break as a young dancer in *Jerome Robbins' Broadway*, then established his own respected career as a choreographer, most recently revisiting Robbins territory as he choreographed the critically acclaimed 2009 revival of *West Side Story*.

Muses also fall into this category. Early dance pioneer and Broadway choreographer/director Jack Cole passed along his unique jazz dance idom to his dancers, specifically his two dance captains/muses Carol Haney and Gwen Verdon, who both, in turn, became muses of iconic director/choreographer Bob Fosse. In a reverse mentoring example, the two muses passed their "Cole" lessons to their new choreographic boss, Fosse, who incorporated some of Cole's dance technique into his own "Fosse style." In a cyclical fashion, Fosse's style became its own school of dance/choreography and performance, codified and passed to future generations by the same muses

(Haney and Verdon), as well as his final muse, Ann Reinking, all of whom became directorial and choreographic artists in their own right (notably Reinking, who helped create and direct 1999's *Fosse*, the homage to her mentor).

Lastly, there are some mentors who are not hands-on nor are they first-person exemplars, but serve instead as **career inspirations and models to future artists**. For instance, Richard Rodgers "worshipped" Jerome Kern, regularly attending the Princess Theatre musicals and informally schooling himself in the integrated songwriting of Kern and company. Irving Berlin often cited George M. Cohan as his idol, wishing to model his career after him (and succeeding on almost all fronts, minus the directing/choreographing), while Loesser felt the same about Berlin's business acumen and was inspired to start his own music publishing company. Sondheim is probably one of the most potent indirect mentors today, offering encouragement or serving as a professional and artistic inspiration to numerous modern composers/lyricists. For instance, he corresponded with Jonathan Larsen (*Rent*), who, after meeting him in college, often submitted drafts of his work to Sondheim for critiques. Sondheim wrote letters of recommendation to producers for Larson, serving as an early advocate, albeit from a distance. (Larson paid sly homage to this mentor by riffing on a Sondheim song, "Sunday," in his musical *tick, tick ... BOOM!*, reconfiguring the dense anthem to suit a harried Sunday brunch setting.) Even more indirect, however, is Sondheim's mentoring of the "new Sondheim generation" (as designated by critics and scholars), that is, younger composers and lyricists who either specifically cite his influence or show significant vestiges of his technique and aesthetic in their work. This group includes Michael John LaChiusa, Adam Guettel, Andrew Lippa, Jason Robert Brown, and the young authors in the Dramatists Guild Fellows Program.

In short, in its many forms and functions, mentorship has been a constant in musical theatre history, with the mentor's presence and influence vividly felt still today.

JULE STYNE

In a televised retrospective of Jule Styne's career, long-time collaborators Betty Comden and Adolph Green likened the diminutive and extroverted composer to the eponymous boy-hero of one of the trio's canonical works, *Peter Pan*, citing Styne's spritely enthusiasm, energy, and enduring presence on the American musical theatre scene. Indeed, Styne was omnipresent on Broadway for almost three decades as a prolific composer, as well as a prominent producer, who was a tireless champion of the artistic and commercial merit of the traditional book musical. In his prime, Styne was the most-produced composer of original musicals during the Golden Age. His output was legendary, with eighteen musicals in all debuting on Broadway (many lasting years, some lasting days), not to mention the numerous Broadway shows backed by Styne as a producer, as well as the many revues, dansicals, and other Broadway works that have used his songs in their compiled scores. Due to the new norm of longer Broadway runs that coincided with Styne's musical theatre ascendance, his work received a record number of performances on the Great White Way (that is, until the advent of the modern mega–musical and its epically lengthy Broadway engagement). Add to this phenomenon Styne's tireless output, which consisted of almost a musical a year during his most productive period, and it is easy to appreciate his imprint on Broadway. From 1949–74, a new show with a Styne score premiered on Broadway almost every season. Further, he was able to reap the benefits of a new Broadway business model that exploited and expanded the runs of profitable shows (e.g., the total number of performances of his first sixteen musicals, including flops, exceeds that of the entire twenty-five musicals written by Rodgers and Hart).

Given his contributions to and achievements in musical theatre, it is even more impressive that these contributions and achievements came on top of his work as a significant composer of the American songbook (much like predecessors George Gershwin, Irving Berlin, Richard Rodgers, and Cole Porter). His years in Hollywood, during which he wrote songs for a multitude of films, fueled and cemented his legendary place in the pop music canon. For instance, with lyricist Sammy Cahn, he wrote songs for more than seventy films, with fifteen of the compositions becoming #1 hits. Styne also worked with other lyricists (including Frank Loesser),

Jule Styne (at piano) with Barbra Streisand and *Funny Girl* lyricist Bob Merrill, 2/8/1964 © Bettmann/CORBIS

preferring a collaborative practice in which he wrote the music first. By the time of his death, he had composed an astounding 1,500 published songs. Given Styne's success as a Hit Parade composer, it is little wonder that once he began writing Broadway musicals, his scores were marked by their pop music sensibility; for Styne employed a Tin Pan Alley ethos in his application of hummable tunes and melodic hooks, novelty and specialty numbers, extroverted (almost brassy) musicality, and an ability to evoke time and place in an audience-friendly way. He loved show business, and some of his most successful productions addressed certain aspects of the "biz," be it Hollywood, Broadway, vaudeville, or the recording industry. As an artist who is often cited as one of the architects of the Golden Age book musical, Styne usually worked in a traditional mode. He was especially conventional in his exploitation of a longtime revered Broadway institution: the star vehicle. He wrote scores for musicals that effectively showcased and/or introduced star talents such as Phil Silvers, Carol Channing, Bert Lahr, Mary Martin, Judy Holliday, Ethel Merman, Barbra Streisand, Carol Burnett, and Leslie Uggams. Employing his oft-repeated philosophy that a "rendition" is what "makes" a song, Styne was a master at providing signature songs for stars (e.g., "Everything's Comin' Up Roses" for Ethel Merman) and, in some cases, liftable tunes capable of elevating Broadway neophytes to stardom (e.g., Carol Channing's "Diamonds Are a Girl's Best Friend," Barbra Streisand's "People," and Judy Holliday's "The Party's Over"). In such cases, Styne's hits have been dominated by the star's persona; yet, such performances also secured the songs' places in the American songbook for future generations. Styne's unflagging industriousness, keen sense of showbiz, and musical accessibility kept him on Broadway long past many of his contemporaries, with a musical theatre career that began triumphantly in 1947 (*High Button Shoes*) and ended disappointingly in 1993 (*The Red Shoes*). As seen by these career bookends, Styne's Broadway output varied in terms of quality and commercial success. Nonetheless, a run of forty-six years in any profession is nothing short of phenomenal.

Julius Kerwin Stein was born on December 31, 1905, in London to Jewish parents, Isadore and Anna Stein, who had emigrated from the Ukraine. When he turned 8, the family moved to Chicago, where young Julius, now known as Jule, gained notice as a piano prodigy, performing as a soloist with the Chicago, St. Louis, and Detroit symphonies, all before his tenth birthday. At 13, Jule attended Chicago College of Music on scholarship, receiving an advanced education in piano performance, composition, and theory. As a 16-year-old, Jule wrote his first song, which was commissioned for a musical act by another teenager, Mike Todd (who would later become a powerful Broadway and film producer); the song was titled "The Moth and the Flame" (1921). With this endeavor, Jule became a bona fide composer. Furthermore, while dabbling in songwriting for the popular stage, Styne was bitten by the Tin Pan Alley bug; he turned away from his classical roots and endeavored to study the works and idioms of young Tin Pan Alley composers, especially those who were also writing for Broadway. Styne's classical genius was channeled into popular music as he became one of America's premier hit-makers, starting with his first minor hit, "Sunday," in 1926. At the onset of his pop career, Styne was also a pianist in a dance band (at the time, such bands were at the forefront of American popular music); in 1931, he formed his own dance orchestra, serving as leader, arranger, and occasional composer. During this period, he changed his last name from Stein to Styne, reportedly to avoid being confused with another musician (Jules Stein). It was not long before his songwriting caught the attention of the movie studios, and Styne

disbanded his orchestra to work as both a composer and vocal coach for Twentieth Century-Fox, finding success in the Hollywood studio system. Styne's songwriting during this time was championed by Frank Sinatra, who popularized his early numbers on radio, film, and in concert. Further, Styne teamed with talented lyricist Sammy Cahn, forming a close partnership during the Hollywood years that resulted in many chart-toppers, including the holiday classic "Let It Snow! Let It Snow! Let It Snow!" (1945). Styne's tenure in Tinseltown also resulted in a record number of critically acclaimed scores and songs for the movies (many written with Cahn, as well as other lyricists); and his film output included such hits as "It's Been a Long, Long Time," "I'll Walk Alone," "It's Magic," and "Three Coins in the Fountain," which in 1954 won the Academy Award for Best Original Song.

Despite Styne's impressive success in Hollywood, he was more interested in becoming a Broadway artist than a safely established and acclaimed pop music/Hollywood figure. His move to Broadway may also have been a result of his oft-stated belief that writing songs for Hollywood was not as artistic an endeavor as writing for the stage; in Styne's opinion, one was a "songwriter" in the movie business, while one was a "composer" on Broadway. In 1944, Styne was able to realize his "composing" ambition; for he and Cahn were hired to write the score for *Glad to See You*, a show bound for Broadway. Unfortunately, the production never made it past its Boston try-out. Only three years later, Styne and Cahn were given another chance, and they helped create the hit musical that would establish Styne as a Broadway composer and begin his longtime tenure on the Great White Way. *High Button Shoes* (1947), a star vehicle for comedian Phil Silvers, was a musical adaptation by director George Abbott (unofficial librettist) of a semi-autobiographical novel, *The Sisters Liked Them Handsome* (1946), by Stephen Longstreet, who was credited as the show's official librettist. In this good-hearted, nostalgic comedy, Silvers played an inept conman who loses, recovers, and then loses forever in foolish gambles the profits gained from the sale of worthless property swindled from a trusting family. Set in New Jersey in 1913, one of the highlights of the critically acclaimed production was choreographer Jerome Robbins' "Mack Sennett Ballet," a comic dance segment in which bungling burglars, Keystone Kops, swimsuit lovelies, and a gorilla chase one another in and out of bathhouses on the Atlantic City boardwalk. Other numbers were praised for their period flavor and infectious melodies, including the polka-inspired domestic duet "Papa, Won't You Dance with Me?" and the sweetly tuned and sentimental "I Still Get Jealous." Running for 727 performances, the show was one of the year's top box office draws. Cahn returned to the movie-making capital shortly after the triumph of *High Button Shoes*, but Styne remained in New York and started another Broadway project with lyricist Leo Robin: *Gentlemen Prefer Blondes* (1949).

Based on the selfsame titled 1926 novel and play by Anita Loos, *Gentlemen Prefer Blondes* is a comic romp that tells the tale of a gold-digging heroine, Lorelei Lee, who lives a free-spirit, decadent life at the height of the Roaring Twenties. Most of the musical's action takes place aboard an ocean liner, as Lorelei and a female buddy travel to Paris, courtesy of Lorelei's "sugar daddy," all the while enjoying amorous misadventures with various male passengers. Once in Paris, the two women are embroiled in more madcap escapades, all incited by a questionable gift of a diamond tiara given to Lorelei by an admirer. Part of the musical's appeal (740 performances) and legendary status is that it launched Carol Channing's musical theatre career (Channing would go on to originate and define for a generation the role of Dolly Levi in Jerry Herman's *Hello, Dolly!*). As Lorelei, Channing captivated audiences and critics, particularly with her renditions of smartly crafted star-vehicle numbers, such as "A Little Girl from Little Rock" and "Diamonds Are a Girl's Best Friend." (As a result of Marilyn Monroe's performance of "Diamonds Are a Girl's Best Friend" in the 1953 film version of the musical, the song has become an American pop culture classic.)

Shortly following his two early Broadway triumphs, Styne began work on *Two on the Aisle* (1951), teaming with lyricist/librettists Betty Comden and Adolph Green. With lyrics and sketches by Comden/Green and music by Styne, the revue revolved around showbiz and starred Dolores Gray and musical comedy personality Bert Lahr (most fondly remembered today for his portrayal of the Cowardly Lion in MGM's The *Wizard of Oz*). Given Styne's previous box office hits, the revue was a disappointment, running for 281 performances. On a more positive note, it would mark the first of nine collaborations with Comden/Green. If *Two on the Aisle* proved to be somewhat of a letdown for Styne, his next project, *Hazel Flagg* (1953), was an even bigger disappointment, especially given that the musical was adapted by Ben Hecht from his own screenplay of the 1937 screwball classic, *Nothing Sacred*. With lyrics by Bob Hillard, Styne's score did not connect with audiences and failed to capture the charm of its source material. Critics found nothing notable in the music, the book, or the overall production. *Hazel Flagg* only stayed on Broadway for 190 performances. The failure of *Hazel Flagg* was two-fold for Styne; for he also produced the musical, in association with Anthony B. Farrell. Around this time, Styne had expanded his role in the theatre to include that of producer, beginning with the short-lived *Make a Wish* in 1951 (music and lyrics by Hugh Martin). In this capacity, Styne increasingly made his mark on Broadway. For instance, he and Leonard Key produced the landmark 1952 revival of *Pal Joey*, the production that is credited with turning the Rodgers and Hart musical into a box office success, cementing its place in the canon. Another notable producing venture by Styne was *Mr. Wonderful* (1956), which he not only produced but also "conceived." The show proved that powerful nightclub performer Sammy Davis Jr. could be a major box office draw on Broadway, and the star vehicle ran for a profitable 383 performances. Around 1959, Styne formed The Jule Styne Organization, and he continued to produce his own and others' works on Broadway (like Rodgers and Hammerstein).

In addition to his producing ventures and in spite of his 1953 flop, *Hazel Flagg*, Styne dominated the Broadway stage as a composer throughout the 1950s. When director/choreographer Jerome Robbins opted to expand his musical play version of J. M. Barrie's *Peter Pan* into a full-fledged musical during its out-of-town tryouts, he called on reliable pros—Styne, Comden, and Green—to expand the musical numbers initially provided by Carolyn Leigh (lyricist) and Moose Charlap (composer). Thus, Styne, with Comden and Green, supplemented the Leigh/Charlap score with classic compositions, such as the sweet, surging "Never Never Land" and the melancholy "Distant Melody," as well as numerous specialty numbers; for example, "Captain Hook's Waltz" and "Mysterious Lady" (songs written specifically to showcase the voice and comedy of Cyril Ritchard and Mary Martin, respectively, Broadway stars for whom the musical was created). When the show debuted in 1954, it only ran for 149 performances, possibly because another *Peter Pan* production, musicalized by Leonard Bernstein, had just played on Broadway in 1950. In addition, Broadway catered more to adults than young audiences at the time. Today, however, the Styne/Comden/Green/Leigh/Charlap version has been canonized as "the" musical version of *Peter Pan*.

Two years after *Peter Pan*, Styne rejoined Comden and Green to write *Bells Are Ringing* (1956), the tale of a New York City telephone operator who becomes involved in the lives of her answering service clients, taking on a variety of personas and falling for a playwright/client. When it debuted, Comden and Green's book was deemed trite, but the show's score proved delightful in several respects. First, Styne successfully employed a pop sensibility in the songwriting, providing stand-alone Billboard hits, such as the heart-rending "The Party's Over" and the swinging, romantic "Just in Time." *Bells Are Ringing* was designed as a star vehicle for a young comedienne, Judy Holliday, with its score designed to suit her talents. As a result, many of the show's numbers are active songs, geared to compensate for Holliday's limited vocal range while showcasing her extensive comic abilities, combining effective melodic hooks with character development (e.g., "It's a Perfect Relationship" and "I'm Going Back (Where I Can Be Me, at the Bonjour Tristesse Brassiere Factory)"). Upon its opening, the musical proved to be a box office smash (924 performances); further, it stands as the longest-running musical by Styne, Comden, and Green. The next year, the team embarked on *Say, Darling* (1957), a "musical play" version of Richard Bissell's same-titled novel in which he chronicled, using pseudonyms and proxy characters, his own experiences in adapting his earlier novel (*7½ Cents*) into the hit 1954 musical, *The Pajama Game*. Bissell wrote the libretto, while Comden and Green supplied lyrics to Styne's music for a minimal score that, unfortunately, was not particularly memorable. Nevertheless, the production enjoyed a healthy box office (333 performances), most likely due to its timely backstage content and guessing game regarding the real-life theatre personalities suggested by the show's cast of characters.

Styne created scores for numerous hit musicals throughout the '50s; yet none would have the impact, longevity, and artistic merit of the Styne show that ended the decade: *Gypsy* (1959). The musical is considered to be the composer's masterpiece; further, many musical critics and scholars claim it to be one of the finest book musicals ever written. The idea for the musical originated with producer David Merrick, inspired after reading a chapter of the 1958 autobiography of famed stripper Gypsy Rose Lee. Ethel Merman was contracted to play Gypsy's driven stage mother, Rose. Jerome Robbins was signed as the production's choreographer/director, and he brought his past *West Side Story* collaborators to the project: Arthur Laurents (as librettist) and Stephen Sondheim (as composer/lyricist). Unfortunately for Sondheim, Merman rejected the novice composer. After auditioning several composers, Styne was chosen, who then wrote a score that was not only custom-made for the brassy voice of Merman, it also evoked the garish world of Mama Rose and her daughters.

During the writing process, Styne was challenged as never before, often required to supply music to Sondheim's already written lyrics (not Styne's usual composing practice) and to ensure that every song either furthered or supported the story and character development, while also creating a nonstop sound of overt theatricality to suggest and underpin the show's milieu (starting in vaudeville and moving to burlesque). As a result, Styne's showbiz aesthetic shines in Rose's extroverted anthems ("Some People" and "Everything's Coming Up Roses"), as well as the thematic "Let Me Entertain You," used throughout the musical as a prop song while illustrating the evolution of Gypsy Rose Lee. Styne's potent and diverse score includes tender ballads ("Little Lamb"), lyrical waltzes ("If Momma Was Married"), syncopated soft-shoes ("All I Need Is the Girl"), specialty songs ("You Gotta Have a Gimmick"), and one of the most powerful "eleven o'clock" numbers in the musical theatre canon: "Rose's Turn."

With the critical and popular success of *Gypsy*—a work that brought Styne the greatest critical acclaim of his career and ran for 702 performances—his Broadway prestige and presence continued unabated throughout the 1960s. For his next project, he teamed again with Comden and Green, composing the music for another vehicle for his earlier *High Button Shoes* star, Phil Silvers. The show, *Do Re Mi* (1960), comically deals with scams and schemes involving jukeboxes in the music industry and boasts an engaging score that includes a pop classic, "Make Someone Happy." Despite running 400 performances, the production lost money.

The following year, Styne and Comden/Green created *Subways Are for Sleeping* (1961), which disappointed creators and audiences alike. The score received some positive notices but Comden/Green's libretto was deemed a weak adaption of Edmund G. Love's same-titled autobiographical account of his experiences as a self-made New York vagrant, spending his nights on subway trains. When the show debuted on Broadway, the negative reviews could not be overcome, and the production closed after 205 performances.

Styne's next endeavor would make up for the failure of *Subways Are for Sleeping*. In the early '60s, movie producer Ray Stark had conceived the idea of a musical based on the rise to fame and troubled marriage of *Ziegfeld Follies* star Fanny Brice and he asked Styne to work on the show. (Not coincidentally, Stark happened to be married to Brice's daughter, Frances.) Styne thought the project had potential and agreed to compose the score, working with lyricist Bob Merrill (who was also a composer). The project went through various working titles, including *A Very Special Person*, *The Luckiest People*, and *My Man*, only to be ultimately titled *Funny Girl*. Similarly, the show went through numerous female stars during the writing process (Mary Martin, Anne Bancroft, Carol Burnett), all of whom were either rumored or announced to have been cast in the lead role. Broadway legend has it that Styne, upon seeing a young Barbra Streisand singing in a New York jazz club, was so transfixed by Streisand's voice and stage personality that he could no longer envision (or hear) any other performer in the role of Fanny. So he made his compositions progressively difficult to sing, deterring and defeating those who had originally been considered for or preliminarily cast in the role. Ultimately, Styne got his star; and Barbra Streisand, a raw 21-year-old with only two notable New York theatre jobs under her belt (performer in a failed Off-Broadway revue and a Tony-nominated supporting role in 1962's *I Can Get It for You Wholesale*) set Broadway ablaze in a star vehicle custom made for her talents. In the process, Streisand would also become forever associated with the role of Fanny Brice and the musical itself as well as the American song standards generated by its score (the soul-searching "People," the stirring "Don't Rain on My Parade," and the declamatory "I'm the Greatest Star"). The musical, however, suffered a tumultuous development period. Styne, Merrill, and librettist Isobel Lennart spent a year and a half writing before rehearsals finally commenced in November of 1963.

Four months later, the production had changed director four times (Jerome Robbins to Bob Fosse to Garson Kanin and then back to Robbins). Styne was one of the few Broadway artists who could hold his own with Robbins, and the two knew how to work together. Lennart, however, was required to repeatedly rewrite the libretto, including forty rewrites of its final scene. Consequently, the show's premiere was postponed five times. In the end, however, the score by Styne and Merrill, as well as the definitive performance by Streisand (a performance that would become iconic as she replicated it in the 1968 film adaptation, garnering an Academy Award), overcame whatever weaknesses the libretto may have had. The musical's score echoed Styne's achievement in *Gypsy*, as he balanced integrated and comic relationship/character numbers such as "You Are Woman" with metatheatrical excursions (the showy prop number "Coronet Man" and torch song "The Music That Makes Me Dance"), placing the jazzy/bluesy, atmospheric, and metatheatrical compositions alongside one of his most successful chart-topping, show-stopping ballads, "People." Given the show's star-vehicle merits and the score's pop music sensibility (which was becoming rarer for musicals as American mainstream music entered the rock 'n' roll era), it is no surprise that after its opening on March 26, 1964, *Funny Girl* ran for 1,348 performances.

Directly on the heels of *Funny Girl*, Styne opened his second Broadway production of 1964: *Fade Out— Fade In*. He reunited with Comden and Green (who wrote both the book and lyrics) to create another comic star vehicle that spoofed the world of show business, this time, 1930s Hollywood. Styne also composed the score for another "funny girl," Carol Burnett, who starred as a kooky usherette who is made an unlikely film star due to a "mistaken identity" goof. Along with various specialty numbers customized to fit Burnett's comic strengths, the score includes many spirited and up-tempo numbers evocative of the period and spirit of early Hollywood. Unfortunately, the tailoring of *Fade Out* to Burnett also resulted in its premature demise. Opening to rave reviews, the show's box office surged, out-grossing other hits in its first weeks, such as *Hello, Dolly!* and *Funny Girl*. When an injured Burnett had to take a hiatus from the show, the production shut down temporarily as it readied her replacement, Betty Hutton. Upon reopening, the show could not regain its momentum, especially when Burnett returned, only to leave again shortly thereafter. Such is the downside of a star vehicle; and as financial losses mounted, the producers (one of whom was Styne) gave up and closed what should have been a long-running moneymaker after only 271 performances.

Three years later Styne teamed again with Comden and Green, plus librettist Arthur Laurents, for a work that is a curious footnote in musical theatre history: *Hallelujah, Baby!* (1967). Admired by some critics, viciously panned by others, and all-but-ignored by audiences, the show went on to win the Tony Award for Best Musical. Yet today, there are few musical theatre fans who have any recollection or knowledge of the Tony-winning work. In one of Styne's few experiments with concept musicals, he composed a score to work alongside Laurents' libretto which tells the tale of a young African American woman, Georgina, who moves through historical periods in America, never aging, while experiencing varying degrees and episodes of racism as she tries to attain the American Dream. According to numerous critics, Styne's score is considered weak in that he failed to authentically or effectively incorporate crucial idioms such as blues, jazz, gospel, or spirituals in a musical that claimed to illustrate the black experience in America. Tony Award notwithstanding, the show was a letdown for its creators, closing after only 293 performances.

As the 1960s came to a close, Styne faced even more career disappointments. First, he worked with respected lyricist E. Y. Harburg to write the score for *Darling of the Day* (1968), a historical musical set in turn-of-the-century London. Even though the score received positive notices (Styne considered it one of his best), the show's development period was messy, going through three directors and five librettists, and resulted in a production that received mixed reviews overall and ran for a mere 31 performances. Next, Styne reunited with his old lyricist pal Sammy Cahn to compose the score for *Look to the Lilies* (1970), a musical version of the novel and 1963 film *Lilies of the Field*. Neither critics nor audiences were impressed with the show, which closed after 25 performances. As a result, Styne returned to pure madcap comedy for his next venture, composing his last original hit, *Sugar* (1972). Working once again with Merrill as lyricist, Styne composed a score for an audience-pleasing musical that was an adaptation of the popular Billy Wilder film, *Some Like It Hot* (1959). With a book by Peter Stone, the show is a drag comedy in which two men witness a gangland

slaying and pretend to be women to hide in plain sight as part of an all-girl orchestra, travelling with the women to Miami, where peril follows (in the guise of pursuing gangsters), and enjoying unconventional romantic adventures. Even though the show's development period was rocky and combative (at one point, the producers threatened to fire the entire creative team), *Sugar* proved to be profitable and appealing, running for 505 performances. *Sugar* may have been Styne's last stage success, but not his last Main Stem venture. In 1974, he revisited *Gentlemen Prefer Blondes* and wrote a new version of his popular classic, retaining ten original songs but adding five songs written with Comden/Green. The revamped musical was titled *Lorelei*, and even though Carol Channing returned (24 years older) in the title role, the new version did not repeat the box office success of the original, lasting on Broadway for a modest 320 performances. For the next twenty years, Styne continued to work on projects, none of which made it to Broadway; then, in 1993, the octogenarian composed the score for *The Red Shoes*, an adaptation of the 1948 film, with lyrics by Marsha Norman and Paul Stryker (a pseudonym for Bob Merrill). The production was unanimously panned, however, and proved to be an infamous flop, as well as a money loser, closing after 5 performances.

The Red Shoes was a disappointing end to Styne's legendary career. Yet, he needn't have fretted over the failure of this last show, for Styne had already received the Kennedy Center Award for Artistic Achievement, as well as two Grammys, a Tony, an Oscar, and an Emmy before his death in 1994, apt recognition for having spent seven of his life's nine decades immersed in music and contributing to both the American song catalogue and musical theatre canon. As an inductee in the Songwriters Hall of Fame as well as the Theatre Hall of Fame, Styne lives on through his significant achievements in both popular music and on Broadway. Even his most notorious flop, *The Red Shoes*, generated a triumphant concert dance work, as choreographer Lar Lubovitch fashioned material excerpted from the musical into a ballet for the American Ballet Theatre in 1994. In terms of musical theatre, Styne was a constant presence on the Great White Way for almost three decades, with some years seeing multiple Styne shows playing in Broadway theatres. Many were disappointments but even more were modest-to-massive successes. And while some of his popular hits (*High Button Shoes*, *Say, Darling*, and *Do Re Mi*) and award-winning works

(*Hallelujah, Baby!*) have fallen by the wayside, there is a chance that they may be rediscovered in revival form at some future point. More significant are those Styne musicals that continue to thrive. *Peter Pan* has become a family classic. *Bells Are Ringing* enjoyed a Broadway revival in 2001 (with a concert version recently presented by New York City Center *Encores!* in 2010). *Funny Girl's* film version has achieved cult status. And *Gypsy*, considered musical theatre's equivalent of *King Lear*, is repeatedly revived on Broadway as a star vehicle for the latest "grand dame" of the theatre, most recently winning the 2008 Tony Award for Best Revival of a Musical (with Patti LuPone winning the Tony for Best Actress in a Musical for her portrayal of Rose). Given these examples, it seems certain that scores and songs created by Jule Styne, through his unflagging energy, vision, and workmanship, will continue to hold a significant place in American popular culture.

FEATURED PRODUCTION: *Gypsy* (1959)

Music by Jule Styne; Lyrics by Stephen Sondheim; Book by Arthur Laurents

Original Broadway Run: Opened May 21, 1959; Broadway Theatre; 702 performances

When an audience first meets *Gypsy*'s Mama Rose, she is a disembodied voice yelling from the darkened auditorium at her daughter, Louise, who is auditioning with a children's vaudeville act on stage. Next, in a moment that was revolutionary in 1959, Rose materializes from the audience, charging down the aisle and onto the stage to direct the audition. As crafted by *Gypsy*'s collaborative team and first brought to life by the indomitable Ethel Merman (in her last original Broadway role), Rose embodies all that is desperate, driven and delusionary in the entertainment business as she exploits her daughters, June (the younger "star") and Louise (the older, plainer sidekick), for financial gain. Rose ruthlessly attempts to live out her own dreams of stardom through her children. Based on the autobiography of burlesque star Gypsy Rose Lee (née Louise), *Gypsy*'s story is archetypical in its content: parent-child conflict, blind ambition, wasted potential, and survival. The stage adaptation heightened the potent, dramatic material by joining separate components (story, score, performance) into one of the most tightly and effectively constructed book musicals in the American canon.

The musical was the brainchild of producer David Merrick. Upon reading one excerpted chapter of the famous stripper's autobiography in a magazine, Merrick secured the rights to the book in 1958. Megastar Ethel Merman, upon finishing the book, petitioned for the role of Gypsy's stage mother, Rose, and was immediately cast. (She facetiously threatened to shoot other contenders for the part in a publicity stunt. By that time, Merman had enough clout on Broadway to claim any role she desired.) Even with Merman on board, the project hit a roadblock. The score and book were to be written by the team of Jule Styne, Betty Comden, and Adolph Green, but they were stymied by the difficult source material. They gave up, thinking the book (and complex depiction of Rose) could not be musically adapted, and Comden/Green returned their writing advance. Nonetheless, director/choreographer Jerome Robbins (along with Merrick, co-producer Leland Hayward, and Merman) believed the autobiography could be adapted; further, Robbins knew a librettist able to handle such challenging material: his *West Side Story* collaborator, Arthur Laurents. Laurents was intrigued and agreed to write the libretto. The search was still on for a songwriting team (Cole Porter and Irving Berlin had turned the project down); thus, Merrick auditioned numerous artists, including the team of composer Cy Coleman and lyricist Carolyn Leigh (who wrote four songs for their tryout) as well as another *West Side Story* alum (at the suggestion of Robbins), composer/lyricist Stephen Sondheim. Sondheim came out on top; he was hired and immediately set to work with Laurents and Robbins.

All was not copacetic; for when "Ms. Merman" heard that the entire score for her star vehicle was to be written by an unproven Broadway composer (Sondheim), she descended on Merrick, insisting that she had just suffered through a star role in a failed show, *Happy Hunting*, written by novices and would not do it again. Through her agent, Merman suggested that Styne be re-contracted as composer. The other collaborators (especially Laurents) were resistant to Sondheim's demotion. They stated that they would only work with Styne if Sondheim was amenable to the change. Sondheim initially refused, not wanting to be seen only as a lyricist, which would undermine his composing aspirations. His mentor, Hammerstein, intervened, convincing Sondheim his career would be facilitated by again working with

Robbins and Laurents and that he might pick up some valuable songwriting tips from a composer as successful as Styne. Finally, all parties began work on the musical; and when *Gypsy* debuted on May 21, 1959, the production was celebrated by critics and audience, alike.

Merman, magnificently served by Laurents' deft libretto, brought humanity and dimension to the demanding role of Rose, preventing the character from devolving into a stereotypical villain who exploits her children, while Styne and Sondheim provided a score that supported and developed the humanity of the story (mother-daughter friction, sibling rivalry/love, long-suffering romantic relationships, unrealized dreams, and shattered delusions). The collaborators also made sure that the score evoked the bawdy, brassy milieu of vaudeville and burlesque. Every number furthered the plot or metatheatrically commented on its themes and dramatic action, with numerous active songs developing and illuminating the character of Rose. The hard-driving "Some People" serves as Rose's opening "I Am" song; in it, she explains her need to rise above the drudgery of common existence, even if it means acquiring stardom secondhand via her daughters (especially her favorite, Baby June). Once June can no longer abide living and performing under her mother's thumb, she elopes with a young hoofer, leaving her older, milquetoast sister, Louise, to satisfy her mother's ambitions. In the pivotal "Everything's Coming Up Roses," Rose rides a wave of adrenaline and desperation as she deludes herself into seeing Louise as her new "star," asserting her will on the weak girl. Louise cannot replicate June's vaudeville stardom and is ultimately demoted to burlesque houses where, ironically, she ascends to stardom as the stripping Gypsy Rose Lee. Rose ultimately finds herself discarded by a successful daughter, who has finally declared independence from her destructive and demanding mother. In the cathartic "Rose's Turn," one of musical theatre's most revered 11:00 numbers, Rose sings a powerful soliloquy, built on past musical themes, baring her soul as she struggles to deal with the sad truths of her own life. In all three of the above-mentioned iconic active songs for Rose, Styne and Sondheim brilliantly incorporated the "I had a dream" leitmotif, building and echoing it as an evocation of Rose's psyche. Along with the powerhouse numbers for Rose, the songwriting duo also provided diverse metatheatrical numbers, which range from the sweetly tuned and idealistic showbiz anthem "All I Really Need Is the Girl" to the raunchy and comic "You Gotta Have a Gimmick" and multifaceted "Let Me Entertain You." This last song provides another significant leitmotif that appears throughout the score, serving as onstage music for Louise as she moves from young, unnoticed vaudeville ensemble trouper to sexy, successful burlesque star. In addition to the metatheatrical songs, integrated numbers are used throughout the score to develop the plot and illustrate the characters' motives and mindsets. Contrasting Rose's hard-driving numbers are the songs performed by her daughters as they express their optimism or pain, for example, "If Momma Was Married" and "Little Lamb." "Little Lamb" was almost cut from the show as Jerome Robbins disliked it; he felt it stopped the production's momentum. When he took the initiative to omit it during an out-of-town tryout, however, the authors, who felt the song was crucial in depicting Louise's youthful alienation and loneliness, threatened legal action against Robbins. The song remained (and still remains) in the score, much to Robbins' disgruntlement.

Retaining "Little Lamb" was not the only artistic challenge for Robbins; he had originally envisioned the production as a concept musical, with the story loosely told through vaudeville and burlesque acts. Ultimately, he agreed to work with a traditionally linear libretto; a good thing, given that Laurents' book is viewed as one of the most sophisticated and finely crafted in the musical theatre canon. Laurents' libretto flows from dramatic book scenes to integrated songs to metatheatrical numbers, effortlessly shifting gears. Rose is written as one of musical theatre's most complex characters: a woman easy to hate, but also easy to understand and pity. To this end, "Rose's Turn" represents a high point of musical dramaturgy, as Sondheim and Robbins extended the libretto into a seamless and potent stream of consciousness for Rose as she teeters on the brink of sanity. After the grandiose 11:00 number, *Gypsy* closes with a quiet scene of forgiveness and understanding between Rose and Louise; yet, currents of loss and regret hang in the air, ending the show on a melancholy note, as opposed to the traditional musical theatre happy ending.

Gypsy was a hit when it debuted on Broadway in 1959, running for 702 performances, even though it did not win any of its nine Tony Award nominations (*The Sound of Music* and *Fiorello!* swept the awards that season). *Gypsy*'s most significant triumph may be its longevity and relevance for modern audiences. It has become sacred ground and a crowning career achievement for any musical theatre leading lady who is cast as Rose. Broadway revivals have featured such stars as Angela Lansbury (1974), Tyne Daly (1989), Linda Lavin (1990), Bernadette Peters (2003), and, most recently, Patti LuPone (in a 2008 production directed by Arthur Laurents at age 90). The revivals and their leading ladies have garnered major awards while continuing to find audiences wishing to revel in *Gypsy*'s muscular and masterful score as well as its exploration of identity, sacrifice, show business, and survival, all placed within the conflicted context of the American Dream.

Vicki Lewis as Mama Rose in North Shore Music Theatre's production of *Gypsy*, 2010
Photo by Paul Lyden. Used by permission of Paul Lyden.

PULLING BACK THE CURTAIN:

Hooking the Audience:
Formulaic Constructs and Components in Musical Theatre

How to grab the audience's attention and how to maintain the audience's interest are two of the major challenges faced by any storyteller. In the attempt to engage, or "hook," audiences and keep their engagement, musical theatre creators have exploited a number of constructs and components that have become codified and formulaic in designing a conventional audience-pleaser. Five of the most common hooks are: (1) the star vehicle, (2) the "I Am"/"I Want" song, (3) the opener, or "grabber," (4) the intermission teaser, and (5) the 11:00 number.

The **star vehicle** harkens as far back as the musical itself (George M. Cohan helped invent musical comedy with his own star vehicles). The construct is defined as a show designed to serve and showcase the particular talents of either an already-proven star or a unique talent who will hopefully become a new star. Often, these shows place an inordinate amount of the performance load on the star, asking them to "carry" the show. Sometimes, a telltale sign of a star vehicle is that the lead character, played by the star, is named in the show's title. A box office success can be hedged or facilitated when a popular or well-loved artist is showcased to her/his advantage, assuring a built-in fan base and a high degree of audience engagement at the onset. Even more exciting is the vehicle that lets the audience in on the ground floor of an exciting "star" discovery; i.e., the show that so serves an artist that he or she almost overwhelms the production with his or her performance and becomes identified with the lead role. Famous star vehicles include canonical works by the star-maker, star-vehicle king, Jule Styne (e.g., *Gentlemen Prefer Blondes*, *Peter Pan*, *Bells Are Ringing*, *Gypsy*, and *Funny Girl*), along with famous musicals by many other artists (e.g., *Annie Get Your Gun*; *Where's Charlie?*; *Call Me Madam*; *The Music Man*; *Fiorello!*; *Little Me*; *Hello, Dolly!*; *Fiddler on the Roof*; *Golden Boy*; *Mame*; *Sweet Charity*; *Evita*; *Song and Dance*; *Sunset Boulevard*; *Bring in 'Da Noise, Bring in 'Da Funk*; and *Thoroughly Modern Millie*). As a variation on this construct, there are the shared or duo star vehicles—two stars for the price of one—for example, *Camelot*, *I Do! I Do!*, *The Rink*, *Chicago*, *La Cage aux Folles*, *Sweeney Todd*, *Sunday in the Park with George*, *Wicked*, and *The Producers*. No doubt such works, built on stellar live performances, greatly appeal to musical theatre aficionados. Yet, the star vehicle may contain a paradox or an inherent flaw; that is, a vehicle created for a particular voice or talent may not be able to surmount structural problems or weak content when staged later without the star performer most responsible for the work's success. Some vehicles become so identified with their star that another actor may seem to come up short in a later production. Again using Styne as an example, *Funny Girl* has yet to be revived on Broadway and this may be because the show is greatly defined by the imprint of Barbra Streisand (not to mention the book is considered weak). The star vehicle remains a musical theatre institution, whether in revival or original form, continuing to please audiences by asserting the magnetism and power of the Broadway star in a signature work. For instance, Styne's *Gypsy* still reigns as a favored and timeless revival as it provides a potent star role for any current leading lady, or "diva" of the stage, while original works reflecting new directions and tastes in musical theatre, such as *Hedwig and the Angry Inch*, *Hairspray*, and *Fela!*, continue to be written in the star-vehicle vein.

The **"I Am" song** is a potent instrument in the star-vehicle arsenal as well as an audience-engaging number used throughout the musical canon. In the "I Am"/"I Want" song, a character literally tells the audience who he or she is, what makes him or her tick, and why the audience should care. It is often the introductory number by the character and provides an opportunity to display the performer's virtuosity. "I Am" songs can be as direct as Fanny Brice's declaration in "I'm the Greatest Star" or oblique, as Mama Rose's comparison of herself to others in "Some People." (The lyricist of "Some People," Stephen Sondheim, regularly uses oblique "I Am" songs, saying that in real life most people do not have true self knowledge, but reveal themselves through their reactions to external circumstances and other people.) Other classic examples of "I Am"/"I Want" songs include Dolly Levi's "I Put My Hand In" (*Hello, Dolly!*), Annie Oakley's "You Can't Get a Man with a Gun" (*Annie Get Your Gun*), Peter Pan's "I Gotta Crow" (*Peter Pan*), Princess Winnifred's "Shy" (*Once Upon a Mattress*), Eva Peron's "Buenos Aires" (*Evita*), Norma Desmond's "With One Look" (*Sunset Boulevard*), Tevye's "If I Were a Rich Man" (*Fiddler on the Roof*), Mrs. Lovett's "Worst Pies in London" (*Sweeney Todd*), Dot's "Sunday in the Park with George" (*Sunday in the Park with George*), Tracy Turnblad's "Good Morning, Baltimore" (*Hairspray*), and the sequential "I Am" songs in *My Fair Lady*, first by Henry Higgins ("*Why Can't the English?*") and then Eliza Doolittle ("*Wouldn't It Be Loverly?*").

The **show opener/"grabber"** can also be an "I Am" song, especially in the case of a star vehicle. More often a large production number is used at the top of the show as a moment of exposition and an attention grabber. Prior to the 1940s, there was scarcely a musical show that did not open with a grandly staged ensemble song and dance. The opening numbers of these early shows usually had little to do with what followed, as their chief functions were to settle the audience, assure them of plenty of beautiful girls, and identify the performers. Later, the grabber became more integrated and sophisticated; but it was still used to capture the audience's attention by setting the stage, providing exposition, introducing the main players, and infusing the stage with energy, color, and sound. Especially effective examples include "Tradition" (*Fiddler on the Roof*), "Willkommen" (*Cabaret*), "All That Jazz" (*Chicago*), "Jellicle Songs for Jellicle Cats" (*Cats*), "Into the Woods" (*Into the Woods*), "We Are What We Are" (*La Cage aux Folles*), "Rent" (*Rent*), "Circle of Life" (*Lion King*), "It Sucks to Be Me" (*Avenue Q*), "In the Heights" (*In the Heights*), "Just Another Day" (*Next to Normal*), "American Idiot" (*American Idiot*), and "Hello!" (*The Book of Mormon*).

The **intermission teaser** is a construct often employed to keep an audience hooked. This powerhouse number is a cousin to the 11:00 number (*see following*), which leaves spectators on the edge of their seats and wanting more. This teaser (right before the end of Act One) ranges from a confessional moment of crisis to a musicalized pivot point for a single character. It can also be a celebratory or rallying production number that invigorates the musical at its halfway point. The goal is for audiences to enter the lobby with a tune in their head, raised pulse rates, and a need to know more. Styne provides classic models with Rose's crazed exhibition of blind ambition in "Everything's Coming Up Roses" (*Gypsy*) and Fanny's survivalist declaration in "Don't Rain on My Parade" (*Funny Girl*). Given its theatrical effectiveness, the teaser is formulaic and codified in many hit musicals, exemplified by iconic numbers such as "Soliloquy" (*Carousel*), "A Little Priest" (*Sweeney Todd*), "A New Argentina" (*Evita*), "Before the Parade Passes By" (*Hello, Dolly!*), "Mame" (*Mame*), and "Defying Gravity" (*Wicked*). One of the canon's most powerful teasers, on many levels, is the pivotal and confessional performance of "I Am What I Am" in *La Cage aux Folles* by lead character Albin, which serves as a delayed "I Am" song (literally), as well as a variation of the show's "grabber," "We Are What We Are."

The **11:00 number** is a tried-and-true score construct that reengages an audience by closing a production on a dramatic high note. The number has acquired its nickname because it is an original composition (not a reprise) generally sung at or toward the end of the musical, therefore close to 11:00 p.m. Often it is a tour de force for the leading performer, a showstopper that hopefully corresponds to the play's climax. In this respect, the song facilitates the star vehicle, providing the character/performer a moment of truth, insight, and/or virtuosic self-expression, for example, "Rose's Turn" (*Gypsy*), "The Music That Makes Me Dance" (*Funny Girl*), "I'm Going Back" (*Bells Are Ringing*), "Being Alive" (*Company*), and "Cabaret" (*Cabaret*). As this list illustrates, the 11:00 number can be personal and confessional; however, it can also provide an entertainment high when written as a big production number (possibly not even sung by the lead character) that grabs and reinvigorates the audience as the show comes to an end. Examples of this model include "You Can't Stop the Beat" (*Hairspray*), "Superstar" (*Jesus Christ Superstar*), "Sit Down, You're Rockin' the Boat" (*Guys and Dolls*), "Brotherhood of Man" (*How to Succeed in Business Without Really Trying*), "One" (*A Chorus Line*), and "Freak Flag" (*Shrek the Musical*).

JERRY BOCK AND SHELDON HARNICK

Any musical theatre fan would be able to hum the melody of at least one number from *Fiddler on the Roof* (1964); many could even sing an entire song. But if asked to cite the songwriters, even ardent fans might pause before naming Bock and Harnick. This is neither unusual nor surprising, because *Fiddler's* songwriting team never flaunted themselves nor sought notoriety as artists apart from their works. Instead, Jerry Bock (composer) and Sheldon Harnick (lyricist) sublimated their identities to create heartfelt, nuanced musical renderings of endearing characters, life-affirming stories, and cultural moments in time, with each score in accordance with a show's content and criteria. That said, it is still curious that the Bock and Harnick partnership is not more familiar to American theatergoers and music lovers, given that many scholars and critics cite the duo as the dominant musical theatre team of the 1960s, with seven musicals playing on Broadway from 1959–70. Some of the works were disappointments, but others were hits and one, *Fiddler*, was an international phenomenon. The team won numerous Tony Awards as well as that rare distinction in musical theatre, the Pulitzer Prize for Drama. Yet, Bock and Harnick's mission was never to call attention to themselves; their first priority, in the tradition of Rodgers and Hammerstein and Lerner and Loewe, was to serve the show's story, characters, and milieu. Given this mission, alongside the sundry and unique material

they chose to musicalize (e.g., trajectory of a New York mayor, romance of pen pals, persecution of Russian Jews, fall of Adam and Eve, rise of a European banking dynasty), their scores could not help but be divergent. Although many Bock/Harnick musicals are epic in scope, the works also manage to be intimate and rooted in human struggle. They compassionately reflect the rise, or at least the perseverance, of the common man who, along with family and community, uses hope, humor, faith, and resolve to find peace, love, success and/or enlightenment when coping with difficulties or persecution. Often set in distant lands or times, Bock and Harnick musicals continue to resonate with modern audiences, as they contain heart, honesty, and musical integration, representing the pinnacle (as well as, ironically, the final chapter) of musical theatre's Golden Age.

Sheldon Harnick was born in Chicago on April 30, 1924. Young Sheldon was a musically gifted child, playing the violin and writing lyrics for family gatherings. Upon graduation from high school, he served in the Army during World War II, where he wrote songs and performed them for USO shows. After the war, Harnick attended Northwestern University and then had a short-lived career as a dance orchestra violinist. Failing to find success and often stressed by the performance demands of dance band work, Harnick decided to pursue songwriting for the Broadway theatre. In 1950, he moved to New York City where he found modest employment by supplying songs for entertainment

Jerry Bock and Sheldon Harnick with Alfred Molina (Tevye) and cast of Broadway revival of *Fiddler on the Roof*, 2/26/2004 © Joseph Marzullo/Retna Ltd./CORBIS

venues at summer resorts. Harnick's big break came two years later, when his song "The Boston Beguine" was added to a Broadway revue, *New Faces of 1952*, and proved to be a showstopper. This accomplishment led to opportunities to write for other minor revues throughout the 1950s. During this period, lyricist E. Y. (Yip) Harburg convinced Harnick to concentrate on his lyrics and find a composer/partner to supply the music. Harnick took this advice to heart. (Harnick said that as a young man he had been inspired by Harburg's lyrics for *Finian's Rainbow*, claiming that the show changed his life and lured him to the theatre.) Once he became a lyricist, Harnick continued to be inspired by Harburg, using similar wit and wordplay in his work, often turning a phrase at the end of a song to shade or change the meaning of the number. Fortunately, Harnick did not have to wait long for a composer/collaborator; while at a bar in 1956, he was introduced by actor Jack Cassidy to Cassidy's friend, a young composer named Jerry Bock.

Jerry Bock was born in New Haven on November 23, 1928, but grew up in Flushing, New York. As a boy, he not only studied piano but could also play songs by ear and vary their themes. In high school and at the University of Wisconsin, Bock wrote songs, creating some local and touring shows (*My Dream*, a war bonds show, and *Big as Life*, an original amateur musical). After graduation, Bock got a job in New York writing for television revues, as well as composing and musically directing revues for Tamiment, a famous summer resort in the Poconos. Bock supplied ten scores each summer season for three years. Soon, he found a lyricist partner, Larry Holofcener, and the two men contributed three songs to a Broadway revue, *Catch a Star* (1955). The next year, they worked with successful songwriter George David Weiss to provide the majority of songs for *Mr. Wonderful* (the score also included samplings and compilations of songs previously written by other artists). As a star vehicle for Sammy Davis Jr., *Mr. Wonderful* was an extension of Davis' popular nightclub act, with a book co-written by Joseph Stein and Will Glickman that centered on the struggles of a nightclub entertainer. (The show also starred Davis' father, Sammy Davis Sr., and his uncle, Will Mastin, two men with whom he had famously performed as a youth on the vaudeville circuit.) Co-produced by Jule Styne, the show was popular and proved that the talented and charismatic song-and-dance man Sammy

Davis Jr. could hold his own on Broadway in a book musical. It was also the first time Bock would work with Stein, a librettist who would figure prominently in Bock's career. Three months after the show's opening, Bock was introduced to Harnick over drinks in a bar.

The first outing for the new team of Bock and Harnick was less than auspicious. Foreshadowing their adventurous nature when it came to selecting material, they wrote a musical about prize-fighting. Bock was happy to reteam with the librettist team of Joseph Stein and Will Glickman. The new show, *The Body Beautiful* (1958), was widely panned, running for only sixty performances. On a brighter note, the Bock/Harnick score was impressive enough to catch the attention of director George Abbott, who was just starting on a musical project based on the life of Fiorello LaGuardia (1882–1947). The show, titled *Fiorello!*, was to be a mix of romance and politics, illustrating the personal and professional sides of LaGuardia, who served three terms as mayor of New York City from 1934–45, becoming one of America's best-known and most powerful politicians. Young producers Robert Griffith and Harold Prince, having just triumphed with *West Side Story*, secured the rights to musically dramatize the mayor's life, but they needed artists to actually write the show. Griffith lived next door to librettist Jerome Weidman and asked him to work on the show. Weidman agreed to co-write the libretto with Abbott, and the producers began their search for songwriters, preferably artists who could evoke the time periods, integrate the score with the book, and bring a singing/dancing LaGuardia to life. At Abbott's suggestion, Bock and Harnick auditioned for the job, providing a waltz that captured the World War I era. Based on the strength of that one number, they were hired. (The song, "Til Tomorrow," became a highlight of the realized production.) One last search remained: to find an actor to play LaGuardia, a tough, savvy politician who stood only 5' tall but boasted an oversized personality. After many auditions, the producers chose Broadway neophyte Tom Bosley. In looks, energy, and mannerisms, Bosley was eerily similar to the real LaGuardia (whom many in the audience remembered vividly), and upon its opening in 1959, *Fiorello!* made Bosley a Broadway star. (Bosley is mainly remembered today as having played Howard Cunningham, the father in the long-running television series *Happy Days*.)

Along with Bosley, Bock and Harnick's *Fiorello!* score was also greatly praised. Bock had taken pains to create a musical tapestry that relayed the passage of time through different musical idioms (marches, waltzes, schottisches, and Charlestons), while also suggesting the dramatic atmosphere of politics and campaigns. Harnick's lyrics meshed with each musical style, working in tandem with Weidman/Abbott's book to convey the personal and political world of LaGuardia. For example, Weidman/Abbott's dialogue was often converted to song lyrics (or *Sprechstimme*) by Harnick, creating numbers that were self-contained dramatic scenes (e.g., "Politics and Poker"). Critics showered praise on the show and audiences were enamored. The show ran for 795 performances, won the Tony for Best Musical, and received that year's Pulitzer Prize for Drama.

Hoping to replicate the success of *Fiorello!*, Bock and Harnick reteamed with producers Griffith and Prince for a new musical. Weidman was also reenlisted to again co-write the libretto with director Abbott. However, the production, *Tenderloin* (1960), did not measure up to its heralded Bock-Harnick-Griffith-Prince-Weidman-Abbott pedigree. The venture's failure was surprising, given that its content and context were similar to *Fiorello!*. *Tenderloin* is another biographical adaptation, recounting the exploits of an 1890s crusading clergyman and social reformer, Dr. Charles Parkhurst, who endeavored to clean up New York City's infamous and sin-ridden district, the Tenderloin, and expose political corruption. Comparisons to *Fiorello!* were inevitable; Dr. Parkhurst, as a musical theatre character, lacked the charm of LaGuardia. Further, the production was not as smartly written or tightly crafted; consequently, it ran for only 216 performances, even though Bock and Harnick's score received positive notices for its evocative and authentic sound.

For their next major Broadway production, Bock and Harnick worked again with producer Prince, who also served as director. The project's source material came from Ernst Lubitsch's classic 1940 romantic comedy film, *The Shop Around the Corner*, itself based on *Parfumerie*, a 1937 Hungarian play by Miklos Laszlo. (In another configuration, the play's plot would be updated for the hit 1998 film, *You've Got Mail*.) The musical, titled *She Loves Me*, reflects both Laszlo and Lubitsch's works. The musical features a pair of squabbling coworkers in a Budapest perfumery who, unbeknownst to each other, are one another's pen pal, and each has fallen in love with their respective correspondent. In addition to the love/hate conflict—which, of course, ends in love, once identities are revealed—there are several subplots involving the pen pals' fellow shop clerks, their boss, and even the bicycle delivery boy, all of whom are dealing with their own life dramas (infidelities, career aspirations, romantic discoveries, even an attempted suicide). The librettist, Joe Masteroff, was so attentive to the dramatic purity of the show that he wrote a complete play for the work at the beginning of the development process instead of supplying a musical libretto. Given their talent and instinct for score integration, Bock and Harnick used Masteroff's "play" for their score, substituting songs for scenes and monologues. Where spoken scenes were retained, the songwriters seamlessly meshed the scenes with musical excursions and elaborations. As a result, *She Loves Me* contains one of the most tightly integrated scores in the canon. The score is also varied, as it reflects a well-developed and idiosyncratic suite of characters and dramatic situations, with numerous active songs ("Where's My Shoe?" and "Try Me"), character numbers ("A Trip to the Library"), romantic ballads ("Will He Like Me?"), duets ("I Don't Know His Name"), contrapuntal group numbers ("Good Morning, Good Day" and "Twelve Days to Christmas"). The musical is a completely realized musical play, with no less than twenty-three musical interludes and songs, all founded on and creatively exploiting sweet melodies and motive variations reflecting the warmly romantic plot, delightful milieu, and charming, though flawed, characters. Two of the more potent numbers that highlight the melodic renderings of Bock and the character-defining lyrics of Harnick are "She Loves Me" (where the male shop clerk delights in the knowledge that his sniping coworker is actually his "dear friend" pen pal) and "Ice Cream" (where the female shop clerk struggles with her affections for her maddening coworker—as opposed to her "dear friend"—unaware that they are the same person [see fig. 5.5]). *She Loves Me* represents one of the earliest examples of a chamber musical, that is, it has a small cast, and almost every cast member has at least one featured moment or song; there are no large, anonymous singing and/or dancing choruses. Maybe it was the novel form or the lack of bombast and large-scale production numbers, but the show experienced a disappointing box office on its 1963 Broadway debut (301 performances). On the other hand, it received unanimous raves from the critics, was nominated for several Tony Awards (including Best Musical), and is still regarded as a Bock/Harnick gem. Thirty years later, *She Loves Me* was revived on Broadway, with critics once again singing its praises. Even though the 1993 revival ran longer than the original (354 performances), given its intimate treatment of interpersonal relationships, it had difficulty competing against neighboring "razzle-dazzle" mega–musicals.

Bock and Harnick's most celebrated and successful musical, *Fiddler on the Roof* (1964), was in the works before *She Loves Me*. The two were inspired by a novel written by Sholom Aleichem (pen name of Yiddish author and playwright Solomon Naumovich Rabinovich) and approached Joseph Stein to adapt the story into a musical. Stein didn't think it showed promise; but Bock and Harnick refused to give up on the idea of an "Aleichem" musical. When a friend introduced them to a collection of Aleichem's short stories titled *Tevye's Daughters*, they again asked Stein to collaborate on the project. This time Stein agreed, and *Fiddler* was born. This was the first time that Bock and Harnick had initiated a project of their own choosing. The team once again looked to their old friend Harold Prince to produce and possibly direct (his fourth Bock/Harnick musical). They knew Prince would be adventurous enough to tackle a show with such unconventional content and uncertain commercial merit. The musical is set in 1905 Tsarist Russia and depicts peasants scraping by in a *shtetl* (a village called Anatevka), who face persecution and are forced into exile. Prince agreed to produce the musical but felt inadequate to direct a show so steeped in Jewish content. However, he knew of an artist who was conversant with Judaism and was one of the few director/choreographers capable of bringing such challenging material to life on stage: Jerome Robbins. Prince was not mistaken. As *Fiddler*'s directorial/choreographic auteur, Robbins triumphed; he was able to fashion a musical with mainstream "Broadway" appeal, while imbuing the work with cultural authenticity (to this end, he researched distant Yiddish culture, music/dance idioms, and *shtetl* life). Similarly, Bock and Harnick wrote musical numbers that merged audience-pleasing melodies with Hebraic overtones (e.g., "Tradition," "Matchmaker, Matchmaker," "L'Chaim," "Miracle of Miracles," "If I Were a Rich Man," and "Sunrise, Sunset"). Lastly, Stein's literary themes proved to be universal, with audiences connecting to the messages of family, religion, tradition, persecution, and survival. *Fiddler* won almost every major

Tony Award in 1965, including Best Musical and made history with a record-breaking 3,242 performances; it also became one of the first international hit musicals, successfully playing in thirty countries.

Riding high off the success of *Fiddler*, Bock and Harnick searched for a new project which would stretch their songwriting talent and challenge Broadway in terms of content and form. While taking a detour in 1965 to contribute three songs to a modestly successful Sherlock Holmes musical titled *Baker Street*, Bock and Harnick arrived at an innovative concept: combining three one-act musical plays into an evening of thematically linked musical theatre. As they began to develop the show, eventually titled *The Apple Tree*, the songwriters looked for short stories that they could adapt. Initially, the three stories were linked by the theme of woman, man, and the devil, but once director Mike Nichols came on board (his first work on a Broadway musical), he replaced two of the original stories with his own choices. As a result, *The Apple Tree* does not contain a discernible link between the acts, except perhaps, the idea of fulfilled desires that differ from what was wished for and imagined—and a repeated reference to the color brown. The libretto was first contracted to Jerome Coopersmith but later taken over by Bock and Harnick, in another unconventional move for them. The first act is based on Mark Twain's *Diary of Adam and Eve*, a satirical look at domestic, gendered conflict between Adam and Eve that evolves into a tale of love as they negotiate the early days of creation, Eve's bite of the apple, and expulsion from the Garden of Eden. The next act is a musicalization of Frank Stockton's *The Lady or the Tiger?*, depicting a balladeer's tale of a warrior whose fate lies behind two doors. He must choose one of the doors. Behind one door is a woman he would be forced to marry, even though he is in love with another; behind the other door is a tiger that will kill him. His choice is not revealed at the end. *The Apple Tree*'s last act is a musical adaption of Jules Feiffer's *Passionella*, which centers on a female chimneysweep who dreams of becoming a movie star. Courtesy of a modern-day fairy godmother, she is turned into the "gorgeous" Passionella for a few hours every day, is discovered by a movie producer, and made a star—only to realize true happiness with a man who loves her as her chimneysweep self. Vague thematic connections in the libretto and the use of the same actors as the major characters in all three stories link the acts together. Another linkage is the music by

Bock, which contains themes quoted throughout the three vignettes. For example, a melody found in a lullaby and another in the snake's song in the Adam/Eve segment are reprised in the final song of the Passionella act and are reconfigured in the balladeer's song in the Lady/Tiger act. Upon its Broadway debut in 1966, *The Apple Tree* was a moderate hit (463 performances). Its unconventional form and content paved the way for the concept musical, popularized in the late '60s, as well as the "compiled" musical, comprising self-contained, thematically linked stories or plays (e.g., 2000's *Contact*). Largely forgotten, a much-anticipated revival of *The Apple Tree* premiered on Broadway in 2006 as a star vehicle for Kristen Chenoweth. Even though the critics lavished praise on Chenoweth, overall, they felt the show's content was too dated, and it ran for only ninety-nine performances.

Bock and Harnick's last original production on Broadway, *The Rothschilds* (1970), would prove to be the show/straw that broke the team's back (most biographers and historians say the men were never very close or fond of each other, so the dissolution of their partnership was not a surprise). While working on *Fiddler* in 1963, Bock and Harnick were offered the chance to provide the score for an adaptation of Frederic Morton's *The Rothschilds* (1962), a historical account of the Jewish family that founded a European banking dynasty. Worried that the European Jewish content might hew too closely to *Fiddler* and that the show would incur critical comparison or be deemed derivative, Bock and Harnick hesitated. They relented five years later, due in part to the work by Sherman Yellen, who supplied a new libretto that the songwriters thought was workable and could stand up to *Fiddler* comparisons. (Six prior librettists had failed to adapt the book in a way that suited Bock and Harnick.) Yellen's libretto focused on the struggles of a large Jewish family (five sons headed by patriarch Mayer Rothschild) against anti-Semitic sentiment and persecution in Europe, only to triumph over oppression by acquiring power and prestige as bankers, becoming titans of the European financial industry. For their part, Bock and Harnick provided a richly authentic and evocative score to convey place and

time, exploiting European formal and popular musical expressions of the eighteenth and nineteenth centuries. Bock and Harnick consciously used these idioms to differentiate the Rothschild story—one of Western European ascent—from that of Tevye and peasant life on a Russian *shtetl*. Upon its opening on October 19, 1970, *The Rothschilds* had what could be considered a hit run (507 performances), but lost money. Further, Bock and Harnick's fears were realized, for the production was overshadowed by the artistic and commercial phenomenon of *Fiddler*; *The Rothschilds* was dismissed by critics as a weak and derivative follow-up to the 1964 masterpiece. The work is rarely produced today.

After *The Rothschilds*, there was no more "Bock and Harnick." Although they never gave a formal reason for ending the partnership, it was later revealed that conflicts during the show's writing contributed to their separation. Afterward, neither artist had comparable Broadway success working on projects with other partners. For instance, Harnick worked with Richard Rodgers, only to realize the failed 1976 *Rex* (forty-eight performances). Such unsuccessful ventures did not rob them of their places on Broadway, for the Bock/Harnick canon continued to make its presence felt in the form of successful revivals and individual songs featured in revues. When Bock died on November 3, 2010, his death was preceded a week earlier by *Fiddler* librettist Joseph Stein. Although Harnick claimed that he considered Stein a best friend and mourned his death, he also recounted that before Bock's death, the old partners had become close again. Unfortunately, their reconciliation did not result in additional musical theatre projects. Regardless, their body of work lives on. Few may be able to identify the songwriters behind *Fiddler* and *She Loves Me*, but this could be considered a triumph for the artists who sought to "disappear" into their work. That Bock and Harnick musicals are more closely associated with the characters for which they wrote and the stories they helped convey is a testament to their ability to create scores that depict honest and empathetic portrayals of the human condition.

Figure 5.5

ICE CREAM

Music by Jerry Bock; Lyrics by
Sheldon Harnick (1963)

Amalia: (Spoken) *Dear Friend:*

(Sung)
I am so sorry about last night.
It was a nightmare in every way,
But together, you and I
Will laugh at last night someday . . .

Ice cream.
He brought me ice cream,
Vanilla ice cream,
Imagine that!

Ice cream,
And for the first time,
We were together
Without a spat!

Friendly,
He was so friendly.
That isn't like him
I'm simply stunned.

Will wonders never cease?
Will wonders never cease?
It's been a most peculiar day!
Will wonders never cease?
Will wonders never cease?....

(Spoken) *Where was I? Oh . . .*

(Sung – rapidly as possible)
I am so sorry about last night it was a nightmare
in every way
But together you and I will laugh at last night
some day . . .

I sat there waiting in that cafe
And never guessing that you were fat –
That you were near –
You were outside looking bald –
(spoken) Oh, my!

Dear Friend:
I am so sorry about last night....

Last night
I was so nasty!
Well, he deserved it!
But even so . . .
That George
Is not like this George.
This is a new George
That I don't know!

Somehow
It all reminds me
Of Dr. Jekyll
And Mr. Hyde.

For right before my eyes
A man that I despise
Has turned into a man I like.

It's almost like a dream,
And strange as it may seem,
He came to offer me
Vanilla ice cream!

FEATURED PRODUCTION: *Fiddler on the Roof* (1964)

Music by Jerry Bock; Lyrics by Sheldon Harnick; Book by Joseph Stein

Original Broadway Run: Opened September 22, 1964; Imperial Theatre; 3,242 performances

Tradition! During the development of *Fiddler on the Roof*, director/choreographer Jerome Robbins constantly pestered librettist Joseph Stein, composer Jerry Bock, and lyricist Sheldon Harnick to elucidate what the new musical was *about*—not its plot or cast of characters, but the meaning and impetus of the show. Robbins demanded the information so he could fashion a potent opening number (or "grabber") that would viscerally convey the musical's key message. When the writers decided that the crux of the musical was milkman Tevye's personal crisis, that is, his conflict between religious and cultural traditions and the necessity of change, Robbins knew that he not only had his opening number but also had a theme he could use to underpin every moment in the show. Thus, "Tradition," with its Hebraic harmonies by Bock, served as Robbins' ten-minute "grabber" and became *Fiddler*'s musical foundation and touchstone. During the number, Robbins employed circular folk dances of Jewish origin to introduce the audience to Tevye's world of 1905 Anatevka. From that point, the landmark musical established a distinctive milieu, potent themes, and dramatic tensions, familiarizing the audience with the community and the ethos of a conflicted leading character, only to later dramatize the way in which the communal circles were broken, tradition was confounded, and Tevye's world dissolved.

Fiddler is based on material culled from *Tevye's Daughters*, a compilation of Yiddish short stories written between 1894–1914 by Sholom Aleichem. The musical is set in the Jewish *shtetl* of Anatevka at the turn of the twentieth century in Tsarist Russia, a period during which violent anti-Semitism was institutionalized by a Tsarist government wanting to deflect populist dissatisfaction and revolutionary sentiment by blaming the country's Jews, setting "pure" Russians against the Jewish "Other." At the center of *Fiddler*'s story is Tevye, the jocular, yet pious milkman, who tries to eke out a living, while dealing with his long-suffering wife, Golde, and three headstrong daughters (out of five) as they seek to marry the men of their choosing. Tzeitel, the eldest, is the first to challenge Tevye as she wants to choose her own husband, a poor tailor (Motel), instead of an arranged marriage to the financially stable, middle-aged butcher Lazar Wolf. Even though Tevye finally agrees to let Tzeitel marry her tailor, he must convince Golde to accept the union. In a crafty move, he pretends to suffer a nightmare (the dream ballet) in which Lazar's late wife, Fruma-Sarah, rises from the grave to warn against marrying Tzeitel to her husband. The Tzeitel-Motel wedding is a celebratory Jewish affair, only to be ruined by a pogrom led by Russian soldiers, ending Act I on an ominous note. In the next act, the second daughter, Hodel, tests Tevye further by choosing to marry a revolutionary (Perchik). Tevye once again resists the idea of marriage by choice and for love, but finally gives his blessing as they do not ask his permission, conceding that the world is changing and that he must change with it. The events lead to a discussion between Tevye and Golde on the subject of love—"the new style"—and they muse about the twenty-five years of their arranged marriage, realizing that they have grown to "love" each other. Next, Tevye must say goodbye to Hodel as she chooses to follow Perchik when he is exiled to Siberia for his revolutionary activities. When the third daughter, Chava, falls in love with the gentile Fyedka, she elopes with him, having been forbidden by Tevye to marry outside of the faith. Given this ultimate breach of tradition, Tevye is pushed to his breaking point. He cannot forgive Chava, disowning her and cursing God for his family's disintegration and for testing his faith. Coinciding with Tevye's spiritual and familial crisis is the and familial crisis is the governmental decree that the *shtetl* of Anatevka is to be dissolved, giving the villagers three days to pack and go. In the final scene, farewells are said; and Tevye, Golde, their two youngest daughters, and the remaining villagers leave the village, with many (including Tevye's family) heading to America, hoping for a new start. They are followed by the omnipresent Fiddler, playing his violin.

The material for *Fiddler* was very unconventional for the musical stage; that is, the dramatization of an ugly historical event and depiction of a harsh existence, as well as the tale's flawed protagonist and its tragic ending without justice. The original production contained little glamour, with the *shtetl* brought authentically to life by scenic designer Boris Aronson (with roughhewn edifices set against backdrops inspired by and evoking the Expressionist and Symbolist paintings and iconography of Russian-Jewish artist Marc Chagall). Costume designer Patricia Zipprodt meticulously researched her historically, culturally accurate costumes. Potentially most controversial and noncommercial of all were the Jewish content and context of *Fiddler*, with creators and backers worrying that the show would be "too Jewish" for Broadway—not only its libretto, but also the score steeped in Hebraic melody and sentiment. The fear was ironic, given the prevalence of Jewish artists and their influence in the musical theatre world; yet such Jewish presence and influence had yet to be overtly celebrated on Broadway (exemplified by the commonplace practice of musical theatre artists changing their Yiddish family names to gentile approximations).

When Bock and Harnick embarked on their self-described "labor of love," they knew it was a gamble. After recruiting librettist Joseph Stein, the team called on Harold Prince to help them realize their vision on stage. Instead of acting as director/producer, Prince opted to only produce the show (indeed, raising $375,000 capital for such a musical would prove to be a Herculean task), recommending Jerome Robbins for the directing job. Prince convinced Bock and Harnick that only Robbins could bring a visceral and kinetic unity and authenticity to the production, making the difficult subject matter work for a Broadway audience. Further, Robbins had his own Jewish heritage to draw on (including firsthand knowledge of a *shtetl*) and was seeking to acknowledge and celebrate his Jewish identity (having changed his last name from Rabinowitz to Robbins, to the disappointment of his father, whom he spent a lifetime trying to please). Robbins rigorously researched the 1905 world of Russian Jews, asking his actors to do the same. Robbins also employed numerous improvisational exercises and extensive character development work for the cast during the eight-week rehearsal period. As director and choreographer, Robbins was also in a position to use dance to tell stories and physically illustrate the communal ethos of this lost world. He was so insistent on the import of his *Fiddler* choreography that he copyrighted it as a legally scripted component of any future professional production. Examples of Robbins' contributions, beyond the integrated aesthetic and the conceptual world created on stage, include the circular folk dances at the top of show, the ritualistic bottle dance at the wedding, the explosive and dramatic physicality of "L'Chaim" (which evolves from a wary competition between Russian soldiers and the Anatevka villagers into one of culture-sharing and celebratory solidarity), and a dream ballet ("Tevye's Dream") that is more an exercise in expressionism than classical dance. One glitch was Robbins' relationship with the strong-willed, larger-than-life performer who was cast as Tevye: Zero Mostel. Mostel, who was blacklisted during the 1950s for refusing to name names during the HUAC hearings, disdained Robbins for having cooperated with HUAC and for having fingered some of Mostel's friends. In the end Mostel agreed to work with Robbins, as long as he didn't have to have "lunch" with the man or shake his hand. The working relationship was difficult (Mostel was also famous for ad-libbing and ignoring direction when on stage), but the original conception of Tevye was shaped by the talents and personality of the flamboyant Mostel. Bock and Harnick had initially conceived of Tevye as a thin, wasted man, but rethought it once the burley Mostel was cast, specifically creating "If I Were a Rich Man" for him.

The richness of *Fiddler*'s writing was key to the musical's original success, as well as its sustained canonical status and popularity. First, there is the depth, diversity, and appeal of Bock's musical compositions, for he was adept at translating historically and culturally authentic styles of music into

Broadway tunes with mass appeal. In terms of authenticity, *Fiddler*'s music, rooted in Hebraic tones, modes, and melodies, suggests spontaneous folk revelries and solemn ceremonies (e.g., "Tradition," "If I Were a Rich Man," "L'Chaim," "Sabbath Prayer," "Sunrise, Sunset," "Anatevka"). This aspect is reinforced by orchestrations (originally written by Don Walker) that reflect the sound of the klezmer, a traditional Eastern European Jewish musical ensemble that mixes vocals with instruments such as violin and clarinet. Bock also created a conventional musical theatre score, providing leitmotifs for Tevye and the Fiddler (a signature violin riff), while exploiting popular music forms such as the waltz ("Matchmaker, Matchmaker"), hummable up-tempo numbers ("Miracle of Miracles"), and haunting minor-keyed ballads ("Far From the Home I Love"). The success of Bock's compositions also relied on Harnick's lyrics; *Fiddler* contains many active songs that work as one-act musical plays. They are rooted in place, time, and character, often with a whimsical turn of phrase at the song's end that adds a twist to a character's sentiment or a new level of self-discovery (e.g., "If I Were a Rich Man" and "Do You Love Me?"). Serving an equally important role in the show's drama is the libretto by Stein, who worked so closely with the songwriters that some of his scenes were eventually turned into musical numbers (e.g., "Do You Love Me?"). While tinged with wry humor (especially in the case of Tevye), Stein's book also explores the human condition, employing sophisticated dramatic devices such as the soliloquy. In these moments, Tevye talks aloud to God and wrestles with his own soul, while the audience witnesses his doubt. The level of lyricism in Stein's libretto was new at the time, especially his use of symbolism with the Fiddler. This other-worldly character, seen only by Tevye (in his imagination?), is a dramatic symbol of perseverance and precariousness, as well as the balance and adjustments needed to survive in a shifting world.

Once *Fiddler* opened at the Imperial Theatre in September 1964, the creators and backers realized their worries regarding box office failure due to the show's "Jewishness" had been pointless. Audiences embraced what they viewed as the musical's universal themes of family, community, faith, persecution, tradition, change, and survival. The work's reflection of a "generation gap" paradigm, which was just beginning to be addressed in mid-1960s America, also resonated. *Fiddler* became the first musical to top 3,000 performances (3,242, to be exact) and held the record for the longest-running Broadway musical until 1979, when it was surpassed by *Grease* (1971). *Fiddler*'s popularity was not limited to America; it also enjoyed thirty international productions, becoming the first musical to capture a global

Photo of the MUNY production of *Fiddler on the Roof.*
Jim Herren. Photo Coutesy of MUNY.

audience. (Interestingly, the musical found a great following in Japan. Stein was told by an audience member that he was surprised at how popular it was in the United States, given that the work was so "Japanese.") In 1971, Norman Jewison directed a film version of the musical, which starred Israeli performer Topol (who also played Tevye on Broadway) and was nominated for eight Academy Awards, winning three (music, sound, and cinematography).

By the time of *Fiddler*'s film debut, Broadway had come to the end of its musical theatre Golden Age, and many scholars cited *Fiddler* as the last significant work of the Age. Nonetheless, numerous Broadway revivals since its 1964 debut (the latest being in 2004, running for 781 performances), as well as regional and community productions worldwide, reassert *Fiddler's* timeless message and universal appeal.

PULLING BACK THE CURTAIN:
A Golden Age for the Librettists of American Musical Theatre

Once an often-neglected or perfunctory collaborator, the librettist gained prominence as the book musical became the prevalent and aesthetically preferred musical form during the Golden Age. Instead of being relegated to providing thin storylines by which songs by dominant composers and "bits" by star performers could be strung together, the Golden Age librettist, under the newly integrated model, was required to tell a riveting story, be true to character development, and merge the disparate elements of score and dance into an artistic whole. Given this challenging criteria, librettists furthered their craft by introducing new forms and content to the genre. Listed below are some of the notable and prominent librettists of this period. Most writers had careers that spanned film, radio, television, and nonmusical drama. Yet they also chose to apply their talents to the uniquely collaborative medium of musical theatre. Some successfully branched into directing and performing. In all cases, they pioneered the librettist's role as a literary and dramatic artist who could bring stories to life on stage, effectively integrating them with song and dance.

Abe Burrows (1910–85): This librettist/playwright/director/performer was born Abram Solman Borowitz in New York City. He grew up in Brooklyn and attended both City College and New York University. After brief stints in finance and accounting, he turned to comedy writing, mounting a successful career in radio as a writer and performer, earning his own CBS radio show in 1948: *The Abe Burrows Show.* Two years later, Burrows moved to Broadway to team with director George S. Kaufman and composer/lyricist Frank Loesser to write the book for *Guys and Dolls*, for which Burrows (with Loesser) was selected as winner of the Pulitzer Prize in Drama. Burrows was experiencing troubles with HUAC at the time, however, so the Pulitzer committee decided to avoid almost certain controversy by not awarding the prize for drama that year. Nonetheless, Burrows became a Broadway institution over the next two decades, writing or directing such hit shows as *Two on the Aisle* (director), *Can-Can* (director/librettist), *Silk Stockings* (librettist), *Say, Darling* (director/librettist), *How to Succeed in Business Without Really Trying* (director/librettist), *What Makes Sammy Run?* (director), *Cactus Flower* (director/playwright), plus a dozen other less successful Broadway works. A decade after his Pulitzer win was negated, Burrows (again with Loesser) was vindicated, making up for the committee's slight, by being formally awarded the Pulitzer for *How to Succeed* (1961). In addition to a modest amount of screenwriting for film and television, Burrows served as a notable Broadway script doctor (e.g., for many years, the phrase "Get me Abe Burrows!" was showbiz code for a script or libretto that needed repair). A failed book adaptation for a 1974 revival of *Good News* was Burrows' last Broadway outing as a librettist. In 1980, Burrows published his memoir, which recounts his mentoring of other comedy writers, such as Woody Allen (a distant cousin). Burroughs continued to direct on Broadway until 1981, when he staged a revival of *Can-Can.*

Arthur Laurents (1917–2011): This playwright/librettist/director/screenwriter was born Arthur Levine and raised in Brooklyn, New York. After graduating from Cornell University, Laurents wrote radio scripts, putting his career on hold when he was drafted into the Army during World War II. Upon completion of his military service, Laurents returned to radio but soon began writing for the theatre. His first play was *Home of the Brave*, a military drama about anti-Semitism, which opened on Broadway in 1945. (Although Laurents rejected his familial religion of Judaism, he identified with his Jewish heritage throughout his life.) During the 1950s, he wrote four more plays: *The Bird Cage*, *The Time of the Cuckoo*, *A Clearing in the Woods*, and *Invitation to a March*. More significant were his contributions to musical theatre during this decade, specifically, his landmark librettos for *West Side Story* and *Gypsy*. During the 1960s, Laurents not only wrote librettos but also began to direct Broadway productions (amazingly, he continued to direct into his 90s). Some of his more notable successes and failures included *I Can Get It for You Wholesale* (as director, he introduced Barbra Streisand to Broadway in a featured role), *Do I Hear a Waltz?* (a disappointing collaboration with Richard Rodgers for which he, as librettist, adapted his own play, *The Time of the Cuckoo*), *Hallelujah, Baby!* (as librettist, he shared the Tony Award for Best Musical, although the show received negative reviews and a negligible box office), *Anyone Can Whistle* (an infamous flop, with a Stephen Sondheim score, for which he was director and librettist). Laurents was also a recognized Hollywood screenwriter, with hits that included *The Way We Were* (1973) and *The Turning Point* (1977), even though he suffered a period of blacklisting during the late '40s and early '50s due to HUAC/FBI investigations and accusations of communism for which he was eventually cleared. Given his mixed record of Broadway successes throughout the '60s and '70s, Laurents reasserted his power and artistry in 1983, winning the Tony Award for Best Director for the original production of *La Cage aux Folles* (only to follow it up, as director/librettist, with the much-publicized 1991 failure of *Nick & Nora*). The new century saw Laurents again lauded as a director, as he mounted critically acclaimed revivals of his own written masterpieces: *Gypsy* (in 2008, starring Patti LuPone) and *West Side Story* (in 2009, employing an ambivalently received bilingual concept, with Spanish translations of some dialogue and lyrics provided by Lin-Manuel Miranda). Toward the end of his life, Laurents wrote two memoirs, published in 2000 and 2009. On May 5, 2011, the estimable Laurents died in Manhattan at age 93. (Laurent's final memoir, *The Rest of the Story*, was published posthumously in 2012.)

Moss Hart (1904–1961): This multi-talented artist was not only a librettist, but also an accomplished director, playwright, screenwriter, actor, and play-doctor. The grandson of impoverish Jewish immigrants, Hart grew up poor in the Bronx. In order to support his family, Hart dropped out of school at 15 and worked various jobs, until lying his way into a position at a theatrical booking office. Even though he made his Broadway debut as an actor (in Eugene O'Neill's *The Emperor Jones*) in 1926, Hart focused on writing. While his first play to be professional produced closed out of town, and his first musical theatre libretto (*Jonica*, 1930) only lasted a month on Broadway, he struck gold when he began to collaborate with the venerable playwright and director George S. Kaufman. Their comedy, *Once in a Lifetime* (1930), was a major hit with audiences, running 406 performances during the Depression. Kaufman and Hart went on to pen the popular hits *You Can't Take It With You* (1936, Pulitzer Prize) and *The Man Who Came to Dinner* (1939), as well as the musical *I'd Rather Be Right* (score by Richard Rodgers and Larry Hart, 1946). Hart would write the librettos to *Face the Music* (score by Irving Berlin, 1932), the ground-breaking *As Thousands Cheer* (score by Berlin, 1933), *Jubilee* (score by Cole Porter, 1935), and the early concept musical *Lady in the Dark* (score by Kurt Weill and Ira Gershwin, 1941), and direct such blockbusters as *My Fair Lady* (1956) and *Camelot* (1960). As an author, Hart had great respect for writers, so when he began to direct, he was known for honoring the work of playwrights and librettists, in contrast to auteur directors who impose their vision on a text.

Howard Lindsay (1889–1968) and Russel Crouse (1893–1966): This writing team, referred to as simply "Lindsay and Crouse" collaborated successfully and prolifically from 1935–62 on a series of Broadway musicals and comedies. Crouse mostly confined his Broadway role to playwright and librettist, while Lindsay started his career as an actor before moving to directing and writing, while continuing to perform on Broadway. In short, Lindsay was featured or starred in almost a dozen Broadway shows from 1917–52 and directed almost two dozen Broadway productions throughout his career. As writers, Lindsay and Crouse's first collaboration came in 1935, when the team, out of necessity, rewrote the libretto for Cole Porter's *Anything* Goes (which Lindsay also directed). The musical became a major hit (despite its haphazard libretto) and is still a canonical favorite, often revived. Lindsay and Crouse subsequently wrote librettos for hit musicals, including Cole Porter's *Red, Hot and Blue*, Irving Berlin's *Call Me Madam*, and Rodgers and Hammerstein's *The Sound of Music*. As nonmusical playwrights, they were equally successful. In 1939 they wrote *Life With Father*, which starred Lindsay and his wife, Dorothy Stickney; the production ran for over seven years to become the longest-running nonmusical play on Broadway. In 1946, the duo was awarded the Pulitzer Prize in Drama for their play *State of the Union*. After writing fifteen Broadway works (seven of which were musicals), their last libretto collaboration was in 1962 for the failed Irving Berlin musical, *Mr. President*. In addition to their own works, Lindsay and Crouse were also called on to doctor numerous flawed Broadway shows written by others. The team also wielded great business clout, producing countless Broadway shows from 1921–60, as well as owning and operating The Hudson Theatre during the 1940s, staging such hit plays as Joseph Kesselring's *Arsenic and Old Lace* (which they also produced), John Van Druten's *The Voice of the Turtle*, and their own *State of the Union*.

Joshua Logan (1908–1988): This librettist/playwright/director/actor was born in Texarkana, Texas, and mostly reared in Mansfield, Louisiana. After high school, he attended Princeton University, where he studied acting but failed to receive his diploma, as he accepted a scholarship to study in Moscow with Konstantin Stanislavsky. After returning to the United States, Logan debuted on Broadway as an actor in 1932, performing in numerous Broadway plays throughout the 1930s. His first major Broadway success as a director came in 1938, when he staged Rodgers and Hart's *I Married an Angel*. Over the next few years, he directed hit musicals such as *Knickerbocker Holiday*, *Charlie's Aunt*, and *By Jupiter*, along with numerous comedies. In 1942, Logan was drafted and served in the Army during World War II. Discharged with the rank of Army Captain, he returned to Broadway and finished the decade by directing a blockbuster musical (*Annie Get Your Gun*) and a hit comedy (*John Loves Mary*). Logan both wrote and directed the popular play *Mister Roberts*, and he co-wrote, co-produced, and directed the landmark musical *South Pacific*, for which he won not only the Tony Award for Best Director of a Musical but also the Pulitzer Prize in Drama, with collaborators Richard Rodgers and Oscar Hammerstein II. In addition to co-producing *South Pacific*, he also produced numerous Broadway works during the '50s, '60s, and '70s. In 1952, Logan co-wrote, co-produced, directed, and created dances for lyricist/composer Harold Rome's *Wish You Were Here*, rewriting much of the musical after a less-than-stellar opening, with the new and improved production selling out for the next year and a half. Two years later, he co-wrote, co-produced, and directed another hit musical with a score by Rome: *Fanny*. At the height of his Broadway career, Logan also worked successfully as a Hollywood director of numerous films (many of which were adaptations of his Broadway productions); they included *Mister Roberts* (a film adaption of his play), *Picnic* (which he originally directed and co-produced on Broadway), *Bus Stop*, *Sayonara*, and *South Pacific*. The last two movies also merited Academy Award nominations for Logan. In the 1960s, he had less success with his direction of musicals, both on Broadway and in film (e.g., the failed stage productions of *All American* and *Mr. President*, as well as disappointing movie adaptations of *Camelot* and *Paint Your Wagon*). In the 1970s, he published two autobiographical and anecdotal books, and he appeared in *Musical Moments*, a revue of his most popular Broadway numbers. Although he stopped writing for

Broadway in the mid-1950s, Logan directed until 1980. His last play was *Horowitz and Mrs. Washington*; he spent his later years teaching theatre at Florida Atlantic University (1983-86).

Joe Masteroff (1919–present): This librettist/playwright/actor was born in Philadelphia. After graduating from Temple University, he served in the United States Air Force during World War II. Afterward, he studied with the American Theatre Wing from 1949–51 and in 1953 made his Broadway debut as an actor in *The Prescott Proposals*. Six years later, Masterhoff wrote his first play, *The Warm Peninsula*, which had a modest Broadway run of 86 performances. In 1963, he wrote his first Broadway libretto, for Bock and Harnick's *She Loves Me*, which garnered him a Tony Award nomination and still stands as a superlative example of fully realized and tightly crafted musical playwriting (Masteroff innovatively wrote the libretto as a stand-alone play prior to the score). Masteroff's next triumph as a librettist came three years later, when Hal Prince acquired the rights to John Van Druten's *I Am a Camera* and Christopher Isherwood's *The Berlin Stories* in order to create a musical, *Cabaret*. As the show's producer/director, Prince replaced original librettist Sandy Dennis with Masterhoff, who supplied a groundbreaking "concept musical" book, which splits time and space between a cabaret chanteuse's personal story and the metatheatrical milieu in which she performs. Due in great part to Masteroff's libretto and Kander and Ebb's score, *Cabaret* won the Tony for Best Musical and ran for 1,165 performances. Masteroff's next and final Broadway project, *70, Girls, 70*, was less successful, closing exactly one month after it opened in 1971. Even though he has all but left Broadway, Masteroff continues to write, having supplied the libretto for an operatic adaptation of Eugene O'Neill's *Desire Under the Elms*, as well as the book and lyrics for the musical *Paramour*, based on Jean Anouilh's *The Waltz of the Toreadors*, performed regionally in 1998.

Joseph Stein (1912–2010): This playwright/librettist was born in New York City, son of Jewish immigrants from Poland. He grew up in the Bronx and graduated in 1935 from City College of New York, then earned a Master's degree in social work from Columbia University in 1937. After spending six years as a psychiatric social worker (1939–45), he began to write comedy for radio personalities such as Jackie Gleason, which led to writing for television. Stein worked on *Your Show of Shows* alongside comic writers such as Mel Brooks, Neil Simon, and Carl Reiner. In 1948, Stein made his Broadway debut, writing sketches with Will Glickman for a revue, *Lend an Ear*. After more revues, the two collaborated on their first book musical in 1955, *Plain and Fancy*, researching the Pennsylvania Dutch culture to create a story of Pennsylvania's Amish communities. The unconventional Broadway show ran for 461 performances and is currently an annually featured production at The Round Barn Theatre at Amish Acres in Nappanee, Indiana (the theatre is now dedicated to Stein). Other popular works by Stein during the '50s included *Mr. Wonderful* (again co-written with Glickman) and *Take Me Along* (nominated for a best musical Tony and co-written with Robert Russell). In 1963, Stein wrote his most popular play, *Enter Laughing*, based on Carl Reiner's comic novel inspired by Reiner's experience of working on *Your Show of Shows*. The next year, Stein had the greatest success of his career, writing the libretto for *Fiddler on the Roof*, for which he earned two Tonys (Best Musical and Author of a Musical), as well as international acclaim. (Stein also wrote the screenplay for the film adaptation.) While Stein had success with later librettos, such as *Zorba* (1968) and *Irene* (1973), he had many more disappointments, such as *The Baker's Wife* (which never made it to Broadway) and Broadway flops *Juno*, *Rags*, *Carmelina*, and *So Long, 174th Street* (a musical version of the play *Enter Laughing*). Many of these works eventually received renewed interest due to revivals by regional theatres, Center *Encores!*, and other Off-Broadway venues, as well as the West End.

Until his death in 2010, Stein continued to write original works, such as the libretto for *All About Us*. With a score by Kander and Ebb, the musical is based on Thornton Wilder's *The Skin of Our Teeth* and premiered at the Westport Country Playhouse in 2007.

Michael Stewart (1924–87): Born Myron Rubin in Manhattan, this librettist, lyricist, and playwright attended Queens College and advanced to Yale School of Drama, graduating in 1953 with a Master of Fine Arts. As with many of his compatriots, he spent the first part of his writing career supplying sketches for Broadway revues during the 1950s, until he turned to television, joining the staff writers for Sid Caesar's program, *Caesar's Hour*. At the start of the 1960s, Stewart turned to Broadway book musicals and became one of the most prolific writers of musical comedies, with a string of hits over the next two decades. (Although Stewart dabbled in playwriting, his plays did not succeed on Broadway and he ultimately concentrated on musical theatre.) Starting with *Bye Bye Birdie* in 1960, for which he wrote the book and won a Tony Award for Best Musical, he provided the librettos for a number of box office and critical successes throughout the decade, including *Carnival!*, *Hello, Dolly!* (winning two more Tonys, one for best musical and one for best author) and *George M!*. Stewart's work during the 1970s and '80s was more uneven; but significantly, he began writing lyrics as well as librettos during these decades. Some successes included *I Love My Wife* (librettist/lyricist), *Barnum* (lyricist), and *42nd Street* (co-librettist). Some box office failures, such as *Mack & Mabel* (librettist) and *The Grand Tour* (co-librettist), still managed to merit a modicum of positive critical notice. Some, however, were out-and-out flops (e.g., 1981's *Bring Back Birdie* and 1985's *Harrigan 'n Hart*). Up until his untimely death at the relatively young age of 63, Stewart stayed active and relevant in the theatre. He won three Tonys, having been nominated eight times, a record of achievement that left the theatre community wondering how many more musicals he could have written if he had only lived longer.

The librettist found his or her voice during the Golden Age, asserting power and dramatic, dramaturgical expertise in the industry. The burgeoning role of the librettist and his or her art in the musical theatre genre during the Age informed and spurred the careers of future artists, furthering the development and sophistication of the modern musical libretto. Artists who have followed in the wake of the Golden Age pioneers include some who have mostly concentrated their talents to the genre, such as the prolific and successful **Peter Stone** (*1776, Sugar, Woman of the Year, My One and Only, The Will Rogers Follies, Titanic, Curtains*, and the 1999 *Annie Get Your Gun* revisal). As the musical moved from the Golden Age into the 1970s, '80s, '90s, and the twenty-first century, the proven and celebrated comedy writer, versed in theatre, film, and/or television, asserted prominence on the Great White Way. The impressive comedic roster includes **Neil Simon** (*Little Me*; *Sweet Charity*; *Promises, Promises*; and *The Goodbye Girl*), **Larry Gelbart** (*A Funny Thing Happened on the Way to the Forum* and *City of Angels*), **Harvey Fierstein** (*La Cage Aux Folles, A Catered Affair, Newsies, and Kinky Boots*), **Mel Brooks** (*All American, The Producers*, and *Young Frankenstein*), and, most recently, **Matt Stone** and **Trey Parker**, with co-writer **Robert Lopez** (*The Book of Mormon*). In addition to comedy, the "serious" playwright has also persisted in making his or her significant mark on the musical theatre genre; examples include **Marsha Norman** (*The Secret Garden, The Red Shoes*, and *The Color Purple*), **Arthur Kopit** (*Nine*), **Tony Kushner** (*Caroline, or Change*), **David Henry Hwang** (co-writer of *Aida* and a new book for the 2002 revival of *Flower Drum Song*), and **Quiara Alegría Hudes** (*In the Heights*). The most prominent of these artists, in terms of musical theatre output and acclaim, is multi-award-winning playwright and librettist **Terrence McNally**, who has authored librettos for seven Broadway book musicals: *The Rink, Kiss of the Spider Woman, Ragtime, The Full Monty,* and *Catch Me If You Can,* winning Tony Awards for both *Kiss of the Spider Woman* and *Ragtime.* Along with the "serious" playwright contingent, there are powerful theatre auteurs who have lent their writing talents to the musical theatre stage, for example, director/producer/conceiver **George C. Wolfe** (*Jelly's Last Jam, Bring in 'Da Noise, Bring in 'Da Funk,* and *The Wild Party*) and director/librettist **James Lapine**, who not only won Tony Awards for his librettos for *Falsettos, Into the Woods,* and *Sunday in the Park with George,* but also the Pulitzer Prize for *Sunday in the Park with George,* continuing in the footsteps of Burrows and Logan. This Pulitzer torch was most recently passed in 2009 to librettist **Brian Yorkey** for his first Broadway foray, *Next to Normal,* signaling that the unique dramatic art of the musical libretto continues to be recognized and awarded in the world of theatre.

Actor Spotlights

Ethel Merman (1909–84)

She was Broadway's favorite diva: a frank, folksy, effervescent star who reigned on the Great White Way for four decades. Her idiosyncratic voice, full of brass and sass, was impossible to forget and became iconic in its own right (George Gershwin famously told her early in her career to never take a voice lesson or let anyone tinker with her natural sound). Merman almost singlehandedly popularized the musical theatre "belt" for women, a forceful, full singing style originating from the torso and chest, as opposed to the lighter, more lyrical soprano technique placed higher in the head. The brazen quality of her voice was matched by her acting style, as she provided the musical theatre world with a new archetype: a female "Johnny" (the straight-talking stock character who has little use for affectation or elitism). Audiences loved Merman, as did composers and lyricists. Cole Porter wrote five musicals for her, citing her as his favorite "voice." Irving Berlin created two hits for her, including the biggest smash of his career, *Annie Get Your Gun*. Much of their appreciation and praise was due to the fact that Merman delivered their melodies forthrightly, and in a pre-amplification age, sang each lyric so it could be heard in the auditorium's last row. She got directly to the heart of the song, delivering lyrics without affected flourish, allowing every word to be understood and the songwriter's sentiments to be channeled through an enthusiastic, extroverted and honest conduit.

Ethel Merman (Annie Oakley), shows *Annie Get Your Gun* co-star Ray Middleton (Frank Butler) an authentic Oakley Winchester rifle backstage, 8/9/1946 © Bettmann/CORBIS

Born Ethel Agnes Zimmerman, Merman was raised in the neighborhood of Astoria, Queens. Although enamored with showbiz and wishing to become a singer, she pragmatically took secretarial classes and worked as a stenographer by day while moonlighting as a singer in New York nightclubs. Eventually she caught the attention of the Gershwins, who cast Merman in their 1930 musical, *Girl Crazy*. Her minor role kept growing as the Gershwins became more excited by her talent. Merman ultimately stopped the show with her rendition of "I Got Rhythm" in which she held a single belted note for sixteen bars (approximately ten seconds), much to the audience's delight and amazement. Afterward, Merman was no longer considered a supporting player; she soon starred in a series of Cole Porter musicals, beginning with 1934's *Anything Goes*, where in the role of Reno Sweeney, she introduced such

Porter standards as "Anything Goes," "You're the Top," and "I Get a Kick Out of You." In the next three decades, she reached new musical theatre heights as she originated canonical roles such as Annie Oakley (*Annie Get Your Gun*) and Sally Adams (*Call Me Madam*), both written especially for her by Berlin. Her Broadway career culminated with her landmark performance in 1959 as Mama Rose in *Gypsy*, her thirteenth original Broadway musical, although she would continue to perform for many more years on stage in revivals and national tours, as well as on television and film. (Although 1964's, *Hello, Dolly!* was written for Merman, she turned it down. She eventually joined the cast in 1970, however, making this the fourteenth Broadway musical written for the "Merm.")

As a true stage and music legend, Merman's voice will be associated with some of the most famous songs in the musical theatre canon, while humorous stories regarding her career have become theatre lore (including one in which she scolded a cast mate for interfering with her performance by trying to "react" to her on stage). Although much of her career occurred prior to the creation of the Tony Awards, she was nominated three times once the awards were in place, winning for 1951's *Call Me Madam* (surprisingly, Merman did not win for *Gypsy*, although it was and still is considered her greatest performance). In 1972, Merman was bestowed a Special Tony Award, for which she thanked the audience in a most "Ethel" fashion, singing selections from some of her past hit performances, "I Got Rhythm," "No Business Like Show Business," and "Everything's Comin' Up Roses," reaffirming her status as one of Broadway's—and America's—musical icons.

Alfred Drake (1914–92)

A leading man in the most traditional sense, Alfred Drake was the very picture of the dashing hero, the witty *bon vivant* and the rakish cad, his rich baritone beautifully serving every musical in which he starred. A multifaceted theatre artist, Drake was a trained singer and actor who felt equally comfortable in a musical comedy (*Kismet*) and a Shakespearean tragedy (*Hamlet*), successfully starring in both on Broadway, while also directing and writing for the stage.

Born Alfred Capurro in the Bronx, he broke into the professional ranks in 1935 as a chorus member in a series of Gilbert and Sullivan operettas at New York City's Adelphi Theatre. At the age of 22, he got his Broadway break as an understudy in 1936's *White Horse Inn* and soon moved into

Alfred Drake (Curly) in surrey with Joan Roberts (Laurey), surrounded by original *Oklahoma!* cast, 1943 © Bettmann/CORBIS

featured roles (Rodgers and Hart's *Babes in Arms*). In 1943, he became part of musical theatre history as he originated the role of Curly in the landmark production of *Oklahoma!*. This was not the last canonical musical in which he would play a lead role. As Fred Graham in 1946's *Kiss Me, Kate*, he was adept at handling the romance and sophistication of Cole Porter's score, and smoothly mastered the satiric comedy, romping through the character songs with panache. Drake also flexed his "classical actor" muscle, believably assuming the role of Petruchio in the play-within-the-musical (*The Taming of the Shrew*). It would be decades before another actor could measure up to Drake's comprehensive ownership of the role. As a Broadway powerhouse, Drake mastered a dozen starring roles (both musical and nonmusical), as well as directing and writing numerous productions. As an actor he was nominated for three Tony Awards, winning Best Actor in a Musical for his portrayal of the rascally poet in *Kismet* (1953). In 1990, shortly before his death, he was awarded a Special Tony Award, honoring him for Excellence in Theatre. Indeed, this "actor's actor" in the musical theatre arena was an exemplar of the Golden Age and its emphasis on the musical play.

Mary Martin (1913–90)

As a leading lady who epitomized the can-do vigor and "cockeyed" optimism of midcentury America, Mary Martin graced the Broadway stage for several decades in roles that ranged from a feisty Navy nurse who overcomes ingrained racism to a boy from Never Never Land who refuses to grow up to a singing postulant who forsakes her vows in order to "follow her dream." Martin's appeal for her many fans was not only her warm voice and musical sensibility, but also her talent for embodying characters who brought hope, grit, humor, and triumph to the stage (along

Mary Martin as Peter Pan, c. 1955 © CORBIS

with a touch of fantasy through her portrayals of Peter Pan and the goddess Venus).

Mary Virginia Martin was born in Weatherford, Texas, where she demonstrated an early gift for music and mimicry. After a failed teen marriage to Benjamin Hagman (which resulted in the birth of her son, television star Larry Hagman), Martin decided to go for broke and pursue a professional performing career. Although she faced more than two years of trial and rejection, especially in Hollywood—where she acquired the nickname of "Audition Mary"—she slowly found minor singing gigs on radio, film, and stage. (An anecdote from her early years entails an audition for Oscar Hammerstein II in which she sang his "Indian Love Call," explaining that he probably wasn't familiar with this "soprano" song. He slyly waited until after the audition to inform her that he had written it.) In a real-life demonstration of the determination and talent that characterized many of her future stage roles, Martin plodded and persevered until she got her big break in 1938 as a featured performer in Cole Porter's *Leave It to Me!*, bringing down the house with her suggestive, tongue-in-cheek rendition of "My Heart Belongs to Daddy." With that song, Martin's star began to rise. (In fact, the performance was so significant that she was later cast to play herself and reprise the number in the 1940 film *Love Thy Neighbor* and 1946's *Night and Day*, the Hollywood biopic of Cole Porter.)

Martin became a true Broadway leading lady in 1943 when she was cast as the eponymous goddess in *One Touch of Venus*, playing a statue come to life while singing a sophisticated Kurt Weill score. Her performance garnered praise and awards; it was followed by a successful stint as Annie Oakley in the national tour of *Annie Get Your Gun*, which was also filmed for a live television broadcast. For her work on various configurations of *Annie Get Your Gun*, she was given a special 1948 Tony Award for "spreading theatre" nationwide. By the end of the 1940s, Martin was a Broadway fixture and would remain so for decades. She originated beloved canonical characters such as Nellie Forbush in *South Pacific*, Peter in *Peter Pan*, and Maria Von Trapp in *The Sound of Music*, winning Tony Awards for all three roles (as well as an Emmy Award for her portrayal of Peter in the 1955 televised version of the musical, a version that would be filmed again in 1956 and 1960). Both *Peter Pan* and *The Sound of Music* were developed especially for her, as was the two-person musical *I Do! I Do!*. At the height of her career, Martin had become a Broadway insider, married to producer Richard Halliday. Their partnership lasted for over thirty years and was instrumental in the development of many of her star vehicles. Although Martin appeared in nine films during her career (all prior to her Broadway reign), she was generally passed over for the movie versions of her signature stage works. According to reports, this did not seem to disturb Martin, who capped her impressive array of theatre awards with the distinction of becoming a 1989 Kennedy Center Honoree. Martin claimed that she was most driven by and dedicated to the immediate and reciprocal affection and energy of *live* theatre. It was a mutually beneficial paradigm; her Broadway fans were similarly invested in her spritely, spirited performances, which are still viewed as highlights of the Golden Age as well as examples of midcentury American positivity.

CHAPTER 6

SWINGING '60S TO THE EARLY '90S: RETHINKING AND REVOLUTIONIZING MUSICAL THEATRE

● ●

During most of the 1960s, it would be tempting to see the musical as hopelessly out of touch with contemporary America. Even with three Broadway blockbusters opening in the same year (1964)—*Fiddler on the Roof*, *Hello, Dolly!*, *Funny Girl*—and the film version of *My Fair Lady* walking away with eight Academy Awards—it could appear that musical theatre's Golden Age had staged its own grand finale as these works neither reflected nor commented on the turmoil of the 1960s. In short, the aforementioned Broadway triumphs were escapist and nostalgic. With the assassinations of President John F. Kennedy (1963), Martin Luther King (1968), Senator Bobby Kennedy (1968), and the escalating war in Viet Nam, the world was a different place from the comparative calm of the 1950s. And in 1964, the Beatles appeared on *The Ed Sullivan Show* for the first time, heralding, with electronic chords, that the British Invasion was in full force and rock 'n' roll was here to stay. As urban centers across the country fell into disrepair, many theaters were abandoned (and left to the wrecking ball); consequently, the road business of touring musicals almost ceased altogether. The Great White Way was also seeing a major shift, as a population and industry of hustlers, hucksters, streetwalkers, drug dealers, and others looking to make a quick buck off of the tourism and spectacle of Times Square soon permeated the district. Financially and artistically, musical theatre—oft termed the "fabulous invalid"—was not in very good shape.

But theatre is nothing if not resilient, given its ephemeral, flexible, adaptable, and ever-shifting nature. And as times were "a-changin'," musical theatre began to reflect the shift, experimenting with novel sounds and exploring revolutionary trends. When *Hair* arrived on Broadway in 1968, the Great White Way finally embraced a musical with songs and sentiments that mirrored some of the headlines of the day. Further, its staging aesthetically placed the work light years away from other musicals playing around Times Square. Then, with the New York premieres of Stephen Sondheim's *Company* (1970), Andrew Lloyd Webber's *Jesus Christ Superstar* (1971), Michael Bennett's *A Chorus Line* (1975), and John Kander, Fred Ebb, and Bob Fosse's *Chicago* (1975), musical theatre saw the emergence of new artists who not only delighted critics but also found audiences for their disparate visions of what musicals could be in a post-Golden-Age era. Throughout the 1960s, '70s, and '80s, experimentation continued as the integrated book musical's dominance was challenged by innovative forms such as the concept musical, the rock opera, the jukebox musical/revue, the dansical, the sung-through musical, and the mega musical. Despite rising ticket prices, theatre attendance began to climb both in New York and on the road. While movie musicals virtually disappeared from the silver screen after *Cabaret* (1972) and *Grease* (1978), the stage musical continued to attract audiences even as it pioneered new forms and structures. Truly, rumors of musical theatre's demise were grossly exaggerated.

Of the many areas explored and developed as a result of the genre's expansion and experimentation during the latter half of the twentieth century, issues of racial, ethnic, and gender disparity/difference were at the forefront. For instance, the "black musical" became a staple on Broadway in various configurations. In many respects, the black musical is a subdivision of the pop/rock musical, featuring music that reflects jazz, blues, gospel, funk, reggae, rap, or Motown, with a libretto that centers upon the struggles, advances, and exploits of African Americans. Importantly, not all creative artists behind works categorized as black musicals have been African Americans. Further, some musicals have been placed in the category because they center upon the African American experience, even if they do not feature the aforementioned music idioms. In short, the category's connective tissue is an attempt to tell a story of race in America (or assert new racial paradigms), placing black characters at the work's forefront. As musical theatre entered the mid-1960s, the black musical slowly became a fixture on Broadway, beginning with *Golden Boy* (1964). With a score by notable composer/lyricist team Charles Strouse and Lee Adams and a book adapted by William Gibson from Clifford Odets' 1937 boxing drama, the musical tells the tale of an African American's struggle to break out of his poor New York City environs to become a professional fighter (the original play's protagonist was Italian American). The signature role was performed to great acclaim by song-and-dance star Sammy Davis, Jr., resulting in a run of 569 performances. Following *Golden Boy*, numerous other musicals arrived on Broadway that addressed issues of race and racism in the United States, with many totally or partially written by black artists. The sleeper hit of the 1970 Broadway season was *Purlie*, an adaptation of the 1961 play *Purlie Victorious*, with music by Gary Geld, lyrics by Peter Udell, and a libretto by Ossie Davis, Philip Rose, and Udell. The musical centers on the exploits of a self-ordained, determined black preacher (Purlie) who outfoxes a bigoted plantation owner in order to buy a church in a rural Georgia town. Purlie not only wins the church, but also a wife in the process; and the show's progressive, positive nature delighted audiences, running for 688 performances. Two years later, the revue *Don't Bother Me, I Can't Cope* (1972), with music and lyrics by Micki Grant, good-naturedly illustrated and even satirized contemporary social problems faced by African Americans, using gospel, rock, calypso, and folk music in its infectious score. *Don't Bother Me* ran for 1,065 performances and was followed by another successful but more serious work: Judd Woldin and Robert Brittan's *Raisin* (1973 / 847 performances). Closely adapted from Lorraine Hansberry's landmark 1969 play, *A Raisin in the Sun*, the musical concerns a black family's internal conflicts and external challenges as they attempt to buy a home in a white neighborhood. On the heels of these works came one of the most popular black musicals of the period: composer/lyricist Charlie Small's *The Wiz* (1975). Riffing on a classic (*The Wizard of Oz*), *The Wiz* provided a unique 1970s take on the iconic story, featuring a book by William F. Brown that included contemporary jargon and a street-smart sensibility, as well as an all-black

cast and a rock, blues, and funk score. Although the work's sight and sound might have been altered, *The Wiz*'s basic story still centers on Dorothy as she teams with the Scarecrow, Tinman, and Lion to find her way home from Oz, seeking help from a bogus Wiz and finding a pathway through self-discovery. The spirited re-envisioning of the work resulted in a four-year run (1,672 performances), although last-minute adjustments and a strong publicity/advertising campaign helped save the production in its early stages, when many had dismissed it as a likely flop. Further, the success of the Broadway musical resulted in a 1978 film version starring entertainment luminaries Diana Ross, Michael Jackson, Lena Horne, and Richard Pryor.

Following *The Wiz*, the black musical continued to draw audiences, yet many were not as successful as their immediate predecessors, e.g., composer/lyricist Alex Bradford's *Your Arms Too Short to Box With God* (1976), Michael Butler's *Reggae* (1980), and Gary Sherman's *Amen Corner* (1983). But *Dreamgirls* (1981)—music by Henry Krieger, book and lyrics by Tom Eyen, and direction/choreography by Michael Bennett—lit up Broadway for years, running for 1,521 performances. Further, when addressing the black musical during the '80s, special mention should be made of *Mama, I Want to Sing!* (1983), an Off-Broadway phenomenon that played the 632-seat Heckscher Theater in Harlem for 2,213 performances. Written by Vy Higginsen, Ken Wydro, and Wesley Naylor, the original production closed after eight years only because of a lease dispute, costing $35,000 but grossing $25 million in its first five years.

During the late 1970s and '80s, the jukebox musical also proved to be a popular format for African American songwriters and performers. Notable examples include *Ain't Misbehavin'* (1978), a celebration of songs by Fats Waller; *Sophisticated Ladies* (1981), showcasing the music of Duke Ellington; and *Black and Blue* (1989), an anthology of songs by African Americans that were popular in Paris between the two world wars. In addition, Broadway saw a non-traditional casting trend by which early musicals were remounted with all-black casts, beginning with the well-received *Hello, Dolly!* revivals (1967 and 1969) that starred Pearl Bailey in a highly acclaimed performance of the title role, as well as less successful all-black revivals of *Guys and Dolls* (1976) and *Oh, Kay!* (1990).

In addition to new racial paradigms on Broadway, musical theatre underwent revolutionary shifts in regard to its portrayals and explorations of gender. As the "swinging '60s" moved into the '70s and '80s, anti-heroines and other nonconventional female characters (including sexual, flawed, powerful, voracious, and/or morally ambivalent women) were spotlighted on Broadway in works such as *Sweet Charity*; *Mame*; *Promises, Promises*; *Applause*; *Follies*; *Chicago*; *The Best Little Whorehouse in Texas*; *Sweeney Todd*; *Evita*; and *Dreamgirls*; while even the convention of the "trouser role" (a prominent male character played by a cross-dressed woman) was resurrected ala composer/lyricist/librettist Rupert Holmes' *The Mystery of Edwin Drood* (1985). Overt feminist points of views were also musicalized, most notably by *I'm Getting My Act Together and Taking It on the Road* (1978), created by lyricist/librettist Gretchen Cryer and composer Nancy Ford. This women's liberation tale of a divorced 39-year-old pop singer (played by Cryer) ran at the Public Theater (and later at Circle in the Square) for 1,165 performances. More than a decade later, another all-female writing team created a more traditional musical: *The Secret Garden* (1991). The critically lauded and popular work features music by Lucy Simon and lyrics by celebrated playwright Marsha Norman, as well as a libretto by Norman based on the classic children's novel. The Broadway production ran for 709 performances and was nominated in six Tony categories, winning three (including one for Norman's book). Another aspect of gender was playfully addressed in 1983 via the drag content and aesthetic of Jerry Herman's *La Cage aux Folles*; in addition, the extremely popular production exemplified a new Broadway openness towards topics once considered outside the mainstream and unfit for the musical stage, i.e., sexual orientation.

But *La Cage* was just the latest in a long line of musicals containing subject matter that bucked the predominantly traditional character and content of musical theatre—a trend ignited by the genre's move into the Age of Aquarius. *Hair* (1968) and its rock musical contemporaries (*Jesus Christ Superstar* and *Two Gentlemen of Verona*) set the stage for a new musical theatre era that questioned and challenged conventional mores and exploited a mischievous spirit, exploring previously taboo topics. In addition, sex itself became a touchstone for the modern musical revolution. Along with transgressive rock musicals,

the era saw sex-centered Broadway works with more conventional scores, e.g., the wife-swapping *I Love My Wife* (1977). Of special note was the phenomenon of *Oh! Calcutta!* (1969), billed as an "erotic entertainment revue" due to its all-nude ensemble and sketches by various writers (e.g., Sam Shepard, John Lennon, and Samuel Beckett) that dealt with hot-button sexual issues such as masturbation and fetishism. Multiple composers contributed to *Oh! Calcutta!*'s score; and the show became a Broadway tourist sensation, running for 1,314 performances. Providing another take on rebellion, sex, and rock 'n' roll was one of the biggest hits of the era: *Grease* (1972), co-created by writing/composing partners Jim Jacobs and Warren Casey. The musical places cultural and sexual revolution in a time machine, dealing frankly and raunchily with sex, class, and teen angst in the codified 1950s, while also contrarily and satirically suggesting that conformity may prove more advantageous than an empty posture of rebellion when pursuing one's heart's desire. The satirized romance between a greaser (Danny Zuko) and a virgin (Sandy Dumbrowski) is set at fictional Rydell High School in 1959 and is accompanied by a nostalgic doo-wop and early rock 'n' roll score that counters some of the more vulgar and raw elements of the book (today, alternative sanitized versions of the musical are available). *Grease* was first performed as a five-hour amateur production in 1971 in a Chicago theater located in an old trolley barn. From there, it moved to Off-Broadway and, ultimately, to Broadway's Broadhurst Theatre in 1972 (and then the Royale), running for 3,388 performances and earning the title of longest running Broadway show until it was surpassed by *A Chorus Line*. Today, the "little cult musical that could" still stands as Broadway's fourteenth longest-running show and, more importantly, has become iconic in American pop culture, due in great part to its wildly successful screen version in 1978, starring John Travolta and Olivia Newton-John, as well as two popular revivals in 1994 and 2007.

As evidenced by the extremely profitable run of *Grease*, only to be topped by *A Chorus Line* (6,137 performances), which was then surpassed by *Cats* (7,485 performances), the last few decades of the twentieth century saw the bar increasingly raise in regards to the run of a musical, as well as the cost and profit motive. In this respect, the business of theatre and, therefore, the producer/s became ever more crucial in the overall creation and implementation of a Broadway show. As costs to mount a new musical increased, producers, beginning in the 1960s, started to experiment with often bold strategies in order to secure a profit from their ventures. Celebrity casting became a major marketing tool as producers not only aimed to get patrons to buy a ticket once, but to create reasons for them to return. By showcasing a succession of wildly divergent stars in a long-running musical's main roles (instead of lesser known replacements, as had once been the norm), producers also tried to attract different demographics to the show. A pioneer in this respect was producer David Merrick as he employed celebrity replacements for Carol Channing in *Hello, Dolly!*. Merrick's alternate star roster included Ginger Rogers, Martha Rae, Betty Grable, Bibi Osterwald, Phyllis Diller, Ethel Merman, as well as Pearl Bailey in an all-black version of the show. Other modern-era business exploits and experiments were even more innovative and unconventional. For example, once composer Andrew Lloyd Webber assumed the role of producer, he sought to eliminate the backer's audition and became the first to sell shares of his production company (Really Useful Group) on the stock exchange, inviting investors to gamble on his future works. And as part of the new producing model, advertising also changed radically. Recognizing that the primary strength of *Pippin* (1972) was Bob Fosse's choreography, producer Stuart Ostrow created the first television commercial to feature clips of an actual Broadway production. Running 1,944 performances, *Pippin* owed a great deal of its longevity to this commercial. Further, in the 1980s, "branding" and the exploitation of marketing logos began to be instigated and promoted by mega-producer Cameron Mackintosh, as well as Really Useful Group (Webber). Lastly, realizing the strong economic impact of live theatre in New York City, the New York State Department of Commerce launched the "I Love New York" commercials in 1978. Promoting Broadway as a must-see tourist attraction, these commercials not only increased audience attendance but are also credited with assisting the economic recovery of New York City in the 1980s. And those who journeyed to Broadway were also made aware of the Off-Broadway scene; for in the late 1960s, this district and producing entity became vital to the art and industry of musical theatre. *Hair* and *A Chorus Line* got their starts in Off-Broadway workshops and experimental venues before becoming Broadway smashes. Other hits became almost exclusively associated with Off-Broadway, ultimately becoming canonical classics, e.g., 1982's *Little Shop of Horrors* (which ran for 2,209 performances Off-Broadway, only to see a disappointing run on Broadway in 2003) and *The Fantasticks* (which has never been staged on Broadway but its original Off-Broadway run, beginning in 1960, lasted 42 years and 17,162 performances, still holding the record for the world's longest running musical). All in all, during the post-Golden Age, musical theatre broke barriers and promoted diversity in areas that included race, gender, business, geography, and genre. One might say that the cultural/socioeconomic revolution had finally reached Broadway, with reverberations reaching far into the future.

JOHN KANDER AND FRED EBB

In the 1960s and early '70s, the groundbreaking concept musical was making waves on Broadway; and one songwriting team—composer John Kander and lyricist/librettist Fred Ebb—not only rode the wave, but helped usher in the new era, eventually creating scores for some of the most influential, innovative, and audacious concept musicals in American musical theatre. Kander and Ebb are distinguished by their experiments with form and their musical treatments of cutting-edge content as well as by their close and long-lasting relationship. Rising to prominence at a time when the musical theatre industry was becoming fragmented, they were a throwback to the tradition of the Gershwins, Rodgers and Hart, Rodgers and Hammerstein, and Comden and Green, that is, close-knit teams who loved working together (although, one can also see current examples of this writing model, for example, Marc Shaiman and Scott Whitman, or Trey Parker and Matt Stone). Kander and Ebb's collaboration was fruitful, resulting in seventeen musicals, written over forty years, as well as scores for television and films, including *New York, New York*, which introduced a theme song that has become the city's unofficial anthem. For their efforts, the pair won numerous Tony, Emmy, and Grammy awards. Their notable career was one of submerging their own identities to write differently and specifically for each of their musicals. Kander and Ebb's sound and style may not be easy to recognize at first hearing (although Kander has often been deemed the "king of the vamp"); but their meticulous attention and dramatic prowess at musically creating some of the most unique "worlds" in the musical theatre canon is indisputable.

John Harold Kander may have composed one of New York City's most iconic themes, but he was a transplant to the city. Born in Kansas City to parents Bernice and Harold Kander, on March 18, 1927, John was a Midwesterner who did not hit New York until he was in his 20s, attending Columbia University (after Oberlin College) where in 1953 he received a Master's in music. As a highly trained musician/composer, he spent nine years learning the theatre ropes and making important Broadway connections. This included lucking into a job as a substitute rehearsal pianist for *West Side Story*, which led to his playing for the original *Gypsy* auditions. There, he met and impressed Jerome Robbins, who suggested that Kander also write

John Kander and Fred Ebb with Chita Rivera and Liza Minnelli at rehearsal for *The Rink*, December 1983 © Bettmann/CORBIS

the dance arrangements for the show. The assignment was followed by another job as dance arranger for *Irma la Douce* (1960). Having found his Broadway footing, Kander soon teamed with co-librettists James and William Goldman to write *A Family Affair* in 1962. For the show, Kander not only composed the music but also shared lyricist duties with the Goldmans. The production, originally directed by Harold Prince (his first Broadway directing assignment), only lasted sixty-five performances; but it was long enough for Kander to garner some positive notice from formidable critics and contemporaries (including Prince). At the same time, he was introduced to his soon-to-be lifelong writing partner, Fred Ebb, by their mutual publisher, Tommy Valando—an auspicious introduction, to be sure.

Fred Ebb, unlike Kander, was a native New Yorker, having been born in Manhattan on April 8, 1932, to Jewish parents, Anna Evelyn and Harry Ebb. While attending New York University, he worked odd jobs, including stints as a baby-shoe-bronzer and a trucker's assistant. Graduating in 1953 with a Bachelor's in English literature, he—like Kander—progressed to Columbia University, earning his Master's. Before working with Kander, Ebb had some success with early collaborators such as Paul Klein, his first theatrical songwriting partner. The team wrote a number of nightclub songs that were declared fresh and comic. He also collaborated with lyricists such as Norman Leyden and Phil Springer on pop songs that were recorded by several notable artists (e.g., Springer/Ebb's "Heartbroken" was recorded by Judy Garland in 1953). In the 1960s, Ebb continued to write material for theatrical revues, including a number of songs with composer Norman Martin. In fact, Ebb collaborated with both Martin and early partner Klein (as well as a young Jerry

Herman) to supply numbers for the modest Broadway revue *From A to Z* (1960). In 1962, Ebb teamed with Kander; and in a modern Tin-Pan-Alley fashion, the two immediately started cranking out tunes, hoping to have one or two published and recorded. They didn't have to wait long: their first song, "My Coloring Book" (1962), became a long-running hit record for Sandy Stewart. The song was then recorded by a young Barbra Streisand, who was also responsible for the success of Kander/Ebb's second published song, "I Don't Care Much," adding the atmospheric, torchy number to her repertoire. Beginning with the early Streisand connection, Kander and Ebb—like Jule Styne—were adept at writing songs and scores for specific voices and the stylized talents of musical or theatrical stars—especially women—who became forever associated with iconic Kander/Ebb tunes. One such star, whose career has often been linked to Kander and Ebb, is Liza Minnelli. In 1965, when she was 19 years old, Minnelli joined the duo for their first of many Broadway musicals together: *Flora, The Red Menace*.

It was not surprising that Kander and Ebb moved directly from writing pop songs to musical scores, for both artists had been drawn to the musical theatre at early ages, aspiring to Broadway careers. *Flora, the Red Menace*, their first collaboration that made it to Broadway after a failed attempt with a work titled *Golden Gate*, was a disappointment for the duo, although it did make a star out of the teen-aged Minnelli. The whimsical satire was produced by Hal Prince (who recommended Kander and Ebb for the job) and directed by George Abbott. Its book, by Abbott and Robert Russell, depicts the adventures of a sassy wannabe fashion designer, Flora, who is a bohemian free spirit, befriending like-minded artists during the Great Depression. Conflict ensues when she finally lands a much-needed job and must decide between her professional ambition and her personal ideals, both of which are complicated by her burgeoning romance with an avowed Communist. Although it had become "safe" to satirize the Red Scare and McCarthyism in the mid-1960s, *Flora, the Red Menace* failed to connect with audiences. The show opened at the Alvin Theatre on May 11, 1965, and closed after eighty-seven performances. Minnelli, on the other hand, delighted both audiences and critics, winning a Tony Award for her lead performance, the youngest recipient of the award to that time.

In addition to the close relationship between Kander/Ebb and Minnelli that began with *Flora*, the songwriting duo saw another positive association grow as a result of the show, that with wunderkind producer/director Hal Prince. In a crucial development, given his earlier experience with Kander/Ebb, Prince was responsible for signing the team to write the songs for *Cabaret* (1966), which he produced and directed. The show would change the lives of the duo, as well as the musical theatre genre. Freely adapted by librettist Joe Masteroff from Christopher Isherwood's *Berlin Stories* (based on Isherwood's own experiences in Berlin in the early 1930s) and John Van Druten's play adaptation, *I Am a Camera* (1951), *Cabaret* is a concept musical (although the term "concept musical" was not yet coined in '66). Set in 1931 Berlin, the work metaphorically and metatheatrically explores the decadence and decline of the Weimar Republic as the National Socialist Party (Nazis) begins its rise to power. As seen through the microcosm of a cabaret—the Kit Kat Klub—the musical exploits metatheatre on several levels, using overtly presentational numbers inside the club to reflect and comment on events in the outside world. Such events include a futile affair between a self-absorbed, self-destructive Kit Kat Klub performer, Sally Bowles, and a disillusioned American writer, Cliff, as well as an ill-fated romance between a German landlady and a Jewish fruit seller. The Broadway production jarred audiences with its dramatic structure that includes abrupt shifts between book scenes and the garish cabaret numbers as well as its dark content. The show also titillates with a Kander and Ebb score rooted in place and time, evoking musical forms, styles, and constructs such as the vamping "oompah" of the German drinking song, the torchy ballad of the chanteuse, the naughty satire of the Weimar cabarets, the waltz of popular music, and the assertive march time of Germanic folk tunes. Given the score's specificity and referential nature, it is a major achievement that the title song [see fig. 6.1] became a takeaway hit and an American song standard. As a result of its many merits, *Cabaret* won eight Tony Awards, including Best Musical and Best Score for Kander and Ebb, and ran for a phenomenal 1,165 performances.

After *Cabaret*, Kander and Ebb returned to the more traditional book musical with *The Happy Time* (1968). This coming-of-age musical was adapted from Robert Fontaine's 1945 novel of the same name and a 1950 dramatization by Samuel Taylor. Its tender and nostalgic libretto, by N. Richard Nash, features a young French-Canadian boy who wants to run off and see the world with his flamboyant uncle, who is visiting the boy's family. Despite the folk-inspired and integrated score by Kander and Ebb, the Broadway production lasted less than a year (286 performances). In the same Broadway season and seemingly without taking a breath, Kander and Ebb premiered another musical: *Zorba* (1968). The show is often framed as a Greek *Fiddler on the Roof*, partly because its book was supplied by *Fiddler*'s librettist, Joseph Stein, and the show itself was developed by many of *Fiddler*'s original production team members (including producer Harold Prince). Stein adapted the libretto from a Nikos Kazantzakis novel, *Zorba the Greek* (1952), as well as its same-titled 1964 film version. It focuses on an aging, larger-than-life Greek villager, Zorba, and his evolving relationship with a young American fellow who has inherited an abandoned mine on Crete. Although the robust, earthy nature of the title character contains vestiges of *Fiddler*'s Tevye, the village in which Zorba lives is a darker, more sinister place than Anatevka. The plot includes acts of suicide and a murder by vengeful Crete villagers; while the inherited mine, after setting off such tragedies, is found to be inoperable. On a brighter note, Kander and Ebb's score contains a spirited, ethnic sound that reflects celebratory Greek music and folk life ("Y'assou" and "No Big Boom-Boom"), while balancing the bluster with moments of tenderness ("Happy Birthday"). In addition to producing *Zorba*, Harold Prince served as the production's director and was credited with exploiting the show's "concept musical" aspect. The musical begins as a tale told by a group of entertainers (a Leader and singers) in a café, who then periodically interrupt the linear book action with sung commentary. Upon its debut, *Zorba* was nominated for, but did not win, the Tony Award for Best Musical, while running 305 performances (a 1983 Broadway revival did a little better, running for 362 performances).

Kander and Ebb's modest success with *Zorba* was followed by the failure of *70, Girls, 70* in 1971. Based on a play by Peter Coke, *Breath of Spring* (1958), and adapted by Ebb, Norman L. Martin, and Joe Masteroff, the plot concerns a group of wily old-timers who find their Upper West Side retirement hotel in danger of being sold to developers. They proceed to steal furs from New York City stores to resell them and use the proceeds to buy the hotel themselves. In addition to its cast of Broadway veterans (one of which, David Burns, died during the Philadelphia try-outs), the original production also boasted a Kander and Ebb score that affectionately referenced the yesteryear music styles of Tin Pan Alley, while evoking a senior citizen point of view (e.g., "Coffee in a Cardboard Cup"). The show did not click with audiences and closed after a measly thirty-five performances. Although *70, Girls, 70* was a disappointment for the pair, the '70s proved to be happy times for one Kander/Ebb "girl," Liza Minnelli. In 1972, Ebb wrote the program for a televised concert special for Minnelli, *Liza with a Z*, which featured original songs by Kander and Ebb. For their effort, the duo won an Emmy Award. Even before this television achievement, Kander and Ebb had begun work on the Academy Award–winning 1972 film version of *Cabaret*, directed by Bob Fosse (who also directed and choreographed *Liza with a Z*). The story was significantly changed for the film (with the romance between the landlady and fruit peddler omitted). This meant that Kander and Ebb had to contribute new songs for the movie, which starred Minnelli, who won an Academy Award for her portrayal of Sally Bowles. And in 1974, Kander and Ebb contributed to *Liza*, a Broadway concert for Minnelli.

One year later, the team wrote the score for the musical film *Funny Lady*, an unsuccessful sequel to the earlier smash hit, *Funny Girl* (both of which starred Barbra Streisand). Although Kander and Ebb's work on *Funny Lady* was not particularly notable, their score for the Broadway musical *Chicago* that same year is considered to be one of their masterpieces. This highly positive view of *Chicago* was a few decades in the making, however, for the show had a mixed reception in 1975 due to its concept-musical format, biting tone, theme, and alienating performance style. The songwriters reteamed with director/choreographer Fosse, while Ebb also worked as a co-librettist (with Fosse) to fashion an ahead-of-its-time book in which a murderess, Roxie Hart, exploits criminal celebrity in hopes of attaining vaudeville stardom. The show starred Broadway song-and-dance divas Gwen Verdon and Chita Rivera (who would soon become another Kander/Ebb favorite). The creators decided to have all the musical numbers presented as overtly presentational and stylized vaudevillian turns by the performers. Thus, Kander and Ebb created musical numbers that referenced specific acts, stars, and conventions of the vaudeville stage, including a "razzle-dazzle" number, as well as a vamping burlesque turn, a "sad clown" soliloquy, a soft-shoe shuffle, a "sister" specialty act, a ventriloquist bit, and numerous sardonic character numbers. The musical may have been beat out of every one of its ten Tony Award nominations (mostly by the phenomenon of the season, *A Chorus Line*), but it still ran for more than two years. And although rumors had circulated regarding a Fosse-directed film, the show did not seriously resurface until its 1996 Broadway revival (which is still playing after more than 7,000 performances), while the film version was produced in 2002 and won the Academy Award for Best Picture, igniting hopes for a resurgence of the movie musical.

Chicago exemplifies a Kander/Ebb show in that it contains several features that define the team's work. First, along with highlighting stars, a Kander/Ebb musical often allows its director to shine (e.g., Prince and Fosse). As Kander and Ebb often disappeared into their works, they created shows that were, and remain, "directors' mediums." This is especially so in the case of the concept musical, which is more open than a linear book musical, allowing for signature interpretation and staging by the director, bringing him or her to the forefront of the production. Above and beyond the power of the director, however, is the power of the Kander/Ebb score, as it dictates overall tone, atmosphere, and theatricality. In short, Kander/Ebb scores are not always integrated but they are always dramatic, facilitating or commenting on the action while providing authentic-feeling musical evocations of place and time. A final signpost of a Kander/Ebb work is its protagonist, who is not always likable and is often flawed, but is, nonetheless, a survivor. And to survive, Kander/Ebb characters frequently have self-knowledge. They may sometimes appear cynical and manipulative, but when fighting to win in a dark world, the characters are almost forced to play the game in unprincipled, immoral ways.

After *Chicago*, Kander and Ebb created another musical tailored specifically for Minnelli. Previously, the team had written the score for the unsuccessful film *New York, New York*, directed by Martin Scorsese and starring Minnelli (while generating possibly their best-known song). Wishing to work with Scorsese and Minnelli again, they wrote *The Act* (1977), a musical about a fading film star and her attempt to reinvent herself as a Las Vegas nightclub performer. In truth, the show, with a book by George Furth, was an excuse for

Minnelli to perform one lavish Vegas-style production number after another. The production was directed by Scorsese in his only Broadway foray, although he had to be replaced during previews by seasoned director/choreographer Gower Champion. The score was not notable, generating no standout songs, but audiences loved Minnelli and were not only willing to pay $25 a ticket (a new high for ticket prices), but were also amenable to the fact that she had to prerecord some of the numbers, due to the strenuous dance sequences (another first for Broadway). The show ran for just under ten months, and Minnelli won another Tony Award.

Kander and Ebb's next Broadway musical, *Woman of the Year* (1981), was another vehicle for another diva, movie star Lauren Bacall. In this romantic battle of the sexes, librettist Peter Stone updated the 1942 movie of the same name to feature a female television news personality who feuds with a male cartoonist, demeaning his profession while he lampoons her in his cartoon. Ultimately, the feud turns to love, then marriage, then more feuding, then a resolve to work on the marriage. Told in flashback, the show features a wry and pleasing score (tailored to Bacall's limited vocal range), with standout comic numbers such as the "The Grass Is Always Greener." For their work, Kander and Ebb won their second Tony Award for Best Score, and audiences flocked to see the show, which ran for 770 performances. Regarding the duo's subsequent Broadway foray and tenth collaboration, *The Rink* (1984), they not only wrote another star vehicle but made it a two-for-one, creating a musical that co-starred Liza Minnelli and Chita Rivera. The book was written by award-winning playwright/librettist Terrence McNally and centers on a mother, Anna, and her prodigal daughter, Angel. Anna owns a broken-down roller skating rink on a seaside boardwalk that she plans to sell to developers. A restless and emotionally lost Angel has returned home, searching for answers by reconnecting with her past, represented by the rink. As the mother and daughter work to repair their relationship and move forward with their own lives, a series of flashbacks and revelations set the stage for each woman's emotional growth and catharsis. Kander and Ebb felt that the character-driven score was one of their most dramatically effective and versatile. For example, at the top of the show, Angel sings of her current detachment and yearnings in the confessional, up-tempo waltz "Colored Lights," then later finds a moment of reconnection with Anna as the two women share the conversational duet

"The Apple Doesn't Fall (Very Far from the Tree)." Critics were not as fond of the show as its songwriters, and negative reviews trumped the show's star power. When *The Rink* closed after 204 performances, Kander and Ebb were crushed, taking the harsh criticism of the show personally and feeling as though they had let down their "best friends" (Rivera and Minnelli). They would not create another musical for nine years.

In 1991, the revue *And the World Goes 'Round* opened Off-Broadway and ran for 408 performances, reminding audiences of the genius and theatrical potency of Kander and Ebb. The production, an eclectic compilation of Kander/Ebb songs, was conceived by director Scott Ellis, choreographer Susan Stroman, and librettist David Thompson. The numbers were pulled from past works, with some being tender, some dramatic, some pure showbiz, and some just outright funny (the current, revised version features more up-tempo numbers than ballads). Although it has never played Broadway, the revue is a regional and community theatre favorite.

Kander and Ebb triumphantly reemerged on Broadway in 1993 with their musical adaptation of *Kiss of the Spider Woman*. The production reunited them with one of their favorite stars, Chita Rivera, as well as their longtime collaborator/director Prince and playwright McNally (in its pre-Broadway configuration, Susan Stroman was connected to the project as well). Regardless of the mutual admiration and history among production team members, the show went through an arduous development process, not surprising, given its edgy and unconventional subject matter and concept. First it appeared as a workshop production at State University of New York at Purchase in 1990, where it received tepid reviews. Nonetheless, it piqued the interest of Canadian mega producer Garth Drabinsky, whose company, Livent, in 1992 produced the show in Toronto. This version, directed by Prince, featured the main cast and the content and format that would later debut on Broadway. It would enjoy a Broadway run of more than two years, while winning Kander and Ebb another Tony Award for Best Original Score.

McNally's libretto for *Kiss of the Spider Woman* is an adaption of the 1976 novel by Manuel Puig (and its 1985 film version). It tells the tale of a transgendered, gay window dresser, Molina, who has suffered three years' imprisonment under military rule in an unnamed Latin-American country, for having "corrupted" a youth. He finds fantastical escape, however, through his reoccurring visions of Aurora, his favorite star of numerous B movies, whose many roles include the Spider Woman, a seductress who kills men with a kiss. Given this plot point, Aurora (originally played by Rivera) often materializes and interrupts the action on stage with theatrical song-and-dance numbers that comment on themes and events that have happened or are yet to come. The crux of the musical is the relationship that develops between Molina and his new cellmate, a revolutionary named Valentin. Molina falls in love with Valentin, and Valentin disgustedly rejects Molina's attentions at the onset. More than once Molina nurses a tortured and even poisoned Valentin back to health in their cell, sacrificing his own wellbeing for the hard-shelled dissident. Soon, the two men develop a sexual relationship. When Molina is given a brief furlough, Valentin persuades Molina to make some phone calls for him. When caught by the military police, Molina, threatened with death, must name the operatives he called for Valentin. Molina not only refuses but proclaims his love to Valentin and is shot dead. In a surreal final scene, the figure of Aurora comes to Molina, bestowing her final kiss. The Broadway version, directed by Prince and choreographed by Vincent Paterson and Rob Marshall, opened on Broadway on May 3, 1993, only closing after an impressive 904 performances, despite an initial negative review from *The New York Times*. And although there were no stand-alone or breakout hits by Kander and Ebb, their score was atmospheric and dramatic, moving between tender, confessional moments to expressions of angst and anger, often interrupted by razzle-dazzle showbiz and surrealism (e.g., "Where You Are" and "Morphine Tango"). In the end, the *Times* was outvoted, for not only did Kander and Ebb win a Tony for their work, but the musical itself won seven Tony Awards, including one for Best Musical. Further, *Kiss of the Spider Woman* was eventually produced worldwide, including a Spanish-speaking version that played in Buenos Aires (a major feat, given its subject matter).

The team's last original work to reach Broadway during Ebb's lifetime was *Steel Pier*, which opened in 1997. Given the pedigree of the production team (Kander and Ebb, as well as *World Goes 'Round* director Ellis and choreographer Stroman), there were high expectations for the show, but the results were disappointing. Combining a linear book format with a fanciful premise,

David Thompson's libretto concerns a dance marathon set in 1933. And although there are subplots with other dance contestants, the plot centers on a dancer, Rita Racine, who has once again been positioned as a publicity "ringer" by her unscrupulous husband and marathon manager. In this instance, however, she is forced to partner with a novice who (little does she know) is a pilot who had originally won a raffled dance with her in better times, but then suffered a fatal plane crash and has been granted an afterlife opportunity at having his wish fulfilled. In the end, Rita falls for her unearthly partner who, in his final act, provides her with the strength to move beyond the dance marathons and her destructive marriage. The show exploits a metatheatrical structure and offers an invitation, as with *Cabaret*, to dance away one's demons and realize one's dreams at the "Steel Pier" (the show's title song). Kander and Ebb provided a score rich in period Tin Pan Alley flavor. The satirical and affectionate pastiche of a score contains driving ballads, syncopated up-tempo numbers, comic novelty songs, tender duets, and all-out production numbers. Opening on Broadway on April 24, 1997, *Steel Pier* received mixed reviews. Most critics faulted the book but praised the performances (the cast included Broadway luminaries and soon-to-be luminaries such as Karen Ziemba, Debra Monk, and Kristin Chenoweth), as well as the nostalgic and dance-heavy score by Kander and Ebb. Running for only 76 performances, the show was, surprisingly, nominated for 11 Tonys; unsurprisingly, it won none.

During the 1990s, Kander and Ebb were also busy creating musicals that were developed and workshopped outside New York City, being staged, with some notoriety, by regional theatres at the beginning of the twenty-first century. *Over & Over*, an adaptation of Thornton Wilder's play *The Skin of Our Teeth* (1942), debuted at the Signature Theatre in Arlington, Virginia in 1999 and was revamped for a 2007 staging by the Westport Country Playhouse under the title *All of Us*. *The Visit*, a musical adaptation of the 1956 expressionist play by Friedrich Dürrenmatt, enjoyed a positive reception when presented by the Goodman Theatre in Chicago in 2001, later playing at the Signature in Arlington in 2008 (both productions starred Chita Rivera). Due to the buzz created by these Kander/Ebb musical adaptations, hopes still exist that they can be further refined and reach a wider audience, possibly via a New York venue. The fact that such works would

debut on Broadway posthumously for Ebb would not be unusual; for the two most recent critically praised Broadway musicals by Kander and Ebb did not premiere until after Ebb's death on September 11, 2004. They are *Curtains* (2007) and *The Scottsboro Boys* (2010).

When Ebb died of a heart attack at his home in New York City at age 76, he and Kander were working on a new musical titled *Curtains*, subtitled "A Backstage Murder Mystery Musical Comedy." Developmentally, the show was hindered and haunted by the death of not only Ebb, but other initial collaborators; it lost its conceiver and original librettist, Peter Stone, who died in 2003 and was replaced by Rupert Holmes (who supplied new lyrics where necessary after Ebb's death). The show's orchestrator, Michael Gibson, died while the project was under way. Thus, it is darkly ironic that the plot of this musical comedy—a send-up of backstage musicals and murder mysteries—centers on death. *Curtains'* action, set in Boston in 1959, unfolds when an untalented star of a dismal musical takes her curtain call on opening night only to be murdered instead of applauded (or, more likely, booed). One police detective (and musical theatre fan) takes the case, unraveling the mystery, finding the murderer, and rescuing the show, all the while risking his own neck and finding romance. *Curtains'* musical theatre setting provided an opportunity for delightful metatheatrical numbers (which, by this time, had become a signature aspect of a Kander/Ebb show), although the production was more of a traditional book musical (as opposed to "concept") than many in the Kander/Ebb oeuvre. After its 2006 world premiere in Los Angeles to mixed but encouraging reviews, *Curtains* opened on Broadway (directed by Scott Ellis) in March 2007 and ran through June 2008. Mixed reviews persisted, but the musical garnered eight Tony Award nominations, with David Hyde Pierce, as the detective, winning the award for Best Performance by an Actor in a Musical.

In 2007, the Drama Desk honored Kander and the late Ebb with a special award for their forty-two years of contributions to and advancement of the art of musical theater. Posthumous awards are commonplace in the musical theatre world, but posthumous original productions, debuting to great critical acclaim on Broadway, are rare. But in 2010, Broadway saw the premiere of another controversial and innovative concept musical by Kander and Ebb (six years after his death): *The*

Scottsboro Boys. With a book by David Thompson, this musical dramatizes the 1931 real-life succession of trials, convictions, reversals, and retrials of nine black teenagers who were falsely accused of gang-raping two white girls on the Southern Railroad freight train run from Chattanooga to Memphis. For two decades, the Scottsboro Boys' struggle for justice symbolized a culture a systemic racist persecution in America, while becoming a cause célèbre for civil rights activists and a nightmare for the young men accused and incarcerated. The musical was eight years in the making. In 2002, Stroman reunited with Thompson, Kander, and Ebb as the team began looking to develop a new "American" musical. After researching famous American trials, they arrived at the "Scottsboro Boys" tragedy and felt compelled to tell the story. After Ebb's death in 2004, the work was put on hold; but in 2008 Kander appealed to Stroman and Thompson to revisit the project. To facilitate the production, Kander supplied lyrics in Ebb's place where necessary. To provide further social critique to the content, the creators framed the musical as a minstrel show, adhering to the archaically codified format while including a cast of all African Americans, save one Caucasian in the symbolic role of "Mr. Interlocutor." As a result, the musical uses the music styles and entertainment forms of America's past to provide salient commentary and point a possible way forward. At its Broadway opening on October 31, 2010, the show's resurrection of the minstrel show as its framework caused controversy and some audience discomfort. Yet no one could deny the score's energy and effectiveness, as well as the vigor of Stroman's choreography and direction. Most theatre critics praised the production and despite closing on December 12, 2010, after only 49 performances (and a petition drive to keep it open), *The Scottsboro Boys* was nominated for twelve Tony Award nominations, including one for Best Musical, but failed to win any (possibly a result of having closed before the voting and having the smash hit *The Book of Mormon* open in the same season). Regardless, the musical again demonstrated the audacity and innovation of Kander and Ebb, providing a fitting farewell to one of the most significant songwriting teams of the American musical theatre, a duo who creatively exploited past constructs, musical styles, and narratives to, paradoxically, revolutionize the genre, moving it forward into the twenty-first century.

Figure 6.1

CABARET

Music by John Kander; Lyrics by Fred Ebb (1966)

What good is sitting alone in your room?
Come, hear the music play.
Life is a cabaret, old chum,
Come to the cabaret.

Put down the knitting, the book and the broom.
Time for a holiday.
Life is a cabaret, old chum,
Come to the cabaret.

Come taste the wine,
Come hear the band.
Come blow a horn, start celebrating;
Right this way, your table's waiting.

No use permitting some prophet of doom –
To wipe ev'ry smile away.
Life is a cabaret, ole chum,
Come to the cabaret!

I used to have a girlfriend known as Elsie,
With whom I shared four sordid rooms in Chelsea.
She wasn't what you'd call a blushing flower.
As a matter of fact she rented by the hour.

The day she died the neighbors came to snicker:
"Well, that's what comes of too much pills and liquor."
But when I saw her laid out like a Queen,
She was the happiest corpse I'd ever seen.

I think of Elsie to this very day.
I'd remember how she'd turn to me and say:
"What good is sitting alone in your room?
Come hear the music play.
Life is a cabaret, old chum,
Come to the Cabaret.

Put down the knitting, the book and the broom.
Time for a holiday.
Life is a cabaret, old chum,
Come to the cabaret."

And as for me, as for me,
I made my mind up, back in Chelsea,
When I go I'm going like Elsie.

Start by admitting, from cradle to tomb –
Isn't that long a stay.
Life is a cabaret, old chum,
Only a cabaret, old chum,
And I love a cabaret.

FEATURED PRODUCTION: *Cabaret* (1966)

Music by John Kander; Lyrics by Fred Ebb; Book by Joe Masteroff

Original Broadway Run: Opened October 18, 1966; Broadhurst Theatre; 1,165 performances

In 1966, an unsuspecting Broadway audience entered a theater to see a bare, blackened stage, flanked by dim, distant streetlamps, and dominated by an oversized, downward-slanting mirror (reflecting the seats in the theater auditorium) and a sign overhead that would read in lights "Cabaret." Such a stage environment signaled to spectators that they were soon to experience a Broadway musical unlike any other. The concept musical exploited an "alienation effect" in which the theatrical elements were laid bare. Musical set pieces (prop numbers) were metatheatrically employed to jolt the audience into awareness and comment on and metaphorically frame the action, while providing the connective tissue and thematic underscoring of the show. The unique theatrical journey was conducted by a Master of Ceremonies, an androgynous character who, as originally played by Joel Grey, ominously appeared in tuxedo, face powder, and rouge, with lips painted in a pucker. After he entered and welcomed the audience to the Kit Kat Klub, using a variety of languages in the lightly vamping opener "Willkommen," he was joined by a gaudy, brassy all-girl orchestra and the Kit Kat Girls. The women confrontationally strutted their bodies and world-weary attitudes, in their costumes (by Patricia Zipprodt), replete with garters and natty black stockings. As the number built to a discordant, almost orgiastic level, the Master of Ceremonies assured the audience that everything at the cabaret would be beautiful. And therein lies one of the ironies of *Cabaret*. For things turn very ugly, as evil encroaches on the outside world (a decaying Germany) and the performative world (a decadent Kit Kat Klub) of *Cabaret*. In metaphoric, metatheatrical fashion, *Cabaret* asserts there is no difference between the garish, nasty acts on the Kit Kat stage and the sins being perpetuated in Berlin society at the time. As the title song sardonically states, "Life is a cabaret."

Much of *Cabaret's* concept and style can be attributed to the show's original producer and director, Hal Prince, who began by working with librettist Joe Masterson on an adaptation of John Van Druten's 1951 play, *I Am a Camera*. As they worked, however, they were drawn more to the play's original source, Christopher Isherwood's *Berlin Stories*, especially in terms of the debauched, deteriorating milieu of the early 1930s Weimar Republic. Thus, little was left from *Camera* in the libretto, except for the role of Sally Bowles, a British cabaret chanteuse who, although just one of the many figures in *Camera* and Isherwood's original writings, became a central character in the musical. Next, Prince and Masterson had to find a dramatically effective way to link the external events with the self-contained world of the Kit Kat Klub. There were many starts and stops as they struggled to bring the libretto to the stage, ultimately conceiving the idea of the Master of Ceremonies. This omniscient, mocking creature emcees the Kit Kat Klub proceedings, overseeing numbers that offer jazzy, naughty entertainment (evocative of the Berlin cabarets at the time), while commenting on and echoing real-life events outside the club and in Sally's life. Prince and scenic designer Boris Aronson physically compartmentalized the show, providing separate narrative areas on stage. One area was a blank space delineated by light in which the Kit Kat Klub came to life, with emcee, band, and Kit Kat Girls performing directly for the audience in front of the giant, slanted fun-house mirror. The other was a realistic, representational space in which the book scenes and integrated songs were performed, telling of the self-absorbed, self-destructive Sally, who seduces an expatriate American writer, Cliff, only to have the romance unravel when she cannot change her selfish ways, aborting a pregnancy and turning a blind eye to the dangerously shifting events around her. Cliff, who clearly sees the menace of Hitler's Nazi Party, finally retreats, wiser and sadder, to America. Since Sally figures prominently in both worlds, her performance in both narrative spaces bridges the gap. (Cliff attends the cabaret, but as an outsider.) The other scenes played in the representational area belong to the subplot, which depicts another ill-fated love affair between two older Germans: Cliff's boarding house landlady, Fraulein Schneider, a pragmatic widow trying to survive difficult times, and a sweet-tempered, Jewish fruit shop owner, Herr Schultz, who courts her. They plan to marry, but as Fraulein Schneider becomes aware of the rising tide of anti-Semitism, she breaks off the engagement. At the end of *Cabaret*, it is implied that Schneider's fears were legitimate and that Schultz has been "relocated" to a Jewish concentration camp. There is no happy ending for any of the characters in *Cabaret*.

When Prince approached Kander and Ebb about writing the score for *Cabaret*, they eagerly accepted. The match between content, concept, and songwriters was perfect; for they were able to write in an integrated fashion, as well as in a stylized metatheatrical mode, creating showbiz numbers that evoked the sound and spirit of 1930s Berlin cabarets (echoing the cabaret and theatre stylings of one of the most prominent German composers of the time, Kurt Weill). What was startlingly innovative, however, was how dramatic the presentational cabaret songs proved to be, highlighting *Cabaret*'s themes and undertones. One of the most potent examples is "If You Could See Her." This light Kit Kat Klub number at first appears to be a campy song and dance between the Master of Ceremonies and a performer in a "girl" gorilla suit, during which he sings of his attraction to the primate and their problematic romance. It is only at the end, as the audience has enjoyed the silliness, that the emcee abruptly announces that the gorilla is "Jewish" (due to misunderstandings and protests from Jewish anti-defamation groups, this line was altered to "a meeskite" to be less "offensive" in the original Broadway production, but was reinstated for revivals). In just one line, the audience is reminded of the real-life romance between Schneider and Shultz; and the song suddenly becomes an ominous warning about their relationship and Germany's growing anti-Semitism. Sally's final solo, "Cabaret," is another example of the dramatic dimensions provided by the cabaret performances. At first, the song appears to be a full-on confessional eleven o'clock number, with a beer-hall sing-along chorus. What is different, however, is that Sally's lyrics are not confessions in the traditional sense. Although never overtly declared, she decides during the song to abort her pregnancy. Through her lyrics she justifies her choice to ignore real-world consequences and responsibilities, inviting all to deny reality, to "taste the wine, hear the band," and to live life in a cabaret. In terms of subtext, the number is fraught with discord and heavy with metaphor, as it can be seen to represent a segment of the German populace at the time, enjoying Weimar decadence while ignoring the dangers of Hitler's rise.

In addition to the cabaret numbers, Kander and Ebb provided integrated book songs that were equally effective. Five of these songs were given to Schneider and Shultz, helping develop their characters and highlight their romance and its sad end. The sweetest melodies in the Kander/Ebb score are saved for their duets, that is, a gentle waltz, "Married," and a comic courtship song that revolves around a pineapple, "It Couldn't Please Me More." In fact, Schneider's songs are the most powerful in the show with regard to character development. Early on, she sings a minor-keyed waltz ("So What?"), as she explains her clear-eyed view of life and survival to her new tenant, Cliff. Her last solo, however, is a dirge-like ballad during which she defends her decision to break off her engagement with Schultz, again citing her survival philosophy that has now been tested to its tragic end ("What Would You Do?"). The two songs not only illuminate her mindset and actions, but also speak for the wider German population in 1931 (and even those in the 1966 Broadway audience, seeing themselves reflected in the large stage mirror). The songs also suggest the German cabaret music of the day, especially the melodic structure and tone of Kurt Weill, which was made even more significant given that his real-life widow, the iconic German actress Lotte Lenya, came out of retirement to originate the role of Schneider on Broadway. One other *Cabaret* song exemplifies Kander and Ebb's gift for writing numbers that sound true to time and place, but also provide drama and meaning. "Tomorrow Belongs to Me" is an anthem sung twice in the show, once by the Master of Ceremonies and club waiters and a second time at a party attended by Sally and Cliff. As the party-goers join in the song (with Cliff, Sally, Schneider, and Schultz looking on), their fervor grows and the song acquires Nazi overtones, ominously ending *Cabaret*'s first act with the characters' arms outstretched in Sieg Heils to the audience. (The song is framed as a Germanic folk song and sounds so authentic that Kander has often had to explain that it is an original composition.)

Cabaret may have shocked 1966 audiences with its bleak narrative, unconventional structure, and "alienation" aesthetic, but its artistry and innovation pleased them even more. The original production ran for 1,165 performances and won eight Tony Awards. The 1972 film version, stylistically directed and choreographed by Bob Fosse, was equally successful, becoming one of the biggest hits of the early 1970s, winning eight Academy Awards. The film's script and score were revised, however, with the role of Sally changed to be American (to better suit the film's star, Liza Minnelli), while Cliff was renamed "Brian" and became British. The Schneider and Schultz subplot was omitted. Kander and Ebb contributed new songs to the film score to replace the many that were cut; the additions included iconic hits such as "Mein Herr" and "Money, Money," as well as one of their trunk songs, "Maybe This Time." The revised score became instrumental when the added film songs, as well as another old Kander/Ebb number, "I Don't Care Much," were combined with all the original songs to create the score for the most recently acclaimed Broadway revival in 1998. Directed by Sam Mendes and co-directed/choreographed by Rob Marshall, this revisionist revival retained the original plot and subplot, but added scenes to suit the expanded score, while moving the show in an even darker direction. For instance, the Master of Ceremonies was given an aggressive and sexually deviant air, with military boots, rouged nipples, and leather braces framing his crotch. Most dramatic was the reinterpretation of this mysterious role. Whereas the original production suggested the emcee was an omniscient, evil presence, the 1998 revival presented him as a malevolent presence but one who appears to be deteriorating. It is ultimately revealed that he represents evil, but from the perspective of the Jewish victims. In the revival's libretto, the show ends with the Master of Cere-

monies removing his black leather coat to reveal the ominous "striped pajamas," as he turns to enter the ovens of Auschwitz that have appeared against the stage's back wall. Broadway audiences may have thought that they "knew" *Cabaret*; yet they were stunned and stirred by Mendes' re-interpretation. The 1998 production garnered four Tony Awards (including Best Revival of a Musical) and played for an astounding 2,377 performances, proving that *Cabaret* is a musical theatre classic that persists as potent theatrical territory, still ripe for contemporary exploration and experiment.

Ali Dunfee and Brian Mallgrave in Boulder's Dinner Theatre production of *Cabaret*. Used by permission of Boulder's Dinner Theatre.

PULLING BACK THE CURTAIN:
Metatheatre Reaching Metaphoric, Reflexive Heights

Many a musical theatre professional and aficionado would agree with the title sentiment of Irving Berlin's iconic song "There's No Business Like Show Business." Unsurprisingly, many musical theatre artists prior to and during the Golden Age reinforced the adage, along with Shakespeare's old axiom "All the world's a stage," as they exploited **metatheatre** in their musicals, creating shows that illustrated and celebrated the world of theatre. Such metatheatrical works contained rehearsal segments, audition scenes, and shows-within-the-shows, employed as parts of the narrative and/or musical highlights. A representative roster of the canonical musicals that employ metatheatre in this fashion includes *Sally*; *Show Boat*; *Girl Crazy*; *On Your Toes*; *Babes in Arms*; *Pal Joey*; *Anything Goes*; *Kiss Me, Kate*; *Annie Get Your Gun*; *The King and I*; *Flower Drum Song*; *The Sound of Music*; *Guys and Dolls*; *Gypsy*; *Funny Girl*; *The Book of Mormon* … and the list goes on. These early musicals' use of metatheatre falls into a traditional or classic category; that is, the librettos include scenes or overall contexts in which characters become scripted, overt performers within the plot, allowing opportunities for pure exhibitionism (be it vocal and/or dance). Such performative moments signify that the boundaries between the musical fiction and real life (that is, between the audience in the show and the audience in the theater auditorium) are fluid and can be blurred, further suggesting that some showbiz aspects may actually serve as metaphors for real life (think of how many "auditions" occur every day: job interviews, blind dates, etc.). One must recognize—at the expense of rejecting the esoteric reading of metatheatre—that a performance-within-the-performance can simply be used as a utilitarian device, providing an entertaining diversion to reinvigorate a faltering libretto, giving a star his or her showcase turn, or featuring a new song in hopes of generating a breakout hit. Regardless, the fact that, from its earliest days, musical theatre often reflects on itself is indisputable. And one might look at this paradigm through a pragmatic lens; for in the most basic sense, writers often write about what they know. For many musical writers, that would be theatre and show business.

As musical theatre moved into the second half of the twentieth century, writers started to see and revel in the power of metatheatre and its reflexive nature. The device and strategy of metatheatre became more overt and **conceptually metaphoric** in many modern musicals; that is, the works began to make the most of the idea that "life is a cabaret." Some theatre artists moved beyond providing a few serviceable and representational performances/shows-within-shows to create entire worlds defined by mindful, stylized metatheatrical numbers that could comment on and metaphorically represent the musical's theme and dramatic action. In some cases, the musical was constructed as a concept work filtered through and founded upon a certain theatrical style or genre (e.g., storytelling, cabaret, vaudeville, revue, clownish improv, environmental theatre, *Commedia dell'Arte*, circus, British music hall, film noir, minstrelsy, and rock concert). Such a construct and underpinning could use nonintegrated and/or highly theatrical musical numbers to interrupt and then expand on a narrative while reinforcing ideas of life-theatre fluidity and interchangeability. A sampling of these formative and formidable works include *Man of La Mancha*, *Cabaret*, *Hair*, *Chicago*, *I Love My Wife*, *Follies*, *Godspell*, *Pippin*, *Barnum*, *The Will Rogers Follies*, *The Mystery of Edwin Drood*, *City of Angels*, *Kiss of the Spider Woman*, *Jelly's Last Jam*, *The Scottsboro Boys*, and *Tommy*. Some musicals during this period did not overtly use a theatrical style or genre in concept-musical style to disrupt the narrative and voice a metatheatrical message, but, nonetheless, there existed an unmistakable metaphor behind their theatrical milieus. Many of the numbers (or in the case of *A Chorus Line*, its complete narrative book) evoked parallels between real life and theatre, for example, *La Cage Aux Folles* and *Dreamgirls*. Other hit musicals written during the 1980s, '90s and early twenty-first century were less centered upon the life-theatre metaphor and retained the traditional construct of the linear book musical; yet their prime or intermittent theatrical settings still allowed for prop songs and overall meta-theatrical constructs. To varying degrees these works relied on nostalgia and "insider" musical theatre knowledge for their audience appeal. In this respect, the musicals exploited a reflexive paradigm, arousing a sense of community and connection, using librettos that referenced and, more important, celebrated the genre's history, artists, conventions, constructs, and myths (e.g., *George M!*, *42nd Street*, *The Tap Dance Kid*, *The Phantom of the Opera*, *Crazy for You*, *Victor/Victoria*, *Hairspray*, *The Drowsy Chaperone*, and [*title of show*]).

As is usually the case, such a trend resulted in what could be deemed a new category: **the reflexive musical**, with one of the earliest examples occurring in 1968: *Dames at Sea*. This tongue-in-cheek homage to the backstage musical not only deals in nostalgia, but overtly lampoons the fact that its entire composition is a pastiche of the endearing conventions and tired clichés of old-school musical comedy. *Dames'* debut was prescient, for a few decades later, theatre entered the postmodern era (defined by pastiche and irony), and the reflexive musical took root, becoming the style *du jour* on Broadway at the turn of the twenty-first century. The form pokes fun at itself, inviting knowledgeable viewers to enjoy the inside joke of parodied musical conventions, while reinscribing the legacy and cultural import of the American musical. The reflexive musical represents a mutual pat on the back, a shared wink and nod among musical theatre aficionados, who are energized by a broader acknowledgment that the genre has become so codified and culturally imprinted on the American psyche that a musical can performatively comment on itself. In other words, the genre has risen to the level of an American institution, worthy of being parodied. Included in this model is the use of outrageous source material and content, with incongruous material being musicalized ironically according to the standard practices, styles and dictates of the musical theatre genre. Overt examples of this reflexive form include Tony Award nominees and winners *Urinetown*, *The Producers*, *Monty Python's Spamelot*, and *Rock of Ages*, as well as Off-Broadway works such as *Debbie Does Dallas*, *Bat Boy*, and *Reefer Madness*, the last three being subtitled "*The Musical.*" The postmodern movement has also incited a new sensibility in which a book musical with a traditional linear narrative can contain elements of the reflexive musical, alerting audiences to the fact that the work is a "musical," often in a tongue-in-cheek fashion. Often, this aspect may come in the form of a quick acknowledgment of the "musical" moment in the libretto or a breaking of the fourth wall by the cast to sardonically remind the audience of the musical's conventions and theatrical identity (e.g., *The 25th Annual Putnam County Spelling Bee* and *Shrek the Musical*).

As these instances have become more common in contemporary musical theatre, it has become the norm for a trendy musical comedy to signal that it is aware of its "musical" nature. But there are complaints that this reflexive vogue detracts from the genre's traditional paradigm in which audience members buy into a self-contained musical world and are lifted to new heights through a willing suspension of disbelief, journeying with the characters through an uninterrupted musical narrative. Such a possible loss of invest-ment by all involved, as well as a tendency to rely on insider shtick, engenders much consternation and debate amongst members of the musical theatre community. Yet it can be difficult not to reference (and affectionately satirize) one's art, especially when it is a place of employment, pride, identity, and passion. Both points are significant ones to ponder as the metatheatrical, metaphoric, and reflexive musical moves further into the twenty-first century.

BOB FOSSE

When addressing the rise of the choreographer/director on Broadway, as well as the function, power, and aesthetic of dance in the musical, one must look to those dance artists, authors, and auteurs who helped write this new choreographic chapter in musical theatre history. Topping the list would be Bob Fosse. During Fosse's thirty-two-year Broadway career, he choreographed twelve Broadway musicals; of those twelve, he directed seven, unofficially conceived the book for one, and officially wrote (or co-wrote) the librettos for two. He won nine Tony Awards for his choreography and direction. Few biographies of stage aspiration and fame can equal Fosse's quick ascension on Broadway. As an über director/choreographer, he helped usher in a new era of musical theatre while solidifying, through the codification of his own aesthetic and dance "style," his place as one of Broadway's most iconic musical theatre artists.

Born Robert Louis Fosse in Chicago in 1927, he began dancing at age 9 and started his professional career at age 13 as part of a tap dance duo, the Riff Brothers. Trained, managed, and mentored by an old vaudevillian dancer, Fred Weaver, the two boys performed in talent contests and vaudeville, but when gigs became scarce, they resorted to performing in burlesque clubs around the city. This early association with sex and burlesque was a great influence on Fosse's later

work. After serving two years in the U.S. Navy in the entertainment division, Fosse got his first big break as a "gypsy" dancer on the road. With his recent military service, he was perfectly suited for a new Broadway musical by composer/lyricist Harold Rome titled *Call Me Mister* (1946). The hit show, which was a good-natured satire of World War II servicemen's readjustment to civilian life, purposely cast ex-GIs and ex-USO performers. Fosse landed a spot in the musical's national tour, which lasted just over a year. After the tour, he returned to the successful "dance duo" formula of his youth, forming the dance team "Fosse and Niles" with his new wife, Mary Ann Niles. Fosse & Niles worked mostly in nightclubs and early television, making guest appearances in variety shows, such as Sid Caesar's *Your Show of Shows*, until they were noticed and hired in 1950 for a new Broadway revue, *Dance Me a Song*. The show ran for only thirty-five performances but played an important role in Fosse's early career for two reasons: (1) He started to garner notice on Broadway as a "choreographer," devising the witty and thematic dances for Fosse & Niles and (2) he began an affair with star Broadway dancer Joan McCracken. Fosse divorced Niles to marry McCracken, thus ending his Fosse & Niles period (1946–52).

Another decisive event was a 1952 industry night/variety show for which Fosse was asked to provide choreography. Although he had yet to be credited with

Bob Fosse rehearsing *Pleasures and Palaces*, February 1965
© Bettmann/CORBIS

a formal "choreographer" title, he was gaining a reputation as a dancing talent who would rather devise his own steps than use the inventions of others. Fosse used his choreography to highlight his own physical strengths, hide his weaknesses, and showcase the impressive vaudevillian and burlesque vocabularies he learned as a youth. When stage managers decided to spotlight the best and brightest new talent on Broadway in a one-night union benefit, they asked Fosse to choreograph and dance in what would prove to be a significant industry showcase. The variety show was called *Talent 52*; and Fosse's work impressed many people in the audience, including a Hollywood scout who offered him an MGM movie contract as a dancer. With stars in his eyes, Fosse took the leap and moved to Hollywood to follow in the steps of his self-proclaimed idol, Fred Astaire.

After a few less-than-memorable movie roles, Fosse took a bit part as one of Bianca's suitors in the 1953 film version of *Kiss Me, Kate*. The movie's choreographer was the prolific Hermes Pan, famous for his work on countless movie musicals, including *The Gay Divorcee* (1934) and *My Fair Lady* (1957). Fosse asked Pan for permission to choreograph his own section of "From This Moment On." In this forty-eight-second dance duet with Carol Haney, Fosse created his first show-stopping moment as a self-expressive choreographer, that is, a choreographer who calls attention to himself/herself and his/her designed movement, as opposed to completely serving plot and character. In a further display of virtuosity, Fosse not only stepped out of Pan's choreographic world, but isolated his segment with no intention of melding his dance into Pan's framework. The segment reflected Fosse's personal style, borne of his own physicality and aesthetic preference, and featured a sexualized Fosse and Haney. They slunk across the stage, turning in their feet, gyrating their hips, snapping their fingers, and keeping their centers of gravity low to the ground, until Fosse executed an explosive back flip at the end. The *Kate* segment piqued the interest of two Broadway artists: George Abbott and Jerome Robbins. And at McCracken's suggestion (she was still in New York), Abbott hired the inexperienced Fosse to choreograph his 1954 Broadway musical about romance and union complications in a pajama factory. The musical was based on the Richard Bissell novel *7½ Cents* and titled *The Pajama Game*. For the production, Fosse teamed with the new composer/lyricist duo Richard Adler and Jerry Ross, novice co-producers Frederick Brisson, Robert Griffith,

and Harold Prince, and Abbott's directing partner, Jerome Robbins. Robbins assured Abbott that, if made co-director, he would oversee Fosse's work, helping with the choreography if necessary. Reportedly, Fosse staged all the big dances himself (having designed them in a six-week period before rehearsals began, earning Robbins' respect), but he did need Robbins' help with a few songs.

Fosse's choreography for *Pajama Game* was critically and popularly lauded (resulting in his first Tony Award for Choreography). One of the most celebrated aspects of the production was his first Broadway showstopper, "Steam Heat." Fosse had originally envisioned an elaborate dream ballet to start the second act, but Abbott vetoed the notion, suggesting that the act start with something smaller featuring the factory workers. Adler and Ross supplied a new novelty song about steam pipes and radiator noise, and Fosse fashioned a number for three dancers in an amateur talent show at a union rally. Abbott was unhappy when he saw the Fosse interpolation, viewing the number as nothing more than a dance showcase that interrupted the plot's forward momentum and had little to do with the story. However, Robbins and Prince supported Fosse; the dance stayed in the show.

"Steam Heat" represents a seminal moment in Fosse's career in which he successfully deployed a strategy to separate and spotlight his choreography, making no attempt to integrate the number into the narrative. The dance represented what could be termed a "superfluous showstopper." Throughout his career, Fosse would specialize in the superfluous showstopper, often in the form of a "prop number," that is, a musical number in which characters are required to sing or dance as part of a scripted "performance" scene (e.g., an audition, rehearsal, or excerpt from a show-within-the-show). In addition to the showstopping character of "Steam Heat," there were other characteristics of the dance that would become Fosse calling cards with regard to his choreography and style. First, Fosse's "Steam Heat" erased and depersonalized its individual performers (two men and one woman) in service of the choreography, using identical, androgynous costumes, with hats that partially hid their faces and served as visual props. (Fosse loved to use hats, gloves, feathers, and other costume accoutrements.) In this respect, Fosse significantly advanced the concept of non-gendered choreography; that is, men and women dancing the same movement. Later in his career, he would heighten the degree of sexuality in his dances, until it became one of his work's defining components; but both sexes would exploit the "bump and grind," not just the women. "Steam Heat" also reflects the genesis of Fosse's signature movement by which characters become abstract, mechanized bodies, using jazz dance isolations (moving one part of the body in opposition or isolation from another), as well as body percussion (finger snaps, hand claps, thigh slaps, whistles, tongue clicks, etc.). The movement is bound, quirky, and anti-classical (i.e., instead of upright, extended, and turned out, the center of gravity is low with movement turned in: pigeon-toed, knock-kneed, torso collapsed).

In addition to "Steam Heat," Fosse contributed a diverse number of dances to *Pajama Game*, including an athletic production number, "Once a Year Day"; a tango spoof, "Hernando's Hideaway"; and a dream ballet (the "Jealousy Ballet") that depicts the comic male lead's fantastical delusions regarding the promiscuous behavior of his secretary/girlfriend, Gladys. Audiences loved the show, which was extremely profitable, running for 1,063 performances, and launching Fosse's Broadway career.

Fosse was hired for *Damn Yankees* the next year, reteaming with Abbott (director/librettist), Adler/Ross (composer/lyricist team), and Brisson/Griffith/Prince (producers). *Damn Yankees'* Faustian baseball tale offered Fosse a diverse landscape for his choreography, from comic, acrobatic, and simulated sports movement by players in a "baseball ballet" ("Shoeless Joe") to a campy, sexy striptease for the devil's seductress, Lola ("Whatever Lola Wants"). The musical contained another superfluous showstopper by Fosse: "Who's Got the Pain?" Framed as a number in a show-within-the-show, the mambo parody was performed by two dancers in hats who became an abstract, symbiotic dancing duo, executing showy and eccentric choreography set to Latin rhythms. *Damn Yankees* was another big hit (1,019 performances) for which Fosse won another Tony Award. He also met his third wife, dancer/singer Gwen Verdon, who began her own Broadway star trajectory in the role of Lola. Fosse would ultimately leave McCracken and marry Verdon. And while Verdon became Fosse's muse and the star of many of his most significant triumphs (e.g., *New Girl in Town*, *Redhead*, *Sweet Charity*, and *Chicago*), she became a Broadway legend in her own right. In the next two years, Fosse enjoyed a succession of choreographic triumphs, including the Styne/Comden/Green smash hit *Bells Are Ringing* (1956) and *New Girl in Town* (1957), a musical version of Eugene O'Neill's *Anna Christie* (1921) with a score by composer/lyricist Bob Merrill. Fosse caused a sensation in *New Girl* with the "Red Light Ballet," a sexualized dream ballet showing Anna's past as a prostitute in a brothel. Given censor concerns, the number was cut from the show. *New Girl* ran for 431 performances, due in great part to Fosse's choreography and the performance of Verdon as Anna.

In 1959, Fosse the choreographer became Fosse the choreographer/director as he helmed the musical *Redhead*, with music composed by Albert Hague and lyrics by Dorothy Fields, who also wrote the book with Sidney Sheldon, David Shaw, and her brother Herbert (who died during the writing). Originally created as a star vehicle for Bea Lillie, by the time it was offered to Verdon, she insisted that her husband, Fosse, be given the chance to direct it, *Redhead* is a mystery set in London in the early 1900s. The main plot centers on Essie Whimple, a wax figure maker who becomes an amateur sleuth and tries to solve a Jack-the-Ripper–type murder. In addition, the show's metatheatrical subplot is set in a music hall, which allowed Fosse the opportunity to choreograph showstopper numbers such as "The Uncle Sam's Rag" and "Erbie Fitch's Twitch" (framed as rehearsal and audition numbers, respectively) and "Essie's Vision" (a 30-minute dream ballet in which Essie envisions herself as a music hall headliner). The dances used Fossean props and costumes, such as bowler hats, canes, gloves, etc., while showcasing Fosse's idiosyncratic jazz dance style alongside numerous other idioms (e.g., the cancan, gypsy folk dance, acrobatic military/precision movement, and period music hall eccentrics). Some critics noted that *Redhead's* dance was not always integrated and sometimes called too much attention to itself at the expense of the book and score. Regardless, *Redhead* proved popular with audiences, running for 452 performances and garnering Fosse his third Tony Award for Choreography, as well as his first Tony for Direction of a Musical. Like *New Girl*, however, it is probable that *Redhead's* success was mainly due to Fosse's choreography and Verdon's performance, for the musical has fallen into obscurity today.

After his triumph with *Redhead*, Fosse had moderate success during the next five years, with a couple significant failures sprinkled in. First, he suffered the humiliation of being fired during rehearsals as director/

choreographer for the failed *The Conquering Hero* (1961) due to conflicts with the producers, writers, and show's star. Then, when some of his original choreography was retained for the finished show but not maintained in its original form, Fosse sued the producers (this was prior to the 1976 ruling by the U.S. Copyright Office that designates choreography as property suitable for copyright). Regarding the misuse of his choreographic property, on a matter of principle, Fosse asked for and won a settlement of six cents. Fosse's next job was with Frank Loesser's *How to Succeed in Business Without Really Trying* (1961). Initially, he was asked by producers Feuer and Martin to assist the show's choreographer, Hugh Lambert. The novice Lambert was in over his head and was demoted, serving as Fosse's assistant. Fosse, credited with "musical staging," supplied the quirky and humorous choreography for such standout numbers as "Coffee Break" and "The Brotherhood of Man," as well as a soft-shoe interpretation of "A Secretary Is Not a Toy." The next year, Fosse co-directed, with producer Feuer, and choreographed *Little Me* (1962), a star vehicle for television star Sid Caesar, who played a variety of roles in several comic situations, varying in place and time. With a score by Coleman (music) and Leigh (lyrics) and a book by popular American playwright Neil Simon, the show was a disappointment, running for 257 performances. Nonetheless, Fosse's choreography was again a standout, especially his "Rich Kids Rag," for which he requested four original ragtime variations (all punctuated by whistles, trombone slides, bass drums, and other percussive sound effects). The number was a choreographic highlight in which adults, posing as snobby children, danced in party dresses, short pants, knee socks, and white gloves, wiggling about with knock-knees, pigeon-toes, noses in the air, and arched bums. *Little Me* may have underwhelmed audiences and critics, but for his efforts, Fosse won another Tony Award for Best Choreography.

In 1965, Fosse experienced both highs and lows. First, he functioned as director/choreographer for *Pleasures and Palaces*, a musical with a Loesser score that never made it to Broadway due to negative reviews and problems during its out-of-town tryouts. Fosse had also begun work on his next triumph, drafting the libretto for a one-act musical based on Federico Fellini's film *Nights of Cabiria* (1957). Fosse titled the work-in-progress *Sweet Charity* and intended it to be part of a Broadway evening comprised of unrelated one-acts by different authors. Instead, his producers opted to develop the *Charity* concept into a full-length musical and commissioned Neil Simon to help finish the libretto. By the time the show opened in 1966, Simon was given full credit for the book. The loosely designed libretto was tailored to fit Gwen Verdon's talents and features Charity Hope Valentine (played by Verdon), an optimistic and idealistic taxi dancer in New York with a sordid past who repeatedly and unsuccessfully searches for love.

Although *Sweet Charity*'s score by the composer/lyricist team of Cy Coleman and Dorothy Fields garnered critical praise (with popular stand-alone hits such as "If My Friends Could See Me Now" and "Big Spender"), its book was derided by the same critics. In the end, it was the musical's dances, direction, and Verdon's performance that were most lauded. Fosse's staging and choreography embellished the plot and created an "aesthetic" world, while cementing and codifying his signature dance technique (now becoming known as "Fosse style"). Three numbers from *Charity*—"The Rich Man's Frug," "Big Spender," and "If My Friends Could See Me Now"—illustrate this development. With "The Rich Man's Frug," Fosse realized a mini dance concert within an integrated book musical, exploiting Charity's visit to a nightclub as an opportunity to surround her with abstract characters who executed non-narrative Fossean choreography, rooted in popular 1960s dance trends. The number was divided into four sections, designated as The Frug, The Aloof, The Heavyweight, and The Big Finish, in which dancers with frozen faces and no psychological motives employed stylized movements such as snaking arms, isolated hips, swayed backs, angular, ricocheting torsos, and tight-fisted boxing motions. In "If My Friends Could See Me Now," Fosse continued to use theatre props and showbiz style, giving Charity a top hat and cane to execute a giddy vaudevillian dance as she revels in her chance encounter with an Italian movie star. In "Big Spender," performed by Charity's fellow taxi dancers, Fosse moved into a pelvic-oriented, erotic dance mode and he asserted what is termed his "mannequin" or "broken doll" choreography; that is, a depersonalized automation for women (and men, occasionally), represented by crooked torsos, locked limbs, thrust hips, and quirky isolations that periodically erupt, as if controlled by an erratic puppeteer, into thrusts and contortions, all accompanied by confrontational, knowing, or blank faces. Fosse also introduced his codified choreographic device termed the "Fosse amoeba," another depersonalized dance moment in which all performers clump together to create one dancing organism that is brought to life by the sequential, ruptured, echoed, and contrapuntal movement of the dancers' individual limbs and torsos.

Although critics complained about *Sweet Charity*'s weak book and lack of musical cohesiveness, Fosse's choreography was praised and the production was popular, running for 608 performances. The 1969 film version of the musical was a monumental failure. The disappointment was two-fold for Fosse, as he was both the director and choreographer (his first stint as a Hollywood director, although he had film experience as the choreographer of the hit movie versions of *The Pajama Game* and *Damn Yankees*). Despite the setback, Fosse's stage, film, and now television career did nothing but skyrocket during the 1970s. The extent of his power and reach (some might say overreach) did not always set well with collaborators. Fosse's next Broadway triumph was *Pippin* (1972). Through its creation, he found himself at odds with, and legally challenged by, the show's composer and lyricist, Stephen Schwartz. Roger Hirson wrote the book for *Pippin*, a metaphorical tale of a medieval lad (Pippin) born to royalty, who journeys through politics, war, sex, and domesticity in search of identity and fulfillment. The musical's story is mostly told through the songs of Schwartz, who had developed the work as a college project. When director/choreographer Fosse took over the show, he overrode the legitimate writers, stylistically and choreographically controlling and shaping *Pippin*'s narrative and content by putting much of the show's emphasis on his caustic chorus of Fosse dancers (the "Players"), stylized as a *Commedia dell'Arte* troupe, who lead Pippin on his life journey in metatheatrical fashion. Most significant was Fosse's creation and insertion of the Leading Player (originated by dancer/singer Ben Vereen), a Mephistophelean emcee who oversees and comments on the corruption and Pippin's disillusionment. The musical became a darker, more sexual, and dance-centric incarnation (lasting 2¼ hours with no intermission) than the one the writers had envisioned. The proceedings on stage often reconfigured and undermined Schwartz's idealistic, pop-infused score, composed of catchy, tuneful numbers (e.g., "Magic to Do," "Corner of the Sky," and "Love Song").

Once *Pippin* opened, most New York critics gave Fosse credit for the show's success. Schwartz, however, publicly denounced Fosse's cold and cynical version and sued for rights to his original *Pippin*. In a two-to-one ruling by the American Arbitration Association in November 1973, it was decided that Schwartz could lease the Australian rights to the show to his chosen producer and could revise this production's script according to his initial concept. As a result, there are two versions of *Pippin*: Schwartz's Australian production and Fosse's version which appeared in the U.S. (Broadway and tours), London, and Vienna. Fosse's version was awarded Tonys for both direction and choreography in 1973, while becoming the highest-earning Broadway musical in history and running for 1,944 performances, a run facilitated by the show's television commercial, a first for Broadway. That same year—1973—proved to be historic for Fosse, as he won the "triple crown": that is, a directing Tony, Oscar, and Emmy for, respectively: *Pippin*, the film version of Kander and Ebb's *Cabaret* (which he also choreographed), and a television special for Liza Minnelli (*Liza with a Z*). This trifecta of directing awards in a single year is a feat that has yet to be replicated.

After *Pippin*, Fosse directed and choreographed *Chicago* (1975), as well as co-authored the book with Fred Ebb. Although *Chicago*'s score is one of composer John Kander and lyricist Ebb's most acclaimed, the musical was Fosse's baby. Upon acquiring the rights to Maurine Dallas Watkins' 1926 play by the same name, Fosse and Ebb turned the material into a concept musical, built on Fosse's idea of framing each scene and number as a vaudeville turn. The show was designed for Verdon, who was a creative force behind the play adaptation, even though Fosse had recently found another muse and "girlfriend" in Ann Reinking (an original chorus member of *Pippin*). Rehearsals were seriously jeopardized when Fosse suffered a heart attack midway, requiring open-heart surgery. It seems that his lifestyle (chronic smoking, alcohol, sex, and amphetamine addiction) had finally caught up with him. After his brush with death, Fosse returned to work with a pronouncedly darker view of life and human nature. Given this mindset, he emphasized the dark and cynical aspects of the libretto. *Chicago* tells the tale of Roxie Hart, a murderess aspiring to stardom based on her criminal celebrity, who, cleared of charges through the shenanigans of her shady lawyer, realizes her dream with a fellow murderess as part of a vaudevillian "sister" act.

Fosse was able to again showcase his vaudeville and burlesque dance expertise, employing everything from ventriloquist acts, sister acts, soft-shoe numbers, and fan dances. Given the show's core themes of sex and sin, the "Fosse style" dominated as women and men shimmied about the stage with sexually suggestive jazz moves in numbers such as "All That Jazz," "Roxie," and "Razzle Dazzle." *Chicago* debuted in 1975. Reviews were mixed, as the critics were not sure what to make of the musical's cynical depiction of America. Even though *Chicago* ran for 893 performances, it wouldn't be until its 1996 revival that the show would be regarded as the iconic mega-hit that it is today.

During the 1970s and into the '80s, Fosse continued his work as a film director, often exploiting avant-garde camera techniques (e.g., tracking, panning, and oblique shots), bold cinematographic choices (filming in black and white for certain projects), and cutting-edge editing (including montage, jump cuts, and abruptly interjected close-ups). His film roster includes the moderately successful *Lenny* (1974), a biopic of controversial comedian Lenny Bruce that was nominated for six Academy Awards, and his self-referential masterpiece, *All That Jazz* (1979). Fosse not only conceived, directed, and choreographed this dance-heavy, somewhat surreal, semi-autobiographical film, but he also co-wrote the screenplay. *All That Jazz* chronicles a director/choreographer's (i.e., Fosse's) life, focusing on a thinly disguised depiction of Fosse's crisis period (the heart attack) during the development of *Chicago* and editing of *Lenny*. The film was nominated for the Academy Award for Best Picture, as well as nine others (winning four for costume design, editing, art direction, and score). Fosse's film career ended on a disappointing note, as his last movie, a stark biopic of a murdered Playboy playmate titled *Star 80*, was met with a meager box office and negative reviews when it opened in 1983.

Also included in this period is Fosse's involvement with *The Little Prince* (1974), a failed musical film that he choreographed and in which he played The Snake, performing the role as a caricature of himself, slinking and posturing about with "Fosse style" moves, costumed in all black clothes, gloves, and derby hat. (Fosse never relinquished his quest to be a dancing musical star, mixing his choreographer/director career with Broadway performing stints. He understudied the role of Joey in Broadway's 1952 revival of *Pal Joey*; eventually starring in the show's 1963 New York revival.)

Back on Broadway, however, Fosse created a production that did not attempt to reconcile dance within an integrated, or "Golden Triangle" musical paradigm. With *Dancin'* (1978), Fosse eliminated the libretto, librettist, and composer to create the first "dansical;" that is, a musical dominated by dance, with a diminished score and libretto. By transforming a dance concert into a "musical," Fosse found the perfect vehicle to showcase his signature choreography and aesthetic; it was his attempt to create a ballet on Broadway. The show was one Fosse dance number after another; and its only linking theme was Fosse's choreographic art. Instead of an original score, Fosse used already-written songs for the numbers, with composers ranging from Bach to Benny Goodman to Cat Stevens, and only random moments of dialogue by the dancer/singers, including a prologue to the show in which a dancer informed the audience that they were about to see a musical with no story, only dancin'! Standout numbers included "I Wanna Be a Dancin' Man" (a soft-shoe number performed by the entire company as "Fred Astaires" in white suits and ties), "Mr. Bojangles" (a bittersweet jazz shuffle by an old dancer, shadowed by his younger self), and "Sing, Sing, Sing" (a flashy Vegas-style number, complete with sexy "Fosse style" jazz alongside acrobatic movement). Critics seemed to either love or hate the show, depending on their view of the new dansical form. Indeed, there was concern over whether a "dance concert" should be considered a "musical." Audiences did not share the critics' ambivalence. *Dancin'* ran for years (1,774 performances), appealing to dance lovers and Fosse fans as well as legions of foreign tourists who could see a Broadway show without worrying about language barriers. The musical was a forerunner to a later hit dansical based on Fosse choreography, *Fosse* (1998), a career retrospective of Fosse's work (including many numbers from *Dancin'*). It was co-conceived and co-directed by Ann Reinking (with Richard Maltby, Jr.) and played for 1,093 performances, again promoting the idea that a successful musical could be composed solely of dance numbers.

In 1986, Fosse created his last original musical, *Big Deal*, for which he served as director, choreographer, and the sole librettist. In his musical adaptation of the 1958 Italian film *Big Deal on Madonna Street*, Fosse kept the basic story of small-time hustlers bungling a heist, while moving the action to Depression-era Chicago and changing the characters to African Americans. He worked once more without original songs or music, choosing to compile a score of period Tin Pan Alley hits, such as "Life Is Just a Bowl of Cherries" and "Me and My Shadow." In this respect, *Big Deal* is one of the earliest jukebox *book* musicals; that is, not a revue or theatricalized concert treatment of one artist's song catalogue but an "integrated" book musical with already-written songs by multiple artists inserted into a narrative. *Big Deal* received scathing reviews, with much of the ire aimed at Fosse's book. It closed after only 69 performances, although Fosse won one more Tony for his choreography. In 1986, Fosse staged a Broadway revival of *Sweet Charity*, starring Debbie Allen. The next year, while overseeing rehearsals of the national tour, Bob Fosse suffered a fatal heart attack; and he died with Verdon at his side. Thus ended a career that had unabashedly asserted the authority and authorship of the Broadway choreographer/ director, culminating in the creation of the dansical, a new form in the musical theatre genre. The import of Fosse's career is evident in that his iconic dance idiom and aesthetic have persisted into the twenty-first century, informing television (especially the music video), film, and Broadway, with the first revival of *Pippin* making a splash on the Main Stem in 2013, and the 1996 revival of *Chicago* (choreographed by Reinking in "Fosse style") still running. What's more, any musical theatre performer dressed in black, wearing white gloves and a tilted derby, while slowly lifting a hand, wiggling fingers, and isolating a hip is universally recognized as a purveyor of Fosse's art and a symbol of the man himself.

FEATURED PRODUCTION: *Chicago* (1975)

Music by John Kander; Lyrics by Fred Ebb; Book by Bob Fosse and Fred Ebb

Original Broadway Run: Opened June 3, 1975; 46th Street Theatre; 898 performances

Chicago is considered one of the most prescient works in the American musical canon, debuting in the mid-1970s. The show was originally deemed gratuitously dark, cynical, and experimental, given its depiction of America's legal system, tabloid media, and celebrity-obsessed culture, intersecting criminality with fame, capitalism, and corruption (all decades before the O. J. Simpson murder trial, Court TV, Bernie Madoff, and the sensationalized jail sentences of celebrities such as Martha Stewart, Paris Hilton, and Lindsay Lohan). *Chicago* not only weathered but trumped the test of time, demonstrating its resilience as it remained in the canon for two decades, only to artistically resurge with the phenomenal success of its 1996 Broadway revival. The new production was embraced by a mass audience that, in the 1990s, was not only undisturbed by its content and construct but enthusiastically applauded the musical's dark snapshot of "contemporary" American culture.

Another aspect of *Chicago*'s resilient nature is the fact that its musical adaptation took nearly thirteen years to realize. In the early 1960s, Gwen Verdon developed an interest in a 1926 play by Maurine Dallas Watkins titled *Chicago*. Verdon saw its musical theatre potential, as well as a starring role for herself as the protagonist Roxie Hart. Verdon's husband, director/choreographer Bob Fosse, became equally enamored with the idea. By this time, Watkins had become a born-again Christian and renounced her former life, in which she had been a *Chicago Tribune* court reporter, assigned to cover the 1924 trials of real-life adulterous murderesses Beulah Annan and Belva Gaertner. The popularity of her news articles inspired Watkins to write *Chicago*, loosely based on the sensational trials. The play ran for 172 performances on Broadway and became fodder for successful Hollywood adaptations. In her later life, however, Watkins wanted to distance herself from the scandalous, sin-ridden *Chicago* and she wanted to keep it from being performed again in any fashion; thus, she refused numerous requests by Fosse to buy the rights to the

play. Only after Watkins's death in 1969 did her estate sell the rights to Fosse, Verdon, and Richard Fryer (who produced the show with James Cresson). The composer/lyricist team of John Kander and Fred Ebb began work on the musical score. Fosse, who would direct and choreograph, began co-writing the book with Ebb. Their work resulted in a concept musical in which all the numbers were framed as vaudevillian turns, with the songs and performances modeled after signature acts of bygone stars. This format allowed Fosse to layer the work with Brechtian "alienation" techniques (e.g., breakage of the fourth wall, incongruous elements, heightened and stylized theatricality, and lack of integration), while creating surrealist moments that interrupted the narrative to highlight or comment on a theme/concept that equated America's legal system with showbiz.

North Shore Music Theatre's production of *Chicago*, 2002
© Paul Lyden. Used by permission of Paul Lyden.

Chicago, set in the Windy City in the 1920s, revolves around the scandalous adventures of murderess Roxie Hart. First, however, *Chicago*'s theatrical world is introduced by another murderess, Velma Kelly, who sneeringly welcomes the audience to the show with a seductive performance of the vampy, hot jazz number "All That Jazz." Velma, it turns out, is an ex-vaudevillian who, after finding her husband in bed with her sister (who was her performing partner), murdered them both. With the milieu established, the narrative focuses on the saga of Roxie Hart, a married chorus girl who has just murdered her illicit lover. Hart, however, soon talks her husband, Amos, into taking the blame, claiming the lover was a burglar; she caps her deceit with a cynical torch song, extolling Amos' gullibility in "Funny Honey." Eventually, Amos realizes he has been had and Roxie ends up in women's prison where Velma and other murderesses reside, justifying their criminal acts in "Cell Block Tango"—a rhythmic, hard-driving number consisting of monologues (as each murderess sardonically recounts her crime), contrapuntal vocals, and the pounding, relentless riff of the chorus, which repeatedly asserts that the male victims deserved their fates. Soon Roxie encounters the jail's matron, "Mama" Morton, who financially benefits from the "showbiz" management of inmates accused of tabloid-worthy crimes, explaining her exploitative policy of quid pro quo in a brassy solo, "When You're Good to Mama." Pushing her celebrity project, Velma, aside in favor of Roxie, Morton sets up Roxie with Velma's star lawyer, the corrupt and manipulative Billy Flynn. And after Roxie convinces Amos to pay for Flynn's services (a con job depicted in "A Tap Dance"), Flynn addresses the audience with his theme song, "All I Care About (Is Love)." In one of the most cynical and alienating moments in the show, Flynn is backed by sexually suggestive dancers wearing little clothing and employing burlesque feather fans as he strips to his underwear, all the while proclaiming his devotion to pure love, justice, and the American way.

Once Flynn takes Roxie's case, the musical goes to even further absurdist lengths. Flynn cons tabloid columnist Mary Sunshine into believing a sympathetic and tantalizing retelling of Roxie's crime. Sunshine publicizes the sob-story version in "A Little Bit of Good" (in the production, Sunshine's character is played by a man in drag). Then, in an arranged press conference, Flynn literally puts words into Roxie's mouth during "We Both Reached for the Gun," turning her into a ventriloquist's dummy as she mouths his words to the media, while sitting on his lap and being physically controlled by him. Once Roxie finds her criminal celebrity growing, she aspires to turn her fleeting fame into vaudeville stardom. She imagines herself flanked by a dancing male chorus, performing the glitzy dream number "Roxie." Velma, on the other hand, sees her celebrity usurped and tries to recruit Roxie as the other half of her old sister act by singing and dancing "I Can't Do It Alone." Roxie refuses, only to see her own stock plummet when a new murderess grabs the headlines. As both Roxie and Velma come to the realization that they are on their own in a cold, cruel world ("My Own Best Friend"), Roxie decides to fake a pregnancy to recapture her tabloid fame.

Velma starts the second act by welcoming the returning audience with disdain and detailing Roxie's new wave of celebrity ("I Know a Girl"), while Roxie continues to embellish her tales of prospective motherhood and innocence ("Me and My Baby"). The ever-gullible Amos believes the baby is his but recognizes his insignificance in the overall scheme of things, singing a woeful lament interspersed with dialogue ("Mr. Cellophane") in a vaudevillian "sad clown" fashion. After Velma tries to upstage Roxie, showing Flynn all the showbiz tricks she has planned for her own trial ("When Velma Takes the Stand"), and after Roxie egotistically dismisses Flynn, only to hire him back when she sees a fellow inmate convicted and executed, Flynn coaches Roxie for her trial, recommending that she use Velma's suggested flashy showbiz stunts to dazzle her jury ("Razzle Dazzle"). Using the strategies, Roxie is acquitted. Victory is bittersweet, however, as she discovers that she has become old news, deserted by the media, Flynn, and even Amos, once she confesses there is no baby. Roxie, the ultimate survivor who may have deluded others but never herself, sings "Nowadays," a torchy ballad extolling her life's potential and prospects. The number morphs into a final flashy flapper dance, "Hot Honey Rag," performed by Roxie and Velma, suggesting that they have successfully achieved vaudeville stardom. Whether or not this number represents reality is left up to the spectator; yet it is a theatrical vindication of two criminals who have triumphed, courtesy of a corrupt culture of celebrity worship, greed, and crime.

Subtitled "A Musical Vaudeville," *Chicago* was defined by its vaudevillian concept and aesthetic, for Fosse, Ebb, and Kander purposely referenced iconic vaudeville stars such as Helen Morgan, Sophie Tucker, Texas Guinan, Ted Lewis, and Bert Williams in both the construct and style of numbers performed by Roxie, Morton, Velma, Flynn, and Amos, respectively. The vaudevillian concept reinforced the idea that no character in the musical was authentic but was a performer who had to con, morph, and "razzle-dazzle" to survive. The dark concept and cynical view of human nature, as well as Fosse's alienating production strategies, elicited mixed reviews from the critics. Even though the score was engaging and tuneful, even nostalgic in its referencing of Tin Pan Alley and vaudevillian song idioms, many audience members echoed the critics' sentiments, being put off by the Brechtian production techniques and content that they found distasteful and overly caustic.

Nonetheless, the show was nominated for Tony Awards for direction, choreography, score, actor and actress in a musical, and best musical, being beaten in every category that year by *A Chorus Line*. The musical had a lengthy run, due in great part to its stars and subsequent lead role replacements, such as Liza Minnelli. *Chicago* was seen as a misunderstood and underappreciated musical; that is, until it was revived on Broadway in 1996 to fantastic acclaim. The revival's libretto was modified by David Thompson, while it was directed by Walter Bobbie and choreographed "in the style of Bob Fosse," as noted on all program materials, by Ann Reinking, who also starred as Roxie Hart (interestingly, she had been a cast replacement for the role in the 1975 original). It took a couple decades, but audiences finally "got" the musical, reveling in its dark themes, jarring theatricality, sneering commentary, and blatant sexuality (one critic equated the Broadway revival to a dose of Viagra). The 1996 *Chicago* won six Tony Awards, including Best Revival, and to date, has enjoyed numerous national tours and international productions. The still-running production holds the box office record for Broadway musical revivals, also reigning as the longest-running "American musical" in Broadway history, having recently topped 6,900 performances. In 2002 the hit film version, directed and choreographed by Rob Marshall, ushered in a new age for the movie musical, winning the Academy Award for Best Film, among numerous other awards. More than three decades after its debut, *Chicago* continues to feel timely and relevant; and today, the prescient musical stands as one of Broadway's most significant postmodern reflections of American culture in the twenty-first century.

PULLING BACK THE CURTAIN:
Fosse and the "A-Effect" in Musical Theatre

When chronicling musical theatre history, much is made of the integrated book musical. Modeled after the representational well-made play, this traditional form asks that audience members lose themselves in a linear narrative, emotionally investing in the travails and triumphs of heroes, ingénues, villains, and comic sidekicks. Unlike the play, however, the book-musical journey is one of integrated song, dance, and text, an amalgamation of components resulting in a powerful, united whole, able to transport audiences to moments of heightened intellectual, emotional, spiritual, and aesthetic awareness. This construct and concept has been deemed the "Total Work," which was advocated, elucidated, and codified in the mid-1800s as the *Gesamtkunstwerk* by opera auteur and theorist Richard Wagner (1813–83). The modern era spawned other theatre auteurs, however—rebels who had the audacity to question and oppose Wagner's ideal of the *Gesamtkunstwerk*. German playwright, librettist, director, and theorist Bertolt Brecht (1898–1956) extolled the use of music, dance, and text in dramatic works. But contrary to Wagner, Brecht asserted that the components, when melded together, lose individual power and potential, undermining the work overall. He argued that an integrated work's audience becomes numbed, inert, and disempowered, caught up in the morass of the melding. Brecht advocated that music, dance, and text be made independent of each other in a theatre work, calling attention to their own unique character.

In addition to the segregation of elements, Brecht believed that a "calling of attention" could be accomplished by what he termed *Verfremdungeffekte*, literally translated as the "making strange" effect. In the American theatre, we refer to this effect and device as the "alienation effect," or "A-effect." The A-effect can be exploited many ways in a musical; three of the most prevalent are as follows:

Fracturing of narrative and fragmentation of overall construct. One of the most prevalent strategies in this category is the "breaking of the fourth wall," which is a moment, often scripted, when the actors break from a scene or song to indicate they are aware of the audience (addressing them, referencing them, etc.). Once audience members realize that they are seen, they become active participants instead of removed observers. Another crucial dramaturgical technique, especially with musicals, is the abrupt division of a work into scenes, songs, and dances, with no attempt at integration, often alerting the audience to the separation and conscious lack of cohesion (using narrators, prologues, etc.). The desired effect of these structural and theatrical strategies is the alleviation of suspense for the audience (they are constantly made aware of the theatrical construct and dramatic progression).

Alienating performance techniques. Here, a performer aims to jolt audiences into awareness of the theatrical event and create a sense of alienation instead of empathetically enlisting them into "believing" his or her character's narrative. For instance, in an acting, singing, or dancing moment, the performer does not try to be "realistic" or "in character," but instead, may execute the scene/song/dance in an overtly theatrical, distanced, stylized, reflexive, or presentational manner.

Exploitation of technical design and stage craft to "make strange." To create an A-effect and illustrate theatricality instead of replicating reality, a Brechtian play or musical may expose the lighting equipment and other scenery mechanics, as well as use microphones, signs, masks, film projections, anachronistic costumes, etc., to interrupt and subvert the illusion of "realism" on stage.

These strategies and devices challenge the willing suspension of disbelief that has been the norm in American musical theatre spectatorship since the genre's earliest days. This willing suspension is the phenomenon in which an audience member agreeably leaves the real world to immerse him or herself in a theatrical and lyrical narrative and performance, often rewarded by emotional catharsis and aesthetic pleasure in the process. Brecht felt this paradigm equated to a lobotomy and state of paralysis for the spectator. He wanted spectators to think critically about what they were viewing on stage and be spurred to act once they left the theatre. Thus, if a theatre moment "makes strange," it can awaken audience members and ask them to contemplate the whys and wherefores of the theatrical proceedings, that is, to look curiously at the work instead of taking it for granted, to become an active participant and interpreter. This leads, in Brecht's view, to a more invigorating and transformative experience for all and a higher purpose for the theatre.

One of Broadway's chief practitioners and purveyors of the A-effect was choreographer/director Bob Fosse. In many productions, he spotlighted his choreography as isolated, non-integrated showcase dance numbers (e.g., *The Pajama Game*'s "Steam Heat"), separating the dance from the other components, as Brecht advocated. These numbers had little to do with the libretto and actually stopped its narrative progress. They also called attention to themselves as pure dance, the movement stamped with an idiosyncratic style that set it apart and seemed "strange" and distant from the surrounding material. Such dances were neither rooted in character nor reflective of place or time. Instead, they were intended to stand apart and to alert the audience to the power and meaning of the dance.

Another aspect of Fosse's A-effect paradigm was his acquired control of the musical's book, often co-writing or "rewriting" the librettos of his later productions. As part of this development, many Fossean productions, to one degree or another, incorporated dramatic moments that broke the fourth wall, a revolutionary practice in musical theatre at the time (i.e., at the height of the integrated book musical era). Many critics and scholars credit Fosse with introducing and furthering a musical theatre construct in which actors stepped out of character to confront the audience and make it clear that the musical numbers were only performances, nothing more. What made the moments so powerful was their juxtaposition within the narrative of a musical, fragmenting an otherwise integrated work. For example, *Chicago*'s numbers broke the linear, dramatic thread of the show as the actors broke from each scene to turn out to the audience and perform their numbers. Instead of creating dances that organically arose from a scene or song, Fosse staged these numbers as isolated, "announced" choreographic displays comprising dancers who employed the Fosse style knowingly and confrontationally.

In a similar vein, director Fosse employed a Brechtian "narrator" device in many of his productions to break the fourth wall, fragment the overall construct, and employ the A-effect, even if a narrator did not originally exist in the libretto. For instance, Fosse reconfigured the Leading Player in *Pippin* (initially a minor role) into a dancing Mephistophelean emcee who addresses the audience and comments on the action. One of the most powerful examples of the Leading Player's function in Fosse's *Pippin* was the Player's performance of "Glory," a number that exalts the glories of war, which morphed into a dance segment nicknamed "The Manson Trio" (a reference to cult murderer Charles Manson). In Fosse's "Manson Trio," the Leading Player appeared with a cane and straw hat set at an angle, accompanied by two leggy female dancers costumed in sexually suggestive armor and breastplates. The smiling trio performed an eerily mechanical and contorted version of a vaudevillian soft shoe, while scenes of war violence played behind them. It ended with the Leading Player's exclamation to the audience that they hadn't seen "nothing" yet. It was a moment of campy showbiz, sex, and artificiality, juxtaposed against bloodshed, providing an A-effect aimed to disconcert audiences and alert them to the insanity, brutality, and "theatre" of war.

Fosse did not always have to refashion librettos written by other parties to employ the A-effect. In the case of *Chicago*, he co-wrote the libretto with Fred Ebb, which often relied on narrative devices that broke the fourth wall (vaudevillian turns and cast members sharing narrator duties), while employing alienation performance techniques for the actors. For instance, at the end of *Chicago*, lead characters Velma and Roxie finish their big finale, "Hot Honey Rag," then acknowledge the actual audience in triumph, thanking them by tossing roses. The original Broadway performance was one of alienation, however, infused with irony. Numerous accounts report that although the performers were smiling and extravagantly expressing gratitude at the number's end, Fosse directed them to use a subtext of profanity, imaginatively hurling obscene retorts at the real-life audience along with the roses. Thus, the women's caustic presentation, objective distance, contrary inner dialogue, and fourth wall-breaking reinforced the character and themes of *Chicago*. Their actions also indicted a Broadway audience who had been tricked by "razzle dazzle" into cheering for two sociopaths.

Fosse also employed, courtesy of his designers, certain design components that facilitated the A-effect. In 1966's *Sweet Charity* (which started with a libretto by Fosse), signs flashed above the stage informing the audience, in abbreviated captions, of Charity's hopes, state of mind, and emotional journey. In *Pippin*, Fosse incorporated extroverted effects, including a wall of fog, lights, and illuminated gloved hands in the opening number, "Magic to Do." He also called for anachronistic costumes, placards, sound effects, and voice-overs throughout the show. There is no clear evidence that Fosse consciously knew he was using Brechtian A-effect techniques when he was working on his most "Brechtian" projects. He was not versed in the actual theory and practice but seemed, instead, to use the techniques and overall aesthetic instinctively, resulting in work that critics and scholars deemed "Brechtian." It is also important to note that Brecht developed his theory and employed his techniques to incite sociopolitical awareness and action, while most musical theatre artists—with Fosse leading the way—have exploited aspects of Brecht's *Verfremdungseffekte* to create heightened theatrical experiences, as opposed to promoting sociopolitical agendas.

As Fosse's "alienation" elements proliferated on the musical theatre stage, an acceptance of non-integrated, Brechtian musicals grew among American audiences. This is not to suggest that there had been no A-effects in musicals before Fosse. Indeed, pioneering Brechtian works on Broadway include Marc Blitzstein's *The Cradle Will Rock* (1937), a musical modeled after Brecht's works and agitprop plays that indicted the Depression-era evils of capitalism and the corrupt corporatist culture of America, as well as Brecht's own *The Threepenny Opera* (1928), with music by Kurt Weill. *Threepenny* is another indictment of capitalism and corruption that in a translated version enjoyed a run of 2,611 performances at the Theatre de Lys in the mid-1950s, plus numerous Broadway revivals (the latest being a failed 2006 version). Immediately predating Fosse's *Pippin* were musicals such as Kander and Ebb's *Cabaret* (1966), which featured a Master of Ceremonies who served as an ironic commentator and metaphoric agent of "strangeness," along with an overall structure that was purposefully divided into book scenes and meta-theatrical songs and dances. (Fosse, who had no hand in the Broadway show, exploited these aspects even further in his 1972 film version of the musical, while director Sam Mendes made the most of the A-effect in his significant 1998 revival.) Then there is 1968's *Hair*, which not only dismissed integration and linear storytelling, but also purposefully aimed to discomfit the audience, jolting spectators into awareness through "alienation" devices such as exposed microphones, nudity, masks, confrontational language, overt symbolism, theatricalized ritual, and breaking of the fourth wall, including actors addressing audience members while climbing over their seats.

Nonetheless, it was Fosse who significantly helped codify the A-effect in commercial musical theatre, while promoting the idea that a director might utilize such devices and strategies to reconfigure any musical into a work of Brechtian non-integration and alienation. His influence is evident today, as he predated the postmodern era, which thrives on irony, fragmentation, subversion of theatrical pretense, and referentiality (e.g., pastiche). Given this new climate, the Brechtian A-effect has gone mainstream in the American musical theatre genre. For instance, the 1996 revival of *Chicago*, with its alienation aspect heightened (actors sitting on stage, waiting to assume their roles), no longer confused but thrilled audiences who felt familiar with and appreciative of the musical's "strangeness." Today, there are musicals that have increasingly distorted and fractured the *Gesamtkunstwerk* ideal as they isolate one component as a core constituent (e.g., dansicals such as 2002's *Movin' Out*). Further, there are musicals in the *Chicago* mode, using the A-effect or Brechtian techniques to evoke cynicism and/or sociocultural criticism; they include such Broadway works as *The Wild Party* (2000), *Spring Awakening* (2006), *Next to Normal* (2009), and *The Scottsboro Boys* (2010). Some examples fall more in line with Brecht's original intent, representing political calls to action (e.g., 2009's *Fela!*); while some seek to help audiences confront serious issues, such as AIDS (e.g., 1996's *Rent*). In a postmodern twist on the Brechtian model, there exist twenty-first-century musicals that have satirically, smartly, and referentially used alienation techniques to get laughs, such as *Urinetown* (2001), *The 25ᵗʰ Annual Putnam County Spelling Bee* (2005), *Spamalot* (2005), and *Rock of Ages* (2009). Americans have become, in many ways, more cynical, questioning, and referential—not a bad thing, as such an evolution is mirrored by a musical theatre populace that can not only embrace the heightened "reality" of the integrated book musical but can, on the other hand, also rigorously explore, comprehend, and delight in the many forms of the A-effect on the musical theatre stage.

MICHAEL BENNETT

Michael Bennett assumed many roles during his theatre career, for example, director, librettist, and producer; yet it was his earliest passion and profession—dancing—that underpinned, informed, and still distinguishes much of his immense contribution to musical theatre. As Bennett rose meteorically through the Broadway performing ranks to attain the title of musical theatre auteur, he never forgot his roots: the world of the chorus dancer, i.e., the gypsy. He created dance-centric musicals while inspiring and mentoring a new generation of Broadway dancers and directors. A Bennett musical "danced" in terms of its overall production aesthetic and concept. As director, he translated a cinematic look and feel (e.g., the roving camera "eye") to the stage, combining scenery, lights, and staging to create a fluid presentation that appeared to be in constant motion, both in terms of people and technical elements. In his tribute to the dancing chorus from which he hailed, he created one of the most successful, groundbreaking, and iconic works in the musical theatre canon, not to mention the American theatre: *A Chorus Line*. All of which bespeaks the passion, talent, vision, import, and legacy of director/choreographer/dancer Michael Bennett.

Reflecting a now-familiar musical theatre paradigm, Bennett was not Michael's given last name. Instead, he was born Michael Di Figlia on April 8, 1943, in Buffalo, New York, where he grew up with his old-world Sicilian father, Salvatore, and Russian Jewish mother, Helen. Showing talent as a toddler, Helen enrolled Michael in a dancing school when he was only 3 years old. By age 12, he was a star dance pupil and performer, versed in numerous idioms (jazz, ballet, tap, contemporary) and landing gigs in local hospitals and orphanages as part of a select youth performing troupe. He also spent summers in New York City, studying dance and dreaming of becoming a choreographer. During Michael's early teen years, he began choreographing many of his own routines and performing semiprofessionally as Mickey Di Figlia at weddings and Bar Mitzvahs, contributing his earnings to his financially struggling family. During high school, Michael participated in little else than theatre and dance, with summers spent apprenticing in a touring stock theatre company, where he landed the role of Baby John in a production of *West Side Story*. At 16, Michael got his big break. Hearing that his idol Jerome Robbins was casting a European tour of *West Side Story*, Michael headed to New York to audition, hoping to replicate his stock theatre success by landing the role of Baby John. To his delight, he got the job. To

Michael Bennett stands before the celebration cast of *A Chorus Line*, 1983.
© Bettmann/CORBIS

his parents' dismay, he dropped out of high school to take the job (with graduation only a few months away). But, Michael Di Figlia—soon to be Michael Bennett—never regretted his decision and never looked back. Bennett was not only the youngest cast member on the tour but was also one of the most focused, determined, and ambitious performers that many of his cast mates had ever encountered.

One such cast mate was Bob Avian, who was eight years older than the brash teenage Bennett. Avian admired Bennett and bonded with him. He would eventually become one of Bennett's closest career associates, a frequent collaborator on many of his most successful works, and a lifelong best friend. The year-long European tour was a milestone for Bennett in other respects as well, for he learned the ropes of professional musical theatre, made industry connections, and impressed his peers and superiors. Afterward, he returned to New York and immediately hit the audition circuit, soon landing his first Broadway show, the second-rate *Subways Are for Sleeping* (1961), where he proved his merit as an energetic and idiosyncratic chorus dancer. His next show may have been an all-out Broadway flop titled *Nowhere to Go But Up* (1962), but it provided him a priceless career opportunity. Bennett had never been shy about his desire to move out of the chorus and become a choreographer/director (vowing to become the next Jerome Robbins). In *Nowhere to Go*, Bennett had only been hired for the show's preproduction phase but was soon tagged to replace the assistant choreographer and work directly with seasoned choreographer Ron Field. Thus, at 19 years old, Bennett was able to oversee and contribute to the choreography of a major Broadway production. In 1963, he was hired for the chorus of the marginally successful *Here's Love* (1963). Directed and choreographed by venerable artist Michael Kidd, with a score by *The Music Man*'s Meredith Willson, the show (an adaption of the popular 1947 movie *Miracle on 34th Street*) allowed Bennett another chance to shine. He was not only featured in the show's major dream ballet, but Kidd allowed him to choreograph his own pas de deux section. *Miracle* was followed by another modest hit, *Bajour* (1964), in which Bennett again excelled as a chorus member. During *Bajour's* run, Bennett auditioned for a popular music television show, *Hullabaloo*, and got the job. As one of the *Hullabaloo* Dancers, he performed routines comprising trendy dance steps, which spotlighted the chart-topping pop hits of the week. The show ran for two

years and proved a formative experience for Bennett in two respects: (1) Popular, populist dance forms, as were danced on *Hullabaloo*, would significantly inform Bennett's choreographic style. He often merged dance steps and styles from the streets of New York with classical, formal idioms such as ballet, jazz, tap, and modern (it helped that his shows would mostly be set in contemporary, urban milieus). (2) On *Hullabaloo* he was paired with another young dancer named Donna McKechnie. The two would embark on a lifelong relationship, including a short-lived marriage in 1976 (lasting only several months and proving a curious sidebar for Bennett, given that he openly declared and embraced his homosexuality). McKecknie also became his muse and star dancer/performer in several of his landmark shows.

While working on *Hullabaloo*, Bennett began to design dances for variety television shows, such as *The Ed Sullivan Show* and *The Dean Martin Show*. Before long, Broadway took note of how far the young "gypsy" had come. Bennett was contacted by producer Edward Padula to choreograph a musical he was developing based on the novel *The Insolent Breed*, *A Joyful Noise* (1959), by Borden Deal. The musical, titled *A Joyful Noise*, depicts the rise to fame of a Tennessee country singer who rejects the corrupt music industry in Nashville to return to his small-town roots. *A Joyful Noise* was panned at its 1966 opening and closed after only twelve performances. Bennett's choreography, as well as his company of dancers, received positive notices (the dancing chorus included Baayork Lee and newcomer Tommy Tune, both of whom would become select members of a core group of performers repeatedly used by Bennett in his shows). For *Noise*, Bennett innovatively employed contemporary movement alongside period, stylized dance idioms to tell the story; consequently, he was nominated for his first Tony Award. Bennett's next Broadway choreography gig, *Henry, Sweet Henry* (1967), was another box office failure. The show, a musical adaptation of Nora Johnson's novel *The World of Henry Orient* (1958), features a middling orchestra conductor who chases women and then finds himself, ironically, chased by two infatuated 15-year-old girls. With a libretto and lead actor that failed to capture the magic of the original novel and its popular film adaption, as well as a weak score by lyricist/composer Bob Merrill, *Henry* played for only eighty performances. Once again, though, Bennett's career was not hurt by the show's failure; his work on *Henry* garnered another Tony nomination.

As Bennett's choreographic star rose, he worked more in television and film. He also donned the show doctor cap, serving as an uncredited choreographer for productions such as the Off-Broadway hit *Your Own Thing* (1968), as well as the Broadway failure *How Now, Dow Jones* (1967). Significantly, the latter musical had been produced by David Merrick, who was impressed enough with Bennett to offer him the official role of choreographer for Merrick's next project, an adaptation of Billy Wilder's Academy Award-winning film *The Apartment* (1960). The new musical, titled *Promises, Promises*, proved to be a satiric and dark depiction of corporate and sexual gamesmanship as well as a humorous and human look at contemporary urban romance. The libretto, adapted by Neil Simon, tells the story of a single white-collar patsy, Chuck Baxter, who tries to promote his career by lending his bachelor apartment key to business higher-ups for their extramarital trysts. Complications ensue when one of the office girls is summarily dumped by a philandering executive and attempts suicide in Chuck's apartment. After Chuck nurses her back to health, the two bruised survivors begin a tentative friendship that turns into a bittersweet romance. The score contains a 1960s pop sound and feel; not surprising, given that it was written by Broadway newcomers, but proven pop-chart champs, Burt Bacharach (composer) and Hal David (lyricist). The show spawned a major radio hit, "I'll Never Fall in Love Again" (an occurrence that was becoming rare in the modern musical theatre era). For Bennett's part, his choreography combined technical dance steps with pedestrian stage movement that was character-driven and told a story. He also continued to develop his signature choreographic style, merging popular dance trends with formal dance idioms and composition. Exemplifying this strategy was *Promises'* most lauded dance number, "Turkey Lurkey Time," during which tipsy secretaries go wild at an office Christmas party dancing on desktops, with choreography that incorporated steps such as the Jerk and Pony. (Bennett highlighted chorus member/dancer Donna McKechnie in this number, and she eventually moved into the lead for national tours and the London production.) In addition, Bennett exploited the idea of making stage action continuous and cinematic, that is, one scene or number seamlessly blending into another through movement and choreographed transitions, as opposed to blackouts or dropped curtains. In *Promises, Promises*, he choreographed scene changes by having performers "dance" the scenery onstage while other pieces were danced off.

Audiences loved the fresh-sounding and -looking musical when it opened on December 1, 1968. As a result, *Promises, Promises* ran for 1,281 performances, and at the age of 25, Bennett earned his third Tony nomination for choreography.

The next year Bennett was hired to choreograph the high-profile star vehicle *Coco* (1969). The libretto and lyrics were written by the celebrated Alan Jay Lerner and classical conductor/composer/pianist André Previn composed the music. As the show aimed to celebrate and chronicle the career of fashion designer Gabrielle "Coco" Chanel, it called for an icon of equal stature to play the title role. The creative team was able to recruit legendary film star Katharine Hepburn, and the musical was developed around her. Unfortunately, Hepburn was neither a singer nor a dancer. Bennett, especially, had a contentious relationship with the resistant star as he tried to choreograph her, as well as impart his vision and concept of haute couture via the overall dance aesthetic of the show. (Bennett had spent two weeks visiting Coco Chanel in Paris, immersing himself in the world of high fashion.) Hepburn had insisted on a director of her own choosing, Michael Benthall, who was a celebrated British director with whom she had worked successfully in the 1950s. Benthall, however, had little experience with staging musicals, so Bennett found himself repeatedly making staging suggestions, finally taking over most of the large ensemble scenes. According to numerous reports, Bennett directed most of *Coco*, without formal credit. He did get credit, however, for his inventive choreography, including one highlighted segment in which Coco's fashion scrapbook came to life, with dancers as fashion models given individuality and panache through Bennett's movement design. In the end, *Coco* did not receive many positive reviews, given that it was hampered by a lackluster score and significant production problems. Regardless, the show had the biggest box office advance in Broadway to that time; and Hepburn reaffirmed her star power, with the show selling out nightly. When she left the production after nine months, however, ticket sales disappeared and *Coco* closed nine weeks later.

Although Bennett's directorial efforts were not formally acknowledged on *Coco*, it was well known to industry insiders that he was a formidable talent. One musical theatre giant who had been watching and admiring Bennett's work since *A Joyful Noise* was Harold Prince. The powerful director/producer had begun work on a new musical to be based on a series of vignettes about urban relationships (or lack thereof) by playwright George Furth, with a score by lyricist/composer Stephen Sondheim. The project was to be titled *Company*, and Prince invited Bennett to join the production team as choreographer. Although Bennett was thrilled at the prospect of working with Prince, he didn't see much dance potential in the intimate material. The ever-astute Prince, however, offered to make a place for Donna McKechnie in the cast as a featured dancer, providing more choreographic possibilities for Bennett. So Bennett became a part of one of the most significant concept musicals in American musical theatre history—many cite it as the show that propelled the concept musical to the genre's forefront during the latter part of the twentieth century. *Company* deals with a bachelor, Bobby, on his thirty-fifth birthday, who observes the troubled, complex relationships of his coupled friends, causing him ambivalence regarding his own single status. In the end, however, he realizes that finding an intimate connection with another human being is the key to personal fulfillment. Bennett was proved correct in that *Company* was not a "dance show," for the characters, with their dramatic or physicalized songs, carried most of the movement, as opposed to specified dancers. Furthermore, much of his choreography went unnoticed, given his efforts to seamlessly integrate designed movement with Prince's direction and concept. He did, however, get the dance spotlights for McKechnie as promised. In the dance number "Tick Tock," McKechnie performed a two-part jazz routine, "Having Sex" and "Making Love," which figuratively suggested the activities going on between Bobby and his newest conquest in an unseen bedroom. The number received attention for its inventiveness and content, as did the entire musical. When *Company* opened on April 26, 1970, reviews were positive. The show ultimately ran for 706 performances and won six Tony Awards, including one for Best Musical, and Bennett was once again nominated for his choreography.

So successful was Bennett's teaming with Prince and Sondheim on *Company* that he was offered the position of co-director with Prince, as well as choreographer, for their next project, *Follies*. Bennett offered the position of associate choreographer to his friend Bob Avian (who had worked with him on previous shows such as *Coco* and *Company*). The assistance/collaboration was necessary, for Bennett was going to be kept busy with the challenging show. *Follies* began as an original story idea by its librettist James Goldman. A venerable Broadway theatre, that was once home to the lavish *Weismann Follies* (a fictional *Ziegfeld Follies*), faces imminent destruction. The demolition spurs a farewell reunion of its old-time stars, all haunted by unfulfilled dreams and ghosts of the past. Although the concept musical contains a myriad of specialty numbers, side plots, and time/space disturbances (the musical moves between and occasionally merges the past and the present), its libretto centers on the failing marriages of two couples. Exemplifying *Follies*' overall atmosphere of disappointment and ennui is the fact that two of the married characters had had youthful affairs with one another; now they live with regrets over their alternate choices of spouse. Matching its grand concept and theme, the original staged production of *Follies* was epic in size, with 140 scenic and costume designs, a large orchestra, and a cast of fifty, which included an ensemble of showbiz veterans (whereby real life imitated fiction), a dance chorus of "Weismann Girls," and youthful counterparts for the married characters. To reflect the intermingling of past and present, designer Boris Aronson created a set that replicated the interior of a grand, yet aged and worn Broadway theater of yesteryear.

As the collaborator responsible for staging the musical numbers, Bennett deftly played with the past/present concept. He often placed both the elderly *Follies* chorines onstage with their youthful "ghost" counterparts, who were (at least) 6'2" showgirls made into otherworldly visages with black and white makeup and costumes, six-inch heels, and towering headdresses. One particularly effective Bennett number was "Who's That Woman?," nicknamed the "mirror number," in which the elderly chorines awkwardly try to revive a Weismann dance number from memory. In Bennett's configuration, they gradually sang and danced the routine while their younger showgirl selves were placed in the background, simultaneously dancing the combination with elegance. The entire effect was that of a time-lapse mirror. Bennett merged the two groups at the song's climax, creating one singing, dancing ensemble while suggesting the continuity between the past and present. The mirror number exploited both movement and metatheatre to serve as a metaphor for one of *Follies*' major themes. Importantly, going forward, the triumvirate of metaphor, movement, metatheatre, and their interactivity would become a defining paradigm in a Bennett musical, e.g., *A Chorus Line*.

Bennett insisted on a continuous, integrated movement and dance design to complement the show's unbroken flow of dialogue and score (with constant activity often in the background during a song or scene). He also required that the show's scenic component be similarly designed and choreographed, reflecting the fluid nature of time, space, and action. Thus, *Follies*' technical design employed travelling set pieces and backdrops, including a moving dolly with a performing band, and lighting techniques (e.g., spotlights, slow fades, travelling spots, and soft filters) that combined to create a cinematic effect for stage focus and transitions. As with the exploration and exploitation of metaphor and metatheatre, this ceaselessly "alive" stage would also become a Bennett trademark.

Upon *Follies*' opening on April 4, 1971, it received mixed reviews, many praising the score, concept, and staging, while criticizing the book, specifically, its convoluted plot and structure. The show's death knell, however, was that audiences did not connect to the dark themes, unsympathetic characters, and challenging construct. As a resultant, *Follies* closed after 522 performances and lost money, even though it was awarded seven Tony Awards. It was not a loss for Bennett, however, as he won his first two Tony Awards, sharing one with Prince for direction and another for his choreography. Bennett, still in his twenties, was being hailed as a "genius" by collaborators, underlings, and industry insiders. Bennett was not happy with the ultimate structure of *Follies*, however, for he had futilely lobbied Prince for a more traditional format during the musical's development. The experience with Prince provided Bennett with another career lesson, that is, he needed to more fully control his projects. Bennett would get his wish with his next musicals. But first, he took a detour from the musical stage to direct George Furth's play *Twigs* (1971), a work of four linked vignettes with minor storylines about a mother and each of her three daughters (all played by the same actress). Reviews were positive, and the Broadway production ran for eight months, adding a nonmusical accomplishment to Bennett's résumé.

For his next project, *Seesaw* (1973), Bennett assumed the role of director/choreographer and librettist. He was called in to save the failing show (replacing director Ed Sherin and choreographer Grover Dale) and he insisted that the libretto be re-written (necessitating the withdrawal of librettist Michael Stewart). *Seesaw* was adapted from the play *Two for the Seesaw* (1958) by William Gibson. It tells the tale of a short-lived extramarital affair between a Waspish Midwestern lawyer in New York City and a free-spirited, yet insecure aspiring Jewish dancer. Although the show's original production team was composed of experienced Broadway artists and the score was written by venerable songwriters Cy Coleman and Dorothy Fields, the out-of-town try-outs were dismal. Panicked, the producers turned to wunderkind Bennett who demanded total control before taking over the troubled project. When demands were met (only six weeks before the Broadway debut), Bennett wasted no time in reconfiguring the production, rewriting the book with contributions by the cast and some uncredited doctoring by Neil Simon. He also re-auditioned the entire cast, firing the female lead and half the show's chorus and recasting with many of his own "gypsy" favorites (e.g., Baayork Lee and Tommy Tune). When *Seesaw* opened on March 18, 1973, the critics were underwhelmed, feeling the production was a disjointed, schizophrenic affair, with its intimate relationship drama undermined by the interpolation of big showbiz/New York City production numbers. Consequently, the show ran for 296 performances and failed to recoup its million-dollar advance. Bennett, however, earned another Tony Award for his choreography, which ranged from jazzy show dance to waltzes, polkas, mambos, ballet, tap, and popular dances such as the Twist and Hustle. The choreography was a collaborative effort with associate choreographer Avian and, especially, cast member Tune. The song "It's Not Where You Start" became a tour de force number for Tune, who played a gay choreographer who celebrates a Broadway job, dancing amid a stage filled with multi-colored balloons. The number and show helped launch Tune's choreographic career as he, with Bennett's approval, designed the dance himself.

Bennett's work with Tune on *Seesaw* exemplifies another defining aspect of Bennett's career: a lifelong practice of mentoring and championing Broadway dancers and aspiring choreographers (although he also developed a reputation for being manipulative and controlling). Starting with his longtime partnership with associate choreographer Avian, Bennett never shied away from working collaboratively with cast members and assistants who, under his mentorship, began their own careers as choreographer/directors (e.g., Tune and Graciela Daniele). Bennett was also a loyal supporter and promoter of his favorite dancers (e.g., McKecknie), building his own Bennett "troupe" through the years. Thus, Bennett stands as one of the most collaborative and facilitative choreographers of the 20th century. The most potent example of this Bennett paradigm is his masterpiece *A Chorus Line* (1975). The landmark musical started with a casual conversation between Bennett and two dancers who lamented the current lack of job opportunities on Broadway. This was in 1974, and it resulted in Bennett conducting a series of late-night group sessions with Broadway dancers (gypsies), during which they shared personal and professional stories, all of which were tape-recorded. To shape the taped conversations, Bennett began to assemble librettist collaborators, and eventually a composer and lyricist. Owing to the new industry paradigm of Off-Broadway development in the form of workshops, the "dancers" project was backed by Joseph Papp and his Public Theater. During the musical's workshop period, Bennett also managed to direct an original Broadway comedy, *God's Favorite* (1974), by Neil Simon. But the "dancers" project was Bennett's top priority; and from its modest, experimental beginnings, Bennett's homage to the chorus dancer became a Broadway juggernaut, breaking box office records by running for 6,137 performances. (Further blurring the line between reality and fiction, the show was basically without stars.) Although Bennett again teamed with Avian for much of the choreography, it was Bennett who was credited with conceiving, directing, and choreographing the show (his second time receiving this triple billing, following in the footsteps of his idol, Jerome Robbins). In 1976, *A Chorus Line* was nominated for Tonys in ten categories, winning nine (including Best Musical and two for Bennett's direction and choreography), as well as the Pulitzer Prize in Drama; Bennett, at 32 years of age, became a rich man and one of Broadway's top powerbrokers.

After *A Chorus Line*, Bennett wasted little time capitalizing on his industry power and prestige. In 1978, he purchased 890 Broadway and turned the building into an arts center, with the first two floors converted into a 299-seat theatre, along with studios that he leased to professional dance companies (American Ballet Theatre is housed there). Additionally, venerable set designer Robin Wagner moved his offices here, as well as Barbara Matera, Ltd., a legendary costume shop which supplied costumes for many Broadway productions from 1967 to 2010. Two other floors were allocated to Bennett's newly created production company, Quadrille Productions. Quadrille's first project was also its first failure: *Ballroom*. Disappointment in the show was magnified because it was the long-awaited Bennett follow-up to *A Chorus Line*. Based on a 1975 television movie, *Queen of the Stardust Ballroom*, the musical tells the story of a mature widow in the Bronx who falls in love with a mailman at the Stardust Ballroom (a local dance hall), only to discover that he is married. The libretto was adapted by the original movie scriptwriter, Jerome Kass, and contains a score by composer Billy Goldenberg and co-lyricists Alan and Marilyn Bergman. In a concept reminiscent of *Follies*, Bennett filled the cast with past dance and stage stars. Working again with Avian, he created a completely choreographed world for the musical, researching ballroom dance forms in order to incorporate the foxtrot, Viennese waltz, tango, cha cha, samba, swing, and rumba. Ironically, one of the major complaints against the show was that the polished and professional dance executions did not always ring true, given the musty and amateur nature of the dance hall at which they were performed. To its credit, the musical was unique in its focus on mature characters, its authentic replication of a specific dance genre, and its continuous movement in staging and scenery. It was also an awkward throwback to earlier times, comprised of dance sequences that did nothing to reflect character or move the plot forward. It did not help that the plot was maudlin and the score was undistinguished. Bennett suffered a professional and monetary setback when the production opened in December 1978 to dismal reviews and a nonexistent box office. After workshopping the production for over a year and spending $2 million of his own money, Bennett lost his entire investment when *Ballroom* closed after only three months.

The *Ballroom* fiasco did not defeat Bennett, however, for he was back on top in 1981 with the launch of his new Broadway musical, *Dreamgirls*. The musical was the brainchild of Off-Off-Broadway playwright Tom Eyen and composer Henry Krieger. It concerns the tumultuous rise to fame of a fictional 1960s African American girl group called The Dreams. (Even though the plot and cast of characters reflect the real-life Supremes, the authors repeatedly denied any correlation.) Beginning in 1978, the musical had been developed as a showcase for musical actress Nell Carter and was given an early workshop by Joseph Papp. When Carter left the project to take a job in television, further development was put on hold. A year later, thanks to Bennett, the musical was resurrected. Upon hearing the fourteen songs that had been written by Eyen and Krieger, Bennett agreed to finance a six-week workshop of the production at his studios. After the first workshop, he took over as director (and co-choreographer with Michael Peters) and reconfigured the work into a concept musical. The development process, consisting of multiple workshops, took over a year at a cost of $3.6 million, with Bennett's financing greatly supplemented by backers such as Geffen Records and the Shubert Organization. In addition, *Dreamgirls* went through a number of cast changes and challenges in regard to the important character of Effie, the full-figured, dynamic, and difficult member of The Dreams, who is dropped from the group when the manager (who is her cheating lover) decides to transform the trio into a more mainstream and glamorous commodity. After Carter left the show, a 20-year-old gospel singer, Jennifer Holliday, was cast in the role. Holliday was displeased with the libretto's treatment of her role, however, repeatedly quitting and necessitating replacements during the project's workshop phase. Bennett finally appeased her, working with librettist/lyricist Eyen on script changes. When *Dreamgirls* opened on Broadway on December 20, 1981, Holliday set the stage ablaze with her amazing vocals and no-holds-barred performance style, imprinting her original vocal rendition of "And I Am Telling You, I'm Not Going" as the definitive performance of the song. (For her efforts, Holliday won a Tony Award for Best Actress in a Musical and a Grammy Award for Best Vocal Performance for her recording of "And I Am Telling You" on the cast album.)

Dreamgirls' libretto chronicles a ten-year span, from 1962 to 1972, during which a fledgling girl group from Chicago rises from being back-up singers for a popular R&B singer (Jimmy "Thunder" Early) to having their own act, "The Dreams," ultimately becoming a chart-topping vocal trio with a celebrated front-woman, "Deena Jones and the Dreams." In the process, there are payola scandals, extramarital affairs, internal power-plays, artistic sellouts, and music industry corruption, with two major victims of the scandal, corruption, and commercialization being Effie and Jimmy Early. Effie triumphs in the end, however, as she resurrects her career after being dumped from The Dreams; Jimmy's career, on the other hand, ends when he cannot agree to the demands of the music industry and transform himself from an R&B artist into a mainstream commercial crooner. *Dreamgirls'* story is told in an almost completely sung-through fashion, with more than thirty songs in the Eyen/Krieger score. Krieger's music is not only Motown-influenced, with catchy pop and funk-infused numbers such as "Cadillac Car" and "Steppin' to the Bad Side," but his score also combines R&B with gospel (e.g., soul-stirring anthems such as "And I Am Telling You" and "I Am Changing"), while ranging from lyrical ballads to disco (with the take-away radio hit, "One Night Only," presented as both a ballad and an up-tempo dance mix). One of the most successful aspects of the production, however, was Bennett's "cinematic" staging of the show's twenty locales (as well as its metatheatrical construct in which most numbers are positioned as recording or performing gigs, thereby played "out" to the audience). Bennett's concept was brought to life by gifted scenic designer Robin Wagner and lighting designer Tharon Musser. Wagner provided five massive towers that were remote-controlled so that they could move across the stage. There were also three extensive lighting bridges that were raised and lowered in sequence with the towers, all of which provided a dynamic array of locales on the mostly blank stage, allowing scenes and transitions to seamlessly flow in choreographed, cinematic concert. Facilitating the constantly shifting focus and theatrical drama were the travelling spots, washes of color, and other dynamic lighting effects by Musser. Given the polish and pizzazz of the production, reviews were generally positive when the production opened in 1981, and audiences loved the visual and auditory energy of the show. *Dreamgirls* ran for almost four years (1,521 performances). More than one critic began to cite *Dreamgirls* as proof of Bennett's mastery with regard to kinetic energy, fluidity, and the realization of "total theatre," claiming him to be the heir to Jerome Robbins (even though his kinetic/integrated theatre had become linked to technology, as opposed to the purely physical dance and choreography of Robbins). *Dreamgirls*, a phenomenon in its time, has yet to enjoy a successful Broadway revival, although its 2006 film version, starring Jamie Foxx, Beyonce Knowles, and Eddie Murphy, was nominated for the Academy Award for Best Film. (A 2009 national tour of *Dreamgirls* started in Harlem's historic Apollo Theatre, which, while it is in Manhattan, is not a Broadway theatre.).

Dreamgirls was Bennett's last realized production on Broadway—not the smash 1981 version, but a disappointing 1987 revival (only 177 performances). In the interim, he developed other projects such as *Scandal*, a musical that dealt with a woman's embrace of sexual exploration. Bennett produced and workshopped *Scandal* from 1980–85 but abruptly ended the project during its Broadway planning stage, possibly worried about the controversial themes and content. In addition, Bennett worked on a massive, environmental children's theatre event, *A Children's Crusade*, from 1983–86. The production, which called for 400–500 New York City schoolchildren, never reached the workshop stage. Bennett was then hired to direct the stage production of *Chess*, a sung-through musical adaptation of the 1984 concept album by composers Benny Andersson and Björn Ulvaeus (of the pop group ABBA) and lyricist Tim Rice. The musical deals with a high-stakes chess game between an American and Soviet champion as well as its surrounding romantic and political gamesmanship. Bennett never saw *Chess* to fruition, however, for he had to leave the project in 1986 when his battle with HIV/AIDS (contracted in the early 1980s) necessitated that he focus on his health. Prior to this, Bennett had sought medical treatments around the country. In 1986, he turned to a Tucson medical center's experimental drug program and relocated to the Arizona desert with his partner, Gene Pruit. The drug program was unsuccessful and Bennett died on July 2, 1987, of AIDS-related lymphoma. He was only 44 years old. Having been hailed as the most promising contemporary torchbearer of the director/choreographer tradition on Broadway, it was a tragedy that Bennett's flame was extinguished prematurely. Although the musical theatre community would look to a new generation of artists to follow in his footsteps, (e.g., Tommy Tune), there was little doubt that Bennett's death had left a directorial/choreographic void on the modern musical stage.

FEATURED PRODUCTION: *A Chorus Line* (1975)

Music by Marvin Hamlisch; Lyrics by Edward Kleban
Book by James Kirkwood and Nicholas Dante

Original Broadway Run: Opened May 21, 1975; Shubert Theatre;
6,137 performances

In an industry rife with anecdote and mythology, Michael Bennett's *A Chorus Line* holds a distinctive place in musical theatre lore. When two struggling Broadway dancers found themselves kvetching to successful director/choreographer Michael Bennett in the winter of 1974, they had no idea that they were about to make Broadway history. After the fiasco of *Rachael Lily Rosenbloom (And Don't You Ever Forget It)*, the chorus dancers, Tony Stevens and Michon Peacock, were dispirited over the dwindling job prospects due to the economically depressed climate on Broadway. They had set up something of a support meeting for two dozen of their dancing comrades who were also "gypsies" (a term for dancers in the chorus whose careers consist of migrating from one Broadway show to another). Stevens and Peacock asked Bennett to conduct the next session. The meeting occurred in a midtown gym and was kicked off by Bennett as he relayed his own "gypsy" history. Then he asked each dancer his or her name, where he or she was from, where he or she was born, and why he or she chose to become a dancer. Twelve hours (midnight to noon the next day) ensued of tape-recorded confessions and discussions about what it meant to be a Broadway gypsy. The session proved so fruitful that Bennett decided to conduct a second session, in a rehearsal studio, resulting in thirty total hours of taped material. Seeing theatrical potential, Bennett spent a month shaping the material with the help of Nicholas Dante, a dancer and aspiring writer who had been at the first meeting. With a five-hour drama in hand, Bennett appealed to producer Joseph Papp of the Public Theater to back the new production. Papp had reportedly wanted Bennett to direct a revival of Kurt Weill's *Knickerbocker Holiday* (1938) for the New York Shakespeare Festival but was persuaded to back the "dancers" project instead, lending Bennett one of the Public's performing spaces (the Newman Theater) so he could develop the work. Bennett's cast members and creative team were paid a measly $100 a week, but the scenes and dance segments produced in five weeks for the initial workshop were impressive enough to elicit further financial support from Papp. This "workshop" paradigm was a novel concept at the time, for Off-Broadway theatre companies had recently branched into the territory of musical theatre. In a low-cost, low-risk fashion, companies could fund and nurture new musicals, rehearsing and staging showings of the works at various developmental stages, taking the place of high-stakes and costly out-of-town tryouts.

Between the first and second Public workshop, Bennett directed a Neil Simon comedy, *God's Favorite* (1974), on Broadway. During the play's preview, he was chatting with playwright James Kirkwood and, before long, Kirkwood became another writer on the "dancers" project. In this same period, composer Marvin Hamlisch and lyricist Edward Kleban were secured as songwriters for the show. Although Hamlisch had recently won multiple Academy Awards for his work on the films *The Way We Were* (1973) and *The Sting* (1973), he had never composed an entire Broadway score, while Kleban only had Off-Broadway experience. The duo wrote a score that was engaging, contemporary, and dramatic, reflecting the show's libretto, which was further shaped and polished by Kirkwood. All together, the team worked on the second workshop of a musical that would soon be known as the Broadway smash *A Chorus Line*.

Completing the picture was *A Chorus Line*'s cast of real-life gypsies. Initially, the creative team had signed Kevin Kline to play Zach, the director. Kline, however, couldn't handle the dance component.

After considering Christopher Walken (given his dance experience) but signing Barry Bostwick, who dropped out after three weeks of rehearsal, they hired trained dancer and actor Robert LuPone. This casting saga proved to be an overblown issue. Zach may conduct the audition (often as a disembodied voice emanating from an unseen location), but the focal point of *A Chorus Line* is the gypsy. In the libretto, twenty-four dancers vie for eight spots in a Broadway musical chorus line. After the show's first ten minutes of dance combinations, the auditioning group is narrowed to seventeen finalists. As part of the final audition process, Zach asks them to tell their life stories and how and why they became dancers. The ensuing personal stories and, most especially, the characters delivering them are at the heart of *A Chorus Line*. Although many of the original production's cast members were pulled from the first taped sessions, not all were included in the project; some were not deemed good theatrical fits for their dramatized stories, so their stories were reassigned to others. Of the original group, some were given their first feature Broadway roles, while some were seasoned Broadway performers who were raised to a new level of prominence (e.g., Donna McKecknie, Baayork Lee, Wayne Cilento). In the end, three of the performers received Tony Awards for their performances (McKecknie, Sammy Williams, and Carole Bishop).

When *A Chorus Line* opened in 1975, no one had ever seen anything like it. The intermission-less show was deemed a concept musical, for even though the audition plot occurs in a linear fashion, many of the numbers become dreamlike or serve as flashbacks. Further, the focus of the musical is not its thin storyline but its theme, which combines metaphor and metatheatre. In a famous anecdote, Bennett started one rehearsal by drawing a line on the floor with chalk, explaining the metaphor of the dancers being "on the line" in terms of their need to get the job, as well as the larger metaphor that all humans, to one degree or another, are "on the line" at times in their lives. Bennett's white line evolved into one of the iconic components of *A Chorus Line*'s original set, behind which the dancers often stood as they told their stories and were interrogated by Zach. The scenic design by Robin Wagner was startling in its use of a stark, mostly blank stage (theatre's "blank slate"), decorated only by a set of mirrors at the rear, which were used effectively throughout the show, especially during the final number in which all the dancers reappear, with their personas multiplied by the mirrors' reflection. In concert with Wagner's abstract design, Tharon Musser's lighting cinematically created focus, atmosphere, and movement, while the production was the first on Broadway to utilize a computerized light board. The technical elements reinforced the musical's unique and metatheatrical structure, which contains one number after another played "out" to the audience. While the audition occurs in real time, it dramatically jumps to the future for the final number ("One"), which veers into surrealism as those who were ultimately cast in the musical are joined by the previously rejected auditioners, all performing in a glittery, robotic chorus line.

Despite its experimental style and structure, *A Chorus Line*'s tale is basically an old-fashioned homage to the backstage musical, with the curtains pulled back to an unprecedented degree. The show's opening number is a voyeuristic view of a real-time Broadway dance chorus audition, with twenty-four dancers warming up and then put through their paces, learning and competitively executing show jazz and classical ballet combinations. After the initial dance component, as well as a contrapuntal vocal number in which the dancers sing aloud their internalized fears and hopes regarding the audition ("I Hope I Get It"), seven auditioners are eliminated. Thereafter, the show begins in earnest as the remaining dancers compete for eight spaces—four women and four men—and bare their souls to the director Zach in the form of song, dance, and monologue. In many respects, the characters represent archetypes of the Broadway "gypsy." For instance, there is the aging and embittered chorus dancer (Sheila), the guy who fell into dancing by following his sister to class (Mike), those who escaped unhappy home lives by losing themselves in the fantasy of the ballet (Sheila, Bebe, Maggie), the ingénue who embarks on cosmetic surgery to land roles (Val), the dancer who has had to deal with ethnic stereotyping (Connie), the dancer who has to "fake" the vocals (Kristine), the resilient gypsy who has had to weather naysayers (Diana), the gay man who has hidden his sexual orientation from his parents (Paul), and the one who "made it," only to "lose it" and return to the chorus (Cassie, a prominent role originated by Donna McKechnie). Through their songs and monologues, such archetypes come alive and evolve into more fully realized characters. Respectively, their revelatory numbers include "I Can Do That," "At the Ballet," "Dance: Ten; Looks: Three" (originally titled "Tits and Ass"), "Sing," "Nothing," and "The Music and the Mirror." Hamlisch and Kleban's score is infused with a pop-rock sensibility, ripe with hummable melodies and plainspoken lyrics. Kleban's sentiments are both street-smart and lyrical, while Hamlisch's musical compositions range from up-tempo numbers to tender ballads, as well as one generic/liftable power ballad ("What I Did for Love"). He also composed a plethora of pure dance music, driven by groove beats and catchy rhythms, for example, the opening musical segment for the dance audition. The spoken monologues in *A Chorus Line* are as pithy and poignant as the score (not the usual case for traditional musicals). This is especially true for the character of Paul, who painfully relates the story of having his parents inadvertently witness his performance in a drag show. The honest and heartfelt monologue established Paul as one of the first sympathetic and realistic gay characters in a Broadway musical.

By the end of *A Chorus Line*, the archetypical gypsies acquire the identities of true survivors. Through their song, dance, and stories, they appear to be idiosyncratic, damaged, hopeful, vulnerable, sassy, funny, sensitive, and talented people who dare to dream. The ultimate irony, however, is that these fleshed-out characters have been fighting for places in a chorus line that actually robs them of individuality and authentic identity. At its end, *A Chorus Line* flashes forward to show the winners of the chorus line slots, dancing and singing their show's final number, "One." Soon they are joined by all the *A Chorus Line* cast members, forming a company of performers who now look alike, dance alike, and sing alike. In the original production, the company sparkled in gold costumes and top hats, a stark contrast from the dog-eared leotards and tights worn for most of the show. These disparate individuals had merged to become a synchronized background, highlighting an unseen star. (Bennett originally toyed with the idea of pulling someone from the audience to be the star at the head of the number every night.) In short, the gypsies bared their souls for a job that demanded that they sublimate their identities once again to serve the show and its star.

When *A Chorus Line* began previews on April 15, 1975, at the Public's Newman Theater (299 seats), word of mouth and rave reviews ensured that the production's run would sell out. After only 101 performances, the show transferred to one of Broadway's largest theatres, the Shubert (1472 seats). The musical acquired legendary status, becoming Broadway's longest-running show in September 1983, finally closing in 1990 after 6,137 performances. In addition, the original production won nine Tony Awards, including Best Musical, Best Book, Best Score, Best Director, Best Choreography, Best Actress, Best Featured Actor, Best Featured Actress, and Best Lighting Design. The Public Theater also saw a profit of almost $50 million, in exchange for their original $500,000 investment. Michael Bennett similarly reaped great financial rewards (and gave a small percentage of his earnings to the dancers in the original recording sessions). The musical toured the country and the world, becoming a sought-after theatre ticket in every place it landed. Further, it served as the template and inspiration for a new way to develop musicals, with workshops taking the place of out-of-town tryouts and becoming standard operating procedure on Broadway.

Besides the show's impressive numbers and awards, *A Chorus Line* stands as a testament to the power and potential of musical theatre to speak to many issues and provide a multifaceted theatrical experience. The musical was, and continues to be, innovative and distinctive in a variety of ways:

(1) It provided one of the earliest and truest looks behind the scenes at the musical theatre industry (a novel level of voyeurism); (2) The musical is a textbook example of theatrical reflexivity (reinforced by the metaphoric mirrors used on its original stage set), as well as metatheatre. While theatre-specific, the show's theme is also universal, as it speaks to anyone who has had to put it all on the line to get a job or assert self worth, while conforming to the wishes of others; (3) The musical paid unprecedented attention to an unsung hero of the Broadway stage, the gypsy. While this role is specifically highlighted, it is also used to represent the universal, that is, the "little guy" who has lived life in the shadows. The irony of this aspect also stands as one of *A Chorus Line*'s greatest achievements in terms of thematic complexity, for after the assertion of identity, the gypsy is swallowed into the anonymity of the chorus line; (4) In a mythic and real-life ironic twist, *A Chorus Line* was the result of true-life gypsy Bennett leaving the ranks to chase his own star, only to return to his "gypsy" roots to acquire that stardom. The tale of the man behind *A Chorus Line* and his rise to Broadway power stands in stark contrast to the dancer's story he dramatized, however, for the show is the antithesis of musical theatre's conventional "Cinderella" paradigm. Instead of being lifted from the chorus and made into stars, the central characters become stars for a moment, only to return to the chorus (a situation most exemplified by the plight of returning chorus member, Cassie); and (5) The show reinvigorated the art and practice of show dance at a time when musicals were providing fewer employment opportunities for dancers, inspiring an interest in dance across America, while providing jobs for hundreds of Broadway triple threats during its record-breaking run. In a powerful demonstration of this situation, the show's 3,389th record-breaking performance was treated as a celebratory event during which Michael Bennett took the stage with 332 past *A Chorus Line* alums.

Ten years after its debut, *A Chorus Line* was adapted to film. Directed by Richard Attenborough and starring Michael Douglas, the movie had little to do with the original stage incarnation. Bennett was not involved, the libretto was significantly altered, and the score was minus some original numbers, replaced by others that had been written especially for the film by Hamlisch and Kleban. In 2006, *A Chorus Line* was revived on Broadway, a much-anticipated event for the musical theatre community. Directed by Avian, with original choreography restaged by Baayork Lee, the production was treated as an archival tribute to Bennett's original. Yet the audiences (many of whom were not old enough to have seen the original) delighted at the time travel. The show was nominated for a Tony Award for Best Revival and ran for a healthy 759 performances. Almost as important was the film documentary made of the revival's production process: *Every Little Step* (2008). The film documents the casting of the revival, beginning in 2005 with 3,000 hopefuls gathered for the open call, and traces the journeys of the finalists who won (and lost) the coveted roles. It also includes audio of the original taped sessions with Bennett, interviews with original cast members, and footage from the original production. In 2013, a new revival of *A Chorus Line* opened in London, again directed and choreographed by Bob Avian. If there was any doubt as to the surviving myth and seductive call of the gypsy, the notoriety and success of recent revivals provide testament to the power and pull of this Broadway artist, especially as he and she are potently dramatized and paid homage via *A Chorus Line*.

PULLING BACK THE CURTAIN:
Triple Threats and Broadway Gypsies

"Gotta sing, gotta dance, gotta act" —words of advice when asked what it takes to "make it" as a musical theatre professional. This is a relatively recent mandate. In the genre's early days, one could rise to musical theatre stardom as a specialist in only one area (e.g., George M. Cohan was an extraordinary dancer but had to talk-sing his musical numbers). Such a "specialty" paradigm was even more pronounced for members of the chorus during the first half of the twentieth century. Separate singing and dancing choruses were used for typical musical comedies, and a performer was most often hired for one or the other. Acting training had yet to become widespread and institutionalized in the United States during this time; thus, few musical theatre performers had what might be considered formal actor training or technique (as was the case with most theatre performers at the time). As the industry moved into the second half of the century, the musical environment and working model began to change. Many cite Jerome Robbins' *West Side Story* (1957) as a turning point for the genre and profession. Robbins had been influenced by a new system of acting being taught in New York City and around the country, a codified technique originated in the late nineteenth century by Russian director/actor/teacher Konstantin Stanislavksy and promoted in the United States as "The Method" by master acting teacher Lee Strasburg and others. Robbins became an advocate of "method acting" and as a director/choreographer used many of its precepts and encouraged the use of its techniques when rehearsing *West Side Story*. Further, instead of dividing his show into dance choruses to handle his technically demanding choreography and singing choruses to handle composer Leonard Bernstein's challenging music, Robbins demanded that his performers be able to both sing and dance, omitting the need for separate choruses. With the success of *West Side Story*, the actor/singer/dancer, or **"triple threat"** was on its way to becoming the norm on Broadway.

This is not to suggest, however, that many of today's musical theatre stars do not excel in one area over another, with their work on Broadway focusing on their strengths and specialties (e.g., classically trained singer/actor Audra McDonald is rarely asked to dance). But, the musical theatre genre has evolved to the point that artists are expected to have had some training (formal or informal) in all three disciplines. As a result of the complicated and often character-driven librettos in the modern canon, most contemporary musical theatre performers undergo formal actor training as they realize that simply singing (or dancing) in the show is not enough. It is crucial that performers have acting skills, while most need to be able to both sing and dance to some degree. Even if not a triple threat, a musical theatre lead is often asked to exhibit "threat" credentials by doing all three when necessary (e.g., Patti LuPone donning tap shoes in the 1987 revival of *Anything Goes*). True triple-threat stars are specifically trained or highly competent in multiple areas. This list includes Broadway legends and current headliners such as Gwen Verdon, Chita Rivera, Liza Minnelli, Tommy Tune, Ben Vereen, Joel Grey, Bernadette Peters, Bebe Neuwirth, Karen Ziemba, and Sutton Foster. Even if not a triple threat, a skilled performer in the musical profession can often "fake" the discipline in which he or she is not formally trained or has not specialized. In this case, the singer/actor or dancer/actor will dance or sing, respectively, with such aplomb that the audience believes it is witnessing a triple threat in action, given the artist's commitment to the performative moment (e.g., singer/actor Norbert Leo Butz's prize-winning eccentric dancing in *Catch Me If You Can* and dancer/actor Ann Reinking's performance of lead roles that have demanded serious vocals, for example, *Chicago*).

In many cases the triple-threat evolution on Broadway drastically changed what was being asked of musical theatre dancers, especially those who were working in the chorus. These performers were known as Broadway's **"gypsies."** They were the dancers who haunted the Great White Way, moving from show to show, from chorus to chorus, willing to pay any dues necessary to stay employed and maybe, just maybe, move from the chorus into a featured or lead role on Broadway. As the idea of the triple threat caught hold in the musical theatre industry, the gypsy soon found that dance alone was often not enough to land a job. Instead of being highly trained movers on stage, who could concentrate on executing the choreography in the chorus, they were now required to sing and act (e.g., to become "characters" in their numbers). Performers wishing to have the most employment opportunities and a hand-up in auditions began to strengthen their skill sets, training as singers *and* actors, as well as dancers. The gypsy, by necessity, became a triple threat on Broadway. The additional training was not in vain, for Broadway is rife with legendary tales of those who have moved out of the chorus to become stars or powerful directors and choreographers in their own right, for example, Ann Reinking, Chita Rivera, Grover Dale, Gwen Verdon, Wayne Cilento, Graciela Danielle, Jerry Mitchell, Tommy Tune, Donna McKecknie, Cady Huffman, Karen Ziemba, Sutton Foster, etc. Some gypsies did not have to wait long for their big break. For instance, Sutton Foster, Gwen Verdon, and Shirley MacLaine became stars almost overnight when, as understudies in the chorus, they took over lead roles to great acclaim. And some gypsies have been singled out while in the chorus (e.g., Tune's lanky 6'7" frame and dancing style often got him noticed and featured early in his career).

Some gypsies, however, slogged it out in the chorus for years before being given a chance to prove themselves in featured roles or at a musical's helm as directors and/or choreographers. Some gypsies never leave the chorus; it is the life they lead as triple threats in the theatre. *A Chorus Line* brought these unsung heroes to the attention of the wider public, while the Broadway industry has its own, insular ritual by which the gypsy is spotlighted and honored. Specifically, the conveyance of the gypsy robe is a tradition (started in the 1950s) by which the chorus member with the most Broadway credits in a new production is bestowed a robe on opening night that has been passed down from show to show, with mementos and artifacts added to it through the years. As the honored chorus member wears the robe, he or she circles the stage in front of the other cast members, while they touch the robe for luck. What started as an informal acknowledgement and good luck ritual has become an institutionalized practice. The passing of the robe now has rules as to how it is presented, worn, and displayed. When a robe can no longer hold any more mementos, a new robe is begun and the old one is retired to prominent display at sites such as the Lincoln Center library and the Smithsonian. In many ways, it is a metaphoric and fitting tribute to the resilient, eternal spirit of the gypsy, whose triple-threat talents have long provided the lifeblood for the American musical theatre.

GALT MACDERMOT, JAMES RADO, AND JEROME RAGNI

In the late 1960s, America was experiencing a cultural shift (some might call it a revolution), ushered in by young radicals and their embrace of sex, drugs, and rock 'n' roll, as well as a rejection of social and class strictures, capitalist and corporate greed, and the Vietnam War. One art form, however, had yet to be significantly influenced by the counterculture movement: musical theatre. No one would have used the words "radical" or "revolutionary" (or even "groovy") to describe the musicals playing on Broadway during this tumultuous period. Then, in 1968, *Hair* hit the Great White Way, and the musical theatre world joined the "Be-In." Looking at the show's antiwar, anti-establishment, pro-drugs, pro-sex, humanist, and tribal sentiments, along with its electronic, in-your-face rock score, one would suspect that *Hair* was the brainchild of experimental theatre artists and/or taboo-testing, free-loving flower children. The assumption would be partially correct. In the grand tradition of serendipitous unions between opposites, the trio that created the genre-rocking *Hair* was a diverse and, at first glance, contradictory group. Co-librettists/lyricists Jerome Ragni and James Rado were each the epitome of the hippy-era wild child, having spent most of the decade as actors and writers who were intrigued, inspired, and (in Ragni's case) employed by the experimental theatre

companies of the day. In a concerted effort to realize a musical event that could effectively and theatrically express their worldview, Ragni and Rado joined forces with a classically trained "square," that is, Canadian composer Galt MacDermot. Together, the three artists surprised audiences and critics alike with the breadth of the work they achieved as they merged their diverse backgrounds, differing temperaments, and divergent ways to approach their craft. For all three, *Hair* would become and remain their greatest musical theatre achievement. The men would continue to influence the genre, however, be it through re-visitations of *Hair*, other moderately or marginally successful projects, or infamous flops, all of which pushed the Broadway musical envelope and suggested the potential of new theatre constructs, sounds, and experiences.

The eldest of the *Hair* trio, Galt MacDermot, was born in Montreal on December 18, 1928. He was an upper-class, well-educated son of a diplomat and spent much of his youth formally studying violin and piano. As he pursued his musical passions, he also earned a degree in history and English from Montreal's Bishop University. Afterward he found himself drawn toward jazz and swing dance idioms (e.g., boogie-woogie). In 1950, MacDermot's father received a diplomatic assignment to South Africa; and MacDermot accompanied the family to the continent where he earned his second degree from Capetown College of Music, this time in organ and composition. This education included exposure to and immersion in African and other world music idioms

James Rado and Jerome Ragni, 1960s Photo used by permission of Photofest.

that would influence much of his compositional work. After his studies at Capetown, MacDermot returned to Montreal with his new wife, Marlene, where he spent the next seven years as the organist at a Baptist church, composing pieces for the choir and slipping them into the Sunday services. He also organized a calypso band and played piano for a jazz trio. In 1955, he was signed to a small record label in Quebec, releasing the album *Art Gallery Jazz* a year later. In the work, he included a number titled "African Waltz," which had originally been part of a dance opera he composed while a student in South Africa. A cover version of the song by British bandleader Johnny Dankworth became a surprise hit in London in 1961. When the composition was covered by American jazz saxophonist Cannonball Adderley in the same year, the song earned MacDermot a Grammy. Hoping to capitalize on the success of "African Waltz," MacDermot relocated to London for a few years in the early '60s. Finding little financial success, however, he and Marlene migrated to Staten Island, New York, in 1964, where he paid the bills by writing songs and moonlighting as a pianist in local bars. Then, in 1967, MacDermot was put in touch with a couple of actors and aspiring lyricists/librettists, Gerome Ragni and James Rado, by music publisher and mutual acquaintance Nat Shapiro. Ragni and Rado had already written a rough draft of *Hair* and presented it to producer Joseph Papp, who offered to mount the work as the inaugural production of his new Off-Broadway space, The Public Theater, if the show could be realized as a complete musical. MacDermot, the consummate craftsman and professional, composed enough tunes in two weeks that Papp agreed to produce a limited run of the show.

Here, it is important to take a quick detour and explain the evolution, make-up, and significance of Off-Broadway, especially since this New York theatre scene, as well as its overall philosophy, has crucially informed and developed the musical theatre genre. Many musical scholars and historians cite *Hair* as the flagship and formative moment of the Off-Broadway movement for musical theatre (although one could argue that the successful and landmark Off-Broadway runs of *The Threepenny Opera* in the mid-1950s and *The Fantasticks*, which opened in 1960, precipitated the phenomenon of *Hair*). The Off-Broadway movement got its start during the 1950s and '60s when a group of small Manhattan theatres (100–499 seats) provided experimental theatre offerings targeted to select audiences. (Off-Off-Broadway theatres have fewer than

100 seats.) The venues were deemed "professional," that is, in compliance with the theatre unions, even though they were outside the "Broadway Box" (the theatre district ranging from 40th to 54th streets, and between Sixth and Eighth avenues, including Times Square and 42nd Street). Given the absence of commercial pressure to please a large ticket-buying populace, Off-Broadway theatres were free to experiment with form, content, and aesthetics, while challenging conventions and audiences. Today, an Off-Broadway theatre can be situated within the "Broadway Box," as long as it has a seating capacity limited to the 100–499 range and maintains full professional status, adhering to union contracts.

In general, *Hair* owes its existence to the Off-Broadway movement. And a deciding factor in Papp's historic decision to offer his Off-Broadway venue and producing efforts to *Hair* was the breadth, diversity, and accessibility of MacDermot's music. Referencing the African sounds and rhythms to which he was exposed in South Africa, as well as the divergent Western European and American music idioms in which he was versed, MacDermot was able to merge the spirit and sound of contemporary pop/rock music with classically hummable melodies and theatrically effective constructs. Such a proficient mix produced standalone radio hits such as "Let the Sunshine In," "Easy to Be Hard," "Aquarius," "Good Morning, Starshine," and "Hair" [see fig. 6.2]. In many ways, however, he left the true rock sensibility and *Hair*'s edgiest, most provocative content to his collaborators, Rado and Ragni.

Born James Radomski on January 23, 1932, Rado grew up in Rochester, New York, and Washington, D.C. As a creative youth, he was drawn to music and the theatre. Once he became a speech and drama major at the University of Maryland, he dabbled in songwriting, co-authoring a couple of musical shows. Upon graduation, he spent two years in the U.S. Navy, then attended graduate school at The Catholic University of America in Washington, D.C., co-authoring a musical revue (writing both lyrics and music for his songs). Finished with academia, Rado moved to New York City and became one of the many aspiring actor/artists in the city. To further his craft, he studied acting with the famous purveyor of the "method" technique in America, Lee Strasberg (and with other famous "method" teachers Uta Hagen and Paula Strasberg), while continuing to write and record pop songs with his own garage band, James Alexander and the Argyles. In his early 30s, he landed a Broadway gig in June Havoc's *Marathon '33* (1963). The next year, he was cast in the Off-Broadway play *Hang Down Your Head and Die*, an anti-capital punishment musical that played one performance at the Mayfair Theatre before being shut down by the government. The musical begat a passionate and creative relationship between Rado and fellow cast mate, Gerome Ragni; the two would become partners in art and life (e.g., in 2008, Ragni asserted in interviews that he and Rado also shared a sexual relationship during their writing partnership).

Ragni's childhood differed from Rado's. Gerome Bernard Ragni was born on September 11, 1935, in Pittsburgh, one of ten children in a poor Italian family. After attending Georgetown University he, like Rado, spent time at The Catholic University of America, where he indulged his dramatic side and seriously studied acting. After making his professional acting debut in 1954 in a regional Washington, D.C. production of *Shadow and Substance*, he found his way to New York, where his first significant performance was the hit play *War* (1963) at the Village South Theatre, for which he received positive notices. On May 18, 1963, Ragni married his longtime girlfriend Stephanie (together, they had a son, Erick). Like Rado, he found his way to Broadway around his thirtieth birthday, being cast in a bit part in the 1964 Broadway production of *Hamlet*, directed by John Gielgud and starring Richard Burton (which also led to Ragni's appearance in a movie version of the Burton production that same year). In addition to getting his feet wet on the Broadway stage, he debuted Off-Broadway in 1964, working with Rado for the first time as part of the cast of the short-lived, radical *Hang Down Your Head and Die* at the Mayfair.

Ragni and Rado reunited the next year as Chicago cast members of Ann Jellicoe's popular play, *The Knack*, produced by Mike Nichols and directed by Brian Bedford. Ragni had played the role of Tom in the 1964 New York City production and had received rave reviews in the Chicago production, which included Rado in role of Tolan. Soon, the two men gained some notoriety as an acting duo, not only for their work on stage, but for other projects they developed while in Chicago. Most notable was their attempt to revive *Hang Down*, from memory, collaborating on new songs and material with rock musicians Corky Siegel and Jim

Schwall. Reformatting the production to be a four-man show, the group planned to stage their performances as environmental theatre in unusual venues, such as homes and apartments in the Chicago area. (Environmental theatre is a style and method of theatre presentation and performance that breaks down the boundaries between performers and audience, mingling the two spaces. Environmental theatre techniques were widely used and popularized by the avant garde theatres of the 1960s.) With future productions in mind, Rado and Ragni rented the Harper Theatre, where *The Knack* was currently playing. Unfortunately, once *The Knack* closed, the duo had to abandon all prospective Chicago projects and return with the company to New York. This did not deter Rado and Ragni from their plans to create a musical and theatrical event through which they could espouse their political, social, and cultural views and indulge their artistic aspirations.

Ragni, besides being an actor, was a painter and poet. He had been involved since 1962 with The Open Theater, an offshoot of the avant garde Living Theatre, which employed experimental, physical, and environmental theatre techniques. (According to most reports, Ragni, as a company member, was responsible for coming up with the "Open Theater" name.) In 1966, upon returning to New York City, Ragni took a leading role in The Open Theater's successful production of Megan Terry's *Viet Rock*, an experimental, confrontational, and satirical anti-Vietnam War rock musical. While Ragni was shaking things up in the city's avant garde theatre community, Rado's career had taken a more conventional turn, originating the Broadway role of Richard Lionheart in James Goldman's historic play *The Lion in Winter* (1966). The two men did not lose touch with one another, however, and they continued to be drawn to the emerging hippie scene of New York's East Village. Both Rado and Ragni were inspired by the counterculture's pleas for class/race/gender equality, free love/sex, drug-induced enlightenment, and social tolerance, as well as the mounting anti-war protests in the streets. They had initially hit on the idea of a musical that would encompass these ideas when they were in Chicago; and Ragni's experience in *Viet Rock* only strengthened his belief that a musical employing the bold techniques and aesthetics of the Open Theater, accompanied by a rock music score, could create an electrifying, communal, and politically mobilizing event.

Ragni and Rado began seriously writing the musical that would soon be known as *Hair*. After uniting with composer Galt MacDermot, their work was deemed stage-worthy by producer Joe Papp. With regard to their differing backgrounds, lifestyles, and methodologies, the writing process between MacDermot and the two librettists/lyricists was not a face-to-face collaboration. Instead, MacDermot preferred to receive lyrics and descriptive requirements from the duo and then send them the composed music.

After its limited run at Papp's Public Theater in 1967, *Hair* played shortly at Cheetah, a large nightclub in mid-town, drawing interest from a wealthy backer, Michael Butler. He moved the production to Broadway's Biltmore Theatre, where it opened on April 29, 1968. Subtitled "The American Tribal Love-Rock Musical," the Broadway show was an experimental, experiential, often improvisational, and even ritualized celebration of the counterculture mindset and existence, performed by a long-haired "tribe" of flower children who sang, danced, and otherwise theatricalized their alternative lifestyles, satirizing and exploiting hot-button topics such as race, sex, war, drugs, capitalism, environmentalism, and religion. The Broadway production starred both Ragni and Rado as the two lead members of the tribe. The score had been expanded to contain thirty songs, while the content had been made even more incoherent and inflammatory by director Tom O'Horgan. One of O'Horgan's more infamous additions was the Act I finale, which featured full frontal nudity by both male and female cast members (an overblown scandal at the time, given that the nudity was voluntary for the cast and occurred behind a scrim with such low lighting as to be hardly visible). Regardless (or maybe because of) the provocative elements, *Hair* became a Broadway sensation, running for 1,750 performances and spawning many productions worldwide. Some of *Hair*'s songs (recorded by numerous artists) became Top 10 radio hits, while the Broadway cast album was widely released, resulting in the music of *Hair* being added to the American songbook.

Soon after making waves on Broadway, Ragni and Rado left New York's *Hair* to play their signature roles in the Los Angeles production for five months, frequently changing the show during the run. While in LA, Ragni and Rado, along with one of the "superstars" of Andy Warhol's Factory, Viva, also starred in the improvised, experimental movie *Lions Love* (1969).

When Ragni and Rado returned to the Broadway production of *Hair*, the duo continued their habit of revising and destabilizing their signature show, often implementing radical changes mid-performance. Their bad-boy behavior was not appreciated by Broadway backstage and industry professionals, but it did provide publicity. In one instance, Ragni and Rado were arrested for walking nude down the theatre aisle during a performance; at another point, the duo's antics necessitated guards being placed outside the theatre, barring their entry. The antics paid off. When the legal and professional conflicts were resolved, all their changes were written into the script and the duo rejoined the show.

In the meantime, MacDermot moved from *Hair* on to new projects; but he was still closely associated with producer/director Papp. He worked as composer for a new musical debuted by Papp's New York Shakespeare Festival: *Two Gentlemen of Verona* (1971). The Shakespeare play was planned as part of the company's free presentations in Central Park. MacDermot had composed background music for two previous Shakespeare in the Park productions. When Papp hired Mel Shapiro as director, however, Shapiro felt that the production should not only have underscoring but, instead, have a full score, complete with a modern musical sound and feel. Thus, *Two Gentlemen of Verona* was turned into a rock musical, and playwright John Guare was hired as the work's lyricist, while also teaming with Shapiro to write the libretto. The result was a high-energy production performed by a racially diverse cast, with the milieus of Milan and Verona being re-presented as Puerto Rico and New York. Guare and Shapiro mostly replaced Shakespeare's words with modern-day and ethnic slang equivalents; yet they retained Shakespeare's verse when theatrically effective (e.g., the lyrics for "Who Is Sylvia?" are lifted directly from Shakespeare's play). Such anachronisms and adaptations provided the show with a modern and ironic flavor. The production's language and atmosphere were more than matched by MacDermot's exuberant rock score. In the end, the Central Park run proved so popular that *Two Gentlemen* moved to the St. James Theatre, playing 614 performances, winning the Tony Award for Best Musical (beating out Sondheim's *Follies*), and furthering the belief that the rock musical had arrived.

While MacDermot was enjoying success with *Two Gentlemen*, Ragni was not only continuing to play Berger in the touring companies of *Hair* but he was also writing *Dude, The Highway Life*, a new musical that he had been developing ever since the opening of *Hair*. Ragni approached MacDermot to write the music, but the composer was already committed to *Two Gentlemen*. Once finished with the *Two Gentlemen* score, however, MacDermot wrote the music to fifty of the songs in Ragni's show (only half of the numbers would be retained for the final Broadway version). Unfortunately, Ragni's unwieldy libretto was practically incomprehensible on stage, even though he had cut his original rough draft of 2,000 pages down to a "mere" 200. The libretto tells a metaphorical tale in which forces of good and evil attempt to win the soul of a young man, Dude, who ultimately indulges in a life of sex and drugs, causing his parents (Adam and Eve prototypes) much pain and worry. Capitalizing on his *Hair* success and notoriety, Ragni was able to make extreme demands to realize his vision of Dude's life journey on stage. Specifically, he insisted that the entire interior of the Broadway Theatre be emptied and reconfigured, at a cost of $800,000, to create an environmental theatre-in-the-round performance space that was representative of Earth, along with Heaven and Hell. Further, to represent Earth, the emptied theater floor was covered with fake dirt (real dirt caused problematic dust and mud) and flanked by the audience; the entire space was then embellished by ramps, runways, trapdoors, pillars, trapezes, bleachers, and mechanical set pieces/devices. Ragni's designers, technicians, and producers drew the line, however, at some of his more outlandish requests, including his wish for 100 butterflies to be released at the top of each show. Not surprisingly, *Dude's* rehearsal/preview period was a nightmare.

Tom O'Horgan was brought in during previews to take over *Dude* (the original director and choreographer had resigned). Actors were replaced, including an almost surreal development in which the lead, a white 23-year-old who couldn't sing, was replaced by an 11-year-old African American in the role of Dude. Due to the boy's age, another man was cast as "Big Dude" in order to retain the songs containing mature content. All resulted in a mutiny by the cast and director during previews, and they demanded that Ragni rewrite much of the show (especially the second act). Many actors ultimately provided much of their own dialogue.

After the show opened at the Broadway Theatre in October 9, 1972, it closed after sixteen performances, greeted by scathing reviews and disgruntled audiences. MacDermot's score was also panned, due, in great part, to the fact that it couldn't be heard, because the acoustics were horrible in the "dirt pit" and members of the orchestra were separately suspended in chairs above the audience.

Shortly after *Dude* closed, MacDermot experienced another major failure with the flop rock musical *Via Galactica* (1972). With lyrics by Christopher Gore and a book by Gore and Judith Ross, the musical was a futuristic depiction of a community of outcasts (with special focus on a space-age garbage man) and their life on an asteroid in the year 2972. The special effects and pyrotechnics used to convey the "space" aspect were more laughable than effective; and the plot was so unclear that a synopsis was included in the show's program. Nonetheless, audiences were still baffled when the show, conceived and directed by respected British director Peter Hall, opened on Broadway on November 28, 1972. Those who did comprehend the material didn't like it. After fifteen previews and seven performances, *Via Galactica* closed. Savaged by critics and audiences alike, the musical's sole distinction was that it was one of the first Broadway shows to lose more than $1 million.

While Ragni and MacDermot collaborated on *Dude* and MacDermot experienced further failure with *Via Galactica*, Rado continued to explore the themes and theatrical forms of expression that he had begun with *Hair*. Specifically, he created a score and collaborated with his brother, Ted, on a book for a musical entitled *The Rainbow Rainbeam Radio Roadshow* (*Rainbow* for short). *Rainbow*, which features a character called "Man who was killed in the Vietnam War and now lives in Rainbow Land," opened at Off-Broadway's Orpheum Theater in December 1972. Often regarded as a sequel of sorts to *Hair*, the show received a positive review in *The New York Times*, with Rado lauded for his music and lyrics. Since then, *Rainbow* has been revised numerous times, some versions explicitly reflecting *Hair* (e.g., *Rainbow: The Ghost of Vietnam* which was staged in the late 1990s) and others appearing as more abstract, standalone works (e.g., the newest rendition, initially titled *Billy Earth: The New Rainbow* and then renamed *American Soldier: The White Haunted House*).

In 1974, Rado reunited with Ragni to co-write *Sun: An Audio Movie*, a show with music by Steve Margoshes, based on a play by New York writer Joyce Greller. The musical (later titled *YMCA*) centers on environmental and political themes, decrying pollution and the devastation of the rain forests. It was presented as a workshop for backers in 1976. One year later, Rado and Ragni wrote another musical together, again with Margoshes, titled *Jack Sound and His Dog Star Blowing His Final Trumpet on the Day of Doom*. The show had an Off-Broadway staging in 1977, playing a short run alongside an ill-fated Broadway revival of *Hair* that ran for forty-three performances in total and featured Ragni and Rado as the bogus cops who bust the show. The team would continue to revisit both *Sun/YMCA* and *Jack Sound*, creating new versions until Ragni's death from cancer at age 55 in 1992.

While Rado and Ragni experienced a reunion of sorts, MacDermot continued his own career trajectory, realizing one more original Broadway work in 1984: *The Human Comedy*. With book and lyrics by William Dumaresq, the show was an adaption of William Saroyan's 1943 novel, which, in a backward fashion, had begun as a Saroyan screenplay for the 1943 movie of the same name. Described by many scholars and critics as an American folk opera, this sung-through musical is a coming-of-age tale set during World War II in a small Californian town. The show centers on a young telegram messenger, Homer, who witnesses the wartime struggles, along with the emotional highs and lows experienced by the citizens in his town and, especially, his family members. For instance, Homer's mother works tirelessly to support the family, having lost her husband in the war; his brother is enlisted in the Army; his sister is a love-starved teen; and his little brother, Ulysses, yearns to travel the rails while grappling to understand his father's death (and, yes,

the allusions are literary responses to and reflections of Homer's ancient Greek works). *Human Comedy* is epic in scale, with a large cast of characters and numerous subplots, as well as a through-composed score by MacDermot. MacDermot's work not only includes traditional show tunes, it also exploits the idioms of gospel, pop, swing, and folk, all appropriate to mood, character, plot, and period (1940s). Again working with Joseph Papp, the show debuted at his Public Theater in 1983, garnering enough positive feedback to motivate a move to Broadway. Unfortunately, unlike its Public Theater musical predecessors *Hair* and *A Chorus Line*, the musical was dismissed by audiences when it opened at the Royale Theatre in 1984. Even though critics applauded MacDermot's score and the overall dramatic range and achievement of the work, *Human Comedy* closed after only thirteen performances. To date, *Human Comedy* was MacDermot's last original work to debut on Broadway.

An end to the MacDermot/Rado/Ragni chapter came with Ragni's death in 1992. Today, Rado continues to be associated with *Hair*, having directed national tour productions and a 2006 Canadian stage version in Toronto; he has also further redeveloped *Sun/YMCA*. MacDermot continues to compose music for a variety of venues (concert, recording, film, theatre), performs with the New Pulse Jazz Band, and is enjoying a contemporary resurgence as a number of his compositions have been sampled by rap and hip-hop artists. But the three men will mainly be remembered for the revolutionary work and spirit they engendered within the musical theatre genre with *Hair*, proving that a modern "rock" musical could not only succeed on Broadway but also become a social and cultural phenomenon while simultaneously speaking to and reflecting a specific moment in America's history.

HAIR

Music by Galt MacDermot;
Lyrics by Gerome Ragni and James Rado (1967)

She asks me why
I'm just a hairy guy,
I'm hairy noon and night,
Hair that's a fright.
I'm hairy high and low,
Don't ask me why, don't know,
It's not for lack of bread,
Like the Grateful Dead. Darlin' …

Give me a head with hair,
Long beautiful hair,
Shining, gleaming, steaming, flaxen, waxen,
Give me down to there hair,
Shoulder length or longer,
Here baby, there mama,
Ev'rywhere, daddy, daddy

Hair, hair, hair, hair, hair, hair, hair, hair
Flow it, show it,
Long as God can grow it, my hair.

Let it fly in the breeze
And get caught in the trees,
Give a home to the fleas in my hair.
A home for fleas, (yeah) a hive for bees, (oh yeah)
A nest for birds, there ain't no words,
For the beauty, the splendor, the wonder of my

Hair, hair, hair, hair, hair, hair, hair, hair
Flow it, show it,
Long as God can grow it, my hair.

I want it long, straight, curly, fuzzy
Snaggy, shaggy, ratty, matty
Oily, greasy, fleecy,
Shining, gleaming, steaming, flaxen, waxen,
Knotted, polka-dotted, twisted, beaded, braided,
Powdered, flowered and confettied,
Bangled, tangled, spangled and spaghettied.
Oh, say can you see my eyes

If you can then my hair's too short.
Down to here, down to there.
I want hair down to where it stops by itself
Doo-doo-doo-doo …

They'll be "gaga" at the "go-go"
When they see me in my toga
My toga made of blond, brilliantined,
Biblical hair.
My hair like Jesus wore it,
Hallelujah, I adore it.
Hallelujah, Mary loved her son.
Why don't my mother love me?

Hair, hair, hair, hair, hair, hair, hair, hair
Flow it, show it,
Long as God can grow it, my
Hair, hair, hair, hair, hair, hair, hair, hair
Flow it, show it,
Long as God can grow it, my
Hair, hair, hair, hair, hair, hair, hair, hair
Flow it, show it,
Long as God can grow it, my hair.

FEATURED PRODUCTION: *Hair* (1968)

Music by Galt MacDermot; Lyrics and Book by Gerome Ragni and James Rado

Original Broadway Run: Opened April 29, 1968; Biltmore Theatre; 1,750 performances

You've taken your seat in the Biltmore Theatre on an April evening in 1968, waiting for the lights to dim, the overture to start, and the opening number (i.e., the "grabber") to welcome you to the production, inviting you to sit back, relax, and enjoy the musical theatre entertainment on stage. What you did not expect, however, was to be "grabbed" or touched in the literal sense of the word. But then again, the show you were about to experience was not just any Broadway musical; it was *Hair.* And your invitation at the top of the show was not to sit back and observe, but to join the Be-In, to be part of a cultural revolution, and to "drop out and drop in" as an inductee of the *Hair* tribe. Specifically, as the opening refrains of the psychedelic anthem "Aquarius" played, cast members roamed through the audience and climbed over seats, engaging with the audience and inviting them to join the movement, let go of judgment and release inhibitions, and celebrate love, peace, beads, happiness, flowers, and *Hair.* In this manner, the landmark rock musical, composed by Galt MacDermot, with lyrics and libretto by Gerome Ragni and James Rado, signaled to Broadway its aim to challenge every conventional aspect of musical theatre, be it music, content, style, and/or performance. As a result, the production, in all its shaggy glory and flower-child exuberance, lived up to its subtitle, "The American Tribal Love-Rock Musical."

Since working together as actors during the mid-1960s, co-librettists and lyricists Rado and Ragni had toyed with the idea of writing a musical about the emerging hippy movement and its worldview, using experimental and environmental theatre techniques. After hanging with a group of young drop-outs, Vietnam draft-dodgers, long-haired rebels, and counterculture flower children in the East Village, Rado and Ragni, according to their own reports, were even more committed to the idea of transmitting the experiences and ideologies, as well as the energy and freedom, of this community to the stage. Further, they began to adopt the lifestyle as their own. Soon, the writing team had lyrics to thirteen songs, including "Ain't Got No," "I Got Life," "Don't Put It Down," "Colored Spade," "Manchester," "Frank Mills," "Hair," "Aquarius," "Easy to Be Hard," "Good Morning Starshine," and "Where Do I Go?." Industry professionals, however, were not willing to finance and produce the Rado/Ragni draft of the show, given that the material was only in text form (this work was to be a musical, after all). To facilitate the project, however, music publisher Nat Shapiro introduced the writers to a trained and gifted composer, Galt MacDermot, who quickly supplied music for a handful of songs.

Producer Joseph Papp, who had been initially interested in the work, was impressed enough with MacDermot's completed songs to sign the show, titled *Hair,* as the inaugural production at his new Off-Broadway venue, The Public Theater. Gerald Freeman, as the theatre's artistic director, was signed to direct the musical's debut, which included both writers in the performance. Specifically, Ragni starred as the hippy tribe's flamboyant leader, Berger; Rado was briefly allowed to play the more sensitive role of Claude (ten performances). MacDermot even made a brief appearance as one of the phony cops who busts the show at the end of the first act. One of the fans of the Off-Broadway production was financial backer Michael Butler, who ultimately bought the rights from Papp for $50,000, with plans to move *Hair* to Broadway. He signed a new director, Tom O'Horgan, who was versed in avant garde theatre techniques, styles, and content. As the show was being readied for its Broadway close-up, it was moved to a nightclub in Midtown, called Cheetah, for a month's worth of performances.

With O'Horgan at the helm, the show underwent numerous cast and production team overhauls, while Ragni was slated to reprise his role of Berger and Rado was permanently cast as Claude. Further, O'Horgan emphasized the more controversial and unconventional aspects of the show. He encouraged improvisation and audience-engagement by the cast, muddied the linear narrative with non sequiturs and hallucinogenic sequences, and pushed even more hot buttons with incendiary language and acts on stage, including inflammatory songs such as "Hashish" and full frontal nudity at the end of Act I (having been inspired by a nude antiwar protest he saw in New York City at the time). O'Horgan "invited" the cast to shed inhibitions and material belongings, such as clothing, to join in a humanist and naturalist plea for peace. The segment, which came on the heels of Claude's lyric ballad "Where Do I Go," triggered major legal/censorship challenges. Yet the musical triumphed over the long-held "indecency" statutes of New York City (it is important to note, however, that *Hair* may have beat the courts in New York, but the show continued to face similar challenges, as well as protests, as it toured the country). The entire nudity brouhaha could also be seen as a throwback to the *Ziegfeld Follies* in regard to sex and publicity, given the fact that *Hair's* nudity was obscured (it was behind a scrim and the lighting was low; similar to Ziegfeld's "tableaus"), while audiences were intrigued and titillated by the concept and the controversy.

In its new Broadway configuration, the sprawling content of *Hair's* libretto was matched by an expanded score by MacDermot, who had also become the production's music director. In moving from the Public to the Biltmore, the number of songs in *Hair* increased from twenty to more than thirty (to put this in perspective, most Broadway musical scores at the time had around fifteen numbers, *Oklahoma!* had thirteen). The breadth and diversity of MacDermot's score is extraordinary. Specifically, MacDermot's compositions range from psychedelic pop ("Aquarius") to British Invasion pop ("Manchester") to rocking anthems ("Hair" and "I Got Life") to gentle folk ballads ("Frank Mills") to easy-listening folk-rock ("Good Morning Starshine") to Hindu mantras ("Hare Krishna") to Motown ("White Boys/Black Boys") to a Renaissance madrigal ("What a Piece of Work Is Man") to the blues ("Easy to Be Hard"), and a bring-down-the-house gospel revival ("Let the Sunshine In"). Many of the songs were influenced by the sounds and rhythms that MacDermot heard while living and studying in Capetown, South Africa. He has often described his score as being rooted in African rhythms and music forms. Some music critics, however, disparaged the use of the term "rock" with regard to the musical. Specifically, they applauded the score for its diversity, comprised of sounds and rhythms not yet heard on the Broadway stage. They also remarked, however, that the traditionally structured and hummable compositions did not really reflect the current sounds and content being heard and hailed as cutting-edge or "acid" rock on the radio, for example, Jimi Hendrix, The Doors, Cream, Janis Joplin, The Who, etc. Critics' quibbling aside, some songs from *Hair* began to win radio play and popularity even before the show's Broadway debut, with several numbers being recorded by a range of artists, resulting in top radio hits for acts such as Three Dog Night, The 5th Dimension, and Oliver. Further, the Broadway cast album topped the U.S. charts for a year.

Once the expanded *Hair* opened on April 29, 1968, at the Biltmore Theatre on Broadway, it brought new, younger, and more adventurous audiences into the Broadway district, as well as offered conventional ticket buyers a voyeuristic view of the hippy lifestyle and mindset that they might have, otherwise, hesitated to experience firsthand in the East Village or Ashbury Heights. To explicate the libretto here would be difficult, given that it is a sprawling, experiential "happening" and has also undergone many changes and reconfigurations since its Broadway debut. Overall, the production is a performative celebration of counterculture concerns and beliefs in the late 1960s, as lived by a tribe and led by its flamboyant leader, Berger. The loosely structured plot includes the travails of tribe member Claude, who, as he searches for a higher purpose in life, discovers his draft number has been called and refuses, unlike his cohorts, to burn his draft card. Ironically, he is tragically and symbolicallly presented as a casualty of war at the end of the production. Other subplots include free-love triangles, as well as an extended psychedelic drug trip that theatrically suggests, through song and dance, the American id, ego, and superego, specifically addressing concepts and historical examples of the nation's military complex, war tragedies, and underlying racial tensions. In its mission to expose and denounce America's hang-ups and hypocrisies toward sensitive or taboo subjects, *Hair* addresses race, racism, and miscegenation ("Colored Spade" and "Black Boys/White Boys"), antimaterialism and anticorporatism ("Ain't Got No" and "I Got Life"), youth rebellion ("Hair"), sex ("Sodomy"), and drugs ("Hashish"), while also using confrontational, controversial verbiage, slurs, and imagery to illustrate how words, concepts, and symbols can become appropriated, warped, and used in discourse as weapons by a bigoted, intolerant establishment. Other *Hair* themes and topics include indictments of war, most dramatically expressed through "Three-Five-Zero-Zero," which references Allen Ginsberg's 1966 poem, *Wichita Vortex Sutra*, in which an army general gleefully spells out the number of enemy soldiers killed in one month. Pacifism is further evoked through the uplifting anthems of "Hare Krishna" and "Let the Sunshine In." Environmental concerns are also broached in the score, specifically by the whimsical tune "Air," sung by a character in a gas mask who satirically greets the pollutants of carbon monoxide and sulfur dioxide. Significantly, Judeo-Christian religiosity is confronted and exploited throughout the work, whether in oblique reference or obvious satire (e.g., Berger is looking for "my Donna" in the song "Donna," a tongue-in-cheek reference to the Madonna). Despite the tribe's ambivalence and irreverence regarding formal religious doctrines and practices, they form their own religion, with rites and rituals practiced and observed during the show. Alternative forms of spirituality and belief systems are explored in *Hair*, including astrology ("Aquarius" and "Good Morning Starshine") and Hinduism ("Hare Krishna"). Lastly, literary themes are smartly exploited throughout the libretto. In addition to the aforementioned Ginsberg reference, *Hair*'s lyrics and libretto often cite Shakespeare, with the humanist lyrics of "What a Piece of Work Is Man" being pulled directly from *Hamlet*. Indeed, the sprawling content of *Hair* is complex, sometimes convoluted, and often controversial; but the subject matter and its subversive treatment on stage did not turn off Broadway audiences. *Hair* became a phenomenal box office hit in 1968. The show ultimately ran for 1,750 performances, while furthering the counterculture movement in America during the late 1960s and early '70s as the show became an iconic theatre work and poster child for a new age, successfully touring nationally and internationally.

In later years, however, the canonical status and future for *Hair* seemed bleak. In 1977, a revival flopped on Broadway, lasting for only forty-three performances; other special engagements and concert versions were unenthusiastically received (including a disappointing 2001 City Center *Encores!* version). This suggested that *Hair* was simply a curious and dated artifact that could no longer speak to a contemporary audience. It did not help that the 1979 film adaptation, directed by Milos Forman and choreographed by Twyla Tharp, was a box office disappointment, possibly because it debuted a decade after the hit Broadway production and substantially differed from the original plot, earning Rado and Ragni's disapproval. Then, as the first decade of the twenty-first century was winding down, a revival proved to Broadway audiences that the "granddaddy" of the rock musical still had life and legs. Beginning in 2007, Joe's Pub and the Public Theater presented a 40th anniversary production of the show for three nights at the Delacorte Theater in Central Park. The concert version, directed by Diane Paulus and featuring MacDermot on the keyboards, was a big hit with audiences (actors from the original production were even included in the encore of "Let the Sunshine In"). Nine months later, The Public Theater staged a full production for a limited summer run at the Delacorte, again directed by Paulus and with many cast members carried over from the concert version. Reviews were so positive and audience members so enthusiastic that the Public decided to transfer the show to Broadway. Backers were hard to find, however, with the country in the depths of a major recession and many investors wary about putting their money behind such a risky work. Yet with the addition of new partners, the producers finally raised the $5.5 million necessary and worked to keep production costs low. The initially hesitant investors were smiling when the revival opened at the Al Hirschfeld Theatre on March 31, 2009. Reviews were mostly raves, with many lauding the show's energy and ability to connect to a new generation. Audiences agreed. By August the entire production investment had been recovered, being one of the fastest recoups in Broadway history. Ultimately, the latest *Hair* revival ran for 519 performances (sales began to suffer when the original cast transferred to the London production). It also won the Tony Award for Best Revival of a Musical, as well as other major awards, and a Grammy Award for its cast album. On the heels of a successful 2010 national tour, the revival re-landed on Broadway for a limited run during the 2011 summer/autumn season. It was the first show to have a free streaming live cam on the stage so that audiences all over the world could experience the nightly spectacle. Given this latest box office success, it seems that *Hair* not only stands as a landmark in America's musical theatre history, but can still push buttons and inspire audiences to dance in the aisles.

PULLING BACK THE CURTAIN:
Dawning of the Age of the Rock Musical

Up until the 1960s, musical theatre had not only reflected the most current musical movements, idioms, and sounds in America but had also produced many of the top radio hits of the day. All of this changed with the advent of rock 'n' roll. The musical theatre industry was slow on the uptake with regard to the new music genre, a curious situation, given that Broadway had previously been at the musical forefront with the popularization and proliferation of trendy dance crazes and swing rhythms, as well as other cutting-edge and innovative idioms (e.g., ragtime and jazz). But when the electric guitar, hard-hitting vocals, long hair, and groove beat began to dominate popular music, Broadway all but ignored the new sound and aesthetic. For instance, the biggest hits on Broadway during the 1964 season were the traditional book musicals *Hello, Dolly!*, *Funny Girl*, and *Fiddler on the Roof*—all backward-looking works with scores consisting of traditionally constructed and hummable show tunes (even though *Fiddler* also exploited a Hebraic folk sound). Listening to these hit musicals, no one would suspect that America's popular music scene was undergoing a revolution and reeling from the "British Invasion." Specifically, Beatlemania had hit America, and other rock groups, such as The Rolling Stones and The Animals, had young audiences screaming, jamming, and dancing. The years that followed saw an even more radical revolution in the rock scene, as artists and bands such as The Byrds, Jimi Hendrix, Cream, The Doors, Janis Joplin, Buffalo Springfield, and Jefferson Airplane upped the counterculture appeal of rock 'n' roll with further sound amplification, sociopolitical commentary, musical experimentation, and world-music assimilation. Rock 'n' roll became grouped with sex and drugs, and the new sound embodied a youthful movement of rebellion and revolution (as has always been the way of popular music evolutions).

Then, in 1967, a couple of counterculture actors and writers, James Rado and Gerome Ragni, teamed with a classically trained composer who was also versed in African music, Galt MacDermot, to create Broadway's first rock musical: *Hair*. MacDermot may have not been as hard-rocking as the most progressive bands on the radio; but he employed the groove beat and amplified, electronic sound, as well as psychedelic, Motown, and tribal touches, to demarcate his score as "rock"—the first to have been so designated on Broadway. (*Rolling Stone* magazine derisively compared his score to a collection of commercial jingles, ignoring the fact that the soft-rock sound of The Monkees also topped the charts at the time.) *Hair* was not delineated as "rock" only by its score, however. Equally instrumental to its overall "rock musical" character was a combination of aesthetic, construct, and themes, all informed by and reflective of youthful rebellion and the counterculture.

Thus, *Hair* became an archetype for the rock musical. And today, similar criteria exists with regard to pure "rock musical" status; for a musical work most widely considered to be of the subgenre not only has the necessary rocking, electronic score, characterized by rawness, amplification, and use of synthesizers, but it also contains the following components, content, themes, and aesthetic:

Youth Culture: While the writers of rock musicals are not always young (even though they closely identify with the age group), the musical's cast is predominantly young (often professional novices), personifying the demographic most targeted and explored in the work. The production's overall aesthetic exploits and reflects popular, cutting-edge mediums of entertainment (i.e., an array of aural and visual elements that include rock music idioms, amplified sound design, hyperkinetic staging, and edgy, high-tech costume/scenic design), as well as the sociopolitical and cultural concerns of youth.

Counterculture: Relative to the youth-culture emphasis is the rock musical's access, illumination, and advocacy of a counterculture. The characters in a rock musical are often alienated from contemporary social, political, and cultural norms. Crucial to the characters' alienation from and rejection of mainstream values is the added dimension that they are bound to one another by their lifestyle choices and misfit status. The counterculture becomes its own community (even a tribe), bound by youthful angst, anger, and antisocial behavior as well as its noisy celebration of freedom, choice, and enlightenment.

Rebellion in Search of Identity: In direct correlation to the rock musical's counterculture character is the form's major themes of rebellion and identity. Rock musical characters often take the rebellious path of sex, drugs, and rock 'n' roll, testing boundaries as they search for a sense of identity and authenticity. This crisis of identity and authenticity may be a result of youthful alienation incited and complicated by other components such as sexual orientation, gender, race, religion, ethnicity, or ideology. In any case, the path forward is one that includes rebellion, along with a plea for tolerance of the alternative lifestyle, the revolutionary, the "Other," the outcast, the misfit. Hearkening back to *Hair*, tolerance and understanding, as answers to rebellion and identity, are key themes in any rock musical.

Since *Hair*, there have been many works dubiously deemed by critics, scholars, artists, and audiences to be rock musicals. Thus, it may be helpful to consider another classification for borderline works: the pop rock musical. This category includes musicals that contain a modern-sounding score, replete with electronic instrumentation and contemporary vocal styles. Yet the overall sound is not as aggressive, amplified, and alternative as the rock musical score. The score is more situated within the radio-friendly, pop rock genre; it is often nostalgic, maybe even a jukebox compilation (e.g., *Grease, The Wiz, Little Shop of Horrors, Aida, Mamma Mia, Jersey Boys, Million Dollar Quartet, Movin' Out, Priscilla Queen of the Desert*). Other works may espouse a more experimental and hard-driving rock score, yet the subject matter misses the rebellious, alienated, and especially, youth-centric aspect of the rock musical (e.g., *Next to Normal*). With regard to these subtle differentiations, the following works fall within the "rock musical" category, while having enjoyed significant and/or influential runs on Broadway:

- *Hair* (1968); 1,844 performances; Book/Lyrics by Gerome Ragni/James Rado; Music by Galt MacDermot
- *Jesus Christ Superstar* (1971); 711 performances; Lyrics by Tim Rice; Music by Andrew Lloyd Webber
- *Two Gentlemen of Verona* (1971); 627 performances; Book by John Guare/Mel Shapiro; Lyrics by Guare; Music by Galt MacDermot (Tony Award Best Musical)
- *The Rocky Horror Show* (1975); 45 performances; Music/Lyrics/Book by Richard O'Brien
- *The Who's Tommy* (1993); 899 performances; Based on 1969 concept album by The Who; Book by Pete Townshend/Des McAnuff; Lyrics/Music by Pete Townshend
- *Rent* (1996); 5,123 performances; Music/Lyrics/Book by Jonathan Larson (Tony Award Best Musical; Pulitzer Prize for Drama)
- *Spring Awakening* (2006); 859 performances; Book/Lyrics by Steven Sater; Music by Duncan Sheik (Tony Award Best Musical)
- *Passing Strange* (2008); 165 performances; Book/Lyrics by Stew; Music by Stew/Heidi Rodewald
- *In the Heights* (2008); 1,184 performances; Book by Quiara Alegría Hudes; Music/Lyrics by Lin-Manuel Miranda (Tony Award Best Musical)
- *Rock of Ages* (2009); still running; Music/Lyrics by multiple artists; Book by Chris D'Ariengo

- *American Idiot* (2010); 422 performances; Music by Green Day; Lyrics by Billie Joe Armstrong; Book by Armstrong/Michael Mayer
- *Bloody Bloody Andrew Jackson* (2010); 94 performances; Music/Lyrics by Michael Friedman; Book by Alex Timbers
- *Spider-Man: Turn Off the Dark* (2011); still running; Music/Lyrics by Bono/The Edge; Book by Julie Taymor/Glen Berger/Roberto Aquirre-Sacasa

In addition to the above list, numerous rock musicals have found homes and even cult statuses Off-Broadway, with two notable, long-running examples being *Your Own Thing* (1968) and *Hedwig and the Angry Inch* (1998).

With a glance, one might note that the heralding of a new "rock musical" age, due to the phenomenon of *Hair*, was premature. *Jesus Christ Superstar* and *Two Gentlemen of Verona* contributed to the prediction that the rock musical was on Broadway to stay, but then the form seemed to fizzle out. With colossal, costly flops such as *Dude* and *Via Galactica* in 1972, the willingness to risk money on the edgy, rock-scored musicals dissipated and Broadway audiences seemed to lose interest. Case in point, *The Rocky Horror Picture Show* only lasted forty-five performances (the work was formative, however, given the iconic cult status of its film adaptation). It would be almost twenty years before another successful rock musical premiered on Broadway (i.e., *Tommy*). But not until *Rent* in 1996 did the excitement over the subgenre genuinely resurface. In many ways, *Rent* is hailed as the true heir to *Hair*. A Pulitzer-winning and Tony-winning hit (with rabid followers called RENT-heads), Jonathan Larson's musical is an iconic celebration of a "new" East Village counterculture, a tribe for the 1990s, whose members shun materialism and rebel against social norms in search of freedom, artistry, and love. In a '90s twist, however, the characters also battle lethal repercussions of the drugs/sex lifestyle (addictions and AIDS). With Larson's untimely and sudden death by an aortic dissection (aortic tear) the day before the show's highly anticipated Off-Broadway premiere, the musical acquired almost mythic status, with new urgency and depth given to its message of searching for connections and meanings in life, as well as living each moment as fully, authentically, and positively as possible (e.g., "One Song Glory,"

University of Colorado at Boulder's production of *Rent*, 2011
Used by permission of Nathan Rist.

"Seasons of Love," and "Another Day"). The show was hailed as the beginning of a new rock musical era. Yet again, the pronouncements were premature. The true rock musical renaissance would not happen for another decade, beginning with the 2006 debut of *Spring Awakening*. The Tony-Award-winning adaptation by librettist/lyricist Steven Sater of the 1891 Frank Wedekind play was given an anachronistic and edgy treatment by its director, Michael Mayer (including a staging concept in which audience members could sit on the stage throughout the show), and contains a score composed by alternative rock musician Duncan Sheik. Now, more than forty years after *Hair*, it seems that the rock musical has finally found its place on Broadway with regard to critical recognition and box office. Most rock musicals that have debuted on Broadway after *Spring Awakening* have been nominated for Tony Awards. Further, *In the Heights*, a musical that examines intergenerational conflicts and the assimilation struggles (i.e., identity searches) of young adults in the Dominican-American neighborhood of Washington Heights, not only won the Tony for Best Musical but its score, by Lin-Manuel Miranda, helped popularize rap and hip-hop on Broadway. *In the Heights* was not alone in contributing new sounds to the musical theatre genre. Recent rock musicals on Broadway have showcased such diverse rock music styles/idioms as "punk" rock (*American Idiot*), "hair-band" rock (*Rock of Ages*), and "Emo" rock (*Bloody Bloody Andrew Jackson*). The current production of *Spider-Man: Turn Off the Dark* takes the rock musical themes of youthful alienation, rebellion, and identity to soaring heights (literally) while proving to be the most infamous and expensive musical of the twenty-first century. In short, the new styles/idioms, diverse subject matter, and technological advances of the current rock musicals have invigorated the Great White Way, bringing in new audiences and helping to restore the musical's status as an art form that authentically and inclusively reflects the sights and sounds of contemporary America.

JERRY HERMAN

How does one solve a paradox like Jerry Herman? When surveying the artists who have achieved greatness and distinction during the modern era of American musical theatre, it is difficult to categorize lyricist/composer Herman. His career lacks a certain level of experimentation and innovation achieved by his peers. Yet his musicals have proved capable of speaking to modern audiences and generating great box office, an ironic development given that most of his works are placed squarely in the past and rely heavily on old-school musical tricks and techniques. Herman himself understood the conundrum, admitting that he didn't really understand current songwriting trends (i.e., rock 'n' roll, dissonant/atonal experimentation, and ironic prose), but felt most comfortable with the conventional sounds and sentiments of the 1930s and '40s. Exemplifying this admission, his works can appear to be musical theatre throwbacks, often taking the form of the formulaic crowd-pleaser or star vehicle, ripe with flashy, hummable, loosely integrated production and specialty numbers. In this respect, the most renowned Herman scores often lack sophisticated integration and specificity, as they are composed of generic songs that are easily liftable, built on melodic lines and time signatures that are direct and infectious. A Herman song often employs the timeless, hypnotic waltz (3/4) time as well as the marching or "cakewalking" time signature of 2/4, a meter that almost begs a clap-along from its audience and strutting kicks from its performers. Another signpost of a Herman score is his exploitation of the "bombastic ballad," his signature soul-stirring anthem that is given further dramatic impetus by simply increasing the song's tempo or modulating its key. Lastly, Herman (an admitted acolyte of Irving Berlin) has never tried to be self-expressively witty, urbane, or intricate in his lyrics, choosing, instead, to use simple, straightforward lyrics, often repeating one refrain several times in the chorus or "big finish" of a song.

All of these characteristics of Herman's works have led many a detractor to dismiss his shows as big, empty vehicles, ripe with caricatures that are given little distinction and development as they sing his bombastic, repetitive, formulaic, and generic compositions. If this view seems overly harsh, that is because it *is* overly harsh. In the same breath that one might

Jerry Herman in rehearsal of *Hello, Dolly!* with Carol Channing, March 1964 © Bettmann/CORBIS

criticize the throwback character of a Herman show or score, one must also cite the captivating degree of buoyant optimism and the resulting entertainment value provided by his most popular works. Meanwhile, the generic nature of his scores resulted in many direct, exuberant, hummable, and liftable songs that moved beyond the boundaries of a specific Herman show to find places on the pop charts and, ultimately, become musical theatre standards in the American songbook. As a composer/lyricist, Herman has often reported that he sees his primary role to be that of a "heightener" of a libretto's emotions through song. To this point, the bombastic ballad may be a simple device but it effectively serves such a heightening purpose, while also occasionally providing an iconic musical theatre moment. Further, Herman's productions represent a rarity in the musical theatre canon in that they center on a middle-aged female, providing great starring vehicles for mature Broadway divas (and diva drag queens). These musicals fly in the face of the old "matron" stereotype, for Herman's "big ladies" drive their overall shows and are shown in powerful and positive lights. And in an industry that lives or dies by the box office, Herman's hits have been bonanzas for Broadway (as well as for regional, community, and educational theatres across the country). This "leading traditionalist," as Herman is often called, is also a musical theatre title holder; he is the only American composer/lyricist to have had three of his musicals play over 1,500 performances on Broadway, i.e., *Hello, Dolly!* (1964), *Mame* (1966), and *La Cage aux Folles* (1983). In short, love him or leave him, there is no denying the indelible imprint made by Jerry Herman on the American musical theatre genre.

Gerald Herman was born in New York City on July 10, 1932, and raised in Jersey City. His mother was a piano teacher but young Jerry never took a lesson from her or anyone else; instead, he taught himself to play, picking out tunes by ear (a practice that hearkened back to the likes of Cohan, Berlin and Loesser—all idols of Herman). After high school, Herman attended Miami University, intent on becoming a drama major. He was active in the musical theatre arena, writing songs (music and lyrics) and librettos for college revues, as well as serving as a director and/or designer for student productions. So popular were his college revues that one, *I Feel Wonderful* (1954), was backed by local enthusiasts and produced at an Off-Broadway theatre after Herman had graduated from Miami. It was the first of a series of revues during the early 1960s by Herman to play Off-Broadway and in nightclubs (where Herman also found work as a pianist, having relocated to New York City). During his struggling days in the Big Apple, Herman kept busy writing musical numbers for television. When Herman's agent introduced him to playwright Don Appell, the two men set their sights on Broadway, musing over concepts for an original show. Appell suggested a musical about Israel; and as unlikely a topic as that might have seemed, Herman was intrigued by the idea. With no specific story in mind, the two men headed to Israel for research, where they spent five weeks immersed in Israeli sounds, sights, and culture. There, they came up with a plot, and Herman began writing songs to turn the narrative into a musical, titled *Milk and Honey* (1961).

The libretto of *Milk and Honey* features a late-blooming romance between a middle-aged man, Phil (who is separated from his wife), and a younger widow, Ruth. Both characters meet and fall in love while visiting Israel as American tourists. Ruth is distraught over their romance, however, given that Phil is still married. As a result, the show ends with Phil committing to a future with Ruth and travelling back to America to finalize his divorce. In many ways, *Milk and Honey* is a unique musical. First, instead of the traditional love story between an ingénue and leading man, *Milk and Honey* contains a complex romance between conflicted middle-aged characters. Second, it stands as the only successful Broadway show to have been set in Israel. When *Milk and Honey* opened on Broadway in October 1961, critics were pleased by the original storyline and setting, as well as the performances and Herman's score. Specifically, it had been Herman's wish to make the lead characters Americans instead of Israelis so that he wouldn't be limited to minor-keyed Hebraic melodies and idioms; yet, he managed to infuse his score with the sounds of Israel, most notably with the songs "Shalom" and "Milk and Honey," while supplying more traditional compositions that boasted both exuberant and tender melodies. Running for 543 performances, the musical proved to be a positive career launch for Herman.

One of the few downsides to having achieved early success with *Milk and Honey* was that the musical theatre industry pegged Herman as a composer/lyricist most suited to writing scores for serious, romantic musicals dealing with mature characters. This was a mistaken assumption, given that Herman felt most at home writing in the old-fashioned musical comedy style, with snappy show tunes and simple, declamatory lyrics. It is no surprise that he leapt at the chance to provide the score for a new musical being developed by über-producer David Merrick—an adaptation of Thornton Wilder's popular farce *The Matchmaker*. The project's throwback nature was a perfect fit for Herman. Further, in various incarnations, the source material had been tickling audiences' funny bones and warming their hearts for more than a century. *The Matchmaker*'s basic storyline had originated in 1835 as *A Day Well Spent*, a popular British play by John Oxenford. Seven years later, the farce was revisited by Johann Nestory, who penned a Viennese adaptation under the title *He Wants to Have a Lark*, which was also a hit with audiences. The plot received a musical theatre treatment in 1891, resulting in one of Broadway's first blockbuster musicals, *A Trip to Chinatown*. This early musical featured the top-selling song of the Tin Pan Alley era, "After the Ball," by Charles K. Harris. Moving into the twentieth century, a novice playwright, Thornton Wilder, wrote his own Americanized version, *The Merchant of Yonkers*, which had a disappointing run on Broadway in 1938. Committed to the appeal and potential of the timeworn storyline, Wilder revisited his own work fifteen years later with the more maturely written and styled *The Matchmaker*, which not only became a major Broadway hit in 1955 but also an American classic.

Herman, ever attuned to the smell of a populist hit but still a new kid on the block, aggressively auditioned to write the score for the most recent reinterpretation of the classic comedy: a musical titled *Hello, Dolly!*. To win the job, he wrote four songs that so pleased producer Merrick that he verbally contracted Herman on the spot. Herman joined proven librettist Michael Stewart and prestigious director/choreographer Gower Champion, along with flamboyant star Carol Channing, who took the title role after Ethel Merman turned it down. Surprisingly, given the pedigree of the production team and star, *Hello, Dolly!* struggled mightily during its out-of-town tryouts. Merrick even threatened to shut down the production before its Broadway debut. In a panic, revisions ensued, with writers called in and some significant cast replacements made. For his part, Herman worked overtime to fix the show musically, deleting some numbers and writing three new ones on the road (including the full throttle ballad and Act I intermission teaser "Before the Parade Passes By," which became a standalone hit). The creators also heightened the drama and spectacle in Act II by delaying Dolly's reappearance until the show's title song, a showstopping production number in which she is welcomed back to an old favorite restaurant. Dolly's entrance down the grand staircase of the Harmonia Gardens, in plumed, red-gowned profligacy, while a chorus of dancing, singing, and adoring waiters saluted her, became (and continues to be) the pinnacle of the show. The song, given its form and function, was the first of many "staircase" numbers for Herman and became a trademark of his musicals. The Herman "staircase" number is usually an interpolated and lavish salutatory song comprising simple, exclamatory lyrics (with the saluted character's name used repetitively) and a catchy melody, often intensified by brassy instrumentation, mass volume, kinetic energy, a presentational performance style, and major star power.

Although structural changes were made to the libretto by Stewart (and others), the plot still adhered closely to Wilder's *Matchmaker*. The musical farce tells a turn-of-the-century tale of a curmudgeonly Yonkers merchant, Horace Vandergelder, who has forbidden his ward and niece, Ermengarde, to marry an impoverished artist, Ambrose. Ever ready to meddle, the matchmaker Dolly Levi talks Ermengarde and Ambrose into eloping, knowing that Vandergelder is leaving on a scheduled trip to New York City. Further, Vandergelder's trip has been arranged by Dolly, for she has been hired by the lifelong bachelor to find him a wife. Little does he know that Dolly, a widow, has decided to make Vandergelder her next husband. Adding to the fun, Dolly convinces Vandergelder's head clerk, Cornelius Hackl, and second shop clerk, Barnaby, to play hooky from the store during their boss' absence; for she has arranged for the two romance-hungry men to meet a dressmaker, Irene Malloy, and her assistant, Minnie Fay. Per Dolly's machinations, the three young couples converge for dinner at her old New York City haunt, Harmonia Gardens, unaware that Vandergelder will be dining there with Dolly, who has hijacked his originally arranged blind date. Frantic, antic comedy ensues as the dining couples try to avoid being seen by Vandergelder. The restaurant escapades result in all parties being arrested and hauled into court, where Cornelius appeals to the judge, citing "love" as the culprit. The judge releases the group; once back in Yonkers, love triumphs as everyone is mated in the end, including Dolly and Horace.

When *Hello, Dolly!* opened on January 16, 1964, reviews were not unanimously positive. The musical was appreciated and applauded by many for its old-school charm, vigor, showmanship, humor, and spectacle as well as the indisputable magnetism of Channing in the role of Dolly. But there were also criticisms over what some saw to be the vulgar exploitation of flash and dash over substance, especially in terms of score/libretto integration. Specifically, much grousing and head scratching occurred over the title song at Harmonia Gardens, "Hello, Dolly!," which did not advance the story or develop character; instead, it appeared to be a purely exhibitionist song and dance for the sake of spectacle (even today, critics often ask why the heck there is such an epic celebration over a widow's return to a restaurant). Yet critics could not deny the catchy appeal and versatility of Herman's score. And even if the songs themselves often veer toward the generic, failing to specifically reflect the show's time and place, Herman's score is nevertheless ripe with music and dance forms that were popular in the late 1800s, for example, waltzes ("Dancing"), military marches in 2/4 time ("It Takes a Woman"), and strutting cakewalks ("Put on Your Sunday Clothes" and "Hello, Dolly!"). In addition, the score includes lyrical ballads ("Ribbons Down My Back" and "It Only Takes a Moment"), character songs ("I Put My Hand In" and "So Long, Dearie"), as well as "Before the Parade Passes By," a solo ballad that grows into an all-out production number as it transitions from slow tempo to march tempo, along with a volume increase and key modulation. As a testament to the score's strength in its day, Herman's title song, "Hello, Dolly!," as recorded by jazz great Louis Armstrong, won the Grammy Award for Song of the Year in 1965, beating out "Hard Day's Night" by The Beatles.

Audiences paid little notice to the nitpicking critics and were overwhelmingly won over by the charms of *Hello, Dolly!*—a phenomenon possible explained by the show's feel-good, nostalgic, and escapist nature at a tumultuous moment in American history (the mid-60s). The musical placed second only to *Fiddler on the Roof* as one of the top-selling musicals of the decade, running for 2,844 performances. And eventually, the critics' ambivalent views shifted to reflect that of the general public, with the musical sweeping the Tony Awards, winning eleven in all (including Best Musical as well as Best Score for Herman). *Hello, Dolly!* was also a star-maker; for it not only catapulted Herman to fame, but also cemented Channing as a musical icon in the role of Dolly Levi. She would continue to be identified with the role throughout her life, repeatedly reprising it on Broadway and on tour, never missing a performance. (It is musical theatre lore that to have been Ms. Channing's understudy for Dolly was to be guaranteed a life of waiting in the wings, never to go on stage.) Channing, however, left the original Broadway production to headline the national tour; and a series of leading ladies (Ginger Rogers, Martha Raye, Betty Grable, Phyllis Diller, and original choice Ethel Merman) took on the role that has proved, along with Mama Rose, to be one of musical theatre's most enduring powerhouse vehicles for mature women. The role of Dolly Levi also became groundbreaking with regard to the concept and practice of nontraditional casting, for African American Pearl Bailey assumed the role after Channing's departure, accompanied by an all-black cast. In 1975, this revisionist all-black version, headlined again by Bailey, became the first Broadway revival of *Hello, Dolly!*—a significant development, even though the show played for only forty-two performances. Channing would headline future Broadway revivals but would lose the one chance to make her incarnation of Dolly immortal on the screen when it was decided by Hollywood powers-that-be that she was not right for their film adaptation. Instead, the part of Dolly was given to Barbra Streisand, who was decades younger than the title character as written. The film was a disappointment, because movie musicals had begun to lose popularity by the time it debuted (1969).

Not long after *Hello, Dolly!*, Herman enjoyed another theatrical triumph, once again capitalizing on proven source material, a popular play that glorifies another strong-willed, free-spirited, meddling matron who triumphantly lives life on her own terms. Herman's musical adaptation was titled *Mame* (1966), and it became the fifth longest running musical of the 1960s. The show was written by Jerome Lawrence and Robert E. Lee, who had earlier adapted the novel *Auntie Mame* (1955) by Patrick Dennis (not autobiographical but "inspired" by his eccentric aunt) into a winsome Broadway play by the same title in 1956. Feeling that their work almost begged to be musicalized, Lawrence and Lee approached Herman and the three began to develop *Mame*. After Mary Martin turned down the lead role, more than forty women were auditioned. Finally, a British singer/actress named Angela Lansbury won the part. With her critically acclaimed performance as the larger-than-life aunt, Lansbury began her reign as one of Broadway's favorite leading ladies. Herman solidified his reputation as a Broadway hit-maker when the musical opened to positive reviews and began a phenomenal run of 1,508 performances (Herman's second show to top 1,500).

The libretto of *Mame* spans almost two decades (1928–46), placing much of the action at 3 Beekman Place, the New York City home of Mame Dennis. The story revolves around the eccentric, idealistic, and strong-willed Mame, who lives according to the philosophy that one must seize the day, seek adventure, and live life to its fullest, otherwise risk becoming just another poor "son of a bitch" who wastes his or her life. At the crux of Mame's story is her relationship with her orphaned nephew, Patrick, who becomes her ward. Through the years, Auntie Mame raises Patrick in an unconventional household, exposed to the constant drama of her life. First, as a widow, she is wiped out by the stock market crash. She then turns to show business for money, exploiting her best friend, stage star Vera Charles. She lands a role in Vera's latest musical comedy, but brings it to ruin. Ultimately Mame finds financial security through marriage to Southern aristocrat Beauregard Jackson Pickett Burnside, only to return to widowhood when he dies in a freak climbing accident in the Alps. Indomitable and ever positive, she looks beyond her own tragedy to help her nephew, now an adult, by meddling and matchmaking. Mame steers Patrick away from an unsuitable social-register snob and toward a modest, sincere girl who can offer him true love, bringing the musical to a happy end.

Along with a stellar cast and smart libretto, Herman's bouncy, hummable score helped create the infectious, energetic world of *Mame* on stage. Although the score lacks authentic reference to the sounds of America's Great Depression and World War II (two epic periods spanned by the musical), Herman's songs successfully reflect the sunny, determined, straight-talking nature of Mame. Most of the tunes are composed of simple meters and formulaic, catchy melodies, paired with generic lyrics that aggressively assert can-do optimism. Examples include "It's Today," "Open a New Window," and "We Need a Little Christmas," with the latter becoming a contemporary Christmas classic (another instance where Herman was able to follow in the footsteps of his idols Berlin and Loesser). Further, Herman provided the showstopping "Mame," another "staircase number" for his leading lady, replete with cakewalking meter and a salutatory chorus lyric that exclaims her name over and over in its rousing finale refrain. In addition to these stereotypical Herman numbers, his score includes other touches; specifically, a telling character duet in which Mame and Vera exchange smartly satiric barbs ("Bosom Buddies"), as well as the tender ballad "If He Walked Into My Life" (this number, which is sung by Mame as she ponders her guardian role with Patrick, does little to further or illuminate their relationship; instead, it reads as a generic torch ballad and has frequently been lifted from the musical and used, out of context, as such). After its Broadway opening, *Mame* was nominated for numerous Tony Awards, including Best Musical, but only the "Herman ladies" won their respective Tonys: Lansbury for Best Actress in a Musical and Bea Arthur (who originated the role of Vera) for Featured Actress. The musical has lived on to become a favorite on the regional and community theatre scene, while a Broadway revival was staged in 1983, again with Lansbury in the lead (and "supervised" by Herman), but it only ran for forty-one performances. Nonetheless, the musical stands as one of the more significant star

vehicles for its female-driven content and the powerful, multifaceted "matrons" at its center.

It would be a long time before Herman would replicate the success of his first two hits, although not for lack of trying. Three years after *Mame*, Herman opened his new Broadway production, *Dear World* (1969), inspired by Jean Giraudoux's 1943 play, *The Madwoman of Chaillot*. For the musical, Herman again teamed with librettists Jerome Lawrence and Robert E. Lee, with Lansbury in the lead role. Like the play, the musical centers on the theme of dehumanizing industrialization, capitalism, and science being trumped by idealistic poets, misfits, and lovers, that is, dreamers committed to a world of beauty, passion, and fantasy. In *Dear World*'s libretto, a corporation discovers oil directly under a Parisian bistro, where a "countess" (a.k.a. The Madwoman) lives in the basement, consumed by delusions and memories of a lost love. In a complicated twist, one of the corporation's executives has fallen in love with the bistro's waitress. When it is decided that the bistro will be blown up to obtain the oil, the executive teams with the waitress and the countess to foil the plan. In her ultimate act of defiance and victory, the countess lures the corporate bosses to her underground world, where they become lost in the sewer system. To reflect and support the unconventional story, Herman's score includes some sophisticated touches, including a lyrical, evocative waltz, "I Don't Want to Know," and the contrapuntal "Tea Party," as well as authentic references to period Parisian cabaret music. There are also Herman interpolations of trademarks such as the title song, "Dear World," which veers into pure showbiz as it evolves into a strutting, high-kicking anthem (saluting a philosophy rather than a leading lady, however). The disjointed score was just one of the reasons for *Dear World*'s negative reviews when it opened on February 6, 1969. Many critics felt the musical was overblown and artificially "Broadway," given the intimate and poetically nuanced source material. Herman and his collaborators agreed, lamenting that they had felt pressured to turn the work into another Broadway blockbuster. Thus, *Dear World* closed after only 132 performances, while Herman, Lawrence, and Lee proceeded to rewrite the show in later years, restoring the intimacy they felt had been undermined on Broadway. Herman continued to tinker with the show up through 2000 for regional theatres, adding three new songs and even bringing in another librettist, David Thompson, for further book revisions.

Dear World was followed by another ambitious, yet disappointing failure for Herman: *Mack and Mabel* (1974). With music/lyrics by Herman and a libretto by *Hello, Dolly!*'s Michael Stewart, the musical details the tumultuous romance between slapstick movie pioneer Mack Sennett (originator of the Keystone Cops) and his famous star Mabel Normand. One might have expected a romantic screwball comedy in the vein of *On the Twentieth Century*. Instead, Stewart chose to play up the bittersweet and conflicted nature of the affair between the two film icons, treating the relationship so seriously that the book often seemed at odds with the musical's overall milieu (i.e., the comic antics of the Sennett movies and the flirty sexiness of Normand in her starring roles). One positive aspect of the sober and probing treatment, however, was the chance it gave Herman to flex his songwriting muscles. At the time, he was being pigeon-holed as a one-trick-pony who often resorted to simplistic, repetitive lyrics and formulaic melodies that lacked nuance and complexity, not to mention a lack of character/place/time specificity. As a rebuttal, Herman wrote some of his most potent and thoughtful lyrics for *Mack and Mabel*'s score, as well as compositions that played with minor keys, chromatic and challenging melodies, and diverse balladic styles, ranging from Mabel's pained and poignant "Time Heals Everything" to Mack's ironic quasi love song, "I Won't Send Roses." Most critics (as well as Herman) deemed the music of *Mack and Mabel* to be his most sophisticated. This is not to suggest that there weren't some Herman trademarks in the 1974 production. They included the toe-tapping (literally) homage to the optimism and escapism of early musical talkies, "Tap Your Troubles Away," as well as the "staircase" number for the show's diva ("When Mabel Comes in the Room"), which is sung by well-wishers on the movie set. Instead of descending a staircase to great aplomb, however, Mabel (originally played by Bernadette Peters) got to ride a camera crane over her adoring crowd. Upon *Mack and Mabel*'s debut, however, audiences and critics were unimpressed, and the production ran for sixty-six performances.

Mack and Mabel was not the last flop for Herman in the '70s. In 1979, after two disappointing revivals of *Hello, Dolly!* (1975 and 1978), Herman wrote the score for a new musical, *The Grand Tour*. With a libretto by co-authors Mark Bramble and Michael Stewart (Herman's third collaboration with Stewart), the musical

is an adaptation of Franz Werfel's novel, *Jacobowsky and the Colonel* (1944). In short, the work is a satire in which an anti-Semitic aristocrat, desperate to escape the encroaching Nazis, must team with an optimistic, assertive Polish-Jewish intellectual who owns a car, but cannot drive it. The rest of the libretto covers their travel adventures, including an eventual love triangle. As far as the critics were concerned, Herman's score was undistinguished; and the musical had the dubious distinction of being Herman's weakest box office draw to date, running for sixty-one performances. Herman started the next decade by supplying a few songs for *A Day in Hollywood/A Night in the Ukraine* (1980). The two-part nostalgic, metatheatrical homage to early musicals and the Marx Brothers was conceived, directed, and choreographed by Tommy Tune. Dick Vosburgh wrote the clever libretto, while the numbers written specifically for the project were supplied by composer Frank Lazarus, with lyrics by Vosburgh. In addition, the score contains numbers contributed by other artists (e.g., Herman) as well as already-written period songs. Although the show was a popular and critical hit, running for 588 performances, it was not much of a boon to Herman's career as he was only one of many contributors.

By the early 1980s, Jerry Herman was in danger of being relegated to footnote status in musical theatre history, embodying the cautionary tale of the quick-rising star who fails to live up to early promise. A disappointing revival of *Mame* on Broadway in 1983 did not help matters, suggesting that Herman's best years were decades behind him. Then, in the same year, he again earned his showman stripes and cemented his place in the musical theatre canon with a new work that not only recaptured his Broadway audience but also tapped into a broader cultural consciousness, breaking new ground as the first Broadway homosexual musical. The landmark work was *La Cage aux Folles* (1983). Based on the same-titled 1973 French farce by Jean Poiret, the musical adaptation has a libretto by playwright/actor Harvey Fierstein and was initially directed by director/librettist Arthur Laurents. The musical is set at a contemporary drag-queen nightclub in St. Tropez, run by a pragmatic owner, Georges. The club's star attraction is a drag diva, Zaza, performed by the flamboyant and dramatic Albin, Georges's gay lover for over twenty years. When Georges and Albin's longtime domestic world is disrupted by the discovery that

Georges' son (resulting from a long-ago youthful tryst) plans to marry the daughter of a well-known social conservative and morals crusader, they decide that they must conceal the intimate nature of their relationship. As Albin is specifically forced to alter his persona and hide his homosexuality, he is angry and hurt. Once he acquiesces, however, he goes the extra mile, posing in drag as Georges' matronly wife. Unfortunately, the ruse is discovered; but in the end, Albin and Georges are able to use a little creative blackmail to convince the conservative father to allow the marriage.

Given that *La Cage aux Folles* centers on a homosexual couple and deals with gay themes, the musical was considered a pioneering achievement in musical theatre. Still, there were detractors who felt, regardless of the subject matter, that the musical was not exactly groundbreaking. First, the love affair and domestic partnership between Georges and Albin was treated in a clichéd and sterile fashion, as opposed to an in-depth exploration of an authentic long-time relationship. Second, the musical, in many ways, reflected past Herman box office hits, that is, a large, splashy musical comedy in the old-school Broadway tradition. Specifically, the show featured a glamorous drag chorus (the Cagelles), which came in handy since the score was ripe with big, catchy production numbers, such as "La Cage aux Folles," "The Best of Times," and "We Are What We Are." The last song provided Herman with another bombastic ballad, as he reprised the melody and much of the lyrics for Albin, who expresses his frustration over being forced back into the closet, singing "I Am What I Am" [see fig. 6.3]. Along with Herman's trademark cakewalks/marches and hummable melodies, he provided some delightful character numbers, such as "With You on My Arm" and "Masculinity," as well as sentimental Parisian touches (e.g., "Song on the Sand"). Overall, the appealing book, characters, design, and score (Herman's tenth) meshed to create a world on stage that delighted audiences. Word of mouth was so positive during out-of-town tryouts that *La Cage* was almost guaranteed hit status before it reached Broadway. As a result, when the show opened on August 21, 1983, it was able to demand record ticket prices for orchestra seats ($47.50) and won six Tony Awards (in all major categories), with Herman winning his second Tony for his score. *La Cage* became Herman's third Broadway musical to pass the 1,500-performance mark, running for 1,761 performances.

As Herman entered the latter part of his career, riding high on his success with *La Cage*, he began to enjoy and exploit his status as a Broadway icon, revisiting his extensive body of work in various reconfigurations. First, there were the revues. On December 18, 1985, he opened *Jerry's Girls*, which celebrated his "Big Lady" shows, as well as the Herman songbook. A second Herman revue, *An Evening with Jerry Herman*, played on Broadway from July to August in 1998. This production was even more personal, as Herman starred as pianist and performer, supported by two cast members. And then there were the revivals. Herman has never been shy about reviving his works, with his major hits being revived on Broadway more frequently than almost any other artist's. In 1995, he brought *Dolly* back to Broadway, the third New York revival of his original mega-hit. The production depended heavily on nostalgia, starring Channing (now in her seventies), and ran for 116 performances before beginning what was deemed Channing's "farewell" tour. The first decade of the twenty-first century proved to be even more lucrative for Herman in terms of revivals, with two successful new productions of *La Cage* opening on Broadway only six years apart (2004 and 2010). In a fun twist on the revival phenomenon, Herman also saw two of his *Hello, Dolly!* songs, as clips from the 1969 film, interpolated into Pixar's animated *WALL-E* (2008) as a major component of the storyline, reasserting the musical's iconic American status and immortalizing its songs in a new form for a new audience. Immortalization was further guaranteed a couple years later when Herman received the Tony Award for Lifetime Achievement in the Theatre in 2009 and was a recipient of the Kennedy Center Honors in 2010. Given this flood of career accolades and tributes, it seems that although Jerry Herman may still be regarded by some as an old-fashioned throwback to musical theatre's past, his musicals and songbook will live far into the future.

Figure 6.3

I AM WHAT I AM

Music and Lyrics by Jerry Herman (1983)

I am what I am –
I am my own special creation.
So come take a look,
Give me the hook or the ovation.
It's my world that I want to take a little pride in,
My world, and it's not a place I have to hide in.
Life's not worth a damn,
'Til you can say, "Hey world, I am what I am."

I am what I am,
I don't want praise, I don't want pity.
I bang my own drum,
Some think it's noise, I think it's pretty.
And so what, if I love each feather and each spangle,
Why not try to see things from a diff'rent angle?
Your life is a sham 'til you can shout out loud
I am what I am.

I am what I am
And what I am needs no excuses.
I deal my own deck
Sometimes the ace, sometimes the deuces.
There's one life, and there's no return and no deposit;
One life, so it's time to open up your closet.
Life's not worth a damn 'til you can say,
"Hey world, I am what I am!"

FEATURED PRODUCTION: *La Cage aux Folles* (1983)

Music and Lyrics by Jerry Herman; Book by Harvey Fierstein

Original Broadway Run: Opened August 21, 1983; Palace Theatre; 1,761 performances

Jerry Herman was sorely disappointed. Having seen the French film *La Cage aux Folles* (1978) in 1981, the composer/lyricist had fallen in love with the style and spirit of the romantic farce, which is set in the heart of the drag-show entertainment milieu and is centered on an old-fashioned love story between two longtime spouses of disparate temperaments who face and ultimately overcome a challenge to their relationship. In the case of *La Cage aux Folles*, however, the couple happens to be homosexual and the instigating source of conflict stems from their own beloved family member, a son who has been raised from infancy by the two men and who eventually asks that they pretend to be something other than their domestic, committed gay selves. Herman saw musical potential, positivity, and "heart" in the material; but its adaptation was already in progress, assigned to other musical theatre artists, director/choreographer Tommy Tune and composer/lyricist Maury Yeston. Fortunately for Herman, the original project faltered after three months of fitful starts. The composer/lyricist leapt at the chance to replace Yeston, ultimately making history with his fellow collaborators as he helped to realize the first "homosexual musical" on Broadway.

The idea to adapt the film version of *La Cage aux Folles* into a stage musical originated with successful movie producer Allan Carr, who was looking to make his mark on Broadway. Unable to secure the rights to the film, however, Carr settled for the rights to the movie's original source, the French farce written in 1973 by Jean Poiret. With dramatic rights secured, he then contracted Jay Presson Allen to devise a libretto and Maury Yeston to compose the score. Originally titled *The Queen of Basin Street*, the Allen/Yeston musical was to be relocated to New Orleans, with Mike Nichols and Tommy Tune set to direct and choreograph, respectively. Next, Carr teamed with executive producers Fritz Holt and Barry Brown, both of whom had Broadway credentials and could bring significant financial backing to the project. Holt and Brown were underwhelmed by the creative team, however, given that *The Queen of Basin Street* had stalled in the development phase; and the executive producers fired all of Carr's original picks (the dismissed artists filed lawsuits, but only Yeston won his case, collecting a small royalty from the profits of the realized *La Cage aux Folles*).

Starting anew, with source material in hand, Holt and Brown turned to librettist/director Arthur Laurents to direct the project, having worked successfully with him as a director (and original librettist) of their 1974 revival of *Gypsy*. Initially, Laurents hesitated to take on the project. He seriously doubted that a gay musical could work on Broadway, even though he himself was an outspoken and politically active gay man who enjoyed a longtime domestic partnership, and had written other groundbreaking musicals that dealt with challenging content and themes of intolerance (e.g., *West Side Story*). He was unenthusiastic about the show's "drag" component, aware of a current heightened degree of homophobia in America due to the emergence of a newly transmitted disease in the gay community termed GRID (gay-related immune deficiency), soon to be known by its official name, HIV/AIDS. Reservations aside, Laurents ultimately took the job, mostly as a favor to the executive producers. He became more enthusiastic, however, when he learned that he would be working with songwriter Jerry Herman and librettist Harvey Fierstein (who had recently won two Tony Awards for writing and starring in 1982's touching, honest, and humorous gay-life saga, *Torch Song Trilogy*). As with all artistic collaborations, the members of the creative team offered differing accounts regarding the early development of the show. According to Laurents, Herman had written the show's triumphant and defiant anthem regarding identity and self-acceptance, "I Am What I Am," before anything else was put on paper. The song so moved Laurents that he developed his entire directorial concept around it, envisioning the scene that would showcase the number at the end of Act I, while also directing Fierstein and Herman to use it as the inspiration and underpinning for their writing. Herman, however, has stated in various accounts that the show was far along when Fierstein supplied the climactic scene for Act I, which included the line "I am what I am." Herman was so taken with the line that he asked Fierstein if he could turn the phrase into a song; the next day Herman supplied a full bombastic ballad based on the sentiment.

Although there may be ambiguity surrounding key aspects of the show's beginnings, there is consensus that the artists purposefully chose not to frame the show as a diatribe or mission statement regarding gay rights. Instead, the Herman/Fierstein/Laurents musical, titled *La Cage aux Folles*, would simply position the homosexual couple at its center as a matter of fact and play up the relationship's universal character. The musical is set in St. Tropez, where a successful drag-queen nightclub, La Cage aux Folles, is owned and operated by a savvy, conservative businessman, Georges. Much of the club's success is due to Georges' longtime lover, Albin, a flamboyant drag performer whose alter ego, Zaza, is La Cage's main attraction. At the top of the show, the audience is welcomed to the club (and the world of *La Cage aux Folles*) by Georges. He introduces the floor show and its glamorous drag chorines known as Les Cagelles, who perform "We Are What We Are," a wry, seductive grabber that builds to a full-throttle production number. (Several women are always included in Les Cagelles' chorus line to tease the audience further with playful gender-bending). Next, Albin is shown getting ready to perform as Zaza, with the jaunty character number, "With a Little Bit of Mascara." Meanwhile, Georges' 24-year-old son, Jean-Michel (the result of long-ago brief sexual encounter by Georges), announces that he has proposed marriage to Anne Dindon, the daughter of a local political zealot who heads the Tradition, Family and Morality Party. After Jean-Michel convinces Georges that he is in love with Anne (singing the lilting "With Anne on My Arm"), he admits that he has lied to his fiancée about Georges' profession and sexual orientation. He also asks that Albin not be present when his future in-laws visit for dinner and that all indicators of "homosexuality" be removed from Georges and Albin's home. Georges agrees and attempts to break the news to Albin, while also trying to soften the blow with affectionate, tuneful playfulness (turning "With Anne on My Arm" into a soft-shoe song and dance, "With You on My Arm"), as well as nostalgic romance (singing the sentimental "Song on the Sand," redolent of a heart-tugging French *chanson*). However, it is only after the club's next production number starring Zaza (the driving, extroverted "La Cage aux Folles") that Albin realizes Georges and Jean-Michel's plan. Stunned and hurt, Albin rejoins Les Cagelles onstage, only to ask them to leave and then launches into his own version of the opening number, revamped as "I Am What I Am." The ballad builds to an emotional climax as Albin pronounces his intention to stay true to himself and his refusal to return to a "closeted" homosexual existence, ending the song by furiously removing his wig, throwing it at Georges, and departing the theatre. (In the original production, Laurents had Albin actually exit the real theater building, all the way through the aisles and into the street outside.)

Act II begins with the reconciliation between the two lovers, as Georges apologizes and Albin agrees to assume the macho heterosexual identity of "Uncle Al" for dinner with the potential in-laws. After a training session via the comic character number "Masculinity," Albin is hurt again by Jean-Michel, who not only rejects the "Uncle Al" idea, but disparages Albin's overall homosexual character, earning Georges' ire as he reminds Jean-Michel of how good a "mother" Albin has been to him for years, singing the tender ballad "Look Over There." A new plan presents itself, however, when it turns out that Jean-Michel's birth mother will not be able to attend the dinner. As a result, Albin decides to pose in drag as Georges' matronly wife. As the dinner party verges on success, Albin, in his female guise, charms the Dindons and is talked into performing a song, the infectious and Parisian-influenced "The Best of Times." Unfortunately, Albin is so overtaken by the fevered pitch and enthusiasm of the number that he tears off his wig at the song's climax, revealing his identity. All seems lost; but in an ingenious and unscrupulous move, Georges and Albin threaten to publish pictures of the Dindons at their establishment, socializing with known homosexuals, unless they relent to the marriage between their daughter and Jean-Michel (who has shame-facedly apologized to Albin). And in a final ironic twist, after agreeing to the wedding, the Dindons dress in drag as members of Les Cagelles to disguise themselves and escape negative publicity as they exit through the stage door of La Cage aux Folles.

The musical was to be, at its core, an old-fashioned love story between two opposites who weather outside threats to their longtime commitment and domestic stability, finding new strength and sense of identity as they triumph over bigotry and their own shortcomings. Nonetheless, some consternation occurred over the fact that the two men in love barely touched each other in the original production. Nor did Herman's lyrics really address the homosexual nature of the relationship (aside from an oblique reference to the "closet" in "I Am What I Am"). Regardless, a heartfelt love story between two gay men at the center of a musical was groundbreaking in the 1980s. There were genuine love songs shared between the two men, as well as their embrace and dance into the sunset at the show's end. In short, there was a "kill 'em with kindness" attitude to the show, emphasizing the charm of its characters and relationships, the razzle-dazzle of its nightclub milieu (including the Tony Award-winning drag costumes by Theoni V. Aldredge), and the ear-pleasing appeal of its score, filled with Herman trademarks such as straightforward lyrics, toe-tapping rhythms, and evocative, hummable show tunes. The song line-up includes full-throttle anthems, lyrical ballads, humorous character songs, and lavish production numbers, many of which have a Parisian flavor. Herman also provided a clever twist on the traditional reprise as he reconfigured certain songs to create completely new musical and dramatic moments, for example, the reconfiguration of the slyly provocative "We Are What We Are" into the furious anthem of "I Am What I Am," as well as the heterosexual ode "With Anne on My Arm" into the homosexual duet "With You on My Arm."

When La Cage aux Folles opened on Broadway on August 21, 1983, the show was one of the most anticipated events of the season, commanding a new premium ticket price for choice seats. Yet the preceding tryouts in Boston had been nerve-wracking for its creators. First, they had serious concerns over one of their leads, Gene Barry, who had been cast as Georges. His co-star, George Hearn, was proving to be revelatory in the flashier role of Albin (an impressive feat, given that Hearn's most recent Broadway triumph was as the tortured, malevolent Sweeney in Sweeney Todd). Hearn would win a Tony Award for his performance. Barry, on the other hand, was proving lackluster in his crucial role and might have been replaced, if the creators could have found a suitable and willing replacement. Instead, Laurents directed Barry, as Georges, to add operatic flourishes to his introductions of the nightclub numbers and to maintain intense eye contact with Albin, thereby suggesting the deep commitment between the two men. The direction worked, and the passion between Georges and Albin appeared heightened on stage, as well as nuanced. However, this led to another qualm among the creative team. How would Middle America accept the love story at the heart of the musical? The creators' anxiety was so pronounced that Herman actually had panic attacks during the Boston try-outs. Yet in numerous accounts, his nerves were calmed when he observed a staunch, middle-aged Bostonian husband and wife take hold of each others' hands as they watched the sentimental love song ("Song on the Sand") between Georges and Albin early in the first act.

At that point, Herman felt that the team had a hit on its hands, and he was correct, for the original Broadway production eventually ran for 1,761 performances, an achievement all the more amazing given that the production was shadowed by the early and highly charged days of the AIDS epidemic. In fact, in the spring of 1984, the *La Cage* cast became the main event in a charity evening to raise funds to fight the disease and help those suffering, beginning the enormously successful and impactful Broadway Cares/ Equity Fights AIDS program, which has raised tens of millions for the cause since that time. Further, the notoriety and success of the musical did not end with its initial run in the 1980s, which garnered six Tony Awards, including one for Best Musical. Specifically, the twenty-first century saw a resurgence of the musical on Broadway. A celebrated revival in 2004 pleased both ticket buyers and critics, winning the Tony Award for Best Revival of a Musical. As if that feat were not enough, it was repeated only six years later when another *La Cage* revival (transplanted from London) won another Tony Award for Best Revival (the only musical to have ever won this award twice), while being nominated in ten other categories, winning three awards total and running for 433 performances. Given this latest triumph, it appears that the refrain of "I am what I am" still holds power and delivers a punch, while its drag-queen milieu still delights, and a once-taboo love story between two men has proved to be iconic and timeless.

Arvada Center's production of *La Cage Aux Folles*, 2007
© P. Switzer. Used by permission of Patricia Switzer.

PULLING BACK THE CURTAIN:
Homosexuality on the American Musical Theatre Stage

Even though Jerry Herman is generally considered by many audiences and critics to be "old-fashioned" and a "leading traditionalist," he, nevertheless, was one of the earliest twentieth-century musical theatre authors to write a Broadway musical about Jewish people (i.e., *Milk and Honey*, 1961). Similarly, his *La Cage aux Folles* (1983) is generally acknowledged to be the first "homosexual musical" on Broadway. In an industry known for being inclusive and supportive of LGBTQ artists, why did it take so long for a Broadway musical to feature gay characters?

As Mel Brooks once famously intoned, "Without Gypsies, Jews and Faggots, there would be no theatre." But while many of the composers, librettists, lyricists, directors, and producers who created America's musical theatre were Jewish and/or gay, these artists generally wrote works which featured and celebrated a WASPish world (white, Anglo-Saxton, and Protestant), to which could be added the assumption that its population was heterosexual, able-bodied, and (preferably) upper-class. Interestingly, the early years of American musical theatre celebrated minority, ethnic communities in works by such authors as Harrigan and Hart, Williams & Walker, George M. Cohan, etc.; but by World War I, a more homogenous view of America was being created by Broadway and Hollywood. It is important to note that this was not the result of an organized movement or the tenets of some political group. Rather, it was a collective vision of an American ideal created by writers (and funded by producers) in their attempts to broadly appeal to mass audiences.

What is ironic is that this WASP ideal of America, as expressed in American musical theatre, has been created by many artists who were (and are) neither heterosexual nor Protestant: Howard Ashman, Leonard Bernstein, Marc Blitzstein, Fred Ebb, William Finn, Harvey Fierstein, Lorenz Hart, Jerry Herman, Elton John, John Kander, Arthur Laurents, John Cameron Mitchell, Terrence McNally, Mark O'Donnell, Cole Porter, Marc Shaiman, Stephen Sondheim, Jeff Whitty, Scott Wittman, and the list goes on. Of course, artists are not limited by their identity; they can create any kind of character they choose. Indeed, when the talented homo- and bi-sexual artists Jerome Robbins (director/choreographer), Leonard Bernstein (composer), Stephen Sondheim (lyricist), Arthur Laurents (librettist), Oliver Smith (set designer), Jean Rosenthal (lighting designer), and Irene Sharaff (costume designer) collaborated on *West Side Story* in 1957, they created a musical adaptation of that most heterosexual of all love stories: *Romeo and Juliet*.

Many historians mark the beginning of the modern gay rights movement with the 1969 riots outside of the Stonewall Inn (a gay bar in Greenwich Village) which occurred when a group of patrons fought back against routine police raids. These riots led to the formation of many groups and organizations that argued for an end to discrimination against gay and lesbian people; they brought GLBTQ people and stories literally "out of the closet." Within a couple of years, creators such as Al Carmines (Off-Off-Broadway, *The Faggot*, 1973) and Richard O'Brien (London, *Rocky Horror Show*, 1973) began to experiment with musicals that featured same-sex desire between characters. Their box office successes no doubt led other writers and producers to take a chance on material which previously had been deemed too "niche" to turn a profit. (Homosexuals are thought to comprise anywhere from two to ten percent of the general population, so most producers would consider it foolish to invest their time and backers' money in a musical that would only appeal to such a small demographic.) Off-Off-Broadway musicals such as *In Gay Company* (1974), *Lovers: The Musical That Proves It's No Longer Sad to Be Gay* (1974), *Fascination* (1975), *Gulp!* (1976), *Joseph McCarthy Is Alive and Living in Dade County* (1977), and *In Trousers* (1979) began to appear on the boards, proving that there was a general audience for works that featured gay characters.

Given that the maximum seating capacity of an Off-Broadway theater is 499 seats, presenting in such a venue is less risky, financially, than booking a gay-themed musical into a theater designated as being on "Broadway" (most seating 1,000 to 1,500).

Broadway producers took notice of the increased popularity of gay characters/plots in Off-Broadway and Off-Off-Broadway musicals and slowly began to test the waters on Broadway. In 1969, the Main Stem musical *Coco* featured a stereotypically snippy gay designer, Sebastian Baye (the musical is a biography of the great French fashion designer Coco Chanel). While nominated for seven Tony Awards, the production won only two; but notably, one was awarded to René Auberjonois for his portrayal of the homosexual Baye (Best Performance by a Featured Actor). Three subsequent Broadway musicals in the '70s provided much more positive looks at homosexuality, however: *Applause*, *Seesaw*, and *A Chorus Line*. In 1970, *Applause* (the musical adaptation of *All About Eve*) not only included a gay character—the hairdresser Duane—but also featured a production number that took place in a Greenwich Village gay bar ("But Alive"). This positive depiction of GLBTQ people continued with the homosexual character of David (played by Tommy Tune) in 1973's *Seesaw*. In a classic Cy Coleman/Dorothy Field showstopper, Tune belted out "It's Not Where You Start, It's Where You Finish," all the while dancing on a stage filled with balloons. Two years later, the Pulitzer Prize-winning *A Chorus Line* started his historic fifteen-year long run. Included in the cast of 19 characters auditioning for a Broadway musical are two men who identify themselves as gay: Greg and Paul (notably, their characters are doubly "othered" by being Jewish and Puerto Rican, respectively). While the two dancers are not mocked for being gay, neither is hired to be one of the eight cast members in the upcoming production.

Inspired by the sexual revolution of the 1970s, several "adult" musicals appeared on Broadway and Off-Broadway which celebrated the body and "free love:" *Oh! Calcutta!* (1969), *Let My People Come* (1974), *I Love My Wife* (1977), and *The First Nudie Musical* (1978). Although *Let My People Come* included two "gay" songs ("I'm Gay" and "And She Loved Me") and *The First Nudie Musical* included a brief LGBTQ song ("Lesbian, Butch, Dyke"), the scope of the sex-centric works were (mostly) resolutely heterosexual. Thus, audiences would have to wait until 1983 for Jerry Herman, Harvey Fierstein, Arthur Laurents, and Alan Carr to bring *La Cage aux Folles* to Broadway and feature homosexual characters in leading roles. Critics are quick to point out that *La Cage* does not show much same-sex desire (the two leading men never kiss on stage) and the thrust of the musical is the homosexual couple's facilitation of a wedding between young heterosexuals. But Herman shaped his musical traditionally for a 1980s Broadway audience, knowing that theatre-goers at the time were not ready for an in-your-face approach to a marginalized group negatively linked to the current AIDS pandemic.

Certainly, one element which helped propel *La Cage* to a very impressive original run of 1,761 performances on Broadway was the elaborate costumes and production numbers featuring Zaza and Les Cagelles. So other producers took *La Cage*'s lead and funded musicals which featured a character (or characters) in drag: *Pageant, the musical* (1991), *Whoop-Dee-Doo* (1993), *Splendora* (1995), *When Pigs Fly* (1996), *Taboo* (London, 2002), *Priscilla, Queen of the Desert* (2007), etc. This list arguably includes *Chicago* (1975), *Hairspray* (2002), and *Matilda* (2012), all of which feature male actors in drag. But, the tranvestism in these productions is employed as a theatrical device and has nothing to do with the character's psychology, sexuality, and/or gender identity. Edna Turnblad and Miss Trunchbull are meant to be seen as women in *Hairspray* and *Matilda* (respectively), and *Chicago*'s Mary Sunshine is an homage to vaudevillian female impersonators. Similarly, in a nod to the "Best Boy" tradition in British Pantomime, the title role in *The Mystery of Edwin Drood* (1985) is written to be performed by a woman in drag.

Starting in the 1990s, gay characterizations were more realistic and less stereotypical than their counterparts in the 1970s. In works such as *Falsettos* (1992), *A New Brain* (1998), *Kiss of the Spider Woman* (1993), *The Full Monty* (2000), *A Man of No Importance* (2003), *Avenue Q* (2003), and *Glory Days* (2008), the gay male characters are multi-dimensional and their sexuality is no longer their primary defining character trait. And as the impact of the AIDS crisis became more public, musicals such as *Elegies for Angels, Punks, and Raging Queens* (1989), *An Unfinished Song* (1991), *All That He Was* (1993), *C'est la Guerre!* (1994), *AIDS—The Musical* (1995), *Rent* (1996), and *The Last Session* (1997) incorporated this plague into their portrait of America. In a similar vein, some musical biographies appeared which sought to explore the life of a well-known GLBTQ person. Examples include *Faggot* (Oscar Wilde, 1973), *The Boy From Oz* (Peter Allen, 1998), *Fela!* (Fela Anikulapo-Kuti, 2009), *Thrill Me* (Leopold and Loeb, 2006), and *Loving Repeating* (Gertrude Stein, 2007). While the overall musical theatre evolution has been from gay stereotypes to three-dimensional characters, it must be noted that several early twenty-first-century Broadway hits retain gay subplots with gay characters who are not integral to the overall trajectory of the play (or message) but, rather, are two-dimensional characters simply defined by their sexuality. This roster includes *Mamma Mia!* (1999), *The Producers* (2001), *Spring Awakening* (2006), *Spamalot* (2005), *Rock of Ages* (2009), and *Lysistrata Jones* (2011).

Of course, the subject missing from this discussion thus far is the depiction of same-sex desire between female characters in musicals. One of the first musicals to focus on lesbians was developed in London's Gay Sweatshop Women's Company, *I Like Me Like This* (1979). Lesbian characters began to appear in musicals on Broadway and Off-Off-Broadway, but not nearly in the same numbers as their brothers, e.g., Raffaela in *Grand Hotel* (1989), Giulietta Trapani in *Aspects of Love* (1989), Cordelia and Charlotte in *Falsettoland* (1992), Maureen and Joanne in *Rent* (1996), Madeline in *The Wild Party* (2000), Shug Avery and Celle in *The Color Purple* (2005), Trix in *The Drowsy Chaperone* (2006), and Enid in *Legally Blonde* (2007).

Likewise, musicals about trans-people (transvestites, transsexuals, transmen, transwomen, etc.) are even rarer. While Albin (*La Cage aux Folles*) performs in drag as Zaza, this foray into transvestism is not part of his identity; rather, it is his profession (ditto for the drag queens in *Priscilla, Queen of the Desert*). There have been significant musicals containing transsexuals, however: *The Knife*, *Hedwig*, *Bombay Dreams*, *Priscilla*, and *Billy Elliot*. With a book by David Hare and a score by Tm Rose Price and Nick Bicat, *The Knife* (1987) explores a biological man as he undergoes surgery to realize her female body. More interesting, and successful with audiences, is John Cameron Mitchell and Stephen Trask's popular *Hedwig and the Angry Inch* (1998) which gives Hedwig, with her botched sex change operation, the opportunity to talk (and sing) about the necessity, and difficulty, of breaking down binaries. Although there is no explanation as to the identity of the character of Sweetie in *Bombay Dreams* (2002), as a *hijira*, this bio-man has adopted feminine gestures, clothing, and gender roles, but most South Asian cultures do not consider such persons as women, rather a third sex. The transsexual character of Bernadette in *Priscilla, Queen of the Desert* is given precious little backstory, but the character is treated seriously as she starts a relationship with Bob, a mechanic the performers meet on their journey from Sydney to Alice Springs, Australia. Lastly, in Elton John and Lee Hall's *Billy Elliot* (2005), Billy's friend Michael introduces him to the glorious world of dressing up in women's clothing in "Expressing Yourself." In the stage musical, while we don't know what eleven-year-old Michael is going to "grow up" to be, he clearly has same-sex attraction for Billy. Given the traditionally taboo aura surrounding children's sexuality and non-conventional gender choices, the popularity of *Billy Elliot* in London (2005, still running), Australia (2007), New York City (2008, for 1304 performances), Toronto, Chicago, Seoul (2010), etc., makes the handling of this subject matter all the more noteworthy.

In the 1920s, Broadway earned a new nickname, "The Great White Way," due to the proliferation of bright electric lights and signs lining Broadway, especially in the theatre district. The moniker also seemed to imply that the theaters were full of plays and musicals about white people. Indeed, the bulk of twentieth-century American dramatic works focused on a homogenous WASPish view of the United States. But with the revolutionary social movements of the 1960s and '70s, musical theatre began to reflect a broader view of America with a perspective that was less about a "melting pot" ideal and more about a gumbo, that is, a dish where one can easily see its diverse contributing components. And with this crucial sociocultural shift, the climate became supportive of a gay character in drag taking center stage and belting out a Jerry Herman anthem, "I Am What I Am," to thunderous applause.

CY COLEMAN

Throughout his long and prolific career, Cy Coleman was hailed in musical theatre circles as a musician's musician. Not only was he a consummate composer versed in pop, jazz, and classical music, often writing his own vocal and dance arrangements, he also spent much of his career as a concert hall soloist, as well as a sought-after nightclub and cabaret performer (reportedly enjoying this role as much as or more than that of composer). In recognition of his prodigious gifts, Coleman was awarded three Tony Awards for Best Score, three Emmys, two Grammys, an Academy Award nomination, and in 1981 was inducted into the Songwriters Hall of Fame. Despite the rewards, however, he has never been particularly well known or celebrated by the wider theatre-going populace, even though many of his songs became popular standards in the American songbook of the 1960s and '70s. Ironically, his musical versatility confounded an easily recognizable musical fingerprint in his oeuvre. For instance, when writers describe Coleman's work, they sometimes pigeonhole him as a jazz composer; yet he also wrote an entire show, *On the Twentieth Century*, that used not a lick of jazz, but instead told a Jazz Age story entirely in comic opera style. Coleman never shied away from innovative or experimental projects, often drawn to musicals with unique concepts, constructs/forms, and compositional demands (e.g., the cabaret form of *I Love My Wife*, the circus format of *Barnum*, the vaudeville/revue structure/content of *The Will Rogers Follies*, the witty one-man-show concept of *Little Me*, and the juxtaposition of reality and fiction in *City of Angels*). It would be correct, however, to appreciate and recognize the "jazziness" of much of Coleman's work, given his ease with pop riffs, syncopated bounciness, and brassy, muscular melodies, as well as his own performing career as a jazz pianist. And if there is a Coleman trademark, it is the rousing traditional musical theatre showstopper that moves beyond its show origins to become a popularized anthem of positivity and determination (even if the positive sentiment is ironic). Coleman was often inclined to compose for properties that dramatize hard-luck, heartbroken, or frustrated characters (most often women) who draw on inner reserves of idealism, optimism, and resilience to—if not actually triumph— at least find hopeful resolution at the end of their

Tony Bennett, Chita Rivera, and Cy Coleman at celebration honoring Coleman, April 6, 1982 © Bettmann/CORBIS

journeys. Many of their songs have become recognized and often-performed numbers that celebrate good-natured American optimism and pragmatism.

Contributing to Coleman's multifaceted and hard-to-pigeonhole body of work in the musical theatre arena may be the fact that his music was consistently influenced by the flavor and energy of his collaborators. And in an age when musical theatre composition was, and still is, almost completely a male reserve, Coleman worked with nearly all the female lyricists of his generation: Betty Comden, Dorothy Fields, Barbara Fried, and Carolyn Leigh. (Not coincidentally, many of the most memorable and heartfelt characters in Coleman shows are women.) Paired with Carolyn Leigh, Coleman composed music that tended to be feisty and brittle, like her lyrics. Dorothy Fields' verses were world weary and wry, so Coleman gave her music for those colors. Betty Comden and Adolph Green brought Coleman flamboyant, educated lyrics; he responded with the eloquent vigor of *On the Twentieth Century* and *The Will Rogers Follies*. Even when working with male lyricists, his music matched the character of their writing. In short, the musician's musician was also the collaborator's collaborator, consummately shaping his compositions to reflect the aesthetic, intent, and content of his partner's work.

Cy Coleman was born Seymour Kaufman to Russian immigrant parents Max and Ida Kaufman in the Bronx, New York, on June 14, 1929. He was hailed as a musical prodigy at an early age, teaching himself to play the piano as a 4-year-old on an abandoned piano in a vacated apartment in the Kaufman's tenement building. By age 6, young Seymour had performed concert recitals at Steinway Hall and Town Hall, ultimately playing Carnegie Hall as a seasoned 7-year-old pianist. Continuing his "prodigy" trajectory, Seymour studied classical piano under scholarships, attending New York College of Music while still in high school. Soon, however, he became interested in jazz while playing in servicemen canteens during his mid-teens. Consequently, his life took a turn from the classics to jazz and pop; further, he officially changed his name to Cy Coleman at age 16. After high school graduation, he formed the Cy Coleman Trio, found steady bookings in New York jazz clubs, teamed with lyricist Joe McCarthy, and had some modest success with pop hits (e.g., "Why Try to Change Me Now," recorded by Frank Sinatra). He also had a few songs added to Broadway revues such as *John Murray Anderson's Almanac* (1953).

Such was Coleman's career throughout the early '50s, until McCarthy's drinking problems pushed him into looking for a new writing partner. Fortuitously, Coleman ran across lyricist Carolyn Leigh on a New York City street. They were familiar with one another's work and joked that they should start writing together … immediately! The joke turned serious when they followed up on the idea and wrote a song in two days, "A Moment of Madness," which was immediately published and recorded by popular songster Sammy Davis, Jr. Following this auspicious start, the two wrote some of the biggest non-rock hits of the 1950s and '60s, including "Witchcraft" and "The Best Is Yet to Come" (both of which became Frank Sinatra standards). As Coleman and Leigh were acquiring fame as a writing duo, albeit one complicated by legendary disagreements, they auditioned to write the score for *Gypsy*. They didn't land the job, but one of their four audition songs, "Firefly," became a hit song on its own merits. Not long thereafter, the team debuted on Broadway with their first musical, *Wildcat*. They were talked into writing the score for the show by its director/ choreographer Michael Kidd and librettist N. Richard Nash, who were also acting as co-producers. Developed as a star vehicle for iconic comedienne Lucille Ball, the musical chronicles the adventures of Wildcat "Wildy"

Jackson as she attempts to strike oil in the territory of Centavo City in 1912. Initially, Ball's narrow vocal range proved limiting for Coleman. Nonetheless, he and Leigh were able to combine a simple, brassy melody with sassy, declamatory lyrics to produce an audience-pleasing opener/grabber for the star ("Hey, Look Me Over!"), which also became a standalone hit. Coleman and Leigh further managed to balance the assertive nature of this "I Am" opener with more introspective numbers, such as "That's What I Want," shedding light on the "unhappy-in-love" character of Wildy (an early prototype of the heartbroken, frustrated female that would dominate many of Coleman's future musicals). Although *Wildcat* opened in December 1960 to unenthusiastic reviews, Ball's star power spurred a decent initial box office. Conversely, because the show's success depended on Ball, its run was ultimately cut short (only 171 performances) once she fell ill and could no longer perform.

Two years after *Wildcat*, the team of Coleman and Leigh wrote a second musical, *Little Me* (1962), another star vehicle, this time for television comedy luminary Sid Caesar. Based on Patrick Dennis' novel *Little Me: The Intimate Memoirs of That Great Star of Stage, Screen and Television: Belle Poitrine* (1961), the show is a farcical rags-to-riches biography of a beautiful sexpot, tracing her rise from humble beginnings as Belle Schlumpfert, a girl from the wrong side of the tracks, to Belle Poitrine, a rich, royal diva. *Little Me*'s librettist, Neil Simon, stayed true to Dennis' work by focusing on Belle's adventures. He also shaped it to show off the comic genius of Caesar, who played Belle's husbands and lovers, many of whom suffer ridiculous untimely deaths. Caesar's seven roles included Belle's first love, Noble Eggleston (a snobby suitor from the "right" side of the tracks to whom she returns in the end), as well as an 88-year-old banker, a narcissistic French entertainer, a poor-sighted hick soldier, a bigwig Hollywood director, a pitiful prince, and Noble's son (Noble Jr.). While Coleman and Leigh's score for *Little Me* smartly and humorously furthers the plot, it is rooted in flamboyant character depictions. Redolent of much of the Coleman canon, the musical features Belle as a repeatedly heartbroken, yet eternally idealistic and resolute girl from "The Other Side of the Tracks" (the opening number), who is determined to achieve success and romance, only to realize that the only person on whom she can truly depend is herself ("Little Me"). When the show debuted in 1962, it generated hit songs such as the period World War I waltz "Real Live Girl" and the smooth "I've Got Your Number," a come-hither song/dance, performed by Belle's longtime male friend. The original production of *Little Me* benefitted from the creative choreography and co-direction (with producer Cy Feuer) of Bob Fosse. The initial reviews were mixed or lukewarm, resulting in a run of only 257 performances. Nonetheless, the show was nominated for ten Tony Awards, with Fosse being the sole winner for his choreography. *Little Me* continues to resurface on Broadway; specifically, there was a 1982 Broadway revival (thirty-six performances), for which Coleman and Leigh, having ended their partnership twenty years before, reunited temporarily to contribute two new songs. In 1998, a second revival, starring Martin Short, lasted for only ninety-nine performances. Both revivals kept the tradition of having male stars play multiple roles and also echoed the original as they, despite weak box offices, merited numerous Tony nominations, only to receive one win (Martin Short for Best Actor in a Musical).

After *Little Me*, Coleman and Leigh acrimoniously ended their five-year partnership, which, although contentious, produced two Broadway shows and over twenty published songs, with a hefty supply of popular hits, as well as several numbers for motion pictures. Following the team's split, Coleman would write almost exclusively for musical theatre. But first, he needed a new lyricist. He thought of the venerable and legendary Dorothy Fields, placing a phone call to her and suggesting they write some songs together (some accounts cite the songwriting proposal as happening during a conversation between the two at a party). Fields agreed, and in no time, the team embarked on writing the score for a new musical conceived by *Little Me*'s choreographer/co-director, Bob Fosse, titled *Sweet Charity* (1966).

Throughout his professional life, Coleman was evasive about why he frequently chose to work with female lyricists. His only public comment regarding this unique (and defining) aspect of his career was that he simply sought to work with "the best," whether he had to approach such artists or whether they approached him. In any case, his partnering with Fields, who was twenty-five years his senior, seemed to bring out the brassy, sassy best in both artists; their score for *Sweet Charity* is an iconic archetype of the 1960s musical. Loosely based on the Federico Fellini film *Nights of Cabiria* (1957), the musical was the brainchild of Bob Fosse (although the libretto was ultimately written by Neil Simon), who envisioned an adaption suited to the star talents of his wife, Gwen Verdon. Fosse moved the action from Italy to New York City and replaced Fellini's prostitutes with taxi dancers. It is no wonder that Coleman was drawn to and inspired by the material; for the tale of taxi-dancer Charity and her search for "love" afforded another opportunity to musicalize a hard-luck, heartbroken, yet eternally idealistic, female protagonist. Happily, Fosse's stylized direction and choreography (e.g., numerous extended signature dance numbers), as well as Verdon's star power, were more than matched by Coleman's jazz-influenced compositions and Fields' ironically modern lyrics. In addition to the wide-ranging dance music and underscoring composed by Coleman (including a leitmotif for Charity), the show generated hit numbers such as "Big Spender," "If My Friends Could See Me Now," and "There's Gotta Be Something Better Than This." The musical was a hit with audiences and critics, running for 608 performances.

Although the duo flirted with a follow-up project about Eleanor Roosevelt, Coleman and Fields' next musical would not hit Broadway until seven years after *Sweet Charity*. The work was *Seesaw* (1973), a romantic musical comedy whose heroine might well have been Charity's sister. Based on William Gibson's play *Two for the Seesaw* (1958), with a libretto reworked by director/choreographer Michael Bennett (who replaced original librettist Michael Stewart and director Edwin Sherin) and again doctored by Neil Simon (who refused official credit), the musical depicts the romantic adventures of Gittel Mosca, another trusting, tarnished, kooky, and serially disappointed sweetheart in New York City who braves a brief affair with a "square" lover. The musical failed to impress critics, who lamented its awkward juxtaposition of intimate scenes and over-the-top production numbers, spearheaded by Bennett. Given its humdrum reviews, *Seesaw* would have closed earlier but a gimmick of having an onstage appearance by the city's mayor, John Lindsay, helped the show run for 296 performances. Also contributing to its success was the jazzy and hummable score by Coleman and Fields, which includes a signature Coleman anthem, "Nobody Does It Like Me," comprised of a vampy, catchy melody and ironic lyrics for Gittel as she details chronic romantic failure, as well as "It's Not Where You Start (It's Where You Finish)," a cakewalking homage to can-do optimism and razzle-dazzle showbiz. (The original number featured future star director/choreographer Tommy Tune in a breakout Broadway role, singing, dancing, and high-kicking his way up a flight of stairs through a stage floor of balloons.)

The Coleman/Fields partnership ended with Fields' death in 1974. Finding himself once again without a writing partner, Coleman turned to his first male lyricist/librettist collaborator, Michael Stewart, with *I Love My Wife* (1977). Stewart initiated the project, having been inspired by a French farce with music, *Chez Moi, J'Habite Chez une Copine* (*Come to My Place, I'm Living with a Girlfriend*), as well as the show's unconventional staging, in which actors simply took to the stage with microphones, interrupting their scenes, to lip-synch songs. Coleman was also excited by the material; thus, the two men designed a concept musical centered on the idea of spouse-swapping in Trenton, New Jersey. In the musical, two couples, restless in marriage, flirt with the idea of engaging in the sexual revolution. In the end, they realize that "swinging" is not for them because they love their respective spouses too much to engage in non-marital sexual trysts. The libretto also includes an evolved Coleman prototype, that is, the hard-luck, heartbroken girl translated into the frustrated, disappointed wife (and husband). In the original production, four musician/singer/dancers shared the stage with the couples, often participating in musical numbers (presented purely as "songs") that commented on the action and theme instead of being integrated into the plot. The musical itself received mixed reviews, mostly due to the subject matter, which some felt was tasteless and outdated, while others found it warm and fresh. Coleman's music was cheered as he ventured through a variety of idioms: his signature jazz as well as country ballads, vaudevillian romps, romantic waltzes, and cabaret tunes. Overall, however, the naysayers may have proved prescient. Even thought *I Love My Wife* ran for an astounding 872 performances and received six Tony Award nominations (with Gene Saks winning a Tony for his direction), the musical has yet to be revived or to cement a place in the American musical canon. Further, no songs from its score have survived as standards in the musical theatre or American popular music catalogue.

Even before Coleman started work on *I Love My Wife*, he had joined forces with librettists/lyricists Betty Comden and Adolph Green to write numbers for an Off-Broadway

workshop revue. Enjoying their collaboration, the team decided to write a Broadway musical, settling on *On the Twentieth Century* (1978), a work based on a 1932 farce by Ben Hecht and Charles MacArthur, which had spawned the classic 1934 Howard Hawks film. Mostly set on a train, the show depicts a desperate ploy by the declining, yet flamboyant, theatrical impresario Oscar Jaffee to persuade the high-strung film star Lily Garland (his ex-lover and old protégée) to star in his latest stage production, thus reviving his career. During the ride from Chicago to New York on the famous Twentieth Century Limited, comedy ensues due to the animosities between Oscar and Lily, as well as the activities of three other colorful passengers: a "religious nut," a rival producer, and Lily's jealous lover. In the end, after Oscar fakes shooting himself to manipulate Lily and Lily fools Oscar by signing a fake name to his contract, the two again exchange screaming insults, only to fall into each other's arms. Given the material, Coleman decided to move away from his jazz and pop music roots and compose a score completely in the comic opera genre, feeling that the largess of the classical idiom matched the highly stylized, emotional, and presentational nature of the characters, as well as the contrived and over-the-top plot. Coleman's score for the screwball work played with styles, forms, and constructs pulled from operetta, comic opera, and even grand opera. The song list includes contrapuntal numbers, passionate soliloquies, patters, and romantic ballads harkening back to works of past operetta composers such as Victor Herbert, Rudolf Friml, Jacques Offenbach, and Gilbert and Sullivan (with some critics also citing echoes of opera composers such as Puccini). The brilliantly composed, integrated, and pastiche nature of the score was highly praised by critics, while Hal Prince's smartly satiric, spirited direction and the high-tech, art-deco train set designed by Robin Wagner created a special on-stage world. The free-wheeling comic opera won five Tony Awards and ran for 449 performances. Although *Twentieth Century* has yet to be revived on Broadway, it is considered a masterwork in Coleman's canon, with many in the Broadway community anxious to see it staged again.

After the financially successful *I Love My Wife* and *On the Twentieth Century*, Coleman teamed with his fourth female lyricist, Barbara Fried, on a failed follow-up project, *Home Again, Home Again*, which closed out-of-town in 1979. Moving into the 1980s, Coleman reestablished his winning streak, which lasted into the early '90s. First, after the failed *Home Again*, Coleman turned again to lyricist Michael Stewart to collaborate on the musical biography *Barnum* (1980), which tells the tale of P. T. Barnum, the nineteenth-century impresario and promoter of celebrity attractions and oddities such as Tom Thumb and the elephant Jumbo, as well as spectacles and the three-ring circus (a.k.a. "The Greatest Show on Earth"). The show's libretto, written by Mark Bramble, spans 45 years of Barnum's life (1835–80). Constructed as a concept musical, the lavish and flashy Broadway production portrayed the impresario's life through a series of musical numbers presented as circus acts, with performers required to juggle, twirl, high-step, tumble, and fly across the stage (as well as impersonate famous personalities promoted by Barnum, for example, Tom Thumb and operatic diva Jenny Lind). The title character, as originated by Jim Dale, performed numerous circus tricks, including tightrope-walking, while singing. On a quieter note, *Barnum* also included a tender depiction (by Glenn Close) of Barnum's wife, Chairy, another conflicted, long-suffering spouse in the Coleman canon who compromises her own desires to go along with her husband's extravagant, restless ambitions and lifestyle. The flamboyant showbiz spirit and world of *Barnum* is reflected in its brassy, assertive score, which is chock full of syncopation and brisk tempos, as well as catchy melodies. The snappy tunes match Stewart's smart rhymes, huckster patter, and overt expression. Emblematic of the entire score is Barnum's anthem, the strutting, vigorous "There Is a Sucker Born Ev'ry Minute," while the character of Chairy shows a softer musical side, exemplified by her introspective "The Colors of My Life." In the end, critics and audiences cheered *Barnum*; the show merited ten Tony Award nominations, winning three, while running for 854 performances. Its success proved to be two-fold for Coleman, for he was also the show's co-producer.

Although Coleman suffered significant failure on Broadway in 1989 with *Welcome to the Club* (twelve performances), the prolific composer managed to triumph in the same year with *City of Angels*, a jazz-infused spoof of hard-boiled detective novels, 1940s Hollywood, and the "tortured artist" syndrome. It won six Tony Awards including Best Musical and Best Score, running for 878 performances. With a book by Larry Gelbart and lyrics by David Zippel, *City of Angels* explores the travails of a novelist, Stine, who is trying to adapt his detective novel for the movies. The subplot (actually, a side-plot that exists alongside Stine's story) concerns Stine's fictional private eye, Stone, who has been hired to track down a missing heiress. Gelbart's book is a creative mash-up of Stine's real life in Hollywood and Stone's fictional adventures in Los Angeles (the "City of Angels"), as written by Stine. Specifically, Stine's marriage is falling apart because of his infidelities and his wife's disillusionment with their life; further, Stine's pandering to his new Hollywood studio boss results in constant rewrites of Stone's adventure, causing the fictional detective much frustration and bewilderment. (One of the most creative moments in the musical is the rewinding of a scene with Stone in which both movement and language reverses on stage as it is being erased by Stine.) When Stine's life is in complete freefall, he is aided by Stone in rewriting his own story, creating a happy Hollywood ending.

City of Angels is an iconic Coleman work in many respects. First, Coleman not only composed his purest jazz score, but he also wrote the vocal arrangements. Especially impressive in this regard is his work for the "Angel City 4," a vocal jazz quartet that acts as a 1940s Greek chorus, scatting and providing harmonic commentary throughout the show. Second, *City of Angels* features the two female archetypes to which Coleman was drawn throughout his career: Stine's wife, Gabby, and Stone's secretary, Oolie. Gabby is the disillusioned, disgruntled wife who sings a rueful marriage lament, "It Needs Work," when she catches Stine cheating. Meanwhile, Oolie is the habitually unlucky-in-love character who sardonically recounts her repeated history of unacceptable partners in "You

Can Always Count on Me." Highlighting these female archetypes, Coleman and Zippel created a shared number for Gabby and Oolie: "What You Don't Know About Women." Here, the real-life wife and the fictional girl Friday, each in their own "world," imaginarily chew out their respective male counterparts in a sassy jazz duet. Helping with the theatricality of this number was the creative scenic and lighting design by Robin Wagner and Paul Gallo, respectively, who created black and white sets with grayish lighting for Stone's world and full-color sets, creamily lit, for Stine's reality. Florence Klotz's costumes were also crucial to the concept, with black/white/gray wardrobes for the fictional characters and color for the others. Similar to the Gabby/Oolie duet is another number that bridges both worlds: "You're Nothing Without Me." In this barbed duet between Stine and Stone, each man argues why he is the crucial one in their relationship. In addition to the aforementioned up-tempo numbers, Coleman supplied the show with torchy, bluesy ballads (e.g., "With Every Breath I Take" and "Lost and Found"). Deservedly, along with the six Tony Awards won by the musical, Coleman received one for his multifaceted and sophisticated score. Curiously, this much-lauded 1989 musical has yet to be revived on Broadway, and its scenic conventions (black/white versus color) have proved to be prohibitive in terms of cost for regional and community theatres. Yet *City of Angels* remains in the canon as a gem of a book musical, containing one of the more authentic jazz scores in the musical theatre genre.

Two years later, Coleman was back on Broadway with another popular and critical triumph, *The Will Rogers Follies* (1991), teaming again with lyricists Betty Comden and Adolph Green. The musical was another show business biography. The libretto, by Peter Stone, tells the life story of Will Rogers as he rose from a vaudeville trick roper and comic monologist to a *Ziegfeld Follies* star, retaining his rope tricks while his ironic commentaries and observations became adored and quoted by all America. The show ends with his untimely death in a 1935 airplane crash. As Coleman's longest-running musical on Broadway, *The Will Rogers Follies* enjoyed 983 performances, due in great part to the vision of its director/choreographer, Tommy Tune. Tune staged the entire story as one elaborate vaudeville and *Follies* number after another, many of which included beautiful Ziegfeld Girls in lavish and risqué costumes performing flashy and stylized dance numbers up and down a lit staircase, as

well as vaudevillian touches (e.g., a novelty dog act). Rogers emcees the "show" of his life, making his first appearance as he is lowered to the stage on a rope. With the character of Betty Rogers, the show contains another representation of the disgruntled, disappointed wife, struggling with a showbiz husband. In fact, Betty blatantly laments her choice of Will in the brassy "My Big Mistake"; but like the wives in *Barnum* and *City of Angels*, she finally admits, in the uplifting "Without You," that her life would have been colorless without Will. Betty's character also gave Coleman a chance to balance his muscular and extroverted score with more lyrical, heartfelt ballads ("My Unknown Someone") and torchy blues ("No Man Left for Me"). Providing an overall sound and aesthetic for the showbiz homage, Colman created a vast array of color and dimension by way of seemingly simple tunes. The trumpeting sound of "Will-a-Mania," sung by the entire chorus in a "bring-down-the-house" opener, was a throwback to the crowd-pleasing grabbers of yesteryear, speaking directly to an audience and raising its collective pulse, especially when coupled with high-energy, colorful staging. Similarly, "Our Favorite Son," a patter song and elaborate precision dance performed by Will and the Ziegfeld lovelies (in suggestive red/white/blue costumes and jingle hats), satirized presidential politics with its campaign song and dance. In contrast to such razzle dazzle, Coleman supplied Will with a signature song and leitmotif, "Never Met a Man I Didn't Like." The song's simple, straightforward melody and strolling country feel musically personified Rogers' warm, wry, and relaxed character. *The Will Rogers Follies* won six Tony Awards, including Best Musical and Best Score (Coleman's third Tony in the "score" category). Some critics and scholars celebrated the work as an overall reaffirmation of the American musical theatre when it defeated the heavily nominated *Miss Saigon* in the Best Musical category at the height of what many saw as the British/European mega-musical invasion of Broadway.

Coleman's last original Broadway musical, *The Life* (1997), was a moderate success. Although it ran for 466 performances and received eleven Tony nominations, winning two for featured performances, many critics felt that Coleman's work on the show seemed uncharacteristically awkward and forced. Coleman was heavily involved in all aspects of the show, composing the score and contributing to the dance and vocal arrangements, as well as co-producing the work and co-writing the book with David Newman and Ira Gasman (who was also *The Life*'s lyricist). Based on an original idea by Gasman, the musical is a down and dirty walk on the wild side of Times Square's 42nd Street in the 1970s (before it was cleaned up for tourists). Dealing with pimps, prostitutes, runaways, drug addicts, drug dealers, and street people, the libretto centers on Queen, a prostitute who works the street to support "her man," a Vietnam veteran named Fleetwood, with dreams of escaping her seamy life. Ultimately, in a bus-stop showdown where Queen finally attempts to leave town, a rival pimp stabs and kills Fleetwood in an effort to reclaim Queen; then she shoots the rival pimp and kills him. When a fellow prostitute agrees to take the rap for Queen, she boards her bus, finally (or hopefully) leaving "The Life" for good. The production's sordid depictions of sex and drugs, as well as a level of misogynistic brutality, were not typical for a Coleman musical; his most popular works have a spirit of can-do optimism and positive drive, even when the characters are under duress and suffering disappointments. Coleman worked to revamp his traditional brassy and jazzy (or classic) sound to suit the contemporary milieu. For instance, the prostitutes' anthem, "My Body," incorporates a groove beat and an electronic rock sound, while retaining Coleman's knack for the melodic hook. Reviews of the show were generally good, but some quibbled with the content,

which they felt tried too hard to be gritty and realistic, while Coleman's score, although incorporating an electronic pop/rock component, still seemed rooted in a traditional musical theatre mode, minus a true edge or contemporary sound to match the setting.

It is ironic that Coleman, with such a proclivity for female collaborators, spent most of his life as a bachelor. However, in the same year as *The Life*'s debut, Coleman married Shelby Brown, with whom he had a daughter, Lily Cye, in 2000. After enjoying family life for the next four years, Coleman died of heart failure in 2004 at the age of 75. He continued to work up until his death, leaving behind several unfinished projects, including *Pamela's First Musical*, with a libretto by celebrated female playwright Wendy Wasserstein. Fortunately, Coleman's music still pervades the musical theatre canon and the American psyche. His music bespeaks confidence—conviction in forward motion—and moments of optimism in which the sky's the limit. A Coleman character is proud to proclaim "It's Not Where You Start (It's Where You Finish)," underscored by a melody that builds through chromatic shifts, lifting the entire musical to new heights. And in a like fashion, Coleman's overall body of work, along with his musical prowess and consummate professionalism, lifted the musical theatre genre.

FEATURED PRODUCTION: *Sweet Charity* (1966)

Music by Cy Coleman; Lyrics by Dorothy Fields; Book by Neil Simon

Original Broadway Run: Opened January 29, 1966; Palace Theatre; 608 performances

Charity Hope Valentine: No character name in the musical theatre canon is more telling and descriptive. As a taxi dancer at the seedy Fan-Dango Ballroom in New York City, Charity is an exemplar of the repeatedly heartbroken and eternally romantic gal. As her name implies, she lives for others, in perpetual hope of finding love, even though she has often "prostituted" herself in pursuit of such an ideal. She wears her heart on her sleeve, literally (in the form of her famous arm tattoo). And most important, although she is mostly surrounded by hardened, cynical characters and has been robbed, jilted, and even pushed in a lake, she soldiers on, armored with her good intentions, love to give, resilient idealism, and faith in human nature. It is no wonder that audiences in 1966 fell in love with this character; for she represented an amalgamation of the live-and-let-live, easygoing hippy (whose movement was burgeoning at the time), as well as a throwback to the sweet, romantic, in-need-of-rescue ingénue of yesteryear. As a result, the original production of *Sweet Charity* not only ran for 609 performances, but the show and its title character still stand today as deft musical representations of the 1960s *Zeitgeist*.

The musical was the brainchild of Bob Fosse, who chose to adapt Federico Fellini's *Nights of Cabiria* (1957), an Italian film that tells the tale of a waiflike prostitute's search for love and her eventual heartbreak. After Fosse wrote a rough libretto for a one-act version of the work, moving the action to New York City, changing Cabiria's name to Charity, and cleaning up her act by making her a taxi dancer (although, it is understood in the musical that her paid-for dances often extended to "other services"), he was overly challenged by the task of writing a full-length libretto. Neil Simon took over the librettist reins, even though Fosse was billed as having "conceived" the work. The production was shaped into a star vehicle for Fosse's wife and Broadway star, Gwen Verdon. For the score, composer Cy Coleman joined with legendary lyricist Dorothy Fields. Given Coleman's gift for writing syncopated and expressive music that bespeaks can-do optimism, brassy assertiveness, and jazzy coolness, he was the perfect composer to devise a score that not only facilitated Fosse's elaborate, extensive, and numerous dance numbers, but also musically reflected the buoyant character of Charity, the arc of her unsuitable romances, the gritty world of the Fan-Dango Ballroom, the dreams of the other taxi dancers, and the 1960s milieu. As part of his evocative score, Coleman managed to create a whimsical leitmotif for Charity, which underscores her stage entrances and exits. Fields, decades older than her collaborators, was paradoxically responsible for the fresh, modern language and jazzy slang that peppers the score, creating a world of "chums" who are "top-notch," who eat "chow," and "pop their corks." And Fosse flooded the stage with "Fosse style" movement.

Simon's book for *Sweet Charity* is a trifling affair (and, consequently, the component most derided by critics). In a series of loosely connected and abruptly sequenced scenes, Charity moves through her adventures, some romantic, some pathetic, some thrilling, some tangential, and some heartwarmingly, heartbreakingly revelatory. At the start, she meets her current beau in Central Park who is a shady character, literally, for his only defining feature is his dark sunglasses. Charity, ever-blinded by her own rose-colored glasses, extols the virtues of her bored and shifty fellow in the syncopated, jaunty "You Should See Yourself," only to then be pushed into the lake by him as he snatches her purse. Such is the life of Charity.

Next, audiences are introduced to Charity's "working" world, as her fellow taxi dancers at the Fan-Dango beckon to customers in "Big Spender," a musical exercise of seduction and boredom, expressed by sinuous choreography as well as jaded vocals. Charity's luck improves as she runs into Italian film star Vittorio Vidal, who recruits her as his escort for an evening at an über-exclusive nightclub, a milieu evoked through the stylized dancers and choreography of the epic dance number "Rich Man's Frug." She then innocently accompanies Vidal back to his penthouse apartment, where she celebrates her unexpected, unbelievable good fortune in the high-energy "If They Could See Me Now." Although Vidal reunites with his Italian starlet lover that same night (with Charity hidden in the closet), Charity still embraces her adventure, relating the tale to her two best friends, Nickie and Helene, at the Fan-Dango. All three revel in the possibilities suggested by Charity's night, singing and dancing the cathartic "There's Gotta Be Something Better Than This." Yet Charity is still searching for love and eventually meets the claustrophobic, conservative Oscar Lindquist, when they are comically trapped in an elevator. And even though Charity is full of insecurity because of the way she's been treated throughout her life, she sings "I'm the Bravest Individual" to Oscar, someone who is a bigger mess than she is, rising to the occasion, ready as ever to provide the kind of emotional "charity" that no one needs more desperately than she.

As the relationship between Charity and Oscar grows, they enjoy several adventures, including a brief encounter with a religious/hippy cult, joining them on the grooving, contrapuntal "The Rhythm of Life." Emboldened by her new romance, Charity quits the Fan-Dango, yet shows a moment of introspection and insecurity as she sings the minor-keyed ballad "Where Am I Going?." Once Oscar tells her that he is seriously in love with her, she hits emotional heights, dancing with a strutting and brass-instrument-playing male chorus while singing the full-throated "I'm a Brass Band." At the end, the romance is short-lived. Oscar, haunted by thoughts of the other men who have been in Charity's life, breaks off the relationship. One might see the crisis as a conflict between the "free love" vibe of the 1960s and the traditional moralities of the past. After the heart-wrenching break-up, Charity bookends the musical by again falling into the same park lake, this time by accident. But Charity proves resilient, looking on the bright side while expressing thanks that, at least, her purse was still intact. She dances into the sunset, with her leitmotif lingering in the air.

The original Broadway production of *Sweet Charity* ran for several years. It merited eight Tony nominations, even though Fosse was the only winner (for his choreography). And this musical, so rooted in a specific era/mindset, has proved to be a revival favorite. Specifically, a 1986 revival, which was directed and choreographed by Fosse and featured Debbie Allen as Charity, ran for 369 performances and won four Tony Awards, including one for Best Reproduction (Play or Musical)—the revival category at the time. In 2005, another much-publicized revival starred Christina Applegate in the title role. Directed by Walter Bobbie and choreographed by Wayne Cilento (a Fosse protégé), the production ran for 279 performances and was Tony-nominated for Best Revival. In short, the well-received Broadway revivals, as well as the frequent staging of the show by community and regional theatres, proves that the musical rendering of Charity's travails, as well as the signature Coleman/Fields score, has remained a "sweet" musical experience for American audiences.

PULLING BACK THE CURTAIN:

Words of Women: Major Female Lyricists/Librettists in American Musical Theatre

It is a cold, hard fact that writing a musical has been and continues to be a task most often assumed by men. Why this is so is baffling, especially given the extraordinary careers of those few women who broke the gender ceiling to reign alongside men as established and prolific musical theatre librettists/lyricists. The most prominent of these women are **Rida Johnson Young** (1875–1926), **Dorothy Fields** (1905–74), **Betty Comden** (1917–2006), and **Carolyn Leigh** (1926–83), all of whom defied the odds, not only of a male-dominated musical theatre industry (in terms of authorship), but of America itself, rising to professional heights during an era in which the American woman was, most often, restricted to the home and relegated to the domestic role of wife and mother. These women worked closely and successfully with some of the biggest male composer names in the business: Victor Herbert, Jerome Kern, Jimmy McHugh, Leonard Bernstein, and Jule Styne, just to name a few. Further, Comden had a lifelong male writing partner (Adolph Green), while Fields, Comden, and Leigh all had successful, steady collaborations with composer Cy Coleman. Yet all women retained autonomy and power as they imprinted works with their own indelible stamp of lyrical romance, wry subversion, witty repartee, and/or sassy libido, providing a multifaceted rendering of female sensibility, psyche, and experience. In the process, these women created some of the most endearing, engaging, extroverted, and interesting central female characters in the musical theatre canon. The roster includes "naughty" Marietta, sharpshooter Annie Oakley, cabby Hildy Esterhazy, sisters Ruth and Eileen, amateur sleuth Essie Whimple, telephone operator Ella Peterson, taxi dancer Charity Hope Valentine, diva Lily Garland, celebrity wife Betty Rogers, and even Peter Pan, who is traditionally played by a woman. These pioneering lyricist/librettists represent "boys club" interlopers and anomalies who, through effort and talent, matched their male compatriots as they also became household names. However, looking to the current state of Broadway, there are not as many successors to these pioneers as one might suppose; for a new generation of female lyricists has not yet materialized on a major scale. The closest thing the modern theatre has to a Young/Fields/Comden/Leigh torchbearer in terms of visibility and longevity is **Lynn Ahrens**, who has a respectable list of box office successes and critical merit to her name, working mostly alongside men as she has written words and stories for strong, complex female characters in works such as *Once on This Island* and *Ragtime*.

As both Fields and Comden have sections dedicated to them in this book, it would be redundant to chronicle their careers here. It is sufficient to note that **Dorothy Fields** was one of the first women to triumph not only on the musical theatre stage but also in Hollywood and as a Tin Pan Alley songwriter, initially working with composer Jimmy McHugh from 1928–35, creating iconic pop hits such as "I Can't Give You Anything but Love, Baby" and "On the Sunny Side of the Street." Her slangy vernacular and jaded, wry style introduced a modernist temperament to American songwriting, as well as a new, spirited voice for the American female. Throughout her multifaceted career, she wrote lyrics for more than 400 published songs. She also proved herself as a talented librettist. Maybe it was her upbringing as the daughter of famed vaudeville/revue star and producer, Lew Fields, but Dorothy Fields seemingly transitioned smoothly into becoming "one of the boys" as she mastered the art of writing the book, as well as the lyrics, for musical comedy. Joining with her brother, Herbert Fields (a successful librettist in his own right), she co-wrote several Cole Porter hits in the 1930s, followed by the mega-hit *Annie Get Your Gun*, then provided the lyrics and co-wrote with Herbert, up until his death, the libretto for *Redhead* (1959). In the 1960s, Fields reemerged as a lady lyricist of note, giving voice to a newly modern female prototype in *Sweet Charity*.

Also exploring the sexual liberation (or at least the gendered power) of the female character in musicals was the lyricist/librettist **Betty Comden** (1917–2006). With her constant writing partner of six decades, Adolph Green, Comden contributed highbrow, showy, and witty lyrics to many a successful and canonical musical, including *On the Town, Bells Are Ringing, On the Twentieth Century, Wonderful Town,* and *The Will Rogers Follies,* while providing the clever and comic librettos for the first three works (as well as numerous lesser productions). Further, the duo wrote screenplays for some of the most beloved and successful Hollywood musicals of the mid-twentieth century, including *Singin' in the Rain* and *The Band Wagon.* In addition to her intricate rhyme schemes, showbiz-insider perspective, classical literature/ music allusions, and smart use of slang and conversational patter, Comden played a significant role in creating female characters for the musical stage who have smarts, libidos, and gumption—a far cry from the weepy, dreamy, sweet-spoken ingénue found in many early Broadway works.

Speaking of such early female stock types, however, there was a woman who preceded both Fields and Comden in terms of power and prestige on the burgeoning American musical stage by putting heightened poetry into the mouths of classical ingénues and naughty soubrettes, while also penning many of their fantastical and highly popular tales. **Rida Johnson Young** (1875–1926) was a playwright, lyricist, and librettist who wrote more than thirty plays and musicals, as well as lyrics for over five hundred songs, with major hits including "Italian Street Song" and "Ah! Sweet Mystery of Life" from *Naughty Marietta* (composer Victor Herbert's most successful operetta, for which she wrote the lyrics and book) and "Will You Remember?" from another Broadway smash, *Maytime* (written with another operetta champ, composer Sigmund Romberg). Further significant Broadway musicals/operettas with lyrics and/or librettos supplied by Young include *The Red Petticoat* (Jerome Kern's first complete Broadway score in 1912), *Lady Luxury* (1914), *Her Soldier Boy* (1916), *His Little Widows* (1917), *Sometime* (1918), *Little Simplicity* (1918), and another operetta with Herbert, *The Dream Girl* (1924). As a prolific playwright, Young's Broadway catalogue includes dramas such as *Next* (1911), *The Girl and the Pennant* (1913), *The Isle o' Dreams* (1913), *Shameen Dhu* (1914), *Captain Kidd, Jr.* (1916), *Little Old New York* (1920), and *Cock o' the Roost* (1924). In 1935, the film version of *Naughty Marietta* was nominated for the Academy Award for Best Picture; and in 1970, Young was posthumously inducted into the Songwriters Hall of Fame.

While Young predated Fields and Comden, another powerhouse talent, **Carolyn Leigh** (1926–83), came on their heels. As a lyricist of pop songs and Broadway and film scores, Leigh was best known for her partnership with composer Cy Coleman, generating such American classics as "The Best Is Yet to Come," "Firefly," and "Witchcraft." She was born on August 21, 1926, in the Bronx, New York; and after she graduated from Queens College and New York University, she got her professional start as a copywriter for ad agencies and radio programs. Soon, Leigh's smartly worded jingles and ad copy caught the attention of a music publisher, who gave her a one-year lyricist contract. Her career took off after she supplied the nostalgic and innocent lyrics, set to Johnny Richards' music, for "Young at Heart" (1953), which not only became a pop hit (and eventual American song classic) but was heard on the radio by musical theatre star Mary Martin, who felt the simple, youthful, and heartfelt lyrics would be perfect for her newest project with Jerome Robbins, *Peter Pan.* Thus, Leigh teamed with composer Mark "Moose" Charlap to write some songs for the show (their score was later supplemented with songs by fellow lyricist, Betty Comden, along with Green and Jule Styne). Leigh's gifts were not limited to simple evocations of youthful emotion, however, for she was also adept at penning wry and pointed adult sentiments. Once she teamed with Coleman, she became a regular name on the pop charts, while the duo created scores for two Broadway shows: *Wildcat* and *Little Me.* Their Broadway scores generated stand-alone hits and cabaret/revue favorites such as "Hey, Look Me Over!" and "Real Live Girl," songs enhanced by Leigh's adroit rhyme schemes and direct, conversational, colorful language. After splitting with Coleman, her Broadway career waned, with only one notable work to her lyricist credit, *How Now, Dow Jones* (1967), a "Wall Street" musical derived from an original idea by Leigh (although Max Shulman wrote the libretto), with music by Elmer Bernstein. Along with Broadway, Leigh provided lyrics for the scores of such lauded films as *The Cardinal* (1963) and *Father Goose* (1964). At the time of her death from a heart attack in 1984, she was working with celebrated composer Marvin Hamlisch on the musical *Smile*. One year later, Leigh was inducted into the Songwriters Hall of Fame.

Although few musical theatre historians and scholars have applied the label of "feminist" to Fields, Comden, and Leigh, as their works most often reinscribe traditional gender roles, one must also appreciate the female perspective and insight that they contributed to the American musical theatre canon. All three writers created works that feature strong, funny, flawed, and overall, multidimensional women. This model is also exemplified by the later works of their successor Lynn Ahrens. As previously noted, although there have been a number of women writing for the musical theatre since the Golden Age (i.e., Carole Bayer Sager, Gretchen Cryer, Marsha Norman, and Mindi Dickstein), Ahrens stands apart as the most celebrated and prolific female lyricist/librettist working today who has relegated much of her career to the musical theatre sphere.

Born October 1, 1948, **Lynn Ahrens** grew up in New York City and New Jersey, graduating from Syracuse University with a degree in Journalism and English. In the 1970s, she was asked to be one of the songwriters for ABC-TV's *Schoolhouse Rock!*, while also performing many of her own songs (e.g., the "Preamble" to the United States Constitution). Meanwhile, she achieved steady success as a freelance writer, composer, and singer of commercial jingles (e.g., "What Would You Do for a Klondike Bar?"). In 1982, Ahrens turned to musical theatre, meeting her future longtime partner, composer Stephen Flaherty, at the BMI Musical Theatre Workshop in New York City. The next year, they wrote their first musical, *Lucky Stiff* (1988), with book and lyrics by Ahrens, which premiered Off-Broadway at Playwrights Horizons. The duo's next musical, *Once on This Island* (1990), established the team on Broadway. Ahrens wrote both the book and lyrics for this Afro-Caribbean fable, which delighted audiences, running for 469 performances. The musical also received eight Tony Award nominations. After the team's failed Broadway follow-up, *My Favorite Year* (1992), Ahrens took a brief departure from Flaherty to team with composer Alan Menken to write the score for *A Christmas Carol*. This musical version of Dickens' famous tale debuted at Madison Square Garden's Paramount Theater, becoming an annual New York holiday event; Ahrens also wrote the teleplay for the 2004 television version. Reuniting with Flaherty, Ahrens found success in Hollywood, collaborating on songs for the animated movie *Anastasia* (1997) and receiving Academy Award and Golden Globe nominations for Best Song and Best Score. The next year, the duo returned to Broadway to realize the biggest critical success of their partnership to date, *Ragtime* (1998). Based on the 1975 novel by E. L. Doctorow, Ahrens wrote the lyrics for this epic and historical musical, which not only ran for 834 performances but was also nominated for twelve Tony Awards. Ahrens and Flaherty won the Tony for Best Original Score; while Ahrens received critical acclaim for her poignant, sharp, and deft lyrics, rooted in honest human expression. In 2009, *Ragtime* was revived on Broadway. Although it only played for 65 performances, the work was still a critical darling, nominated for seven Tony Awards. Ahrens/Flaherty's follow-up to *Ragtime* was *Seussical* (2000), with a book co-written by Ahrens (with Flaherty) as well as the lyrics. The show suffered lukewarm-to-negative reviews and played for only 198 performances. Yet it has become one of the most performed musicals across America due to its young audience appeal. Ahrens and Flaherty's next three musicals, *A Man of No Importance* (2002), *Dessa Rose* (2005), and *The Glorious Ones* (2007), were staged at the Mitzi E. Newhouse Theatre in

Lincoln Center. Although they did not make it to Broadway, they received impressive critical notices. In addition to musicals, Ahrens has written for feature films, documentaries, theatrical concert pieces, and revues. There is little doubt that she still has much to offer the musical theatre genre in coming years. Ahrens, along with a new generation of contemporary female writers (e.g., Amanda Green / *Bring It On*), will continue in the tradition of her predecessors, keeping the words of women alive and potent on today's musical stage.

ANDREW LLOYD WEBBER

He is the modern musical "maximalist"—a composer, producer, businessman, and showman who is responsible for some of the biggest hits in musical theatre history, repeatedly working on a grand scale in terms of spectacle, size, sound, gravitas, hype, marketing, and profits. His name is Andrew Lloyd Webber (or Sir Lloyd Webber or Lord Lloyd Webber, given his awarded knighthood and peerage, respectively). His *Phantom of the Opera* is currently Broadway's longest-running musical, having overtaken his *Cats* in 2006. Both musicals, along with many others, succeeded in making Lloyd Webber the contemporary box office "king" of Broadway and London's West End. The record-breaking works are also linked by the fact that each is a "sung-through musical," an innovative form that consists of a continuous vocal and instrumental score (including the use of recitative in place of dialogue), which was propagated and evolved by Lloyd Webber in the late 1970s and early '80s.

While Lloyd Webber has redefined the musical genre (categorizing an operatic construct as a "musical"), he has famously argued that music, accompanied by images and gesture, can tell a story in a more sophisticated manner and more effectively than words. The powerful Lloyd Webber can get away with such a grand and biased assertion, for his music is a heady mix of liftable tunes (e.g., his iconic power ballads), dramatic orchestrations (written by him, a rarity in the industry), stylistic exploits, and classical applications/references. In short, Lloyd Webber has a knack for finding the sweetest sounds and powerful melodic hooks (sometimes tending to "borrow" from others, which will be discussed later), while employing an array of compositional styles and genres. He exploits the timeworn tradition of using reprises and leitmotifs to ingrain such digestible melodies into the collective psyches of his audiences. As a result, in the '70s and '80s, when musical theatre had stopped being the pop music of its generation, Lloyd Webber managed to have several songs from his musicals top the music charts (e.g., "I Don't Know How to Love Him," "Don't Cry for Me, Argentina," "Memory," and "The Music of the Night"), with such standalone numbers becoming contemporary song standards, as their various recorded versions became ubiquitous on both coasts and around the world.

Given that Lloyd Webber's sung-through philosophy/construct contradicts or complicates musical theatre's longtime ideal of a collaborative, integrated, interactive model, built upon *both* music and dialogue/text (as well as dance), many critics have faulted the works of Lloyd Webber, charging that his music overshadows and dominates the other components. (To this point, Lloyd Webber also controls the collaborative writing process of his musicals, changing and/or adding lyricists midstream if he is dissatisfied.) Such criticisms may seem like serious charges, but they have had little impact on Lloyd Webber's import and influence, especially when his most popular musicals ruled the West End (London's premiere theatre district near Piccadilly Circus and Trafalgar Square, comparable to New York's Broadway) and traveled overseas, where they reigned on Broadway during the 1980s in what was termed a theatrical "British invasion." Lloyd Webber moved beyond "mere" composition during this period to become, in many respects, the most powerful man in the musical theatre industry. His production company, originally set up in 1977 to support his own works, Really Useful Group (R.U.G.), became a publically traded corporation in 1986. While ownership of the entity was purchased back by Webber, with the company becoming a private enterprise again in the 1990s, R.U.G. remains an international powerhouse, producing and licensing the Lloyd Webber canon around the world, plus profitable works by others. The company is also one of the largest theater operators in London and is active in almost every aspect of the entertainment arena, e.g., stage, television, film, publishing, and recording. As a result of Lloyd Webber's phenomenal rise to power and celebrity, some scholars have quipped that the musical theatre genre/industry at the height of his influence could have been divided into two eras: pre-Webber and post-Webber.

Andrew Lloyd Webber was born in Kensington, London, on March 22, 1948, to nurturing, mentoring musical parents. His father, William Lloyd Webber, was a classically trained professional organist and music composition and theory teacher. His mother, Jean Hermione, was an accomplished violinist and pianist. (The official family surname is Lloyd Webber; William merged his last name, Webber, with one of his middle names, Lloyd, while a student at the Royal College of Music.) During Andrew's formative years, he was immersed in the world of music, along with his younger brother, Julian, who became a renowned concert cellist. Much to the delight of his parents (especially his resolute, admiring mother who tirelessly promoted both her sons), young Andrew showed early musical promise. As a 4-year-old, he learned to play piano, moving on to viola and the French horn by age 9, an age at which he also began to compose his own works (the first reportedly being a suite of six short pieces). Although he had an early interest in architecture, he soon found a way to build and design works of art through music, preferring to play his own compositions rather than the old master classics. He also saw his compositions in theatrical terms, putting on his own musical shows in a homemade toy theater, collaborating with Julian and his beloved Aunt Viola (Jean's sister), a theatre aficionado whom he credits for instilling in him his lifelong love of musical theatre as she took him to many live stage productions.

As a teen, Lloyd Webber was an unhappy boarding student at Westminster Underschool (an exclusive prep school, for which he won a full-tuition scholarship), due in great part to his aversion to the school's rabid sports culture. By this time, Lloyd Webber was already committed to pursuing a career in music and was studying music theory and composition, learning at the hands of his father. While he enjoyed pop music and loved opera and other classical works, his main goal was to compose for the theatre, naming Richard Rodgers as his idol. After prep school, Andrew won a scholarship to Oxford in 1965, only to drop out after one semester, feeling that the institution offered him little in the way of musical training and focus. It was in this same year that Lloyd Webber began one of the defining relationships of his early career, teaming with a young, aspiring writer named Tim Rice, who was three years his senior and similarly at loose ends, having left Sorbonne to pursue his literary dreams. Rice contacted Lloyd Webber at the suggestion of a literary agent who was familiar with the composer and unimpressed with a book idea pitched by Rice, thinking his talents might lie in songwriting. The Lloyd Webber/Rice meeting went well, and the two young men immediately set to work, hoping to establish themselves as the new kids on the musical theatre block.

Their path to fame was anything but traditional, however, even though their first collaboration, in 1965, was a conventional book musical (as opposed to the sung-through form that their future musicals would take). The work was a musical adaptation of a true story by Thomas John Barnardo titled *The Likes of Us*. The show stayed on the page, however, as they could not find a venue or backers for a public performance. (The work was resurrected in 2005 and given a stage production at Lloyd Webber's Sydmonton Festival.) Although Rice was happy to work on musicals, he also had serious pop music aspirations. For the next two years, the partners wrote a series of mediocre pop songs that were recorded as minor singles by various British artists, but the writers saw little in way of recognition or financial gain. Then, in 1968, a teacher at Colet Court (a prep school for boys aged 7–13) asked them to write a cantata for the school choir to perform at the annual concert. The duo was allowed creative freedom with regard to musical style, but the subject matter needed to be a biblical story for children. Neither Lloyd Webber nor Rice was religiously inclined (in fact, Lloyd Webber asserts that he just skimmed *The Children's Wonder Book of Bible Stories* for material). They chose the Jewish Testament tale of Joseph, favored son of Jacob, who rises to great power, being blessed with the gifts of dream interpretation and prophesy. In the libretto, Joseph is sold into slavery by his jealous brothers after being bestowed a flamboyant coat of many colors from his doting father. Joseph becomes a seer for the Pharaoh and ultimately assumes great Egyptian power, seated next to the ruler. He also forgives his brothers, showing them mercy during a time of great famine. For the cantata's musical style, Lloyd Webber worked in the realm of homage and pastiche (with a pop flavor), composing a continuous string of stylized numbers to depict episodes and characters in Joseph's life. The choir piece lasted only twenty minutes, but made a big impact. So positive was its reception that it received a second staging, this time impressing a *Sunday Times* jazz and pop critic in the audience (his son happened to be in the choir), who glowingly reviewed the cantata in the *Times*. Riding this wave of positive publicity, Lloyd Webber and Rice decided to make an album recording of the work, now titled *Joseph and the Amazing Technicolor Dreamcoat*, which was released to highly favorable reviews.

Joseph put Webber and Rice on the map, but it would be years before the concert piece would become the musical that is performed today. The two men continued to add numbers and lengthen the work until it became a full-length production, although still completely sung through (the musical was ultimately stretched to two hours by adding at its end a fifteen-minute danced medley, or "mega mix," of every song performed earlier in the show). *Joseph*'s score is a mesh of popular music styles and genres, including country-western, rock 'n' roll, calypso, French chanson, and doo-wop, with a singing narrator to keep the tale moving briskly along, and an eponymous hero who performs the show's emotional minor-keyed ballad, "Close Every Door." After its choral and recorded versions, plus extensive tinkering and expansion, *Joseph* debuted on the West End in 1973. By the time *Joseph* arrived on Broadway in 1982, Webber and Rice had become musical theatre powerhouses, all but assuring the show's box office success; indeed, it ran for 747 performances in New York. Since then, *Joseph* has had numerous national and international tours, including a successful version starring Donny Osmond, and revivals on both Broadway and the West End. The "little cantata that could" is now one of the most performed musicals by Lloyd Webber in professional and amateur theatres around the world. Furthermore, it was the first notable work by the two writers to suggest their unique and soon-to-be characteristic techniques and styles, that is, Lloyd Webber's through-composed and eclectic mix of classical, traditional, and pop/rock music, paired with Rice's ironic, smart, modern, and pointed lyrics.

But in the late 1960s, *Joseph*'s mega success was still years away, and Webber and Rice were little more than a struggling songwriting team, having made little money off the initial performances and recording of *Joseph*. The artists did manage to secure an agent, however, while landing another gig that would cement their reputations as fresh visionaries (and subversives)

in the musical realm. After *Joseph*, Webber and Rice hit upon the idea of writing another song cycle about, of all things, Jesus Christ. Aware of the sensitive subject matter, they approached prominent clergies, including the Dean of St. Paul's Cathedral, for their opinions and approval early in the process. Given the success of the *Joseph* album, they decided to record a series of rock songs based on Christ's last days. The process included buying back a previously written song, "I Don't Know How to Love Him," from a publisher to include in the work. In spring 1969, they had their recording, which was rejected by all major record companies except MCA (Music Corporation of America). The company took a risk and released a few test singles in America and England. Despite lackluster sales, MCA gave the green light to Webber and Rice to write an entire score for a concept album, which they completed in a year. The finished work, titled *Jesus Christ Superstar*, was released in 1970 to great media speculation and controversy. (One of the most humorous and overblown episodes occurred when it was rumored, falsely, that John Lennon would be singing the title role in a concert performance planned by St. Paul's Cathedral. Given the past brouhaha that had erupted over Lennon's assertion that the popularity of the Beatles superseded that of Jesus Christ, the media had a feeding frenzy over the fictional Lennon performance and the public was outraged until the rumor was put to rest.)

With a couple of live concert presentations under their belt (often met with picketing protestors), Webber and Rice searched for producers willing to give *Jesus Christ Superstar* a full theatrical staging. None could be found. Then the album started rising on the American pop charts, hitting #1 by February 1971, with breakout singles getting significant radio play. Broadway producers gave the material a second look. Webber and Rice's new manager, Robert Stigwood (who would have major control over their career for nine years), pressured the men to finalize a stageable score, especially because unlicensed, ad hoc theatrical productions of the album were beginning to pop up. With score in hand and producers on board, Stigwood hired director Tom O'Horgan to spearhead the much-anticipated Broadway debut (after firing an earlier director). O'Horgan had a reputation as a "bad boy" director, due mostly to his revolutionary and notorious Broadway staging of *Hair*. He applied his same aesthetic of heightened and incendiary theatricality to *Jesus Christ Superstar*. The production became an overblown spectacle, with campy, gauche, and confrontational elements that twisted the piece into what many deemed to be a highly offensive depiction of Christ, his last days with his apostles, and crucifixion. Lloyd Webber was not happy with O'Horgan's interpretation, and the Broadway experience would be one of the last times that he would let control of his property be wrested from him. Further, when O'Horgan's production debuted at the Mark Hellinger Theatre on October 12, 1971, reviews were lukewarm; the public reception was mixed, many being outraged by what they saw as homoeroticism, blasphemy, and an exploitation of sensitive material. Thus, the production closed after 711 performances (yet made a profit).

Jesus Christ Superstar wouldn't find unqualified success until it was staged more closely to Lloyd Webber's vision by Jim Sharman at the West End's Palace Theatre one year later. Although still edgy and theatrical in places, Sharman's concept and staging of *Superstar* was, overall, more modest and restrained than O'Horgan's, with the priority being a sincere interpretation/performance of the score. The show received rave reviews, audiences loved it, and it ran for a phenomenal 3,358 performances. *Superstar* eventually achieved "superstar" status, playing in thirty-seven countries and reaping a fortune in profits. Today, the work, deemed a "rock opera," is revered (along with *Hair*) as a forebear of the rock musical movement. Lloyd Webber's rock opera also became the prototype for the modern sung-through musical, dominated by a score that had an already-established fan base due to pre-released hit pop singles such as "Superstar." In terms of its score, *Jesus Christ Superstar* is singular in many ways, containing an opener ("Heaven on Their Minds") that consists of an electric bass guitar groove, which serves as one of the work's many leitmotifs. In addition to wailing rock vocals and throbbing riffs, the score incorporates Hebraic music references, funk rhythms, and stylistic nods to other genres, with some of the more emotive moments treated as arias, that is, surging power ballads such as "I Don't Know How to Love Him" and "Gethsemane." Matching Lloyd Webber's anachronistic and hip sounds, Rice's lyrics for *Superstar*'s songs and its recitative are curt, ironic, slangy, clever, and current. The production presents a biblical story through a modern lens, speaking in the vernacular of the 1970s youth movement, musically and textually. In 1973, a film version, directed by Norman Jewison, garnered several Oscar nominations

for Webber and Rice. In addition, numerous prominent revivals and tours have been seen by millions of fans around the world, with the most recent Broadway revival opening to critical acclaim in March 2012, garnering a Tony nomination for Best Revival of a Musical.

In the years that followed *Superstar*'s theatrical debut, Lloyd Webber wrote music for a film, *The Odessa File* (1974), and bought a country house in Sydmonton Court, with his first wife (of three marriages). At the estate, he founded what has now become a top music and theatre festival that he often uses to workshop and debut his own pieces: the Sydmonton Festival. In addition, Webber and Rice returned to *Joseph*, expanding the cantata into a forty-minute theatre piece that debuted in 1973 at the West End's Albery Theatre, running for 243 performances. But the two men were most concerned with finding a new project that would prove to be a significant successor to *Superstar*. The only problem was that they had different projects in mind. This is not surprising, given the disparate temperaments of the two young partners. Reportedly, Lloyd Webber was a driven workaholic, perfectionist, and controlling personality, while Rice was a more free-wheeling spirit who reveled in the messy creative process, working in a relaxed manner and dismissive of his collaborator's taskmaster tendencies. These differences would only grow over the years, but an early rift occurred in the mid-1970s when Lloyd Webber wanted to try another traditional book musical, opting to adapt the *Jeeves and Wooster* novels by P. G. Wodehouse. Lloyd Webber had been a longtime fan of the early twentieth-century literary adventures of the brilliant, acerbic valet Jeeves and his foppish employer Bertie Wooster, set among the British upper classes. Rice had little interest in the Wodehouse tales as he was looking for edgier material that would suit his mode of expression, as well as the modernist/pop genre he wanted to further explore. Rice did some early work on the lyrics of the new musical, titled *Jeeves*, but he soon left the project. Lloyd Webber recruited lauded playwright Alan Ayckbourn to write both the book and lyrics (Ayckbourn had never written a libretto and didn't especially like musicals). When *Jeeves* opened on the West End in 1975, it received scathing reviews, closing after only three weeks. It still stands as one of the few book musicals with dialogue written by Lloyd Webber to receive a major stage debut. (Lloyd Webber, never one to give in to failure, revisited *Jeeves* with Ayckbourn decades later, producing a slightly more successful 1996 version in London, titled

By Jeeves. The version was completely reworked, with only two songs from the original production retained. It still failed to impress, running only seventy-three performances in 2001 when it debuted on Broadway.)

Rice then talked Lloyd Webber into pursuing Rice's pet project, a musical biography of the conflicted and controversial Eva Perón. For years, Lloyd Webber had been reticent to tackle the Perón project, unsure that the Argentine political figure was a suitable and commercially viable subject for a musical. Nonetheless, Rice was drawn to her life story, feeling that there were common threads to *Superstar* that could be further explored, specifically, the cult of personality, and the high costs, contentions, and ambivalences of celebrity and power. Once Lloyd Webber finally committed to the project, the two men wrote what would turn out to be their second bicoastal sung-through hit: *Evita*. The work chronicles the life of María Eva Duarte de Perón, an ambitious guttersnipe who meritoriously and manipulatively escapes the lower-class provinces to become an Argentine radio and movie star in the late 1930s and early '40s, ultimately seducing and marrying the powerful military officer Juan Perón. Juan is elected Argentina's president in 1946, with Eva at his side and over his shoulder, steering many of his political moves. While his fascist regime brutally squashes dissidents and funnels money into hidden offshore banking accounts, Eva duplicitously stands with the common people, "her *descamisados*," who declare her to be their savior, their "Santa Evita." Her influence is such that she solicits the office of vice president, but her ambitions are cut short when she is stricken with cancer, dying at the premature age of 33. In addition to Eva and Juan, an anachronistic character is also featured in Rice's libretto. Employing a Brechtian "alienation" strategy, Rice inserted Argentine revolutionary Che Guevara into the storyline as a metaphoric narrator, even though his path did not cross that of the Peróns in real life (his most famous actions were aimed at a different military dictator, Cuba's Fidel Castro, and occurred years after Eva's death). Assuming various guises in his role as provocateur, Che not only criticizes and confronts Eva throughout the musical, he also offers scathing commentary with regard to the Argentine people and the sociopolitical climate that allowed such manipulation, corruption, and exploitation.

Following the example of *Jesus Christ Superstar*, Webber and Rice opted to first record *Evita* as a concept album in 1976. The album did not have the same impact of *Superstar*, but it rose to number twenty-four on the British pop charts and produced a hit single, "Don't Cry for Me, Argentina," another emotive, soul-bearing power ballad. The modest success of the recording was enough to warrant further theatrical development. In a surprising move, Webber and Rice, along with their powerful agent/manager, Stigwood, signed American director Harold Prince to spearhead the work's West End debut (Prince had been a longtime Broadway producer but was achieving a new level of notoriety as a bold visionary and highly "conceptual" director of cutting-edge musicals such as *Cabaret*, *Company*, and *Follies*). Starring British musical theatre star Elaine Page, *Evita* debuted on the West End in 1978 to great fanfare, where it ran for a phenomenal 3,176 performances. Its success greatly helped pre-sell the show for its New York debut, with some insiders declaring that the work was almost "critic-proof" by the time it moved overseas. Prince's production hit the Broadway stage in 1979, with the roles of Eva and Che taken by American performers Patty LuPone and Mandy Patinkin, respectively. Although both performers had some Broadway credits to their names, the show made them major theatre stars almost overnight (where they would continue to reign for decades). The production itself was an imaginative mix of conceptual and metaphoric staging by Prince and scenic/costume designers Timothy O'Brien and Tazeena Firth. While most of the scenery consisted of evocative, mobile set pieces on a blank stage (e.g., a lavishly adorned bed for Eva and Juan, a cluster of "musical chairs" for military officers, a balcony with a microphone for Eva), spectacle was added via screen projections and large, energized crowd scenes. The score was the production's dominant and most-remarked-on component, a situation that is basically unavoidable in the case of sung-through works. To reflect the Argentine milieu, Lloyd Webber veered away from the electric rock "groove" of *Superstar* to write music that contained a pop sensibility, flavored by a variety of Latin rhythms and styles. *Evita*'s wide-ranging score includes driving up-tempo production numbers ("Buenos Aires" and "Rainbow High"), bombastic and tender ballads ("Don't Cry for Me Argentina" and "Another Suitcase in Another Hall"), atmospheric, Latin evocations ("On This Night of a Thousand Stars," "Goodnight and Thank You," "I'd Be Surprisingly Good for You"), and epic, complex ensemble numbers, some with classical, choral overtones ("Oh What a Circus," "Requiem for Evita," "And the Money Kept Rollin' In," "Santa Evita," and the climactic Act I finale/teaser, "A New Argentina"). Along with the book (a flexible term in the case of sung-through musicals), Rice provided the savvy and often barbed lyrics, depicting Eva as both a sympathetic protagonist and ruthless, ambitious, duplicitous egomaniac. Despite Rice's ironic and ambivalent treatment, some critics were initially skeptical of the work, feeling *Evita* glamorized an exploitative villain. (Some critics went so far as to quip that a "Hitler musical" would be next for the songwriting pair.) Initial New York reviews were mixed. As predicted, however, *Evita* didn't need raves from the press, for it soon won over American audiences (and holdout critics), winning seven Tony Awards (Best Musical, as well as Score, Actress, Featured Actor, Lighting, Book, and Director) and running for 1,567 performances (twice as long as Broadway's *Superstar*). Given LuPone's iconic performance, it has taken decades to revisit the work on Broadway, which is why the theatre community was excited when a long-awaited revival opened at the Marquis Theatre on April 5, 2012. The show starred pop singer Ricky Martin as Che, as well as acclaimed Argentine actress Elena Roger in her Broadway debut as Eva; it ran for 337 performances, garnering several Tony nominations.

Lloyd Webber's next work to reign on Broadway would not only become a record-breaker and a universal phenomenon, but would also reinvent the idea of what constitutes a "canonical" musical. Shortly after *Evita*'s triumph in London, Lloyd Webber met with the relatively new, but already successful, West End producer Cameron Mackintosh. During the meeting, Lloyd Webber expressed his interest in musicalizing the collection of poems in T. S. Eliot's *Old Possum's Book of Practical Cats* (1939). He had been working on individual poems for years, playing some of the compositions at his annual Sydmonton Festival.

Initially, it was thought that *Cats* would be one half of a two-part evening of theatre dance, as Lloyd Webber had also written a set of pop-infused variations on Paganini's A-minor Caprice No. 24, titled *Variations on a Theme of Paganini*, for his brother, Julian, the celebrated cellist. Julian recorded *Variations* in 1978, and the single became a chart-topper in Great Britain, as well as the theme for London's *South Bank Show* (a popular British arts television show). Later,

Lloyd Webber felt that *Variations* could be staged as an all-dance work, paired with a one-act version of *Cats*, but the combined concept could not find backers (investors saw promise in *Variations* but derided the idea of a bunch of dancing kitties). Thus, Lloyd Webber shifted gears. He had also written an episodic song cycle (with libretto idea and lyrics by Don Black) for British actress Marti Webb, chronicling the romantic trials and tribulations of an English girl in the States. The sung-through theatre piece, titled *Tell Me on a Sunday*, debuted at the Sydmonton Festival and was then filmed in 1980 as a one-hour BBC television special. The production was a success and two of its songs, "Tell Me on a Sunday" and "Come Back with the Same Look in Your Eyes," became hit singles in England. So when no support could be found for the *Cats/Variations* match-up, Mackintosh and Webber reconfigured and retrofitted *Tell Me* and *Variations* into a thematically linked musical theatre event, with Webb's vocal performance of the *Tell Me* songs constituting the show's first half and a 45-minute dance segment set to *Variations*, portraying her character's conflicted love story, constituting the second half. The hybrid musical was titled *Song and Dance*. John Caird was recruited from the Royal Shakespeare Company to direct and Anthony Van Laast was hired as choreographer. The West End production opened in 1982 at the Palace Theatre to mixed reviews, running for 781 performances. More significant, however, was the fact that a year before this debut, Lloyd Webber and Mackintosh made history with their groundbreaking and odds-defying standalone production of *Cats*.

Cats is a sung-through, heavily danced, and loosely connected musical interpretation of the characters and poems from the T. S. Eliot collection. Original choreography was by Gillian Lynne, and Eliot's own words were used as the lyrics, except for the breakout song, "Memory," another emotive, bombastic ballad by Lloyd Webber, with lyrics supplied by the work's director, Nunn. Much of the excitement over the original production concerned its visual spectacle, especially the scenic and costume designs by John Napier. The set design was not restricted to the stage area. Indeed, Napier covered almost all of the walls of the interior of the New London Theatre with scenery, surrounding the audience with a fantastical junk yard. Napier's anthropomorphic feline costumes, along with the makeup designs by Candace Carell, resembled nothing that had ever graced the musical stage before and were soon to become iconic imagery for a new generation of theatre-goers. *Cats* opened at the West End's New London Theatre in May 1981, and ran for a chart-topping 8,949 performances, standing as London's longest running musical until it was surpassed in 2006 by another Mackintosh mega production (with Napier designs), *Les Misérables*. When the show moved to Broadway and opened at the Winter Garden Theatre in 1982, Napier again designed an environmental set which filled the entire auditorium, and the orchestra was moved to an unseen location behind the playing space. The Broadway production would run for a record-breaking 7,485 performances, standing as Broadway's longest running show until the torch was passed in 2006 to *The Phantom of the Opera*, another Lloyd Webber creation that included Mackintosh as a partnering producer. Beginning with *Cats*, the entrepreneurial Mackintosh revolutionized the marketing and "sale" of a musical, as he began licensing the original look and sound of his mega-musicals on a global scale. A Mackintosh production (i.e., its concept, scenic/costume design, staging, choreography, orchestrations, music direction, etc.) could be replicated, for a licensing fee, by major theatres and companies around the world, enabling the creator/licenser to reap great profits from the many simultaneously playing reproductions. Mackintosh would not only institutionalize this practice for successful Lloyd Webber creations but also for his other mega-hits by other artists, such as *Les Misérables*, *Miss Saigon*, and *Mary Poppins*. Mackintosh would also be one of the few producers to be prominently named on all billing materials, alongside his iconic marketing logos, which were effectively employed to transcend language differences (e.g., the "eyes" of *Cats*, the "waif" of *Les Misérables*, the "helicopter" of *Miss Saigon*, and a stylized redeployment of the "nanny with umbrella" for *Poppins*).

Lloyd Webber was also instrumental in the marketing and production of *Cats*, as he would continue to be for all his works, gaining more and more property control throughout his career. Mackintosh shared producing duties and profits with Really Useful Company, Lloyd Webber's production company. *Cats* not only made Lloyd Webber a bona fide celebrity, but also made him very rich, changing his life forever and rewarding courageous early backers with a 200 percent profit on individual investments. Unfortunately, *Cats* also spelled the end for Webber and Rice. Previously, the two writing partners had weathered tensions during *Evita*,

when Lloyd Webber began editing and rejecting some of Rice's lyrics for the show. When Rice found he was not especially needed for *Cats*, having his only submitted lyrics (for the song that would become "Memory") turned down in favor of Nunn's, he reportedly felt disrespected and discarded, finally ending his relationship with Lloyd Webber. Post-Rice, Lloyd Webber has yet to establish a lasting partnership with another librettist/lyricist, mostly preferring to rotate lyricists while giving preference to the music in his works. (Rice has enjoyed a fruitful second chapter to his career, finding great success working for Disney as he produced lyrics for contemporary hit musicals such as *Beauty and the Beast*, *The Lion King*, and *Aida*.)

The 1980s proved to be a decade of astronomical success and excess for Lloyd Webber. During 1982, alone, Broadway saw a full-length theatrical version of *Joseph* arrive at the Royale Theatre (which ran for 747 performances), *Cats* made its triumphant Broadway premiere (winning the Tony Award for Best Musical), and *Song and Dance* debuted on the West End. One sad interruption in late autumn of that year was the death of Lloyd Webber's father (and lifelong mentor). In the next year, 1983, Lloyd Webber realized a lifelong dream by purchasing a London theater, the Palace. He also began an affair with a young cast member from the London production of *Cats* named Sarah Brightman and divorced his first wife. In 1984, he married Brightman and started working on his next grand musical to move to Broadway, *Starlight Express*, with the term "mega-musical" now being used to denote the large-scale, spectacle-driven works that followed in the wake of the *Cats* phenomenon.

In 1973, Lloyd Webber attempted, unsuccessfully, to provide a score for a British children's television show based on Rev. W. Awdry's Railway Series books. A decade later, Lloyd Webber finally realized his locomotive fantasy on stage and called it *Starlight Express*. Conceived by Lloyd Webber, with lyrics by Richard Stilgoe (as well as Don Black and David Yazbek in later configurations), the musical is a cross between Cinderella and the Little Engine That Could. The libretto revolves around Rusty, a scruffy little steam engine who is given inspiration and guidance by his Poppa and, consequently, wins an all-important race against the mighty diesel-powered Greaseball and the sleek electric-motored Electra. Under the guidance of director Trevor Nunn (still basking in the glow of *Cats*), Lloyd Webber's sung-through, pop-rock spectacle debuted on the West End in 1984 to mostly negative reviews. Audiences ignored the critics and flocked to the extravaganza, resulting in a record-breaking box office for the London show (7,461 performances). Given the public's enthusiasm, Nunn felt emboldened to take on the critics, unabashedly declaring the show to be a "Disneyland" for adults. Many in the press derisively deemed the show to be "*Cats* on wheels," and any praise of the production was mostly directed toward John Napier's scenic and costume designs, which created a transcontinental railway system on stage and turned actors into trains, putting them on roller skates and outfitting them in stylized costumes. When *Starlight Express* moved to Broadway in 1987, the production's cost had grown to over $8 million. The Gershwin Theatre was transformed into a massive, high-tech roller-skate park, containing a labyrinth of tracks that went over and around the audience, as well as a hydraulic steel bridge that raised and revolved in numerous patterns. The show ran for 761 performances, but it was unable to make a profit. The Broadway show was also a disappointment for Lloyd Webber, given the critics' panning of what they deemed to be an overworked, clichéd, and vacuous score. Although *Starlight Express* never overcame the slings and arrows cast by critics and others in the musical theatre arena, it managed to live on and prosper, enjoying numerous American and international tours (a current production of the show has been running continuously since 1988 in a custom-built theater in Bochum, Germany).

Between *Starlight's* popular (yet critically attacked) 1984 debut in London and the show's less popular (and still critically attacked) transfer to Broadway in 1987, Lloyd Webber continued to dominate the musical theatre stage. In 1985, *Song and Dance* opened on Broadway with its American star, Bernadette Peters, proving effervescent in the one-woman "Song" segment. Although reviews ranged from lukewarm to severely critical of the show's awkwardly merged two-part song/dance construct, there began to be an almost unspoken resignation by theatre critics that Lloyd Webber was critic-proof and could practically walk on theatrical water. In the same year, Lloyd Webber, dispirited by the negative response to *Starlight*, composed a concert choral work, *Requiem*, a mass dedicated to his recently deceased father. The recording won a Grammy Award in 1986, while "Pie Jesu" from *Requiem* ranked high on the British pop charts. During this period, Lloyd Webber also started work on a musical that he would view, along with *Requiem*, as an "artistic" assertion and redemption for what was deemed to be the "empty" excess of *Starlight Express*. The show, *The Phantom of the Opera* (1986), would also provide a star vehicle for his new wife and muse, Brightman. The work ultimately became Lloyd Webber's most successful musical.

In 1984, Lloyd Webber happened upon an intimate stage adaptation of the 1911 Gaston Leroux novel, *The Phantom of the Opera*, at an East London fringe theatre. The modest but bold production used musical excerpts from public-domain operas; Lloyd Webber was inspired to try his hand at creating a musical version for the West End, having also been a longtime fan of the tale and its many film adaptations (especially the classic 1925 silent version starring Lon Chaney). He approached his compatriot producer, Mackintosh, with the idea of co-producing a theatrical adaptation, thinking along the campy lines of *The Rocky Horror Show* or maybe in the vein of a satiric penny dreadful. After reading the original novel, however, Lloyd Webber chose to treat the material in a manner more in tune with the novel, that is, to play up its darkly romantic and tragic overtones. Instead of using opera excerpts, Lloyd Webber decided to compose the music himself, working again with Stilgoe as a co-adapter and lyricist. After the project's first act was positively received at the Sydmonton Festival, it was agreed that the work should be expanded into a full musical, heightening its romantic aspects. Lloyd Webber enlisted another lyricist, Charles Hart, to give the musical a more romantic spin. (Lloyd Webber first approached Alan Jay Lerner, who subsequently wrote the lyrics to "Masquerade" but had to quit the project due to failing health. The composer then appealed, to no avail, to his estranged partner, Rice, before Hart was signed.) In short, *Phantom's* book and lyrics are composites by various artists (with Lloyd Webber controlling the libretto), and all is dominated by Lloyd Webber's imposing and singularly constructed/conceptualized music. To directorially bring the gothic love story to life, he once again appealed to Prince, confident in his ability to balance stage concept with spectacle, metaphor, musicality, and drama, while paying attention to the human tragedy at its center.

Phantom is the tale of a half-masked, disfigured man (Erik, aka, the Phantom) who haunts the Paris

Opera House, tortured by his past and obsessed with music. Living in the Opera's catacombs, the Phantom is smitten with the golden voice of a chorus girl, Christine Daaé, taking her to his secret subterranean dwelling where, in Svengali fashion, he molds her talents. With his coaching, she moves beyond her fear and bewilderment of the otherworldly Phantom to fall under his tutelage and spell, his "Music of the Night." As the Phantom works to ensure Christine's stardom by terrorizing the Opera and murdering obstructive detractors, his muse falls in love with a traditional suitor, Raoul. And in the end, she must choose between the two men: Raoul (who has vowed to bring the Phantom to justice) and the Phantom (who has written an opera especially for her). At the musical's climax, she is kidnapped by the Phantom, and Raoul discovers the Phantom's underground lair, only to be captured by him as well. The Phantom offers to spare Raoul if Christine will agree to stay with the Phantom forever. With a kind kiss, Christine assures the Phantom that he is loved and melts his heart. He avows his eternal love to Christine; allows the young lovers to escape; and prepares to meet his tragic end at the hands of an angry mob. In the end, however, he vanishes under his cloak, with only his mask discovered by the group.

Lloyd Webber custom-tailored the role of Christine Daaé to suit Brightman's coloratura voice and ethereal stage presence, with many a theatre critic and insider alluding to the real-life love/muse affair between Lloyd Webber and Brightman. Brightman originated the part in London (with Michael Crawford as the Phantom) and put her definitive stamp on the musical, which debuted on October 9, 1986, at Her Majesty's Theatre. Given the magnitude of *Phantom's* West End success, the creative team (most notably, Lloyd Webber and Prince) decided that Brightman was essential to the production and should travel with the show to Broadway. There were resistors, however, who insisted that an American actress could successfully take over the role, as had been proven by Patti LuPone, Betty Buckley, and Bernadette Peters in the Broadway translations of *Evita*, *Cats*, and *Song and Dance*, respectively. In an unprecedented move, Prince (backed by Lloyd Webber) presented a thinly veiled threat to Actors' Equity and Broadway producers that he and the musical's producers (Mackintosh and Really Useful Theatre Company) might not take *Phantom* overseas unless Brightman was allowed to play Christine, thereby jeopardizing the great buzz and presold $18 million

box office. Not surprising, when *Phantom* premiered on January 9, 1988, at Broadway's Majestic Theatre (where it is still running), it starred Brightman, along with other original players such as Crawford and Steve Barton as Raoul. Its reviews were positive and audiences were delighted by the panoramic sound and epic look of the production, especially its scenic/costume designs by Maria Björnson, which provided jaw-dropping spectacle (e.g., a boat ride by Christine and the Phantom to his cavernous lake dwelling, as well as a chandelier that plunges to the ground over the heads of the audience at the climactic end of the musical's first act).

Phantom is a sung-through musical defined by its melodrama, theatrical spectacle, gothic aesthetic, and most significant, its complex score that combines classical composition, operatic flavor, and pop sensibility. For example, the title song is introduced by a baroque organ rendition of the musical's leitmotif, only to be brought into the 1980s with a pop-synthesizer treatment and ending with an operatic display of coloratura vocals by Christine. The musical's lauded score boasts another emotional anthem which became a ubiquitous standalone hit, "Music of the Night." With this haunting ballad, the Phantom plaintively expresses his musical passion and obsession in aria style.

Here, another significant aspect of Lloyd Webber's career must be addressed: the charges and insinuations of plagiarism laid against the composer. "Music of the Night' contains a central theme markedly similar to the refrain of *Brigadoon's* "Come to Me, Bend to Me," by Lerner and Loewe. Lloyd Webber has acknowledged this resemblance, stating that he purposefully composed "Music of the Night" as an homage to the Lerner and Loewe work. The *Brigadoon* writers took no umbrage, but the same could not be said for other composers who felt they had been plagiarized in the past by Lloyd Webber (with a growing number of critics pointing out his unmistakable melodic references to and outright borrowings from classical composers such as Mendelssohn, Puccini, and Paganini). In the case of *Phantom*, however, accusations were overt and lawsuits surfaced. Although Roger Waters, formerly of the band Pink Floyd, publically accused Lloyd Webber of using short riffs from one of the band's songs in his score for *Phantom*, he declined to sue. Another songwriter, Ray Repp, did sue Lloyd Webber for "lifting" one of his thematic compositions for *Phantom's* title song, but lost the court case. (Another rock composer, Rick Wakeman, asserted in 2008 that the same song's riff had actually been stolen from him.) Complaints came from the dead as well, as the Puccini estate brought suit against Lloyd Webber over various themes used throughout *Phantom*; the case was settled out of court. The controversy and argument over this aspect of Lloyd Webber's oeuvre is complicated and elicits divided sentiment, with some Lloyd Webber critics claiming that the composer is limited in the realm of "original thought," while his supporters assert that he has a postmodern gift for pastiche and homage, taking familiar themes and reinterpreting them with new stylistic treatments, rhythms, harmonies, and theatrical conventions.

Most audience members were unaware of the controversies when *Phantom* triumphantly opened on Broadway in 1988, winning seven Tony Awards, including one for Best Musical and Best Director of a Musical (Prince), dominating almost every technical category (with Lloyd Webber, however, conspicuously snubbed with regard to his score and book). Further, with this production joining *Cats* and *Starlight Express* on Broadway, Lloyd Webber made history, becoming (and still reigning as) the only composer to have ever had three musicals simultaneously playing on the West End and Broadway. Mackintosh and Lloyd Webber also saw enormous financial profits by licensing over a dozen productions of *Phantom* around the world. In January 2006, *Phantom* overtook *Cats* to become Broadway's longest-running musical, with more than 10,000 performances at the Majestic as of this writing.

In the interim between *Phantom*'s West End opening and its Broadway transfer, Lloyd Webber became the first musical theatre composer on the London Stock Exchange. In 1986, his Really Useful Company went public under the new corporate name of Really Useful Group (R.U.G.), with its stock issued at £3.30 per share. The share price doubled in two years while Lloyd Webber retained 38 percent of the company. During this time, a savvy investor might buy a piece of the Lloyd Webber enterprise, gambling that his next musical would be another *Cats* or *Phantom*. (R.U.G. would go private again in 1990, with Lloyd Webber staging his own leveraged buyout, and then in 1999, Webber would buy back 30 percent of the company, which had gone into the hands of Universal Pictures.)

In many ways, Lloyd Webber's next musical was one of his most adventurous and uncharacteristic; however, the show also proved to be the beginning of the end of his Broadway reign. Lloyd Webber was uncomfortably aware of the critical respect and acclaim accorded contemporary composer/lyricist Stephen Sondheim and his edgy chamber musicals, a level of prestige still denied Lloyd Webber. Thus, he departed from the mega-musical format in the late 1980s to try his hand at an experimental, intimate chamber piece, *Aspects of Love* (1989). As producer, composer, and book adapter, Lloyd Webber created *Aspects* as a musicalized version of an autobiographic novella by David Garnett (who was a writer, bisexual bon vivant, member of the literary Bloomsbury Group, and nephew of Virginia Woolf). Again recruiting Trevor Nunn as director and commissioning lyrics from Don Black and Charles Hart, Lloyd Webber's adaptation was a bed-hopping, sung-through soap opera. The book covers a seventeen-year period (1947–64), centering on the romantic and intimate exploits of Alex Dillingham and his familial milieu. In a series of flashbacks, Alex reflects on how he, as an infatuated 17-year-old, became sexually involved with a worldly 25-year-old actress, Rose, only to lose her to his wealthy Uncle George, who, despite a longtime affair with a free-spirited lover, Giulietta, ultimately marries Rose. (Prior to the marriage, Rose and Giulietta also formed a friendship that evolved into a brief affair.) Later, the elderly George and Rose have a daughter, Jenny, who, in her early teens, becomes infatuated with the adult Alex (who may or may not be her real father). In the end, after curtailing inappropriate relations with Jenny, Alex meets and falls in love with Giulietta.

In summary, the tale sounds sordid and convoluted, and most critics derided the work as such. Despite tepid reviews, the show, which opened in April 1989 at the West End's Prince of Wales Theatre, ran for 1,325 performances. However, the London production of *Aspects* did not recoup its investment, while the musical's 1990 Broadway transfer ran for only 377 performances, opening to harsh reviews and closing at a loss of $8 million. Audiences were possibly expecting another Lloyd Webber spectacle and, instead, received a small-scale production with a handful of performers and a dark, moody, intimate setting, which may account for its negative reception. Nonetheless, many critics felt that *Aspects*' music was estimable (although a bit overwrought, with overused leitmotifs and "trunk" compositions taken from early, unrealized Lloyd Webber works). Given its combination of character expression and seductive melodies, the sung-through score boasts a plethora of musically dense and dramatically effective numbers, e.g., the confessional ballad "Anything but Lonely" and the thematic framing song "Love Changes Everything" (which became a hit pop single in Great Britain). *Aspects* has been given a second look in recent years, with a successful re-envisioned 2010 London revival, again directed by Nunn.

After *Aspects*, Lloyd Webber returned to the "big" musical, but true to form, his new project was steeped in controversy and negatively targeted by critics. As early as the 1970s, Lloyd Webber had wanted to adapt the critically acclaimed Billy Wilder film *Sunset Boulevard* (1950). Lloyd Webber was intrigued by its dark tale of a has-been silent film star, Norma Desmond, who lives in a delusional fantasy, planning her movie comeback via her original *Salome* screenplay that she has coerced a young writer, Joe, to put to paper. In the end, Norma discovers that "new Hollywood" has no place for her and that Joe, who has also assumed the role of her gigolo, has begun a genuine love affair with a woman his own age. The incidents push Desmond over the edge. In a fit of passion, she shoots Joe (the film begins with a voiceover by Joe, paired with an image of his corpse floating in a swimming pool). She then descends into a fog of madness, allowing the authorities to take her into custody as they feign a fully lit movie set in her home and she infamously prepares for her cinematic "close-up." Once Lloyd Webber secured the film rights from Paramount Pictures, more than a decade after he had begun tinkering with the concept, he set to work with director Nunn and two librettist/lyricist writing collaborators, Christopher Hampton and Black (the practice of multiple lyricists had become standard practice for a Lloyd Webber show). One must also cite the writers of the original film (including Wilder) as contributors to Lloyd Webber's mostly sung-through musical, as much of its text was lifted directly from the movie. When *Sunset Boulevard* opened at the West End's Adelphi Theatre on July 12, 1993, it starred Patti LuPone as Norma Desmond. Although the production received ambivalent critical reviews, it ran for 1,529 performances. Similar to *Aspects*, however, the long-playing London show lost money (mostly due to its lavish production demands). In

December 1993, *Sunset Boulevard* had its American premiere at Los Angeles' Shubert Theatre, starring Glenn Close. This is where things got messy for Lloyd Webber and his musical. Given the unanimous raves for Close's Los Angeles performance, as well as her prominent American film profile, it was decided that she would premiere the role on Broadway instead of LuPone (who had been contractually guaranteed the New York run). LuPone threatened to sue but was appeased by a financial arrangement with Lloyd Webber's Really Useful Company, accompanied by a press release proclaiming that the casting change was in no way related to her stellar talent. In a further complication, film icon Faye Dunaway was slated to take over the lead role in Los Angeles after Close moved to Broadway. However, Dunaway proved so disappointing in rehearsals that the producers closed the show at the Shubert and sold the scenic elements to Toronto for another production, prompting the actress to sue for breach of contract and defamation. All was eventually resolved, but the entire litigious episode caused many a critic and theatre insider to joke that, with *Sunset Boulevard*, Lloyd Webber had proven invincible to both critics and lawyers.

Sunset Boulevard opened at the Minskoff Theatre on December 17, 1994, with the largest box office advance that had yet been seen on Broadway, running for 977 performances. The production won seven Tony Awards, but the Best Musical win was against only one other nominee (a jukebox musical, *Smokey Joe's Cafe*) and its win for Best Original Score was because there were no other nominees in the category that year. This scenario caused a myriad of musical theatre scholars, critics, practitioners and fans to dispiritedly ponder the future of the Broadway musical. Adding further insult to injury, the award-winning score was given little acclaim by music critics who deemed Lloyd Webber's jazz/swing compositions to be derivative and his use of reprises and leitmotifs overly heavy. This is not to suggest that the score lacks appeal, for it not only contains driving, infectious numbers ("Sunset Boulevard"), but also stirring ballads ("With One Look," "New Ways to Dream," and "As If We Never Said Goodbye"), which have been successfully recorded by top artists. Awards and kudos were also given to scenic designer Napier, who again brought his technical brilliance to the stage, starting the show with an aerial view of Joe's corpse in the swimming pool, following with an exciting car chase, and topping it all with the awe-inspiring materialization of Desmond's mansion, a multi-leveled baroque structure capable of rising into the air to allow scenes in other locales to occur underneath. In short, *Sunset Boulevard*, as Broadway spectacle, was stunning—and so was the cost. At its close in 1997, three years after opening, *Sunset Boulevard* had yet to recoup its reported $13 million investment.

At this writing, *Sunset Boulevard* stands as the last significant musical by Lloyd Webber to have made an impact on Broadway. Nonetheless, his power and prestige in the musical arena has not waned; in fact, Lloyd Webber's output and influence in the industry proceeds at a dizzying pace. During the '90s, he was knighted and elevated to a peerage in Great Britain for his "music" service. He continues to write and produce, yet no work has achieved the success of his earlier musicals. *Whistle Down the Wind* (1998), based on a 1961 film by the same name, with lyrics by Jim Steinman, has yet to make a successful move to Broadway (although a recording of its takeaway ballad, "No Matter What," by the boy band Boyzone became a #1 hit on the UK pop charts). Another show that has not made it to the States is *The Beautiful Game* (2000), which revolves around soccer and a group of teenagers coming of age in 1969 amid The Troubles in Belfast, Northern Ireland. The show had a noteworthy run at The Cambridge Theatre in London and was recently revisited by Lloyd Webber under a new title, *The Boys in the Photograph*, receiving a world premiere at The Liverpool Institute for Performing Arts in 2008. For the Lloyd Webber shows that made it across the pond early in the twenty-first century, Broadway proved inhospitable. The aforementioned failed revamp of *By Jeeves* (1996) played for only 73 performances when it moved to Broadway in 2001, and an original musical, *The Woman in White* (2004), proved to be a major disappointment. With lyrics by David Zippel and a book adaptation by Charlotte Jones, *The Woman in White* is loosely based on the same-titled 1859 epistolary mystery novel penned by Wilkie Collins. With Nunn once again at the helm of a visual Lloyd Webber feast (with cutting-edge use of media projections), the production suffered several set-backs but ultimately ran for over a year (500 performances) at London's Palace Theatre. When a tweaked version arrived at Broadway's Marquis Theatre on November 17, 2005, Lloyd Webber

fans were enthusiastic, having waited over a decade for a new work; but critics were lukewarm, deeming the musical to be lackluster and mediocre. The show closed after only a few months (109 performances), making it the shortest run for an original Lloyd Webber musical on Broadway.

In recent years, Lloyd Webber has been busy promoting and exploiting a new frontier of musical theatre production: the televised reality show. By way of a talent competition on British television titled *How Do You Solve a Problem Like Maria?*, Lloyd Webber, acting as a judge, cast the winner (Connie Fisher) in the lead role for a revival of *The Sound of Music* that he was producing. He would follow suit with 2007's *Any Dream Will Do!*, casting the role of Joseph for a West End revival of his *Joseph and the Amazing Technicolor Dreamcoat*. In 2008, he would return as a judge for BBC's talent show *I'd Do Anything*, finding leads for a London revival of the musical *Oliver!*. In 2009, Lloyd Webber spearheaded a search via the BBC series *Over the Rainbow* for a novice musical theatre performer to play Dorothy (as well as a dog to play Toto) in his West End production of *The Wizard of Oz*. He cast the winner, Danielle Hope, as the young Kansas heroine and, in a significant development, worked again with Tim Rice to create a number of new songs for the show, which opened in March 2011 at Lloyd Webber's Palladium Theatre. The production closed after eighteen months, and a hoped-for transfer to Broadway has failed to materialize at present. History was to repeat itself with *Love Never Dies* (2010), the highly anticipated sequel to *The Phantom of the Opera*, which was scheduled to arrive in the U.S. in 2011. With music by Lloyd Webber and lyrics by Glenn Slater (as well as Hart, who joined the team later), the musical was given an original plotline (veering from the original Gaston Leroux novel) by Lloyd Webber, Slater, and Ben Elton. The musical places Christine Daaé, with husband Raoul and son Gustave, at Coney Island in 1907, where she has travelled to perform at the behest of an anonymous impresario (the Phantom who, it turns out, is very much alive). The rest of the tale is a potboiler, full of romance, intrigue, and discovery. Directed and choreographed by Broadway favorites Jack O'Brien and Jerry Mitchell, respectively, *Love Never Dies'* initial West End run was troubled. After opening at the Adelphi Theatre on March 9, 2010, the production was put on hiatus for a "revamp" in November and re-opened under the hand of a new director (Bill Kenwright), with some lead performers replaced. Reviews were still mixed, however, and the West End production closed in August 2011, while a planned Broadway version has been postponed "indefinitely." A reworked Australian production has been filmed, however, and is available on DVD.

When categorizing a Lloyd Webber production as a "failure," it is important to keep such a descriptor in context. Lloyd Webber, despite disappointments over recent Broadway ventures, for several months in 2012 he enjoyed "déjà vu all over again" on the Great White Way. That year the arrival of two highly anticipated revivals (*Evita* and *Jesus Christ Superstar*) joined *Phantom of the Opera* to put Lloyd Webber's name once more atop no fewer than three Broadway marquees. A brief list of Lloyd Webber's career output and accomplishments is dizzying, and his wealth and power in the musical theatre industry are unmatched. He has been named one of the top 100 richest men in Great Britain, where he currently lives with his third wife, Madeleine Gurdon (he divorced Brightman in 1990). In addition to his triumphs as a composer, producer, and impresario, he is a West End theater owner many times over. *Phantom of the Opera* reigns today as Broadway's longest-running show. Overall, Lloyd Webber's body of work consists of thirteen musicals, a set of variations, a song cycle, two film scores, and a Latin Requiem Mass, all of which have garnered him seven Tony Awards, three Grammy Awards, an Academy Award, seven Olivier Awards, a Golden Globe Award, and the 2006 Kennedy Center Honor. There can be little doubt that this musical theatre maximalist will continue to contribute to the canon in a mega fashion, while placing his impressive imprint on the genre and industry.

FEATURED PRODUCTION: *Cats* (1981)

Music by Andrew Lloyd Webber; Lyrics by T. S. Eliot

Original Broadway Run: Opened October 7, 1982; Winter Garden Theatre; 7,485 performances

Who will ascend to the Heaviside Layer? If one has read T. S. Eliot's *Old Possum's Book of Practical Cats* (1939), the question may hold some meaning. If one is familiar with Andrew Lloyd Webber's blockbuster musical *Cats*, however, the query not only strikes a meaningful chord (in more ways than one), but it brings an entire theatrical world to mind. Composer Lloyd Webber, along with producer Cameron Mackintosh, director Trevor Nunn, designer John Napier, and choreographer Gillian Lynne, brought Eliot's fantastical and whimsical children's poems, written in the 1930s for his godchildren, to theatrical life fifty years after their publication. At the hands of Lloyd Webber and company, the collection of lovingly crafted "nonsensical" verses became both a modern-day extravaganza and a worldwide musical phenomenon, breaking box office records on both coasts and imprinting its anthropomorphic aesthetic and pop-friendly sound on the theatre-going public, while reinventing the look, feel, and concept of the canonical musical.

To the casual observer, Eliot's allegorical works may seem an odd choice on which to build a musical, but to Lloyd Webber, who loved both cats and Elliot's poems (which were a children's classic in Great Britain), the writings begged to be musicalized. As early as the mid-1970s, he began experimenting with adaptations of the poems, approaching producer Cameron Mackintosh at the end of the decade with his concept to combine the pieces into a musical theatre work. Prior to this meeting, Lloyd Webber had impressed Eliot's widow, Valerie, with some early compositions in concert form at his annual Sydmonton Festival, and she, in return, had supplied him with some previously unpublished thematic ideas regarding the cats, penned by her late husband. It was this connective tissue that helped Lloyd Webber "see" the musical, and he relayed his vision to Mackintosh. To Mackintosh's credit, he not only agreed to produce the effort but became an active player behind the scenes, recommending and convincing the artistic director of the Royal Shakespeare Company, Trevor Nunn, to helm the work (his first assignment as a musical theatre director).

Together, the three men solidified the musical's concept, creating a thinly linked storyline that revolves around the scheduled sunrise arrival of Old Deuteronomy, the patriarchal cat, at the Jellicle cat junkyard, where he will escort a chosen feline to the Heaviside Layer, granting the lucky cat a new Jellicle life. The plot's intrigue and conflict lies in the question over which cat will become the chosen one. Amid a garbage heap and nocturnal setting, Jellicle cats attend the Jellicle Ball, waiting for the ultimate gift of resurrection (T. S. Eliot was also a literary heavyweight who often addressed Judeo-Christian themes and content in his works). After the exposition, a colorful parade of cats begins, as each Jellicle shares, through song and/or dance, his or her fanciful life story and character portrait. The list is expansive, but a condensed sampling includes Jennyanydots (the Old Gumbie Cat, whose plump physique and lazy daytime demeanor belies her nighttime hunting prowess), Bustopher Jones (the spiffy, well-fed, upper-crust kitty), Rum Tum Tugger (the sexy, rebellious, rockin' tomcat), Mungojerrie and Rumpleteazer (a team of cat burglars who showboat vaudevillian clowning and dexterity), Mr. Mistoffelees (the mysterious, magical cat who can appear and disappear at will), and Gus (the old theatre cat, declining and suffering from dementia). Similar to Gus is another aging character, Grizabella, the Glamour Cat. She is the faded, spurned, bedraggled cat who has seen better days and wistfully relives her starry past, as conveyed through her eleven o'clock number, "Memory." And at the end of *Cats*, it is Grizabella (the downtrodden outcast) who is chosen to ascend to the Heaviside Layer.

The power ballad "Memory" is the score's only number to contain lyrics by someone other than the late Eliot. The song's development has become musical theatre legend, given its convoluted and discordant history. Originally, the Eliot poems were to be used for all of *Cats*' lyrics; however, when Mackintosh asked Lloyd Webber for a pivotal number for Grizabella, given her character's significance in the plot's resolution, the music came easily but the men could not find a suitable poem from which to draw lyrics. Thus, director Nunn dove into Eliot's book of poems for a week and penned a reflective lament for Grizabella, which pleased both Lloyd Webber and Mackintosh. A complication ensued, however. Tim Rice, Lloyd Webber's previous writing partner (who had opted not to be involved in the project), unexpectedly showed an interest in *Cats* by offering to supply lyrics for the new song. (It happened that Rice's significant other, West End musical star Elaine Page, had just been cast to replace theatrical icon Judi Dench in the role of Grizabella, due to Dench's fall and serious injury during rehearsals; thus, Page would be singing the crucial song.) Rice wrote lyrics that, according to the collaborators, were good but lacked the feel, intent, and aesthetic of the climactic scene, as well as the musical overall. Mackintosh and Lloyd Webber decided to go with Nunn's initial offering. Given the phenomenal success of *Cats* and the takeaway hit "Memory," Nunn made a fortune on his sole foray into lyric-writing. Rice, on the other hand, bitterly parted ways with Lloyd Webber after the debacle—an unfortunate end to an artistically potent musical theatre partnership.

In most respects, however, *Cats*' lyrics are beside the point when it comes to its sung-through score; Lloyd Webber's lush and melodic compositions are at the heart of the show's aural, aesthetic world, often superseding Eliot's obscure poetry. Underpinning the entire work is a connective leitmotif (a searching series of minor-keyed chromatics) that evokes and develops the mysterious Jellicle milieu. The enigmatic leitmotif opens the musical as the lead-in to "Jellicle Songs for Jellicle Cats." This expositional number grows from cryptic, staccato solos into a full-bodied opener, with all cats singing and dancing in classic showbiz style. The leitmotif reappears throughout the show; for example, variations of it underscore chanted/*Sprechstimme* lyrics in numbers such as "The Naming of Cats" and "The Jellicle Ball," with the leitmotif turning into a sung vocal line in the latter. Along with the leitmotif, as well as numerous thematic reprises and variations, the musical through-line and character of *Cats* is asserted and strengthened by the many specialty numbers provided by Lloyd Webber. Most are melodically infectious and range in style from vaudevillian to classical, depending on the character of the featured cat. Lloyd Webber's compositional diversity and dexterity are evidenced by songs such as "The Old Gumby Cat" (a narrative ballad punctuated by swing-time, harmonic choruses), "The Rum Tum Tugger" (a rock 'n' roll romp), "Macavity" (a jazzy blues number), "Gus: The Theatre Cat" (a sweet, sad lullaby), and the aforementioned "Memory."

Although, the score played a significant part in *Cats*' landmark success, one must note the other crucial factor: the spectacle. *Cats* would become the genesis from which the mega-musical movement would spring, due, in great part, to the contributions of scenic/costume designer John Napier. Napier created the oversized junkyard in which the cats roamed and romped. He also designed their costumes (aided by make-up designer Candace Carell), which reinvented what characters in a musical could look like, putting anthropomorphic designs on the musical theatre map more than a decade before *The Lion King*. Napier's work was more than a design; it was a fantasy world created for multigenerational audiences which completely covered the interior of the theatre. The world of *Cats* was also one of almost nonstop movement, given a dance-heavy concept by Nunn who brought in choreographer Gillian Lynne (with whom he had worked at RSC) to create the expressive jazz movement/dance for the show. Many individualized "feline" mannerisms were also incorporated into the cats' characterizations throughout the production.

Thanks to the musical's triumphant reception at West End's New London Theatre (where it opened in 1981 and would run for 8,949 performances), the Broadway production of *Cats* debuted to great fanfare at the Winter Garden Theatre on October 7, 1982. Like the original London staging, the American version featured environmental spectacle, with the Winter Garden's proscenium arch removed and the orchestra relocated behind the action to allow the performers to get up close to the spectators. The junkyard spilled into the audience, surrounding them with oversized garbage and other artifacts, while the ceiling was lowered and given a canopy of twinkling lights, simulating stars and cats' eyes, into which Old Deuteronomy and Grizabella (played by Broadway star Betty Buckley) ascended in a giant tire lit by 4,000 light bulbs. Audiences loved the entire experience, while critics lauded the novel production, awarding it seven Tony Awards (including Best Musical). In June 1997 the show broke the previously held record by *A Chorus Line* for longest-running Broadway musical, with the landmark production playing Broadway until 2000, closing with 7,485 performances (eighteen years) under its belt.

Today, how does one explain the phenomenon and the long-lived, universal popularity of the idiosyncratic *Cats*? First, one might cite the allegorical underpinnings of the piece, including its tale of perseverance, suffering, and eternal life (i.e., a Judeo-Christian ethos with many biblical allusions). Next, there is the infectious score, as well as the simple fact that the material, although whimsically exaggerated, appeals to cat lovers, who recognize and connect to the feline types represented. It must also be noted that in the 1980s, *Cats* predated the "children-friendly" works of Disney and DreamWorks on Broadway, thus appealing to the entire family. And since much of the story was told through dance, one did not one need to understand English to enjoy the show, making it perfect for international tourists. Finally, there was the novelty of Napier's environmental spectacle, with the flashy event directed by Nunn, who had "serious" theatre credentials, adding artistic cachet to the entire enterprise. Speaking of enterprise, *Cats* ignited a commercial revolution within the musical theatre arena, rewarding savvy backers with a 200 percent return on their investment, while Mackintosh instituted a practice of international licensing, underpinned by a global marketing campaign that "spoke" to foreign markets (the "cat's eye" logo needed no translation). In 1998, Lloyd Webber released a film version of the stage production of *Cats* (filmed at the Adelphi Theatre in London), preserving the show for future generations. Thus, even if *Cats* appears to be a curious artifact to some critics and spectators today, one need only reflect on the musical's many distinctions and innovations to conclude that *Cats* will probably prove its marketing slogan true by living "now and forever" on the musical stage and in the musical theatre psyche.

Village Theatre's *Cats* ensemble, 2006. Courtesy of Village Theatre.

PULLING BACK THE CURTAIN:
Boublil / Schönberg and the Sung-Through Mega-Musical

In the early 1980s, two new terms entered the musical theatre lexicon: the "sung-through musical" and the "mega-musical." Both terms describe forms that were setting the musical arena abuzz and would forever change the musical theatre genre and industry. In simple terms, a sung-through musical is a work that contains very little or no spoken text; thus, dialogue is constructed as recitative, and the score tells the entire story. In the 1980s (during the ascent of Andrew Lloyd Webber and his early, triumphant assertions of the form, e.g., *Jesus Christ Superstar*, *Evita*, and *Cats*), many a musical theatre purist groused that the sung-through musical was simply an "opera" by another name. Further, early critics lamented that, in a sung-through work, the music/text/dance paradigm, i.e., the Golden Triangle, was compromised because of the dominance of the score and composer. The Triangle became distorted beyond recognition, and its unique, interactive musical theatre power was diminished. Criticisms along this line have persisted. Some camps still argue that the sung-through musical leaves seemingly little room for the "Bubble Formula," that is, the traditional effervescence that occurs in a musical when a scene evolves from spoken dialogue to song (and dance), with the heightening of emotion within the scene. Yet many others championed the new form. And as the sung-through work gained popularity, there was no denying that the completely sung/musicalized construct transcended language barriers and could speak to a wider populace than had previously been reached by the traditional American musical. For a global audience, a theme or tale could be dramatized through an evocative, emotive, and infectious score, illustrated and embellished through its attendant stage spectacle. Herein lie the foundation and the formula behind the revolutionary success of the mega-musical. This type of production transcended the size and scope of prior Broadway musicals in terms of score, source content, collaboration, technical components, and worldwide market/imprint (driven by a new licensing model, courtesy of pioneering producer Cameron Mackintosh). Lloyd Webber asserted the sung-through form within the musical theatre genre and, with Mackintosh, began the mega-musical movement. Two other men, however, took the revolution to new heights in the 1980s and early '90s: Claude-Michel Schönberg and Alain Boublil. Together, they created innovative, artistic, canonical, and iconic works which were epic in scale and global in nature.

Hailing from France, Boublil and Schönberg are a team in the purist sense, for they work in a highly collaborative fashion. Schönberg is the composer, Boublil writes the lyrics, and they work together on the librettos. Initially, the two men were more interested in writing pop hits than theatre scores, but they were inspired by Lloyd Webber and Rice's *Jesus Christ Superstar*. Thus, they created their own rock opera, *La Revolution Française*, and released it as a double concept album in 1973, selling 350,000 copies. The opera chronicled the French Revolution, indicating that, from the beginning, Boublil and Schönberg were drawn to grand, sweeping historical subject matter. The same year, they presented *La Revolution Française* at the Palais des Sports in Paris, where it became the first staged French rock opera. (Schönberg played the role of King Louis XVI in the production.) The pair's next project was similarly ambitious: *Les Misérables*, based on Victor Hugo's 1861 sprawling 1,200-page novel. Hugo's work, written in exile during the reign of Napoleon III (1851–70), is a critique of the social injustices and living conditions suffered by the poor and downtrodden during Hugo's lifetime. Boublil and Schönberg (plus poet Jean-Marc Natel, who worked with Boublil on the lyrics) released the work as a concept album, selling 260,000 copies. An arena version was staged at the Palais des Sports for sixteen weeks. During this time, the recording reached the ears of Cameron Mackintosh, who greeted the idea of a French musical with skepticism but, after hearing the music, became excited at the prospect of producing an English version of the sung-through work. And after two years of development, *Les Misérables* opened at the

Royal Shakespeare Company's Barbican Theatre in 1985, landing on Broadway two years later in March 1987. True to its "mega" descriptor, *Les Misérables* boasted one of the largest group of collaborators ever assembled for a musical at the time. The team included producer Mackintosh, in partnership with RSC, co-directors and co-adaptors Trevor Nunn and John Caird, co-librettists Schönberg and Boublil, composer Schönberg, and French lyricists Boublil and Jean-Marc Natel, with English lyrics supplied by Herbert Kretzmer ("additional material" is credited to James Fenton, while Nunn and Caird are given some credit for lyrics to "On My Own").

The landmark success of *Les Misérables* (*Les Miz*) is all the more remarkable given the multilayered, historical, and expansive nature of its tale and subject matter. The epic story begins in 1815 and centers on paroled convict Jean Valjean, who served nineteen years in prison, having been wrongfully accused of stealing a loaf of bread. Seeking a new, redemptive life, Valjean rises to become a factory owner with a social conscience, adopting a daughter, Cosette, as a result of a promise made to her dying prostitute mother. Unfortunately, an obsessed gendarme, Javert, does not accept Valjean's piety and has vowed to bring the ex-convict to justice for breaking his parole. Javert's dogged pursuit ultimately forces Valjean and Cosette to flee "underground," where they cross paths with revolutionaries involved in the Parisian civic uprisings (the July revolution of 1830 and the worker riots of 1832–34). Cosette falls in love with the revolutionary student Marius (who is also obsessively loved by the *Les Miz* poster child, Eponine). In the midst of the ill-fated

Alain Boublil and Claude-Michel Schönberg surrounded by cast of *Les Miserables* at Theatre Mogador in Paris © Michael Le Poer Trench/Sygma/Corbis

uprisings, Valjean saves the life of Marius. Marius, however, is unaware that Valjean was his savior and is contemptuous of the old convict. In the end, however, the two men are reconciled, and Valjean dies in peace, assured that Cosette and Marius are happy while also secure in the belief that he is a redeemed man, having lived a life of service, helping to create a better world for posterity. Javert, on the other hand, succumbs to despair and commits suicide, believing that he violated his unforgiving code of absolute justice by failing to capture and punish Valjean.

Having caused a sensation overseas, *Les Miz* was greeted in New York by an immense box office advance, which also included a new top ticket price of $50. The musical did not disappoint, and it swept the Tony Awards in almost every major category, including Best Musical, while running for an astounding 6,680 performances. It currently holds the record as the third longest-running musical on Broadway. The work was lauded for its fluid, cinematic staging by Nunn and Caird (with some theatrical moments, such as the flag-waving, in-place marching to "One More Day," becoming as iconic as the big-eyed waif on the show's marketing materials). Equally impressive was the scene design by top mega-musical designer John Napier, which included a jaw-dropping barricade for the battle scenes, which revolved on a giant turntable to reveal other playing spaces. The stage milieu was atmospheric, flexible, and immense; yet it never seemed incongruently glitzy or showy. But if the *Les Miz* staging and scenery thrilled audiences, the piece's moving and powerful score touched hearts, creating a rabid fan base. Combining contemporary sounds, pop hooks, and operatic constructs in a continuous web of dramatic music, Schönberg's sung-through compositions work much like a film score, driving action, creating big moments, underscoring emotion, musically melding the many subplots, and creating a self-contained, identifiable world. The score can also be seen as a genre/industry outlier, in that it lacks the jazz influence and show-tune character of many conventional (i.e., American) musicals. As opposed to some sung-through works, the score did not rely on overly repetitive themes, awkward recitatives, or pedestrian modulations and variations to link and transition its numbers. Instead, the *Les Miz* "songs" are often emotional high points that have been logically evolved and realized via a complex, varied use of melody in recitatives, sophisticated leitmotifs and dramatic, atmospheric orchestrations. The songs themselves are diverse, atmospheric, and potent. There are emotive and explicatory power ballads that do double duty as despairing laments (e.g., "Who Am I?," "I Dreamed a Dream," "On My Own," "Stars," and "Empty Chairs and Empty Tables"), while stirring, full-throated ensemble anthems ("Do You Hear the People Sing?") are countered by simple and plaintive-voiced prayers ("Bring Him Home"). The many storylines and character expressions are evinced through intricate contrapuntal constructs, for example, "In My Life" (an interwoven confessional shared by Valjean, Marius, Cosette, and Eponine); "A Heart Full of Love" (a juxtaposed love trio between Marius, Cosette, and Eponine); and "One Day More" (the entire company's manifesto and climactic call to arms).

Boublil and Schönberg's first major hit impressively displayed many of the characteristics that would come to define their oeuvre. Specifically, *Les Miz* boasts an open emotionalism, wearing its heart on its sleeve. Numerous characters sing directly to the audience, baring their souls on stage. In this respect, the work lacks qualities that are often cited as hallmarks of the American musical, i.e., irony, cynicism, and outright comedy (although there are some comedic secondary characters, they are overshadowed by the serious nature of the piece). In short, *Les Miz* is honest and heartfelt and it takes itself seriously. It also has the scenic size and musical muscle to match the force of its passions. Lastly, the musical crosses cultural, national, and historical boundaries, appealing to a worldwide demographic. As evidence of this last characteristic, the show circled the globe after its triumphant West End and Broadway debuts, being translated into fourteen languages and produced in nineteen countries (always according to Nunn's direction and using Napier's designs). In this manner, *Les Miz* became a universal signifier and ambassador for the musical theatre genre. The long-awaited film version also proved wildly successful. Released in 2012, *Les Miz* was a critical darling and box office smash, winning the Golden Globe Award for Best Motion Picture—Musical or Comedy, as well as garnering eight Academy Award nominations (including Best Picture), winning three for technical merits and supporting actress Anne Hathaway.

Boublil and Schönberg's next work, *Miss Saigon* (1989), would retain many *Les Miz* characteristics, for example, its sung-through construct, sincere and direct emotionalism, a dense and diverse score, historical subject matter, big themes, and a global perspective. The new show was not placed as far back in history, however, its setting being the final days and immediate aftermath of the Vietnam War. Yet the musical had a significant historical legacy; its storyline contains vestiges of and references to *Madame Butterfly*, a 1900 melodrama by David Belasco, which was turned into a famous 1904 opera by composer Giacomo Puccini. Both the melodrama and opera center on a doomed love story set against a culture clash backdrop of East versus West, ending with the suicide of a lovelorn and betrayed Asian female consort. Boublil and Schönberg, however, found a way to reinterpret the *Madame Butterfly* material, contemporizing its themes. Reportedly, the pair was inspired by a 1975 news photo of a Vietnamese woman offering her child to an American GI during the Fall of Saigon. Thus, they wrote a libretto that deals with an ill-fated love affair between a Vietnamese girl and an American Marine in the days leading up to Saigon's fall. (The Fall of Saigon was the capture of South Vietnam's capital city by North Vietnam's People's Army of Vietnam and the National Liberation Front, signaling the end of the War and necessitating "Operation Frequent Wind," the helicopter evacuation of American personnel and many South Vietnamese loyalists seeking exile—the largest such evacuation in history.) The rest of the tale spans the three years following the War, moving between Saigon, Bangkok, and America. At the beginning of the musical, Kim, a Vietnamese country girl, comes to Saigon to support her family as a "bar girl;" and Chris, a Marine guard at the U.S. Embassy, falls in love with her at first sight and takes her as his "companion," saving her from a life of prostitution in Saigon. Kim also falls in love with Chris; but days later, after a token wedding and intimate co-habitation, their world collapses as Saigon falls. Chris is evacuated during Operation Frequent Wind by way of one of the most famous stage spectacles in musical theatre history, that is, a life-size helicopter landing on stage. Kim is left behind, swept into the frenzied, panicked mob of South Vietnamese citizens held at the gates. Once back in the States, Chris marries but is haunted by nightmares of Vietnam and Kim. He finds that Kim is still alive and working as a bar dancer in Bangkok. Unknown to him, she was pregnant when he left and led a desperate existence in Vietnam (as it was unified and "reeducated" under Communist rule). She was ultimately forced to flee the country after killing a man to protect her racially mixed son (Chris' child). Seeking a sense of closure, Chris travels to Thailand with his wife, Ellen, to find Kim. Upon his arrival, however, Kim suffers the heartbreaking realization that Chris, with wife in tow, has not come to rekindle their relationship. Nonetheless, Kim begs Ellen to take her boy to America, ensuring a better life for him. When it becomes clear that the couple will not separate the son from his mother, Kim performs a final, desperate, and selfless act, committing suicide to force their hand. Inserted into this story, as well as providing commentary and furthering its thematic thrust, is the character of the Engineer, a Brechtian figure who embodies the survivalist, capitalist paradigms of wartime corruption, exploitation, duplicity, and moral relativism. As a seedy pimp and profiteer, as well as a canny dealmaker, the Engineer is the ultimate survivor. He is driven by naked greed, yet his corruption is also fueled by the fantasy of attaining the American Dream.

As described above, Boublil and Schönberg's libretto for *Miss Saigon* is a heady mix of modern history lesson, star-crossed romance, irresolvable cultural conflict, and acerbic sociopolitical commentary. The musical's tragic end is also informed and driven by the age-old theme of maternal love and sacrifice. The sung-through score (Schönberg's compositions with French lyrics by Boublil, translated and Americanized by Richard Maltby, Jr.) reflects the story's high dramatic stakes, sardonic comment, and sprawling content, while providing a tapestry of sound. *Miss Saigon* has a more contemporary pop sound than *Les Miz* (veering toward "jazzy" at times). Schönberg's compositions include a snappy opener with a pulsing groove beat ("The Heat Is On in Saigon"), a bluesy power ballad ("The Movie in My Mind"), a smooth '70s pop duet ("The Last Night of the World"), and a pure showbiz production number ("The American Dream," which blatantly references strutting musical theatre show tunes by the likes of Kander and Ebb, complete with a heavy dose of irony). Still, Boublil and Schönberg's score is rooted in sincere, high-stakes emotionalism, featuring expressive and expansive ballads such as "Why God, Why?," "I Still Believe," "I'd Give My Life for You," and "Bui-Doi" (translated as "Children of Dust," the song sympathetically addresses the plight of marginalized Vietnamese children who were sired and abandoned by American soldiers). There are Southeast-Asian musical evocations by Schönberg in the epic score, ranging from the haunting "Wedding Ceremony" and tender "Sun and Moon" to the militaristic "The Morning of the Dragon." Upon its debut, *Miss Saigon* fans were captivated by the show's poignant and lush score. Further, the Broadway production wowed audiences viscerally, due in great part to the dynamic and cinematically fluid staging by director Nicholas Hytner (like Trevor Nunn, Hytner originally hailed from the classical, nonmusical theatre arena, i.e., London's National Theatre). In this same category (the mega visual/visceral element), *Miss Saigon* became infamous due to what many industry insiders called a gimmicky and ostentatious use of a real-life helicopter by Napier for the show's evacuation scene. What was not as commonly discussed was Napier's otherwise brilliant set that suggested the squalor of Saigon and other pedestrian milieus, juxtaposed against metaphoric pageantry ("The Morning of the Dragon") and surreal spectacle ("American Dream," replete with a life-size Cadillac rolling onstage amid gaudy Star-Spangled showgirls).

In many ways, the oversized story, themes, score, staging, and scenic design of *Miss Saigon* were eerily reflected and heightened by the real-life drama that accompanied the musical's move from its West End origins to Broadway. Given the production's positive reception when it debuted at London's Drury Lane in September 1989, as well as the credentials of its creators, its transfer to Broadway should have been smooth sailing. However, several obstacles almost kept *Miss Saigon* from ever reaching the Great White Way. First, the production's immense spectacle (read: helicopter) required a venue capable of accommodating the technical demands; and no such New York theater was available. As the show's producer, Mackintosh was able to orchestrate a transfer of his still-playing *Les Miz* from the sizable Broadway Theatre to the smaller Imperial Theatre to free up the Broadway for *Miss Saigon*. Then a second major roadblock cropped up. In 1990, Actors' Equity tried to correct years of racial inequity in the casting (or, more accurately, the non-casting) of minorities on Broadway and instated a ruling that minority actors must be given acting opportunities denied them in the past. It was ruled that the Asian characters in *Miss Saigon* must be played by Asian performers; and Caucasian actor Jonathan Pryce, who had brilliantly originated the Eurasian role of the Engineer in London, would not be allowed to repeat his portrayal on Broadway. Mackintosh, offended by the artistic intrusion and supportive of Pryce, threatened to simply cancel the Broadway production, forcing a return of $25 million in advance ticket sales (the advance would ultimately grow to $37 million). Equity members, however, did not want to lose the great employment opportunity presented by *Miss Saigon*; they petitioned the union to change its decision, which it ultimately did, admitting that it had "inappropriately" applied an "honest and moral principle." Later, Equity also challenged the Broadway engagement of Filipino actress Lea Salonga (who originated the role of Kim), citing contractual regulations that require producers to prove that foreign actors in lead roles on Broadway are either certifiable "stars" or providers of "unique services" that cannot be met by an American actor. Mackintosh was forced to prove that he had searched for another U.S. performer, and that none could match Salonga. Ultimately, he won the case in arbitration. When *Miss Saigon* finally landed (no pun intended) on Broadway on April 11, 1991, both Pryce and Salonga headlined the show, winning Tony Awards for their portrayals. Theirs were the few Tonys awarded *Miss Saigon*, however, for the musical was mostly denied wins, although it was nominated in every category. There was some conjecture within the Broadway community that this may have been due to a backlash against the "British invasion" of the mega-musical. Along these same lines, many theatre critics, scholars, and acolytes expressed impassioned negative or positive views as to the merits and influence of the mega show. Most audience members, however, were thrilled with *Miss Saigon*'s larger-than-life theatrical experience, and the production ran for 4,092 performances. In many respects, *Miss Saigon* represents the apex of the mega-musical evolution, as well as the beginning of the end of the imported form's reign. *Miss Saigon*'s status is affirmed by the fact that, once it opened, Mackintosh had four mega productions dominating the boards in New York (*Les Miz*, *Cats*, and *Phantom of the Opera* being the other three). The show also demanded a new top ticket price of $100. The box office success and resilience of concurrent mega shows resulted in jobs for 40 percent of working actors in the United States and England—all in musicals produced by Mackintosh and written by either Lloyd Webber or Boublil/Schönberg.

To date, Boublil and Schönberg have not been able to recapture the magic and success of *Les Miz* and *Miss Saigon* on Broadway. This does not mean that they haven't tried. They spent years developing and grooming their significant follow-up to *Miss Saigon*, another epic, tragic, romantic, and historic sung-through tale: *Martin Guerre*. After its 1997 West End debut, which merited an Olivier Award for Best Musical, the show received numerous try-outs in American regional theatres. Unfortunately, the reputation of Boublil and Schönberg could not overcome the weaknesses of the musical (or, possibly, their past triumphs set a bar too high for the flawed production); and *Martin Guerre* never made it to Broadway. Their only post-*Miss Saigon* Broadway production is *The Pirate Queen* (2007), a sung-through musical about a sixteenth-century Irish pirate chieftain and adventuress, Grace O'Malley. After a lengthy development and tryout period in 2006, in Chicago, during which *Miss Saigon* co-lyricist Richard Maltby, Jr. was called on to work with Boublil and Schönberg on the book and the show's lyrics (writing with Boublil and John Dempsy), the Broadway show opened at the Hilton Theatre on April 5, 2007, under the direction of Frank Galati. Following dismal reviews and poor ticket sales, *The Pirate Queen* closed in June after only eighty-five performances, resulting in a loss of almost $18 million. *The Pirate Queen* has yet to be performed in London.

Critics harped that *The Pirate Queen* felt like a "throwback" to the 1980s and early '90s, a criticism that leads one to consider whether, in many ways, a sung-through musical today cannot help but suggest an artifact of another era. The form is not as prevalent as it was at the height of the "British invasion;" for even those who followed in the footsteps of Lloyd Webber and Boublil/Schönberg have veered away from the strictly sung-through construct. For example, the prolific composer Frank Wildhorn began his career with epic sung-through works such as 1990's *Jekyll and Hyde*; but his more contemporary pieces, although still heavily composed, contain book scenes with dialogue (e.g., 2009's *Bonnie and Clyde* and *Wonderland*). Further, the sung-through form has been removed from its mega framework, having been reinterpreted as a suitable construct for an intimate, immediate, and/or "alternative" work, for example, Jonathan Larson's *Rent* (1996) and Tony Kushner and Jeanine Tesori's *Caroline, or Change* (2004). In fact, the term "mega" has become almost archaic and redundant in today's musical theatre vernacular, for such a categorized musical is no longer the breathlessly awaited exception to the rule but, instead, the expected norm on Broadway. For instance, when *The Lion King* (1994) pushed the visceral/visual component to new heights, the production was not assigned the "mega-musical" moniker but was simply addressed as an example of grand artistry and visionary spectacle. And in its wake, many contemporary mainstream musicals almost demand mega treatment in terms of stage production and scenic splendor (e.g., *Wicked, Billy Elliot, Mary Poppins*), with the bar being set ever higher for state-of-the-art stage effects (e.g., *Spider-Man*). Further, the global exportation and exploitation of a major musical hit has become a matter of course. In short, what artists such as Lloyd Webber, Boublil, Schönberg, and Mackintosh set into motion has become the Broadway model, a development that contains both drawbacks and benefits for the musical theatre genre. Current-day extravaganzas often squeeze out smaller, more experimental shows on Broadway, given the district's limited venue availability and audience draw. But on the other hand, many of the most sizable and impressive hits have helped the genre reach a wider and more diverse audience. And in a crucial twist, the smaller shows that persist on Broadway, despite the muscle and size of their intimidating neighbors, are often works that have succeeded on the basis of their innovation and bravado, pushing the genre in new and exciting directions (e.g., *Avenue Q* and *Once*). Given the active debate that still rages over these considerations, complications, and implications, one fact is clear: the mega-musical cannot be denied as one of the most significant musical evolutions of the twentieth century.

STEPHEN SONDHEIM

Stephen Sondheim has legions of fervent fans who relish his alliterative lyrics, ambivalent sentiments, confounding melodies, experimental aesthetics, and overall challenges to traditional musical theatre. He has had his share of detractors as well, doubters who occasionally deem his clever turn of phrase to be overly worked, his style of composition to be too technical and esoteric, and his aesthetic/content to be elitist and inaccessible (an anathema to musical theatre populism). Such are the duality and paradox of Sondheim, a modern musical theatre lyricist/composer who is almost uniformly lauded by critics and scholars, while the general audience has proved divided regarding his output, either extolling him as a hot visionary or rejecting him as a cold, inaccessible technician. It is not every day that a musical theatre artist inspires such divide and interrogation; but not every composer/lyricist is the revolutionary and enigmatic Sondheim. Today, he is revered as musical theatre establishment (Broadway's Henry Miller's Theatre was renamed the Stephen Sondheim Theatre in 2010), while the "Sondheim style" has become its own recognized and much-copied mode of song and show on Broadway, as well as an entrenched and iconic genre classification in the American musical canon.

The world of Sondheim is a complex, contradictory, and challenging place, informed by the multifaceted art and aesthetic of the composer/lyricist. On one hand, Sondheim can be seen as a throwback to the extroverted, self-expressive artist of Broadway's early, pre-Golden-Age era. Yet he also reveres the integrationist ideal of the Golden Age, criticizing what he deems to be the inferior and one-dimensional nature/construct of the sung-through musical, i.e., the form that took Broadway by storm during the 1980s, overshadowing his own works at the box office. Then again, he is also the ultimate modernist, providing scores that have advanced musical theatre's content/sound revolution, while tackling material that invoked the postmodern future and potential of the American musical. A quick survey of his experimental and challenging subject matter, source material, and concepts includes the following: Georges Seurat, Plautus, *Ziegfeld Follies*, foreign films, Kabuki, cannibalism, imperialism, urban alienation, presidential assassins, defective relationships, fluid time continuums, obsessive passions, the American Dream, and the all-American con. The dramatic themes of the Sondheim musicals are equally dense and multilayered, for they deal in gray areas, addressing the complex, conflicted aspects of human nature. They paint probing and challenging pictures of the world, offering no easy answers. Many of these musicals wallow in the dark, dank underbelly of humanity. They also often offer a glimmer of hope at the end of their unvarnished, analytic journeys. A Sondheim world includes (sometimes fatally) flawed characters, as well as unstable and troubled relationships (resulting

Stephen Sondheim (center) with Arthur Laurents at the Broadway opening of the 2008 revival of *Gypsy* © Walter McBride/Retna Ltd./Corbis

in the deconstruction of romantic ideals); but a great deal of morbid, twisted, and sardonic humor can also be found in such paradigms.

As a lyricist, Sondheim may be seen as more evocative of Hart than Hammerstein, in that his lyrics can be self-expressively ingenious and showy (he has admitted to working with a thesaurus at his side). But in the manner of his life-long mentor, Hammerstein, he also converts his clever rhymes, alliterations, and turns of phrase into crucial components of the musical play, choosing to dramatically serve his characters by way of conversation, testament, referential comment, argument, or denial, with sentiments and language most often rooted in character and situation. Sondheim confronts his audiences with lyrics that can be appreciated as distilled and pungently poetic thoughts voiced aloud, while asking that they be interpreted as multileveled commentary and theatre. Such skill with the written word not only fits but accentuates his work as composer; most of his scores consist of music that is challenging, informing his lyrics as it counterpoints and underscores them. His range as a composer is unmatched by most contemporaries, as he employs experimental and dissonant composition in conjunction with traditional Tin Pan Alley, operetta, "show tune," and other recognizable genre constructs/forms. He also aims to confound the expectations of his listener, often choosing to compose away from the piano to avoid the impulse to write for the ear, as well as deny himself easy melodies and redundancies (in fact, his lack of hummable pop hits places him as the anti-Berlin/Lloyd Webber). Ironically, herein also lies the "Sondheim paradox;" despite his efforts, his alienating, unorthodox melodic phrases, including quirky progressions and unexpected pitches, identify his compositions as "oh, so Sondheim."

One last significant aspect of Sondheim's career is his contribution to the development and growing importance of the concept musical (a musical form in which the style and theme take precedence over a linear story) and the chamber musical (an intimate and modestly scaled work featuring a shared libretto by an individualized ensemble). With a few exceptions, Sondheim's composer/lyricist career has not included grand-scale musicals comprising large choruses and big dance numbers; in fact, his most iconic shows include little dance, if any. Even though some of his early triumphs and experiments with Hal Prince were

extravagantly staged, this aspect began to wane as he moved into the second phase of his career with librettist/director James Lapine. Just as he tried to cut to the cryptic core of the human condition in his scores, he also began to look for less "fuss" in his musicals. It may be Sondheim's surgical scalpel, that is, his paring away of extraneous "stuff" to expose raw and real tissue, that stands as his most enduring contribution to the musical theatre genre, one that has been modeled by a new generation of Sondheimesque writers and composers.

Stephen Joshua Sondheim was born to Jewish parents, Herbert and Etta Janet, in New York City on March 22, 1930. Herbert Sondheim was a successful dress manufacturer, and Stephen's early childhood was spent on the Upper West Side. By his own accounts, his only-child adolescence was one of privilege, but loneliness, which lacked parental closeness and connection. It took a dark turn when Stephen was 10. Herbert abandoned Etta for another woman, and the couple divorced. From that point, Stephen was raised by his mother on a farm near Doylestown, Pennsylvania, in what he has described as a dysfunctional and contentious mother-son household. He learned to lose himself in the arts while a student at George School, a private Quaker preparatory school. His time at the school resulted in the most significant mentoring relationship of his young life and provided him with a surrogate father during his most difficult developmental years. Through his association with classmate James Hammerstein, young Stephen became friends with James' father, Oscar Hammerstein II, who took an interest in the serious boy who, coincidentally, had begun a love affair with musical theatre when he saw *Very Warm for May* (1939) on Broadway as a 9-year-old. The show was composed by Jerome Kern, but its libretto and lyrics happened to be written by Hammerstein. Sondheim cites the production as the formative event that inspired his youthful ambition to write for musical theatre. Having captured Hammerstein's attention, the 10-year-old Sondheim aspired to follow in the lyricist/librettist's footsteps; as a teen, he wrote his first musical, *By George!*, before graduating from George School in 1946. *By George!* was not the only work Sondheim created under the tutelage of Hammerstein, who designed a kind of writing course for Sondheim. Hammerstein assigned Sondheim adaptations and original musical theatre projects, then seriously critiqued the teenager's output, bluntly telling Sondheim how poor the works were, but then mentoring him in ways to improve them. Sondheim has often recounted these informal lessons as the most intense and beneficial of his career, noting that he could gain more in an afternoon with Hammerstein than an entire lifetime of on-the-job experience. Sondheim attributes much of his lyricist craft to Hammerstein, that is, his facile use of rhyme, his emphasis on character expression, and his construction of songs as "mini plays," dramatic numbers that contain potent beginnings, middle complications, and end resolutions. When he was 17, Sondheim saw firsthand the travails and disappointments of Broadway, working as a backstage gopher (errand boy) for Hammerstein and Rodgers on their problem-ridden and less-than-successful *Allegro*.

After prep school, Sondheim attended Williams College in Williamstown, Massachusetts, where he studied mathematics but soon majored in music. He was especially attracted to music/composition theory, with its formulaic elegance, logic, and "mathematic" rules (which, once conquered, were made to be broken). It was here that Sondheim began to acquire, under the early influence of his composition professor, Robert Barrow, a lifelong philosophy that art is not purely the result of inspiration, innate talent, and/or or a muse's blessing but is, instead, a problem to be solved through meticulously studied, developed, and applied craft. After graduating *magna cum laude* from Williams in 1950, Sondheim sought to further explore composition, theory, and harmony, and to pursue his childhood passion of writing for the theatre. But first he wanted to venture beyond the formal classroom. He won the Hutchinson Prize, which allowed him to independently study with avant-garde composer Milton Babbitt, who was not only a leader in modern and atonal composition but had dabbled in musical theatre and appreciated the genre. With Babbitt, Sondheim acquired what he deemed "serious artillery," learning to push the boundaries of tonality, while further exploiting the rules and techniques of theory and composition (leitmotifs, chromatics, motif variations, contrapuntal constructs, playful time signatures). As a result, most Sondheim works although remaining consistently tonal, include a high degree of dissonance, experimentation, and frequent confounding of melodic conventions. During his two-year stint with Babbitt, Sondheim also honed his dramatic writing skills by penning scripts for *Topper* (a CBS television series that ran from 1953–55). In 1954, all of Sondheim's hard work paid off. He

was hired by successful producer Lemuel Ayers to write the score for a musical slated for the 1954–55 Broadway season, titled *Saturday Night*, with a book by brothers Julius J. Epstein and Philip G. Epstein, based on their unproduced play, *Front Porch in Flatbush*. The Epsteins' libretto, set in 1928, dealt with a pack of male friends in Brooklyn, and one member's ill-fated attempt to break out of the neighborhood and upgrade his mediocre life. Unfortunately, Ayers died before the work could be mounted and the show, with its complete Sondheim score, was shelved (although songs have appeared in Sondheim revues and other formats). Sondheim was disheartened by the setback, but excerpts from early drafts of his score caught the ear of playwright Arthur Laurents, who dismissed Sondheim's music but thought his lyrics were wonderful. He suggested Sondheim as a lyricist for the new project he was developing with composer Leonard Bernstein and director/choreographer Jerome Robbins: *West Side Story* (1957). Bernstein had originally planned to write the lyrics himself but was finding the task burdensome and others, such as Betty Comden and Adolph Green, had proved unavailable or unwilling to join the project. Of course, Sondheim was not what one might call a willing participant, seeing himself more as a composer than a lyricist. With urging from Hammerstein, however, Sondheim reconsidered, and the rest, as they say, was history. In this first major Broadway foray, Sondheim not only gleaned invaluable theatre tips and techniques from his senior collaborators, but also managed to imprint his artistic signature on the production. He worked with Laurents to create a street vernacular for the warring gang members, combining slang (much of which was his own invention) with succinct character expression and clever rhymes (some of which he claims, today, were too clever in the mouths of the musical's youths). He also learned from Robbins how every element of the production must contribute to the dramatic action. For instance, Robbins was famously upset with Sondheim when the lyricist declared that "Maria" was written to be sung as a stationary, reflective aria. A disgusted Robbins challenged Sondheim to try and effectively *stage* such a number. A chastened Sondheim became newly convinced that musical theatre songs should carry the show forward in some way and facilitate an expressive, emotional swelling in the process.

With the critical boost from *West Side Story*, Sondheim started his professional career at the top, not

Off-Off-Broadway or in regional theatre. Furthermore, several of the artists who collaborated with him on the production—Robbins, Laurents, and producer Harold Prince—were to play significant roles in his career for many years. Sondheim's next significant foray on Broadway, *Gypsy* (1959), was a reunion with both Robbins (director/choreographer) and Laurents (librettist). In a case of déjà vu, Sondheim had to once again be convinced by Hammerstein to take the lyricist job, a bitter pill to swallow as he had initially been signed as the show's composer/lyricist but was demoted once leading lady, Ethel Merman, balked at working with a "novice" composer. Writing with established composer Jule Styne, Sondheim proved himself to be a proficient and poetic lyricist for the iconic production, establishing a vernacular to fit and enhance the show's brassy and metatheatrical score, milieu, and character. He gave Mama Rose an "I Am" song ("Some People") that innovatively uses references to others to obliquely illustrate her pugnacious and determined nature. He also employed a great deal of metaphor and metatheatre to suggest the emotional/psychological make-up and development of the characters (e.g., "Let Me Entertain You," "Little Lamb," and "You Gotta Have a Gimmick"), with some of his language entering the American slang lexicon ("Everything's Coming Up Roses"). When *Gypsy* triumphantly debuted, Sondheim and the rest of the production team had redefined what the musical biography could be; and in the process, they created an American classic.

It took three more years, but a full Sondheim score (music and lyrics) finally premiered on Broadway. The production was *A Funny Thing Happened on the Way to the Forum* (1962), and it still stands as the biggest box office hit of Sondheim's career, running for 964 performances. Contrary to the material that was soon to be associated with the lyricist/composer, Sondheim's first Broadway score contained no alienating subject matter, challenging construct, or confounding musicality. Instead, the production was, in many ways, a return to the old-fashioned, extroverted musical comedy of yesteryear. The project began as an idea by writer (and Sondheim friend) Burt Shevelove, who wanted to create a farcical musical out of the characters and plots found in the twenty-one extant plays by classical Roman comic playwright Titus Maccius Plautus (254–184 BCE). Given his love of classical literature and the unusual source material,

Sondheim needed little persuading to supply the score for the libretto by Shevelove and his co-writer Larry Gelbart. In the end, the finished product borrowed only a few characters and situations from Plautus' plays, but the spirit of the classic Roman comedies abounds in *Forum*. Specifically, the show is set in ancient Rome and is ripe with characteristically contrived plot devices, slapstick, bawdy humor, puns, social satire, and stock characters such as the clever slave, the boastful warrior, the naive hero, the virginal ingénue, the dotty old man, the sexy courtesan, the cheating husband, and his shrewish wife. The libretto centers on the zany adventures of a crafty slave, Pseudolus, who has been promised his freedom by his young master, Hero, if he can arrange a union between his master and the beautiful, but dim-witted, Philia. (The role of Pseudolus was originated by the larger-than-life Zero Mostel, after comic stars Phil Silvers and Milton Berle turned it down.)

Sondheim has said that writing for the quick-paced and hyperactive *Forum* was a challenge, given that his songs served more as divertissements and moments of repose than as action carriers. Nonetheless, he managed to provide songs that fit the mood, delivered additional comedy, and allowed each character a performative and expressive moment, all resulting in a diverse and tuneful score that evinces an expansive blend of old-fashioned showbiz and classical sound, further enhanced by clever, sardonic lyrics. Sondheim's work includes expressive, narrative songs, e.g., a detailed getaway directive ("Free"), a bouncy contrapuntal dialogue ("Pretty Little Picture"), a vaudevillian soft-shoe ("Everybody Ought to Have a Maid"), a blowhard musical march ("Bring Me My Bride"), an operetta-styled ballad ("Love I Hear"), and a self-soothing waltz for the anxiety-ridden slave ("I'm Calm"). Comedy abounds in most of the numbers, especially the lyrical and ironic "Lovely," in which both Philia and Hero extol her winning looks while excusing her empty head. Given the score's adroitness, it is surprising that the musical seriously floundered during its out-of-town tryout. And when it became clear to director George Abbott and producer Hal Prince that audiences were less than enthusiastic about the new musical, they turned to past collaborator and powerhouse director/choreographer Jerome Robbins for advice and show-doctoring. (Sondheim had originally suggested Robbins as director/choreographer, but Robbins turned down the project.) The problem could have been *Forum's* unusually modest format (only one set and sixteen actors, with no singing or dancing chorus), but Robbins immediately noted that Sondheim and company had missed the boat with regard to the all-important "grabber;" for the musical opened with a lyrical ballad by the romantic lead ("Love Is in the Air"), which did nothing to set up the raucous, infectious comedy that was at the heart of *Forum*. Robbins suggested a new opening number that would hook the audience and serve as a preamble to the true nature of the show. Sondheim understood and wrote the energized and vaudevillian "Comedy Tonight," setting the tone for the satirical and hyperactive romp, along with an underlying reference to man's undying spirit of adventure and quest for freedom. The new number, with Robbins' staging, did the trick, along with Robbins' doctoring of other numbers, originally choreographed by Jack Cole. At 32 years old, Sondheim, as both composer and lyricist, had a major Broadway hit. But while the show garnered several Tony Awards, including a win for Best Musical, Sondheim's score did not even receive a nomination, an anomaly in his career.

Sondheim's next two Broadway endeavors were disappointments, both critically and in terms of audience appeal. Reuniting with Laurents as librettist, Sondheim wrote the score for *Anyone Can Whistle* (1964). Upon its Broadway debut, the show was savaged by critics, who felt its theme of madness as the hopeful answer and alternative to the harsh realities of a sane world was artistically smug, simplistic, and puerile. Audiences agreed, and the production closed after nine performances. *Anyone Can Whistle* contained several significant elements with regard to Sondheim's career, however. It contained an extended dance segment, titled "The Cookie Chase," for which Sondheim composed original music. To date, "The Cookie Chase" stands as the only lengthy instrumental composition that Sondheim has written for the theatre. Further, *Whistle* generated an original cast album after its closing (an almost unheard-of occurrence at the time for a Broadway failure), and many of its songs have since entered the Sondheim canon. This occurrence illustrates the standalone nature and strength of Sondheim's work; even though he sought to follow Hammerstein's integrationist example, his singular approach to lyrics and musical composition has resulted in a song catalogue that is rarely dependent on the shows from which the numbers originate (in fact, a song

from a Sondheim flop is often revered as an example of how his numbers can rise above their circumstances and find a life of their own). Lastly, Sondheim began to employ one of his signature songwriting techniques in *Whistle*, that is, implying a character's psychology, motivations, and emotional state through the nature and style of his or her song's musical composition, often in opposition to what the song lyrics are saying. For instance, in the musical, a corrupt female mayor sings "Me and My Town," lamenting her town's decline, while the number's snappy, syncopated tune reveals her insincerity and hypocrisy. Sondheim has often asserted that in real life, humans rarely relate to one another (or to themselves) without some degree of deception or delusion; thus, audience members must also take into account subtextual musical clues to understand Sondheim characters.

After the disappointment of *Whistle*, Sondheim wrote the lyrics for *Do I Hear a Waltz?* in 1965, collaborating with Hammerstein's most famous partner, Richard Rodgers. *Waltz* was a box office disappointment, running for only 220 performances, and the show was also Sondheim's fourth and last work with Laurents as librettist. (Sondheim has proved to be loyal and steady with his librettists, as well as directors, orchestrators, and music directors, working with only a few in his career and sticking with them for years before moving on to someone new.)

In 1970, Sondheim returned to writing both music and lyrics, as well as working with Harold Prince, who not only directed and produced *Company*, but also hired the production team. In this first-of-many Sondheim/Prince collaborations, the two artists, along with librettist George Furth, strove to exploit a new thematically driven musical form, soon to be labeled the "concept musical." They also kept the show's size to a minimum, resulting in a cast of fourteen characters, with no dancing/singing chorus and all characters being either leads or featured roles. In other words, the production was also a "chamber musical," an intimate construct that would become a frequent format for a Sondheim work. Beginning as a collection of eleven one-act plays by George Furth, Prince envisioned a musical that surveyed modern relationships amid a fractured and frictional urban environment. Furth revised three of his plays and added two more to create a montage of relationship dramas linked by the production's theme, as well as the characters' common friendship with confirmed bachelor Bobby (or as they refer to him in Sondheim's leitmotif, "Bobby, Bobby, Bobby"). The story is nonlinear, as Bobby, on his 35th birthday, reflects in a series of flashbacks on his friends' conflicted marriages (or prospective marriages), as well as his own philandering lifestyle. The original Broadway production was staged on designer Boris Aronson's modernist set, a two-level skeletal construct made of plastic and chrome (complete with two moving elevators) that suggested the cold compartmentalization of high-rise living. Locales were designated by scenic projections, and the entire set framed the actors as specimens under a microscope, exposed in their desperate and ambivalent attempts at intimate connection in a modern-day metropolitan setting.

Furth's libretto is, purposefully, a disjointed affair, while Sondheim's score is the glue that dramatically holds *Company* together, providing a multifaceted musical tapestry of emotion and expression for the divergent characters. Much of the score includes the ironic pairing of ambivalent, strident, or cynical sentiments with lush, sophisticated, and/or referential musical compositions. Such compositions range from catchy riffs and rhythms, often redolent of vaudeville and Tin Pan Alley (e.g., "The Little Things You Do Together," "You Could Drive a Person Crazy," "Side by Side by Side/What Would We Do Without You?"), to lyrical or bombastic ballads ("Sorry-Grateful" and "The Ladies Who Lunch," respectively), as well as modernist musical experiments ("Another Hundred People"). Comedy pervades the score, often arising from the disparity between song style and sentiments. Examples include "Barcelona," a gentle waltz in which Bobby disingenuously talks a one-night-stand into staying a bit longer in his bed, as well as "Getting Married Today," a chirpy patter song that dramatizes a suicidal panic attack by a prospective bride before her "joyous" nuptials. Given its sardonic tone, it is significant that *Company* manages to end on a positive note with Sondheim's final song for Bobby, "Being Alive." Through this active ballad, comprised of a slow musical build and searching, soaring intervals, Bobby discovers that human connection and commitment are necessary for fulfillment. The cathartic song also counters accusations that Sondheim's constant mode of expression is existential angst and darkness. Upon its debut, *Company* was a critical juggernaut, helping to put the concept musical on the map, and stands today as one of Sondheim's more popular works. The original run lasted for 706 performances and garnered six Tony Awards, with Sondheim winning Best Original Score and Best Lyrics (categories were separate at the time). A film was made of the original cast album's recording session; and there have been two Broadway revivals of the production since 1970, including an award-winning revisionist version in 2006, directed by John Doyle.

In less than one year, the *Company* collaborators of Sondheim, Prince, Aronson, and Michael Bennett (*Company*'s choreographer) premiered a new musical on Broadway, *Follies* (1971), which had been in the planning stage before *Company* but was preempted by the earlier show's Broadway debut. With librettist James Goldman (who supplied the original story idea), the team created another concept musical, but definitely not a chamber musical, as *Follies*' size and scope was epic, including 140 scenic/costume designs, a large orchestra, and a cast of fifty. The size of the production reflected the musical's grand themes and multilayered plot, which revolves around a reunion of old-time revue stars and chorines (played by real-life showbiz veterans) as they bid farewell to their soon-to-be demolished Broadway theater, once home to the *Weismann Follies* (a fictional version of the *Ziegfeld Follies*). Throughout the evening, the characters not only attempt to relive old stage glories but also struggle to exorcise demons and reconcile unfilled dreams. Anchoring the anxiety and angst is the show's central storyline, which concerns two unhappy couples of differing socioeconomic statuses (the affluent Phyllis and Ben and the middle-class Sally and Buddy). The four characters had shared early careers and youthful, romantic ideals (illustrated through flashbacks, with other actors playing the young counterparts). Reunited, they ponder their empty lives and the roads not taken (it is notable that Sally and Ben had been a couple in their youth).

One of the production's major challenges was the complexity of presenting two radically different worlds (the past and present) on stage. To facilitate this concept, scenic designer Aronson created, on stage, an elaborate, multilevel replication of a grand old theater in a modern state of decay. His set was enhanced and transformed by costume, lighting, and makeup designs that marked the repeated time travel by juxtaposing full-color palettes (signifying present day) with black and white (the past). Similarly, Sondheim's score reflected the fluidity, tension, and interactivity of the two worlds. While many of *Follies'* numbers boast the musical lyricism, glamour, and pizzazz of Broadway's gilded past ("Beautiful Girls" and "Loveland"), many are also complicated and contemporized by their acerbic and conflicted lyrics, reflecting the colder, harsher modern age. In the original production, no musical number better synthesized this thrilling and nightmarish collision of the past and present than "Who's That Woman?" (also known as "The Mirror Song"). Choreographed by Bennett (who co-directed the production with Prince), it consisted of seven retired chorus girls performing their recollection of an old Weismann routine, while their youthful alter egos elegantly danced the routine on an upstage platform, with both groups ultimately merging at the number's climax. Sondheim loved Bennett's choreographic interpretation, feeling that it perfectly demonstrated the metaphoric thrust and emotional ambivalence of the song. Indeed, these two qualities are Sondheim signposts and imbue his score for *Follies*. Exploiting showbiz nostalgia and pastiche, with the theatre serving as a metaphor for life, Sondheim's score is filled with specialty numbers for the elder chorines, including strident anthems of identity, survivorship, and the stage ("Broadway Baby" and "I'm Still Here"). On a more introspective note, emotional ambivalence is evidenced through lyrical numbers by the leads. For instance, Ben self-questioningly ponders "The Road You Didn't Take," and Sally waxes poetic as she practices self-deception through "In Buddy's Eyes," until finally admitting that she had never stopped loving Ben in "Losing My Mind" (with some musicologists linking this torchy, tortured ballad to Gershwin's "The Man I Love"). In contrast, Phyllis bares her scarred soul in a vengeful and scathing denunciation of her marriage in "Could I Leave You?" [see fig. 6.4]. With its cutting lyrics and pulsing waltz time, the number is a dark parody of traditional romantic ballads. At *Follies'* opening on April 4, 1971, the critics respected the ambition of the production and praised Sondheim's score, but felt that the overall show did not successfully meld its dark themes to the many subplots and tricky time-travelling conventions. Audiences were also left cold and confused by the material. *Follies* closed after 522 performances and lost money, even though it won seven Tony Awards (with Sondheim winning one for his score). Since its initial run, *Follies* has proved to be a favorite for "concert" versions on Broadway,

while its authors continue to tinker with the work to smooth out the libretto/coherence problems. A recent revival opened in the fall of 2011, but ran for just over 120 performances despite the star power of Broadway luminaries such as Bernadette Peters, illustrating that the innovative musical, in spite of its now canonic score, still proves to be a challenge at the box office.

Although many a Broadway artist may have been daunted by repeated mixed reactions to experimental ventures, Sondheim (along with Prince) paid little attention to box office hesitation and continued to push the musical theatre envelope. Specifically, Sondheim and Prince's follow-up to *Follies* was another choice musical morsel for the highly discriminating theatre palate. Joining with librettist Hugh Wheeler, the team tackled foreign film auteur Ingmar Bergman's *Smiles of a Summer Night* (1956). Hewing close to the original film, Wheeler's libretto details an emotional and sexual game of roulette played out in turn-of-the-century Sweden. The plot revolves around a prosperous middle-aged lawyer, his virginal bride, and his son (who pines after his father's young wife), along with the lawyer's former mistress (a worldly actress), her current lover (a count), and the count's suicidal wife. When all parties converge at a country house for a weekend, old loves are rekindled, illicit affairs are pursued, rivalries grow, and new loves are discovered. The musical, titled *A Little Night Music* (1973), is thematically similar to Sondheim and Prince's earlier projects in that it takes a sophisticated look at characters in intimate relationships tinged by regrets, dashed dreams, and restless infidelities. As opposed to *Company* and *Follies*, however, critics deemed *Night Music's* characters to be warmer and more genuine than the earlier urban, contemporary types, with the musical providing a more hopeful view of living and loving, while addressing issues of age and class disparity.

To suggest the musical's setting and time period (with a specific nod to classical operetta), Sondheim innovatively composed the entire *Night Music* score in waltz time or variations thereof. He then countered the romance of the 3/4 time signature with acidic and witty lyrics. Loves and relationships are observed and dissected in numbers consisting of lush, waltzing melodies played against biting sentiments (e.g., "You Must Meet My Wife," "Every Day a Little Death," and "It Would Have Been Wonderful"). Sondheim once again illustrated his mastery of the expressive contrapuntal character number, brilliantly evidenced by the show's intermission teaser in which all the characters receive and respond to their invitations to "A Weekend in the Country." In addition to the waltz time signature (for a musical that, ironically, had little real dancing and no dance numbers), another innovation by Sondheim was his use of a quintet to sing the overture and whose members reappear throughout the evening in the manner of a Greek chorus, narrating and reflecting the sentiments of the characters through numbers such as the lilting "Remember." When the new chamber musical opened on Broadway on February 25, 1973, the critics waxed rhapsodic in their praise of Sondheim, lauding his merger of brilliant rhyme and vernacular with compositions that evoked the work of such romantic heavyweights as Mahler, Ravel, Rachmaninoff, Brahms, Strauss, and Liszt. Audiences also enjoyed the convergence of sophisticated story and song. The production ran for 601 performances, with backers receiving a 125 percent return on their investment. The show also produced a rare pop hit for Sondheim, "Send in the Clowns," which stands as his best-known song. Set to a haunting, minor waltz, the song's lyrics are wistful and bittersweet, using a clown metaphor and theatre references to lament the farcical and futile state of a relationship (while ending on a note of hope for "next year"). Even though *Night Music* proved to be both a commercial and critical success (winning six Tony Awards, including one for Best Musical and one for Sondheim's score), it would not be until 2009 that a Broadway revival would be staged. Starring film star Catherine Zeta-Jones and Broadway legend Angela Lansbury, this revival received positive critical notices and ran for 425 performances.

In the year after *A Little Night Music*'s premiere, Sondheim reunited with *Forum* librettist Burt Shevelove to create a "freely adapted" version of another ancient classic, Aristophanes' *The Frogs*, innovatively performed in a Yale University swimming pool. Sondheim's next Broadway foray was even more adventurous, as he brought Kabuki to the Great White Way. Sondheim and Prince, together for a fourth time, looked to the stylized and ancient form of Japanese theatre to provide a framing device, staging concept, and musical/performance style for their new work, *Pacific Overtures* (1976). With a book by John Weidman (and Hugh Wheeler, who supplied additional material), *Pacific Overtures* centers on the emergence and modernization of Japan, while

critiquing the insidious, destructive and corrupting effects of capitalism and imperialism. The challenging libretto spans 120 years, beginning in 1853 with the arrival of Commodore Matthew Perry on the shores of isolated nineteenth-century Japan (the Floating Kingdom). Given Perry's gift of persuasion and threat of aggression, the Japanese slowly agree to trade with the West. Consequently, the country sells its soul and achieves affluence, modernizing its dress, manner, social order, and belief systems as it evolves into a commercial and industrial powerhouse. The transformation and jarring juxtaposition of East and West is reflected in the show's final number, "Next," performed by Asian performers in Western dress, executing traditional Broadway choreography, against a scenic display of industrialized, urban Japan, replete with noise, pollution, skylines, and billboards. While the show's creators sought to unpack the clashes and conciliations between ancient, traditional cultures and outside modernizing forces, they also tried to humanize the theme by placing it within a more personal and intimate framework. Thus, *Pacific Overture*'s libretto focuses on two men who respond differently to the culture shock (specifically, a custom-bound samurai is converted to Western decadence while a Westernized fisherman resists the new direction, reverting to the traditions of the samurai).

To stage such epic and tricky material, the production team sought to present the story from the Japanese point of view, with a Western theatrical spin. They created a Broadway facsimile of the ancient form of Kabuki, with a cast of over two dozen male performers, most of whom played multiple roles, both male and female, in traditional Kabuki make-up and manner (contrary to popular belief, there were a couple women in the show, but they were used only in the chorus and as scene-change servants). In what was to be his final and most highly lauded design, Boris Aronson gave the production a Japanese flavor with authentic touches. A low border framed the proscenium in the Winter Garden Theatre to approximate the horizontal look of a Kabuki stage, as well as a full-stage stylized "curtain" of kimonos and a runway from stage right to the back of the auditorium for entrances and exits through the house (a version of the traditional Kabuki *hanamichi*). A Kabuki consultant, hired by producer/director Prince, worked with the Asian-American cast on the overall movement and performance style. Sondheim also sought to replicate a Japanese music aesthetic. Exploiting the Asian pentatonic scale (its minor modal tone), the composer mixed this Japanese tonality with Western melodic conventions and harmonies (even though harmonies are not employed in traditional Japanese music). Sondheim used simplicity and elegance in his lyrics, evoking the style of Haiku poetry, while combining the poesy with dramatic and smart sentiments. The resulting score contains numbers that range from careful deliberations ("There Is No Other Way") to narrative descriptions ("Someone in a Tree"), as well as complex dialogic constructions ("Chrysanthemum Tea") and lilting meditations ("Pretty Lady"). In the end, however, the collage of Broadway and Kabuki confused many critics, who were unsure how much of the show was artistic interpretation and how much was authentic, feeling that both styles suffered from the co-mingling. Some critics complained that the historical panorama, scenic spectacle, and heavy themes overwhelmed the human story, while much of the Broadway populace simply didn't know what to make of the show's Kabuki aesthetic. The production ran for only 193 performances. Though it garnered ten Tony nominations, it won only two for its scenic and costume designs. The show still stands as one of the bravest musical theatre experiments to have run on Broadway, and it was revived in 2004 (a scaled-down production that retained the Kabuki concept and all-male cast). The revival, however, remained a difficult box office draw, closing after only 69 performances.

In 1979, Sondheim and Prince teamed again with librettist Hugh Wheeler to create one of the more morbid and sardonically twisted musicals in the American canon: *Sweeney Todd, The Demon Barber of Fleet Street*. Drawing on the Grand Guignol story of a murderous barber in mid-nineteenth-century London and its dramatic renderings (e.g., 1847's *A String of Pearls, or the Fiend of Fleet Street*, by George Dibdin Pitt, and 1973's *Sweeney Todd*, by Christopher Bond), Wheeler's libretto centers on a barber, Sweeney Todd, who has returned to London from an unmerited prison sentence to exact revenge on the judge who ruined him as well as his family by raping his wife and then taking his daughter as a ward and prospective bride against her will. Sweeney is abetted by an infatuated pie shop owner, Mrs. Lovett. As Todd's rage continues unabated, he begins to slit the throats of his customers, taking revenge against a society that was complicit in his ruin. In a grisly development, Lovett helps Sweeney hide the

evidence of his crimes by enterprisingly cooking the victims into meat pies, devoured by her customers. Plot twists abound and the cannibalistic, vengeful world implodes, with all guilty parties meeting gruesome ends. Complementing and facilitating the overwrought and disturbing material, Sondheim's mostly through-composed score is a brilliant mesh of wry, cutting, and poignant lyrics, set to lush compositions that reflect both the classical concert stage and the popular British music hall. Numbers range from narrative, active character numbers to soaring arias and elegantly constructed contrapuntal pieces. Leitmotifs abound and the entire musical is bookended by the operatic chamber number "The Ballad of Sweeney Todd," which thematically foreshadows and then moralistically concludes the sordid tale. With its Industrial Revolution themes of class warfare and capitalist cannibalism, *Sweeney Todd* was as adventurous as *Pacific Overtures*; yet audiences were more accepting of its alienating world. Thus, the 1979 production is now seen as a high point in the Prince/Sondheim oeuvre, running for 557 performances and meriting eight Tony Awards (including Best Musical, plus wins for direction, book, score, and lead performances by Len Cariou and Angela Lansbury as Sweeney and Lovett, respectively); all of which proved that startling and dark subject matter, combined with a brilliant score, visual excellence, and iconic performances, could succeed on Broadway.

Two years after *Sweeney Todd*, Sondheim teamed again with Prince on what would turn out to be their last Broadway production together: *Merrily We Roll Along* (1981). Although the musical was another bold experiment, it was one of Sondheim's more notable Broadway flops. The production ran for only sixteen performances after an unusually long and contentious try-out period of fifty-two previews held in New York City (instead of the customary out-of-town venues), during which the choreographer and lead actor were replaced. Many cite *Merrily*'s failure as the breaking point that prompted the end of Sondheim and Prince's historic relationship. Nonetheless, Prince asserts today that he never stopped trusting or admiring Sondheim, but he does concede that he became overly taxed by the work entailed in producing and directing such demanding and experimental pieces. Given this information, it is interesting to note that *Merrily* had initially been Prince's idea. When his wife suggested that he do a show about "teenagers," he remembered *Merrily We*

Roll Along, a minor 1934 play by George S. Kaufman and Moss Hart. Once Prince recruited Sondheim, the two reunited with librettist Furth. The team kept the play's title and basic storyline, but updated the time period by setting it in the years 1957–76, or, one should say, 1976–57, for the musical follows the conceit of the original play by telling the story in reverse, moving backward from the present until the show ends with the story's beginning.

Merrily We Roll Along tells the tale of a powerful Hollywood producer, using key scenes from his past to chronicle his climb to the top and to trace backward how he abandoned his promising Broadway composing career, longtime friends, early loves, and youthful ideals only to achieve hollow success. Like *Follies*, the show contains the theme of corrupted and dashed youthful ideals and expectations, while playing with fluidity of time. Again critics were confused and disturbed by the libretto's depressing themes, as well as its structure. Conceptual problems haunted the show (e.g., Prince chose to cast performers in their teens/early twenties, then tried to overcome the age incongruities by abstractly dressing everyone in sweatshirts with their names on their chests and placed the action in a distracting and bare-bones suggestion of a high school gym). Despite savage reviews, Sondheim's score was widely praised, with many critics sad that the overall production so disserved the music. Wanting to focus on the intertwining and unraveling relationships and friendships at the core of the piece, Sondheim sought to keep his score similarly interconnected. He exploited the use of a chorus to sing reprises of the title song to transition scenes (a linking device also used in *Sweeney Todd* and *Night Music*), as well as leitmotifs and numerous reprises to comment on time passing and dramatically illustrate the concurrent developments and changes. Two such reprised songs are the chipper, vaudevillian "Old Friends" and the heart-wrenching, balladic "Not a Day Goes By." The range of the two songs, along with other score favorites such as the jazzy and smooth "Good Thing Going," indicates the diversity and depth of the Sondheim score. Consequently, Prince felt he had let Sondheim down when the show failed. The two friends would not work together again until 2003 (for a Chicago production of *Bounce*). Today, *Merrily We Roll Along* continues to be revised by Sondheim and Furth, as numerous regional theatres and Off-Broadway producers have revisited the challenging work. There have also been persistent

plans in the works to mount a revival on Broadway, but at this writing, the production has yet to materialize. A 2012 revival at London's Menier Chocolate Factory moved to the West End for a limited engagement of three months in 2013, after winning the 2012 Critics' Circle Best Musical award.

Sondheim's career can be divided into two chapters, the first consisting of the eight Broadway musicals directed and/or produced by Harold Prince: from *West Side Story* to *Merrily We Roll Along*. The second phase is delineated by Sondheim's work with another director, James Lapine (who is also a librettist), beginning with *Sunday in the Park with George* (1984) and lasting, to date, through *Sondheim on Sondheim* (2010). In June 1982, producer Lewis Allen suggested to Sondheim that he meet with playwright/director Lapine. Sondheim enthusiastically agreed, as he was looking to find a new creative partner and had been impressed with Lapine's *Twelve Dreams* the year before at the New York Shakespeare Festival. Twenty years Sondheim's junior, Lapine had also been a photographer and taught graphic design before he migrated into playwriting and directing. Sondheim was struck by Lapine's visual approach to writing and directing. The two men connected almost immediately and their collaboration reaped great rewards, starting with *Sunday in the Park with George*, which opened on Broadway in 1984. The musical was inspired by the seminal painting by pointillist artist Georges Seurat, *A Sunday Afternoon on the Island of La Grande Jatte* (1884). For their production, Lapine and Sondheim decided to focus on the artist behind (and absent from) the group portrait. They created a fictional life for Seurat that centers upon a failed affair with a fictional mistress/model, Dot (pun intended). The liaison results in a fictional great-grandson, who happens to be a present-day multimedia sculptor at a career crossroads. From this narrative speculation, Sondheim and Lapine's musical evolved into a critique of and meditation on the entire art world, that is, the alienation and emotional sacrifice of the artist/genius, as well as the discrepancy and fluidity between life and art, and the cost of merging art with commerce (i.e., selling out).

Since Sondheim started his career at the top, he had no experience with the Off-Broadway/Off-Off-Broadway/ regional theatre world. But with *Sunday*, Sondheim did not want to revisit the negative experience of going through a formal tryout period in full view of New York critics, as had happened with *Merrily*. Therefore, he agreed to a three-week run of workshop performances at Playwrights Horizon, an Off-Broadway group with which Lapine had worked before. When the workshop production opened in July 1983, it starred Broadway heavyweights Mandy Patinkin as Seurat and Bernadette Peters as Dot. Lapine's libretto contained only a semi-complete first act: a series of scenes centered on Seurat as he creates his famous painting, as well as his neglectful relationship with Dot, who, upon discovering she is pregnant, decides to leave the emotionally unavailable artist. Toward the end of the workshop's twenty-five performances, Lapine added a second act, placed 100 years in the future. Seurat's possible great-grandson, also named George, suffers from artist's block and the pressures of commercialism, only to be shown the light by his grandmother (Dot's daughter) and the ghost of Dot herself. When the musical moved to Broadway's Booth Theatre, it was still being refined up to a couple nights before its official opening. Reviews were mixed. Some felt the book was cold and clumsily constructed (especially the second act), while the visual component was enthusiastically applauded (scenic designer Tony Straiges' miraculous transformation of a white stage space—a blank canvas—into three-dimensional replicas of some of Seurat's famous paintings). More than ever before, lavish praise was bestowed on Sondheim's score. Just as Richard Rodgers' music changed from working with Larry Hart to Oscar Hammerstein, Sondheim adapted his work to fit the poetry, content, and structure of Lapine's libretto. Using Seurat's theories of painting for inspiration, Sondheim worked in an impressionist and modernist vein, flirting with atonality to create staccato and nonlinear leitmotifs and compositions that reflect pointillism, with the separate dots of music and composition merging into a cohesive whole. He also employed cryptic and clever lyrics to tell stories and paint character portraits. In many instances, the staccato leitmotifs and caustic lyrics grow into lush melodies and emotional character expressions (e.g., "Sunday in the Park with George," "Finishing the Hat," "Putting It Together"). Contrapuntal constructs also abound, ranging from comic character pieces such as "It's Hot Up Here" to sweeping, emotional ballads, such as "Move On." When not specifically reflecting character, the score still serves and expands the libretto's themes, replete with deceptively simple

meditations (e.g., "Children and Art"), as well as complex anthems (e.g., "Sunday").

Audiences may not have flocked to the challenging *Sunday*, but it ran for a respectable 604 (albeit money-losing) performances. The show was nominated for ten Tony Awards (winning two for its scenic components). In terms of its merits, the musical won the Pulitzer Prize for Drama. Given its many accolades, it is surprising that it took more than two decades before *Sunday* was revived on Broadway. Specifically, a successful 2005 London revival by Menier Chocolate Factory transferred to Broadway in 2008 (with Roundabout Theatre Company as producer). The revival received positive critical notices and nine Tony nominations, while its significant use of new theatre technologies (digital projection and animation) pushed the musical's visual artistry and themes into the twenty-first century.

The Lapine/Sondheim collaboration continued successfully throughout the 1980s. After *Sunday*, they created what would become their most popular musical, *Into the Woods* (1987). The work is a twisted amalgam of favorite childhood fairy tales, resulting in a modern-day morality play. Choosing to workshop the new musical far away from the Broadway critics, Sondheim and Lapine premiered *Into the Woods* at San Diego's Old Globe Theatre in 1986. Given its positive response, the musical (again directed by Lapine) moved to Broadway, opening at the Martin Beck Theatre on November 5, 1987, where it ran for 764 performances (a big box office for a Sondheim show). Many in the production and design team were carryovers from *Sunday*, including star Bernadette Peters and scenic designer Tony Straiges, whose storybook design included a moving sidewalk downstage to suggest the characters' journeys into the woods. The show garnered Tony Awards once again for Sondheim (Best Score) and Lapine (Best Book).

Lapine's award-winning libretto not only intertwined the plots of several Brothers Grimm fairy tales (e.g., *Little Red Riding Hood*, *Jack and the Beanstalk*, *Rapunzel*, and *Cinderella*), it also takes a satirical look at the characters' fantastical adventures and ultimate wish fulfillments, while exposing the repercussions and harsh realities behind their "happy endings." Lapine linked the disparate fairy tale plots and characters by using the device of a storybook narrator and the metaphorical setting of the forest for the adventures, supplying an original tale in which a baker and his wife seek to break a witch's curse so they can have a baby. All tales resolve happily by the end of the first act. *Into the Woods* drastically changes direction in Act II, as a female Giant (the widow of Jack's beanstalk victim) crashes to earth and exacts revenge and destruction on the fairytale characters. All the characters must once again venture into the woods to protect their community and ensure their safety by vanquishing the Giant. To further complicate the plot, the characters have become restless and dissatisfied with their "happily-ever-after" lives. During the ethical and physical melee that follows, some key characters are killed (either by the Giant or by the desperate actions of their neighbors), and some choose to abandon the chaos (e.g., the Witch). The four remaining characters (The Baker, Jack, Little Red Riding Hood, and Cinderella) work together to slay the Giant, realizing they must remain united and resist wallowing in hate, fear, blame, and isolation. In the end, the four become a quasi family, and the deceased characters are heard reciting the lessons learned from their individual tales. In the denouement, the deceased Baker's Wife reappears to instruct her husband to tell the story of "the woods" to their child; and the Witch asserts, in a final message, that children will listen to such tales and learn from the examples of their elders.

Given *Into the Woods*' jam-packed and interwoven plot, it is no surprise that its themes are vast and complicated, yet convergent. Although the musical centers on parent-child relationships (especially that of parental duties and well-intentioned mistakes, as well as the responsibilities and risks of maturity), it also addresses larger issues of communal interrelations, moral relativity, and the cost of wish or self-fulfillment. Sondheim did not miss a beat as he created a score that not only encompasses the expansive dramatic themes but provides a world of music that travels from child to adult with whimsical flourish, bittersweet poignancy, and dramatic efficacy. He exploited musical motifs throughout the musical, such as the two-note interval that comprises the "I wish" lament of the many characters and the bouncy, chromatic motif that is at the melodic heart of the title tune. Lapine's text for *Woods* often sounds like spoken song, with much of the dialogue heavily metered and syncopated. Sondheim's score seamlessly moves this style into song, as many of his numbers are active and dialogic, for example, the seduction duets between the Wolf and Little Red ("Hello, Little Girl") and Prince

Charming and the Baker's Wife ("Any Moment"), as well as the melodramatic contest between the two Princes ("Agony"), the warm matrimonial affirmation shared by the Baker and the Baker's Wife ("It Takes Two"), the mutual discoveries made by Cinderella and the Baker's Wife ("A Very Nice Prince"), and the castigating, contrapuntal argument between the desperate survivors in Act II ("Your Fault"). In a stylistic nod to children's storytelling, Sondheim also gave the characters narrative songs to literally stand and sing to the audience (i.e., Cinderella's "On the Steps of the Palace," Jack's "Giants in the Sky," Little Red's "I Know Things Now," and the Baker's Wife's "Moments in the Woods"). And capping the score are Sondheim's allegorical ballads, framed as lush lullabies: "No One Is Alone" and "Children Will Listen." In addition to its lengthy run and Tony Awards, the original cast recording won a Grammy and the production was filmed for television in 1991. In 2002, a successful revival found its way to Broadway (again directed by Lapine, with some revisions), running for 279 performances and winning the Tony Award for Best Revival of a Musical. The musical has also been adapted into a child-friendly version for use by schools, with the second act completely removed, as well as certain portions of the first.

For Sondheim's next project, *Assassins* (1990), he briefly separated from Lapine to work again with past collaborator John Weidman (librettist of *Pacific Overtures*). Together, they created a work that stands at the apex of the dark and daring world of Sondheim. The show underwent a protracted journey to Broadway, not landing on the Main Stem until fourteen years after its debut. Sondheim was the instigator and driver of the controversial project when, as a panelist at the Musical Theater Lab, he became intrigued by a rough script by playwright Charles Gilbert. He asked Gilbert for permission to use the play's idea, which centered on assassins and would-be assassins of U.S. presidents. Gilbert agreed and offered to write the libretto, but Sondheim already had Weidman in mind. Playwrights Horizons then supplied the Off-Broadway development/performance space in its 139-seat main theater. Given the scenic and choreographic limitations of the tiny 25-foot stage, director Jerry Zaks treated the musical, titled *Assassins*, as an unadorned, loosely integrated character study, a concept underpinned by Weidman's libretto and, especially, the "revue" and pastiche nature of Sondheim's score. To summarize, the show begins in a fairground shooting gallery, where seven assassins and would-be assassins are introduced (i.e., Leon Czolgosz, John Hinckley, Jr., Charles Guiteau, Giuseppe Zangara, Samuel Byck, Lynette "Squeaky" Fromme, and Sara Jane Moore). They approach the game's Proprietor, who entices them to try their luck, promising them greatness if they succeed at the ultimate challenge: killing an American president. Next, they meet their "pioneer," John Wilkes Booth; and his assassination of Abraham Lincoln is soon heard offstage, after which the Balladeer enters and sings of Booth's terrible and seminal act (the Balladeer continues to interject commentary throughout the production, serving as a personification and seductive cheerleader of the American Dream). From this point forward, the characters jump time and space to commingle and commiserate with one another (ranging from gunplay in a bar to marijuana joint sharing on a park bench). In the process, the characters act as antagonistic catalysts and goading provocateurs with regard to their compatriots' assassination attempts. The musical numbers are often treated as revue-style songs or vaudevillian turns, to express the characters' motives and psychologies, as well as narrate their assassination tales. Further, Sondheim masterfully composed most of the assassins' numbers in styles that reflected the popular music genre of their day. For instance, "The Ballad of Booth" is a banjo-strummed folk song in the manner of Stephen Foster. "The Ballad of Guiteau" combines a gospel anthem with a frantic cakewalk, while a slow 1970s soft-rock groove underpins the twisted love duet, "Unworthy of Your Love," shared by Hinkley and Fromme (sung not to each other, however, but to the objects of their passions, Jody Foster and Charles Manson). Throughout the score, Sondheim pushes the ironic envelope, setting biting lyrics to lush or traditional compositions, a construct especially evinced by "The Gun Song," which includes expletives in its lyrics that extol the gun's power to change the world, set to waltzing rhythms and barbershop harmonies. In Act II of *Assassins*, the action moves to the sixth floor of the Texas School Book Depository, where Lee Harvey Oswald is having second thoughts about his plan to assassinate President Kennedy. Consequently, Booth appears to Oswald and is joined by the other assassins. All entreat Oswald to proceed in order to make history and change the world, thereby affirming their own acts of infamy. So he crouches at the window and shoots, his notorious act marked by song ("November 22, 1963"). In the final scene, the assassins return to the shooting range and pronounce the democratic right of everyone to pursue happiness and his or her "dream," singing the jaunty carnivalesque "Everybody's Got the Right." As they end their anthem, the assassins aim their guns at the audience.

Opening on December 18, 1990, *Assassins* ran for 73 performances Off-Broadway, playing to full, enthusiastic houses, mostly composed of Sondheim fans, but garnering reviews from New York critics that ranged from lukewarm to savage. In defense of the highly charged show, Sondheim has stated that he not only sees the assassins as negative byproducts of America's culture of guns and individualism but hopes the production can incite a purging of this dark American character. Two years later, a London version, with an added song ("Something Just Broke"), was positively received by both audiences and critics in a 76-performance run at the Donmar Warehouse (with the Brits seemingly less offended by the show's "assassin/American Dream" analogy). *Assassins* would not appear on Broadway, however, until 2004, when it was produced at Studio 54 by Roundabout Theatre and directed by Joe Mantello. Significantly, the production was initially scheduled for 2001, but due to the terrorist events of September 11th, *Assassins*' subject matter was deemed too incendiary and insensitive for a nation recovering from the deadly tragedy. Even three years later, the musical was still a difficult pill for Broadway audiences to swallow. It ran for only 101 performances; but the production won five Tony Awards, including one for Best Revival of a Musical.

Four years after *Assassins*' Off-Broadway debut, Sondheim reunited with Lapine to create *Passion* (1994), his last original work to be produced on Broadway. To bring forth his sophisticated score, Sondheim teamed again with orchestrator Jonathan Tunick and conductor Paul Gemignani (these two men have repeatedly and ingeniously brought Sondheim's compositions to full orchestral life and theatrical fruition). Although Lapine wrote the book, it was originally Sondheim's idea to adapt Ettore Scola's 1981 Italian film, *Passione d'Amore* (based on Iginio Ugo Tarchetti's 1869 novel *Fosca*). The work details an unconventional love triangle, set in nineteenth-century Italy, between a handsome soldier (Giorgio), his stunning, married mistress (Clara), and his initially repellent, obsessed, and infirm "stalker" (Fosca). Themes abound in the musical, including those of love, obsession, beauty, infirmity, control/manipulation, and the transmutable nature and transforming power of "passion." The musical begins with Giorgio in a post-coital bed with Clara, where they extol their idyllic love. He is soon transferred to a military outpost where he is frightened and then transformed by the unconditional and fanatical passion of the desperate, wretched, and lonely Fosca (with her lovesickness physically evinced by her chronically ill, bedridden condition). In the end, as Fosca offers him "love without reason," as opposed to Clara who refuses to leave her children to marry him, Giorgio falls under Fosca's manipulative, fevered spell.

Given the complicated themes, content, and construct of the libretto (much of the story is told through Giorgio's letters to Clara, giving the musical the form of an epistolary play), Sondheim needed to provide a complementary world of music, which he did by creating an operatic and atmospheric score tailored to the intimacy of a chamber musical. *Passion* contains one of Sondheim's most lush, romantic, and somber scores, with multifaceted compositions forming a continual web of song that underscores and facilitates the characters' emotional and almost dreamlike journeys. (Reflecting this aspect, *Passion*'s musical numbers were not listed by individual song titles in the original Broadway program.) In the end, Sondheim's efforts went mostly unappreciated by the general public. *Passion* was deemed austere and disturbing by Broadway audiences. After opening on May 9, 1994, it ran for only 280 performances; nonetheless, the production was filmed shortly after closing and televised on PBS. *Passion* holds the distinction as being the shortest-running musical to have won the Tony Award for Best Musical, only one of its many awards in the 1993–94 theatre season (on the other hand, there was a dearth of original staged musicals that year). Besides its ten nominations, the production garnered awards for Sondheim (score), Lapine (book), and Donna Murphy (leading actress who played Fosca). The UK debut of *Passion* ran for 232 performances in 1996, with a revised script/score and new direction; a West End revival in 2010 won the *Evening Standard*'s Best Musical Award. Other than a concert version in 2005, which was met by glowing reviews, there has yet to be a full restaging of the musical on Broadway.

Since *Passion*, no *new* Sondheim work has debuted on Broadway. In 2004, Sondheim's musical theatre version of *The Frogs*—originally debuted at Yale in 1974—received the grand Broadway treatment. The production was directed and choreographed by Broadway powerhouse Susan Stroman and its book was "even more freely adapted" by one of its stars, Broadway funnyman Nathan Lane. Although the musical was highly anticipated and hyped, given the stellar production team, there were creative problems, as well as cast contentions. The finished product did not meet expectations, earning negative reviews and running for only ninety-two performances.

Three years after *Frogs*, Sondheim fans were beside themselves, thinking they might see, after a decade, a new Sondheim work on Broadway. Adding to the insider intrigue and anticipation was the fact that the show had been in development, appearing in various workshop and regional stage versions, for the past ten years. The workshopped musical was originally known as *Wise Guys* (1999), then renamed *Bounce* when it debuted regionally in Chicago in 2003 (directed by Hal Prince in a much-heralded reunion with Sondheim), and, finally *Road Show*, directed by John Doyle for Off-Broadway's Public Theater in 2007. With another libretto by John Weidman (*Pacific Overtures* and *Assassins*), *Road Show* is a chamber musical with nineteen cast members that shows the dark side of capitalism and the American Dream through the dramatized portrayal of real-life brothers Addison and Wilson Mizner. The Mizners were infamous entrepreneurial partners in the late nineteenth and early twentieth centuries. In the musical's libretto, the brothers—one a malleable, sensitive visionary and the other, a controlling, self-indulgent gambler—are shown achieving prosperity through successive speculations, ranging from gold prospecting to land investments. In the end, however, their ambitions and appetites (even a hint at incestuous relations) lead to burnout and self-destruction, illustrating the downside of the American hunger for and single-minded pursuit of success, money, and notoriety. Reactions to *Road Show* were mixed, with critics feeling the production's message was confused and the characters never fully developed. Sondheim's score was deemed to be too narrative and perfunctory, simply serving as a guide by which the brothers' story is chronicled, as opposed to giving nuanced expression to the characters and providing dramatic impetus and color. The highly anticipated production did not make the leap to Broadway.

The failure of *Road Show* to reach the Main Stem is not to suggest, however, that Sondheim has not been a ubiquitous presence on the Broadway stage during the first decade of the twenty-first century. Given the richness of his song catalogue, his compositions have always been favored fodder for successful, canonical revues, e.g., *Side by Side by Sondheim* (1977) and *Putting It Together* (1991). In this vein, the first decade of the new century saw two more Broadway revues by major stars, Barbara Cook's *Mostly Sondheim* (2002) and Mandy Patinkin's *Celebrating Sondheim* (2002). The artist himself capped the phenomenon by creating with Lapine the ultimate "insider" revue: *Sondheim on Sondheim* (2010). Produced by the Roundabout Theatre at Broadway's Studio 54, the revue opened on April 22, 2010, as a limited engagement, running for seventy-six performances. The production featured an intimate ensemble of eight actor/singers who performed signature, obscure, and even student-written numbers by Sondheim culled from his sixty-two-year career. Sondheim himself virtually emceed and contextualized many of the numbers by way of filmed interviews (projected on sixty-four plasma screens), talking about the numbers, the shows, his writing process, and his career. As Lapine has stated, the production became an "impressionistic" view of a multifaceted artist, while the montage brought the man himself into focus.

In addition to the numerous revues, an onslaught of Sondheim revivals hit Broadway at the beginning of the twenty-first century. With the exception of *Passion*, every significant Sondheim musical has been revived on Broadway in the last decade. While many were conventional, two were revelatory in their revisionist garb: *Sweeney Todd* (2005) and *Company* (2006), both directed by auteur John Doyle. These productions were scaled-down, intimate, and presentational (no attempt to hide the work's artifice, theatricality, and performative nature), with a concept that included the performers doubling as musicians. These works were only two of many contemporary Sondheim revisitations; and whether or not the string of revivals attracted large audiences (2004's *Pacific Overtures* lasted for only sixty-nine performances, while 2009's *A Little Night Music* ran for over a year), they managed to garner a lion's share of critical acclaim and awards, reaffirming the immense, timeless contribution made by Sondheim to the musical theatre canon. For over fifty years, Stephen Sondheim has changed not only what the American musical sounds like, but what it looks like and the subject matter it explores. He is the winner of eight Tony Awards (more than any other composer), including the Special Tony Award for Lifetime Achievement in the Theatre. In addition, he has won a Pulitzer Prize, an Academy Award (his original music for 1990's *Dick Tracy*), and multiple Grammy Awards. For Sondheim fans around the world, his soundscapes place audiences in the shoes of characters such as Red Riding Hood and Seurat, that is, canonical Sondheim types who make their way through nebulous terrains, facing uncomfortable truths that expand their world views, while unlocking the multifaceted potential and peril of the blank canvas that is the human experience. In short, Sondheim has forever changed the world and genre of musical theatre by opening it to new possibilities of truth, ambivalence, conflict, and insight.

Figure 4.4

COULD I LEAVE YOU?

Music and Lyrics by Stephen Sondheim (1971)

Leave you? Leave you?
How could I leave you?
How could I go it alone?
Could I wave the years away
With a quick goodbye?
How do you wipe tears away
When your eyes are dry?

Sweetheart, lover,
Could I recover,
Give up the joys I have known?
Not to fetch your pills again
Every day at five,
Not to give those dinners for ten
Elderly men
From the U.N.—
How could I survive?

Could I leave you
And your shelves of the World's Best Books,
And the evenings of martyred looks,
Cryptic sighs,
Sullen glares from those injured eyes?
Leave the quips with a sting, jokes with a sneer,
Passionless lovemaking once a year?
Leave the lies ill-concealed
And the wounds never healed
And the games not worth winning
And—wait, I'm just beginning!

What, leave you, leave you,
How could I leave you?
What would I do on my own?
Putting thoughts of you aside
In the south of France,
Would I think of suicide?
Darling, shall we dance?

Could I live through the pain
On a terrace in Spain?
Would it pass? It would pass.
Could I bury my rage
With a boy half your age
In the grass? Bet your ass.
But I've done that already—
Or didn't you know, love?
Tell me, how could I leave
When I left long ago, love?

Could I leave you?
No, the point is, could you leave me?
Well, I guess you could leave me the house,
Leave me the flat,
Leave me the Braques and Chagalls and all that.
You could leave me the stocks for sentiment's sake
And ninety percent of the money you make.
And the rugs
And the cooks—
Darling, you keep the drugs.
Angel, you keep the books.
Honey, I'll take the grand,
Sugar, you keep the spinet
And all of our friends and—
Just wait a goddam minute!
Oh, leave you? Leave you?
How could I leave you?
Sweetheart, I have to confess:
Could I leave you?
Yes.
Will I leave you?
Will I leave you?
Guess!

FEATURED PRODUCTION: *Sweeney Todd* (1979)

Music and Lyrics by Stephen Sondheim; Book by Hugh Wheeler

Original Broadway Run: Opened March 1, 1979; Uris Theatre; 557 performances

Throughout history, audiences have been drawn to the thrills and chills of a good horror story. A notable example is the British population's fascination with murderous villains during the Victorian era, when the deeds of bloodthirsty characters were retold or fictionalized through popular penny-dreadfuls. Although many in America had heard of Jack the Ripper (a real-life example of a dreadful archetype), only a few may have heard of the fictional Sweeney Todd, a similarly favorite cautionary creep tale of nineteenth-century England. More than 100 years later Broadway audiences were made unnervingly familiar with this barber and his sordid crimes. And in a most unlikely scenario, the vehicle for retelling Todd's tale was a musical. Given the masterminds behind the work—composer/lyricist Stephen Sondheim and director Hal Prince—one might not have been surprised. The musical was titled *Sweeney Todd* (subtitled *The Demon Barber of Fleet Street*). Audiences who attended the original 1979 production were warned of the unconventional events that were soon to unfold on the Uris Theatre stage. A ragtag chorus confronted the audience with a discomfiting "grabber" in the form of a folk ballad that implored spectators to "attend the tale" of the eponymous character, building to an operatic frenzy (evoking Wagner's Valkyries) and climaxing with the appearance of Sweeney Todd himself raised from the grave. Todd menacingly took the stage and dared the audience to look away as he prepared to reenact his vengeful journey. The audience stayed for the journey, possibly realizing they were witnessing a new chapter in the history of American musical theatre.

The idea of musicalizing the legend of Sweeney Todd originated with Sondheim in 1973 after he attended a contemporary play version of the tale, produced in an intimate black box theatre in London. As early as 1847, George Dibdin Pitt had theatricalized the "demon barber" and his evil deeds with *A String of Pearls, or the Fiend of Fleet Street*, staged in Grand Guignol fashion (a style of theatre presentation that might be compared to today's horror or "slasher" film). Sondheim was inspired by the stark adaptation he saw in the small London theatre, written by Christopher Bond. Bond's *Sweeney Todd* presented the barber not only as a blood-thirsty killer and bogeyman, but also a doomed victim of his environment and class constraints. In the voracious climate of the Industrial Revolution, Bond positioned the plot's cannibalism as a metaphor for the eat-or-be-eaten survival ethos of the time. It was the Industrial Age milieu, metaphor, and molding of Todd that ultimately drew Prince to the project after a period of resistance. Once Sondheim had his director on board, the two men, with recruited librettist Hugh Wheeler, tackled the dark tale, chronicling Todd's doomed path from victim to mad avenger.

At the beginning of *Sweeney Todd*, after the thundering choral rendering of the minor-keyed "The Ballad of Sweeney Todd" (which ominously opens with a factory whistle and pulsing orchestration), a young sailor, Anthony Hope, is seen on a boat sailing to London. Here, he meets Sweeney Todd, a brooding man haunted by demons, who has been released from an Australian prison. After the two men share greatly disparate views of the city on the horizon ("No Place Like London"), Todd alludes to his own tortured history, telling the idealistic sailor the tragic tale of Benjamin Barker (Todd in his past life). Through the haunting "The Barber and His Wife," it is revealed that Barker was a barber who had been unjustly sentenced to prison by a judge seeking to steal his wife. Todd and Anthony part ways, wishing each other well. It isn't until the next scene that the audience learns the full extent of Todd's betrayal at the hands of Judge

Turpin. Upon returning to his old neighborhood, Todd meets Mrs. Lovett, the proprietress of a failing meat pie shop below the barber's vacant apartment. After she swoops down on Todd with a manic "I Am" patter song ("The Worst Pies in London"), she finishes the story for him, singing an escalating waltz in which she describes how Barker's wife, Lucy, was duped and then raped by Turpin, leading to her suicide by poison ("Poor Thing"). Further, the judge took Todd's young daughter, Joanna, as his ward and now that she has come of age, plans to force her to marry him. An enraged Todd vows to avenge his ruin and his wife's death, as well as save his daughter from the judge's clutches. Lovett, who recognizes Todd as Barker, is infatuated with the man and offers to become his "partner," helping him reopen his barber establishment above her shop. From here, the plot continues straightforwardly, as Todd plans to lure Turpin to his place and slit his throat. Meantime, young Anthony happens on Joanna on a London street where she is singing to a caged bird ("Green Finch and Linnet Bird"), a metaphor for her own predicament at the hands of her lustful guardian, Turpin. Immediately smitten, Anthony is forbidden to see her by the judge. Anthony pours out his heart in the overwrought aria "Joanna," vowing to rescue her. Back in Todd's barber shop, things have taken a complicated turn. Not only has Anthony appeared and told Todd about Joanna, prompting him to offer his shop as a sanctuary if Anthony can free her, but Todd has had to turn his scalpel on a blackmailing rival barber in order to silence him and keep his revenge plan on track. With the blackmailer's corpse still fresh in his apartment, Todd is finally visited by Judge Turpin seeking a shave. In a twisted and seductive duet between Todd and Turpin during the shave, the two men share a soaring, ironic revelry extolling the virtues of women and beauty, "Pretty Women," with vocals that mesh and counter in a fugue-like structure. Just as Todd goes in for the kill, however, he is interrupted by Anthony, who bursts in and blurts out his plans to elope with Joanna. Turpin is outraged and blames both Todd and Anthony for conspiring against him, then storms out, vowing never to return. Todd turns on Anthony, chasing him out and despairing that he has again been defeated in life. Descending into madness, Todd launches into a soliloquy, "Epiphany," vowing vengeance on society as a whole. Here, the musical introduces its darkest plot development; for Mrs. Lovett suggests a grisly, yet economical, solution to the dilemma of the corpse still hidden in Todd's trunk. If he must satisfy his bloodlust, then she can do away with the evidence and boost the profits of her shop by baking his corpses into tasty meat pies. The idea is introduced and solidified in the duo's manic and comic waltz, "A Little Priest."

In melodramatic fashion, Act II of *Sweeney Todd* gets even more convoluted, with events escalating at fever pitch. Todd continues to slash the throats of his customers (choosing those who will not be missed) and Lovett's shop becomes prosperous as customers devour her pies ("God, That's Good"). Lovett has also taken in an addled young boy, Tobias, who was the abused apprentice of Todd's first victim. Lovett hopes for a matrimonial future with Todd (the picture of domestic bliss is painted through her music hall ditty "By the Sea"). Meanwhile, Turpin has committed Joanna to Fogg's Asylum for lunatics, and Anthony plans to disguise himself as a wigmaker to enter the asylum and rescue her. Throughout the show, a strange and demented Beggar Woman makes erratic appearances, begging for alms, warning of "mischief," and making lewd advances to onlookers. Finally, the show comes to its climax, incited by Tobias, who is now devoted to Lovett (evidenced by his vow to protect her in the gentle ballad, "Not While I'm Around"). Tobias is suspicious of Todd's activities, obliging Lovett to lock him in the basement, where he discovers the nature of the ingredients in her meat pies and escapes into the cellar's catacombs. As Todd and Lovett search for Tobias, Anthony rescues Joanna, freeing the lunatics as well. All events are musically interwoven and enacted through the contrapuntal choral number, "City on Fire." Following this large-scale scene are a quick series of crises that lead to the demise of all the evildoers (and one innocent). First, the Beggar Woman intrudes on Todd as he prepares for his last chance to kill Judge Turpin (he sends Turpin a letter, advising him to come to his quarters to catch Anthony and Joanna). To quiet the Woman's ranting, he slits her throat. Next, Todd succeeds in killing Turpin (Turpin recognizes "Benjamin Barker" just as his throat is slit). Anthony and Joanna escape the carnage. In a tragic discovery, however, Todd realizes that the Beggar Woman he has killed is actually his wife, Lucy, who had not died from her poison but, instead, had gone insane. Enraged, Todd turns on Mrs. Lovett, who he realizes has lied to him. Lovett insists that she was only trying to protect him, and Todd appears to forgive her as the two waltz to a reprise of "A Little Priest." However, he waltzes her right into her own pie oven, slamming the door and burning her alive. He cradles his dead Lucy in anguish, singing a reprise of "The Barber and His Wife," while behind him a demented Tobias approaches and slits Todd's throat with his own razor. At the scene's end, the chorus (a constant throughout the show) reappears, singing the final reprise of "The Ballad of Sweeney Todd," joined by Lovett and Todd from the grave, daring the audience one last time to "attend the tale of Sweeney Todd."

Sondheim's score for *Sweeney Todd* is probably the most complex through-composed and darkly comic of his career, definitely one of his more operatic works. However, it also contains lilting, hummable tunes redolent of the British music hall and tavern folk songs (e.g., "The Ballad of Sweeney Todd," "Poor Thing," and "By the Sea"), although such "hummable" numbers are often taken to classical heights, as they have complicated melodic and compositional structures. The score is both stark and comic, perfectly serving Wheeler's humorously macabre book. Although dialogue exists, it is almost completely underscored, with much of it weaving in and out of recitative (e.g., "The Contest" and "Ladies in Their Sensitivities"). Many of the songs are narrative, active, and rooted in character, while steeped in irony as they range in style from comic patter song ("The Worst Pies in London") to soliloquy ("Epiphany") to waltz ("A Little Priest") to tender ballad ("Not While I'm Around"). Yet in operatic fashion, there also exist numerous reflective "stand and sing" arias such as "Johanna," "Green Finch and Linnet Bird," and "My Friends" (an eerie paean sung by Todd to his razor blades), as well as contrapuntal duets ("Pretty Women" and "Kiss Me"). The classical flavor of *Sweeney Todd* is even more evident during ensemble numbers such as "City on Fire," an homage to the ancient Furies which reprises and spoofs snippets of other songs in newly ominous contexts (for example, Mrs. Lovett reprises refrains of "Not While I'm Around" during the number as she and Todd hunt for Tobias to kill him). Sondheim's use of leitmotifs in *Sweeney Todd* is without equal in the musical theatre canon. The most potent example is his use of the "Johanna" leitmotif, introduced by a lovesick Anthony in his signature aria, then hauntingly referenced by Todd as he murders his victims, obsessing over his lost daughter (countered by Anthony who reprises the song as he searches for her). In the leitmotif's most twisted exploitation, Judge Turpin turns the name/refrain into a frenzied chant during a scene of self-flagellation (omitted from the original production for censorship worries).

Another impressive component of the production, conceptualized by director Prince, was its scenic design by Eugene Lee (even though it went contrary to Sondheim's original "chamber musical" vision). When *Sweeney Todd* was booked into the biggest theatre in New York at the time, the Uris, Prince asked Lee to create a setting that would dominate the cavernous auditorium. To contextualize this nineteenth-century melodrama, Prince not only wanted a factory on stage (to symbolize the Industrial Revolution), he wanted a *real* factory on stage. (Lee found one in Rhode Island that he moved into the Uris Theatre, removing the theater's proscenium arch to make the imported factory parts seem even larger.) The monumentality of Lee's set for the Broadway premiere aggressively announced itself. A catwalk bridge and enormous traveling girder delivered Todd's new barber chair, but was mainly there to create atmosphere, looming over the large revolving center-stage scenic unit that contained Todd's barbershop upstairs, with Mrs. Lovett's pie shop and the basement on the lower level. In point of fact, the musical has nothing to do with the Industrial Revolution. But when asked why he wanted a factory setting for the story, Prince replied that it was such a milieu that produced "Sweeney Todds." With the industrial framework and the socioeconomic inequalities it created, Prince hoped to give the production a social commentary, making it more than a revenge story. Prince's concept, combined with the Sondheim score, Grand Guignol excess, twisted humor, and luminary lead performances (Len Cariou and Angela Lansbury) resulted in a production that won eight Tony Awards, including the season's prize for Best Musical, and ran for 557 performances, a lengthy run by Sondheim standards (although the production still finished in the red).

Sondheim would have to wait until 1989 to see a production of *Sweeney Todd* that was closer in scale to his original vision, that is, a simple, metaphoric staging with a few streetlamps and fog (produced by Off-Broadway's Circle in the Square Theatre). Most recently, British director John Doyle reduced the scale even more dramatically for his 2004 Tony-Award-winning revival, which featured only ten performers (who also performed the score as musicians since his version did not have a separate orchestra). Audiences have also had the option to see versions of *Sweeney Todd* that retain its original grandeur. In 1984, Prince, using Lee's Broadway design, staged *Sweeney Todd* for the Houston Grand Opera. The director also used a simplified (although still large) Lee setting for his production for the New York City Opera, where it became part of the company's repertoire. These revivals are only a few of the many stagings by opera companies, regional theatres, Off-Broadway theatres, etc., that have occurred since the production's 1979 debut. Regardless of its size and spectacle, or lack thereof, the musical has proved to be a Sondheim masterpiece, telling a grisly, but strangely universal, tale of destruction, revenge, and one man's battle against fate, society, and the demons of his past.

Timothy Nolen and Barbara Marineau in Goodspeed Musicals' *Sweeney Todd* at the Goodspeed Opera House, 1996. Photo by Diane Sobolewski. Used by permission of Goodspeed Musicals.

PULLING BACK THE CURTAIN:
The Chamber Musical

No splashy "grabber," no dropping chandeliers or landing helicopters, no long kick line or epic chorus number. It is a "small" show, which may be described as a black box musical or intimate musical or low-budget musical. All descriptors are correct, but the definitive categorization for a musical that is small in scale, but lacks nothing in the way of score sophistication, book complexity, and audience fulfillment, is the "chamber musical." Given the diverse nature of this economical form, it is difficult to pigeonhole. However, one might describe a chamber work as an intimate musical (book or concept form) that does not require extravagant staging and has a small cast (the number ranging from single digits to the teens). Most performers play significant, individualized roles. This is not to suggest that there are no ensemble players, but they are few in number and may be featured as a reappearing narrative group (e.g., a mini Greek chorus) or used to creatively fill out the cast by handling multiple smaller roles. Such a compact, personalized paradigm contrasts with the conventional large-scale musicals of the Golden Age and earlier, which featured stars and supporting roles (or sidekicks), surrounded by largely anonymous dancers and singers, who were relegated to sizable choruses that served to fill the stage with sound and movement. In short, a chamber musical does not contain spectacle or extraneous choruses and supernumeraries as part of its aesthetic or need them to musically convey content. Neither does it include big, flashy chorus numbers, the types of which were paid homage in *A Chorus Line* (a musical that, except for its illustrative opening and closing numbers, could ironically be deemed, at its heart, a chamber musical).

Even though obscure and modest attempts at intimate musicals were made in the first half of the twentieth century (e.g., Kurt Weill and Alan Jay Lerner's *Love Life* in 1948), the trend toward smaller, more economical works never found footing until the 1960s, when producers and artists became more experimental (and budget conscious), seeking to change the look and feel of the traditional Broadway show. Further facilitating this development, Off-Broadway began to develop musicals, calling for more modest productions to fit their smaller spaces and stage/design limitations. As chamber musicals grew in popularity throughout the '60s, '70s, and '80s, many notable early Broadway and Off-Broadway works were whimsical and "cute," often with light pop or sweetly digestible scores to match their compact aesthetic, content, and production scale. Examples include *The Fantasticks* (the Off-Broadway hit that still holds the record for longest-running musical); *She Loves Me*; *You're a Good Man, Charlie Brown*; *Dames at Sea*; *Godspell*; *I Love My Wife*; *Little Shop of Horrors*; *Baby*; and *Romance/Romance*. During this period, composer/lyricist Stephen Sondheim (working with directors Hal Prince and James Lapine) created many chamber musicals. In the process, he took the form in another direction, providing complex (and, at times, operatic) scores to match daring material on an intimate scale. Canonical examples include *Company*, *A Little Night Music*, *Sweeney Todd*, *Sunday in the Park with George*, *Into the Woods*, *Assassins*, and *Passion*. (It should be noted that not all the aforementioned Sondheim productions were originally staged modestly, but they are written as compact, ensemble-driven pieces that do not require elaborate scenic trappings or grand dancing/singing choruses). Even Andrew Lloyd Webber, king composer of the mega-musical, tried his hand at the chamber musical in the late 1980s with *Aspects of Love* (which received disappointing reviews on its 1990 Broadway debut), as well as his reconfigured *By Jeeves* (which flopped mightily on Broadway in 2001).

When addressing the chamber musical, one should note that there is an even smaller, more intimate musical form in the genre, the two-hander. With a cast of only two characters, this musical is rare and provides a unique experience (and challenge) for the performers and their audience. Early popular Broadway examples include *I Do! I Do!* and *They're Playing Our Song*, while Off-Broadway has been the home to more current successes such as *The Last Five Years* and *john and jen*.

The chamber musical continues to hold a prominent place in the musical theatre genre (proving to be a budget-conscious choice for small theatres). The following list of notable contemporary examples illustrates the growing diversity of the form: *Rent*; *The Wild Party*; *Urinetown*; *The 25th Annual Putnam County Spelling Bee*; *Caroline, or Change*; *The Light in the Piazza*; *The Drowsy Chaperone*; *[title of show]*; *Little Women*; and *Next to Normal*. Most of the aforementioned works have had successful box office runs and merited prestigious nominations and rewards, including two Pulitzer Prizes, all of which goes to show the prominence, potential, and permanence of the "little show" on Broadway.

Actor Spotlights

Angela Lansbury

Considered by fans and scholars alike to be the Grand Dame—and "Mame"—of the modern musical era, Angela Lansbury currently reigns on Broadway as one of its most beloved and enduring stars. Yet, her triumphant career extends to film and television as well, with her multifaceted talent meriting a nearly unparalleled degree of recognition in the entertainment industry. She has earned three Academy Award nominations, six Golden Globes, and eighteen Emmy Award nominations, and, most notably, a record number of Tony Awards for Best Actress in a Musical (four wins in all). In addition, she won a fifth Tony in 2009 for her nonmusical

Angela Lansbury performing at New York City Center Gala Celebration honoring Stephen Sondheim, April 26, 2010 © Walter McBride/Retna Ltd./Corbis

work in the Broadway revival of Noel Coward's classic comedy, *Blithe Spirit*. At the time, Lansbury was in her eighties, proving that age had not diminished her stage prowess and affirming the timeless appeal and artistry of a venerated icon who has thrilled Broadway audiences for more than a half century, conquering genres spanning drama, comedy, and musical theatre.

Angela Brigid Lansbury was born on October 16, 1925, in the London Borough of Poplar, UK, to a British actress mother, Moyna MacGill, and a merchant/politician father, Edgar Lansbury. The family was theatrical, with her younger twin brothers becoming producers in later life. Moyna had the most influence over young Angela, given Edgar's untimely cancer death in 1934. She encouraged her daughter's theatre ambitions, taking her to numerous plays and enrolling her in the Webber Douglas Academy of Dramatic Art from 1939–40 and the Feagin School of Dramatic Art in New York from 1940–42 (the family, with stepfather Leckie Forbes, had moved to New York City in August 1940, narrowly evading the London Blitz). Lansbury's first major success came in film, as the family ultimately moved to Hollywood due to her mother's career. At one of her mother's industry parties, the 18-year-old Lansbury made an impression on a casting director who gave her a supporting role as a devious maid in his upcoming major studio film, *Gaslight* (1944). For her notable movie debut, she earned an Academy Award nomination and jumpstarted her career as one of Hollywood's most reliable and versatile character actresses. With over 50 films to her credit, she would go on to earn two more Oscar nominations for increasingly varied roles, including the fanatical mother and Communist agent in 1962's The *Manchurian Candidate* (playing against an actor only three years her junior in the role of her brainwashed son).

Given Lansbury's theatrical training, it is no surprise that she would quickly find her way to Broadway. Again, her consummate ability to sincerely, humorously, and colorfully portray wildly divergent, larger-than-life characters served the musical stage well. In addition, her vocal dexterity set her apart, for while not a classically trained instrument, Lansbury's idiosyncratic singing voice is full of passion, flair, and nuance—in short, there is no mistaking the sound of Angela Lansbury. After debuting on Broadway in nonmusical plays such as *Hotel Paradiso* (1957) and *A Taste of Honey* (1960), Lansbury made her musical debut as a duplicitous mayoress in Stephen Sondheim's early failure, *Anyone Can Whistle* (1964), where she received positive reviews, despite the show's overall negative reception. Then, in 1966, Lansbury landed a musical vehicle perfectly suited to her talents: Jerry Herman's *Mame*. In the title role, Lansbury sparkled as the eccentric, audacious free spirit, Auntie Mame, who takes her nephew under her wing, trying to teach him how to live life to its fullest. In what could have been a gauche, cliché performance, Lansbury humanized the adventurous matron and charmed audiences in the marathon role, earning her first Tony Award for Best Actress in a Musical. It would be the beginning of a momentous musical theatre career. A few years later, Lansbury would reunite with Herman for *Dear World* (1969). Playing a dowager living in a world of dreams and delusions, Lansbury won her second Best Actress Tony, although the musical itself would be deemed a failure.

Gypsy has long been a career benchmark for any top musical theatre actress; but for years, the production was mostly identified with and attributed to the formidable Ethel Merman, who originated the iconic role of Mama Rose. Due to this situation, Lansbury was hesitant to take on Merman's signature role when she was offered the part in the first high profile revival of the production. She ultimately relented, however, and the production debuted in London's West End, eventually making it to Broadway in 1974. Having created her own definitive version of Rose, Lansbury was hailed for her performance and earned a third Tony Award, while her triumph also suggested interpretative and performative possibilities for future leading actresses. Lansbury's next musical feat would reinforce her reputation as one of Broadway's most daring artists, shape-shifting into the maniacal pie-maker, Mrs. Lovett, for Stephen Sondheim's *Sweeney Todd* (1979). Skillfully mastering Sondheim's multifaceted score, including tongue-twisting patter songs and tonally complex ballads, she also imbued her murderous character with heart and soul (albeit, both were deluded and twisted). Sporting disheveled pigtails, over-rouged cheeks, and smudged bee-stung lips, many critics likened her creepy, campy portrayal to that of a macabre "Raggedy Ann," while waxing rhapsodic over the humor she injected into the otherwise dark and depressing proceedings. For the role, Lansbury won another Tony, while her performance in the national tour was taped for a 1982 televised broadcast. Further, given the *Sweeney* award, Lansbury holds the record for most Tonys for Best Actress in a Musical (she is also a contender regarding most overall Tony Awards for women).

After her *Sweeney* triumph, Lansbury took a hiatus from the New York stage while she again focused on film and television. She provided the voices for popular animated films such as 1991's *Beauty and the Beast* and 1997's *Anastasia* and found great success on the small screen playing the lovable and crafty small-town detective Jessica Fletcher in the long-running television series *Murder She Wrote* (1984–1996). In total, Lansbury has eighteen Primetime Emmy award nominations to her credit, most accorded to her work on *Murder*, for which she was also awarded a Golden Globe and People's Choice Award. After an absence of twenty-three years, Lansbury delighted audiences when she returned to Broadway in a play by Terrence McNally, *Deuce* (2007). Two years later, Lansbury received her *fifth* Tony Award for her portrayal of Madame Arcati in a 2009 revival of *Blithe Spirit*. In the same year, she played another "Madame," this time Madame Armfeldt in the first Broadway revival of *A Little Night Music*, officially returning to the musical stage and receiving another Tony nomination, as well as a warm "welcome home" from her legions of musical theatre fans. In 2012, the tireless Lansbury starred in the Broadway revival of Gore Vidal's *The Best Man*, reminding audiences as to why she is revered today as the First Lady of Broadway.

Bernadette Peters

As a professional child actor, Bernadette Peters grew up on the musical stage, and luckily for the musical theatre genre, it continues to be her home. In a career that has spanned five decades, Peters currently stands as one of musical theatre's most popular and lauded stars; she has been the recipient of two Tony Awards for Best Actress in a Musical (out of seven total Tony nominations) and three Drama Desk Awards (out of nine nominations). In addition, Peters has lent her talent to over twenty films, with a Golden Globe to her credit, and appeared in numerous television shows, earning several Emmy nominations. She is also known for her concert performances at such landmark venues as Carnegie Hall, Hollywood Bowl, Radio City, Sydney Opera House, and Lincoln Center, in addition to numerous solo albums and Grammy-awarded original cast recordings. If this isn't enough, she is also an author of children's books. First and foremost, however, Peters is most revered as a modern-age "Broadway Baby."

Peters was born Bernadette Lazzara in February 1948 to an Italian-American family in Queens, New York, the youngest of three children. The family had no entertainment background or connections (her father, Peter, drove a delivery truck); but her mother saw promise in little Bernadette and got the three-year-old a spot on the television show *Juvenile Jury*. From there, Bernadette regularly appeared on stage and screen, earning her Actors' Equity card by age nine under the name of Bernadette Peters to avoid ethnic pigeonholing, using her father's first name as her stage name. Throughout the late '50s and early '60s, an adolescent Peters appeared in numerous network television shows and stage productions, making her New York City debut at the ripe old age of ten in the New York City Center revival of *The Most Happy Fella* (1959). As a teen, Peters attended Quintano's School for Young Professionals while furthering her stage career. Although she would go on to play the role of Mama Rose to great acclaim as an adult on Broadway, her first association with *Gypsy* was when she was only thirteen, appearing as one of the "Hollywood Blondes" and understudying June in the production's second national tour. In 1962, she recorded her first single and in the next few years, continued to work in regional theatre, summer stock and, ultimately, Off-Broadway once she graduated from high school (e.g., 1966's *The Penny Friend*). Peters made her Broadway debut in the failed production of *Johnny No-Trump* (1967) but found more success playing Josie Cohan opposite Joel Grey's George M. Cohan in the 1968 hit, *George M!*. But it was her luminescent Off-Broadway turn as the star-struck ingénue in the musical spoof *Dames at Sea* (1968) that accorded her major notice and her first Drama Desk Award. In the production, Peters effortlessly exploited a full range of vocal and acting skills, that is, a bright mezzo belt mixed with warm soprano; comic coyness tempered by honest sentiment; and wide-eyed innocence countered by sassy charm. In addition, she demonstrated solid tap dance skills. Such a stellar triple-threat display would come to define the unique star quality of Bernadette Peters, serving her well as she began to move into lead roles on Broadway. These included Hildy in the 1971 revival of *On the Town*, for which she received her first Tony Award nomination, and silent film star Mabel Normand in Jerry Herman's *Mack and Mabel* (1974), for which she received another Tony nomination, with laudatory reviews extolling her luminary talent and poignant portrayal, despite the musical's box office failure.

In the mid-1970s, Peters moved to Hollywood to focus on film and television work, finding some measure of success in both, with a Golden Globe win for her lead role in the movie-musical homage *Pennies from Heaven* (1981). Her television credits included numerous appearances on variety programs, award shows, musical specials, movies made for television, and televised musicals. (In recent years, she has also become a frequent guest star in sitcoms and drama series.) She missed her first love, however; and Broadway missed her. After an eight-year hiatus, Peters returned to the New York stage in the Off-Broadway play *Sally and Marsha* and then resumed her Broadway musical career in Stephen Sondheim's *Sunday in the Park with George*

Mandy Patinkin, Bernadette Peters, and Stephen Sondheim, 1983 © Bettmann/CORBIS

(1984), originating the dual role of a fictional mistress of George Seurat (Dot) and a sage grandmother (Marie). Her dramatic, artistic interpretation of the production's difficult score and libretto earned her a third Tony nomination. In her subsequent star vehicle, Andrew Lloyd Webber's *Song and Dance* (1985), Peters captivated audiences and critics alike as she brought to life a sardonic, romantic, quirky British expat/milliner in a solo, sung-through tour de force. For her commanding performance, Peters won her first Tony for Best Actress in a Musical. Next, Peters further cemented her reputation as a premier interpreter of Sondheim by creating the role of the Witch in his *Into the Woods* (1987). In 1999, Peters put her own endearingly comic spin on the role of Annie Oakley in the Broadway revival of *Annie Get Your Gun*, for which she won her second Tony. In 2003, Peters took on another iconic Ethel Merman role, again remaking it in her inimitable fashion. The role was Mama Rose and the production was the 2003 revival of *Gypsy*, for which she earned another Tony nomination, along with critical reviews that praised her complex and original performance. After *Gypsy* closed, Peters did not return to Broadway for six years. But in July 2010, to the delight of Sondheim fans, her reemergence was in another Sondheim musical, replacing Catherine Zeta-Jones as Desiree Armfeldt in the revival of *A Little Night Music*. Due to the aforementioned roles, along with her most recent lead performance of Sally in the 2011 Broadway revival of Sondheim's *Follies* and her numerous concerts featuring the composer/lyricist's work, Peters has become closely associated with Sondheim. Further, Sondheim himself has extolled Peters' uniquely symbiotic singer/actor talent, going so far as to call her musical theatre performances "flawless." For the greater part of the modern musical era, audiences couldn't have agreed more.

Mandy Patinkin

Celebrated for his brilliant tenor voice, audacious performance style, and mastery of complex scores (notably, those of Stephen Sondheim), Mandy Patinkin, ironically, did not originally aspire to a musical career. Instead, he set out to conquer the nonmusical stage, but it was only a matter of time before producers, directors, and audiences discovered his vocal gifts, establishing him as one of Broadway's top musical stars. Patinkin need not have worried about being pigeonholed as a Broadway musical performer, however. To date, the versatile actor has managed to succeed in all entertainment mediums, winning a Tony Award (Best Performance in a Featured Role in a Musical), an Emmy Award (Outstanding Lead Actor in a Television Series), cult film status for his portrayal of Inigo Montoya in 1987's *The Princess Bride*, and recording industry merit for his many bestselling albums. The musical theatre arena has benefited greatly from his unique contributions for more than three decades, while the perfectionism and performing bravado of Patinkin puts him in a legendary category that matches the icons of Broadway's golden past.

Mandel Bruce "Mandy" Patinkin was born on November 30, 1952, in Chicago, Illinois; and his middle-class Jewish upbringing included an education in Conservative Judaism, as he attended religious school daily during his adolescence and actively participated in the synagogue choirs. As a result, Patinkin's Jewish heritage would figure prominently in his later life and theatrical career. After high school, he attended University of Kansas and then Julliard. Armed with a prestigious Julliard degree in drama, he entered the professional ranks, landing a few television commercial and radio appearances, as well as a Broadway debut in the 1975 revival of the comedy *Trelawny of the "Wells"* (1898). After a couple more nonmusical Broadway gigs, the twenty-seven-year-old Patinkin became the wunderkind of musical theatre, wowing audiences in 1979 with his portrayal of Che Guevara in Rice and Webber's *Evita* on Broadway. Patinkin went on to win the Tony Award for his vocally and theatrically bold performance (two characteristics which would mark many of his future musical stage endeavors). Soon thereafter, he heeded the siren call of Hollywood and turned his focus to film, earning a Golden Globe nomination for Best Leading Actor for *Yentl* (1983). In 1984, however, he returned to Broadway, starring as George Seurat in the Pulitzer Prize-winning musical *Sunday in the Park with George* (1984) and garnering another Tony Award nomination for Best Actor in a Musical. It also started his longtime association with Stephen Sondheim, as Patinkin would become known for his highly creative and artistic renditions of the Sondheim song canon in concerts and recordings. From this point, he regularly moved between stage and screen, experiencing great success, as well as great turmoil—both attributed to his well-documented uncompromising personality and demanding work ethic. In 1987, he created his most famous (and personal favorite) screen role, Inigo Montoya in *The Prince Bride*, and continued his film work throughout the '90s, while also starring in Broadway's *The Secret Garden* (1991). Patinkin also obtained the lead role on CBS' *Chicago Hope* in 1994, for which he won an Emmy Award but left the show in its second season (only to return to the show in 1999, receiving another Emmy nomination). During this period, he also released numerous solo albums, including an eclectic collection of songs sung entirely in Yiddish, titled *Mamaloshen* (1998), which he later turned into a concert production which played both on and off Broadway and toured the United States. (Patinkin regularly includes Yiddish numbers in his concerts; he is also very active in Jewish causes.)

In the new millennium, Patinkin has shown no signs of slowing down; in 2000, he returned to Broadway in Michael John LaChiusa's *The Wild Party*, earning another Tony Award nomination for Best Actor in a Musical. He then spent two seasons (2005 and 2006) as a lead character in the CBS crime drama *Criminal Minds* and is currently seen as Saul Berenson in the Showtime series *Homeland*, having garnered an Emmy nomination for his role in the award-winning program. Throughout the 2000s, Patinkin has continued to be active on the concert circuit, often providing extroverted and innovative performances, exploiting a combination of vocal prowess and emotional theatricality that thrills his legions of fans (with some critics likening his stage magnetism and over-the-top style to that of Al Jolson). The list of acclaimed Broadway solo shows include 2001's *Mandy Patinkin in Concert* and 2002's *Celebrating Sondheim*. His more recent Broadway foray reunited him with his early *Evita* costar (and co-diva), Patti LuPone, as they joined forces for the limited 63-performance engagement of the highly lauded concert *An Evening with Patti LuPone and Mandy*

Patinkin, ending in January 2012. The evening proved to be another example of how Patinkin is a modern torchbearer, reminding audiences of the live theatrical thrills provided by the consummate stage performer.

Patti LuPone

Patti LuPone in *Sunset Boulevard*, London, July 1993 ©Robbie Jack/Corbis

Often cited as one of modern theatre's reigning "divas," Patti LuPone is a rare talent who has not only dominated the musical stage for decades with her fiery performance style, versatility, and stunning vocals, but she is also acclaimed for numerous nonmusical roles in theatre, as well as film and television. LuPone is a singer/actor for the ages. Although she rose to fame via modern forms such as the sung-through and concept musical, her knockout belt, expansive vocal range, and bold stage manner hearken back to the reigning divas of yesteryear, including Ethel Merman, whose two signature works, *Anything Goes* and *Gypsy*, were revived and claimed anew in the modern era by Ms. LuPone.

Patti LuPone was born on April 21, 1949, on Long Island, New York, to Italian parents and had music in her genes, with her great-grand-aunt and namesake being the renowned nineteenth-century opera singer Adelina Patti. Patti spent her teens performing with her older twin brothers, William and Robert, as part of a song-and-dance ensemble called "The Lupone Trio." (Robert LuPone would achieve stage success in his own right, originating the role of Zach in Broadway's *A Chorus Line*.) Single-mindedly pursuing a professional performing career, LuPone was a graduate of Julliard's inaugural Drama Division. In 1972, her graduating class (including some of theatre's top names today) professionally organized and, at the hand of the legendary director/producer John Houseman, formed The Acting Company, which made its mark on the New York theatre scene with repertory seasons consisting of classical works. LuPone appeared in over a dozen company productions from 1972 to 1976, receiving her first Tony Award nomination (Best Featured Actress in a Musical) for the company's production of *The Robber Bridegroom* (1975). After leaving The Acting Company, she garnered further attention for her work on stage, including a series of plays for David Mamet (she has a longstanding affiliation with the playwright), as well as standout performances in less-than-successful musicals (1976's *The Baker's Wife* and 1978's *Working*). In 1979, she stopped being the promising name known only by theatre insiders and found national celebrity, thrilling audiences with her performance of Eva Peron in the Broadway premiere of Webber and Rice's sung-through epic, *Evita*. Her gutsy interpretation and awe-inspiring vocals resulted in a Tony Award for Best Actress in a Musical and moved her into the upper echelon of musical theatre performers. The work experience was a difficult one, however, and foreshadowed future professional clashes between LuPone and producers, directors, and other powers-that-be due to her uncompromising standards and demand for respect and equity in the industry.

Following *Evita*, LuPone also found opportunities on both the big screen and small, resulting in a résumé that boasts copious film and television appearances, including a lead role in the television series *Life Goes On* from 1989 to 1993. But it is on the live stage that LuPone has acquired star status and a rabid fan base. After originating the role of Fantine in the 1985 London production of *Les Misérables*, she became the first American to win the prestigious Olivier Award (for her work in both *Les Miz* and a touring revival of *The Cradle Will Rock*, produced by the reunited alumni of The Actors Company). Upon her return to America, she took on the daunting task of reviving Merman's signature role of Reno Sweeney in the Lincoln Center Theatre's 1987 revival of *Anything Goes*. For her vocal fireworks and sardonic portrayal (as well as some respectable tap dancing), she nabbed another Tony nomination. In 1993, she returned to London to originate the role of Norma Desmond in Andrew Lloyd Webber's new musical, *Sunset Boulevard*. Her performance merited another Olivier nomination; but the producers replaced her with Glenn Close for the American debut (after LuPone's lawsuit threat, all parties eventually came to equitable terms). The *Sunset Boulevard* setback did not slow LuPone down, however, as she returned to Broadway in an award-winning one-woman show, *Patti LuPone on Broadway* (1995). LuPone also proved her mettle as a nonmusical star, taking over the lead role of Maria Callas in Terrence McNally's *Master Class* (1995) and exploiting her comic sensibilities in the Broadway revival of *Noises Off* (2001). LuPone's latest triumphs have been in the musical sphere, however. First, she garnered another Tony nod for her cynical, postmodern reinterpretation of Mrs. Lovett in John Doyle's 2005 revival of *Sweeney Todd*. (In the production, she was also required to play the tuba and orchestra bells as part of the 10-person acting/orchestra ensemble.) Second, as a career highpoint, LuPone took on the iconic role of Mama Rose in the 2008 Broadway revival of *Gypsy*; and for her electric, imposing performance, LuPone swept the major New York City theatre awards, including the Tony. These days, even when LuPone is not in a major Broadway musical, she is never far from the stage. She is one of the genre's most venerated chanteuses, performing in both intimate cabarets and concert halls (including Carnegie). Her concert output includes a string of successful one-woman singing showcases (e.g., *The Lady with the Torch*) and numerous acclaimed concert versions of iconic musicals, with a select few filmed for television (e.g., *Sweeney Todd*, *Candide*, and *Passion*). Recently, LuPone was nominated for another Tony for her performance in the Broadway musical *Women on the Verge of a Nervous Breakdown* (2010), followed by the lead vocal performance in New York City Ballet's 2011 production of Kurt Weill and Bertolt Brecht's *The Seven Deadly Sins* and an acclaimed 63-performance concert engagement on Broadway with Mandy Patinkin, titled *An Evening with Patti LuPone and Mandy Patinkin*, which closed in January 2012. In short, the diverse talent and star power of LuPone is ubiquitous in the New York theatre scene and continues to reverberate throughout the industry.

CHAPTER 7

THE DAWN OF A NEW MILLENNIUM AND THE CURRENT STATE OF AMERICAN MUSICAL THEATRE

The changes that occurred in the American musical at the end of the twentieth century clearly illustrated that musical theatre had entered a new era. While contemporary works owed much to the past, the genre also saw an acceleration in the development of subgenres that would have been unrecognizable to early musical creators such as Cohan, Kern, Berlin, Gershwin, Hart, and Fields. As summarized in Chapter One, today's musical theatre boasts a number of diverse trends constituted by innovative styles, constructs, and concepts that fall under a newly expanded genre umbrella. Further, the musical theatre industry underwent major changes in the 1990s and early 2000s as media conglomerates increasingly entered the musical production arena, a territory once ruled by independent producers, impresarios, and private investors. In addition to the imprint of Hollywood and corporate entertainment on the Great White Way, especially the ubiquity of musicals adapted from hit films, other forms and influences of new media found their way to the musical stage. Even reality television began to play a role in the casting and development of certain musicals. Meanwhile, issues of race, ethnicity, gender, and sociopolitical concerns continued to permeate award-winning librettos, while new idioms of music (rap, Latin, African) revolutionized and reinvigorated the "lullaby of Broadway." Audiences also became accustomed to new musical forms which confounded and/or morphed the traditional Golden Triangle: all-sung musicals, all-danced musicals, musicals without original scores, musicals without live music, etc. Given the multifaceted nature of the current musical theatre scene, this final chapter will delineate and address the latest (1990s to current) trends and categories, while explicating some of the contemporary era's more prominent and prestigious works, artists, and developments.

Opening of *Mary Poppins* at Broadway's New Amsterdam Theatre, March 2007 © BRENDAN MCDERMID/Reuters/Corbis

CONTEMPORARY SUNG-THROUGH (OPERA) AND OPERETTA MUSICAL

As musical theatre entered the new millennium, it did not turn its back on the past. Instead, in an ironic twist, musical artists continued to reinvent and expand the genre by often employing classical and antecedent forms such as operetta and opera. At the turn of the twenty-first century, derivations of the operetta, with its mix of story, dialogue and dominant lush scores performed by well-trained semi-operatic voices, could be heard in Frank Wildhorn's *The Scarlet Pimpernel* (1997), Jeffrey Stock's *Triumph of Love* (1997), and Michael John LaChiusa's *Marie Christine* (1999). These contemporary operettas were not marketed as such, since producers most likely wanted to avoid anything that might sound old-fashioned and too classical or elitist, thereby limiting the works' Broadway box office appeals. Further, Sondheim did not label his own work thusly (even though 1973's *A Little Night Music* and 1979's *Sweeney Todd* clearly fall into this category), and continued to resist the classification for his last original Broadway musical, *Passion* (1994), despite its perpetuation of the classical form's aesthetic and compositional tradition.

Although Sondheim did not provide Broadway with another original score after *Passion* (only revivals, revues, and re-workings of earlier pieces, such as *Frogs*), his presence was continually felt during the '90s and into the new millennium by way of critically lauded works penned by a new generation of composer/lyricists, often hailed as Sondheim torchbearers. Composer/lyricist successor Adam Guettel broke ground with his first significant work, *Floyd Collins*, which opened

Off-Broadway in 1994. The son of composer Mary Rodgers (*Once Upon a Mattress*) and grandson of iconic composer Richard Rodgers, Guettel certainly enjoys the prestige of belonging to an American musical theatre dynasty. With a libretto by Tina Landau, Guettel's *Floyd Collins* belongs in the operetta category, albeit a "pocket" version with only thirteen performers. The work is based on the true story of a Kentucky man, Floyd Collins, who was trapped in a cave in 1925 for sixteen days and was interviewed during his travail (amidst a media circus) but could not be saved. Beginning with *Floyd Collins*, critics placed Guettel alongside Sondheim and Leonard Bernstein; and while the Off-Broadway musical developed a cult following, Guettel's *The Light in the Piazza* (2005), a musical adaptation of the same-titled novella, actually put his name in Broadway lights. *Piazza* also won Tony Awards for Best Original Score and Best Orchestrations, securing Guettel's place in musical theatre history. With complex harmonics, dense melodic structures, and operatic textures, Guettel's lush, romantic score for *Piazza* provided a soundscape that came much closer to Sondheim's *Passion* than to conventional musical theatre.

A contemporary of Guettel, lyricist/composer Michael John LaChuisa, not only penned the operatic *Marie Christine* (a retelling of the Medea myth, set in New Orleans and Chicago during the 1890s) but also a number of challenging, esoteric, and heavily musicalized chamber works that have played both on Broadway and off. The list includes *Little Fish* (2003), *The Wild Party* (2000), *The Petrified Prince* (1994), *Hello, Again* (1994), and *First Lady Suite* (1993). Along with Guettel and LaChiusa, Jason Robert Brown is cited as a significant Sondheim descendant in regard to his scores that often include complex compositions, densely layered musical landscapes, sophisticated lyrical content, and demanding vocals. In 1998, he entered the ranks of prominent Broadway composer/lyricists, winning a Tony Award for his first Broadway score: *Parade*. Based on a real-life 1913 event, *Parade* addresses issues of anti-Semitism, recounting the unjust accusation, trial, conviction, and ultimate lynching of an innocent Jewish factory manager, Leo Frank, for the rape and murder of a young female teen in Marietta, Georgia. Brown continues to create Broadway and Off-Broadway works. His 2002 Off-Broadway success, *The Last Five Years*, is a sung-through "two-hander" which details a failed marriage from both the man and woman's differing perspectives and timelines, while his more recent

Broadway work, *13* (2008), again illustrates his versatility, centering on a 13-year-old's dilemma over his Bar Mitzvah and featuring a teen cast.

While many of the above works variously evoke a classical aesthetic and musicality, some of the more recent operatic (or sung-through) works to have winningly played Broadway boast a more contemporary sound and feel. For instance, the rock opera was reasserted and reenergized in 1996 by the massive success of *Rent*, as well as current rock successors such as *American Idiot* (2010). Other examples that are practically sung through or continuously underscored are not as hard-rocking, but they explore subject matter and musical composition reflective of a new century (e.g., 2004's *Caroline, or Change* and 2009's *Next to Normal*). And no discussion of opera and the sung-through musical can ignore the work that not only continues to reign on the Main Stem but is the ultimate homage to opera as presented through a musical theatre lens: Andrew Lloyd Webber's *The Phantom of the Opera*. In the last decade, the pioneer and master of the sung-through musical, Lloyd Webber, has had little success with new works (e.g., *The Woman in White* lasted only three months on Broadway in 2005), but his masterwork, *Phantom*, is still drawing audiences and holds the title of longest running musical on Broadway. Further, his early sung-through hits *Evita* and *Jesus Christ Superstar* enjoyed successful Broadway revivals in 2012. Today, it is exceedingly rare that a musical may be labeled or marketed as an "operetta" or "opera," even though the shoe may fit in terms of musical composition or overall character. A tell-tale sign of "operetta/opera" musicals, however, is the fact that opera companies often undertake revivals of them, illustrating the slipperiness and flexibility of the definitions of musical, operetta, and opera.

THE NON-LINEAR OR CONCEPT MUSICAL

By the 1990s, the concept musical no longer represented the avant-garde antithesis to the integrated book musical but had become an accepted norm in the genre. Regardless, there was (and continues to be) plenty of room within the form for experimentation, a fact exploited by a contemporary contingent of musical theatre artists. With its emphasis on character, theme, and/or message, the concept musical's timeline is often nonlinear and its overall aesthetic can be highly, consciously theatrical. Further, since they are "thought pieces," concept musicals are rarely comedies. Sondheim's works during the 1970s and '80s are often cited and hailed as having set the trend in motion. Similarly, the group of "new kids" writing in the tradition of Sondheim have perpetuated and evolved the form. After two successful Off-Broadway works (*First Lady Suite*, a chamber opera featuring past American First Ladies, and *Hello, Again*, a time-jumping montage of sexual liaisons), Michael John LaChiusa was heralded as one of the promising artists who was forging new territory by way of Broadway concept musicals such as *The Wild Party* (2000). Based on Joseph Moncure March's 1926 poem, *The Wild Party* inspired LaChiusa and co-librettist/director George C. Wolfe to musicalize the literary work's depiction of Jazz Age debauchery. The production opened on Broadway in 2000 with a top tier cast (Eartha Kitt, Mandy Patinkin, and Toni Collette) and was nominated for seven Tony Awards. Set in the twilight of the vaudeville era, the show is conceptualized around a series of vaudeville turns, complete with signs announcing the titles of the acts. Unable to find an audience, however, *The Wild Party* closed after 68 performances, losing all of its $5 million capitalization. The box office failure of *Wild Party*, along with that of LaChiusa's *Marie Christine* a year earlier, seemed to indicate that Broadway audiences were not yet ready to embrace his audacious experiments.

The LaChiusa disappointments were not lone events. While the current longest running Broadway revival happens to be a concept musical (*Chicago*) and the form fits very well within the tenets of postmodernism, musical theatre audiences have appeared to be more conservative in their tastes, seemingly preferring a linear story and hummable tunes to radical experimentation. The case seems even more pronounced in today's family-oriented, high-priced, risk-averse Broadway market. The short runs of high profile contemporary concept musicals such as John Kander and Fred Ebb's *The Scottsboro Boys* (2010 / 49 performances) and Jeanine Tesori's *Caroline, or Change* (2004 / 136 performances) serve as warning beacons to those who would argue that audiences want challenging fare. Even though many critics considered these musicals and similar productions to be worthy of great praise and Tony Award nominations, the shows failed to find a loyal, wide audience. In fact, some prominent composers who were first associated with concept or experimental musicals never realized box office success with such works but, instead, with more conventional vehicles. Case in point, although first gaining notice for her evocative and richly textured compositions for the dark and challenging Off-Broadway musical *Violet* (1997), Tesori would not make her mark on Broadway with that piece, nor would she find a large audience for *Caroline*. Instead, she won popular notice for her spirited, nostalgic score for *Thoroughly Modern Millie* (2002 / 903 performances), as well as her pop-infused score for *Shrek The Musical* (2008 / 441 performances)—both movie musicals with traditionally linear storylines. Similarly, composer/lyricist Andrew Lippa enjoyed a modest cult following due to experimental and critically acclaimed Off-Broadway works such as *John & Jen* (1993) and *The Wild Party* (his own 2000 musical adaptation of March's poem, which coincidentally debuted in the same season as LaChiusa's Broadway version). However, Lippa would eventually take his Broadway bow with a conventional and audience-friendly musical comedy: *The Addams Family* (2010 / 722 performances). And one final example of this paradigm is composer/lyricist/librettist William Finn, whose early works were considered pioneering and experimental in terms of sound, content, and structure. His quirky Off-Broadway catalog includes the trilogy of 1979's *In Trousers*, 1981's *March of the Falsettos*, and 1990's *Falsettoland* (works that innovatively and humorously deal with gay themes/relationships and include concept musical elements), as well as 1998's *A New Brain* (a concept musical that recounts in surreal, vaudevillian style Finn's own near-death experience due to brain surgery). In 1992, Finn combined *March of the Falsettos* and *Falsettoland* into *Falsettos* for his Broadway debut, and the surprisingly popular composite ran for 486 performances. The production was also highly praised by critics, with Finn winning a Tony Award for his score, along with one for the libretto, shared with co-writer James Lapine. More recently, in 2005, Finn again delighted both audiences and critics with *The 25th Annual Putnam County Spelling Bee*—a musical satire which targets national spelling bees (placing the contest on stage in real time) while lampooning cultural, racial, ethnic, social, and gender stereotypes. The musical (with a book by Rachel Sheinkin) also includes concept musical devices such as flashbacks, breakage of the fourth wall, and acknowledgement of the audience to the point of incorporating audience members in the spelling bee itself. The production not only garnered Tony Awards but played for 1,136 performances and has become a regional, community, and educational theatre favorite. Finn's persistent use of leading edge content/concepts in musical theatre, along with his ability to move these techniques, sounds, and subject matter into the mainstream, may be seen as today's Broadway template in regard to the concept musical: a mesh of experimental devices and innovative material given a whimsical, tongue-in-cheek treatment that speaks to a contemporary, savvy audience.

THE REFLEXIVE MUSICAL

As referenced above, much of the humor found in William Finn's *The 25th Annual Putnam County Spelling Bee* is a result of its overtly and self-consciously theatrical nature (especially the audience participation segments), serving to lampoon the overall conventions and clichés of musical theatre itself. In this respect, *Putnam* represents one popular contemporary variation of the concept musical: the reflexive musical. While the "backstage musical" has long been a fashionable subgenre, the reflexive (or self-reflective) musical is not just about show business and/or musical theatre. The reflexive musical drops the pretense that it is a believable, sincere self-contained world in which people just happen to break into song and dance. Instead, it makes fun of itself and the genre overall as it lampoons the conventions or very idea of musical theatre. Many reflexive musicals ask the audience to believe that the production is happening in real time in front of them. Further, actors often break the fourth wall to point out the ridiculousness of a musical moment or include the audience in the overall "joke" regarding certain unorthodox musical treatments and/or tired formulas. Interestingly, at the dawn of the twenty-first century, musical theatre saw an onslaught of reflexive musicals, as postmodern irony and pastiche had become all the rage in the entertainment industry. One of the most significant and purest examples of this trend is *Urinetown, the Musical* (2001), a reflexive work based on the farcical premise that, due to water shortage, a town has outlawed private urination and is forcing citizens to use public toll toilets. At the beginning of the show, the not-so-little urchin Little Sally interrupts Office Lockstop as he attempts to introduce the musical, asking why a musical comedy has such an "awful" title. As she attempts to understand the water crisis, Officer Lockstock cuts her off, warning both Sally and the audience that too much "exposition" can often ruin a musical.

Just months before *Urinetown*'s debut, a modern backstage musical with a predominantly reflexive personality arrived on Broadway to great fanfare: *The Producers* (2001). This comic romp derives much of its humor from inside jokes about showbiz and musical theatre. It was adapted by Mel Brooks and Thomas Meehan from Brooks' 1968 film, with lyrics written by Brooks and music composed by Brooks, arranged by Glen Kelly and Doug Besterman. The main storyline centers on two struggling producers who scheme to get

Susan Stroman performing with Nathan Lane and Matthew Broderick at a 2011 gala honoring Stroman at New York City's Hudson Theatre © Walter McBride/Corbis

rich by raising millions of dollars from gullible backers for a cheaply produced show deliberately designed to be a Broadway flop. Once the show closes, the producers can pocket the investment cash. Of course, things do not go as planned... Although caricatures of theatre types provide much of the comedy, the biggest reflexive joke is the planned flop's subject: Adolph Hitler. *The Producers* features over-the-top, campy, and hilarious production numbers from the show-within-the-show, *Springtime for Hitler*, while simultaneously poking fun at the many incongruous plots and conventions found in musical theatre overall. *The Producers* was seemingly the right show at the right moment; for American audiences in 2001 had developed a strong appetite and preference for ironic and irreverent entertainment. Further, Broadway needed a shot in the arm, as many in the industry worried that the good old American musical comedy had become a relic of the past, relegated to Broadway revivals. Directed and choreographed by Susan Stroman and starring Nathan Lane and Matthew Broderick, *The Producers* debuted on April 19, 2001, and proceeded to run for 2,502 performances. During its run, the production broke the record for the largest single-day box office in theatre history, taking in more than $3 million, while the show also swept the Tony Awards. Holding the record for most Tony wins to date (thirteen), *The Producers* became the first musical to win every category in which it was nominated.

With the smash success of *The Producers*, other reflexive musicals (or works that used reflexive techniques such as breaking the fourth wall for "wink and nod" moments) sprung up on Broadway. The roster includes 2005's *Dirty Rotten Scoundrels* and *Spamalot*; and as the trend went to further extremes (e.g., tongue-in-cheek Off-Broadway musical versions of *Reefer Madness* and *Debbie Does Dallas*), some critics worried that the American musical was losing its heartfelt sincerity and guileless charm. Further, the contemporary reflexive musical runs the risk of becoming too much of an insider phenomenon (e.g., *Urinetown* quotes choreography from *West Side Story*), with audiences needing to know a great deal about musicals in order to get all of the allusions and jokes. But musical theatre never gets tired of looking at its own reflection; and writers continue to be drawn to the backstage musical, the show-within-a-show, and the reflexive musical as exemplified by twenty-first-century works such as *The Musical of Musicals: The Musical* (2003), *The Drowsy Chaperone* (2006), *Curtains!* (2007), and *[title of show]* (2008). Further, today's reflexive musical persists in pushing the envelope, e.g., the 2011 Off-Broadway production of *Silence! The Musical*—a satire framed as a musical adaptation of the 1991 movie thriller, *The Silence of the Lambs*—has played over 500 performances.

THE INTEGRATED BOOK MUSICAL

Regardless of the many contemporary subgenres that have revolutionized Broadway, the traditional integrated book musical has not been laid to rest. On the contrary, original Broadway shows built upon coherent, strong librettos that create theatrical worlds focused on story and character, with songs constructed to further plot and character development, are still alive and well. Some fit the traditional Golden Age mode to a tee while others have added a contemporary twist and touch of irreverence to the proceedings. Productions such as *Ragtime* (1998) fall into the first category. This musical adaptation of the same-titled 1975 novel by E. L. Doctorow melds numerous stories and characters to create a narrative of America in the early 1900s. While *Ragtime* chronicles the travails of three families, it also paints a multifaceted historical portrait of immigrant struggle, racial inequality, women's emancipation, industrial revolution, political unrest, early showbiz, and the overall pursuit of the American Dream. With a book by one of the most prolific and successful librettists working today, Terrence McNally, and a score by the team of Stephen Flaherty and Lynn Ahrens, the production debuted in January 1998 and ran for 834 performances. McNally was awarded a Tony for his book and Flaherty and Ahrens won the Tony for their score. Carrying on the tradition of Golden Age teams such as Rodgers and Hammerstein, Lerner and

Loewe, and Bock and Harnick, Flaherty and Ahrens specialize in tight musical integration and evocative use of period styles, storytelling, and character specificity; they also continue to be one of the closest and more prolific writing teams in contemporary musical theatre.

On the other end of the integrated musical spectrum is a modest book musical that debuted in 2003 and resembled nothing Broadway audiences had seen before

(or since): *Avenue Q*. The work was conceived by Robert Lopez and Jeff Marx, who wrote the music and lyrics, while its book was written by Jeff Whitty. Inspired by the idea of a *Sesame Street* for adults, the team created a musical that combines puppet characters with human characters (the puppeteers are also seen by the audience but invisible in terms of the storyline) to relay the journey into adulthood by main character Princeton, recent college graduate and new "Avenue Q" resident. As Princeton faces the real world and learns lessons of maturity, he forges relationships with other Avenue Q residents who are struggling with their own life issues. The musical's mature content, softened by its big heart and buoyed by its cutting comedy, drew a massive audience. Further, its innovative use of puppetry, as well as its unconventional, postmodern, and often politically incorrect take on traditional musical theatre, as well as cultural mores and even children's TV programming, has made the musical one of the most unique works in the canon. The strange "little show that could" ultimately surprised the Broadway establishment, winning the Tony Award for Best Musical and running for 2,534 performances. (A revival is currently enjoying a successful Off-Broadway run.)

Another integrated musical to excite Broadway during the early 2000s while garnering a great box office and affirming (alongside *The Producers*) the resurgent sentiment that modern audiences still hungered for musical comedies was the smash hit *Hairspray* (2002). When the composer/lyricist team of Marc Shaiman and Scott Wittman brought their adaptation of a 1988 John Waters film to Broadway, they created a unique mix of nostalgia, sentiment, sincerity, and camp (*Hairspray*'s matron just happens to be played by a man in drag). The musical tells the tale of Tracy Turnblad, a guileless, idealistic teen in the 1960s who earns a spot on *The Corny Collins Show* (a fictional television dance program, resembling *American Bandstand*), despite her chubby physique that is not the show's ideal. Tracy then uses her newfound celebrity to promote and facilitate the show's eventual racial integration. *Hairspray* deftly and comically addresses cultural and societal issues of body image, identity, generational angst, and racial segregation, while enveloping all in a bubbly pop score and hyperkinetic dance aesthetic. Delighting audiences and critics alike, the Broadway production won eight Tony Awards (including Best Musical) and ran for 2,642 performances. Later musicals such as *The Drowsy Chaperone* (2006) and, especially, the

smash hit *The Book of Mormon* (2011) continued this integrated and narrative musical comedy tradition. Demonstrating how far the traditional musical comedy dare go, *The Book of Mormon* overcame potential controversy to merit a highly lucrative box office, pleasing (and offending) audiences with the satiric tale of two Mormon missionaries sent to Uganda to convert a ravaged village. The musical was the brainchild of Broadway novices Trey Parker and Matt Stone (creators of television's animated series *South Park*) and Robert Lopez (co-creator of *Avenue Q*), who teamed to write the show's book, lyrics, and music. Upon its 2011 debut, *Mormon* became the darling of Broadway, as well as a postmodern rendering of the book musical given its tight score, character-driven story, hopeful ending, and fearless lampooning of taboo topics such as religion, God, AIDS, and sodomy. With nine Tony Awards (including Best Musical) under its belt, the irreverent and highly popular *Mormon* is still playing to packed houses.

Not all notable contemporary book musicals have turned to comedy for success. Another group of distinguished works have carried on the integrated musical tradition while featuring serious, challenging subject matter. This category includes 2006's *Grey Gardens* (music by Scott Frankel, lyrics by Michael Korie, and book by Doug Wright), 2009's *Next to Normal* (book and lyrics by Brian Yorkey, with music by Tom Kitt) and *Memphis* (music by rock musician David Bryan, who co-wrote lyrics with the show's librettist Joe DiPietro). Debuting in the same year, *Next to Normal* and *Memphis* both garnered numerous awards as they challenged audiences with sophisticated, mature themes and won loyal followers, meriting long, profitable Broadway runs (*Grey Gardens* did not enjoy the same commercial reception and notoriety, but was praised by many critics). *Memphis* features a blues, rockabilly, gospel, and rock 'n' roll score as it tells the tale of a white Memphis DJ's attempt to overcome racially segregated boundaries in the recording industry of the 1950s, fighting personal battles and bigotries when he becomes romantically involved with a black singer. *Next to Normal* is often positioned as a rock musical, which isn't altogether accurate in terms of subject matter and overall aesthetic (although its score is electronic and often exploits driving rock grooves). Nonetheless, the musical was groundbreaking in its subject matter, that is, a middle-aged woman's battle with bipolar disorder and her resulting treatment for mental illness (in

a novel plot twist, one of the lead characters is actually the mother's hallucination of her dead son). Reaffirming the potential and portent of the twenty-first-century integrated book musical, *Next to Normal* won the Pulitzer Prize for Drama (the most recent musical to merit this rare honor) and *Memphis* won the Tony Award for Best Musical.

One of the most significant integrated book musicals to take Broadway by storm in the contemporary era is neither farcically comic nor thematically challenging. Instead, *Wicked* (2003) blends both comic and sincere elements, along with a heavy dose of fantasy and spectacle. With a book by Winnie Holzman, based on Gregory Maguire's *Wicked: The Life and Times of the Wicked Witch of the West* (a 1995 prequel to L. Frank Baum's *Oz* books), the musical adaptation boasts an infectious, hummable, and evocative score by composer/lyricist Stephen Schwartz, a proven voice in the modern musical arena. Capitalizing on the ageless appeal of *The Wizard of Oz*, *Wicked* takes its audience on a similarly fantastical journey, illustrating the origins of and relationship between the Witches of Oz (roles originated by Broadway stars Kristin Chenoweth and Idina Menzel). *Wicked* is still running on Broadway and London with strong box office numbers (over 3,600 performances to date), while its reputation and canonical significance continues to be bolstered by numerous national and international tours.

THE REVIVAL AND "REVISAL"

Although many integrated book musicals continue to merit publicity and run successfully on Broadway, such musicals are less likely to be original works and more likely to be "revivals" these days, that is, remounts of previously produced musicals. In an ironic contemporary industry twist, such revivals have become essential to the showbiz and artistry of modern-day Broadway. They provide opportunities for current audiences to see classic or forgotten musicals from the past, as well as chances for artists to reinterpret and reinvigorate such works. Further, a resurrected star vehicle can be used to showcase contemporary performers from various entertainment mediums (e.g., film star Daniel Radcliffe in the much publicized 2011 revival of *How to Succeed in Business Without Really Trying* and pop star Usher's 2006 turn as Billy Flynn in *Chicago*). The diverse actor interpretations enforce the ephemeral and ever-evolving nature of canonical works while also providing much fodder for debate amongst viewers and critics.

Beyond casting and performance, however, the degree by which revivals are newly conceptualized and staged by directors can vary widely. Some revivals may be given "archival" treatments, with the new versions replicating or closely resembling the original. A recent example is the 2006 revival of *A Chorus Line*, the first to have been staged since the landmark musical's initial run (1975–1990). Many of the show's original artists worked on the revival, including director Bob Avion, who had co-choreographed the first production with Michael Bennett. Much of the look and feel mimicked the original, while Bennett's choreography was also reconstructed for the show (re-staged by Baayork Lee). Younger audiences were excited to see the production that they had missed the first time around in much of its original guise, and the revival ran for 759 performances while also spawning a documentary regarding the revival's casting (*Every Little Step*).

Most artists take creative license when staging revivals, however, maintaining the spirit and style of the originals while reinterpreting some aspects and employing new concepts. The resulting works may be termed "traditional" revivals. Contemporary examples include two fairly recent Rodgers and Hammerstein revivals produced by The Royal National Theatre: *Oklahoma!* and *Carousel*. Directed by Richard Eyre, *Carousel*

landed on Broadway in 1994 and painted a grittier and more evocative musical portrait than in the past, with a metaphoric scenic design and nontraditional casting (black actors in traditionally Caucasian roles). The revival of *Oklahoma!*, directed by Trevor Nunn, appeared on Broadway in 2002. Similar to *Carousel*, the production surprised audiences with its more realistic depiction of the rural environs and populace, as well as its reinterpretation of the dance numbers, with permission granted to replace the copyrighted original choreography of Agnes de Mille. The new choreography was designed by Susan Stroman and included the novel concept of having the actors playing Laurey and Curly dance the ballet, instead of using doubles. Both productions, as well as many similar revivals, offered audiences the traditional story, score, and overall spirit of their originals, while introducing new ways by which to view the classic works.

Lastly, there is a "revisionist" category which includes revivals that have had their looks, feels, sounds, and/ or concepts completely reinterpreted by modern artists. In many cases, a revisionist director assumes the role of auteur, conceptualizing, shaping, and realizing a singularly artistic vision for a work. One such auteur in the contemporary musical theatre arena is English director John Doyle. Working in modest British regional theatres for several decades during the belt-tightening years of the 1990s, Doyle began to compensate for orchestra shortages by having actors play musical instruments when their characters were not on stage. Then he began to direct musicals in a way that the characters stayed on stage and in character; thus, their playing an instrument became another facet of their characterization. For this reason, Doyle calls his approach "actor-musicianship." When Doyle's *Sweeney Todd* transferred to the West End in 2004, and then Broadway in 2005, more audiences were exposed to his unique theatrical aesthetic and practice. In Doyle's reinterpretation of the Sondheim classic, the cast was reduced to ten performers who all played musical instruments (in lieu of an orchestra), with the action minimally staged on a postmodern set that was stark and claustrophobic, facilitated by evocative lighting. After he won the directing Tony Award, Doyle returned to New York with a second minimalist actor-musician restaging of another Stephen Sondheim classic, *Company*, which won the Tony Award for Best Revival and enjoyed a 2008 PBS television broadcast. Although not directed by Doyle and not a revival, 2012's *Once*

Kathleen Marshall with Joel Grey and Sutton Foster discussing the award-winning 2011 revival of *Anything Goes*, March 2011 © Walter McBride/Corbis

reflects his influence as the Tony-winning musical (directed by John Tiffany) boasts a company of actors who double as the show's orchestra.

Given the above archival, traditional, and revisionist criteria, it must be noted that revivals can rarely be relegated to just one category. Often, they sit somewhere between traditional and revisionist; and sometimes they move beyond revisionist due to major content alterations. Both cases apply to the revival that features a new (or significantly rewritten) libretto, often termed a "revisal." In some instances, the revisal is so extensive that the work can no longer assume its original title. For example, the "new" Gershwin musical, *Crazy for You* (1992), features an original libretto by Ken Ludwig based on Guy Bolton's basic storyline for the Gershwins' *Girl Crazy* (1930). And the libretto for the recent 2012 revival of *Porgy and Bess* was reshaped to the point of necessitating a new title: *The Gershwins' Porgy and Bess*. In short, it is ahistorical and unethical to present a work to audiences under its old title when it contains significant alterations to its original form / content. Some revisals, however, feature rewritten librettos but do not significantly alter the shape, sound, or intent of a past work; they merely mean to update the textual component, aiming for modern relevance, correctness, and suitability. For instance, a significant rewrite happened when a production of *Annie Get Your Gun* was being prepared for a 1999 Broadway revival starring Bernadette Peters. The original book by Herbert Fields and Dorothy Fields was revised by Peter Stone to remove the jokes and songs aimed at Native Americans. The song "I'm an Indian Too" was cut and the musical's subplot was rewritten to feature an interracial couple. Even though Stone's alterations were made with the permission of Berlin and Fields' heirs, criticism was leveled at Stone and the revival's producers for changing a work of art. On the other hand, no one missed the racial slurs of the original 1946 show; and with Stone's new book and galvanizing performances by Peters and her replacement Reba McIntyre, the revisal had a very profitable run of 1,045 performances.

In 2001, celebrated playwright David Henry Hwang wrote an entirely new libretto for Joseph Fields, Richard Rodgers, and Oscar Hammerstein's *The Flower Drum Song* (1958). The revisal was not only dramatically tightened and improved by Hwang, but his libretto poked postmodern, reflexive fun at America's historic depiction and perpetuation of Asian stereotypes. Although praised during its regional premiere, the Broadway production was less positively received, and it ran for only 172 performances. (Even though Hwang's *Flower Drum Song* is significantly different than the 1958 original musical, it retained the same title when it played on Broadway in 2001.) Lastly, in one of the more intriguing revisal incidences, a 2009 revival of a canonical classic had its book contemporaneously altered by its original librettist. Specifically, when Arthur Laurents directed the most recent revival of *West Side Story*, he chose to translate some of his own dialogue into Spanish. Recruiting composer/lyricist/librettist Lin-Manuel Miranda (*In the Heights*) to supply the Spanish translations for the Puerto Rican characters, the revisal became the first significant bilingual Broadway musical. Opinions over the lingual alterations were mixed. The new book brought *West Side Story* into the new millennium, reflecting a modern American demographic, but also faced some box office backlash. Even though the production ran for 748 performances, the bilingual libretto was adjusted, with the Spanish element edited, after its initial debut.

THE SCREEN-TO-STAGE MUSICAL

For most of the twentieth century, musical theatre writers not only supplied the nation with many of its hit songs, but also many of its top musical films. Indeed, the American Film Institute's list of the 25 "Greatest Movie Musicals" reveals that over half started on the Broadway stage. While the norm has been stage-to-screen transfers, there are a number of Broadway works that were originally conceived and written as musical films, then subsequently reconfigured for the stage. A majority of the significant and/or successful musicals in this category debuted during the contemporary era. Below is a selection of various musical films adapted for the stage during the last two decades, chronologically listed by the year of their Broadway debut:

The Who's Tommy	1993
Beauty and the Beast	1994
Victor, Victoria	1995
State Fair	1996
The Lion King	1997
High Society	1998
Chitty Chitty Bang Bang	2005
Mary Poppins	2006
The Little Mermaid	2008
Newsies	2012

Overall, screen-to-stage musicals are not that much different from other works in the musical theatre canon. Regarding story and characters, relatively few musicals feature an original plot; most are adaptations of source material that first existed as a novel, short story, play, news article, biography, ballet, or even artwork. But according to many critics, the recent trend of screen-to-stage musicals has become epidemic, dominating the contemporary Broadway scene. Further, the majority of works are those that musicalize a film *not* originally constructed as a musical, although it might have featured music in its plot, significant musical sequences, and/or a compilation of catchy background songs. The following sampling of notable stage musicals based on films not written as or intended to be Hollywood musicals provides an overview of this phenomenon (works are arranged chronologically according to the year of their Broadway stage debut):

My Favorite Year	1992
The Goodbye Girl	1993
Sunset Boulevard	1994
Passion	1994
Fame, The Musical	1995
Big	1996
The Full Monty	2000
The Producers	2001
Hairspray	2002
Sweet Smell of Success	2002
Thoroughly Modern Millie	2002
Urban Cowboy	2003
Spamalot	2005
Dirty Rotten Scoundrels	2005
The Color Purple	2005
The Wedding Singer	2006
Tarzan	2006
Billy Elliot: The Musical	2007
Legally Blonde	2007
Young Frankenstein	2007
Shrek The Musical	2008
Women on the Verge of a Nervous Breakdown	2010
Catch Me If You Can	2011
Sister Act	2011
Priscilla Queen of the Desert	2011

Ghost, The Musical	2012
Once	2012
Bring It On, The Musical	2012
A Christmas Story—The Musical	2012
Kinky Boots	2013

As the screen-to-stage musical became more prevalent and popular on Broadway in the late twentieth century, the stage treatments also began to vary greatly. Some of the most prestigious hits in the category are imaginative and theatrical reinterpretations, reinventing the original work for the stage (Julie Taymor's transformative *The Lion King* and Stephen Daldry's visionary *Billy Elliot*), while other successful works have more closely adapted the look, feel, and content of their film sources while effectively heightening such material with elaborate song and dance numbers (*Hairspray*, *The Producers*, *The Full Monty*, *Thoroughly Modern Millie*, *Legally Blonde*, and *Sister Act*). At the same time, there have been less-than-successful movie adaptations, sometimes deemed to be disappointing follow-ups to early smash hits by proven artists (*The Goodbye Girl* and *Sweet Smell of Success*, both composed by *A Chorus Line*'s Marvin Hamlisch, as well as Mel Brooks' *Young Frankenstein* and Shaiman and Whitman's *Catch Me If You Can*). The wide-ranging diversity of the screen-to-stage musical is illustrated by two of Broadway's prominent 2012 entrees: *Once* and *Bring It On, The Musical*. *Once* is an intimate musical based on an independent film that features a minimalist set and a small ensemble, with cast members doubling as the show's orchestra. A critical darling, the production won eight Tony Awards, including Best Musical. *Bring It On* is a big, bright, and spectacle-filled musical adapted from the highly popular mainstream movie about high school cheerleading competitions. With a pop-infused score by co-composers Tom Kitt and Lin-Manuel Miranda (creators of *Next to Normal* and *In the Heights*, respectively) and co-lyricists Miranda and Amanda Green, along with a book by Jeff Whitty (*Avenue Q*), the musical boasts high-energy dances and acrobatics, having supplemented its cast with real-life cheerleaders.

While numerous leading Broadway composers have lent their talents to film musicalizations, one artist has been at the forefront of the screen-to-stage musical

phenomenon: Alan Menken. Menken burst upon the musical theatre scene in 1982 with his lyricist partner Howard Ashman, creating the Off-Broadway hit musical adaptation of the cult film *Little Shop of Horrors*. With the success of *Little Shop*, Disney Studios beckoned and Menken and Ashman wrote Academy-Award-winning scores for two films that were credited with reviving the animated musical on the big screen: *The Little Mermaid* (1989) and *Beauty and the Beast* (1991). Tragically, Ashman died in 1991 from complications from AIDS in the midst of working on *Aladdin* (1992) with Menken. Menken and Ashman (posthumously) won two more Academy Awards for the film (while Tim Rice, stepping in for Ashman and supplying additional lyrics, shared the Oscar). After Ashman's death, Menken worked with numerous lyricists, continuing to provide infectious, stylistically diverse, and melodically rich scores for numerous Disney films (more recently, 2007's *Enchanted* and 2010's *Tangled*), while he also went back to the stage, expanding and adapting his own musical films, as well as numerous other works, for Broadway. The prestigious list includes *Beauty and the Beast*, *The Little Mermaid* and Madison Square Garden's *A Christmas Carol*. In 2012, Menken had three screen-to-stage musicals playing simultaneously on Broadway: the short-lived *Leap of Faith* (19 performances), the well-received *Sister Act* (561 performances), and the still running *Newsies*, for which Menken won his first Tony Award.

Looking at a snapshot of the contemporary Broadway scene, it is telling that in the fall season of 2012, five of the seventeen musicals playing were musical adaptations of films—the aforementioned *Once*, *Bring It On*, *Newsies*, *Mary Poppins*, and *The Lion King* (with *Sister Act* and *Billy Elliot* just recently closed); five others had been made into films (*Chicago*, *Evita*, *Mamma Mia!*, *Rock of Ages*, and *The Phantom of the Opera*), while one was the musical biography of a major film icon (*Chaplin*). Two others were not adaptations, per say, but had significant ties to Hollywood—one to a blockbuster serial enterprise (*Spider-Man: Turn Off the Dark*) and the other, referencing an MGM classic (*Wicked*). And although the screen-to-stage musical capitalizes on name recognition, such a built-in advantage is not always a reliable insurance policy: for every megahit (*The Lion King*, *Hairspray*, *The Producers*), there may be an implosion (*The Goodbye Girl*, *Urban Cowboy*, *Ghost*). Nonetheless, in the last few decades, Hollywood has increasingly viewed Broadway as a new, lucrative market for their properties. In 2002, MGM created "MGM On Stage" to develop and license films from their catalog for stage production. Having started with *Chitty Chitty Bang Bang*, *Dirty Rotten Scoundrels*, *Priscilla Queen of the Desert*, and *Legally Blonde*, this division plans to musicalize over a dozen more films in the coming years. In this respect, MGM now rivals Disney Theatricals, which has been adapting Disney films for the stage for almost two decades, and both companies have been joined by other major film studios such as DreamWorks (e.g., DreamWorks Theatricals) and Universal Studios (e.g., Universal Stage Productions).

In addition to its overall box office impact and dominance, the screen-to-stage musical has significantly affected other aspects of the musical theatre industry as well. Although MGM's *The Wizard of Oz* (1939) was made into a popular stage property in the 1990s, it has yet to play a Broadway theatre (although a 2011 version on the West End, produced by Andrew Lloyd Webber, is tentatively scheduled to open on Broadway in 2013/14). Instead, the show has been performed professionally on the road and in regional theatres, while having been released for amateur productions relatively quickly. This was also the case for Rodgers and Hammerstein's television film *Cinderella* (1957), until it finally took its Broadway bow in 2013. And Disney's megahit *High School Musical* (2006) went from cable television to high school stage productions within its first year, signaling a new era in which a Broadway run is no longer an *absolute* imperative if material has been otherwise validated as profitable property through other entertainment mediums. Another novel trend is the cyclical progression from screen to stage and then back to screen for certain properties. For instance, Mel Brook's original (non-musical) *The Producers* was turned into a hit Broadway musical and then returned to the screen, in its musical form; *Hairspray* went through a similar loop, while numerous other hit screen-to-stage musicals are currently being planned for Hollywood film adaptations.

A preview of the touring production of *Shrek the Musical* at San Francisco's Orpheum on December 1, 2010 © Adm Golub/San Francisco Chronicle/Corbis

THE ROCK/POP ROCK MUSICAL

For most of the twentieth century, musical theatre supplied many of the popular songs of the day. With the advent of rock 'n' roll, a new genre ruled the radio, one in which rhythm replaced melody as the unifying element of a song and lyrics often took a back seat to percussion. For these reasons, most conventional Broadway composers veered away from rock. Instead, composers new to musical theatre have written the majority of pop/rock musicals (and most have tended to create only one successful or notable work). But modern audiences do not seem to care about the "outsider" status of the creators (or, in some cases, prefer the "non-Broadway" sound/style); and rock musicals represent some of the most lauded and groundbreaking works in the contemporary musical theatre era. In 1996, Jonathan Larson's phenomenally successful *Rent* (1996), which is often hailed as *Hair*'s closest progeny, was credited with bringing the rock opera back to Broadway after more than a two-decade hiatus. In the years that followed, more critically acclaimed and/or popular rock musicals affirmed the newly validated Broadway status of the subgenre. This roster includes John Cameron Mitchell and Stephen Trask's *Hedwig and the Angry Inch* (1998 / Off-Broadway), Duncan Sheik and Steven Sater's *Spring Awakening* (2006),

Stew and Heidi Rodewald's *Passing Strange* (2008), Green Day's *American Idiot* (2010), Michael Friedman and Alex Timbers' *Bloody Bloody Andrew Jackson* (2010), and Bono and The Edge's *Spider-Man: Turn Off the Dark* (2011). Along with the rocking, electronic sound and rebellious spirit, the look of the rock musical also transformed the Broadway stage at the turn of the century, helped by a new generation of directors who embraced and exploited cutting-edge technologies to create postmodern landscapes for their musicals' bold theatrics and raw performances. Traditional musical theatre rules became a thing of the past as rock bands often shared the stage with the actors (sometimes joined by audience members), while body mikes were not only visible but flaunted in rock-concert style, and pop culture pervaded the proceedings, sometimes via video screens and digital projections. (For a more detailed analysis of the rock musical, its past and present, see Chapter Six's "Pulling Back the Curtain: Dawning of the Age of the Rock Musical.")

One prominent director who has exploited such technical advances and experimental stage techniques while propelling the musical into the new millennium is Michael Mayer. A lauded visionary and versatile director of both plays and musicals, Mayer has adroitly tackled operettas (*Triumph of Love*) and old-school book musicals (*Thoroughly Modern Millie*), before advancing the rock musical through his revelatory, conceptual,

Director Michael Mayer and Billie Joe Armstrong (Green Day) with producers Ira Pittelman and Tom Hulce celebrating the 300th performance of *American Idiot* at Broadway's St. James Theatre, January 8, 2011
© Walter McBride/Corbis

and aesthetically dense stage treatments of *Spring Awakening* (winning a Tony Award for Best Direction) and *American Idiot*. His more recent Broadway foray was the 2011 revival of Burton Lane and Alan Jay Lerner's *On A Clear Day You Can See Forever* (1965), with a concept that included gender bending and gay themes.

Alongside the hard-rocking musicals, there were also easy-listening or pop musicals that enjoyed (or still enjoy) highly successful runs on Broadway during the 1990s and early 2000s. Many of the works were penned by composers who proved to be exceptions to the one-hit model of the rock artists. This group includes Stephen Schwartz, Elton John, and David Yazbek. As one of Broadway's leading composers in the 1970s, creating hit musicals *Godspell* (1971), *Pippin* (1972), and *The Magic Show* (1974), Schwartz moved to animated film musicals in the 1990s (*Pocahontas*, 1995; *The Hunchback of Notre Dame*, 1996; *The Prince of Egypt*, 1997). Then, in 2003, he reasserted his musical theatre presence, reminding Broadway audiences of his infectious gift of melody and style, combined with theatricality, writing the score (music and lyrics) for the blockbuster *Wicked* (2003).

As one of 1970's top recording and rock concert stars, Elton John was certainly no stranger to pop prestige, but even his most ardent fans were probably surprised by the vengeance whereby he conquered the stage musical. Elton John and Tim Rice's hit Disney film *The Lion King* (1994) became a phenomenal stage

Elton John at the Broadway launch of *Billy Elliot* at New York City's Professional Performing Arts High School, April 2008
© Walter McBride/Retna Ltd./Corbis

sensation in 1997 and then John began writing directly for the stage, starting with *Aida* (lyrics by Tim Rice) in 2000, for which John won a Tony, *Billy Elliot: The Musical* (lyrics by Lee Hall) in 2005, which won the Tony Award for Best Musical, and *Lestat* (lyrics by Bernie Taupin) in 2006. Only *Lestat* failed to connect with critics and audiences, while the other three Broadway productions topped 1,000 performances (the still-running *Lion King* has topped 2,000).

Having been recorded by a number of popular groups and composing numerous scores for television, David Yazbek came to musical theatre by adapting for the stage the 1997 British film *The Full Monty*. Teaming up with veteran librettist Terrence McNally, the stage musical ran for 770 performances. Yazbek returned to Broadway with the popular screen-to-stage musical *Dirty Rotten Scoundrels* (2005), this time collaborating with librettist Jeffrey Lane. The more recent Yazbek work on Broadway, *Women on the Verge of a Nervous Breakdown* (2010), proved to be a disappointment. With both music and lyrics by Yazbek, this musical adaptation of the Pedro Almodóvar film ran for only 69 performances, despite an all-star cast (e.g., Patti LuPone, Brian Stokes Mitchell, and Sherie Rene Scott). Both John and Yazbek are successful pop song writers who made the transition to musical theatre, proving that they can write for character and maintain the award-winning aesthetic of the engaging, contemporary pop song. Grammy-winning pop singer/songwriter Cyndi Lauper has recently joined this group, penning an award-winning score for *Kinky Boots* (2013). With a book by Tony-winning playwright/librettist Harvey Fierstein, buoyed by Lauper's energetic and engaging songs, *Kinky Boots* tells the story of a down-and-out shoe factory that is revived by manufacturing and selling fetish-style ("kinky") footwear for drag artists. The production won the Tony for Best Musical, while Lauper garnered a win for Best Score—the first solo win in this category for a woman. On a side note, there is another pop song composer with significant recording industry credentials who has had success on Broadway: Frank Wildhorn. Contrary to his crossover contemporaries, however, Wildhorn's works often reflect a more classical aesthetic and construct, although imbued with a pop-influenced sound. Many Wildhorn musicals also center on historical figures (both fictional and nonfictional) and works of literature, with the tales being conveyed through completely or semi sung-through scores. Having developed a wide fan base, Wildhorn had three musicals running simultaneously on Broadway in 1999: *Jekyll and Hyde* (1997), *The Scarlet Pimpernel* (1997), and *The Civil War* (1999), while *Dracula, the Musical* followed in 2004 but played for only 157 performances. In 2011, Wildhorn returned to Broadway with two new musicals: *Wonderland* (a modern update of Lewis Caroll's Alice and her Wonderland adventures) and *Bonnie and Clyde* (featuring Depression-era outlaws and ill-fated lovers Bonnie Parker and Clyde Barrow). Neither musical stayed long on Broadway, but *Bonnie and Clyde* received several Tony nominations.

THE JUKEBOX MUSICAL

Related to the pop/rock musical is the jukebox musical, for many rock musicals feature a compiled score by one rock/pop legend or band (e.g., *Lennon* and *American Idiot*). Other rock musicals may boast scores consisting of already written songs by different artists but are rooted in one genre to tell a new and/or reflexive story (e.g., the smash hit *Rock of Ages*, a boy-meets-girl tale with a score consisting of "hair band" songs from the 1980s). In short, a jukebox musical takes advantage of previously written music, as opposed to productions which feature original music. And similar to the revue, the jukebox musical is an assemblage of pre-existing songs where the emphasis may be on the songs instead of plot and/or character.

Unlike earlier elaborate revues put on by the likes of Ziegfeld, late twentieth-century revues tended to focus on the music of one composer and generally did not showcase stars. In the 1990s, most jukebox musicals were small, intimate affairs, e.g., *Five Guys Named Moe* (1992, songs by Louis Jordan), *Smokey Joe's Café* (1995, songs by Jerry Leiber and Mike Stoller) and *Dream* (1997, lyrics by Johnny Mercer). Today, however, the jukebox musical (or modern revue) has not only grown in size and scope, but also in terms of genre significance.

One variation of the jukebox musical, as mentioned above, is the "disguised pop/rock concert." In this format, a series of pop or rock hits are staged as a concert; the evening invariably ends with an uninterrupted series of numbers performed by the cast. Some of these musicals are semi-autobiographical. Others feature less concert performance and more biography, but still contain scores that use the songs a singer and/or songwriter made famous. The list of both concert/biography

variations to have played on Broadway in the last two decades is extensive, and a representative sampling is provided below (the list includes artist/s chronicled in the musical):

Buddy: The Buddy Holly Story
   (1990, Buddy Holly)

Jelly's Last Jam
   (1992, Jelly Roll Morton)

The Boy From Oz
   (2003, Peter Allen)

Good Vibrations
   (2005, Beach Boys)

Ring of Fire
   (2006, Johnnie Cash)

Jersey Boys
   (2006, Frankie Valli & The Four Seasons)

Fela!
   (2009, Fela Anikulapo-Kuti)

Million Dollar Quartet
   (2010, Elvis Presley, Johnny Cash, Jerry Lee Lewis, Carl Perkins)

Baby It's You!
   (2011, The Shirelles)

Let It Be
   (2013, The Beatles)

In this vein, another jukebox musical arrived on Broadway in 2013: *Motown: the Musical*. This musicalized life story of Motown founder Berry Gordon features a score composed of Motown classics and performers who impersonate iconic artists such as Diana Ross, Michael Jackson, Stevie Wonder, Marvin Gaye, and Smokey Robinson.

Another subgenre of the jukebox musical that utilizes pre-existing songs, but creates a plot around them, is the "story album musical" or the "anthology with a story" musical. (These contain plots where the story is not a biography of the songwriter/performer.) Some incorporate songs written originally for musical theatre and others use pop songs (e.g., *Rock of Ages* and *Priscilla Queen of the Desert*). The song catalogue of George and Ira Gershwin has long proved a favorite for this category of musicals, starting with 1983's *My One and Only*. The formula proved even more successful in 1992 with *Crazy for You*—a compiled "Gershwin" book musical that contains five songs from *Girl Crazy*, four from *A Damsel in Distress*, three from the film

Shall We Dance, and six other Gershwin tunes. Ken Ludwig wrote a new libretto; and the musical, directed by Mike Okrent and choreographed by Susan Stroman, played for 1,622 performances. As the latest example of the Gershwin jukebox/story musical, *Nice Work If You Can Get It* (2012) recently pleased audiences with its compiled, nostalgic score, brought to life by Broadway favorites Matthew Broderick and Kelli O'Hara (478 performances).

The Gershwins are not the only artists to inspire narrative jukebox musicals on the contemporary Broadway stage. Jukebox musicals consisting of recycled pop songs and non-biographical plots include the international sensation *Mamma Mia!* (1999, featuring the song catalogue of ABBA), as well as the Twyla Tharp dansical *Movin' Out* (2002, featuring the song catalogue of Billy Joel) and *All Shook Up* (2005, featuring the song catalogue of Elvis Presley). Like the biographical or rock concert forms, musicals in this niche enjoy the fact that many potential theatre patrons already know the scores very well. *Mamma Mia!* has arguably been the most significant and successful example of this modern musical theatre phenomenon. During their ten years of existence as a band (1972–82), the Swedish group ABBA had fourteen singles in the Top 40 (four in the Top 10), and record sales which exceeded 350 million units. British playwright Catherine Johnson took 22 of their greatest hits and fashioned a plot around them about a young woman, Sophie, who wants her father to give her away at her wedding. The problem is that her mom had three suitors in the past, all of whom could be Sophie's dad. *Mamma Mia!* has been performed in ten languages, in 85 cities, and to over 20 million people. Still running on Broadway (over 4,500 performances to date), the show has become an entertainment industry in its own right, also enjoying a hit film adaptation in 2008.

CONTEMPORARY CHOREOGRAPHER/ DIRECTORS AND THE DANSICAL

During the second half of the twentieth century, the choreographer/director not only garnered new power but some rose to the level of musical theatre auteurs, conceiving and creating musicals on Broadway that boasted a heavy dance/movement component. Gone were the days when the choreographer's name was left off the program or the era when the choreographer did not receive a percentage of the weekly gross of a box office hit. On Broadway today, a new group of director/choreographers carry the torch of past pioneers Agnes de Mille, Jerome Robbins, Bob Fosse, Michael Bennett, Michael Kidd, and Gower Champion. Prominent members of the new contingent are listed below, with some of their most significant directed/choreographed (or co-directed/choreographed) works to have played Broadway during the last two decades (the list does not include the artists' numerous and lauded sole choreography credits):

Andy Blankenbuehler   *Bring It On, The Musical* (2012)

Graciela Daniele   *Annie Get Your Gun* (1999 revival), *Marie Christine* (1999), *Chronicle of a Death Foretold* (1995), *Once on This Island* (1990)

Bill T. Jones   *Fela!* (2009)

Kathleen Marshall   *Nice Work If You Can Get It* (2012), *Anything Goes* (2011 revival), *Grease* (2007 revival), *The Pajama Game* (2006 revival), *Wonderful Town* (2003 revival)

Rob Marshall   *Cabaret* (1998 revival), *Little Me* (1998 revival)

Jerry Mitchell   *Kinky Boots* (2013), *Legally Blonde* (2007)

Ann Reinking   *The Look of Love* (2003), *Fosse* (1999)

Susan Stroman   *The Scottsboro Boys* (2010), *Young Frankenstein* (2007), *The Producers* (2001), *Contact* (2000), The *Music Man* (2000 revival)

Lynn Taylor-Corbett   *Swing!* (1999)

Twyla Tharp   *Come Fly Away* (2010), *The Times They Are A-Changin'* (2006), *Movin' Out* (2002)

In addition, ten of the above-listed works have either won or been nominated for the Tony Award for Best Musical: *Contact, The Producers, The Scottsboro Boys,*

Movin' Out, Fosse, Once on This Island, Chronicle of a Death Foretold, Nice Work If You Can Get It, Swing!, Fela!, and *Kinky Boots.*

The new dance musical reaffirms the power of the choreographer/director and incites a new level of diversity in Broadway dance—case in point, the idiosyncratic concert idioms of Bill T. Jones (contemporary and African) and Twyla Tharp (contemporary), as well as hip-hop, courtesy of Andy Blankenbueler. Further, the new millennium ushered in an era of hit dance musicals that placed dance front and center, often at the expense of other components. These works have been deemed "dansicals," that is, musicals that predominantly feature or tell a story through dance, with scores and librettos taking a back seat (often the scores are jukebox compilations and there is little-to-no dialogue). This contemporary phenomenon does not take into account the numerous "special" dance/kinetic events that have also found their way to Broadway and Off-Broadway in recent decades, e.g., *Riverdance, Burn the Floor, Tap Dogs, Stomp, Forever Tango,* etc. While not technically considered musicals, such works helped foster the taste for the all-dance musical; and it is no coincidence that many dansicals incorporate the dance idioms of these Broadway spectacles. There has also been a certain amount of controversy surrounding the rise of the dansical, given its concert dance character. When *Contact* won the Tony Award for Best Musical in 2000, it was clear that the dansical had arrived. Director/choreographer Susan Stroman's work was advertised as a "dance play," comprising three narrative dance vignettes set to completely disparate compositions/recordings that

were loosely linked by the concept of "human contact." And in a postmodern moment of reflection and debate, great consternation was expressed as the lauded "musical" not only lacked an original score but also any live musical component. The entire score was canned, consisting of previously recorded versions of the musical numbers. But Stroman's Tony-winning musical ran for 1,010 performances; plus, it was not a lone phenomenon, for other Broadway dansicals were also drawing sizable audiences. For instance, Lynne Taylor-Corbett's *Swing!* (a celebration of swing music and dance) ran for 461 performances, while also being nominated alongside *Contact* for the best musical Tony. A dance retrospective of the career of auteur Bob Fosse, *Fosse,* ran for 1,093 performances, while containing many numbers culled from Fosse's *Dancin',* the 1979 musical that could be considered the granddaddy of the dansical. And Tharp's coming-of-age story set to the song catalogue of Billy Joel, *Movin' Out,* ran for 1,303 performances and was recently followed by Tharp's less popular but critically acclaimed *Come Fly Away* (a series of dances set to a Frank Sinatra soundtrack). It did not seem to matter that the newly popular dansical did not contain original music, for audiences had become used to jukebox scores and were delighted by the form's top-notch dance and theatrics. While the dance musical is not new (in fact, dance-centric attractions have been around since *The Black Crook*), the dansical is novel in regard to the degree that it blurs the lines between concert dance and a "musical," while allocating ever more power and authorship to the Broadway choreographer.

RACIAL/ETHNIC DIVERSITY AND THE CONTEMPORARY MUSICAL

Although Broadway is nicknamed the Great White Way—a term referring to the district's many theater, marquee, and street lights—the moniker could also be used to describe a musical theatre genre and industry that has been dominated throughout most of its history by white artists and a Western European aesthetic. This homogeneity began to be questioned, challenged, and altered in the 1960s and '70s; and today, the Great White Way boasts numerous examples of racial and ethnic diversity. One of most significant developments in this category is that of the "black musical," a musical category rooted in racial diversity that could also be considered a subdivision of the pop/rock musical, featuring music that reflects African American jazz, blues, gospel, funk, reggae, rap, or Motown. Owing much to antecedents such as Charlie Small's *The Wiz* (1975), contemporary examples include *The Color Purple* (2005), with a book by Marsha Norman and evocative score by Brenda Russell, Allee Willis, and Stephen Bray, as well as *Passing Strange* (2008), with a wry book and raw score by Stew and Heidi Rodewald. Both musicals also address potent issues of racial identity and the legacy of racism and subjugation in America. Complicating the black musical category, however, are the musicals that feature scores built upon or evoking such traditionally African American music genres, yet are written by white artists, while still centering upon issues of blackness, e.g., racial tensions, relationships, and crises. Such prominent examples include David Bryan and Joe DiPietro's *Memphis* (2009), Jeanine Tesori and Tony Kushner's *Caroline, or Change* (2004), and John Kander and Fred Ebb's *The Scottsboro Boys* (2010). Some contemporary musicals feature less African American idioms in their scores, but still voice potent criticisms (both serious and comic) in regard to racial inequality, integration, and interracial relationships, e.g., *The Wild Party*, *Ragtime*, *Parade*, and *Hairspray*. Some might even categorize *The Book of Mormon* as a "learning moment" in regard to racial/cultural understanding, while *Avenue Q* satirically confronts racial/ethnic prejudices head-on with characters lampooning their own minority identities and singing songs such as "Everyone's a Little Bit Racist." On a less overt scale, other shows, such as *Rent* and *The 25th Annual Putnam County Spelling Bee*, are informed by diversity (with casts of color and some allusion to race/ethnicity) but never specifically broach or seek to redress issues of racism and ethnic bigotries.

In the last two decades, the jukebox musical has also proved to be a popular form by which to showcase African American songwriters and performers. In 1992, *Five Guys Named Moe* delighted audiences with an intimate, tightly sung revue that featured the songs of Louis Jordan. Less comfortable for audiences was another jukebox musical in the same year, *Jelly's Last Jam*, which compiled the song catalogue of early jazz great Jelly Roll Morton (portrayed to great acclaim by song-and-dance star Gregory Hines, with his younger self played by tap prodigy Savion Glover). As librettist and director of the production, George C. Wolfe did not take the easy path in regard to the jukebox musical. Instead, he chose to paint an unsympathetic and challenging portrait of Morton (who not only combated racism throughout his career but harbored racist attitudes himself, given his light complexion), while also confronting America's own theatre legacy of blackface. Here, it is important to revisit this once-accepted convention that has long haunted the musical genre, especially given its minstrelsy antecedence. Even after minstrelsy's heyday, the convention persisted in musical theatre, as evidenced by the black-faced antics of Broadway megastar Al Jolson, as well as Tess Gardella (famous for her "Aunt Jemima" stage persona) who originated, in blackface, the role of Queenie in 1927's *Show Boat*, and the insistence by many (but resisted by Gershwin) that *Porgy and Bess* be originally performed by white opera singers in blackface. Such historical artifacts must also include the many "brown-face" portrayals on the musical stage, including that of the Sharks in early productions of *West Side Story*, as well as the disparaging representations of Native Americans in classics such as *Annie Get Your Gun* and "yellow-face" depictions in Rodgers and Hammerstein classics such as *The King and I*, *South Pacific*, and *Flower Drum Song*. In the modern era, such negative systemic practices resulted in the much publicized Actors' Equity 1991 contestation of Caucasian Jonathan Pryce in the role of the Eurasian Engineer in *Miss Saigon*. Thus, it is not surprising that Wolfe's twist on the shameful blackface legacy drew great controversy but addressed the "elephant in the room" when he turned the practice on its head, employing blackface in a surreal and metaphoric segment in *Jelly's*.

In the end, however, the theatrical use of blackface was tempered during *Jelly's* run. But Wolfe found another potent outlet for diversity and racial commentary on Broadway when he reunited, as conceiver and director, with Glover to create *Bring in 'da Noise, Bring in 'da Funk* (1996). The unique Broadway production chronicled the black experience in America through dance, music, and verse, ranging from evocations of slave ships to challenges in hailing New York cabs. The musical was also the first to present elements of rap on Broadway in the form of slam poetry by Reg E. Gaines and music by composers Daryl Waters, Zane Mark and Ann Duquesnay. Given the vision and direction of Wolfe—and more importantly, the innovative choreography and star performance by Glover—the groundbreaking production ran for 1,135 performances, as well as enjoyed numerous well-received national tours. The unique sound of *Bring in 'da Noise* was followed by other musicals more intent on bringing world music to the Broadway stage, especially those idioms representative of African music. For instance, *The Lion King's* score includes compositions by South African Lebohang "Lebo M." Morake. Lebo M.'s music, as well as his musical arrangements and choir direction, imbued the production's overall sound with a degree of authenticity not previously heard in popular musicals. Sub-Saharan African music got even more exposure on Broadway in 2009 with *Fela!*. This jukebox musical depicts the life and career of Fela Anikulapo-Kuti (Fela), a Nigerian musician and composer who created a fusion of funk, jazz and African folk music that he termed "Afrobeat." With a music career that spanned the late 1960s, '70s, and '80s, Fela was also a human rights activist, as well as an outspoken critic of the Nigerian government and military, attempting to run for Nigerian President in 1979 and jailed as a prisoner of conscience in the '80s. In addition to vibrant music and a star-making turn by Sahr Ngaujah in the title role, *Fela!* benefitted from the visionary direction and choreography of contemporary dance auteur Bill T. Jones (who also co-wrote the book with Jim Lewis), resulting in a strong visual aesthetic that exploited highly theatrical lighting and digital projections to showcase a dominant African dance component. The production ran for 463 performances and received eleven Tony nominations, winning three.

During the modern era, Broadway diversity has also been facilitated by the practice of nontraditional casting (once termed "colorblind" casting), with producers, casting agents, directors, and audiences looking past the written race of characters to prioritize the talent that could best serve a role. Of course, such casting practices have also incited debate, criticism, and recrimination in the theatre community (case in point, the aforementioned Actors' Equity/*Miss Saigon*/Jonathan Pryce drama). Nonetheless, while artists of color have headlined Broadway marquees in the past (e.g., Bert Williams, Chita Rivera, Ethel Waters, Jennifer Holliday, Sammy Davis, Jr., Ben Vereen), today's Broadway has repeatedly looked past race and ethnicity when casting stars. Revivals are especially effective in this respect, blurring racial and ethnic divides when they cast performers of color in roles originally

Audra McDonald and Brian Stokes Mitchell at the Tony Awards, June 6, 2004 © Andrew Kent/Corbis

written for Caucasians. A landmark event was the 1975 black version of *Helly, Dolly!*, with Pearl Bailey taking over the title role originated by Carol Channing. What was considered groundbreaking in the 1970s, however, is now rarely viewed as controversial. Two significant African American stars who have crossed the color barrier repeatedly are Audra McDonald (playing Carrie Snow and Lizzy Curry in revivals of *Carousel* and *110 in the Shade*, respectively) and Brian Stokes Mitchell (playing Fred Graham and Don Quixote in revivals of *Kiss Me, Kate* and *Man of La Mancha*).

In 2000, New York City census information indicated that 26.9% of the metropolitan population was Hispanic or Latino, and that 39% of Broadway audiences came from the New York metropolitan region. Given this demographic information, it seems surprising that the Latino musical did not find success on Broadway until the twenty-first century. There were previous disappointing attempts, however, including Luis Valdez's *Zoot Suit* (1979 / 41 performances) and Paul Simon's *Capeman* (1998 / 68 performances). More successful were dance-based "special events" such as *Tango Argentino* (1985, revived 1999) and *Forever Tango* (1997, revived 2004 and 2013). But in 2008, *In the Heights* took Broadway by storm and suggested that the Latino musical had arrived. With a book by playwright Quiara Alegría Hudes and music and lyrics by Lin-Manuel Miranda, *In the Heights* depicts three days in the lives of residents of the Dominican-American neighborhood of Washington Heights in New York City. Rooted in comic, romantic, frictional, and tender intrapersonal relationships, the musical dramatizes the characters' disparate pursuits of the American Dream (be it by college or lottery ticket), as well as intergenerational and familial conflicts informed by issues of Hispanic assimilation in America. Miranda's score also predominantly features rap, hip-hop, and Latin pop alongside more traditional musical compositions, making *In the Heights* the first hit musical to exploit and fuse such cutting-edge music genres in an integrated book form. After tryouts in Connecticut in 2005 and an Off-Broadway stint in 2007, the show opened at Broadway's Richard Rodgers Theatre in March 2008 to rave reviews, resulting in 1,184 performances, 13 Tony Award nominations and four wins (including Best Musical), as well as being named a finalist for the Pulitzer Prize for Drama.

While such shows as Rodgers and Hammerstein's *Flower Drum Song* (1958) and Boublil and Schonberg's *Miss Saigon* (1989) have given Asian-American performers long-running hits in which to perform, there have been very few Asian-American authored musicals. Leon Ko and Robert Lee's *Heading East* (1999), A.R. Rahman's *Bombay Dreams* (2004), and *Maria Maria* (book and lyrics by Hye Jung Yu, music by Gyung Chan Cha, 2006) are rare exceptions. Though the original music was kept, David Henry Hwang wrote a new libretto for *The Flower Drum Song* when it was revived on Broadway in 2002. The "revisal" did not run long, but in Hwang's version, the originally negative Asian stereotypes were either eliminated or treated in a satiric, reflexive manner, reflecting a modern paradigm on Broadway in which past racial/ethnic insensitivities, bigotries, and/or exclusions are often confronted and sometimes corrected by way of revivals.

PRODUCERS AND THE CURRENT BROADWAY MARKET

Producing changed a great deal during the last decade of the twentieth century as the days of the singular theatrical producer disappeared. Legendary solo producers, such as David Merrick, were known for their idiosyncratic tastes, business expertise, and stylistic fingerprints. Indeed, there is a universal sentiment that with the disappearance of the lone producer, there was a corresponding evaporation of significant risk taking on Broadway. Contributing to the current risk-averse climate is the fact that many of today's successful producers no longer aim to "discover" new musicals by independent artists. Instead, they come up with their own ideas for commercially viable musicals (emphasis on "commercial") and then assemble creative teams to develop and realize those ideas on stage. Some musical theatre scholars and historians have groused that this paradigm has cultivated a producing climate in which artistic acumen has been replaced by the quest for cash. Part of this new producing model, however, continues to exploit age-old strategies handed down by predecessors such as Merrick. For instance, producers still play active roles in Broadway casting processes, with an enticing marquee headliner equating investment capitalization and insurance. Such casting strategies include seeking top box office draws (from stage, film, television, and the music industry) as well as rotating wildly different stars in certain lead roles, aiming to attract different demographics throughout a show's run. This "revolving door" star-casting ploy has been engaged by contemporary producers Fran and Barry Weissler with impressive results in the 1994 revival of *Grease*, and later revivals of *Annie Get Your Gun*, *Wonderful Town*, and the most lucrative to date (still running), *Chicago*.

Today's theatre producers have also evolved into corporate entities (and vice versa). An early pioneer in this regard was Andrew Lloyd Webber. Having enjoyed success as a producer throughout his career, in 1986 Lloyd Webber sold public shares in his Really Useful Group in order to replace traditional backers with stock market investors. The strain of maintaining a publicly held company, however, led Lloyd Webber to buy back the outstanding shares in 1990. Nonetheless, his adventure changed the face of the musical theatre industry forever. In fact, Canadian producer Garth Drabinsky similarly took his company, Livent, Inc., public in 1993. Unfortunately, his work, which resulted in the Broadway productions of *Kiss of the Spider Woman*, *Ragtime*, *Parade*, and *Fosse*, was ultimately derailed by convictions of fraud.

Lloyd Webber not only introduced new finance/investment models to the musical theatre industry, but he also exploited trendy twenty-first-century entertainment mediums to publicize and market stage musicals. For a 2006 London revival of *The Sound of Music*, Lloyd Webber hit upon the idea of creating a reality television program centered around the musical's casting. The viewing audience voted on the contestants at each stage, and the actors with the fewest votes were eliminated. Carried on BBC for eleven hours, *How Do You Solve a Problem Like Maria?* was very successful in terms of generating audience interest, as the advance ticket sales topped $11 million before opening. And while 7.7 million viewers witnessed the final showdown between the top three finalists and 2 million voted to extend a six-month contract to Connie Fisher, it seemed nothing more than a publicity stunt. However, 23-year-old Fisher opened to great reviews. Lloyd Webber followed with other reality show castings of West End revivals—all meeting with box office success; thus, it was inevitable that American producers would seek to emulate this successful gimmick. *Grease: You're The One That I Want!* appeared on NBC in 2007, with viewers deciding on the casting of the leads for a Broadway revival of the classic musical, directed and choreographed by Kathleen Marshall. (On a side note, the winner of the role of Sandy, Laura Osnes, has become one of Broadway's leading ingénues, currently starring in the title role of *Rodgers & Hammerstein's Cinderella*.) On cable, MTV held its own reality show competition, *Legally Blonde The Musical: The Search for Elle Woods* (2008), in which producers auditioned hopefuls to replace the Broadway production's lead performer Laura Bell Bundy.

Most significant in regard to the corporatization of Broadway is the fact that by the 1990s, costs had begun to escalate outside the reach of the individual investor. As a result, Broadway musicals are now generally financed by teams of producers and/or corporations (Disney, 20th Century Fox, Clear Channel Entertainment, Suntory International Corporation, Warner Bros., DreamWorks, etc.). The major pioneer and player in this category is Disney Theatrical Productions. Disney made its Broadway debut with little fanfare; for "The Walt Disney Studios" was listed as just one of many co-producers of Bill Irwin's wordless masterpiece, *Largely New York*, in 1989. With their animated film musicals back in popularity, it was only natural that Disney began to look at its own movie catalog for possible stage transfers. Thus, the newly formed Disney Theatrical Productions debuted on Broadway in 1994 with *Beauty and the Beast*. With cross-platform advertising (television, video, internet, etc.) and extensive merchandising, *Beauty and the Beast* had (and continues to have) enormous visibility. Two additional factors contributed to its landmark success (5,461 performances): a reputation as "family entertainment" and occasional star casting.

In short order, Disney decided to not only continue to produce live musicals, but became a theater owner as well. After a $36 million dollar renovation, Disney reopened the New Amsterdam Theatre on 42nd Street to become the home of the next Disney blockbuster: *The Lion King* (1997). With a visionary staging that included puppetry, masks, and larger-than-life spectacle spearheaded by director Julie Taymor (who also designed the costumes/masks), the still-running musical won six Tony Awards (including Best Musical). In 1998, Disney began work on an original musical instead of adapting another existing film musical for the stage. *Elaborate Lives* was not well received in its Atlanta regional premiere, so Disney put the show back into rehearsal before a redesigned, rewritten, recast, and retitled *Aida* opened on Broadway in 2000. Also penned by *Lion King*'s Elton John, *Aida*

was another artistic triumph (four Tony Awards) and box office smash (1,852 performances). In 2004, Disney teamed with British producer Cameron Mackintosh to bring *Mary Poppins* to the stage. Based on stories of P. L. Travers and their own 1964 film version, this was another critically lauded Broadway victory, closing in 2013 after 2,619 performances. While the stage musical version of *Tarzan* (2006; score by Phil Collins) was not well received critically, it found a modest audience. *The Little Mermaid* (2008) fared a bit better with critics and audiences, running for 685 performances. Given Disney's success, it is no surprise that other Hollywood entities have entered the musical theatre forum, especially studios that see theatrical and market potential for their animated and/or other "family-friendly" fare. Most prominent and promising among this new Hollywood contingent is DreamWorks Theatricals; and their first Broadway adaptation, *Shrek The Musical* (2008), portended good things for the company, meriting eight Tony Award nominations (winning one for its costumes) and running for over a year, followed by a popular national tour.

But corporations are not the only producing entities on today's Great White Way. With the disappearance of the individual producer has come the increased importance of transfers arriving to Broadway not only from London but also from American regional theatres. Some of the reigning not-for-profit and regional theatres to have successfully developed and transferred musicals to Broadway include Joseph Papp's Public Theater (the theatre that started the trend with *Hair* in 1967), Lincoln Center, the Goodspeed Opera House in Connecticut, and two major California theatres: LaJolla Playhouse and the Old Globe Theatre. Musicals can also come to Broadway via organizations whose goals are to provide affordable New York visibility for new works; among these, the New York Musical Theatre Festival (NYMT), the New York International Fringe Festival (NYF), and the National Alliance for Musical Theatre (NAMT) are increasingly important development conduits. Numerous notable Broadway and Off-Broadway works got their starts and/or significant development via these organizations and workshops/festivals, including *Urinetown* (NYF), *Altar Boyz* (NYMT), as well as *Thoroughly Modern Millie* and *The Drowsy Chaperone* (NAMT).

As producing in the late twentieth century became more of a corporate enterprise and Broadway production

Director/designer Julie Taymor surrounded by the lion masks she designed for Disney's *The Lion King* on Broadway. © Larry Ford/Corbis costs continued to skyrocket, profit margins and marketing strategies became major showbiz concerns, culminating in a different kind of selling tool introduced by *The Producers* in 2001. Here, the concept of "premium-price" ticketing was implemented in order to counteract the practice of ticket brokers buying the best seats in the house and reselling them at an enormous markup (a profit which did not benefit the original producers of the musical). Thus, *The Producers* designated "premium" tickets, pricing them at $480(!), which meant that few seats ended up with resellers and the profit from the markup went to the producers. Of course, it also contributed to a current environment in which many fear prices, not just for prime seats, are spiraling out of control, discouraging a socioeconomic diversity in its audience—a shame for an art form that has often prided itself on its populist appeal. Ultimately, however, it does not matter whether the musical is produced by an individual or a corporation, whether it boasts an original plot or is a redundant film-to-stage transfer, whether the seats are $20 Off-Off-Broadway or cost $480 for the Premium Broadway experience, whether the show has been in development for years or opens "cold" on Broadway, there is no predicting unqualified success. If focus groups, talkbacks, threaded discussions, blogs, tweets, and questionnaires were one hundred percent effective, there would be no flops on Broadway. Yet the statistics yield a sobering fact: musical theatre remains a high-risk medium where less than one show in five breaks even. But when a show is financially successful, the economic possibilities are staggering.

As the twenty-first century has gotten underway, artists continue to stretch and question many of the assumptions and conventions that have guided musical theatre throughout the previous century. *The Drowsy Chaperone*'s "Man in the Chair" explains to his audience the virtues of the silly (and fictional) 1928 musical they have been watching, explaining that it transports viewers to another world and leaves them with a light tune to lift a heavy mood. Of course, not all musical theatre authors approach the genre with this goal. Nevertheless, whether they are writing a traditional book musical, a concept musical, a jukebox musical, a sung-through musical, a rock opera, a dansical, a screen-to-stage musical, etc., all of these creators would probably agree with the director Julian Marsh when he declares, in *42nd Street*, that the most "glorious" words in the English language are "musical comedy." And such artists, united in their love of the overall genre, are responsible for the multi-faceted nature of today's musical that rarely sits completely within one concrete category. As handy as it is to categorize current trends (as delineated in this chapter), such specifications should only be seen as guidelines; for today's musical often assumes a shifting and/or amalgamated form that takes a little from the past, merges new trends, and pushes into the future. For this reason, the evolutions of and new directions for the twenty-first-century musical remain as elusive as a recipe for creating the fail-proof Broadway show.

Whoopi Goldberg (as Rafiki) joins the cast of Broadway's *The Lion King* at the Minskoff Theatre, taped for *The View* on January 14, 2009 © Walter McBride/Retna Ltd./Corbis